Major Problems
in the Gilded Age
and the Progressive Era

MAJOR PROBLEMS IN AMERICAN HISTORY SERIES

GENERAL EDITOR

THOMAS G. PATERSON

Major Problems
in the Gilded Age
and the Progressive Era

DOCUMENTS AND ESSAYS

SECOND EDITION

EDITED BY
LEON FINK
UNIVERSITY OF ILLINOIS AT CHICAGO

HOUGHTON MIFFLIN COMPANY
Boston   New York

Editor in Chief: Jean L. Woy
Senior Development Editor: Frances Gay
Senior Project Editor: Christina M. Horn
Production/Design Coordinator: Jodi O'Rourke
Senior Manufacturing Coordinator: Marie Barnes
Senior Marketing Manager: Sandra McGuire

Cover image: George Bellows, *New York*, 1911. National Gallery of Art, Washington, D.C. Collection of Mr. and Mrs. Paul Mellon.
Cover design: Diana Coe / ko Design Studio.

Printed in the U.S.A.

Library of Congress Catalog Card Number: 00-103885

ISBN: 0-618-04255-5

123456789-CRS-04 03 02 01 00

TO ANNA AND SIMON—
for helping to preserve a sense of humor
in my historical process

Contents

C H A P T E R   4
Trials of the New South
Page 86

C H A P T E R   5
Rise of the Industrial City: New Places, New Peoples
Page 116

C H A P T E R   6
Politics in the Gilded Age: Mainstream and Periphery
Page 158

C H A P T E R   7
The 1890s: Economic Depression and Political Crisis
Page 188

C H A P T E R   8
Professionalism and the Uses of New Knowledge
Page 225

C H A P T E R   9
The Language of Empire
Page 263

C H A P T E R   1 0
Race and Power Under Jim Crow
Page 295

C H A P T E R   1 1
Consumer Culture and Commercialized Leisure
Page 325

CHAPTER 12
Progressivism: Roots of the Reform Vision
Page 355

CHAPTER 13
Progressivism: Foundations for a New American State
Page 387

CHAPTER 14
Nature Without Nurture: Progressives Confront Environmental Destruction
Page 412

CHAPTER 15
America and the Great War
Page 445

Preface

"The Republic thunders past with the rush of the express," exclaimed steel-company executive Andrew Carnegie in 1885. This volume invites readers to board the mighty train that was the United States around the turn of the last century, and to experience its thunderous ride. The Gilded Age and the Progressive Era, spanning approximately the years 1877 to 1920, form the gateway to the modern America that we have inherited.

The term *Gilded Age* originated in the 1873 novel of the same name by Mark Twain and Charles Dudley Warner. Satirizing the "all pervading speculativeness" and "shameful corruption" rampant during the presidency of Ulysses S. Grant, Twain and Warner set the tone for much future commentary on late-nineteenth-century public affairs. The Gilded Age, in short, identified a period of rapid economic advance simultaneously associated with shady practices in business and politics. The term *Progressive Era,* in contrast, initially summoned up more positive associations. *Progressive*—a label that urban, middle-class reformers applied to themselves (in preference to *liberal, populist,* or *socialist*) in the first decade of the twentieth century—evoked, at least to its defenders, a beneficent and rational reckoning with the excesses of the Gilded Age.

For years, most scholarly debates surrounding the two periods revolved around these initial judgments, essentially trying to separate the "good guys" from the "bad guys." Were the Gilded Age industrialists "robber barons" or "captains of industry," scholars pondered, and they vigorously debated and defended their conclusions. Were American workers supporters or critics of capitalism? Were the populists spouting mere demagoguery, or did they offer a legitimate radical alternative? Was urban government a partial success or an utter failure? Were the progressives enlightened reformers or bigoted agents of social condescension? Recent treatments of the Gilded Age and the Progressive Era, although still addressing earlier historiographic controversies, tend to adopt a more thematic and analytical framework. It is with such newer perspectives in mind that this volume attempts to define the major problems of the age.

Dominated by the new wealth and technology associated with the Industrial Revolution, this period is marked both by stupendous innovation and by stupefying conflicts on almost every front. The transformation of landscape and cityscape was no more dramatic than was the juxtaposition and recombination of peoples in new material surroundings. Just as striking was the metamorphosis of personal values, political ideas, and group identities—with frictions recurringly flashing around poles of race, class, gender, ethnicity, and religious belief. The nation's material progress carried it to the threshold of world superpower, with a growing overseas empire. But

what did power mean at home and abroad? Who benefited from economic development, and who paid the costs? Whose vision defined a new age, and against which
competing visions of social purpose and national well-being?

In applying these overarching themes, I have tried to overcome the fragmentation of perspective and of subfield that too often bedevils the historical discipline.
The rich scholarship in women's and African American history over the past two
decades, in particular, allows this volume to venture further than previous collec-
tions in integrating a discussion of gender and racial differences into the treatment
of political and social issues.

Readers of the first edition of this text will note several changes in the second
edition. New essays or documents—usually both—have been added to each chapter. The essays of the introductory chapter now foreshadow the themes of the entire
volume. The normative as well as oppositional politics of the Gilded Age receive
fuller treatment. There is a sharper sense of chronological development from
beginning to end, highlighted by the focus on the 1890s as a transitional decade.
Finally, Chapter 8's focus on "new knowledge" offers a new perspective on intellectual culture and conflict.

In the second edition, following a preliminary mapping of the period by two
distinguished historians, our journey proceeds in roughly chronological fashion,
though emphasizing themes that continue to resonate even today. We begin with the
great social enigma of the Gilded Age: unparalleled abundance and opportunity on
the one hand, poverty and growing inequality on the other. Looking more closely
at the sweeping material changes, we proceed regionally from the farms and reservations of the once Wild West (Chapter 3) to the post-plantation South (Chapter 4)
to the great new urban-immigrant bulwarks of industrial civilization (Chapter 5).
Chapter 6 emphasizes the norms of the political process in these same years of
explosive economic development. The next three chapters spotlight historical tran-
sitions in full bloom by the 1890s: a challenge to corporate power in the form of the
farmers' crusade and labor unrest unleashed by economic depression; the professionalization of intellectual skills and the application of "scientific" models to both
social and religious questions; and the debate over the expansion of American
power and influence abroad. Finally, Chapters 10–15 highlight the early-twentieth-
century themes that have come to define the Progressive Era. We begin with two of
the most salient social phenomena of the new age—the struggles of African Americans under the Jim Crow system of racial segregation and the triumph of a commercialized consumer culture that redefined American leisure time. Chapters 12 and 13,
in turn, examine the intellectual wellsprings and mixed record of achievement from
the burst of multifaceted governmental activism known as progressivism. One area
of progressive concern, the effort to manage environmental resources, receives special attention in Chapter 14. The final leg of our trip returns us to the world stage:
Chapter 15, "America and the Great War," focuses at once on a president struggling
to reconcile democratic ideals with the realities of world politics, on the coercive
nature of national war mobilization and the ironic outcomes for progressive reforms, and on the cultural impact of loved ones in faraway places.

Following the general format of the Major Problems in American History series,
each chapter brings together historically significant, readable documents and essays
that accent the provocative encounter of the past with the present. In each chapter a

brief introduction sets the historical scene and defines the central issues. Headnotes to the documents and essays place the issues in historical and interpretive perspective. Documents are listed chronologically except where thematic interests dictate an alternate arrangement. Each chapter closes with an invitation to further reading. Although the choice of topics inevitably reflects my own sense of the critical questions and turning points of the period, the array and arrangement of the selections are open-ended enough to encourage readers to debate the issues and to formulate their own understanding of the nation's "major problems" during these years.

Students and professors who wish to continue their study are encouraged to join H-SHGAPE (Society for the History of the Gilded Age and Progressive Era). This group maintains an extensive and well-organized index of thematic websites at <http://www2.h-net.msu.edu/~shgape/internet/index.html>.

In preparing this volume, I have had significant help along the way. For their thematic and bibliographic suggestions, I would like particularly to thank William Barney, Henry Binford, Eileen Boris, Peter Coclanis, Sarah Deutsch, John Kasson, James Leloudis, Susan Levine, Roger Lotchin, David Moltke-Hansen, Malcolm Rohrbough, and Jeffrey Stewart. I am also indebted to the thoughtful advice of the various reviewers consulted by Houghton Mifflin for the revised edition: Lucy Barber, University of California, Davis; Susan Becker, University of Tennessee; Leonard Dinnerstein, University of Arizona; Larry Glickman, University of South Carolina; Cynthia Russett, Yale University. And I would like to thank the reviewers contacted by D. C. Heath for the first edition for their helpful advice and comments: Betty Brandon, University of South Alabama; Priscilla J. Brewer, University of South Florida; John D. Buenker, University of Wisconsin, Parkside; Mark T. Carleton, Louisiana State University; Francis J. Couvares, Amherst College; Jack D. Elenbaas, California State University, Fullerton; Lewis L. Gould, University of Texas, Austin; H. Roger Grant, University of Akron; Martin R. Haas, Adelphi University; D. Alan Harris, Old Dominion University; Gerald W. McFarland, University of Massachusetts, Amherst; Samuel T. McSeveney, Vanderbilt University; Donald W. Rogers, University of Hartford; Jack Tager, University of Massachusetts, Amherst; and Mark Wyman, Illinois State University. These colleagues undertook their task with an impressive sense of responsibility.

In addition, I have profited greatly from the suggestions of Series Editor Thomas G. Paterson and the Houghton Mifflin staff, especially Vice President and Editor in Chief for History and Political Science Jean L. Woy, Senior Development Editor Frances Gay, Senior Project Editor Christina Horn, and Permissions Editor Mary Dalton-Hoffman. From the first edition, I also thank Sylvia Mallory, James Miller, Margaret Roll, and Bryan Woodhouse. Finally, I extend special gratitude to two wonderful research assistants, Katherine Otis and Georg Leidenberger, for their most thoughtful and painstaking contributions across the editorial process.

L. F.

*Major Problems
in the Gilded Age
and the Progressive Era*

C H A P T E R

1

Introducing the Gilded Age

and Progressive Era

In its simplest terms, the history of the Gilded Age and Progressive Era is some-
times considered along a gradient of "accumulating" and "dispensing" resources.
That is, historians often think of the former period as one overwhelmingly defined
by the Industrial revolution and its concomitant accumulation, not to say hoarding,
of great wealth—an era when the social and cultural needs of the population
lagged behind the economic interests of the self-empowering business classes of
the country. By the same token, historians treat the Progressive Era as one of com-
parative improvement—as if the nation suddenly "woke up" to attend in its own
fashion to the stress, and distress, of an industrial civilization. Such metaphorical
constructions, to be sure, do an injustice to the complexities of both periods: the
Gilded Age had its complement of caring public officials, crusading reformers, and
sensitive men and women of letters, just as the Progressive Era reflected the con-
tinuing adventures of rough-and-ready entrepreneurs, financiers, and political
bosses on the one hand and aspiring workers and farmers on the other. Still,
there is justification for beginning with an emphasis on material transformations
and then moving to consider the political, social, and cultural adjustments that
Americans made to such changes. If we err in fastening a "Gilded Age" label to
the former constructions and a "Progressive Era" stamp to the latter topics,
readers should bear in mind that what we are ultimately witnessing in these
years is nothing less than the birth pangs of the world we yet inhabit.

E S S A Y S

In the first essay, writer-historian Sean Dennis Cashman sets the stage for a long
Gilded Age, which he defines as spanning "from the death of Lincoln to the rise of
Theodore Roosevelt." Cashman, like most historians, however, really has his eye on
the spirit of entrepreneurship and material acquisitiveness of the period. Indeed,
he compares late nineteenth-century public life to three other periods of relative
affluence and conservative politics: the 1920s, the post–World War II boom years,
and the 1970s and 1980s terms of office of Presidents Nixon and Reagan. In the

second essay, John Milton Cooper of the University of Wisconsin treats the first two decades of the twentieth century as a "turning point," effectively establishing an agenda "that still dominates American life" at the inauguration of a new century. Cooper's emphasis is on changing social relations and social conflicts—highlighted by racial and ethnic resentments, regional disparities in income, new roles for women, and the rise of a new popular culture shaped by mass media.

Industrial Spring: America in the Gilded Age

SEAN DENNIS CASHMAN

The assassin who ended the life of Abraham Lincoln extinguished the light of the Republic. On April 14, 1865, after the president argued in the cabinet for generous treatment of the South, vanquished in the war between the states, he went to the theater. It was Good Friday and there was a conspiracy afoot to kill him. During the third act of the play at Ford's Theatre in Washington, actor John Wilkes Booth, a fanatical partisan of the southern cause, stole into his box and shot him in the head at close range. Lincoln never regained consciousness and died early the next day. Until his death Lincoln had been a most controversial president—yet his secretary of war, Edwin Stanton, could justly claim, "Now he belongs to the ages." The transfiguration of the murdered president cast a long shadow over American history from 1865 to 1901. In political terms, the period that begins with the assassination of one president ends with the assassination of another, William McKinley, in 1901.

These were formative years. The Industrial Revolution and the development of commercial monopolies, Reconstruction and the New South, the settlement of the West and closing of the frontier—all brought to the fore of politics a cast of characters that was very different from the statesmen, soldiers, and slaves of the Civil War. This was the heyday of the robber barons. Perhaps the most damaging accusation against Lincoln after his assassination was that to win the war he had been ready to sacrifice the ideals of the Republican party to spoilsmen and profiteers. Progressive journalist Lincoln Steffens observed that in England politics was a sport, in Germany it was a profession, but in the United States it was a business— and a corrupt one at that. Yet, in the absence of strong executive leadership during a prolonged period of social, industrial, and economic growth, Lincoln's reputation soared ever higher. At the end of the century New England intellectuals criticized the cult of idolizing Lincoln in an anecdote about an American traveler to England who visited Oxford University. Confused by the architectural similarity between two of the colleges in Turl Street—Jesus and Lincoln—he exclaimed, "I can't tell the difference between Lincoln and Jesus!" A passing student remarked that it was the same with all Americans. The allusion and the confusion were understandable. Lincoln had, after all, saved the Union in war, whereas his successors came close to losing the peace.

————————
Sean Dennis Cashman, *America in the Gilded Age: From the Death of Lincoln to the Rise of Theodore Roosevelt,* 3d ed. (New York: New York University Press, 1984), 1–35. Reprinted by permission of New York University Press.

The West was settled at a fatal cost to Native Americans. The South was tied back to the Union at a humiliating cost to African-Americans. There were two depressions, in 1873 and 1893, each with devastating effects on the economy. The amazing industrial expansion of the United States was accomplished with considerable exploitation of factory artisans. The splendors of the new cities rose amid the squalor of industrial slums. The most damning indictment of this postwar American society was attributed to the future French prime minister Georges Clemenceau, who lived for a time in New York and New England. Noting its undoubted problems, he could claim the United States had gone from a stage of barbarism to one of decadence without achieving any civilization between the two.

Mark Twain paid a different but no less censorious tribute to the aspirations, autocracy, and affluence of the new American plutocracy of industrialists, financiers, and politicians in his utopian satire, *The Gilded Age* (1873). The title takes its cue from Shakespeare. King John is dissuaded from a second, superfluous coronation with the argument, "To gild refined gold, to paint the lily, /. . . Is wasteful and ridiculous excess." And Lady Macbeth implicates King Duncan's sleeping attendants in his murder by daubing them with blood from the dagger Macbeth has used to do the deed. "I'll gild the faces of the grooms withal," she says, "For it must seem their guilt." Mark Twain took this grotesque pun of gold and crime a stage further. His title was to become a triple pun. To gilt and guilt were added guilds in the sense of interest groups, labor unions, and monopolies. Twain's epithet, approved by his collaborator, Charles Dudley Warner, has survived as the most apt description of the period.

If the Gilded Age had a motto it might well have been, "The ayes have it," not only for the celebrated interest in voting stock, but also for the eyes that rejoiced in the glitter of gold, and the I's that define many of the pervasive social themes. Society was obsessed with invention, industrialization, incorporation, immigration, and, later, imperialism. It was indulgent of commercial speculation, social ostentation, and political prevarication but was indifferent to the special needs of immigrants and Indians and intolerant of African-Americans, labor unions, and political dissidents.

Whereas the Gilded Age had no predecessors, we may discern in three subsequent periods some of its features—notwithstanding the considerable differences between them. The first is the 1920s; the second, the period from 1945 to 1960; the third, the 1970s and 1980s. These were periods of predominantly (but not exclusively) Republican administrations. The government, as a whole, in each period was conservative. Accusations of nefarious links between politicians and businessmen and of widespread corruption in public life were rife. The presidency of Ulysses S. Grant in the 1870s is usually represented as a nadir of political probity. But the excesses of so-called carpetbaggers as well as of Congress and the administration in the 1870s pale in comparison with those of the Watergate burglars and White House staff during the presidency of Richard M. Nixon in the early 1970s. Yet the profligacy of the Ohio gang in the 1920s and the Republican chant of K^1C^2 (Korea, communism, and corruption) against the Democrats in 1952 have also remained a notorious part of the legend of the periodic corruption of public life in America.

Each period benefited from a boom in transportation—after 1865, the railroad; in the 1920s, the mass production of the automobile; from the late 1940s on, widespread commercial use of the airplane. Each enjoyed a revolution in communications—in the Gilded Age, telegraph and telephone; in the 1920s, motion pictures and radio; in the 1950s, long-playing vinyl phonograph records and television; in the 1980s, personal computers and compact discs. Innovations in transportation and communications together worked for a more homogeneous culture and a more informed citizenry, as well as having undisputed industrial and commercial significance in their own right.

Each period followed a war that left many Americans disillusioned, bitter, and confused: the Civil War, World War I, World War II, and the war in Vietnam. Their hostility to changed circumstances and the residue of hate engendered by the war but not yet expended partly account for the founding of the racist Ku Klux Klan after the Civil War and for its startling revival during the 1920s. This hostility was also vented against suspect ideologies. In the 1870s and 1880s labor unions were tainted by presumed association with anarchists, and the Haymarket anarchists of 1886 were tried without justice. The Great Red Scare of 1917–1921 against radicals expressed genuine if exaggerated anxiety about the dangers of a communist revolt, which was confirmed in the 1920s by the prejudicial treatment of the anarchists Sacco and Vanzetti. In 1950 Senator Joseph McCarthy lent his name to another wave of anticommunist hysteria that had been growing with the cold war.

The unsuccessful Second Indochina War of 1961–75 left bitter scars on American society. In their anguished protests against its conduct, liberals and radicals hurled accusations of indifference and injustice against the political establishment concerning its attitude toward African-Americans and other ethnic minorities, as well as toward women and the poor. The 1970s and 1980s also revealed society's recurrent obsession with intolerance and indulgence. In the 1970s the Republican party was tarnished by the burglary of the Democratic headquarters in the Watergate complex in 1972 and the stew of self-perpetuating politics by an oligarchy in the Nixon White House. Also tainted were such government agencies as the FBI and the CIA when congressional disclosures mounted about their illegal harassment of American citizens whose political views did not accord with those of the leadership of the two political parties. All this was most disturbing to a people reared in the belief that it was only the rulers of totalitarian regimes who prevented full freedom of expression. Moreover, allegations about overgenerous campaign contributions by big business to Republican coffers, sometimes laundered through Mexican banks, once again roused cries of anger about the overly close relationship between government and business.

In 1986 exposure of the Iran-Contra affair, in which the United States had supplied Iran with guns and munitions in exchange for the release of American hostages as well as for funds that were subsequently diverted to counterrevolutionaries in Nicaragua against the wishes of Congress—all arranged by Republican politicians and military personnel—once again suggested how insidious connections could develop between government, business, and military.

There was also considerable public anxiety expressed by revelations about insider trading on Wall Street, in an escapade in which Ivan Boesky became the principal culprit. A Wall Street crash in 1987 triggered a depression that had been incipient for many years, given the problems of American industry and manufacturing and the increasing debtor status of the United States. The depression deepened in the early 1990s. President George Bush's (1989–93) initial statements about the depression amounted to a doctrine of nonrecognition, and government remedial policies were nowhere in sight. It was like the restoration of an old-world picture of the Republicans as described in the 1930s by Herbert Hoover and in the 1890s by the nominally Democratic Grover Cleveland. The depression of the 1990s occurred in a period when the problems of acute social dislocation for the truly disadvantaged in the inner cities continued to upset liberal confidence in social progress. Meanwhile, the religious right, including southern ultraconservatives and fundamentalists, warned America about liberalism in religion and politics as a subversive threat to the very fabric of society.

In short, some political and cultural attitudes of the Gilded Age long survived the close of the nineteenth century when the period itself had ended.

Industrial Progress

. . . The commemorative Centennial Exhibition, which opened on the banks of the Schuylkill River outside Philadelphia for five months beginning on May 10, 1876, was conceived in a very different spirit from the celebrations for the bicentennial in 1976. Instead of political achievement, it emphasized America's mastery in the application of science. As such, it constituted an industrial revelation of America to the rest of the world.

Memorial Hall in Philadelphia was built in modern Renaissance style to exhibit American arts and culture. But nearby was Machinery Hall, a more austere yet more inviting building. It was guarded by a huge breech-loading cannon, the symbol of war, and by the Corliss steam engine. This enormous 1,400-horsepower machine, designed to furnish power to all the exhibits inside Machinery Hall astonished the 9,910,966 visitors that summer. It weighed nearly 1.7 million pounds and yet ran without vibration or noise. Here was a new symbol of peace and progress. Inside the hall inventions in the fields of agriculture, transportation, and machinery were given special prominence. By its display of drills, mowers, and reapers, of lumber wagons and Pullman sleeping cars, of sewing machines and typewriters, of planes, lathes, and looms, the United States demonstrated its preeminence in mechanics. As the *Times* of London reported on August 22, 1878, "the American mechanizes as an old Greek sculpted, as the Venetian painted." Novelist William Dean Howells gave his verdict to the *Atlantic Monthly* of July 1876. It was in engineering, rather than in art, that "the national genius most freely speaks: by and by the inspired marbles, the breathing canvases . . . [F]or the present America is voluble in the strong metals and their infinite uses. America's destiny lay in industrial development.

Between 1865 and 1901 the American Industrial Revolution transformed the United States from a country of small and isolated communities scattered across 3 million square miles of continental territory into a compact economic and industrial unit. Thus, the rural Republic of Lincoln and Lee became the industrial empire of Roosevelt and Bryan. The United States already had the prerequisites for such a transformation. It was fabulously rich in minerals, possessing about two-thirds of the world's coal; immense deposits of high-quality iron ore; great resources of petroleum; and, in the West, a natural treasury of gold, silver, and copper.

Although in 1860 the United States was still a second-rate industrial power, by 1890 it led Britain, France, and Germany. The value of its manufactured goods almost equaled the total of the others. The accompanying table, adapted from *Historical Statistics of the United States* (1975), shows increases in the production of raw materials between 1860 and 1900. It was precisely because the base of industry before the Civil War was so narrow that its advance seemed so spectacular later on.

There were five keys to America's astonishing industrial success: a superabundant supply of land and precious natural resources; excellent natural and manmade systems of transportation; a growing supply of labor caused by natural growth of population and massive immigration; special facility in invention and technology; and superb industrial organization. Thus what brought the American Industrial Revolution to fruition was human initiative, ingenuity, and physical energy.

The Agricultural Revolution hastened the Industrial Revolution in various ways. An increase in production per farmer allowed a transfer of labor from agriculture to industry without reducing the country's food supply. Moreover, such expanding agriculture did not need the transfer of limited capital from industry to agriculture. Indeed, the profits derived from agriculture could be used for buying manufactured goods, thereby further stimulating industry and manufacturing. There were two manufacturing belts across the nation. One stretched along the Atlantic coast from Maine in the North to Virginia in the South. The other was west of the Allegheny Mountains and north of the Ohio River, extending from Pittsburgh and Buffalo in the East to St. Louis and Milwaukee in the West.

From the middle of the century to the 1890s the railroads were the basis of the new industrial economy. They made possible the development of new areas of commerce as well as that of steel, iron, coal, and other industries. But in the 1890s it was the complex, varied urban market with its demand for a wider range of refined materials and manufactured goods that replaced the railroads as the principal stimulus of the economy as a whole. In the 1890s American cities were modernized, and steel was the essential medium used for building bridges, piping water and sewage, transmitting gas and electricity, and constructing ever higher buildings.

Iron replaced wood; steel replaced iron; and electricity and steam replaced horsepower. In 1870 agricultural production surpassed industrial production by about $500 million. Both were increasing year by year. But by 1900 manufacturing had increased by more than four times. Thus, industrial production now exceeded agricultural production by $13 billion to $4.7 billion. In every decade the levels of production increased in the oil refineries of Ohio and Pennsylvania; the iron and steel mills of Michigan, Illinois, and Pennsylvania; the meatpacking plants of Cincinnati and Chicago; the clothing and shoe factories of New England; and the breweries of Chicago, St. Louis, and Milwaukee. The number of people engaged in manufacturing was 2¼ times as great in 1890 as in 1870; in mining 2½ times as great; in transportation and public utilities 2½ times; in construction 2 times.

Industrial growth and westward expansion were assured by the revolution in transportation and the revolution in communications. There was a spectacular

Table   Industrial Production, 1860 and 1900

COMMODITY	1860 (MILLIONS)	1900 (MILLIONS)	INCREASE (%)
Anthracite coal (short tons)	10.9	57.3	525
Bituminous coal (short tons)	9.0	212.3	2,358
Crude Petroleum (barrels)	.5	45.8	9,160
Pig iron (long tons)	.8	13.7	1,713
Crude steel (short tons)	.01	11.2	11,227
Wheat (bushels)	173.1	599.0	339
Wheat exported (bushels)	4.0	102.0	2,550
Corn (bushels)	838.8	2,662.0	301
Cotton (bales)	3.8	10.1	261

growth in population, from 35,701,0000 in 1865 to 77,584,000 in 1901. Yet these widely dispersed people felt part of a unified whole. A transcontinental railroad network brought farm and factory, country and town closer together. Telegraph and telephone, electricity and press increased public knowledge, business efficiency, and political debate.

By their aptitude for invention and their ability to harness the inventions of others to their own purposes, Americans acquired a facility for turning raw materials into finished industrial products. Between 1860 and 1890 as many as 440,000 patents were issued for new inventions. During the Gilded Age the most significant American inventions, whether new or improved, were those that could hasten and secure *settlement:* the *s*team boilers of Babcock and Wilcox; the *e*lectric lamp of Thomas Alva Edison; the *t*elephone of Alexander Graham Bell; the *t*elegraph stock ticker of E. A. Callahan; *l*inoleum; the *e*levator of Elisha G. Otis; *m*achine tools of Pratt and Whitney; the *e*lixirs of John Wyeth; the *n*ewspaper linotype compositor of Ottmar Mergenthaler; and the *t*ypewriter of Christopher Shoes. The fundamental principles behind many of these and other inventions had long been understood. But not until technology could fashion tools of great delicacy could they be put into practice. Thus, the inventions depended on improved technology and they in turn transformed that technology, making possible ever more inventions of still greater refinement.

One reason why American technology in general became so advanced was the relatively high cost of labor in America that encouraged industrialists to invest in mechanizing. Moreover, the large domestic market allowed for great economies of scale. In addition, Americans in general were far less bound than Europeans by tradition and thus far more willing to try out new methods. Contemporary editor Mark Sullivan traces this facility to a natural ingenuity and determination in the people: "Intellectual freedom and curiosity about the new, the instinct of the American mind to look into, examine, and experiment—this led to, among other things, a willingness to 'scrap' not only old machinery but old formulas, old ideas; and brought about, among other results, the condition expressed in the saying that 'American mechanical progress could be measured by the size of its scrapheaps.'"

Pivotal Decades 1900–1920

JOHN MILTON COOPER, JR.

For the United States, the first two decades of the twentieth century marked a turning point. During these twenty years a political, economic, social and cultural agenda was set that still dominates American life as we enter the century's final decade. To begin to grasp the pivotal character of this era, one need only recall certain salient facts about the United States in 1900. The airplane had not yet been invented, nor had radio, much less television. Automobiles were few and expensive, and there were no paved roads. In the development of nuclear energy, only the most basic discoveries had occurred and only the first tentative theories were being advanced. In 1900, women could vote in only four states. Throughout the entire period, black Americans suffered segregation, discrimination, disenfranchisement, racist political demagoguery, and racial violence that nearly always went unpunished and often won applause from whites. The United States Army in 1900 numbered fewer than 100,000 officers and enlisted men (and, except for nurses, who held separate and lower ranks, no women). The United States Navy in 1900, though modern in equipment, ranked far behind the navies of Great Britain and Germany in size and firepower.

Two decades later, the airplane had proven itself as a weapon of war and was about to be launched as a means of civilian transportation. As "wireless telegraphy," radio had long since become a major medium of communication and was now transmitting the sound of the human voice, making it a potential medium of information and entertainment as well. Automobile manufacturing had mushroomed into one of the nation's biggest businesses, and over a million cars and trucks traveled thousands of miles of asphalt and concrete roads through cities, towns, and even the countryside. Discoveries in electromagnetism and radiation, and theoretical advances concerning the atomic system and relativity, were unlocking the basic secrets of matter and energy. By 1920, four new amendments had been added to the Constitution: one stipulating that United States senators be elected by popular vote; one authorizing the federal government to levy income taxes; one prohibiting the manufacture, sale, and consumption of alcoholic beverages; and one extending the vote to women throughout the nation. Black Americans still suffered from virulent discrimination, and racial violence temporarily escalated around 1920. At the same time, however, blacks and whites had formed civil rights organizations to fight racism, and they had embarked on what would be a long campaign of legal and constitutional challenges to segregation and disenfranchisement. By 1920 hundreds of thousands of blacks had left the South and resettled in Northern cities in a mass migration that would continue for years to come. The United States had just fought a major war in Europe, during which the army had swelled to over four million men (there were still no women except in the nursing corps). The navy was expanding to become the largest in the world.

John Milton Cooper, Jr., *Pivotal Decades: The United States, 1900-1920* (New York: W. W. Norton, 1990), xiii–xvi, 3–16. Copyright © 1990 by The John Cooper Trust and The Elizabeth Cooper Trust. Used by permission of W. W. Norton & Company, Inc.

Optimism was the dominant mood of Americans at the beginning and again at the end of these two decades, and progressivism came to be the banner appropriated by the period's many groups of political and social reformers. Yet between the peaks of optimism and within the calls for progressive reform, fear, social conflict, and hatred flourished as well. Progress in science and technology itself bred discontent. Religious Americans, especially conservative evangelical Protestants, bridled at the public rejection of their beliefs in the supernatural origins of life and the universe, and they fought back through a fundamentalist movement that not only amplified their beliefs but also sought to limit or prevent the teaching of non-religious scientific views. America's industrial development during this period brought with it the rise of economic behemoths, huge trusts that spread fears about the corruption of public life and the stifling of economic opportunity. The major domestic political issues of these decades came increasingly to revolve around how to control private economic power. Regulation and "trust-busting" became the main items on the political agenda at the federal, state, and municipal levels of government. Earlier debates over tariff rates and currency reform were now subsumed under the overriding public concern with the concentration of wealth.

Economic fears fed racial and ethnic resentments as this "nation of immigrants" attracted growing influxes of people from Europe and Asia, particularly to cities in the North and West. With industrial jobs attracting blacks to the North at the same time, many whites felt besieged by the newcomers. Mob violence and movements to pass laws restricting immigration from abroad flourished between 1900 and 1920, while the conflict over the prohibition of alcohol assumed aspects of a clash among ethnic cultures. The labor movement absorbed these tensions as well, with conservative unions seeking to shut off immigration and the more radical unions becoming embroiled in violence and embracing socialist politics.

Gender relations altered significantly in this period as women sought new opportunities in politics, the workplace, the local community, and the world of arts and culture. Some middle-class women, frequently those with advanced educations, not only agitated for women's interests on the vote and other public issues, but also fought for women's interests in the private realm by organizing a movement for birth control. Other middle-class women broke into new fields of employment, such as office and sales work, while poorer women took jobs in the mills of the South and the factories of the North. Women reformers were prominent in the prohibition movement with its roiling social and cultural crosscurrents.

This turbulence inevitably forced its way into the political arena, most markedly at the state and local levels. At the federal level, the United States Supreme Court continued in the role of activist arbiter of economic and social issues that it had assumed earlier and has not yet relinquished. Beyond that the Court began to grapple with fundamental questions of civil rights—involving racial discrimination—and civil liberties—involving freedom of speech—that have likewise persisted as major public concerns. The presidency became the overweening branch of the federal government in these decades through the influence of forceful incumbents such as Theodore Roosevelt and Woodrow Wilson, as well as through the growth of bureaucracy and the prominence of national security issues. The two major political parties fortified their clearly opposing stands on economic issues, and the more ambiguous, overlapping positions on social issues, that they had begun to take just before 1900 and that they have retained with remarkable consistency since 1920. On issues of international activism or isolation for the United States, the parties began during these years to take the respective opposing stands that would largely separate them until the 1940s. With intervention in World War I in 1917, the nation moved to the center of the international stage and ambivalently assumed a role of world leadership.

In all, this was a second golden age of American politics—second only to the generation of the founders of the American republic. Like that earlier golden age, this one sported great leaders, with Theodore Roosevelt and Woodrow Wilson the most prominent among a group that included Jane Addams, William Jennings Bryan, Eugene V. Debs, W. E. B. Du Bois, Oliver Wendell Holmes, Jr., Robert M. La Follette, Henry Cabot Lodge, Elihu Root, and William Howard Taft. This political golden age likewise featured great commentators and analysts of public questions, such as Louis Brandeis, Herbert Croly, Walter Lippmann, and John Reed. These figures debated great questions about the meaning of liberty and equality in this century, as well as the balance of public and private economic power, the extension of rights and opportunities to the excluded, the elements of a national culture, and the proper role for the United States in world affairs—all questions that are today subject to continued, if less forceful, debate. This age encompassed extraordinary events, from the building of the Panama Canal and the impassioned election of 1912, to the vast destruction of World War I and the tragedy of the peace that failed. In all, it exalted a standard of public life that later generations have rarely attained.

As vital as America's political culture during these decades was its popular culture, which took distinctive and lasting shape between 1900 and 1920. Major league professional sports, particularly baseball, produced new popular heroes, such as Ty Cobb and Babe Ruth. Motion pictures, even before the advent of sound, created "stars" in such men as Charlie Chaplin and Douglas Fairbanks and such women as Lillian Gish and Mary Pickford. Movies and radio—still embryonic—foreshadowed the long heyday of electronic "mass media." Mass journalism, already established in large-circulation newspapers, made a great leap ahead with the rise of poplar magazines in this era. These magazines established the first truly national medium of information and entertainment, and in their avid pursuit of critical exposure and analysis—dubbed "muckraking"—they fixed the canons of investigative reporting and set the posture of the press that have endured ever since. . . .

For most Americans in 1900, optimism ran rampant. The scientific and technological revolutions of the nineteenth century had begun to fulfill age-old dreams of human mastery over nature. Thanks to steam and internal combustion engines, sea transportation had grown much less subject to wind and wave, while river traffic could defy the currents. Even more spectacularly, the railroad had transformed land travel. For the first time in history, people and goods could move more swiftly and easily over land than over water. More amazingly still, through applications of electricity to communications, the telegraph could transmit information faster than a person could carry it, and during the previous twenty-five years, the telephone had projected voices virtually instantaneously over any distance. Horizons often seemed unlimited in 1900 because—compared with all previous human experience—they were.

But some Americans' horizons extended much further than others'. Technology gave nearly everybody access to better and cheaper products, but rich Americans benefited much more from this bounty. In cities, prosperous businesses and wealthier homes received electricity, but gas remained the main source of energy for home appliances and street lighting until after 1910. In the countryside, two thirds of farm families would not get either electricity or indoor plumbing until the late 1930s. There were 1,356 telephones in 1900, but only government and business establishments and the residences of the rich had them. The United States counted 8,000 automobiles in 1900, all of them costly curiosity pieces at a time when less than one mile of smooth paved road existed in the country.

The horizons of many Americans were further limited by the uneven distribution of political and social benefits in the United States. Not all of its citizens shared equally in the heritage of American democracy. In theory, the right to vote belonged to slightly less than half the adult population; in practice, it belonged to fewer than that. Over 95 percent of American women could not vote. Only four sparsely populated western states—Wyoming, Idaho, Colorado, and Utah—had extended the franchise to both sexes. The Fifteenth Amendment to the Constitution legally barred racial discrimination in voting, but only a small fraction of adult black males actually voted. Whites, who controlled state governments in the South, where 90 percent of blacks lived in 1900, had barred them from the ballot box through poll taxes, limitations on registration, and literacy tests. Whether by accident or design, those restrictions took the vote away from large numbers of poor southern white males as well. Newly arrived immigrants faced naturalization and registration restrictions, while non-English speaking newcomers suffered from both the language barrier and their unfamiliarity with democratic participation in government. The United States boasted of being the "land of the free," but some Americans enjoyed more freedoms than the majority of their compatriots.

The distribution of resources was uneven not only among the nation's citizens, but among its regions as well. Economically, America was not one country, but three. Less than one-sixth of the continental land area, the regions north of the Potomac and Ohio Rivers and east of the Mississippi, contained 45 percent of the population. This area—the Northeast and Midwest—held an even larger share of the cities and towns, money and banking institutions, schools and libraries, offices and commercial concerns, and factories and railroads. These two regions formed the nation's industrial, financial, and cultural heartland.

The remaining five-sixths of the country was divided into two outlying regions, each culturally and economically dependent on the heartland. The older, less extensive of these sections was the South, which had not overcome the legacy of its defeat in the Civil War thirty-five years before. White Southerners had sustained huge financial losses from widespread battlefield destruction and from uncompensated emancipation of their slaves. Those losses had combined with the retarding effects of cash-crop agriculture to leave the South the least urban, the least industrial, and thereby the poorest region of the country in 1900.

The other outlying section was the West. Although the West sprawled over more than half the continental United States, most of the region struggled with the burdens of sparse population, rugged terrain, and arid climate. Its economy suffered from dependence on quasi-nomadic grazing, agriculture, and the ever-chancy extraction of raw materials for industry. Cowboys made colorful figures for popular literature, but cattle and sheep ranching required vast spreads to produce even modest profits. Miners and lumberjacks also inspired romantic legends, but their work was dangerous, poorly paid, and sporadic. Ranching, lumbering, and mining all failed to foster population growth, high-wage and high-skill jobs, and substantial investment—the necessary conditions for economic development. Only a few parts of the West provided exceptions to this pattern of economic retardation. Ambitious publicly and privately funded irrigation projects transformed extensive areas of California into fertile farmland. Cities such as Los Angeles and San Francisco began to grow too, generating wealth and denser settlement, but California's dependence on scarce water supplies created special problems. Already in 1900, movements had arisen for "conservation" of natural resources and had clashed with westerners who wanted wide-open exploitation of land, timber, minerals, and water.

The comparative poverty and lagging development of the South and West, as compared with the heartland, had already bound these regions in a political alliance in the 1896 presidential election. Together, the South and West had rallied behind two measures—monetary inflation through the coinage of silver and lowered tariffs on industrial products—which they believed would relieve their economic distresses. These two regions had likewise rallied behind both William Jennings Bryan and the Democrats, the champions of those causes. By contrast, the Northeast and Midwest in 1896 had lined up even more solidly behind monetary deflation through a single gold standard, and a protective tariff on industrial products, which they believed would maintain their economic prosperity. The heartland regions had joined to support William McKinley and the Republicans who had passionately espoused those causes. The same issues, candidates, and regional alignments would shape the 1900 presidential election.

Race and ethnicity also contributed to these regional differences. The nine million former slaves and their descendants who lived in the South constituted the bottom rung of society there in every way. They were the poorest in the region: black per-capita income was variously estimated at between a quarter and third of that of whites in the South. They were the least educated: the black illiteracy rate in 1900 stood at 48 percent in the South as a whole, and over 50 percent in the four states of Louisiana, Alabama, South Carolina, and Georgia. Many white Southerners did not fare a great deal better. Southern whites' income averaged around half the national per-capita figure. Their illiteracy rate was over 11 percent, more than double the nationwide rate for native-born whites. New immigrants also occupied low rungs on the social and economic ladder. Because most of them settled in the Northeast and Midwest, they could often get factory work, but their lack of skills and unfamiliarity with English forced them to take the lowest-paying jobs. Because schools were scarce in the parts of Europe from which more and more immigrants were coming in 1900, large numbers were badly educated. Of all the foreign born, nearly 13 percent were illiterate in 1900.

Racial, regional, and ethnic disparities were not new to the United States in 1900, but a heightened sense of alarm about them was novel. Earlier, the nation's least settled areas had provided, in belief if not necessarily in fact, a "safety valve" for social discontent in the older, more densely populated areas. The existence of the frontier was supposed to relieve America of the overcrowding, scarcity, and inequality that plagued Europe. But in 1890 the Census Bureau had declared the frontier "closed." Parts of the South and nearly all the West remained underpopulated, but the great tracts of unoccupied public lands previously marked on the maps by the frontier line no longer existed. That news had immediately aroused fears that something distinct and precious in American life had been lost. Scholars and writers mourned the closing of the frontier by arguing that the availability of vast expanses of open land and pioneering opportunities had been essential to the development of political democracy and individual self-reliance. The need to reclaim an adventurous heritage in the face of new industrial conditions formed the link between domestic concerns and foreign policy issues for political leaders. For many of them, America's greatest need was a new frontier, which they meant in the most literal way.

Nothing aroused more ambivalent attitudes in Americans in 1900 than the cities, especially such metropolises as New York and Chicago. For some, they held out promises of opportunity, glamor, and excitement. Young middle-class men and women from farms, small towns, and the outlying regions were flocking to the cities in pursuit of ambitions to become doctors, lawyers, teachers, journalists, and businessmen. Enough of them had found success to add a new wrinkle to traditional American beliefs in the self-made man and, more recently, woman. The highest-paid corporation lawyer of the 1890s, Elihu Root, was the son of a professor at Hamilton College in upstate New York. The most successful magazine editor of the late 1890s and early 1900s, Samuel Sidney ("S.S.") McClure, had grown up as a fatherless immigrant boy from Northern Ireland on small farms in Indiana and Illinois. The pioneering social worker, Jane Addams, hailed from a medium-sized Illinois town, where her father had been a moderately prominent lawyer.

Yet cities also stirred apprehension. They appeared to threaten the established way of life of Protestant middle-class groups from both below and above. The threat from below lay in the mounting influx of immigrants, particularly from southern and eastern Europe. In 1900, the foreign born in America numbered about eleven million, or 14 percent of the total population. It was the highest proportion of immigrants to "natives" since the 1850s. The newcomers were arriving as part of a massive overseas dispersal of surplus population from all over Europe. They came from many different backgrounds. Some were wealthy and well-educated. Many were Protestants from Britain, the original source of the nation's white population. Large numbers of Germans and Scandinavians went to rural areas, particularly in the upper Midwest and on the Great Plains, where they either bought established farms, worked as agricultural laborers, or brought new land under cultivation as "sodbusters." Increasingly, however, the immigrants settled in the cities of the Northeast and Midwest, in distinct neighborhoods with saloons, stores, and restaurants that catered to their old-country tastes, and with clubs and churches that spoke their own languages. Their exotic languages, unfamiliar customs, different religions, and evidently darker complexions, bred uneasiness in the native white middle class about the country's changing social character.

At first the only institutions that welcomed the immigrants or tried to ease their adjustment to a new culture and environment were the city political machines. In the eyes of many white Protestants, immigrant voting therefore seemed to heighten the nefarious influences of those reputedly corrupt, undemocratic organizations. In the early 1890s organizations were formed to agitate for the restriction of European immigration, just as Asian immigration had been largely shut off in 1881. The restrictionists favored requiring adult immigrants to pass literacy tests in their native language. The intended result of such tests would be to bar the new immigrants from southern and eastern Europe, and admit the predominantly Protestant Nordics from Germany, Scandinavia, and the British Isles. Similarly, the long-standing crusade against alcoholic beverages, allied with certain Protestant churches, was assuming an increasingly anti-immigrant slant. Prohibitionists now denounced saloons and beer halls as threats to morality and arms of corrupt city political machines.

If the alien and debased urban masses seemed menacing to middle-class white Protestants, so did the relatively few at the opposite end of the social and economic spectrum. Ever since the advent of the industrial revolution in the 1820s and 1830s, some observers had voiced misgivings about the resulting vast accumulations of private wealth and their consequences for political freedom and for equality of economic opportunity. Particularly haunting for many Americans was the specter of European society with its entrenched privileges and degraded commoners. Warnings against monopoly and the inordinate influence of wealth had been heard as early as the 1830s, and they had grown more insistent with the nation's fantastic economic growth since the Civil War. The underlying fears had found a classic statement in Henry George's widely read book, *Progress and Poverty,* published in 1879. Despite the "prodigious increase in wealth-producing power," George had declared, ". . . it becomes no easier for the masses of our people to make a living. On the contrary, it is becoming harder. The gulf between the employed and employer is becoming wider; social contrasts are becoming sharper, as liveried carriages appear, so do barefooted children." . . .

Popular fears focused not just on impersonal organizations but on flesh-and-blood tycoons. Some of these tycoons had risen to dominance in manufacturing. They included the puckish, philanthropic, Scottish-born steelmaker, Andrew Carnegie, who had forseen the huge demand for steel to build railroads and cities and had become the largest producer in the industry. When Carnegie sold out to U.S. Steel in 1901—at an outrageously inflated price, critics charged—his profit was over $300 million. The most notable tycoon to arise in manufacturing was the man who singlehandedly ruled an entire industry, the devoutly religious but ruthlessly domineering petroleum magnate, John D. Rockefeller. In the early 1900s, Rockefeller reportedly became the first American to amass a personal fortune worth $1 billion.

The chief initiative for business consolidation sprang, however, not from the manufacturers themselves but from the financiers who sought to eliminate wasteful competition and impose order on the marketplace. The greatest financier and prime mover behind the trusts after 1897 was the New York investment banker, J. Pierpont Morgan. A masterful and coldly rational man, Morgan set out to organize and control virtually every basic American industry, and by the early 1900s, he had largely succeeded. He controlled U.S. Steel, held sway over more than half the nation's railroad trackage, and dominated the electrical, merchant marine, farm machinery, and insurance fields as well. In 1912 a congressional investigating committee found that Morgan and his partners controlled $22 billion in capital, which made them the largest single factor in American economy, not excepting the United States government.

Even the source of all the fantastic technological and industrial progress—scientific discovery—created ambivalence in Americans. In no previous period of human history had science more dramatically unlocked great secrets of the natural world, in physics, chemistry, geology, and biology, than during the nineteenth century. Americans had not led in those scientific advances. The birth of modern biology, chemistry, and physics owed most to the discoveries and theories of Britons, Frenchmen, and increasingly Germans. Not until the third and fourth decades of the twentieth century would American laboratories and universities harbor great contributors to basic science. But Americans unquestionably led the world in technological innovation—the applications of these new discoveries to industry and to everyday life. The Ohio-born, self-taught inventor, Thomas Alva Edison, had made his name synonymous with electrical wizardry, while the Scottish immigrant, Alexander Graham Bell, had developed the telephone. Henry Ford, the Michigan mechanic-turned-manufacturer, had begun, even before 1900, to lay the groundwork for mass production of automobiles, and in December 1903, a pair of brothers who were bicycled mechanics from Dayton, Ohio, Orville and Wilbur Wright, would construct and fly the first heavier-than-air flying machine at Kitty Hawk, North Carolina.

Thrilling as these advances were, they had profoundly unsettling implications. Protestant and Catholic clergymen alike denounced materialism, by which they meant non-spiritual explanations of life and natural phenomena, and decried the growth of religious skepticism—to little apparent effect. Skepticism about religion was not new to the United States in 1900, but materialistic explanations of the natural world had understandably grown in popularity in the late nineteenth century because science and technology could explain and control so much in the world. It had also become fashionable to apply the objectivism of science to art and literature through realism and naturalism, which affected to remove spiritual and morally refined elements in favor of the re-creation of "real life." . . .

Society and politics were likewise subjected to "scientific" studies that purported to yield hard, predictable explanations that stressed the effects of physical and economic forces. These efforts had begun as early as the 1870s with the English sociologist Herbert Spencer's application of concepts borrowed from the sciences—especially his reading of Charles Darwin's theories of biological evolution—to human behavior and institutions. Spencer argued that human society had evolved through the same processes as biological species—through a "struggle for existence" characterized by "survival of the fittest." In the higher stages of this evolution, Spencer believed, governmental controls had given way to unfettered economic competition, which ensured progress through the triumph of the strongest, or "fittest," competitors. Spencer's writings enjoyed a great vogue in the United States, thanks in part to the patronage of Andrew Carnegie. . . .

Scientific approaches to public life, especially Spencer's Social Darwinism, aroused Protestant clergymen in particular to reassert spiritual values. The most significant religious strife lay in the relation between science and the Bible. The major Protestant denominations were already reeling from repeated controversies over the extension of Darwin's theories of evolution to the origin of the human species. These tensions set the stage for a cultural and religious conflict that would last through the first quarter of the twentieth century and beyond.

FURTHER READING

H. W. Brands, *The Reckless Decade: America in the 1890s* (1995)
Charles W. Calhoun, *The Gilded Age* (1996)
Alan Dawley, *Struggles for Justice: Social Responsibility and the Liberal State* (1991)
Vincent P. DeSantis, *The Shaping of Modern America, 1877–1920* (1989)
Sara Evans, *Born for Liberty: A History of Women in America* (1989)
Ray Ginger, *Age of Excess* (1965)
Lewis L. Gould, *The Progressive Era* (1974)
Samuel Hays, *The Response to Industrialism, 1885–1914* (1957)
Richard Hofstadter, *The Age of Reform* (1955)
H. Wayne Morgan, ed., *The Gilded Age* (1970)
Nell Irwin Painter, *Standing at Armageddon: The United States, 1877–1919* (1987)
Mark W. Summers, *The Gilded Age, or the Hazard of New Functions* (1991)
Vincent Tompkins, ed., *American Decades: 1910–1919* (1996)
Alan Trachtenberg, *The Incorporation of America* (1982)
Robert H. Wiebe, *The Search for Order, 1877–1920* (1967)
————, *Self-Rule: A Cultural History of American Democracy* (1995)

CHAPTER

2

The Price of Progress:

Capitalism and Its Discontents

In the late-nineteenth century, American capitalism was more than a means for the production and distribution of goods and services. It was also a system of meanings, imparting purpose and justification to the manifold physical and social disruptions wrought by economic development in a comparatively free, or unregulated, market-place. In place of the economic independence and rough equality widespread among farmers and artisans in the early republic, industrialization—the application of machine processes, fueled by outside power sources, to production—promoted new virtues even as it threatened older ones. Industrialists and their apostles defended capitalism's new order on grounds of natural law, scientific progress, and the expansion of individual economic opportunity. Critics argued that the instruments of technological progress, left in the hands of a relative few, were being used to stifle rather than liberate the potential of a democratic citizenry.

 D O C U M E N T S

As the opening passages of the first two selections suggest, contemporaries sharply disagreed about the gain versus the pain of an industrial, corporate capitalist social order. In Document 1, steel baron Andrew Carnegie marvels at the astounding success of American civilization. Carnegie stresses free labor, public education, and the advantages of British racial stock as key sources of America's Great Leap Forward. What most strikes Henry George, on the other hand, is that "the 'tramp' comes with the locomotive." Document 2 is excerpted from George's introduction to *Progress and Poverty,* one of the nineteenth century's most influential works of social and economic criticism. In this passage, George, a labor reformer whose distinctive nostrum is the "single tax" on unimproved land, promises to get to the root of capitalism's paradox.

The remaining documents present equally vivid contrasts. Amidst the outpouring of self-help literature, the Reverend Alexander Lewis's poem (Document 3) suggests a broad popular and even religious sanction for the ethics of the marketplace. But Mark Twain's acerbic satire (Document 4) of the success ideology reflected in the Reverend Lewis's rhyme and the contemporary stories of Horatio Alger, reveals not only contemporary ambivalence but open conflict about the nation's proper goals and values. The attempt to make "moral worth," not wealth, the measure of worldly success was the transcendent aim of the Noble and Holy Order of the Knights of Labor, as is revealed in its constitutional preamble (Document 5). Part trade union, part political movement, and part fraternal order (but with a nearly universal membership that included women and blacks), the Knights articulated broad aims that contrasted with the subsequent emphasis by the trade unions affiliated with the American Federation of Labor, which concentrated on the defense of skilled, male jobs only (Document 6).

1. Andrew Carnegie Hails the Triumph of America, 1885

The old nations of the earth creep on at a snail's pace; the Republic thunders past with the rush of the express. The United States, the growth of a single century, has already reached the foremost rank among nations, and is destined soon to outdistance all others in the race. In population, in wealth, in annual savings, and in public credit; in freedom from debt, in agriculture, and in manufactures, America already leads the civilized world. . . .

Into the distant future of this giant nation we need not seek to peer; but if we cast a glance forward, as we have done backward, for only fifty years, and assume that in that short interval no serious change will occur, the astounding fact startles us that in 1935, fifty years from now, when many in manhood will still be living, one hundred and eighty millions of English-speaking republicans will exist under one flag and possess more than two hundred and fifty thousand millions of dollars, or fifty thousand millions sterling of national wealth. Eighty years ago the whole of America and Europe did not contain so many people; and, if Europe and America continue their normal growth, it will be little more than another eighty years ere the mighty Republic may boast as many loyal citizens as all the rulers of Europe combined, for before the year 1980 Europe and America will each have a population of about six hundred millions.

The causes which have led to the rapid growth and aggrandizement of this latest addition to the family of nations constitute one of the most interesting problems in the social history of mankind. What has brought about such stupendous results—so unparalleled a development of a nation within so brief a period! The most important factors in this problem are three: the ethnic character of the people, the topographical and climatic conditions under which they developed, and the influence of political institutions founded upon the equality of the citizen.

Certain writers in the past have maintained that the ethnic type of a people has less influence upon its growth as a nation than the conditions of life under which it is developing. The modern ethnologist knows better. We have only to imagine what America would be to-day if she had fallen in the beginning, into the hands of any other people than the colonizing British, to see how vitally important is this question of race. America was indeed fortunate in the seed planted upon her soil. With the exception of a few Dutch and French it was wholly British; and . . . the American of to-day remains true to this noble strain and is four-fifths British.

Andrew Carnegie, "The Upward March of Labor," in *Problems of Today: Wealth, Labor, Socialism* (Garden City, N.J.: Doubleday, 1933 [1908]), 43–46.

The special aptitude of this race for colonization, its vigor and enterprise, and its capacity for governing, although brilliantly manifested in all parts of the world, have never been shown to such advantage as in America. Freed here from the pressure of feudal institutions no longer fitted to their present development, and freed also from the dominion of the upper classes, which have kept the people at home from effective management of affairs and sacrificed the nation's interest for their own, as is the nature of classes, these masses of the lower ranks of Britons, called upon to found a new state, have proved themselves possessors of a positive genius for political administration.

The second, and perhaps equally important factor in the problem of the rapid advancement of this branch of the British race, is the superiority of the conditions under which it has developed. The home which has fallen to its lot, a domain more magnificent than has cradled any other race in the history of the world, presents no obstructions to unity to the thorough amalgamation of its dwellers, North, South, East, and West, into one homogeneous mass—for the conformation of the American continent differs in important respects from that of every other great division of the globe. In Europe the Alps occupy a central position, forming on each side watersheds of rivers which flow into opposite seas. In Asia the Himalaya, the Hindu Kush, and the Altai Mountains divide the continent, rolling from their sides many great rivers which pour their floods into widely separated oceans. But in North America the mountains rise up on each coast, and from them the land slopes gradually into great central plains, forming an immense basin where the rivers flow together in one valley, offering to commerce many thousand miles of navigable streams. The map thus proclaims the unity of North America, for in this great central basin, three million square miles in extent, free from impassable rivers or mountain barriers great enough to hinder free intercourse, political integration is a necessity and consolidation a certainty. . . .

The unity of the American people is further powerfully promoted by the foundation upon which the political structure rests, the equality of the citizen. There is not one shred of privilege to be met with anywhere in all the laws. One man's right is every man's right. The flag is the guarantor and symbol of equality. The people are not emasculated by being made to feel that their own country decrees their inferiority, and holds them unworthy of privileges accorded to others. No ranks, no titles, no hereditary dignities, and therefore no classes. Suffrage is universal, and votes are of equal weight. Representatives are paid, and political life and usefulness thereby thrown open to all. Thus there is brought about a community of interests and aims which a Briton, accustomed to monarchical and aristocratic institutions, dividing the people into classes with separate interests, aims, thoughts, and feelings, can only with difficulty understand.

The free common school system of the land is probably, after all, the greatest single power in the unifying process which is producing the new American race. Through the crucible of a good common English education, furnished free by the State, pass the various racial elements—children of Irishmen, Germans, Italians, Spaniards, and Swedes, side by side with the native American, all to be fused into one, in language, in thought, in feeling, and in patriotism. The Irish boy loses his brogue, and the German child learns English. The sympathies suited to the feudal systems of Europe, which they inherit from their fathers, pass off as dross, leaving behind the pure gold of the only noble political creed: "All men are created free and equal." Taught now to live and work for the common weal, and not for the maintenance of a royal family or an overbearing aristocracy, not for the continuance of a social system which ranks them beneath an arrogant class of drones, children of Russian and German serfs, of Irish evicted tenants, Scotch crofters, and other victims of feudal tyranny, are transmuted into republican Americans, and are made one in love for a country which provides equal rights and privileges for all her children. There is no class so intensely patriotic, so wildly devoted to the Republic as the naturalized citizen and his child, for little does the native-born citizen know of the values of rights which have never been denied. Only the man born abroad, like myself, under institutions which insult him at his birth, can know the full meaning of Republicanism. . . .

It is these causes which render possible the growth of a great homogeneous nation, alike in race, language, literature, interest, patriotism—an empire of such overwhelming power and proportions as to require neither army nor navy to ensure its safety, and a people so educated and advanced as to value the victories of peace.

The student of American affairs to-day sees no influences at work save those which make for closer and closer union. The Republic has solved the problem of governing large areas by adopting the federal, or home-rule system, and has proved to the world that the freest self-government of the parts produces the strongest government of the whole.

2. Henry George Dissects the Paradox of Capitalist Growth, 1879

The present century has been marked by a prodigious increase in wealth-producing power. The utilization of steam and electricity, the introduction of improved processes and labor-saving machinery, the greater subdivision and grander scale of production, the wonderful facilitation of exchanges, have multiplied enormously the effectiveness of labor.

At the beginning of this marvelous era it was natural to expect, and it was expected, that labor-saving inventions would lighten the toil and improve the condition of the laborer; that the enormous increase in the power of producing wealth would make real poverty a thing of the past. Could a man of the last century—a Franklin or a Priestley—have seen, in a vision of the future, the steamship taking the place of the sailing vessel, the railroad train of the wagon, the reaping machine of the scythe, the threshing machine of the flail; could he have heard the throb of the engines that in obedience to human will, and for the satisfaction of human desire, exert a power greater than that of all the men and all the beasts of burden of the earth combined; could he have seen the forest tree transformed into finished lumber—into doors, sashes, blinds, boxes or barrels, with hardly the touch of a human hand; the great workshops where boots and shoes are turned out by the case with less labor than the old-fashioned cobbler could have put on a sole; the factories where, under the eye of a girl, cotton becomes cloth faster than hundreds of

Henry George, *Progress and Poverty* in *Works,* Vol. I (New York: Doubleday, 1904), 3–8, 10–13.

stalwart weavers could have turned it out with their handlooms; could he have seen steam hammers shaping mammoth shafts and mighty anchors, and delicate machinery making tiny watches; the diamond drill cutting through the heart of the rocks, and coal oil sparing the whale; could he have realized the enormous saving of labor resulting from improved facilities of exchange and communication— sheep killed in Australia eaten fresh in England, and the order given by the London banker in the afternoon executed in San Francisco in the morning of the same day; could he have conceived of the hundred thousand improvements which these only suggest, what would he have inferred as to the social condition of mankind? . . .

. . . Out of these bounteous material conditions he would have seen arising, as necessary sequences, moral conditions realizing the golden age of which mankind has always dreamed. Youth no longer stunted and starved; age no longer harried by avarice; the child at play with the tiger; the man with the muck-rake drinking in the glory of the stars. Foul things fled, fierce things tame; discord turned to harmony! For how could there be greed where all had enough? How could the vice, the crime, the ignorance, the brutality, that spring from poverty and the fear of poverty, exist where poverty had vanished? Who should crouch where all were freemen; who oppress where all were peers? . . .

Now, however, we are coming into collision with facts which there can be no mistaking. From all parts of the civilized world come complaints of industrial depression; of labor condemned to involuntary idleness; of capital massed and wasting; of pecuniary distress among business men; of want and suffering and anxiety among the working classes. All the dull, deadening pain, all the keen, maddening anguish, that to great masses of men are involved in the words "hard times," afflict the world to-day. This state of things, common to communities differing so widely in situation, in political institutions, in fiscal and financial systems, in density of population and in social organization, can hardly be accounted for by local causes. . . .

That there is a common cause, and that it is either what we call material progress or something closely connected with material progress, becomes more than an inference when it is noted that the phenomena we class together and speak of as industrial depression are but intensifications of phenomena which always accompany material progress, and which show themselves more clearly and strongly as material progress goes on.

Just as . . . a community realizes the conditions which all civilized communities are striving for, and advances in the scale of material progress—just as closer settlement and a more intimate connection with the rest of the world, and greater utilization of labor-saving machinery, make possible greater economies in production and exchange, and wealth in consequence increases, not merely in the aggregate, but in proportion to population—so does poverty take a darker aspect. Some get an infinitely better and easier living, but others find it hard to get a living at all. The "tramp" comes with the locomotive, and almshouses and prisons are as surely the marks of "material progress" as are costly dwellings, rich warehouses, and magnificent churches. Upon streets lighted with gas and patrolled by uniformed policemen, beggars wait for the passer-by, and in the shadow of college, and library, and museum, are gathering the more hideous Huns and fiercer Vandals of whom Macaulay prophesied.

This fact—the great fact that poverty and all its concomitants show themselves in communities just as they develop into the conditions toward which material progress tends—proves that the social difficulties existing wherever a certain stage of progress has been reached, do not arise from local circumstances, but are, in some way or another, engendered by progress itself.

And, unpleasant as it may be to admit it, it is at last becoming evident that the enormous increase in productive power which has marked the present century and is still going on with accelerating ratio, has no tendency to extirpate poverty or to lighten the burdens of those compelled to toil. It simply widens the gulf between Dives and Lazarus, and makes the struggle for existence more intense. The march of invention has clothed mankind with powers of which a century ago the boldest imagination could not have dreamed. But in factories where labor-saving machinery has reached its most wonderful development, little children are at work; wherever the new forces are anything like fully utilized, large classes are maintained by charity or live on the verge of recourse to it; amid the greatest accumulations of wealth, men die of starvation, and puny infants suckle dry breasts; while everywhere the greed of gain, the worship of wealth, shows the force of the fear of want. The promised land flies before us like the mirage. The fruits of the tree of knowledge turn as we grasp them to apples of Sodom that crumble at the touch.

It is true that wealth has been greatly increased, and that the average of comfort, leisure, and refinement has been raised; but these gains are not general. In them the lowest class do not share. I do not mean that the condition of the lowest class has nowhere nor in anything been improved; but that there is nowhere any improvement which can be credited to increase productive power. I mean that the tendency of what we call material progress is in nowise to improve the condition of the lowest class in the essentials of healthy, happy human life. Nay, more, that it is still further to depress the condition of the lowest class. The new forces, elevating in their nature though they be, do not act upon the social fabric from underneath, as was for a long time hoped and believed, but strike it at a point intermediate between top and bottom. It is as though an immense wedge were being forced, not underneath society, but through society. Those who are above the point of separation are elevated, but those who are below are crushed down. . . .

This association of poverty with progress is the great enigma of our times. It is the central fact from which spring industrial, social, and political difficulties that perplex the world, and with which statesmanship and philanthropy and education grapple in vain. From it come the clouds that overhand the future of the most progressive and self-reliant nations. It is the riddle which the Sphinx of Fate puts to our civilization, and which not to answer is to be destroyed. So long as all the increased wealth which modern progress brings goes but to build up great fortunes, to increase luxury and make sharper the contrast between the House of Have and the House of Want, progress is not real and cannot be permanent. The reaction must come. The tower leans from its foundations, and every new story but hastens the final catastrophe. To educate men who must be condemned to poverty, is but to make them restive; to base on a state of most glaring social inequality political institutions under which men are theoretically equal, is to stand a pyramid on its apex.

3. The Reverend Alexander Lewis Offers an Ode to Upward Mobility, 1902

There is always a way to rise, my boy,
Always a way to advance;
Yet the road that leads to Mount Success
Does not pass by the way of Chance,
But goes through the stations of Work and
    Strive,
through the valley of Persevere;
And the man that succeeds while others fail,
Must be willing to pay most dear.

For there's always a way to fall my boy,
Always a way to slide,
And the men you find at the foot of the hill
All sought for an easy ride.
So on and up, though the road be rough,
And the storms come thick and fast;
There is room at the top for the man who tries,
And victory comes at last.

4. Mark Twain Satirizes the Great American Myth, 1879

Poor Little Stephen Girard

The man lived in Philadelphia who, when young and poor, entered a bank, and says he: "Please, sir, don't you want a boy?" And the stately personage said: "No, little boy, I don't want a little boy." The little boy, whose heart was too full for utterance, chewing a piece of licorice stick he had bought with a cent stolen from his good and pious aunt, with sobs plainly audible, and with great globules of water rolling down his cheeks, glided silently down the marble steps of the bank. Bending his noble form, the bank man dodged behind a door, for he thought the little boy was going to shy a stone at him. But the little boy picked up something, and stuck it in his poor but ragged jacket. "Come here, little boy," and the little boy did come here; and the bank man said: "Lo, what pickest thou up?" And he answered and replied: "A pin." And the bank man said: "Little boy, are you good?" and he said he was. And the bank man said: "How do you vote?—excuse me, do you go to Sunday school?" and he said he did. Then the bank man took down a pen made of pure gold, and flowing with pure ink, and he wrote on a piece of paper, "St. Peter;" and he asked the little boy what it stood for, and he said "Salt Peter," Then the bank man said it meant "Saint Peter." The little boy said; "Oh!"

Reverend Alexander Lewis, *Manhood Making, Studies in the Elemental Principles of Success* (Boston: Pilgrim Press, 1902).

Mark Twain, "Poor Little Stephen Girard," in Anna Randall-Diehl, ed., *Carleton's Popular Readings* (New York, 1879), 183–184.

Then the bank man took the little boy to his bosom, and the little boy said, "Oh!" again, for he squeezed him. Then the bank man took the little boy into partnership, and gave him half the profits and all the capital, and he married the bank man's daughter, and now all he has is all his, and all his own too.

My uncle told me this story, and I spent six weeks in picking up pins in front of a bank. I expected the bank man would call me in and say: "Little boy, are you good?" and I was going to say "Yes"; and when he asked me what "St. John" stood for, I was going to say "Salt John." But the bank man wasn't anxious to have a partner, and I guess the daughter was a son, for one day says he to me: "Little boy, what's that you're picking up?" Says I, awful meekly, "Pins." Says he: "Let's see 'em." And he took 'em, and I took off my cap, all ready to go in the bank, and become a partner, and marry his daughter. But I didn't get an invitation. He said: "Those pins belong to the bank, and if I catch you hanging around here any more I'll set the dog on you!" Then I left, and the mean old fellow kept the pins. Such is life as I find it.

5. The Purposes and Program of the Knights of Labor, 1878

The recent alarming development and aggression of aggregated wealth, which, unless checked, will inevitably lead to the pauperization and hopeless degradation of the toiling masses, render it imperative, if we desire to enjoy the blessings of life, that a check should be placed upon its power and upon unjust accumulation, and a system adopted which will secure to the laborer the fruits of his toil; and as this much-desired object can only be accomplished by the thorough unification of labor, and the united efforts of those who obey the divine injunction that "in the sweat of thy brow shalt thou eat bread," we have formed the [*name of local assembly*] with a view to securing the organization and direction, by co-operative effort, of the power of the industrial classes; and we submit to the world the objects sought to be accomplished by our organization, calling upon all who believe in securing "the greatest good to the greatest number" to aid and assist us.

Objectives

I. To bring within the folds of organization every department of productive industry, making knowledge a standpoint for action, and industrial, moral worth, not wealth, the true standard of individual and national greatness.

II. To secure to the toilers a proper share of the wealth that they create; more of the leisure that rightfully belongs to them; more [social] advantages, more of the benefits, privileges, and emoluments of the world; in a word, all those rights and privileges necessary to make them capable of enjoying, appreciating, defending, and perpetuating the blessings of good government.

III. To arrive at the true condition of the producing masses in their educational, moral, and financial condition, by demanding from the various governments the establishment of bureaus of Labor Statistics.

T. V. Powderly, *Thirty Years of Labor* (Columbus, Ohio: Excelssor Publishing House, 1890), 243–246.

IV. The establishment of co-operative institutions, productive and distributive.

V. The reserving of the public lands—the heritage of the people—for the actual settler. Not another acre [is to be allocated] for railroads or speculators.

VI. The abrogation of all laws that do not bear equally upon capital and labor, the removal of unjust technicalities, delays, and discriminations in the administration of justice, and the adopting of measures providing for the health and safety of those engaged in mining, manufacturing, or building pursuits.

VII. The enactment of laws to compel chartered corporations to pay their employees weekly, in full, for labor performed during the preceding week, in the lawful money of the country.

VIII. The enactment of laws giving mechanics and laborers a first lien on their work for their full wages.

IX. The abolishment of the contract system on national, state, and municipal work.

X. The substitution of arbitration for strikes, whenever and wherever employers and employees are willing to meet on equitable grounds.

XI. The prohibition of the employment of children in workshops, mines and factories before attaining their fourteenth year.

XII. To abolish the system of letting out by contract the labor of convicts in our prisons and reformatory institutions.

XIII. To secure for both sexes equal pay for equal work.

XIV. The reduction of the hours of labor to eight per day, so that the laborers may have more time for social enjoyment and intellectual improvement, and be enabled to reap the advantages conferred by the labor-saving machinery which their brains have created.

XV. To prevail upon governments to establish a purely national circulating medium, based upon the faith and resources of the nation, and issued directly to the people, without the intervention of any system of banking corporations, which money shall be a legal tender in payment of all debts, public or private.

6. A Trade Union Official Enunciates a Restrictive AFL Policy Toward Women Workers, 1897

The invasion of the crafts by women has been developing for years amid irritation and injury to the workman. The right of the woman to win honest bread is accorded on all sides, but with craftsmen it is an open question whether this manifestation is of a healthy social growth or not.

The rapid displacement of men by women in the factory and workshop has to be met sooner or later, and the question is forcing itself upon the leaders and thinkers among the labor organizations of the land.

Edward O'Donnell, "Women as Bread Winners—the Error of the Age," *American Federationist* 4, No. 8 (October 1897). As edited in Eileen Boris and Nelson Lichtenstein, eds., *Major Problems in the History of American Workers: Documents and Essays* (Lexington, Mass.: D. C. Heath, 1991), 232–234. Reprinted by permission of Houghton Mifflin Company.

Is it a pleasing indication of progress to see the father, the brother and the son displaced as the bread winner by the mother, sister and daughter?

Is not this evolutionary backslide, which certainly modernizes the present wage system in vogue, a menace to prosperity—a foe to our civilized pretensions? . . .

The growing demand for female labor is not founded upon philanthropy, as those who encourage it would have sentimentalists believe; it does not spring from the milk of human kindness. It is an insidious assault upon the home; it is the knife of the assassin, aimed at the family circle—the divine injunction. It debars the man through financial embarrassment from family responsibility, and physically, mentally and socially excludes the woman equally from nature's dearest impulse. Is this the demand of civilized progress; is it the desire of Christian dogma? . . .

Capital thrives not upon the peaceful, united, contented family circle; rather are its palaces, pleasures and vices fostered and increased upon the disruption, ruin or abolition of the home, because with its decay and ever glaring privation, manhood loses its dignity, its backbone, its aspirations. . . .

To combat these impertinent inclinations, dangerous to the few, the old and well-tried policy of divide and conquer is invoked, and to our own shame, it must be said, one too often renders blind aid to capital in its warfare upon us. The employer in the magnanimity of his generosity will give employment to the daughter, while her two brothers are weary because of their daily tramp in quest of work. The father, who has a fair, steady job, sees not the infamous policy back of the flattering propositions. Somebody else's daughter is called in in the same manner, by and by, and very soon the shop or factory are full of women, while their fathers have the option of working for the same wages or a few cents more, or take their places in the large army of unemployed. . . .

College professors and graduates tell us that this is the natural sequence of industrial development, an integral part of economic claim.

Never was a greater fallacy uttered of more poisonous import. It is false and wholly illogical. The great demand for women and their preference over men does not spring from a desire to elevate humanity; at any rate that is not its trend.

The wholesale employment of women in the various handicrafts must gradually unsex them, as it most assuredly is demoralizing them, or stripping them of that modest demeanor that lends a charm to their kind, while it numerically strengthens the multitudinous army of loafers, paupers, tramps and policemen, for no man who desires honest employment, and can secure it, cares to throw his life away upon such a wretched occupation as the latter.

The employment of women in the mechanical departments is encouraged because of its cheapness and easy manipulation, regardless of the consequent perils; and for no other reason. The generous sentiment enveloping this inducement is of criminal design, since it comes from a thirst to build riches upon the dismemberment of the family or the hearthstone cruelly dishonored. . . .

But somebody will say, would you have women pursue lives of shame rather than work? Certainly not; it is to the alarming introduction of women into the mechanical industries, hitherto enjoyed by the sterner sex, at a wage uncommandable by them, that leads so many into that deplorable pursuit.

 *E S S A Y S*

In generally more moderate tones than those of their Gilded Age counterparts, historians continue to debate the pros and cons of America's Industrial revolution. In the first selection, with a focus on the literary self-representation of the period, Alan Trachtenberg, professor of American studies at Yale University, stresses the contradictory symbolism of the machine in American life. In the second essay, Professor (and volume editor!) Leon Fink of the University of North Carolina at Chapel Hill examines the particular way in which the labor movement of the 1880s attempted—in vain—to realign American industrial development with democratic principles.

The Machine as Deity and Demon

ALAN TRACHTENBERG

I

Even before the Civil War, the westward trails were destined to be lined with tracks; the pony express and the covered wagon, like the mounted Plains Indian, would yield to the Iron Horse. For if the West of "myth and symbol" . . . provided one perspective by which Americans might view their society, the machine provided another. The two images fused into a single picture of a progressive civilization fulfilling a providential mission. . . . Many Americans before the Civil War had believed that industrial technology and the factory system would serve as historic instruments of republican values, diffusing civic virtue and enlightenment along with material wealth. Factories, railroads, and telegraph wires seemed the very engines of a democratic future. Ritual celebrations of machinery and fervently optimistic prophecies of abundance continued throughout the Gilded Age, notably at the two great international expositions, in Philadelphia in 1876, and in Chicago in 1893.

The image of the machine, like the image of the West, proved to be a complex symbol, increasingly charged with contradictory meanings and implications. If the machine seemed the prime cause of the abundance of new products changing the character of daily life, it also seemed responsible for newly visible poverty, slums, and an unexpected wretchedness of industrial conditions. While it inspired confidence in some quarters, it also provoked dismay, often arousing hope and gloom in the same minds. For, accompanying the mechanization of industry, of transportation, and of daily existence, were the most severe contrasts yet visible in American society, contrasts between "progress and poverty" (in Henry George's words), which seemed to many a mockery of the republican dream, a haunting paradox. Each act of national celebration seemed to evoke its opposite. The 1877 railroad strike, the first instance of machine smashing and class violence on a national scale, followed the 1876 Centennial Exposition, and the even fiercer Pullman strike of 1894 came fast on the heels of the World's Columbian Exposition of 1893.

It is no wonder that closer examination of popular celebrations discloses bewilderment and fear. . . . In the language of literature, a machine (railroad or steamship) bursting on a peaceful natural setting represented a symbolic version of the trauma inflicted on American society by unexpectedly rapid mechanization. The popular mode of celebration covered over all signs of trauma with expressions of confidence and fulsome praise. But confidence proved difficult to sustain in the face of the evidence.

Current events instilled doubt at the very site of celebration. A period of great economic growth, of steadily rising per capita wealth, and new urban markets feeding an expanding industrial plant, the Gilded Age was also wracked with persisting crises. An international "great depression" from 1873 to 1896 afflicted all industrial nations with chronic overproduction and dramatically falling prices, averaging one-third on all commodities. . . . A perilously uneven business cycle continued for more than twenty years, affecting all sections of the economy: constant market uncertainties and stiffening competition at home and abroad for business; inexplicable surpluses and declining world prices, together with tightening credit for farmers; wage cuts, extended layoffs and irregular employment and worsening conditions, even starvation, for industrial workers. . . . Thus, even in the shadow of glorious new machines displayed at the fairs, the public sense of crisis deepened.

No wonder modern machinery struck observers, especially those associated with the business community, as in Charles Francis Adams, Jr.'s words, "an incalculable force." The tempo of crisis accelerated in the 1870's. Farmers agitated through Granger clubs and the Greenback Party against the government's policy of supporting business through deflationary hard money and the gold standard. Industrial unrest reached a climax and a momentary catharsis in July 1877, when fears of a new civil war spread across the country during the great railroad strike. Provoked by a 10 percent wage cut announced without warning by the Baltimore and Ohio line, a measure to halt a declining rate of profit, the strike spread like wildfire to other lines, reaching from Baltimore to Pittsburgh, Chicago, St. Louis, Kansas City, and San Francisco. The apparently spontaneous work stoppages met with approval and support from local merchants, farmers, clergy, and politicians, tapping reserves of anger and wrath against the railroad companies. Workers in other industries joined the walkout, and for a short spell it seemed that the United States faced a mass rebellion, a recurrence of the Paris Commune of 1871 on an even vaster scale. In some communities (St. Louis, for example) committees of strikers briefly assumed control of government and railroad services.

The strike turned bloody and destructive, arousing a vehemence of response from big business and the national government even surpassing the wrath vented by strikers against railroad yards and equipment. . . . The newly inaugurated President, Rutherford Hayes, invoked his powers of military intervention and called out federal troops to protect "by force" (as he noted in his diary) the property of the railroad companies, among whose leaders he counted many of his closest friends and supporters. In the end, the strike left more than a hundred dead, millions of dollars of property destroyed, and a toughened company and government stand against unions. Strikers were very often fired and blacklisted, their leaders fined and jailed. The War Department issued a pamphlet on "riot duty" and constructed for the first time a system of armories in major cities to house a standing "national guard." Industrialization of the state's military force seemed a necessary adjunct to the mechanization of production.

The very extremes of effect lent to the machine an aura of supreme power, as if it were an autonomous force that held human society in its grip. In *The First Century of the Republic,* a book of essays published by *Harper's* magazine in celebration of the nation's centennial in 1876, the economist David Wells observed that "like one of our mighty rivers," mechanization was "beyond control." And indeed the display in Machinery Hall in Philadelphia that summer gave credence to the image of a flood, though without Wells's ominous note. Here, in an exposition of machines removed from their working location, a profusion of mechanisms seduced the eye: power looms, lathes, sewing machines, presses, pumps, toolmaking machines, axles, shafts, wire cables, and locomotives. . . . Alexander Graham Bell here gave the world first notice of the greatest wonder of electrical communication: the telephone. For sheer grandeur and sublimity, however, the mechanisms of communication could not compete with the two most imposing structures in the Hall: the thirty-foot-high Corliss Double Walking-Beam Steam Engine, which powered the entire ensemble from a single source, and its counterpart, a 7,000-pound electrical pendulum clock which governed, to the second, twenty-six lesser "slave" clocks around the building. Unstinted but channeled power, and precisely regulated time: that combination seemed to hold the secret of progress. . . .

II

The idea of an autonomous and omnipotent machine, brooking no resistance against its untold and ineluctable powers, became an article of faith. The image implied a popular social theory: the machine as a "human benefactor," a "great emancipator of man from the bondage of labor." Modern technology was mankind's "civilizing force," driving out superstition, poverty, ignorance. "Better morals, better sanitary conditions, better health, better wages," wrote Carroll D. Wright, chief of the Massachusetts Bureau of Statistics of Labor, in 1882; "these are the practical results of the factory system, as compared with what preceded it, and the results of all these have been a keener intelligence." Wright's paper, originally given as an address before the American Social Science Association, bore the title "The Factory System as an Element in Civilization."

The events of the 1870's and 1880's however, also elicited less sanguine accounts of what the factory system had wrought. . . . Not surprisingly, a growing number of Americans openly questioned whether industrialization was in fact, in Henry George's words, "an unmixed good." As if in pointed rebuke of Wright's arguments and images, George observed the following year, in *Social Problems* (1883), that so-called labor-saving inventions, the "greater employment of machinery," and "greater division of labor," result in "positive evils" for the working masses, "degrading men into the position of mere feeders of machines." Machines employed in production under the present system are "absolutely injurious," "rendering the workman more dependent; depriving him of skill and of opportunities to acquire it; lessening his control over his own condition and his hope of improving it; cramping his mind, and in many cases distorting and enervating his body." . . . George plainly perceived the process of degradation in factory labor as strictly mechanical, experienced as an *effect* of machinery.

. . . George, a native Philadelphian of middle-class birth who had wandered to California in the late 1850's, working as a seaman, printer, newspaperman, failing as a Democratic candidate for office and as the owner of an independent newspaper, wished to arouse the nation to its plight, urging the adoption of a "single tax" against land rents as the solution to the paradox whereby "laborsaving machinery everywhere fails to benefit laborers." His *Progress and Poverty*, written in the wake of the destruction, violence, and frustration of the summer of 1877, fuses evangelical fervor with simplified Ricardian economic theory; its simplicity of analysis and solution, its jeremiad rhetoric of righteousness and exhortation, helped the book find a remarkably wide audience. It reached more than 2 million readers by the end of the century. Appealing to a range of political sentiments and economic interests, George evoked a vision of older republican and entrepreneurial values restored through the "single tax" in the new corporate industrial world. . . .

George's picture of the failures of the machine and of its potential promise corresponded to the perceptions of a significant section of the society, particularly since he promised a change fundamentally within the existing order, the existing relations of capital and labor. Among representatives of older ruling groups, the picture held less promise. "It is useless for men to stand in the way of steam-engines," wrote Charles Francis Adams, Jr., in 1868. Adams, from one of the oldest Eastern families of property and former political status, would soon join forces with the engine as corporate executive of railroad and other enterprises. His less sanguine brother, Henry Adams, wrote later in *The Education of Henry Adams* (1907), regarding his own "failure," that "the whole mechanical consolidation of force ruthlessly stamped out the life of the class into which Adams was born." Devising a theory of history based on "forces," Adams crystallized the technological determinism implicit in both the popular and academic thought of his time. . . .

. . . The familiarization of American society with machinery represents one of the major cultural processes of these years, even in such simple matters as riding in streetcars and elevators, getting used to packaged processed foods and the style of machine-made clothing, let alone growing accustomed to new harsh sounds and noxious odors near factories and railroad terminals. The proliferation of new machines and machine-made tools for industrial and agricultural production marked an even more drastic upheaval in the forms, rhythms, and patterns of physical labor.

Perhaps more expressive of changing cultural perceptions because of its greater diffusion than serious or "high" literature, popular fiction and folklore in these years represented machinery especially in its sheer power and exemption from human vulnerability. In regional folktales and ballads, such figures as the lumberjack Paul Bunyan, the railroad worker John Henry, the locomotive engineer Casey Jones pit their strength and skill and daring against the machine.

Dime-novel Western adventures depict orgies of shootings and killings with every variety of automatic repeating weapons, each named precisely. A magical machine, endowing its owner with ultimate powers of "civilization" against "savagery," the gun not only won the West in such fictions (as it did in fact) but helped make the notion of repeatability, of automation, familiar. Indeed, as recent scholars have remarked, the interchangeability of plots and characters in dime novels parallels the standardization of machine production that became a central feature of factory life in the 1880's. Dime novels also provided a field for technological fantasy; beginning with *The Huge Hunter, or The Steam Man of the Prairies* in 1865, these novels included inventors (often boys) as standard fare, along with robots (like the ten-foot steam man), armored flying vessels, electrified wire, and remote-control weapons. The fiction provided vicarious mechanical thrills along with fantasies of control and power. Machines are imagined as exotic instruments of destruction, only obliquely linked to the means of production revolutionizing the industrial system.

The fictive imagination of terror, of technological cataclysm, served as a form of familiarization. The implications of a technologized world and its potential for explosion were not lost on more troubled observers, who felt themselves on a precarious bridge between an earlier America and the present. . . .

. . . Nervousness provoked by modern mechanical life provided the theme of the widely read medical treatise by George M. Beard in 1884. A pioneering work in the study of neurasthenia, *American Nervousness* builds its case through an elaborate mechanical metaphor: the nervous system is like a machine presently under strain in response to the pressures of the machinery of civilized life. Like Thomas Edison's central electric-light generator, wrote Beard (a friend of the inventor), "the nervous system of man is the centre of the nerve-force supplying all the organs of the body." "Modern nervousness," he explains, "is the cry of the system struggling with its environment," with all the pressures exerted on striving Americans by the telegraph and railroad and printing press. Simply to be on time, Beard argues, exacts a toll from the human system. . . .

. . . [Beard] also discloses another source of severe anxiety prevalent among middle- and upper-class Americans, that of impending chaos, the rule of accident, exigency, and rampant city mobs. . . .

The fear of cataclysm implicit here is not so much technological as social: a fear manifest throughout the popular media after 1877 of uprisings and insurrection, of a smoldering volcano under the streets. For David Wells, writing in 1885, such popular disturbances as the agitation for an eight-hour day and talk of socialism "seem full of menace of a mustering of the barbarians from within rather than as of old from without, for an attack on the whole present organization of society, and even the permanency of civilization itself." Henry George, too, concluded *Progress and Poverty* with a picture of potential collapse, of "carnivals of destruction." "Whence shall come the new barbarians," he asked. "Go through the squalid quarters of great cities, and you may see, even now, their gathering hordes! How shall learning perish? Men will cease to read, and books will kindle fires and be turned into cartridges!" The association of social unrest with the imagery of technological violence, of new city crowds with ignorance and contempt for culture (or regression to "savagery"), fired the imagination with a nightmarish narrative of impending apocalypse. . . .

III

. . . Association of machines with violence suggest profound tensions among Americans who . . . otherwise saluted modern technology as a boon to republican ideals. Metaphors of wreckage and self-destruction seem to express unresolved cultural dilemmas, conflicting value systems such as those described by Leo Marx as "machine" and "garden," the values of mechanical progress and those of pastoral harmony in a peaceful landscape. But the coexistence of figures of destruction, of "dark Satanic mills," with those of unbounded Promethean production, also points in the direction of the Promethean effort itself, toward the character of the mechanization process. Subtle interweavings of destruction and creation formed the inner logic of the industrial capitalist system, a logic less conspicuous but nonetheless compelling in its consequences than the more dramatic versions of contradiction evoked by Henry George. . . . As analysts here and in Europe had begun to discover, that system possessed a baffling unconscious energy which resulted in recurrent cycles of expansion and contraction, inflation and deflation, confidence and depression. Such aberrations seemed to follow from precisely those increases in productive power which marked the industrial world in these years

If Americans seemed especially intense in their response to mechanization, especially obsessed with alternating images of mechanical plentitude and devastation, an explanation lies in the special circumstances of native industrialization, its speed, its scale, its thoroughness within a brief period. Suffering fewer social barriers, possessing the largest domestic region convertible to a national market without internal restriction, by the end of the century American industry rapidly surpassed its chief European rivals, England and Germany. Figures of absolute increase signified the triumph: the production of raw steel rising from 13 tons in 1860 to near 5,000 in 1890, and of steel rails multiplying ten times in the same years; total agricultural output tripling between 1870 and 1900. Agriculture showed the most dramatic and immediate evidence. A single mechanized farmer in 1896 was able to reap more wheat than eighteen men working with horses and hand equipment sixty years earlier. . . .

[The American] propensity [for mechanical improvement] characterized the entire industrial world, but it had been a special mark of American manufacturing since its beginnings. With a scarcity of skilled labor, of craftsmen and artisans with accumulated experience in nascent industrial processes such as spinning, weaving, and milling, American circumstances placed a premium on mechanical invention and improvement. Scarcity of skills together with cheapness of land had maintained a relatively high cost of labor in the young United States. . . . Without an inherited aristocratic social order, the new country held out more hope to entrepreneurs for social acceptance as well as material rewards. Many early industrial entrepreneurs had begun their working lives as craftsmen, mechanics with a knack for invention, and had risen to wealth and status as a result of their mechanical skill and entrepreneurial expertise. . . . By the 1850's the practical Yankee inventor-entrepreneur, the tinkerer with an eye on profit, had come to seem an American type, proof of the republican principle that self-taught men of skill and ingenuity might rise to wealth and social position. . . .

Technological determinism implied that machines demanded their own improvement, that they controlled the forms of production and drove their owners and workers. Americans were taught to view their machines as independent agencies of power, causes of "progress." Machines seemed fixed in shape, definite self-propelled objects in space. In fact, however, machinery underwent constant change in appearance, in function, in design. Machines were working parts of a dynamic system. And the motives for change, the source of industrial dynamism, lay not in the inanimate machine but in the economic necessities perceived by its owners. Higher rates of productivity through economies of scale and velocity, through greater exploitation of machinery and reorganization of both factory labor and corporate structures, were deliberate goals chosen by business leaders out of economic need. . . .

. . . The American fascination with the machine . . . tended to divert attention from the countless small innovations at the work place, changes both in machinery and the design of work. . . . The belief that viewed "progress" as a relation between new machines and old, a matter of replacing the outmoded by the novel, obscured the transformations of labor, of the human relation to production, each mechanical improvement represented. Technological change in these years consisted of a vast interrelated pattern of novelty, developments in metallurgy, mining, chemistry, hydraulics, electricity feeding back into each other. . . . With steam power prevailing in the 1870's, machines grew bigger and faster, and factories resembled jungles of shafts, belts, axles, and gears to transmit power from immense prime movers. . . . Electricity offered new possibilities of conversion of power into heat, light, and motion, and permitted new efficiencies and economics in the design of factories, including decentralization, dispersion of work areas, and assembly lines. In both the transformative (textiles, chemicals, food processing, glass making) and assembling (construction, clothing, shoe, machine making) industries, electricity worked major alterations in the forms of labor. . . .

. . . Unsettled economic conditions made manufacturers obsessed with efficiency, with the breaking of bottlenecks, the logistics of work flow, the standardization of parts, measurements, and human effort. . . . As a result, human effort fell more and more into mechanical categories, as if the laborer might also be conceived as an interchangeable part. Furious efforts to cut labor costs led to the announcement of severe work rules, the replacement of traditional craftsmen by unskilled or semiskilled labor: the effort, that is, to lower the cost of wages by increasing investment in the fixed capital of new machinery. Such developments, . . . set the stage for several of the fiercest labor struggles of the 1880's and 1890's. The process of continual refinement and rationalization of machinery, leading to twentieth-century automation, represented to industrial workers a steady erosion of their autonomy, their control, and their crafts.

In the record, then, of mechanical change lay an intermingling of production and destruction, the scrapping of old machines, old processes, and old human skills. An inevitable wreckage accompanied the "progress in manufacturing" David Wells had described as a "mighty river." That image hinted at unconscious meanings, the figure of speech disclosing more than Wells himself recognized. "Like one of our mighty rivers," he wrote in 1876 about manufacturing, "its movement is beyond control." . . .

IV

. . . In the quest for greater productivity, for more efficient machines, more output per unit of cost, calculation of several kinds played an increasingly significant role. With the enlarged role of the accounting office in decisions relevant to materials and labor, transportation, advertising, and sales, mathematical considerations entered the business world in a major way. . . .

As if called forth by this prime economic motive, Frederick W. Taylor, a foreman at the Midvale Steel Company in Pennsylvania, inaugurated in the 1880's his famous "time-study" experiments, aimed at elimination of waste, inefficiency, and what he called "soldiering" on the part of workers. With his stopwatch—a further encroachment of time on physical movement—Taylor proposed to systematize exactly that process Wells had described as production through destruction: the absolute subordination of "living labor" to the machine. He envisioned a complete renovation of the production process, with standardization of tools and equipment, replanning of factories for greater efficiency, and a "piece-rate" method of payment as incentive for workers. In *The Principles of Scientific Management* (1911), Taylor made explicit the heart of his program: to take possession for management of the "mass of traditional knowledge" once possessed by the workers themselves, "knowledge handed down to them by word of mouth, through the many years in which their trade has been developed from the primitive condition." For Taylor the stopwatch and flowchart were basic instruments whereby management might reduce that knowledge to measurable motions, eradicating their workers' autonomy at one stroke while enhancing their productivity.

Thus, the social distribution of knowledge begins a major shift, a transference (as far as technology and technique are concerned) from bottom to top, in these years of extensive and intensive mechanization. Just as important, and as a symbol of the process, *thought* now appears often in the dumb, mystifying shapes of machines, of standing and moving mechanical objects as incapable of explaining themselves to the unknowing eye as the standing stones of ancient peoples. The momentous event of mechanization, of science and technology coming to perform the labor most significant to the productivity of the system, reproduced itself in ambivalent cultural images of machines and inventors, and in displacements running like waves of shock through the social order.

Class Consciousness American-Style

LEON FINK

Two well-traveled routes into the Gilded Age are likely to leave the present-day visitor with the same puzzled and unsatisfied feeling. One itinerary pursuing the political history of the era begins in 1876 with the official end of Reconstruction and winds through the election of William McKinley in 1896. The other route, this one taking a social prospectus, departs with the great railroad strikes of 1877 and picks its way through the drama and debris of an industrializing society. The problem is that the two paths never seem to meet. Compartmentalization of subject matter in most textbooks into "politics," "economic change," "social movements," and so on, only papers over the obvious unanswered question—what impact did an industrial revolution of unprecedented magnitude have on the world's most democratic nation?

Leon Fink, *In Search of the Working Class: Essays in American Labor History and Political Culture* (Urbana: University of Illinois Press, 1994), 15–29. Used by permission.

The question, of course, permits no simple answer. By most accounts the political era inaugurated in 1876 appears, except for the Populist outburst of the mid-1890s, as a conservative, comparatively uneventful time sandwiched between the end of Radical Reconstruction and the new complexities of the twentieth century. With the Civil War's financial and social settlement out of the way, a society desperately wanting to believe that it had removed its last barriers to social harmony by and large lapsed into a period of ideological torpor and narrow-minded partisanship. Political contests, while still the national pastime (national elections regularly drew 80 percent, state and local elections 60–80 percent of eligible voters, 1876–96), seem to have dwelt less on major social issues than on simple party fealty. Fierce rivalries engendered by the sectional, ethnocultural, and economic interest group divisions among the American people increasingly were presided over and manipulated by party professionals. To be sure, genuine policy differences— e.g., over how best to encourage both industry and trade, the degree of danger posed by the saloon, honesty in government—fueled a venomous political rhetoric. As echoed by both national parties from the late 1870s through the early 1890s, however, a complacent political consensus had emerged, stressing individual opportunity, rights in property, and economic freedom from constraints. The welfare of the American Dream, in the minds of both Democrats and Republicans, required no significant governmental tinkering or popular mobilization. Acknowledging the parties' avoidance of changing social and economic realities, a most compelling recent commentary on the late nineteenth-century polity suggests that the "distinct, social need" of the time was in part filled by heightened partisanship and the act of political participation itself.

In contrast to the ritualistic quality of politics, the contemporary social world seems positively explosive. Consolidation of America's industrial revolution touched off an era of unexampled change and turmoil. As work shifted decisively away from agriculture between 1870 and 1890, the manufacturing sector, with a spectacular increase in the amount of capital invested, the monetary value of product, and the number employed, sparked a great economic leap forward. By 1880 Carroll D. Wright, U.S. commissioner of labor statistics, found that the application of steam and water power to production had so expanded that "at least four-fifths" of the "nearly 3 millions of people employed in the mechanical industries of this country" were working under the factory system. It was not just the places of production but the people working within them that represented a dramatic departure from preindustrial America. While only 13 percent of the total population was classified as foreign-born in 1880, 42 percent of those engaged in manufacturing and extractive industries were immigrants. If one adds to this figure workers of foreign parentage and of Afro-American descent, the resulting nonnative/nonwhite population clearly encompassed the great majority of America's industrial work force. Not only, therefore, had the industrial revolution turned a small minority in America's towns and cities into the direct employers of their fellow citizens, but the owners of industry also differed from their employees in national and cultural background. This sudden transformation of American communities, accompanied as it was by a period of intense price competition and unregulated swings in the business cycle, provided plentiful ingredients for social unrest, first manifest on a national scale in the railroad strike of 1877.

The quintessential expression of the labor movement in the Gilded Age was the Noble and Holy Order of the Knights of Labor, the first mass organization of the North American working class. Launched as one of several secret societies among Philadelphia artisans in the late 1860s, the Knights grew in spurts by the accretion of miners (1874–79) and skilled urban tradesmen (1879–85). While the movement formally concentrated on moral and political education, cooperative enterprise, and land settlement, members found it a convenient vehicle for trade union action, particularly in the auspicious economic climate following the depression of the 1870s. Beginning in 1883, local skirmishes escalated into highly publicized confrontations with the railroad financier Jay Gould, a national symbol of new corporate power. Strikes by Knights of Labor telegraphers and railroad shop craft workers touched off an unprecedented wave of strikes and boycotts that carried on into the renewed depression in 1884–85 and spread to thousands of previously unorganized semi-skilled and unskilled laborers, both urban and rural. The Southwest Strike on Gould's Missouri and Texas-Pacific railroad lines, together with massive urban eight-hour campaigns in 1886, swelled a tide of unrest that has become known as the "Great Upheaval." The turbulence aided the efforts of organized labor, and the Knights exploded in size, reaching more than three-quarters of a million members. Although membership dropped off drastically in the late 1880s, the Knights remained a powerful force in many areas through the mid-1890s. Not until the Congress of Industrial Organizations' revival of the 1930s would the organized labor movement again lay claim to such influence within the working population.

At its zenith the movement around the Knights helped to sustain a national debate over the social implications of industrial capitalism. Newspaper editors, lecturers, and clergymen everywhere addressed the Social Question. John Swinton, the leading labor journalist of the day, counted Karl Marx, Hawaii's king Kalakaua, and the Republican party's chief orator, Robert G. Ingersoll, among the enlightened commentators on the subject. Even the U.S. Senate in 1883 formally investigated "Relations between Labor and Capital." Nor was the debate conducted only from on high. In laboring communities across the nation the local press as well as private correspondence bore witness to no shortage of eloquence from the so-called inarticulate. One of the busiest terminals of communications was the Philadelphia office of Terence Vincent Powderly, general master workman of the Knights of Labor. Unsolicited personal letters expressing the private hopes and desperations of ordinary American citizens daily poured in upon the labor leader: an indigent southern mother prayed that her four young girls would grow up to find an honorable living: an unemployed New York cakemaker applied for a charter as an organizer; a Cheyenne chief sought protection for his people's land; an inventor offered to share a new idea for the cotton gin on condition that it be used cooperatively.

Amid spreading agitation, massed strength, and growing public awareness, the labor issues ultimately took tangible political form. Wherever the Knights of Labor had organized by the mid-1880s, it seemed, contests over power and rights at the workplace evolved into a community-wide fissure over control of public policy as well. Indeed, in some 200 towns and cities from 1885 to 1888 the labor movement actively fielded its own political slates. Adopting "Workingmen's," "United Labor," "Union Labor" "People's party," and Independent" labels for their tickets, or alternatively taking over one of the standing two-party organizations in town, those local political efforts revealed deep divisions within the contemporary political culture and evoked sharp reactions from traditional centers of power. Even as manufacturers' associations met labor's challenge at the industrial level, business response at the political level was felt in the dissolution of party structures, creation of antilabor citizens' coalitions, new restrictive legislation, and extralegal law and order leagues. In their ensemble, therefore, the political confrontations of the 1880s offer a most dramatic point of convergence between the world leading out of 1876 and that stretching from 1877. As a phenomenon simultaneously entwined in the political and industrial history of the Gilded Age, the subject offers an opportunity to redefine the main issues of the period.

The labor movement of the Gilded Age . . . spoke a "language of class" that was "as much political as economic." In important ways an eighteenth-century republican political inheritance still provided the basic vocabulary. The emphasis within the movement on equal rights, on the identity of work and self-worth, and on secure, family-centered households had informed American political radicalism for decades. A republican outlook lay at the heart of the protests of journeymen-mechanics and women millworkers during the Jacksonian period; it likewise inspired abolitionists and the woman suffrage and temperance movements and even contributed to the common-school crusade. . . .

Working-class radicalism in the Gilded Age derived its principles—as grouped around economic, national-political, and cultural themes—from the period of the early revolutionary-democratic bourgeoisie. Implicitly, labor radicals embraced a unifying conception of work and culture that Norman Birnbaum has labeled the *Homo faber* ideal: "an artisanal conception of activity, a visible, limited, and directed relationship to nature." The *Homo faber* ethic found its political embodiment in Enlightenment liberalism. "From that source," notes Trygve R. Tholfson in a commentary on mid-Victorian English labor radicalism, "came a trenchant rationalism, a vision of human emancipation, the expectation of progress based on reason, and an inclination to take the action necessary to bring society into conformity with rationally demonstrable principles." In the late nineteenth century, Enlightenment liberalism was harnessed to a historical understanding of American nationalism, confirmed by both the American Revolution and the Civil War. Together these political, economic, and moral conceptions coalesced around a twin commitment to the citizen-as-producer and the producer-as-citizen. For nearly a century Americans had been proud that their country, more than anywhere else in the world, made republican principles real. In this respect the bloody war over slavery served only to confirm the ultimate power of the ideal.

Certain tendencies of the Gilded Age, however, heralded for some an alarming social regression. The permanency of wage labor, the physical and mental exhaustion inflicted by the factory system, and the arrogant exercise of power by the owners of capital threatened the rational and progressive march of history. "Republican institutions," the preamble to the constitution of the Knights of Labor declared simply, "are not safe under such conditions." "We have openly arrayed against us," a Chicago radical despaired in 1883, "the powers of the world, most of the intelligence, all the wealth, and even law itself." The lament of a Connecticut man that "factoryism, bankism, collegism, capitalism, insuranceism and the presence of such lump-headed malignants as Professor William Graham Sumner" were stultifying "the native genius of this state" framed the evil in more homespun terms. In 1883 the cigar-makers' leader Samuel Gompers, not yet accepting the inevitability of capitalist industry, bemoaned the passing of the day of "partners at the work bench" that had given way to "the tendency . . . which makes man, the worker, a part of the machine." The British-born journalist Richard J. Hinton, an old Chartist who had commanded black troops during the Civil War, also reflected on the sudden darkening of the social horizon. The "average, middle-class American," he complained, simply could not appreciate the contemporary position of American workers: "They all look back to the days when they were born in some little American village. . . . They have seen their time and opportunity of getting on in the world, and they think that is the condition of society today, when it is totally a different condition."

In response the labor movement in the Gilded Age turned the plowshares of a consensual political past into a sword of class conflict. "We declare," went the Knights' manifesto, "an inevitable and irresistible conflict between the wage-system of labor and republican system of government." To some extent older demons seemed simply to have reappeared in new garb, and, as such, older struggles beckoned with renewed urgency. A Greenback* editor in Rochester, New Hampshire, thus proclaimed that "patriots" who overturn the "lords of labor" would be remembered next to "the immortal heroes of the revolution and emancipation."

To many outside observers in the 1880s, the American working class—in terms of organization, militancy, and collective self-consciousness—appeared more advanced than its European counterparts. . . . Eleanor Marx and Edward Aveling returned from an 1886 American tour with a glowing assessment of the workers' mood. Friedrich Engels, too, in the aftermath of the eight-hour strikes and the Henry George campaign, attached a special preface to the 1887 American edition of *The Condition of the Working Class in England in 1844:*

> In European countries, it took the working class years and years before they fully realized the fact that they formed a distinct and, under the existing social conditions, a permanent class of modern society; and it took years again until this class-consciousness led them to form themselves into a distinct political party, independent of, and opposed to, all the old political parties, formed by the various sections of the ruling classes. On the more favored soil of America, where no medieval ruins bar the way, where history begins with the elements of the modern bourgeois society as evolved in the seventeenth century, the working class passed through these two stages of its development within ten months.

Nor was it only in the eyes of eager well-wishers that the developments of the 1880s seemed to take on a larger significance. Surveying the map of labor upheaval, the conservative Richmond *Whig* wrote in 1886 of "socialistic and agrarian elements" threatening "the genius of our free institutions." The Chicago *Times* went so far in its fear of impending revolution as to counsel the use of hand grenades against strikers.

---

*The Greenback-Labor Party (1875–1878) called for an inflated money supply, based on the retention of Civil War greenback dollars and the coinage of silver, to benefit workers and debtor farmers.

Revolutionary anticipations, pro or con, proved premature. That was true at least partly because both the movement's distant boosters as well as its domestic detractors sometimes misrepresented its intentions. Gilded Age labor radicals did not self-consciously place themselves in opposition to a prevailing economic system but displayed a sincere ideological ambivalence toward the capitalist marketplace. On the one hand, they frequently invoked a call for the "abolition of the wage system." On the other hand, like the classical economists, they sometimes spoke of the operation of "natural law" in the marketplace, acknowledged the need for a "fair return" on invested capital, and did not oppose profit per se. . . . The Knights thus modified an earlier radical interpretation of the labor-cost theory of value, wherein labor, being the source of all wealth, should individually be vested with the value of its product, and demanded for workers only an intentionally vague "proper share of the wealth they create." In so doing they were able to shift the weight of the analysis . . . to the general, collective plight of the laboring classes. In their eyes aggregation of capital together with cutthroat price competition had destroyed any semblance of marketplace balance between employer and employee. Under the prevailing economic calculus, labor had been demoted into just another factor of production whose remuneration was determined not by custom or human character but by market price. In such a situation they concluded, as Samuel Walker has noted, that "the contract was not and could not be entered into freely. . . . The process of wage determination was a moral affront because it degraded the personal dignity of the workingman." This subservient position to the iron law of the market constituted "wage slavery," and like other forms of involuntary servitude it had to be "abolished."

Labor's emancipation did not, ipso facto, imply the overthrow of capitalism, a system of productive relations that the Knights in any case never defined. To escape wage slavery workers needed the strength to redefine the social balance of power with employers and their allies—and the will and intelligence to use that strength. One after another the Knights harnessed the various means at their disposal—education, organization, cooperation, economic sanction, and political influence—to this broad end: "To secure to the workers the full enjoyment [note, not the full return] of the wealth they create, sufficient leisure in which to develop their intellectual, moral and social faculties, all of the benefits of recreation, and pleasures of association; in a word to enable them to share in the gains and honors of advancing civilization."

A wide range of strategic options was represented within the counsels of the labor movement. One tendency sought to check the rampant concentration of wealth and power with specific correctives on the operation of the free market. Radical Greenbackism (with roots in Kelloggism and related monetary theories), Henry George's single tax, and land nationalization, each of which commanded considerable influence among the Knights of Labor, fit this category. Another important tendency, cooperation, offered a more self-reliant strategy of alternative institution building, or, as one advocate put it, "the organization of production without the intervention of the capitalist." Socialism, generally understood at the time as a system of state as opposed to private ownership of production, offered a third alternative to wage slavery. Except for a few influential worker-intellectuals and strong pockets of support among German-Americans, however, socialism carried comparatively little influence in the 1880s. . . .

If Gilded Age labor representatives tended to stop short of a frontal rejection of the political-economic order, there was nevertheless no mistaking their philosophic radicalism. Notwithstanding differences in emphasis, the labor movement's political sentiments encompassed both a sharp critique of social inequality and a broad-based prescription for a more humane future. Indeed, the labor representative who shrugged off larger philosophical and political commitments in favor of a narrow incrementalism was likely to meet with incredulity. One of the first, and most classic, enunciations of business unionism, for example, received just this response from the Senate Committee on Labor and Capital in 1883. After taking testimony from workers and labor reformers across the country for six months, the committee, chaired by New Hampshire senator Henry Blair, interviewed Adolph Strasser, president of the cigarmakers' union. Following a disquisition on the stimulating impact of shorter working hours on workers' consumption patterns, Strasser was asked if he did not contemplate a future beyond the contemporary exigencies of panic and overproduction, "some time [when] every man is to be an intelligent man and an enlightened man?" When Strasser did not reply, Senator Blair interceded to elaborate the question. Still Strasser rebuffed the queries: "Well, our organization does not consist of idealists. . . . we do [not] control the production of the world. That is controlled by employers, and that is a matter for them." Senator Blair was take aback.

> *Blair.* I was only asking you in regard to your ultimate ends.
> *Witness.* We have no ultimate ends. We are going on from day to day. We are fighting only for immediate objects—objects that can be realized in a few years. . . .
> *Blair.* I see that you are a little sensitive lest it should be thought that you are a mere theorizer. I do not look upon you in that light at all.
> *Witness.* Well, we say in our constitution that we are opposed to theorists, and I have to represent the organization here. We are all practical men.
> *Blair.* Have you not a theory upon which you have organized?
> *Witness.* Yes, sir: our theory is the experience of the past in the United States and in Great Britain. That is our theory, based upon actual facts. . . .
> *Blair.* In other words you have arrived at the theory which you are trying to apply?
> *Witness.* We have arrived at a practical result.
> *Blair.* But a practical result is the application of a theory is it not?

On a cultural level, labor's critique of American society bore the same relation to Victorian respectability that its political radicalism bore to contemporary liberalism. In both cases the middle-class and working-class radical variants derived from a set of common assumptions but drew from them quite different, even opposing, implications. No contemporary, for example, took more seriously than the Knights of Labor the cultural imperatives toward productive work, civic responsibility, education, a wholesome family life, temperance, and self-improvement. The intellectual and moral development of the individual, they would have agreed with almost every early nineteenth-century lyceum lecturer, was a precondition for the advancement of democratic civilization. In the day of Benjamin Franklin such values may well have knit together master craftsmen, journeymen, and apprentices. In the age of the factory system, however, the gulf between employer and employee had so widened that the lived meanings of the words were no longer the same.

For the Knights the concept of the producing classes indicated an ultimate social division that they perceived in the world around them. Only those associated with idleness (bankers, speculators), corruption (lawyers, liquor dealers, gamblers), or social parasitism (all of the above) were categorically excluded from membership in the Order. Other social strata such as local merchants and manufacturers were judged by their individual acts, not by any inherent structural antagonism to the workers' movement. Those who showed respect for the dignity of labor (i.e., who sold union-made goods or employed union workers at union conditions) were welcomed into the Order. Those who denigrated the laborer or his product laid themselves open to the righteous wrath of the boycott or strike. Powderly characteristically chastised one ruthless West Virginia coal owner: "Don't die, even if you do smell bad. We'll need you in a few years as a sample to show how *mean* men used to be." This rather elastic notion of class boundaries on the part of the labor movement was reciprocated in the not inconsequential number of shopkeepers and small manufacturers who expressed sympathy and support for the labor movement.

Idealization of hearth and home, a mainstay of familial sentimentality in the Gilded Age, also enjoyed special status within the labor movement. For here, as clearly as anywhere in the radicals' worldview, conventional assumptions had a critical, albeit ambivalent, edge in the context of changing social circumstances. Defense of an idealized family life as both moral and material mainstay of society served as one basis of criticism of capitalist industry. The machinist John Morrison argued before the Senate investigating committee that the insecurities of the unskilled labor market were so threatening family life as to make the house "more like a dull prison instead of a home." A self-educated Scottish-born leader of the type-founders, Edward King, associated trade union morality with the domestic "sentiments of sympathy and humanity" against the "business principles" of the age. Almost unanimously, the vision of the good life for labor radicals included the home.

The importance of the domestic moral order to the late nineteeth-century radical vision also translated into an unparalleled opening of the labor movement to women. As Susan Levine has documented, the Knights of Labor beckoned to wage-earning women and workingmen's wives to join in construction of a "cooperative commonwealth," which, without disavowing the Victorian ideal of a separate female sphere of morality and domestic virtue, sought to make that sphere the center of an active community life.

The Knights' self-improving and domestic commitments both converged in the working-class radicals' antipathy to excessive drinking. The oath of temperance, which became known as "the Powderly pledge," appealed in turn to intellectual development and protection of the family as well as to the collective interests of the labor movement. Like monopoly, the bottle lay waiting to fasten a new form of slavery upon the free worker. In another sense, as David Brundage has suggested, the growing capitalization of saloons together with expansion of saloon-linked variety theater directly threatened a family-based producers' community. While most radicals stopped short of prohibition, exhortations in behalf of temperance were commonplace. . . .

In general, then, the labor movement of the late nineteenth century provided a distinct arena of articulation and practice for values that crossed class lines. Two aspects of this use of inherited values for radical ends merit reemphasis. First, to the extent that labor radicalism shared in the nineteenth century's cult of individualism, it established a social and moral framework for individual achievement. The culture of the labor movement stressed the development of individual capacity but not competition with other individuals; while striving to elevate humanity, it ignored what S. G. Boritt has identified as the essence of the Lincoln-sanctified American Dream—the individual's "right to rise." The necessary reliance by the labor movement upon collective strength and community sanction militated against the possessive individualism that anchored the world of the workers' better-off neighbors. By its very nature, the labor movement set limits to the individual accumulation of wealth extracted from others' efforts and represented, in Edward King's words, "the graduated elimination of the personal selfishness of man."

Second, in an age of evolutionary, sometimes even revolutionary, faith in progress and the future (a faith generally shared by labor radicals), the movement made striking use of the past. Without renouncing the potential of industrialism for both human liberty and material progress, radicals dipped selectively into a popular storehouse of memory and myth to capture alternative images of human possibility. The choice of the name "Knights of Labor" itself presented images of chivalry and nobility fighting the unfeeling capitalist marketplace. Appeals to the "nobility of toil" and to the worker's "independence" conjured up the proud village smithy—not the degradation of labor in the factory system. Finally, celebrations of historic moments of human liberation and political advancement challenged a political-economic orthodoxy beholden to notions of unchanging, universal laws of development. Indeed, so conspicuously sentimental were the celebrations of Independence Day and Memorial Day that Powderly had to defend the Order from taunts of "spreadeagleism" and "Yankee doodleism."

This sketch of working-class radicalism in the Gilded Age raises one final question. Whose movement—and culture—was it? In a country as diverse as the United States, with a labor force and labor movement drawn from a heterogeneous mass of trades, races, and nationalities, any group portrait runs the risk of oversimplification. The articulate leadership of the Knights of Labor and the political movement that sprang from it included brainworkers (especially the editors of the labor press), skilled craft workers, and shopkeepers who looked to the labor movement as a source of order in a disorderly age. The self-conception of the radical labor leadership as a middle social stratum, balanced between the very rich and very poor, was evident in Powderly's 1885 characterization of his own ancestors— "they did not move in court circles; nor did they figure in police courts."

This dominant stream within the labor movement included people who had enjoyed considerable control over their jobs, if not also economic autonomy, men who often retained claim to the tools as well as the knowledge of their trade. They had taken seriously the ideal of a republic of producers in which hard work would contribute not only to the individual's improved economic standing but also to the welfare of the community. So long as they could rely on their own strength as well as their neighbors' support, this skilled stratum organized in an array of craft unions showed economic and political resilience. But the spreading confrontations with national corporate power, beginning in the 1870s, indicated just how much erosion had occurred in the position of those who relied on custom, skill, and moral censure as ultimate weapons. Industrial dilution of craft skills and a direct economic and political attack on union practices provided decisive proof to these culturally conservative workingmen of both the illegitimacy and ruthlessness of the growing power of capital. It was they, according to every recent study of late nineteenth-century laboring communities, who formed the backbone of local labor movements. The Knights were, therefore, first of all a coalition of reactivating, or already organized, trade unions.

For reasons of their own, masses of workers who had not lost full and equal citizenship—for they had never possessed it—joined the skilled workers within the Knights. Wherever the Order achieved political successes, it did so by linking semiskilled and unskilled industrial workers, including blacks and new immigrants, to its base of skilled workers and leaders. Although lacking the vote, the presence of women in the Order also undoubtedly strengthened its broader community orientation. The special strength of the Knights, noted the Boston *Labor Leader* astutely, lay "in the fact that the whole life of the community is drawn into it, that people of all kinds are together . . . , and that they all get directly the sense of each others' needs."

Politically, the Knights of Labor envisioned a kind of producer democracy. The organized power of labor was capable of revitalizing democratic citizenship and safeguarding the public good within a regulated marketplace economy. Through vigilant shop committees and demands such as the eight-hour day, organized workers—both men and women—would ensure minimal standards of safety and health at the industrial workplace, even as they surrounded the dominant corporate organizational model of business with cooperative models of their own. A pride in honest and useful work, rational education, and personal virtue would be nurtured through a rich associational life spread out from the workplace to meeting hall to the hearth and home. Finally, the integrity of public institutions would be vouchsafed by the workingmen in politics. Purifying government of party parasitism and corruption, cutting off the access to power that allowed antilabor employers to bring the state apparatus to their side in industrial disputes, improving and widening the scope of vital public services, and even contemplating the takeover of economic enterprises that had passed irreversibly into monopoly hands—by these means worker-citizens would lay active claim to a republican heritage.

The dream was not to be. At the workplace management seized the initiative toward the future design and control of work. A managerial revolution overcoming the tenacious defenses of the craft unions transferred autonomy over such matters as productivity and skill from custom and negotiation to the realm of corporate planning. Except for the garment trades and the mines, the national trade unions had generally retreated from the country's industrial heartland by 1920. In the local community as well, the differences, even antagonisms, among workers often stood out more than did the similarities. Segmentation of labor markets, urban ethnic and socioeconomic residential segregation, cultural as well as a protectionist economic disdain for the new immigrants, and the depoliticization of leisure time (i.e., the decline of associational life sponsored by labor organizations) all contributed toward a process of social fragmentation. In such circumstances working-class political cooperation proved impossible. The Socialist party and the Progressive slates could make little more than a dent in the hold of the two increasingly conservative national parties over the electorate. Only with the repolarization of political life beginning in 1928 and culminating in the New Deal was the relation of labor and the party system again transformed. By the late 1930s and 1940s a revived labor movement was beginning, with mixed success, to play the role of a leading interest group and reform conscience within the Democratic party.

This impressionistic overview permits one further observation of a quite general nature. One of the favorite tasks of American historians has been to explain why the United States, alone among the nations of the Western world, passed through the industrial revolution without the establishment of a class consciousness and an independent working-class political movement. Cheap land, the cult of individualism, a heterogeneous labor force, social mobility, and the federal separation of powers comprise several of the numerous explanations that have been offered. While not directly denying the importance of any of the factors listed above, this study implicitly suggests a different approach to the problem of American exceptionalism.

The answer appears to lie less in a permanent structural determinism—whether the analytic brace be political, economic, or ideological—than in a dynamic and indeed somewhat fortuitous convergence of events. To understand the vicissitudes of urban politics, we have had to keep in mind the action on at least three levels: the level of working-class social organization (i.e., the nature and strength of the labor movement), the level of business response, and the level of governmental response. During the Gilded Age each of these areas took an incendiary turn, but only briefly and irregularly and most rarely at the same moment. The 1880s, as R. Laurence Moore has reiterated, were the international seed time for the strong European working-class parties of the twentieth century. In America, too, the momentum in the 1880s was great. Indeed, examined at the levels of working-class organization and industrial militancy, a European visitor might understandably have expected the most to happen here first. At the political level, as well, American workers were in certain respects relatively advanced. In the 1870s and in the 1880s they established independently organized local labor regimes well before the famous French Roubaix or English West Ham labor-Socialist town councils of the 1890s. Then, a combination of forces in the United States shifted radically away from the possibilities outlined in the 1880s. The labor movement fragmented, business reorganized, and the political parties helped to pick up the pieces. The initiatives from without directed at the American working class from the mid-1890s through the mid-1920s—part repression, part reform, part assimilation, and part recruitment of a new labor force—at an internationally critical period in the gestation of working-class movements may mark the most telling exceptionalism about American developments.

It would in any case be years before the necessary conditions again converged and labor rose from the discredited icons of pre-Depression America with a new and powerful political message. Workplace, community, and ballot box would all once again be harnessed to a great social movement. But no two actors are ever in quite the same space at the same time. The choices open to the CIO, it is fair to say, were undoubtedly influenced by both the achievement and failure of their counter parts a half-century earlier.*

 F U R T H E R   R E A D I N G

Paul Avrich, *The Haymarket Tragedy* (1984)
Stuart W. Bruchey, *Enterprise: The Dynamic Economy of a Free People* (1990)
Sean Cashman, *America in the Gilded Age* (1984)
Alfred D. Chandler, Jr., *The Visible Hand: The Managerial Revolution in American Business* (1977)
Melvyn Dubofsky, *Industrialism and the American Worker, 1865–1920* (1975)
Leon Fink, *Workingmen's Democracy: The Knights of Labor and American Politics* (1983)
———, *In Search of the Working Class: Essays in American Labor History and Political Culture* (1994)
Herbert G. Gutman, *Work, Culture, and Society in Industrializing America* (1976)
Naomi R. Lamoreaux, *The Great Merger Movement in American Business, 1895–1904* (1985)
Christopher Lasch, *The True and Only Heaven: Progress and Its Critics* (1991)
Bruce Laurie, *Artisans Into Workers: Labor in Nineteenth-Century America* (1989)
Susan Levine, *Labor's True Woman* (1984)
Harold C. Livesay, *Andrew Carnegie and the Rise of Big Business* (1975)
J. Anthony Lukas, *Big Trouble* (1997)
David Montgomery, *The Fall of the House of Labor* (1987)
Richard J. Oestreicher, *Solidarity and Fragmentation: Working People and Class Consciousness in Detroit, 1875–1900* (1986)
C. Joseph Pusateri, *A History of American Business* (1988)
John L. Thomas, *Alternative America: Henry George, Edward Bellamy, Henry Demarest Lloyd and the Adversary Tradition* (1983)

---

*The CIO (Congress of Industrial Organizations), a breakaway from the AFL (American Federation of Labor) in the 1930s, enrolled masses of workers from America's basic industries.

Behind the Bravura

of the Wild West

For many easterners in the late nineteenth century, the spectacle of the Wild West served as a kind of antidote to the increasing routinization and bureaucratization of industrial culture. For years—indeed, in a pattern reaffirmed as recently as the 1980s by the man-on-horseback-as-president—the trials of frontier life, the violent dramas of cowboys and Indians, the irreverence of the mining camps, and the legions of stories of wild men and loose women have exercised a continuing attraction for those living more confined lives. In fact, however, the western tableau represented a projection of the same forces of development that were simultaneously reshaping the more densely settled areas of the country: industrialization, migration, immigration, acculturation, and conflicts of race, class, and gender. These themes were as indigenous to the West as a good horse and a six-shooter. When "civilization" overtook the Wild West, in short, it introduced the same tensions (if sometimes in different forms) between new productive processes and older ideals that gripped the larger culture. The one social feature of the trans-Mississippi West that made the conflicts there most distinct was the concentrated presence of Native American peoples. Here, in the inevitable extension of Euro-American settlement, the drama of "Americanization" took a peculiarly ironic and unheroic twist.

D O C U M E N T S

The socialization process in the West is replete with ironies. In Document 1, a buffalo hunter unselfconsciously depicts the arrival of modernity to the Great Plains as an episode of mass destruction. Attempting to surmount the failure of past Indian removals and the backwardness of reservation life, President Chester A. Arthur (1881–1885), in Document 2, anticipates the reformist themes of the Dawes Act (1887), proposing the radical cultural surgery of breaking up commonly held Indian lands into individually functioning homesteads. Document 3 exemplifies the romantic cult around outlaws like Jesse James. Another instance of violent confrontation over property in the West is cited (Document 4) by Miguel Antonio Otero, a former governor of New Mexico, in his recollection of the Mexican Gorras Blancas, or White Caps, who attempted to defend their land from Anglo encroachment. In Document 5, Oglala Sioux Chief Black Elk reconstructs the tragedy at Wounded Knee at the hands of the Wasichus (or white men) in 1890. In Document 6, excerpted from a famous paper read before the American Historical Association in 1893 historian Frederick Jackson Turner defines the moving boundary of Western settlement as the caldron of American democratic character. The passing of the frontier, he suggests, carries ominous implications. As if to bear out Turner's view of frontier virtues, a happy example of the homesteading ideal on the plains is represented in Document 7 by a Montana woman who finds unexpected cooperation from neighboring cattlemen.

1. A Buffalo Hunter Describes His Business, c. 1875

About this time the hunt had grown to such an enormous business that J. R. Lobenstein [Loganstein], a capitalist of that time, and ram rodder of the buffalo hunt, . . . furnished the capital and contracts were sub-let for robe hides, dry hides, bull hides, etc. Merchants were furnished supplies, equipments, etc., [and] they in turn furnished smaller men, who kept up with hunters ready to supply them. An enormous amount of this business was done on time. As they had begun to make money out of it, they would supply any hunter who had a team and wagon. Now all this while the hunter was pegging away and it was not until afterwards that they got it down to a system to make it profitable over a scant living.

There was several methods to kill [buffaloes] and each [hunter] adopted his own course and plan. They would get together and while one gained a point from another, he, in turn, would gain a point from him. One method was to run beside them, shooting them as they ran. Another was to shoot from the rear, what was termed tail shooting: [always shooting] the hindmost buffalo and when a day's hunt was done, they would be strung on the ground for a mile or more, from ten to fifteen yards apart, and in this way the skinner had so much territory to go over he couldn't make wages. . . .

Another method of hunting was to leave your horse out of sight after you had determined the direction and course of the wind, and then get as near as possible. If the herd was lying at rest, he would pick out some buffalo that was standing up on watch and shoot his ball in the side of him so that it would not go through, but would lodge in the flesh; as on many times it had been proven by men [who were] well hid and the wind taking the sound of the gun and the whizz of the bullet off, [that] if a ball passed through a buffalo the herd would stampede and run for miles. A buffalo shot in this manner would merely hump up his back as if he had the colic and commence to mill round and round in a slow walk. The other buffalo sniffing the blood and following would not be watching the hunter, and he would continue to shoot the outside cow buffalo; if there were old cows they would take them as

"The Buffalo Hunt," in Rex W. Strickland, ed., "The Recollections of W. S. Glenn, Buffalo Hunter," *Panhandle-Plains Historical Review* no. 22 (1949), pp 20–26. Approved by the Board of Trustees, Panhandle-Plains Historical Society.

there would be some two or three offsprings following her. If she would hump up, he would know that he had the range, and in this way hold the herd as long as they acted in this way as well as the well trained cowpuncher would hold his herd, only the hunter would use his gun. This was termed mesmerising the buffalo so that we could hold them on what we termed a stand, which afterwards proved to be the most successful way of killing the buffalo.

It was not always the best shot but the best hunter that succeeded, that is, the man who piled his buffalo in a pile so as to be more convenient for the skinner to get at and not have to run all over the country. . . .

The hunter was hired by the piece: if robe hides were worth $3.00, [he was] given twenty-five cents for every one that he killed and was brought in by the skinners—was tallied up at camp. It was the camp rustler's business to keep tally of the number of hides killed each day. If the hides were worth $2.50, he [the hunter] got 20 cents; $2.00, he got 15 cents; $1.50, he got 10 cents; and $1.00, he got 5 cents. . . .

. . . At the Doby Walls fight [the Adobe Walls, June 27, 1874], the hunters [used] all classes of guns, such as the Spencer, Springfield, Winchester and six-shooters, also all classes of buffalo guns, including a new sample 45, which Sharp had just sent out, . . . [Billy Dixon's famous long shot, so Glenn says, was made with the new 45-caliber Sharp.] Still some were not satisfied, so went outside and stepped off a 150 yards and commenced to pile dry bull hides ten in a bunch, and began to shoot with all four guns—as they went through so easily, they added more and continued to add until they had shot through 32 [hides] and one bullet stook in the thirty-third one and it proved to be the new gun. All had to have a shot with the new gun and as it gave entire satisfaction, they sent word back that this was the gun for the buffalo, and all of them ordered a gun. Sharp began to manufacture these rifles as fast as he could in various lengths and this gun, as it afterwards proved, was the cause of the extermination of the buffalo, as before this they had increased faster than killed out as it took too many shots to get a buffalo.

[Mean] while the hunter would be looking over his dead and wounded and cutting out the tongue, hump, and sometimes the tallow, it being the hunter's business to take these out while the buffalo was fresh, throwing them on some tree or rock where the wolves could not get them. In some instances if the hunter did good work the skinner could not keep up with him. Where the buffalo would be killed one day and skinned the next, [they] would be called stinkers. A buffalo left with his hide on will sour even in freezing weather, if skinned right after killing, would not smell for months if his entrails were removed.

I have seen their bodies so thick after being skinned, that they would look like logs where a hurricane had passed through a forrest [sic]. If they were lying on a hillside, the rays of the sun would make it look like a hundred glass windows. These buffalo would lie in this way until warm weather, drying up, and I have seen them piled fifty or sixty in a pile where the hunter had made a stand. As the skinner commenced on the edge, he would have to roll it out of the way to have room to skin the next, and when finished they would be rolled up as thick as saw logs around a mill. In this way a man could ride over a field and pick out the camps that were making the most money out of the hunt. . . .

2. President Chester A. Arthur Aims to Turn Indians into U.S. Citizens, 1881

Prominent among the matters which challenge the attention of Congress at its present session is the management of our Indian affairs. While this question has been a cause of trouble and embarrassment from the infancy of the Government, it is but recently that any effort has been made for its solution at once serious, determined, consistent, and promising success.

It has been easier to resort to convenient makeshifts for tiding over temporary difficulties than to grapple with the great permanent problem, and accordingly the easier course has almost invariably been pursued.

It was natural, at a time when the national territory seemed almost illimitable and contained many millions of acres far outside the bounds of civilized settlements, that a policy should have been initiated which more than aught else has been the fruitful source of our Indian complications.

I refer, of course, to the policy of dealing with the various Indian tribes as separate nationalities, of relegating them by treaty stipulations to the occupancy of immense reservations in the West, and of encouraging them to live a savage life, undisturbed by any earnest and well-directed efforts to bring them under the influences of civilization.

The unsatisfactory results which have sprung from this policy are becoming apparent to all.

As the white settlements have crowded the borders of the reservations, the Indians, sometimes contentedly and sometimes against their will, have been transferred to other hunting grounds, from which they have again been dislodged whenever their new-found homes have been desired by the adventurous settlers.

These removals and the frontier collisions by which they have often been preceded have led to frequent and disastrous conflicts between the races.

It is profitless to discuss here which of them has been chiefly responsible for the disturbances whose recital occupies so large a space upon the pages of our history.

We have to deal with the appalling fact that though thousands of lives have been sacrificed and hundreds of millions of dollars expended in the attempt to solve the Indian problem, it has until within the past few years seemed scarcely nearer a solution than it was half a century ago. But the Government has of late been cautiously but steadily feeling its way to the adoption of a policy which has already produced gratifying results, and which, in my judgment, is likely, if Congress and the Executive accord in its support, to relieve us ere long from the difficulties which have hitherto beset us.

For the success of the efforts now making to introduce among the Indians the customs and pursuits of civilized life and gradually to absorb them into the mass of our citizens, sharing their rights and holden to their responsibilities, there is imperative need for legislative action.

James D. Richardson, ed., *A Compilation of the Messages and Papers of Presidents, 1789–1897,* Vol. XIV (Washington, D.C.: Government Printing Office 1896–1899), 6923ff.

My suggestions in that regard will be chiefly such as have been already called to the attention of Congress and have received to some extent its consideration.

First. I recommend the passage of an act making the laws of the various States and Territories applicable to the Indian reservations within their borders and extending the laws of the State of Arkansas to the portion of the Indian Territory not occupied by the Five Civilized Tribes.

The Indian should receive the protection of the law. He should be allowed to maintain in court his rights of person and property. He has repeatedly begged for this privilege. Its exercise would be very valuable to him in his progress toward civilization.

Second. Of even greater importance is a measure which has been frequently recommended by my predecessors in office, and in furtherance of which several bills have been from time to time introduced in both Houses of Congress. The enactment of a general law permitting the allotment in severalty, to such Indians, at least, as desire it, of a reasonable quantity of land secured to them by patent, and for their own protection made inalienable for twenty or twenty-five years, is demanded for their present welfare and their permanent advancement.

In return for such considerate action on the part of the Government, there is reason to believe that the Indians in large numbers would be persuaded to sever their tribal relations and to engage at once in agricultural pursuits. Many of them realize the fact that their hunting days are over and that it is now for their best interests to conform their manner of life to the new order of things. By no greater inducement than the assurance of permanent title to the soil can they be led to engage in the occupation of tilling it.

The well-attested reports of their increasing interest in husbandry justify the hope and belief that the enactment of such a statute as I recommend would be at once attended with gratifying results. A resort to the allotment system would have a direct and powerful influence in dissolving the tribal bond, which is so prominent a feature of savage life, and which tends so strongly to perpetuate it.

Third. I advise a liberal appropriation for the support of Indian schools, because of my confident belief that such a course is consistent with the wisest economy.

3. A Popular Account of the Death of Jesse James, 1882

*The end of the play—The curtain falls—The lights turned down,
and the King of American bandits makes a hasty exit!*

On the morning of April 3d, 1882, Jesse James "died with his boots on." That it was a cowardly assassination I am forced to admit, but in writing of one that I knew well I have but this to say: he would have done the same to anyone whom he for one moment suspected! He would have killed the man and *inquired into the facts afterwards!* St. Joseph, Missouri, was the scene of his "taking off," and the Ford boys were "in at the death!"

Jesse James: The Life and Daring Adventures of This Bold Highwayman and Bank Robber and His No Less Celebrated Brother, Frank James (Philadelphia, Pa.: Barclay & Co., 1882).

He was shot down by two men who were in his confidence, and who had planned a raid for that very night. After the Blue Cut robbery in September, 1881, James was in hiding at his mother's house at Kearney, near Kansas City. He remained there for a few weeks and kept very quiet. Some time in November he went to St. Joseph and established himself in a little shanty in the southeastern part of the city. His wife, who was devotedly attached to him, and who is young and pretty, went with him. Although there had long been a price upon the heads of the James boys, Jesse paid no attention to it. His many hairbreadth escapades had made him oblivious to danger. Instead of going to Texas, as had been his custom when hunted down too closely, he remained in Missouri, only taking care to keep out of sight. He had been living very quietly in "Saint Jo," always kept himself well armed to guard against surprise, and his shanty was a regular arsenal.

After the shooting it was learned that Jesse had been planning another desperate raid, with the help of two brothers named Robert and Charles Ford. Just who these men were was not then known. It was believed they had been engaged in robberies with him before, but they claimed that they had been on his track for a long time, with the intention of capturing him and claiming the heavy rewards offered by the express companies, that have suffered from his depredations, and the State authorities. However that may be they were in his confidence. Charles had been at his house for several weeks, and Robert came a week or ten days before the assassination. These two men were the ones who shot down their chief without giving him a second's warning. James always wore a belt stuffed full of revolvers of the latest pattern. They were always loaded and he never took a step without them. If the Ford brothers had given him cause for the slightest suspicion he would have shot them down without hesitation. He had often treated detectives who had tried to gain his confidence in just that manner, and he would not have hesitated to do it again. It was thought for this reason that the Fords had been with him before and were well known to him, and it is not impossible that they became frightened at the general breaking up of the band and the many arrests, and sought to cover their own tracks and make themselves right at the same time with the authorities by taking the life of the great outlaw.

At 9 o'clock on the morning of April 3d, 1882, the great outlaw and the two Fords were together in a front room in Jesse James' house. Unconscious of danger James unbuckled his belt and threw it on the bed preparatory to washing himself. He was unarmed. Jesse got upon a chair to arrange a picture. The brothers had determined to kill him and get the reward and this was their chance.

They exchanged glances and silently stepped between the pistols and their victim. Both drew their pistols. The click of the hammers fell on the ear of Jesse, and he was turning his head evidently to see what caused the warning sound when Robert, the youngest brother, sent a bullet crashing through his brain. The murdered bandit fell backward without a cry and rolled in his death agony on the floor.

Jesse's wife, who was in the next room, ran in and saw the two brothers scaling the fence and making off. Hardly had the shot been fired when there was a piercing scream. The dead man's wife flung herself upon the prostrate body and gave way to her grief in a flood of tears. The Fords gave themselves up and were hurried away to the court house and a guard immediately put on duty. The news spread like wildfire. The house was surrounded by excited people and hundreds of persons talked about the bloody deed on the streets. The body was taken in charge by the police and photographed. Persons who had known the outlaw were allowed to view the remains. They declared that there was no doubt this time and at last the great bandit had been killed. The face is fine-looking and intelligent and would not be taken for that of a cruel murderer. The house was searched and found to contain a quantity of firearms and ammunition. In the stable was several splendid horses.

4. Miguel Antonio Otero Remembers the Land Wars of the 1880s

The "Gorras Blanco," [sic] or White Caps, became very active in San Miguel County about this time, burning houses, cutting fences, and resorting to all kinds of intimidations. They stopped teams from hauling railroad ties, because the owners of the teams, usually the driver, were not charging the contractors enough money for the hauling. On these occasions the White Caps would unload the ties and either burn them or chop them up.

At night large parties on horseback, wearing white caps drawn over their faces, would ride through towns and settlements merely for the purpose of intimidating people. Once I saw more than a hundred pass my home at night, two abreast, and on this occasion they rode through both East and West Las Vegas. Numerous complaints had been filed with the county commissioners, asking them to hire detectives and "secret officers" to bring to the courts the perpetrators. . . .

Two nights before our return to Las Vegas it was reported that several haystacks had been burned, miles of fence wire had been cut, and many horses stolen, as well as milch cows, sheep, hogs, and even chickens. It was hard for the county commissioners to secure good and competent men to act as detectives because they were afraid the White Caps would take revenge. Still, a few men agreed to serve, provided their names were not mentioned and they were paid in cash. Very reliable information stated that everything had been properly arranged by S. E. Booth, chairman of the [commission] board, and Placido Sandoval, one of the members. In order that no leak should appear on the horizon, Booth took a fictitious name, "Joe Bowers," while Placido Sandoval assumed the fictitious name, "Baltazar Burmudez." These two county commissioners drew the warrants in their fictitious names, and received the cash which they were expected to pay to the detectives in a secret manner. . . .

. . . Matters were beginning to get hot for the White Caps, and, although no arrests were made, the organization decided to abandon their night rides and commit no further depredations in San Miguel County. They still retained their political organization until most of the leaders either died or left the county.

We had no sooner arrived in Las Vegas from . . . Mora . . . than we were again informed of the dastardly crimes committed by the "Gorras Blanco" or White Caps, under the leadership of two brothers, Juan Jose Herrera and Pablo Herrera. It was common talk that the White Caps had again organized, and that the present

Miguel Antonio Otero, *My Life on the Frontier, 1864–1882* (New York: Press of the Pioneers, 1935), 248–251.

sheriff, Don Lorenzo Lopez, was very closely aligned with them. These rumors were evidently authentic, for, at the next general election, Pablo Herrera was nominated on the Lopez ticket for the House of Representatives from San Miguel County, and was duly elected.

Pablo Herrera spoke perfectly good English, was rather a large man, had dark hair, and always wore a heavy black mustache. Some years before he entered the House of Representatives, he had been convicted of murder and had served his time in the penitentiary.

Pablo was considered a labor agitator, and on his return to San Miguel County he reorganized the "Gorras Blanco," or White Caps, and started to run things. A warrant was soon issued for his arrest and given to Felipe Lopez, a brother of Sheriff Lorenzo Lopez, to serve. He met Pablo very close to the courthouse, pulled his pistol, and without a word shot him through the heart, killing him instantly. Pablo had a bad name, so nothing was ever done to Felipe Lopez.

This killing, however, had a salutary effect on the "Gorras Blanco," and, finding themselves without an aggressive leader, they soon went out of business as an organization, for Juan Jose Herrera was getting too old to take the leadership. Occasionally one would hear of small groups of White Caps cutting fences and burning barns, but nothing more on a large scale, and gradually the roughnecks disappeared, and quiet was restored throughout San Miguel County.

5. Black Elk Remembers the Wounded Knee Massacre of 1890

After the soldiers marched away, I heard from my friend, Dog Chief, how the trouble started, and he was right there by Yellow Bird when it happened. This is the way it was:

In the morning the soldiers began to take all the guns away from the Big Foots, who were camped in the flat below the little hill where the monument and burying ground are now. The people had stacked most of their guns, and even their knives, by the tepee where Big Foot was lying sick. Soldiers were on the little hill and all around, and there were soldiers across the dry gulch to the south and over east along Wounded Knee Creek too. The people were nearly surrounded, and the wagon-guns were pointing at them.

Some had not yet given up their guns, and so the soldiers were searching all the tepees, throwing things around and poking into everything. There was a man called Yellow Bird, and he and another man were standing in front of the tepee where Big Foot was lying sick. They had white sheets around and over them, with eyeholes to look through, and they had guns under these. An officer came to search them. He took the other man's gun, and then started to take Yellow Bird's. But Yellow Bird would not let go. He wrestled with the officer, and while they were wrestling, the gun went off and killed the officer. Wasichus and some others have said he meant to

John G. Neihardt, *Black Elk Speaks: Being the Life Story of a Holy Man of the Oglala Sioux* (New York: Pocket Books, 1959 [1932]), 211–223. Reprinted by permission of the University of Nebraska Press. Copyright 1932, 1959, 1972 by John G. Neihardt. Copyright ©1961 by the John G. Neihardt Trust.

do this, but Dog Chief was standing right there, and he told me it was not so. As soon as the gun went off, Dog Chief told me, an officer shot and killed Big Foot who was lying sick inside the tepee.

Then suddenly nobody knew what was happening, except that the soldiers were all shooting and the wagon-guns began going off right in among the people.

Many were shot down right there. The women and children ran into the gulch and up west, dropping all the time, for the soldiers shot them as they ran. There were only about a hundred warriors and there were nearly five hundred soldiers. The warriors rushed to where they had piled their guns and knives. They fought soldiers with only their hands until they got their guns.

Dog Chief saw Yellow Bird run into a tepee with his gun, and from there he killed soldiers until the tepee caught fire. Then he died full of bullets.

It was a good winter day when all this happened. The sun was shining. But after the soldiers marched away from their dirty work, a heavy snow began to fall. The wind came up in the night There was a big blizzard, and it grew very cold. The snow drifted deep in the crooked gulch, and it was one long grave of butchered women and children and babies, who had never done any harm and were only trying to run away.

6. Frederick Jackson Turner Praises the Frontier as the Source of American Democracy, 1893

In a recent bulletin of the Superintendent of the Census for 1890 appear these significant words: "Up to and including 1880 the country had a frontier of settlement, but at present the unsettled area has been so broken into by isolated bodies of settlement that there can hardly be said to be a frontier line. In the discussion of its extent, its westward movement, etc., it can not, therefore, any longer have a place in the census reports." This brief official statement marks the closing of a great historic movement. . . .

From the conditions of frontier life came intellectual traits of profound importance. The works of travelers along each frontier from colonial days onward describe certain common traits, and these traits have, while softening down, still persisted as survivals in the place of their origin, even when a higher social organization succeeded. The result is that to the frontier the American intellect owes its striking characteristics. That coarseness and strength combined with acuteness and inquisitiveness; that practical, inventive turn of mind, quick to find expedients; that masterful grasp of material things, lacking in the artistic but powerful to effect great ends; that restless, nervous energy; that dominant individualism, working for good and for evil, and withal that buoyancy and exuberance which comes with freedom—these are traits of the frontier, or traits called out elsewhere because of the existence of the frontier. Since the days when the fleet of Columbus sailed into the waters of the New World, America has been another name for opportunity, and the people of the United States have taken their tone from the

Frederick Jackson Turner, "The Significance of the Frontier in American History," in *The Frontier in American History* (New York: Henry Holt, 1920 [1893]), 1–4, 22–35 [with edits], 37–38.

incessant expansion which has not only been open but has even been forced upon them. He would be a rash prophet who should assert that the expansive character of American life has now entirely ceased. Movement has been its dominant fact, and, unless this training has no effect upon a people, the American energy will continually demand a wider field for its exercise. But never again will such gifts of free land offer themselves. For a moment, at the frontier, the bonds of custom are broken and unrestraint is triumphant. There is not *tabula rasa*. The stubborn American environment is there with its imperious summons to accept its conditions; the inherited ways of doing things are also there; and yet, in spite of environment, and in spite of custom, each frontier did indeed furnish a new field of opportunity, a gate of escape from the bondage of the past; and freshness, and confidence, and scorn of older society, impatience of its restraints and its ideas, and indifference to its lessons, have accompanied the frontier. What the Mediterranean Sea was to the Greeks, breaking the bond of custom, offering new experiences, calling out new institutions and activities, that, and more, the ever retreating frontier has been to the United States directly, and to the nations of Europe more remotely. And now, four centuries from the discovery of America, at the end of a hundred years of life under the Constitution, the frontier has gone, and with its going has closed the first period of American history.

7. Catharine Calk McCarty Meets Her Cattlemen Neighbors, 1916

My homestead home, a log house, on the side of a hill on the open range with its dirt floor and dirt roof, seemed a haven that next summer when the hot winds, parching the land as well as the face, seemed never to end. At the back of the house, where the shadows were longest, a hole in the ground, about two feet deep and four feet in diameter served as the "icebox." The water, carried up the hill from my brother's well, and kept covered in the icebox, seemed very cool. . . .

My brother was not on the homestead that summer. Colonel, my dog, followed Tramp and me wherever we went. The old saying, a horse and a dog are man's best friends, I found was true.

As the hot days of July, 1916, neared their end, the wheat as well as the oats were turning yellow. One morning I was awakened by Colonel barking as though something was wrong. Opening the door, stepping out into the morning sun just coming over the hill, I saw a large herd of range cattle pushing against the wire fence around the crop.

This is serious—in a day our crop will be gone and all the feed for winter, I thought. Saddling Tramp and taking my revolver I attempted to round up the cattle. I was not very adept at this. The cattle sensed it. In despair, I shot into the air; this really got them going, and with Colonel helping, the cattle were driven what seemed a long ways away, and I hoped they would not find their way back. Hurrying home, I fed Colonel and Tramp, ate my breakfast, dinner and supper in one.

Catharine Calk McCarty, *Blue Grass and Big Sky* (Phoenix: Stockmore House, 1983), 18–21.

The next day, at daylight the cattle were back. This continued for several days. Shooting in the air and the dog barking seemed to be the only way I could get them moving.

One day when my three-meals-in-one was over, two strange men rode up, came to the door, introduced themselves, and said, "We are representatives of the local stock association. Are you the lady shooting cattle?"

"No," I replied, "I am not shooting cattle. I am just driving them away from that little crop. Every day I think they will lose their way but every morning, there they are."

"Aren't you shooting at them? That's illegal. The stockmen cannot put up with that. The sheriff will serve notice on you if you don't stop."

"I cannot drive them; the only way I can get them away is to shoot in the air."

"You can't do that," they cried. "We are a committee to notify you that this will have to stop."

"Fine, "I said, "if I stop shooting at your cattle, you'll have to help." By that time, they were drinking some coffee. "I'm just a forlorn homesteader trying to protect a little crop while my brother is away. You both have mowers, haven't you, and men, and horses? Well, how about coming here, cutting the crop, and putting up a corral?"

They looked at me.

"If you don't want me to run your cattle, you'll have to cut the crop," I laughed.

They looked at each other. Finally one of them said, "By golly, maybe we could do that."

I said, "Well, if you do that, I'll cook the best dinner I can. You'll have to come early, as those cattle will push in the fence and one hundred head of cattle can do a lot of eating."

We talked awhile about the cattle business, what luck they were having, and how the range had been taken up; and if I were going to shoot and run their cattle, they would not weigh anything in the fall. "They will be nothing but drags if we ever get them to market," they cried.

I listened very attentively, wondering, "Will they really do this? Will they be here tomorrow?" They left with a grin.

Sure enough, next morning, at daylight they were back with a mower and hay rake. There were two men, one mowing, one raking, and two others putting up a corral, taking the wire and posts from the fence. "How wonderful of them," I kept saying to myself.

I cooked everything I had on hand. Making some lemon pies, with lemons and eggs taken from the "icebox" at the back of the cabin, hot biscuits, and the last of some ham and beans, jam, and anything else I could find. I got them filled up. I tried to show them what good sports I thought they were, and how much I appreciated their help, telling them that they were not at all like stockmen who hate honyockers, as homesteaders were called.

They left with mower, hay rake, horses, and bid me a very friendly farewell. I looked at the hay in the corral and the herd having a good feed on the stubble left on the field. That night I slept soundly, way into the next day. No more riding at daybreak, shooting, running cattle. Those days were over.

Shortly I had word from Mr. Hetherington, who seemed to be head of the local stockmen and dominated the association. He wanted to see me. I was afraid that he would want pay for the men who worked and for his rake and mower. I heard he was crippled with rheumatism and I decided to face the lion in his den. I found the way to his home, one day after a long ride. When I knocked at the door, Mrs. Hetherington opened it, and I introduced myself.

"Oh yes," she greeted me, "Mr. Hetherington thought you would be coming one of these days." She brought me into the room where a large man, with shaggy greying hair and heavy eyebrows, sat on a chair.

"Did you want to see me?" I meekly asked.

He fairly shouted, "I sent for you, didn't I? I wanted to see the red-headed girl who rides around shooting cattle."

"But, Mr. Hetherington," I began.

"No, I know. When the local association sent two men to order you to stop shooting and running cattle, what did the weak fools do? Nothing to make you stop, but you talked them into bringing our machinery, horses, and men, cutting your crop, and even building a corral for that handful of hay."

"Did you want to see me?" I began again.

"Yes, I wanted to see what you looked like," he bellowed. Then he threw back his head and laughed and laughed. "This is the best joke on us I ever heard, stockmen cutting honyocker's hay. If it gets around, we'll be the laughing stock of the country."

I laughed, too. Mrs. Hetherington came in with coffee and cake, and we talked and talked. I told him what fine men I thought stockmen are, not at all like homesteaders pictured them, and that my brother hopes in the future to join their crowd.

We parted friends. During that summer, some of the stockmen now and then rode by the house to see how everything was. I thought that the resentment they bore to homesteaders was highly exaggerated.

E S S A Y S

The following essays offer revisionist angles on three classic themes of western history: the official quest for law and order, women's "taming" influence on the frontier, and the domestication of nomadic Indian peoples. First, Stanford University Professor Richard White sets the storied past of popular outlaws like Jesse James in a larger framework of social banditry and symbolic revolt against authority. In the second essay, Robert L. Griswold of the University of Oklahoma examines the spread of domestic ideology from its secure eastern perches to the wilder settings of western communities. This "cultural system"—particularly its set of expectations for and limitations on women's behavior—drew strength, suggests Griswold, not only because of the direct transfer of dominant thinking westward but also because women were able to manipulate the terms of domestic idealism to meet immediate needs. Equally complicated manifestations of the settling of the West were the federal government's attempts to turn Native American nations into communities of landowning farm families. In a case study of the Northern Utes of eastern Utah, historian David Rich Lewis of Utah State University argues that a combination of political, cultural, and environmental factors wreaked economic chaos, even as the Utes struggled to maintain their identity in a reservation environment.

Outlaw Gangs and Social Bandits

RICHARD WHITE

Americans have often regarded western outlaws as heroes. In popular culture—legend, folksongs, and movies—the American West might as well be Sherwood Forest; its plains and prairies teem with what E. J. Hobsbawm has called social bandits. Driven outside the law because of some act sanctioned by local conventions but regarded as criminal by the state or local authorities, the social bandit has been forced to become an outlaw. Members of his community, however, still consider him an honorable and admirable man. They protect him and are ready to reassimilate him if persecution by the state should stop. The social bandit is a man who violates the law but who still serves a higher justice. He robs from the rich and gives to the poor and only kills in self-defense or just revenge. As long as he observes this code, he is, in myth and legend, invulnerable to his enemies; he can die or be captured only when betrayed by friends.

In the American West, stories of this kind have gathered around many historical outlaws: Jesse James, Billy the Kid, Cole Younger, Sam Bass, John Wesley Hardin, Bob Dalton, Bill Dalton, Bill Doolin, and more. These men exert a surprising fascination on a nation that takes some pride in due process and the rule of law and where the standard version of western settlement is subordination of "savagery" to law and civilization. These bandits, however, exist in more than legend; as actual outlaws many enjoyed substantial amounts of local support. Such outlaws must be taken seriously as social bandits. Their appeal, while complex, is not mysterious, and it provides insights not only into certain kinds of western settlement and social conditions but also into basic paradoxes of American culture itself.

The tendency to justify certain outlaws as decent, honorable men despite their violation of the law is, in a sense, unique only because these men openly were bandits. In other ways social bandits fit into a continuum of extralegal organizations, such as claims clubs, vigilantes, and whitecaps*—prevalent throughout the United States but most common in the West. In certain situations the differences between social bandits (criminals) and vigilantes (law enforcers) were not great, and although this may offend certain modern law and order sensibilities, it is a mistake to impose such contemporary distinctions on nineteenth-century conditions.

In the American West during this period, concepts of legality, extralegality, and illegality became quite confusing. Well into the late nineteenth century public law enforcement remained weak, particularly in rural areas where a variety of extralegal

---

*A type of vigilante group that sprang up in many different areas of the country toward the end of the nineteenth century and that was given to violence with racist overtones—e.g., flogging blacks in northern Texas and anti-Mexican actions in southern Texas.

Richard White, "Outlaw Gangs of the Middle Border: American Social Bandits," *Western Historical Quarterly,* 12 (October 1981), 387–408. Copyright by Western History Association. Reprinted by permission.

organizations supplemented or replaced the constituted authorities. Members of claims clubs, vigilantes, and whitecaps, of course, proclaimed their allegiance to community norms and saw themselves as establishing order, not contributing to disorder. On many occasions they were probably correct. Often, however, the line between extralegal organizations who claimed to preserve order and extralegal gangs accused of creating disorder was a fine one indeed. Claims clubs using threats of violence or actual violence to gain additional public land for their members, even when this involved driving off legitimate claimants, vigilante committees whose targets might only be economic or political rivals, or whitecaps who chose to upgrade the moral tone of the community through beatings and whippings may not be outlaws, but distinguishing them from criminals on moral or legal grounds is not very compelling. In the West, *criminal* could be an ambiguous term, and vigilantes often became the armed force of one racial, class, or cultural group moving against other groups with opposing interests. In such cases vigilantes often provoked retaliation, and local civil war resulted. . . .

Social bandits, however, did not represent this kind of organized opposition to vigilantes. They, too, arose where law enforcement was distrusted, where criminal was an ambiguous category, and where the legitimacy of vigilantism was questioned. Where social banditry occurred, however, the vigilantes and their opponents did not form two coherent groups, but instead consisted of numerous, mutually hostile factions. . . .

Three gangs that seem most clearly part of a western social bandit tradition are the James-Younger gang of western Missouri and its lineal successors led by Jesse James (1866[?]–1882), the Dalton gang of Oklahoma Territory (1890–1892), and the Doolin-Dalton gang of Oklahoma Territory (1892–1896). Such a list is purposefully narrow and is not meant to be exclusive. These are only the most famous gangs, but an examination of them can establish both the reality of social banditry and the nature of its appeal.

Social bandits are almost by definition creations of their supporters, but this support must be carefully defined. Virtually all criminals have some people who aid them, since there will always be those who find profit and advantage in doing so. Social bandits, too, may have supporters who are essentially confederates. What separates social bandits from ordinary criminals, however, is the existence of large numbers of other people who aid them but who are only technically implicated in their crimes. Such people are not themselves criminals and are willing to justify their own actions in supporting outlaws on grounds other than fear, profit, or expediency. When such people exist in large enough numbers to make an area a haven for a particular group of outlaws, then social banditry exists. For the James-Younger, Dalton, and Doolin-Dalton gangs, this support had three major components: the kinship networks so important to western settlement in general, active supporters, and those people who can be termed passive sympathizers.

That two of these three gangs organized themselves around sets of brothers— the James brothers, the Younger brothers, and the Dalton brothers—is perhaps the most striking illustration of the importance of kinship in social banditry. Centered on blood relations, the James-Younger gang and, to a much lesser extent the Dalton gang depended on relatives to hide them, feed them, warn them of danger, and provide them with alibis. The James brothers recruited two of their cousins—Wood and Clarence Hite—into the gang, and even the Ford brothers, who eventually murdered Jesse, were recruited because they were related by marriage to Jim Cummins, another gang member. Only the Doolin-Dalton gang lacked widespread kin connections, and this forced them to rely more heavily on other forms of support, which were, however, common to all the gangs.

Besides kinspeople, the gangs drew on a larger group of active supporters who knew the outlaws personally and who duplicated many of the services provided by relatives of the bandits. The James-Younger gang recruited such supporters largely from among neighbors and the ex-Confederate guerrillas who had ridden with them in the Civil War. Such "friends of the outlaws" were, according to the man who broke the gang—William Wallace—"thick in the country portions of Jackson County," and many people in the region believed that no local jury would ever convict members of the James gang.

Similar support existed in Oklahoma. The Daltons—Bob, Emmett and Grat—had possessed "many friends in the territory" and had found aid not only among farmers but also on the ranches along the Cimarron River, in the Creek Nation, and in the Cheyenne-Arapaho country. The Doolin-Dalton gang apparently built on this earlier network of support. Frank Canton, who as undersheriff of Pawnee County pursued the Doolin-Dalton gang, distinguished their active sympathizers from the twenty-five to thirty confederates who fenced stolen goods for the outlaws.

> The Dalton gang and especially Bill Doolin had many friends among the settlers south of Pawnee along the Cimarron River, and along the line of Pawnee County. There is no doubt that Doolin furnished many of them money to buy groceries to live upon when they first settled in that country and had a hard struggle for existence. They appreciated his kindness even though he was an outlaw with a price upon his head, and there were plenty of people who would get up at the hour of midnight if necessary to ride to Bill Doolin to warn him of the approach of officers when they were seen in that vicinity.

U.S. Marshal Evett Nix, too, complained that "protectors and friends" of the Doolin-Dalton gang "were numerous." The small town of Ingalls in Payne County became a particularly notorious center of sympathy for the gang. Three deputy marshals died in the disastrous raid officers made on the town in 1893, and when a posse pursued the bandits into the surrounding countryside, local farmers misdirected the deputies. The frustrated officers retaliated by arresting a number of local citizens for aiding the outlaws. Probandit sentiment persisted in the region into 1894 when a local newspaper reported that Bill Doolin was openly "circulating among his many friends in the Sooner Valley" and pointedly remarked that deputy marshals had been absent from the area as usual. Years later, when the state erected a monument to the deputies who fell at Ingalls, at least one old local resident complained that it had been erected to the "wrong bunch." In the case of all three gangs, the network of primary supporters remained localized. The James-Younger gang in its prime drew largely on Clay, Jackson, and Ray counties in Missouri, while the Daltons and the Doolin-Dalton gang relied heavily on people in Payne, Kingfisher, and Pawnee counties, as well as ranchers in the neighboring sections of the Indian nations and the Cherokee strip.

The final category of popular sympathy for outlaws was probably at once the largest, the least important in terms of the bandits' day-to-day activities, and yet the most critical in the transformation of the outlaws into local heroes. This third group consisted of passive sympathizers—people who probably had never seen an actual outlaw, let alone ever aided one. Their sympathy, however, was quite real, and given a chance they publicly demonstrated it. They mourned Jesse James, "lionized" Bill Doolin after his capture, flocked to see Frank James after his surrender, packed his trial, and applauded his acquittal. Such sympathizers appeared even in Coffeeville, Kansas, where the Dalton gang tried to outdo the James-Younger gang by robbing two banks at once. The result was a bloody debacle—the death of most of the gang and the killing of numerous citizens. Yet within days of the fight, some people openly sympathized with the outlaws on the streets of Coffeeville.

The mere existence of support, however, does not explain the reasons for it. The simplest explanation, and one advanced by many anti-outlaw writers, was that the bandits' supporters acted from fear. This is not very persuasive. While arguing that fear brought support, many popular writers have often simultaneously incorporated major elements of the bandits' legends into their own writings. They paradoxically argue against a sympathy that they themselves reflect. Such sympathy seems an unlikely product of fear, and there is little evidence for the reign of terror by these gangs reported by outside newspapers for Missouri in the 1870s and Oklahoma in the 1890s. Both Dalton and Doolin-Dalton gang members were welcomed to the country dances and other community affairs in Oklahoma that they attended. Certainly they had become locally notorious, but fear was not the dominant note in their notoriety. In Payne County, for example, a Stillwater grocer fortuitously named Bill Dalton capitalized on outlaw Bill Dalton's fame in an advertisement with banner headlines proclaiming that:

> Bill Dalton's Gang Are After You And If You Can Give Them A Trial You Will Be Convinced That They Keep The Freshest & Best Goods In The City At The Lowest Prices.

Feared killers are not usually relied on to promote the sale of groceries. Finally, if fear was the only cause of the bandits' support, it is hard to explain the continued expression of public sympathy after the outlaws were dead or imprisoned and no one had much to fear from them anymore.

A social bandit cannot survive through terror alone, and these bandits did not. They had ties to the local community predating their life of crime, and during their criminal careers social bandits reinforced those local ties. Gangs that did not have such connections or did not maintain them remained parasites whose lack of shelter and aid condemned them to destruction. The social bandits needed popular support; they could not undercut it by indiscriminately robbing the inhabitants of the regions in which they lived and operated. Those outlaws who simply preyed on local communities were hunted down like the stock thieves of Indian Territory. No one romanticized, and rarely even remembered, Dock Bishop and Frank Latham, or the more notorious Zip Wyatt-Ike Black gang, for example. The social bandits avoided such a fate by concentrating their robberies on railroads and banks. Thus, they not only avoided directly harming local people, but they also preyed upon institutions that many farmers believed were preying on them.

Beyond this, social bandits often did assist their supporters in at least small ways. There is no need to accept the numerous romantic stories of gallant outlaws paying the mortgages on the farms of poor widows to grant them an economic role in their local communities. Bill Doolin may very well have helped poor settlers through some hard times with groceries and small gifts; the Dalton and Doolin-Dalton gangs certainly did provide oysters and refreshments for local dances, and such small kindnesses were also probably practiced by the James-Younger gang. What was probably more significant to their supporters in chronically cash-short economics, however, was that all these gangs paid very well for the horses, feed, and supplies they needed. Their largess won them friends.

If fear fails as an explanation for what appears to be legitimate social banditry, then the next logical recourse is to the interpretation E. J. Hobsbawm offered to explain European bandits. According to Hobsbawm, social banditry is a premodern social revolt—a protest against either excessive exploitation from above or against the overturn of traditional norms by modernizing elements in a society. It is quintessentially a peasant protest. Hobsbawm mentioned Jesse James himself as following in this European tradition. The shortcomings of a literal reading of Hobsbawm are obvious. Jesse James could not be a peasant champion because there were no American peasants to champion. Yet Hobsbawm's analysis might be retrieved by reinterpreting the western outlaws more generally as champions of a "traditional" society against a "modern" society.

Such evidence as can be recovered, however, indicates that this interpretation, too, is badly flawed. Both the outlaws and their supporters came from modern, market-oriented groups and not from poor, traditional groups. The James-Younger gang had its origins in the Confederate guerrillas of the Civil War who were recruited from the economic and social elite of Jackson and neighboring counties. Usually guerrillas were the "elder offspring of well-to-do, slave holding farmers." The chief members of the James-Younger gang were ex-guerrillas with similar origins. Colonel Henry Younger, the father of the Younger brothers, owned 3,500 acres of land in Jackson and Cass counties before the Civil War. His wife was a daughter of a member of the Missouri legislature. The father of Jesse and Frank James was a Baptist minister who in 1850 owned a 275-acre farm. Their stepfather was a physician who resided with their mother on a Missouri farm worth $10,000 in 1870, and their uncle, George Hite, Sr., was said, probably with some exaggeration, to have been worth $100,000 before losing heavily in the tobacco speculation that forced him into bankruptcy in 1877.

Many of the gang's other supporters enjoyed similar social standing. Joseph Shelby, the Confederate cavalry leader, and members of the large Hudspeth family all aided the James-Younger gang, and all were prosperous farmers with sizable landholdings. The jury that acquitted Frank James of murder was composed of twelve "well-to-do thrifty farmers," and Clay County, in the heart of the bandit country, was "one of the richest counties in the state," inhabited by a people who were "well-dressed, well-to-do, and hospitable." These substantial farmers and speculators seem an unlikely source for premodern rebels or as leaders of a revolt of the rural poor.

Members and supporters of the Dalton and Doolin-Dalton gangs were not so prosperous, but then these gangs did not have such a firmly established rural region to draw upon. The Daltons were, by most accounts, an ordinary midwestern farm family. Three Dalton brothers became farmers; one was a deputy marshal killed in the line of duty; the other four eventually became outlaws. Bill Doolin was a ranch foreman and, according to local residents, a "respected citizen" before becoming a bandit. Bitter Creek Newcomb, Little Bill Raidler, and Dick Broadwell all had middle-class origins in families of merchants and farmers, and Raidler had supposedly attended college. The remainder of these two gangs included equal numbers of previously honest cowboys and small-time thugs and drifters without close family connections. Supporters of the Oklahoma gangs also apparently spanned class lines, ranging from small-scale farmers to large-scale ranchers like Jim Riley, who was locally considered well-to-do.

Neither class nor traditional values seem to be significant factors in the support of bandits, but the tendency of supporters to live in rural rather than urban regions suggest a third possible explanation of social banditry as an exotic appendage of the agrarian revolt of post–Civil War America. Some evidence, taken in isolation, seems to support such a connection with rural radicalism. Both local boosters and government officials interested in attracting capital attacked the gangs. They blamed them for discouraging investment and immigration. Governor Crittenden and Senator Carl Schurz of Missouri, for example, defended the assassination of Jesse James in ridding the state of "a great hindrance to its prosperity and as likely to give an important stimulus to real estate speculation, railroad enterprise, and foreign immigration."

On the other side, positions taken by some of the bandits after their careers were over make them appear to be radicals. Frank James credited his robberies with maintaining local prosperity because they had frightened eastern capital out of Jackson County and thus kept it free of mortgages. And in 1897 he declared: "If there is ever another war in this country, which may happen, it will be between capital and labor, I mean between greed and manhood, and I'm as ready to march now in defense of American manhood, as I was when a boy in the defense of the South. Unless we can stop this government by injunction that's what we are coming to." Frank James was not alone in his swing to the left. James Younger became a socialist while in prison.

Put in context, however, all of this is considerably less compelling. While active criminals, none of the bandits took radical political positions. Nor did agrarian groups show much sympathy for the bandits. Contemporary writers pointed out that politicians and capitalists stole far more than bandits, and individual farmers aided the gangs, but organized agrarians did not confuse banditry with political action. The leading agrarian party in Missouri in the 1870s—the People's party—although it attacked banks and monopolies, also denounced lawlessness, particularly that of the James-Younger gang. It is also instructive to remember that the Farmers Alliance, which eventually spawned the Populist party, started out as a group to combat horse theft. The Populists themselves showed no more interest in banditry as a variant of political action than had the People's party of Missouri. In any case, if banditry were political in nature and inspired by agrarian resentment against banks and railroads, it is hard to explain why support for bandits was largely confined to Oklahoma in the 1890s while Populism spread all over the South and West.

A better explanation of social banditry is possible. It begins with the peculiar social conditions of western Missouri in the 1860s and 1870s and Oklahoma in the 1890s that allowed social bandits to emerge as variants of the widespread extralegal organizations already common in the West. The exceptional situations prevailing in both Missouri and Oklahoma encouraged popular identification with the out-laws whom local people supported not because of their crimes but rather because of certain culturally defined masculine virtues the outlaws embodied. In each lo-cale there were good reasons to value such virtues. This emphasis on the bandits as symbols of masculinity, in turn, made them accessible to the larger culture at a time when masculinity itself was being widely worried over and glorified. The bandit's virtues made him a cultural hero and embarked him on a posthumous career (of a very conservative sort) which is far from over yet. All of this requires considerable explanation.

Public support of bandits can obviously exist only in areas where belief in the honesty and competency of public law enforcement has been seriously eroded. This was the case in both postwar Missouri and Oklahoma in the 1890s. In the Missouri countryside, ex-Confederates hated and feared Union sheriffs, who they believed used their offices to settle old scores from the war, and they regarded the state mili-tia, called up to maintain order, as plunderers and freebooters. Wartime antagonisms and turmoil faded in time, but when the Pinkertons attacked the home of Zerelda Samuel, mother of the James boys, blowing off her arm and killing her young son—the halfbrother of Jesse and Frank—they rekindled hatred of the authorities. Gover-nor Crittenden's subsequent solicitation of assassins to kill Jesse only deepened the prevailing distrust of the equity and honesty of law enforcement.

In Oklahoma settlers similarly distrusted U.S. deputy marshals, whom they often regarded as little better than criminals themselves. During the land rush, deputies used their office unfairly to secure the best lands and later spent much of their time arresting farmers who cut timber on the public domain or on Indian lands and prosecuting settlers who happened to be found with small amounts of whiskey in the Indian nations. Farmers believed that deputies sought only the fees they collected by persecuting "poor defenseless claim holders." On at least two oc-casions in the late winter and spring of 1893, resentment ran high enough for armed groups to attempt to attack deputy marshals and free their prisoners.

Although newspapers praised their bravery when they died in the line of duty, living marshals merited much less sympathy. Local newspapers rarely praised crimes social bandits committed, but they commonly ridiculed and denounced the lawmen who pursued them. In April of 1894, for example, the *Pond Creek Voice* reported that deputy marshals riding past the garden of an old woman who lived near the Cimarron River had mistaken her scarecrow for an outlaw and had riddled it with bullets before riding off in panic to report their ambush by the Doolin-Dalton gang. When Bill Dalton was actually killed, the *Stillwater Gazette* reported that it would come as a great relief to the deputy marshals "who have made it a practice to ride in the opposite direction from where he was every time they got him located." In the eyes of many people, the deputy marshals were simply another group of armed men, distinguished mainly by their cowardice, who rode around the territory posing a threat to life and property. The transition of the Dalton brothers from deputy marshals and possemen to open criminals was no fall from grace. Indeed, it may have gained the brothers support in some areas.

This distrust of law enforcement is particularly significant in the light of the widespread disorder existing in both areas. Following the Civil War, robbery and murder continued to occur in northwestern Missouri with appalling frequency.

Gangs of ex-guerrillas from both sides pillaged and sought revenge for wartime acts; committees of public safety organized, and vigilantes remained active until the mid-1870s. Numerous armed bands, each protecting its own interests, clashed in the countryside. Legal protection was often unavailable. All this was not merely the last gasp of the Lost Cause; it was not a simple reflection of Union/Confederate divisions. Many local ex-Confederates, for example, opposed the James-Younger gang. The Confederate background of the outlaws certainly won them some sympathy, but only within the local context of chaotic, factional disorder.

The situation in Oklahoma in the 1890s was a remarkably similar mixture of predation, personal vengeance, and vigilantism. With the demand for Oklahoma land exceeding its availability, the government resorted to one of the most astonishing systems of distributing resources ever attempted by a modern state. Settlers in Oklahoma raced for their land. The races were spectacular, colorful, and virtually impossible to police. Numerous people—the "sooners"—stole over the line ahead of the starting time to stake claims. Sooners only increased the inevitable conflicts among people who claimed to have arrived first at a desirable plot of land. In the end the land rushes sowed a crop of litigation and violence. Even if nothing else divided a community, bitter factional struggles for land were sure to persist for years. In Payne County, the center of support for the Doolin-Dalton gang, the county attorney claimed, perhaps with some exaggeration, that there were fifty murders as the direct result of land claim cases in the early years. Such murders involved the leading citizens of Payne County. The first representative of Payne County to the Oklahoma legislature and speaker of the assembly, I. N. Terrill, terminated his political career in 1891 by murdering a man in a land dispute.

Given the distrust of local law enforcement, protection in such disputes often demanded organization and violence. In 1893, for example, the *Oklahoma State Capital* reported the presumed lynching of three sooners by a local vigilante committee. Apparently both sides—the alleged sooners and the vigilante committee—were armed and resorting to violence. Such actions, the reported contended, were common: "Reports are coming in every day of whitecap whippings and terrorizing and it is nothing to see the sooner pulling out every day, claiming that they have been threatened with hanging by vigilant committees if they did not go." The large numbers of horse and cattle thieves who had long existed in a sort of parasitic relationship with the large cattle operations and who now turned to stealing from settlers only increased the level of private violence.

The situation in Oklahoma was, however, more complicated than extralegal groups enforcing the laws against thieves and sooners. There was some ambiguity about what constituted theft. For example, Evan Barnard, an ex-cowboy and settler in Oklahoma who wrote one of the best of western memoirs, defended stock theft by his friend, Ranicky Bill: "He was generous and big-hearted . . . if he knew any settler who was hungry, he did not hesitate to rustle beef, and give it to the starving people. In the early days of Oklahoma, a man who did that was not such a bad person after all." According to Barnard, such attitudes were shared by many settlers. When it became clear that the large ranchers would lose their leases on Indian lands, the homesteaders moved in to steal wood, fencing, and stock. All the old-time cattlemen, Barnard contends, would admit that the "settlers were good rustlers." In practice *sooner, rustler, vigilante,* and *outlaw* were ambiguous terms; very often they were only pejorative names for those whose interests were not the same as other citizens.

In both Missouri and Oklahoma, pervasive lawlessness and widespread distrust of public law enforcement divided the countryside not into two clearly opposing groups, but rather into innumerable local factions. Conditions were ripe for factional violence and social banditry. A rather detailed example from Oklahoma is perhaps the best way to illustrate how tangled the relationship of gangs, vigilantes, and other armed groups could become; how supposed, and even demonstrated, criminal behavior might not cost people public sympathy; how private violence could be deemed not only necessary but admirable; and how social bandits garnered support in such situations.

In 1889, Evan Barnard, his friend Ranicky Bill, and other ex-cowboys banded together before the run for Oklahoma Territory to secure and protect land claims. It was a necessary precaution because "just staking a claim did not hold it." Barnard drove one man from his claim by flourishing a winchester and a six-shooter and telling him it was "a hundred and sixty acres or six feet, and I did not give a damn which it was." Bravado was not sufficient to drive off two other challengers, however; for them, Barnard had to demonstrate "the backing I had among the cowboys." This backing was available regardless of the merits of any specific case. One of Barnard's friends failed to secure a claim, but visits from Barnard's associates persuaded the legitimate claimant to sell out to him for $75. The claimant left but declared: "'If I had half the backing that you have, I would stay with you until hell froze over'. . . . He left the claim and Ranicky Bill remarked, 'hits sure hell to get things regulated in a new country.'" Ranicky Bill himself had to stop a contest on his claim by shooting up his opponent's camp. Private force clearly was both a necessary supplement to, and a substitute for, legal right.

Such bullying understandably stirred up resentment against Barnard and his friends, and some regarded them as sooners, which they were not. When these accusations were compounded by charges that Ranicky Bill was a horse thief, the vigilantes struck. They attacked Ranicky Bill's cabin, and although he escaped, the vigilantes threatened to hang Barnard and another neighbor. Ranicky Bill surrendered to authorities to clear himself, but his real protection came from thirty cowboys who gathered a day after the incident and offered to help him. Later, vigilantes seized another neighbor and twice hoisted him off the ground with a rope that cut into his neck. He refused to confess and was released, but now the entire neighborhood armed against the vigilantes, who ceased their operations.

According to Barnard, none of those accused by the vigilantes were thieves, but other incidents narrated in his book indicate how thoroughly such accusations were tied up in land disputes and factional quarrels. Friends and neighbors of Barnard apparently did steal a team of horses and other property from a claim jumper named Sniderwine during a land dispute. They considered this a legitimate means of driving him from his claim and probably perjured themselves to protect each other.

In such an atmosphere, the organization of settlers into armed groups or gangs for protection seems to have been common. The argument made by an actual stock thief to a new settler that in Oklahoma a man's legal rights and property were worthless without friends sometimes led to the corollary that if you were going to be denounced and attacked for supposed crimes, then you might as well have the "game as the name." And in practice, personal quarrels with each side denouncing the other as Sooners and thieves sometimes left local newspapers totally unable to sort out the merits of the case. Personal loyalties and personal qualities in these situations took on larger than normal significance. Law, theft, and even murder became ambiguous categories; strong men who protected themselves and aided their friends could gain local respect transcending their separate criminal activities.

This respect for strong men who could protect and revenge themselves is the real heart of the social bandits' appeal. It is precisely this personal element that gang members and their supporters chose to emphasize. What distinguished social bandits and their supporters (as it distinguished peasant social bandits and theirs) from radicals and revolutionaries was their stubborn refusal to envision the social problems enmeshing them in anything but personal terms. The James and Younger brothers claimed they were hounded into banditry by vindictive Union men who would not leave them alone after the war. They fought only for self-preservation and revenge, not for a social cause. Supporters of Jesse James justified each of his murders as an act of vengeance against men who had attacked his comrades or family. Indeed, the chief propagandist for the James brothers, Missouri newspaper editor John Edwards, made personal vengeance the underlying theme of all their actions from the Civil War onward. Edwards distinguished the guerrillas from regular soldiers by saying these men fought not for a cause but to avenge assaults against themselves and their families. Personal defense and revenge, he claimed, dominated the entire career of the James and Younger brothers. Whether such a claim is accurate or not matters less than that it was credible. When John Edwards claimed these brothers were merely strong men seeking to defend their rights, the appeal could be felt deeply by those who knew that neither they nor the authorities could protect their own rights and property.

The Daltons' grievances, like those of the James and Younger brothers, were personal. They said they became outlaws because the federal government would not pay them for their services as deputy marshals and the express companies had falsely accused them of robbery. They were not radicals who fought against the system itself; they fought against what they regarded as its corruption by their enemies. Emmett Dalton declared that "our fights were not so much against the law, but rather against the law as it was then enforced." At least two members of the Dalton gang asserted that their criminal careers began with land problems, and Bill Doolin, like Cole Younger before him, claimed it was only the personal vindictiveness of his enemies and the corruption of the authorities that stopped him from surrendering. Many of the supporters of the outlaws agreed with these assertions of persecution, and movements for full or partial amnesty for the gangs were common.

Given social conditions in Oklahoma and Missouri, there was a decisive allure in strong men who defended themselves, righted their own wrongs, and took vengeance on their enemies despite the corruption of the existing order. Such virtues were of more than nostalgic interest. In praising bandits, supporters admired them more for their attributes than their acts. Bandits were brave, daring, free, shrewd, and tough, yet also loyal, gentle, generous, and polite. They were not common criminals.

Lon Stansbery, who knew Bill Doolin from the 3-D ranch, was, for instance, forthright about the bandits' heroic stature and masculine virtue:

> The outlaws of that day were not hijackers or petty thieves, and some of them had hearts, even though they were outlaws. They always treated women with respect and no rancher was ever afraid to leave his family on the ranch on account of outlaws. While they would stand up and shoot it out with men, when women were around, they were the first to take off their Stetsons and act like real men. . . .

From the initial exploits of the James-Younger gang until the death of Bill Doolin, appraisals of the outlaws' character by their supporters, while sometimes allowing for an understandable laxity in regard to the sixth and eighth commandments, remained strong and consistent in their praise. The James and Younger brothers were "brilliant, bold, indefatigable roughriders," and in the words of an amnesty resolution introduced in the Missouri legislature, "brave . . . generous . . . gallant . . . honorable" men. The Daltons were "big hearted and generous" in every way, "like the average western man," while Bill Doolin was a "naturally . . . kind-hearted, sympathetic man." A contemporary diary from Ingalls comments that the Doolin-Dalton gang was "as a rule quite (*sic*) and peaceable," even though they moved about heavily armed, and residents later remembered them as "well behaved . . . quiet and friendly," a description close to an Oklahoma schoolteacher's memory of the Daltons as "nice and polite." Some supporters proclaimed them innocent of their crimes, others merely excused them, but all demanded sympathy not so much for the crime as for the criminal. Again it must be emphasized that what is being praised here is not lawlessness per se. Outlaw stories go out of their way to detach the social bandit from the ordinary criminal. Thus, in one story Bill Doolin turns a common thief who tried to join his gang over to a deputy marshal, since "they would have no men in their outfit who would rob a poor man or any individual." . . .

. . . [T]he *Ardmore [Oklahoma] State Herald* made the connections between the Doolin-Dalton gang and Robin Hood explicit:

> Their life is made up of daring. Their courage is always with them and their rifles as well. They are kind to the benighted traveler, and it is not a fiction that when robbing a train they refuse to take from a woman.
>
> It is said that Bill Doolin, at present the reigning highwayman, is friendly to the people in one neighborhood, bestowing all sorts of presents upon the children. It is his boast that he never killed a man.
>
> This is as fully a romantic figure as Robin Hood ever cut. . . .

By the 1890s, in Oklahoma at least, the standards of how proper social bandits should behave seemed clear enough for the *Oklahoma State Capital,* a paper with little sympathy for outlaws, to lecture Bill Dalton on his duties as the heir of a great tradition. Bill Dalton, in an interview with a local reporter only the week before, had claimed he was considering teaming up with Frank James to open a saloon in Chicago to take advantage of their fame and the World's Fair. The saloon never materialized, and Bill Dalton had left Guthrie without paying his board bill. The *State Capital* had complained:

> There is supposed to be honor among thieves. Men who presume to be great in any calling avoid the common faults of men. There is a heroism even in desperadoes, and

the people admire an ideal type of that class. The James and Younger brothers are re-membered as never having robbed a poor family or assaulted an unarmed man. Even the "Dalton boys"—they who really stood up to their "knitten" and looked down the muzzles of Winchesters—did brave and not ignoble deeds. But Bill Dalton—"Board Bill" Dalton—has besmirched the family escutcheon. The brothers, dead, when they hear what he has done, will turn over in their graves and groan—"Oh, Bill."

Bill Dalton's future specialization in bank and train robbery and his violent death presumably redeemed the family honor.

Social bandits thus did exist in a meaningful sense in the American West, yet their actual social impact, confined as it was to small areas with extreme condi-tions, was minor. They never sought social change, and the actual social evolution of Missouri and Oklahoma owes little to them. Nevertheless, their impact on American culture has been immense. The social bandits who metaphorically rode out of Missouri and Oklahoma into America at large quickly transcended the specific economic and political conditions of the areas that produced them and be-came national cultural symbols. The outlaws were ready-made cultural heroes—their local supporters had already presented them in terms accessible to the nation as a whole. The portrait of the outlaw as a strong man righting his own wrongs and taking his own revenge had a deep appeal to a society concerned with the place of masculinity and masculine virtues in a newly industrialized and seem-ingly effete order.

Practically, of course, the outlaw as a model of male conduct was hopeless, and early popularizers of the outlaws stressed that although their virtues and quali-ties were admirable, their actions were inappropriate. Edwards portrayed the James and Younger brothers as men born out of their time, and Zoe Tilghman (whose book ostensibly denied the outlaws were heroic) claimed the Oklahoma bandits were cowboys "who could not bring their natures to the subjection of such a change from the wild free life to that kind that came to surround them. They were the venturesome spirits of the old Southwest and could not be tamed."

Those who seriously worried about masculine virtue in the late nineteenth and early twentieth centuries romanticized toughness, loyalty, bravery, generosity, honor, and daring, but sought to channel it into muscular Christianity or college football, not into robbing banks and trains. The outlaws' virtues were cherished, but their actions were archaic and antisocial. In this paradox of accepted virtue without an appropriate arena in which to exist lay the real power of the outlaws' appeal. The outlaw legend, rather than the childish solutions of reformers who sought to provide for the development of "masculine" virtues through organized sports or the dangerous solutions of chauvinists who praised war, retained the com-plexity, ambivalence, and paradoxes of a personal experience in which accepted male virtue had little relevance to an industrialized, bureaucratized world.

. . . The position of the western hero reflects the paradoxical position most Americans occupy in an industrialized capitalist society. The traits and acts of the outlaw become symbols of the larger, structural oppositions—oppositions of law and justice, individualism and community, nature and civilization—never ade-quately reconciled in American life. Assimilated into the classic western, the social bandit becomes the western hero—a figure of great appeal. The western is not the simple-minded celebration of the triumph of American virtue over evil that it is so often ignorantly and unjustly presumed to be; instead it is the opposite. It plays on the unresolved contradictions and oppositions of America itself.

The entire structure of the classic western film poses the hero between contrasting values both of which are very attractive: private justice and the order provided by law, individualism and community, nature and civilization. The hero, posed between the oppositions, remains ambivalent. Like the actual social bandit, the western hero never attempts to change the structure itself, but rather tries to achieve a reconciliation through his own courage and virtue. Western heroes personify culturally defined masculine virtues of strength, self-reliance, and honor in a world where they have ceased to be effective. More often than not the hero fails or only partially succeeds in his task and like the epitome of the ceased classic western hero, Shane, is left wounded and out of place in a world he has himself helped to create. In the hero's dilemma, viewers recognize their own struggle to reconcile the cultural irreconcilables that society demands of them—individualism and community responsibility, personal dominance and cooperation, maximum productivity and respect for nature. The bandit and the western hero are social failures, and this paradoxically guarantees them their cultural success. It is as a cultural symbol that Jesse James would survive and thrive even though "that dirty little coward, that shot Mr. Howard [had] laid poor Jesse in his grave."

Western Women and the Uses of Domestic Ideology

ROBERT L. GRISWOLD

When nineteenth-century Anglo women left their homes in New England, the South, or the Midwest to live in the West, they took with them more than the material items necessary for survival. They also took a set of values, assumptions, and ideals that enabled them to make sense of their lives. Although the content of this ideological baggage is not altogether clear, very likely these women subscribed to some variant of domestic ideology. Most undoubtedly believed that women's chief responsibilities were homemaking and child rearing, that females represented the moral foundation of the family and society, and that a commitment to family preceded and took precedence over a commitment to self. As a corollary, they also likely believed that women deserved respect and consideration commensurate with their high moral influence both inside and outside the home.

Yet, the key word is variant. Much of the confusion about women's roles and self-perceptions in the West stems from an overly rigid conception of domestic ideology: as a consequence, the historical debate too often turns on whether or not women slavishly adhered to a narrowly conceived conception of domesticity. Were or were not women submissive, pure, domestic, and pious? Did they or did they not subscribe to the cult of true womanhood? But if ideology is understood less narrowly, if ideology is perceived as a cultural system and not as a cult, such questions

Robert L. Griswold, "Anglo Women and Domestic Ideology in the American West in the Nineteenth and Early Twentieth Centuries," in Lillian Schlissel, Vicki L. Ruiz, and Janice Monk, eds., *Western Women: Their Land, Their Lives* (Albuquerque: University of New Mexico Press, 1988), 15–34. Used by permission of the author.

disappear and a more complex picture emerges of western Anglo women who were both brave and timid, resourceful and dependent, aggressive and retiring. In short, domestic ideology in the West was less a rigid set of assumptions than a supple perspective about gender ideals, less a well-defined "cult of true womanhood" than a way common women made sense of everyday existence.

This less rigid definition of ideology allows suspension of the debate on whether or not western Anglo women actually adhered to eastern moralists' conceptions of ideal womanhood. This is not the issue. . . . As Elizabeth Jameson has suggested, "We need to approach western women's history not through the filters of prescriptive literature or concepts of frontier liberation and oppression, but through the experiences of the people who lived the history." Western Anglo women inherited an ideology that arose in the East, but it was an ideology that was fluid, elastic and complex: women explained their own action by its assumptions, sometimes wrestled to align behavior with diverse perceptions of its tenets, and modified it to meet changing realities. In so doing, these migrants became creators as well as preservers of ideology.

The fact that domesticity arose in the East as part of the complex shift from a corporate household economy to a nascent urban, industrial economy would suggest that domestic ideology might have had trouble establishing firm roots in the West; moreover, eastern domesticity arose in conjunction with the separation of men's and women's worlds into two separate spheres, a separation that was virtually impossible to establish on the plains and in the mining towns of the West. Yet domestic ideology—in particular the valorization of motherhood and the emphasis on women's moral responsibilities to their families and communities—was central to the world view of Anglo women in the West. Although the spheres may have overlapped, the cultural values of domestic ideology had a powerful appeal to female settlers: they gave meaning to women's domestic work, made the blurring of sex roles culturally intelligible, helped confirm women's self-worth, offered a sense of stability in an inherently unstable world, and fostered bonds of friendship with other women. Domestic ideology, furthermore, legitimated women's efforts to "civilize" the West and provided a vocabulary with which to redefine the nature of manhood.

Domesticity for western Anglo women cannot be divorced from the productive labor they performed within the home. . . . The lives of all but wealthy women were characterized by hard work, work given cultural meaning by the ideology of domesticity. After all, the physical and moral well-being of the family stood at the core of nineteenth-century domestic social theory, and while a few privileged women could concentrate exclusively on the latter, most nineteenth-century wives, especially western wives, had to direct much of their energies to the former. But domesticity was never a theory of idleness: it always underscored the importance of productive labor, hence Catharine Beecher's efforts to increase the productivity and efficiency of housewives. And though western women, like their eastern counterparts, observed a gender-based division of labor, the spheres overlapped as women often performed labor generally reserved for men and as men occasionally did the reverse.

The labor of farm wives, for example, was indispensable to the success of the family venture. With her labor she produced the goods necessary for survival and often earned what little cash the family could claim by selling produce. Miners' wives likewise performed a seemingly endless number of tasks essential for their families' survival: they cooked, cleaned, hauled water, gardened, cared for live-stock, chopped wood, sewed, canned, slaughtered, cured meat, made candles and soap and, if poor, washed, sewed, and cooked for single men. Despite this numbing work load, "the underlying social ideology of the Victorian era," writes Elliot West, "survived largely intact among Western miners' wives." A virtuous woman used her labor and talents to establish and maintain a proper home: a sphere that would be a refuge for her husband "and a school of strength and virtue for her children." To be successful, West concluded, women had to be assertive, resourceful, dy-namic and skillful. This variant of domesticity had no room for passivity. To what extent such economic indispensability translated into power within the family is unclear, but the variety of work done by women both stretched and confirmed the fundamental belief that women's first responsibilities were to her family and home. When a wife made clothes, took in laundry, slaughtered livestock, mended fences, or harvested wheat, she did so because her family needed her labor.

The private writings of western women reveal that domestic tasks and the ideology that made cultural sense of these tasks validated women's self-worth. Frontier women described their first homes with affection and wrote with pride of their own innovativeness and resourcefulness in maintaining a home. One Iowa frontierswoman could not contain her pride or excitement as she and her family prepared to move into their new home: "It seems real nice to have the whole con-trol of my house; can say I am monarch of all I survey and none to dispute my right." So, too, miners' wives improvised to make their homes comport with Vic-torian standards of taste and often moved a few cherished belongings from mine to mine in an effort to secure symbolically the domestic stability their peripatetic lives so clearly lacked. Many women seemed to gain an artisan's satisfaction from their domestic duties and regarded their work as a craft. Women took understand-able pride in pies well-baked, shirts well-made, and children well-tended. Here was a healthy, instrumental, republican brand of domesticity free of the ornamental parasitism that allegedly plagued elite urban women.

Although the satisfaction women gained from their domestic work should not be overestimated—after all, many women also complained of the drudgery of their lives—work within the home may have also seemed relatively desirable given the alternatives outside the home. In other words, just as factory work confirmed con-ventional life expectations for eastern women at the turn of the century, the even more narrow job choices for western women likely did the same thing. In light of their high cultural status, wifehood and motherhood were very appealing in com-parison to life as an unmarried domestic, seamstress, or laundress. Teaching was probably the most appealing occupation, in part because teachers combined as-pects of domestic ideology with some prospects of autonomy and advancement, but in most towns, life as a teacher required life without marriage and children. That was a sacrifice few women willingly made. Finally, the slow development of industrialization in the West left women there with even fewer job possibilities than in the East.

Given the low level of industrialization, women in far western cities worked primarily in domestic service. For young single working women, this universally despised occupation undoubtedly helped propel them into marriage. The fact that most single working women lived at home also made marriage seem inviting: it was a way to chart an independent course from parents, no matter how illusory the independence might actually be. Thus, for every adventuresome, single, female homesteader, there were scores of overworked and underpaid domestics, sales clerks, and non industrial manufacturers for whom marriage and family represented a genuine hope for a better life.

The significance of domesticity, of course, went far beyond the nature of the work itself. Domesticity represented ties with community, and migration disrupted those ties. Most wives dutifully followed their husbands on the arduous and dangerous trail west. En route, women encountered the sickness and death, hardship and heartache that accompanied almost every overland expedition. But though a woman might have to leave her home, she did not leave behind the thoughts that filled that home. Domestic ideology was a tie to the past, a way one connected new surroundings to older roots. Amidst the uncertainties and upheavals characteristic of life in a new land, domesticity offered a familiar way to describe one's basic attitudes and hopes. Mothers were especially concerned that their daughters receive the lessons of domesticity, thereby validating the mothers' past and providing a sense of continuity between the two generations. External conditions might change without altering, so mothers hoped, the great lessons of life. The bonds of womanhood between mother and daughter, the complex web of obedience and obligation inherent in that relationship, served to mitigate the upheaval beyond the home.

A shared set of ideas about woman's place also bound non-related women to each other. Frontier women missed the company of other women, urged friends from home to migrate, promised repeatedly to visit female friends in the East, and made determined efforts to establish new friendships as quickly as possible. The cement of these bonds was comprised, in part, of a shared belief about women's duties, responsibilities, and prerogatives. Thus, women sought out other virtuous women for company and shunned those who violated the principles of nineteenth-century womanhood. Whether or not domestic ideology was prevalent among working-class women is debatable—evidence from Mormon women, black women, California divorcees, and miners' wives suggest that it was not restricted to the white middle-class—but domestic ideology strengthened the bonds of sisterhood among women. It did so by offering women a cultural system of social rules, conventions, and values . . . that gave meaning to their daily behavior and to their friendships with other women.

Domestic ideology brought western Anglo women together in another way as well. Fired by the moral message of domesticity, women united to "civilize" the West. This effort should not be confused with the influence of ethereal "madonnas in sunbonnets" or bloodless "gentle tamers" who allegedly worked wonders by the sheer force of their pious, self-sacrificing example. These images of western women are useless stereotypes that obscure the real relations between men and women and blind us to women's prolonged battle over what the West was to become, a battle that often brought women into conflict with entrenched male interests. If women were civilizers, they civilized for their families, for themselves, and for their gender: their quest was not to establish a lofty, other-worldly abstraction called *civilization* but to create the institutions—the schools, churches, charity associations, reforms—

that would check male inspired disorder, assist the victims and losers of the male dominated society, and secure a social order within which domestic virtues and family life could flourish.

Sexual struggle was at the core of this quest, a struggle predicated on the fact that western men and women had different conceptions of social order. Where womenless men dominated the West, prostitution and drinking were not only tolerated but were integral parts of the service structure of the community. Men without families in mining camps and cowtowns had little interest in schools and even less in charity associations, benevolent societies, temperance reforms, and churches. "Competitive opportunism" underlay their enterprise, a search for individual gain that often led to sharp clashes and factionalization within the Western communities. This male inspired, competitive, acquisitive ethos created an inhospitable climate for social reform. Most western mining camps, for example, were places of brief but intense economic exploitation occupied by highly transient males who showed open disdain for the domestic morality of the East. These men came for money, not for righteousness, and the laws they passed generally focused on economic matters and practical needs. Only with the arrival of families did the more stable western mining towns witness the emergence of the appurtenances of civilization. . . .

To the farmers and merchants who succeeded the cowboy, brothels, saloons, and gambling dens were open affronts to middle-class economic order based upon hard work and self-restraint: such evils hurt business, or at least the kinds of businesses middle-class entrepreneurs hoped to establish. Brothels and saloons might appeal to lonely cowboys, rowdy cattlemen, and hard luck miners, but the future of the towns lay with solid farmers, craftsmen, merchants, and their families. Thus, law, order, morality, and economic prosperity stood lined against the get-rich-quick immorality of the booming cowtowns and mining camps. Men's support for reform, then stemmed from a conception of morality inextricably linked to bourgeois economic respectability, rather than from a sense that men were primarily responsible for the moral purity of their communities or that frontier vices subverted their ability to rear proper children: hence men's willingness to compromise and to allow other men to pursue their fortunes and pleasures.

The wives of these men, however, likely had a different perception of social order. Entrusted with primary child-rearing responsibilities, intent on protecting and enhancing the morality of their families, women's opposition to frontier vice had roots deep within their own perceptions of self, family, and society. To protect morality, to build churches and schools, to see that sons and daughters grew up morally straight, these were important goals of many, if not most, Anglo western women. For them, compromise with vice—with the sinful indulgences of men— was unacceptable. Building a decent society required the efforts of both men and women, but women had the greater moral leverage to accomplish the needed reforms. They were the gender entrusted with the moral welfare of their home and community, and to protect their homes, middle-class women had to weave domestic morality into the fabric of society. After all, a pious, peaceful, domestic sphere might somehow survive amidst immoral conditions but would flourish only in an environment suffused with Christian morality. Thus women's diaries and letters record their efforts to establish schools, churches, Sunday school classes, benevolent associations, and charities. Some single females, in fact, came to the West intent on rescuing the region from barbarity: hundreds of unmarried female teachers from New England and upper New York state, for example, tried with mixed success to redeem the West with a blend of pietism and pedagogy. . . .

Civilizing the West meant, above all, civilizing men, and nowhere was the clash between male and female cultures more vivid than in the western settlements. To change male behavior and to define the nature of disorder and moral impropriety, women turned to the assumptions of domesticity. They did so not only because the domestic ideal elevated women's status within the family but because it also legitimated the call for a new style of masculine behavior both inside and outside the family. Thus, in building schools, churches, and charities, women recreated eastern civilization and checked a certain style of western masculinity that tolerated drinking, violence gambling, and whoring. With the arrival of mothers and daughters, a struggle between women and men over masculine identity ensued, a struggle involving the sexual double standard, religious commitment, temperance, gambling, men's psychological commitment to their wives and children, and male and female prerogatives within the family. Domesticity's reforming power lay in its ability to dramatize the social importance of a home-inspired morality and to insist that men and women adhere to a single standard of conduct, and a feminine one at that.

For women the choice was clear: either descend to the level of a male culture that tolerated vice—an unthinkable prospect—or align with righteous women and men and destroy these appurtenances of undomesticated masculinity. Thus, it was women who dominated the ranks of those opposed to drink, gambling, and prostitution. Antiprostitution, temperance, and reform campaigns in Kansas illustrate the reform process at work. In the early booming years of the cowtowns, for example, local newspapers viewed prostitution with amused tolerance, and ordinances against the practice simply served to fill the town coffers with collected fines. Local authorities considered prostitution a necessary social service. The arrival of families, however, challenged this vision of prostitution. With the advent of more even sex ratios, a sharp increase in the number of children, and the rise of respectable, middle-class occupations, women (and some men) called for the strict regulation or abolition of brothels. After all, prostitution was an affront to women's moral sensibilities and to Victorian ideas about sexual exclusivity, emotional intimacy, the sanctity of motherhood, and the importance of domestic life. To virtuous women, prostitution degraded men and women and threatened the sexual integrity of husbands and sons.

Nor did Kansas women limit themselves to antiprostitution campaigns. Helped by connections with eastern organizations (a Lawrence, Kansas, study club, for example, evolved directly from a group in Quincy, Illinois) Kansas women settlers in the late nineteenth century established a host of organizations to civilize the new state. Within a year of settlement, both Wichita and Dodge City witnessed the birth of women's benevolent societies. Organizations like the Woman's Relief Corps, the American Association of University Women, the PEO, the Kansas Federation of Women's Clubs, and the Woman's Christian Temperance Union "affirmed the women's sense of the validity and importance of their own values." The meetings helped break down the isolation many women undoubtedly felt, created complex networks among women reformers, offered women useful instruction on frontier living, and, perhaps most importantly, provided a way for women to translate the moral lessons of domesticity into direct social action. One women's club, for example, ran a successful day nursery for working mothers; another group founded the Home for Friendless Women in Leavenworth; a third helped to start what became the Girls' Industrial School in Beloit. Still other women tried to help prostitutes, poor older women and widows, or concentrated on school reforms, including scholarships for poor girls and an end to gender-based teacher pay inequities. Whether fighting for these reforms or for temperance legislation, the right of wives to refuse intercourse with drunken husbands, or protection and relief for female victims of a male-run economy, the women's groups of Kansas offered an implicit and sometimes explicit critique of a social order dominated by men.

Women's efforts at church formation and temperance, antiprostitution, and gambling reforms were public efforts that protected women's families and fostered in women a collective sense of identity and accomplishment. But the female effort to change male behavior also reverberated within the private lives of western women. Here, too, a battle of sorts was being waged. Domestic ideology made sense to Anglo women not only because it offered a moral basis for social reform but because it gave wives, within the privacy of the home, the right to expect, even demand, behavior from husbands commensurate with women's moral position within the family. Thus, a paradox emerges: domesticity was an ideology of social order, a "cultural rationalization for a specific social ordering of the relations between men and women" that helped legitimate male monopolization of economic, political, educational, and legal life. Yet, domestic ideology contained within it elements of a powerful critique of male behavior and prerogatives that could, if pursued far enough, break up the family, the very foundation of Victorian social order. Civilizing men included civilizing the man who headed the household, and if he could not be reconstructed, increasing numbers of western women simply filed for divorce.

Evidence from California divorce courts from 1850 to 1890 suggests that domestic ideology, however vague and imperfectly realized, shaped the ongoing debate on gender by providing a language that checked traditional male prerogatives and called for both intimacy and mutual respect within the family. Helped by California's wide ranging grounds for divorce and expansive interpretations of marital cruelty by the state supreme court, female divorce seekers could use the leverage afforded by domestic ideology to break free of ties with cold, aloof, insensitive, and domineering husbands. Wives took pains to describe their own allegiance to the domestic ideal and to show how their husbands' cruel behavior made the establishment of peaceful, respectable homes impossible. As home guardians and moral exemplars, women deserved better treatment. Thus, a wife might complain about an overbearing husband "who treated me as slave" or about one who insisted that his wife follow his every command. Other wives demanded respect and complained of husbands' selfishness and of husbands who tried to restrict their wives' contacts outside the home; wives also criticized husbands who meddled in their personal correspondence, who ignored them with a "brutal silence," who unfairly denied them credit with local merchants, or who ignored their physical limitations. While such male behavior might have been objectionable in the first half of the nineteenth century, only in the second half do such complaints by women gain standing in divorce suits. Although these particular complaints might not bring a divorce in and of themselves—California law demanded proof of extreme cruelty— they did bolster cruelty complaints and helped to prove that a man's general behavior did not comport with social expectations for husbands. . . .

If the divorce rate is an accurate barometer of rising material expectations, women's claims on men were clearly rising in the second half of the nineteenth century. Women brought almost 70 percent of the suits, and courts showed little inclination to stem the tide of divorce. These trends were especially pronounced in the West, the region with the highest divorce rate, the most expansive statutes, and the most liberal judicial interpretations of matrimonial cruelty in the nation. In fact, California was a leader in this regard—from 1867 to 1906, over seven thousand California wives sued successfully for divorce on the ground of cruelty—and in the late nineteenth century, California courts redefined the nature of marital cruelty to include mental anguish, a definition with far more latitude than traditional interpretations had permitted.

Why western courts adopted such expansive positions is not altogether clear: perhaps women's claims had special appeal in the West where an overwhelmingly male culture (at least initially) met with female demands for a different cultural ethos. This clash of men's and women's conceptions of social order may have lent considerable weight to women's desires to break free of cruel husbands. Far from home and kin and bereft of familiar institutions, harshly treated women likely made strong claims on the sensibility of middle-class jurists. Thus, judges in rural California listened sympathetically to wives who complained about husbands' brutish sexual demands or about husbands who ignored their sick or pregnant wives, who spent too much time away from the domestic hearth, or who were heartless toward the children. With such behavior, husbands stood opposed to women's civilizing influence, thereby threatening to stop the moral progress so necessary to middle-class perceptions of settlement in the West. By their actions, they lost their right to be husbands. The moral leverage of domesticity asked men to reshape their behavior and to treat the opposite sex with more respect, and when men failed to do so, women increasingly turned to divorce courts for relief. . . .

Despite its origins in the East, domestic ideology established a powerful hold on the lives of western Anglo women. En route, and once settled, women kept alive the basic assumptions of domesticity, helped, no doubt, by frontier schoolbooks, newspapers, and magazines that underscored women's duties as child-rearers, housewives, and moral guardians of family and community. The advice was general and vague but also ubiquitous and constant, and the effect was to preempt competing visions of womanhood. A woman who opposed domestic ideology for whatever reasons likely lacked even the language to express alternative views.

Moreover, the very suppleness of the concepts, the fact that domestic ideology was less a cult or a rigid orthodoxy and more a flexible vocabulary about gender ideals, meant that most Anglo women could turn to its values to make sense of their own lives. For most women, eastern migration was a family enterprise, and their commitment to their families defined their sense of self. What gave cultural meaning to these family responsibilities was the ideology of domesticity, an elastic and resilient set of ideas which supplied a much needed sense of stability, community, and generational continuity in a new region and provided an effective critique of immoral, undomesticated men. The last point is especially important. Given the masculine ethos of the early West, domesticity may have been especially appealing to western Anglo women who found in the ideology a powerful counterpoint to male assumptions about family and community life.

Farming and the Northern Ute Experience

DAVID RICH LEWIS

Nineteenth century American Indian policy rested on the belief that Indians were deficient, and that if they were to survive they must be raised through the social evolutionary stages from savagery to civilization. The idea was to transform Indians into yeomen farmers and farm families, settled and self-sufficient market agriculturalists, the backbone of an idealized Jeffersonian democracy. Applied broadly, agrarian-based policies like allotment had disastrous effects on native environments and subsistence systems, in many cases inducing the very dependency that officials hoped to end. What follows is one case study of this agrarian policy applied to the Northern Utes on the Uintah-Ouray Reservation, and their responses to the fundamental cultural changes entailed by a settled agrarian lifestyle.

The Ute (*Núciu*) peoples were a culturally self-identifying group of affiliated Numic-speaking bands inhabiting the intermountain region of modern Utah and Colorado at contact. Utah Ute bands included the Cumumba, Tumpanuwac, Uinta-at, San Pitch, Pahvant, and Sheberetch (later called collectively the Uintah Utes). The Yamparka and Parianuc (White River Utes), the Taviwac (Uncompahgre Utes), and the Wiminuc, Kapota, and Muwac, (Southern and Ute Mountain Utes) comprised the Colorado Ute bands. For most of the year, Utes moved in extended family hunting groups ranging from 20 to 100 people. Band or inter-band congregations for any extended period of time were rare. Notably individualistic, Utes maintained no central councils. Leadership remained local and consensual, based on the proven ability of individuals to perform specific tasks.

Ute subsistence strategies were elegantly adapted to the relative scarcity and local resource concentrations in their environments. The cyclical movements of family groups through familiar, non-exclusive hunting and gathering territories allowed them to exploit the periodic abundance of a wide variety of resources during the season of their precipitous maturation. . . .

Spanish colonial intrusions into the southern reaches of Ute territory were limited, and only a handful of missionary explorers ventured through the heart of the region. Utes readily adopted horses and Spanish trade goods, raided their pueblos and supply lines, aided them against the Comanches, and contracted their diseases, but never submitted to colonial administration. In 1800, at least 8,000 Utes

David Rich Lewis, "Environment, Subsistence, and Dependency: Farming and the Northern Ute Experience, 1850–1940," in C. Matthew Snipp, ed., *Overcoming Economic Dependency,* under consideration for publication by the University of Oklahoma Press.

from twelve major bands inhabited the region. Contacts between Utes and Euro-Americans increased after 1810 as fur trappers appeared bringing trade goods and guns in exchange for Ute furs, hides, and horses. Northern Ute bands remained aloof and independent during this "middle ground" period. Only after the appearance of Mormon settlers in 1847 and the Colorado gold rush of 1859 did Northern Utes experience the full impact of intercultural contact and direct change. . . .

Mormons were the first to offer Utes an agricultural alternative. In 1855, Agent Garland Hurt announced the creation of three "Indian farms," staffed by white farmers. Ute leaders expressed their interest in the projects and desired the promised crops, but resisted the idea of settling down, doing the work themselves, and surrendering their diversified subsistence strategy. They told Hurt that, "they were very poor, and had to hunt most all the time to keep from starving, and if they laid down their bows to work in the fields they would soon be obliged to pick them up again." A few Utes settled near the farms each summer to watch white farmers work for them, but drought and grasshoppers limited the harvest each year, forcing Hurt to encourage the people to go hunting or face starvation.

After closing the farms in 1860, Bureau officials decided to remove Utah Utes to the Uintah Valley of eastern Utah. . . . Since the Mormons did not want it and Utes showed no inclination to farm anyway, officials deemed the valley suited to their "savage" condition and set aside over two million acres as the Uintah Valley Reservation. The Uintah Basin was not exactly a wasteland, but neither was it an ideal year-round environment. Utes led by *Auten-quer* resisted removal and continued a series of subsistence raids against Mormon settlements known as the Black Hawk War (1863–68). Those who did move to the reservation found little waiting for them and refused to settle near the agency as long as they could hunt and gather in the surrounding mountains.

During the 1860s, agents moved the Uintah Agency several times in search of adequate agricultural lands, but the 70 or 80 acres they managed to cultivate suffered from periodic droughts and grasshopper plagues. Most of the agency's annual budget went to feed and clothe the people when they came into the agency each winter. . . . Ute agents managed to attract a few families to settle and work on the scattered "garden-patch" agency fields, but admitted that there existed a "great antipathy to work on the part of the men, the greater part of what [farming] was done being by the squaws and children." Ute men continued to hunt while agency farmers attempted to illustrate "the dignity of labor." The reproduction of Ute social norms in this reservation setting precluded male agricultural labor—digging in the earth for plant foods, after all, was the subsistence province of women.

Ute agents worried about this attitude and the growing dependence on rations. Upon his arrival in 1871, Agent J. J. Critchlow complained that, "There seems never to have been anything more done for them than to keep them quiet and peaceable by partially feeding and clothing them and amusing them with trinkets." He started a campaign to transform the increasingly dependent Uintah Utes into self-sufficient farmers, but he and his staff ran into the same cultural and environmental problems. Utes continued to reproduce their subsistence round in the reduced environment of the Uintah Basin. In 1875, Critchlow reported 80 families with garden patches totaling 200 acres, but that his staff did the plowing and planting. Families would return from their summer travels to harvest what wheat and vegetables managed to grow during their absence. Nor could Critchlow interest them in cooperative farming, for their individualistic traditions precluded extended communalism. Ute men refused to farm calling it "squaw's work," assuring each other and their agent that "Washington did not intend that they should work," and that the "Great Spirit" created whites to "work and plant for the Indian." . . .

By 1880, most of the Utah Ute bands resided within the boundaries of the reservation and were well on the way to a dependent economy. Traditional foods supplemented by agency rations formed their basic diet, and the handful of Uintah families who did any farming became increasingly dependent on agency resources and rations. Ute leaders blamed whites and evil shamans for the disappearance of game animals and for the diseases which plagued them. Hopes for a self-sufficient reservation economy diminished even further after the forceable removal of the Yamparka, Parianuc, and Taviwac Ute bands from their mountain strongholds in Colorado to the Uintah Basin. . . .

Through the rest of the nineteenth century Utes passively resisted a settled agrarian lifestyle and continued to reproduce typically Ute patterns of behavior. Officials described Ute farms as small subsistence gardens of from one to four acres, scattered along the reservation watercourses. They noted that Uintahs appeared to be more "progressive" in their farming efforts than White River or Uncompahgre Utes, but that Ute women continued to perform the bulk of the agri-cultural labor after agency employees prepared their fields. Agent Robert Waugh candidly admitted that Ute men were, "the most practical & least theoretical of any beings I ever came across. He wants the least & enjoys the most with the least care or effort. He views with a jealous eye any & all efforts to intrude the White Mans ways & wants upon him, & would resist them by force only that he thinks that would be harder. . . ."

Agents also complained that Utes maintained horse herds well beyond practi-cal agricultural needs, reproducing their own value system within a changing reser-vation economy. Agent E. W. Davis reported that, "In the matter of stock raising the Indians have a decided preference to ponies over cattle. Four or five Indians of the Uintah tribe own nearly all the Indian cattle on this reserve. Their influence among the tribe is measured by the number of ponies they possess, and as long as this custom obtains among them they will raise horses in preference to cattle." What was worse, he thought, was that they trained the best horses for racing, not plowing, and that their horses allowed them to continue seasonal hunting and visit-ing patterns instead of staying home to farm.

In the mid-1890s as Bureau officials and state game wardens curtailed treaty hunting rights, more Ute families attempted to farm or raise livestock. Agents reported that with the aid of agency employees some 260 families from a popula-tion of 1,800 Utes had farms totaling nearly 2,500 acres (not all planted) on the combined four million acre Uintah-Ouray Reservation. Due to limited irrigation and the physical isolation of the reservation, Utes produced little salable surplus and had virtually no market outside the agency and Fort Duchesne military post. By 1900, alfalfa and hay replaced wheat and oats, reflecting the increase in Ute livestock holdings. . . . Agents estimated that 20 to 30 percent of Ute subsistence came from their own labor in "civilized pursuits" (farming and wage labor), 10 percent from hunting and gathering, and 60 to 70 percent from government rations. Utes also leased their extensive grazing lands in the western Strawberry Valley, earning a small per-capita income which became, in some minds, a viable economic alternative to agricultural labor.

Between 1894 and 1905 federal officials moved to allot Northern Ute lands in severalty—the ultimate realization of their agrarian ideal for American Indians. At Uintah-Ouray, allotting commissioners surveyed the land and found that aside from river bottoms and adjacent benches, little of it was fit for agriculture. Rocky and alkaline soils, climate, and the broken nature of the country would make even the best lands difficult and expensive to clear and irrigate, but they went ahead with their orders to allot each family head 80 acres and each family member 40 acres of arable land.

In councils with Bureau officials, Ute leaders found common voice in opposing allotment. They understood the connection between severalty and farming and in their speeches rejected allotment through metaphorical attacks on things that would separate the people and break up their lands (fences), that would tie them to a specific plot (log houses), that would make their land agriculturally viable (irrigation) an undercut their land use patterns and resistance to farming. "The Indians have lots of horses," Appah, a White River, told his listeners, "and when you tell us that we must take farms, we do not like that on account of our horses." What are my horses going to do when I have only a little piece of land," asked Grant, a Uintah. "Must I tie my horses in that little field?" John Starr, a White River, told the allotting agent, "You see me and I see you. My flesh is black: you have good flesh, you are white like this paper here. My flesh looks like the ground. That's the reason I like this land: my flesh is like the ground. That's the reason I am going to keep it."

Above all, Utes worried about neighboring Mormons who were already encroaching on their land and water, and the flood of new settlers who would destroy their communality. Captain Joe insisted that "The Indian reservation was not put down for nothing. It is held down by something heavy," by the treaties he witnessed as a young man. "This is the Indian's land. . . . We don't want this reservation opened, and we do not want White people coming in among us." Warren, a Uintah, told his listeners that the land "is not buckskin or deer's hide, and I do not want to sell it." Charley Mack concluded, "What are the Indians going to do? It is like sand. You throw water upon sand and it will cave in and wash off: so with Indians, after a while there will be none left." Allotment threatened a more collective Ute identity and lifestyle that had arisen over time as their elders died, as paths to leadership changed, and as individual families found fewer opportunities to live without help from the larger group. Allotment represented an effort to re-individualize Utes economically after years of collectivist policy and of informal cooperation necessitated by a dependent reservation economy.

Utes responded to the allotment threat in several ways. Most continued their passive resistance by refusing to choose or even visit their surveyed allotments. Others, particularly the Uncompahgres, subverted the agricultural intent of allotment by specifically choosing land remote from the agency, fit only for carrying on an independent hunting and herding lifestyle. In other cases, White Rivers threatened band members who accepted allotments, destroyed allotment survey markers, and made life difficult for the survey crews. In 1906 nearly 400 White River and Uintah Utes fled the allotted reservation in protest and remained around Pine Ridge, South Dakota, for two years before returning to the Uintah Basin.

Perhaps the most dramatic response to counter the individualistic thrust of allotment was the adoption of the Sun Dance religion—a collective group ceremony in which individuals danced for "Power" (*Puwa*), not for themselves, but for the welfare of the group. Utes embraced the dance at a point in their history when the real and perceived deprivations of reservation life and allotment threatened to overwhelm them. They danced to counter their economic and political dependency through group unity. In later years Utes even cloaked the Sun Dance in agricultural imagery, calling it a "harvest festival," in order to protect it from official suppression.

Allotment fulfilled Utes' worst fears by immediately reducing their four million acres to only 353,265 acres, including a 250,000-acre tribal grazing reserve. As whites purchased and moved onto opened lands surrounding the checkerboard Ute allotments, disputes arose over boundaries, trespass, and the right to use and divert stream water. In 1906 the government moved to protect Ute water rights and make agriculture more viable by appropriating $600,000 for the Uintah Irrigation Project. Indian Irrigation Service planners expected to bring water to 80,000 allotted acres and reimburse the government for construction through the sale of unallotted reservation lands.

Irrigation officials soon ran into unanticipated problems. Utes roundly rejected both the construction and costs of the irrigation project. Many refused to work on the ditches or to prepare their allotments for water. Others who took canal construction jobs had little time to farm. Perhaps more troubling was an unforeseen deadline. Project officials found that the reservation was opened and water rights established under state law, thus forfeiting federal protection guaranteed by *Winters v. U.S.* (1908). Utah law required "beneficial use" of the water within fourteen years (by 1919) to maintain primary rights over settlers with secondary or tertiary water claims.

While work on the ditches went forward as quickly as possible, agency officials realized that Utes would hardly be able to prove beneficial use in time to save primary rights on even 10 percent of their lands. Without water they would lose the productive capability and resale value of their allotments and any hope of a self-sufficient agricultural economy. Bureau officials decided to act. With or without the consent of allottees, officials leased Ute lands to white homesteaders on condition that they prepare the land for irrigation. Agents suggest that Ute lessors could live on a corner of their allotment and perform wage labor for the white lessee, that they could sell part of their land to raise money for capital improvements, or that elders and those with inherited allotments could sell their land with the primary water right intact in order to gain some immediate benefit. In 1911 alone, agents arranged the sale of 67 (5%) of 1,365 Ute allotments. Many Utes, particularly White Rivers, tried to prevent band members from signing away heirship properties, but the sales and leasing continued. Between 1915 and 1917, Superintendent Albert H. Kneale arranged 1,764 leases totaling 54,000 (52%) allotted acres. In 1916, Kneale reported that they had 85,150 allotted acres under 22 irrigation canals, with 39,760 acres leased (46%), and 17,354 acres sold or pending sale.

Statistically, agricultural activity at Uintah-Ouray increased dramatically. From 131 Ute farms totaling 4,572 acres (most unplanted) in 1905, agents reported 13,260 cultivated acres in 1914. However, Utes [controlled] only 6,147 acres on 222 allotments (again, most unplanted). White lessees worked the [rest] while 68,869 allotted acres (84%) remained idle. Leasing became a common and, in some cases, preferred method of land use for Ute allottees. One extension agent noted that, "The present prevailing custom is for the Indian owner to employ a white man to run the farm, paying him a definite share of the products." Some Ute leaders opposed leasing, arguing that it brought more whites onto Indian land, or, like William Wash, that "This leasing of land to the whites is a swindle. . . . The Indians do not know how to make money off their land. They don't know w[h]ether the white man is handling it right or not." Despite frequent disagreements between Indian landlords and white tenants, many Utes found leasing a comfortable way to earn a living, please agents concerned with statistics, and avoid the routine of agricultural labor.

This attitude frustrated bureau officials who expected Utes to embrace allotment, the Protestant work-ethic, and become self-sufficient farmers overnight. Superintendent Kneale lamented Ute reliance on rations and their "unearned" income from leases and a small land claims settlement, observing that they were "wholly content to make their living expenses conform to this income, so there is little occasion to perform manual labor." Those who farmed did so intermittently, leaving their fields unattended in mid-season to grow as they would. Few actually lived on their own allotments, preferring instead extended family groupings on a single plot. Officials struggled to get even a sight majority to live in frame houses and not use them as horse stables or destroy them in accordance with mortuary practices. In these ways, Utes continued to reproduce cultural elements in the transformed reservation environment.

Aside from the cultural resistance, there were more practical obstacles to successful agriculture—obstacles which contributed to continued Ute economic dependency. Ute farmers lacked the capital or credit necessary to purchase modern farm equipment and relied on older horse-drawn implements loaned or purchased through the agency. Utes received meager instruction in irrigation and dry farming crops and techniques from the handful of agency farmers hired to supervise scattered operations across the region. Even with an irrigation system the Uintah Basin remained a difficult environment for successful, small-scale subsistence farming. Finally, like other reservations, Uintah-Ouray remained physically and economically isolated from the American marketplace. Until the 1910s, the lack of markets was not a problem since Utes traded what little surplus they produced—mainly hay, oats, and wheat—at the agency or Fort Duchesne. But the fort closed in 1912 just as production from irrigated Ute farms and white homesteads increased, flooding local markets. High freight rates kept their forage and grain crops uncompetitive even in a vigorous regional economy.

By 1920, the Uintah Irrigation Project covered 80,306 arable acres at double the original reimbursable cost, but the costs to the Ute people went well beyond that. Agency officials arranged the sale of over 25,000 acres of the best land to non-Utes. Faulty surveys and canal construction left some allotments without adequate water, and improper irrigation techniques increased erosion and brought up alkali rendering other lands worthless. Some white lessees failed to make adequate improvements or abused the land, leaving it barren and alkaline, while others who purchased Indian lands defaulted on their payments. The irrigation project proved to be an expensive benefit to those Utes who actually used the water and a federal gift to those whites who bought Ute allotments or ultimately used their canals. Its legacy was one of tribal and individual indebtedness and further land sales far outweighing, in Ute terms, the economic or cultural worth of the project. . . .

Ranching had the potential of becoming a more successful agricultural enterprise among the Northern Utes in the twentieth century, but the division of the reservation into small allotments and the loss of the best grazing lands in the Strawberry Valley limited its potential success. Agents had little luck encouraging Utes to reduce their horse herds and replace them with cattle and sheep until the 1920s when changing economic values, increased alfalfa production, and per-capita payments from a claims case made livestock purchases more practical. In 1923, a core group of Ute stockmen owned about 4,000 cattle, 6,500 sheep, and over 5,000 horses. By the late 1920s, Ute livestock ownership broadened as sheep replaced cattle—a cheaper, more productive animal in terms of wool, meat, and offspring, especially on an increasingly overgrazed range. Ute livestock production peaked in 1932 with 3,546 cattle and 14,850 sheep, followed by deep herd reductions as overgrazing, drought, and depressed markets caught up with Basin ranchers. Ute participation in ranching faltered after World War II for many of the same reasons farming did. In the 1960s Utes organized a tribal cattle enterprise which continues to date, but it has never proven very profitable nor has it provided a significant number of jobs.

The history of farming on the Uintah-Ouray Reservation is one example of how federal policies, economic and environmental realities, and Northern Ute cultural responses to those changes contributed to a state of dependency. While case specific, this history mirrors the agricultural experiences of many other western native groups and their progression from cultural self-sufficiency to dependency and enforced marginality. . . .

In hindsight it is easy to see why agriculture alone offered Indian peoples in the western United States little more than short-term subsistence and long-term economic dependence. Most refused to simply abandon their diversified subsistence strategy and conform to American agrarian ideals or farming techniques. They saw the failure of early farm efforts and the cultural costs of conforming to that way of life. Their reservations were mere remnants of once vast estates, unable to support the people, so they turned to rations and periodic wage labor. Reservations were generally unwanted, marginal agricultural lands to begin with, often arid and better suited to ranching or some other activity. Most were isolated from transportation facilities and regional or national markets, making it difficult for Indians to become successful market agriculturalists.

Native peoples generally received inadequate agricultural instruction and equipment to work the land. With little access to capital for improvements, they fell further behind and became dependent on the government for reimbursable loans. Resistance, both passive and active, and the reproduction of cultural norms within the altered reservation environment contributed to farming's limited success. Finally, the agrarian nature of federal Indian policy launched Indians into farming smaller allotments at the very time white farmers were expanding their farms, increasing the intensity of cultivation with power equipment, and cooperatively marketing their produce in order to survive in an increasingly corporate, increasingly urban and industrial world. While the Indian Bureau abandoned allotment in the 1930s and encouraged cooperative tribal enterprises in the 1950s, they did little to restore alienated native lands or Indian confidence in future agricultural development.

FURTHER READING

Robert F. Berkhofer, Jr., *The White Man's Indian* (1978)

Sarah Deutsch, *No Separate Refuge: Culture, Class, and Gender on an Anglo-Hispanic Frontier in the American Southwest, 1880–1940* (1987)

Harry Sinclair Drago, *The Great Range Wars* (1985)

Philip Durham and Everett L. Jones, *The Negro Cowboys* (1965)

Robert V. Hine, *Community on the American Frontier* (1980)

Paul Andrew Hutton, "From Little Bighorn to Little Big Man: The Changing Image of Western Hero in a Popular Culture," *Western Historical Quarterly* 7 (January 1976), 19–44.

Peter Iverson, *The Navajos* (1990)

Patricia Nelson Limerick, *The Legacy of Conquest: The Unbroken Past of the American West* (1987)

Sandra L. Myres, *Westering Women and the Frontier Experience, 1800–1915* (1982)

Robert J. Rosenbaum, *Mexicano Resistance in the Southwest* (1981)

Lillian Schlissel et al., eds., *Western Women: Their Land, Their Lives* (1988)

Richard Slotkin, *The Fatal Environment* (1985)

Richard White, *The Roots of Dependency: Subsistence, Environment, and Social Change Among the Choctaws, Pawnees, and Navajos* (1983)

———, *"It's Your Misfortune and None of My Own": A New History of the American West* (1991)

CHAPTER
4

Trials of the New South

With the withdrawal of the last federal troops from the reconstructed South in 1876, the region's white leaders predicted a new era of economic, social, and political progress. Yet the ghosts of endemic problems and older conflicts could not be quickly banished. Economically, the difficulties were rooted in the South's cotton-centered agriculture, which was mired in postwar debt and, by the 1880s, faced plunging world cotton prices. The squeeze on cotton financing rippled down through factors, bankers, and merchants to landowners, sharecroppers, and tenant farmers operating under the crop-lien system of pledging a future crop against a current loan. For the sharecroppers and tenant farmers, black and white alike, the situation verged on catastrophe. It was out of this gloomy milieu that the dream of a "new" South emerged. An idealized version of the northern urban-industrial revolution gripped the imaginations of many southern boosters, including a number of newspaper editors. They initially pinned their hopes on the cotton mill or, more precisely, the recruitment of the textile industry from its traditional New England base to the labor-rich, low-cost South. They got their way but not entirely with the results they expected. "New South" industrialization blossomed, however, as a mostly white-only affair, and black communities struggled against great odds for economic survival. Carrying the legal claim to freedom and citizenship, southern blacks found their entry to material advancement cut off at every turn. Whether massed in Black Belt regions along the Mississippi, without land of their own, or drifting to and within southern cities, where they were denied entry to skilled trades, the freed people and their children were thrown back on their own resources. In this situation, the development of widespread black education proved a significant accomplishment.

DOCUMENTS

In the cash-poor, debt-ridden, post-bellum southern society, landowners worked out "share" arrangements with their agricultural renters (Document 1). Contending at once with severe economic disadvantages and with political opinions still largely divided by bitter wartime memories, post-Reconstruction southern leaders appealed, of necessity, to northern goodwill and northern pocketbooks. No gesture in this direction was more effective than *Atlanta Constitution* editor Henry W. Grady's appeal for national reconciliation, excerpted in Document 2. Appearing before the New England

Society of New York City on December 21, 1886, Grady sings a song of an industrious New South that was music to northern businessmen's ears. Looking back in Document 3 on the cotton-mill campaign that was a cornerstone of New South development, Broadus Mitchell, a young economic historian of the day, accepts the entrepreneurs' view that civic benevolence, as much as self-interest, underlay mill development. By way of contrast, in Document 4, the legendary labor organizer "Mother" Jones portrays the mill village as a feudal barony populated by tyrannical overseers and half-starved millworkers. In the same period, with characteristic outspokenness, former slave Frederick Douglass, speaking before the Louisville National Convention of Colored People in 1883 (Document 5), describes the utter recalcitrance and naked intimidation with which white America was turning back blacks' claims to full citizenship. In the final selection (Document 6), a black Alabama schoolteacher and two of his pupils reflect an earnest striving for group improvement in their testimony before an inquiring Senate Committee on Labor and Education.

1. Sharecroppers' Contracts, 1876–1886

STATE OF NORTH CAROLINA, Wake County

Articles of Agreement, Between *Alonzo T. Mial* of said County and State, of the first part, and *A. Robert Medlin* of the County and State aforesaid, of the second part, to secure an Agricultural Lien according to an Act of General Assembly of North Carolina, entitled "An Act to secure advances for Agricultural purposes";

Whereas, the said *A. R. Medlin* being engaged in the cultivation of the soil, and being without the necessary means to cultivate his crop, *The Said A. T. Mial* has agreed to furnish goods and supplies to the said *A. R. Medlin* to an amount not to exceed *One Hundred and fifty* Dollars, to enable him to cultivate and harvest his crops for the year 1876.

And in consideration thereof, the said *A. R. Medlin* doth hereby give and convey to the said *A. T. Mial* a LIEN upon all of his crops grown in said County in said year, on the lands described as follows: *The land of A. R. Medlin adjoining the lands of Nelson D. Pain Samuel Bunch & others.*

And further, in Consideration thereof, the said *A. R. Medlin* for One Dollar in hand paid, the receipt of which is hereby acknowledged, have bargained and sold, and by these presents do bargain, sell and convey unto the said *A. T. Mial his* heirs and assigns forever, the following described Real and Personal Property to-wit: *All of his Stock horses, Cattle Sheep and Hogs — Carts and Wagons House hold and kitchen furnishings.* To Have and to Hold the above described premises, together with the appurtenances thereof, and the above described personal property, to the said *A. T. Mial his* heirs and assigns.

The above to be null and void should the amount found to be due on account of said advancements be discharged on or before the *1st* day of *November* 1876: otherwise the said *A. T. Mial his* executors, administrators or assigns, are hereby

"Sharecroppers' Contract, 1876–1886," found in the Alonzo T. Millard Mial Papers, North Carolina Division of Archives and History. As edited in Carolyn Merchant, ed., *Major Problems in American Environmental History: Documents and Essays* (Lexingon, Mass.: D. C. Heath, 1993), 218–219. Reprinted by permission of Houghton Mifflin Company.

authorized and empowered to seize the crops and Personal Property aforesaid, and sell the same, together with the above Real Estate, for cash, after first advertising the same for fifteen days, and the proceeds thereof apply to the discharge of this Lien, together with the cost and expenses of making such sale, and the surplus to be paid to the said *A. R. Medlin,* or his legal representatives.

IN WITNESS WHEREOF, The said parties have hereunto set their hands and seals this *29th* day of *February,* 1876.

his
A. Robert × Medlin, [seal]
mark

Witness: *L. D. Goodloe* [signed]   A. T. Mial [signed], [seal]

This contract made and entered into between A. T. Mial of one part and Fenner Powell of the other part both of the County of Wake and State of North Carolina—

Witnesseth—That the Said Fenner Powell hath barganed and agreed with the Said Mial to work as a cropper for the year 1886 on Said Mial's land on the land now occupied by Said Powell on the west Side of Poplar Creek and a point on the east Side of Said Creek and both South and North of the Mial road, leading to Raleigh, That the Said Fenner Powell agrees to work faithfully and dilligently without any unnecessary loss of time, to do all manner of work on Said farm as may be directed by Said Mial, And to be respectful in manners and deportment to Said Mial. And the Said Mial agrees on his part to furnish mule and feed for the same and all plantation tools and Seed to plant the crop free of charge, and to give the Said Powell One half of all crops raised and housed by Said Powell on Said land except the cotton seed. The Said Mial agrees to advance as provisions to Said Powell fifty pound of bacon and two sacks of meal pr month and occationally Some flour to be paid out of his the Said Powell's part of the crop or from any other advance that may be made to Said Powell by Said Mial. As witness our hands and seals this the 16th day of January A.D 1886

A. T. Mial [signed] [Seal]

his
Fenner × Powell [Seal]
mark

Witness

W. S. Mial [signed]

2. *Atlanta Constitution* Editor Henry W. Grady Heralds the New South, 1886

"There was a South of slavery and secession—that South is dead. There is a South of union and freedom—that South, thank God, is living, breathing, growing every hour." These words, delivered from the immortal lips of Benjamin H. Hill, at Tammany Hall, in 1866, true then and truer now, I shall make my text to-night. . . .

"The New South," speech delivered before New England Society of New York City, Dec. 21, 1886, in Edna Henry Lee Turpin, ed., *The North, South, and Other Addresses by Henry Woodfin Grady* (New York: Charles Merill, 1904), 23–42.

. . . The soldier stepped from the trenches into the furrow; horses that had charged federal guns marched before the plow, and fields that ran red with human blood in April were green with the harvest in June; women reared in luxury cut up their dresses and made breeches for their husbands, and, with a patience and heroism that fit women always as a garment, gave their hands to work. There was little bitterness in all this. Cheerfulness and frankness prevailed. "Bill Arp" struck the keynote when he said, "Well, I killed as many of them as they did of me, and now I'm going to work." So did the soldier returning home after defeat and roasting some corn on the roadside who made the remark to his comrades, "You may leave the South if you want to, but I'm going to Sandersville, kiss my wife, and raise a crop, and if the Yankees fool with me any more, I'll whip 'em again." . . .

But what is the sum of our work? We have found out that in the summing up the free negro counts more than he did as a slave. We have planted the schoolhouse on the hilltop and made it free to white and black. We have sown towns and cities in the place of theories, and put business above politics. We have challenged your spinners in Massachusetts and your ironmakers in Pennsylvania. We have learned that the $400,000,000 annually received from our cotton crop will make us rich when the supplies that make it are home-raised. We have reduced the commercial rate of interest from 24 to 6 per cent, and are floating 4 per cent bonds. We have learned that one Northern immigrant is worth fifty foreigners, and have smoothed the path to Southward, wiped out the place where Mason and Dixon's line used to be, and hung out the latch-string to you and yours.

We have reached the point that marks perfect harmony in every household, when the husband confesses that the pies which his wife cooks are as good as those his mother used to bake; and we admit that the sun shines as brightly and the moon as softly as it did before the war. We have established thrift in city and country. We have fallen in love with work. We have restored comfort to homes from which culture and elegance never departed. We have let economy take root and spread among us as rank as the crab-grass which sprung from Sherman's cavalry camps, until we are ready to lay odds on the Georgia Yankee as he manufactures relics of the battlefield in a one-story shanty and squeezes pure olive oil out of his cotton seed, against any downeaster that ever swapped wooden nutmegs for flannel sausage in the valleys of Vermont. Above all, we know that we have achieved in these "piping times of peace" a fuller independence for the South than that which our fathers sought to win in the forum by their eloquence or compel in the field by their swords.

It is a rare privilege, sir, to have had part, however, humble, in this work. Never was nobler duty confided to human hands than the uplifting and upbuilding of the prostrate and bleeding South—misguided, perhaps, but beautiful in her suffering, and honest, brave, and generous always. In the record of her social, industrial, and political illustration we await with confidence the verdict of the world.

But what of the negro? Have we solved the problem he presents or progressed in honor and equity toward solution? Let the record speak to the point. No section shows a more prosperous laboring population than the negroes of the South, none in fuller sympathy with the employing and landowning class. He shares our school fund, has the fullest protection of our laws, and the friendship of our people. Self-interest, as well as honor, demand that he should have this. Our future, our very existence, depend upon our working out this problem in full and exact justice. We understand that when Lincoln signed the Emancipation Proclamation, your victory was assured, for he then committed you to the cause of human liberty, against which the arms of man cannot prevail—while those of our statesmen who trusted to make slavery the corner stone of the Confederacy doomed us to defeat as far as they could, committing us to a cause that reason could not defend or the sword maintain in sight of advancing civilization. . . .

To liberty and entranchisement is as far as law can carry the negro. The rest must be left to conscience and common sense. It must be left to those among whom his lot is cast, with whom he is indissolubly connected, and whose prosperity depends upon their possessing his intelligent sympathy and confidence. Faith has been kept with him, in spite of calumnious assertions to the contrary by those who assume to speak for us or by frank opponents. Faith will be kept with him in the future, if the South holds her reason and integrity. . . .

The old South rested everything on slavery and agriculture, unconscious that these could neither give nor maintain healthy growth. The new South presents a perfect democracy, the oligarchs leading in the popular movement; a social system compact and closely knitted, less splendid on the surface, but stronger at the core; a hundred farms for every plantation, fifty homes for every palace; and a diversified industry that meets the complex needs of this complex age.

The new South is enamored of her new work. Her soul is stirred with the breath of a new life. The light of a grander day is falling fair on her face. She is thrilling with the consciousness of growing power and prosperity. As she stands upright, full-statured and equal among the people of the earth, breathing the keen air and looking out upon the expanded horizon, she understands that her emancipation came because, through the inscrutable wisdom of God, her honest purpose was crossed and her brave armies were beaten.

This is said in no spirit of time-serving or apology. The South has nothing for which to apologize. She believes that the late struggle between the States was war and not rebellion, revolution and not conspiracy, and that her convictions were as honest as yours. I should be unjust to the dauntless spirit of the South and to my own convictions if I did not make this plain in this presence. The South has nothing to take back.

In my native town of Athens is a monument that crowns its central hill—a plain, white shaft. Deep cut into its shining side is a name dear to me above the names of men—that of a brave and simple man who died in brave and simple faith. Not for all the glories of New England, from Plymouth Rock all the way, would I exchange the heritage he left me in his soldier's death. To the foot of that shaft I shall send my children's children to reverence him who ennobled their name with his heroic blood. But, sir, speaking from the shadow of that memory which I honor as I do nothing else on earth, I say that the cause in which he suffered and for which he gave his life was adjudged by a higher and fuller wisdom than his or mine, and I am glad that the omniscient God held the balance of battle in His Almighty hand, and that human slavery was swept forever from American soil— that the American Union was saved from the wreck of war.

This message, Mr. President, comes to you from consecrated ground. Every foot of soil about the city in which I live is sacred as a battle ground of the Republic. Every hill that invests it is hallowed to you by the blood of your brothers who died for your victory, and doubly hallowed to us by the blood of those who died hopeless, but undaunted, in defeat—sacred soil to all of us, rich with memories that make us purer and stronger and better, silent but stanch witnesses in its red desolation of the matchless valor of American hearts and the deathless glory of American arms, speaking an eloquent witness in its white peace and prosperity to the indissoluble union of American States and the imperishable brotherhood of the American people.

Now, what answer has New England to this message? Will she permit the prejudice of war to remain in the hearts of the conquerors, when it has died in the hearts of the conquered? Will she transmit this prejudice to the next generation, that in their hearts, which never felt the generous ardor of conflict, it may perpetuate itself? Will she withhold, save in strained courtesy, the hand which straight from his soldier's heart Grant offered to Lee at Appomattox? Will she make the vision of a restored and happy people, which gathered above the couch of your dying captain, filling his heart with grace, touching his lips with praise, and glorifying his path to the grave—will she make the vision, on which the last sigh of his expiring soul breathed a benediction, a cheat and delusion?

If she does, the South, never abject in asking for comradeship, must accept with dignity its refusal; but if she does not refuse to accept in frankness and sincerity this message of good will and friendship, then will the prophecy of Webster, delivered in this very society forty years ago amid tremendous applause, be verified in its fullest sense, when he said: "Standing hand to hand and clasping hands, we should remain united as we have been for sixty years, citizens of the same country, members of the same government, united, all united now and united forever.

3. Historian Broadus Mitchell Describes a Benevolent Cotton-Mill Campaign of the 1880s

One cannot view the passion with which [the New South] revival was undertaken without realizing how pointed were the lessons taught the South in the war and its aftermath. Convinced of old errors, the remaking of the South was emphatically in response to a moral stimulus, not less real because not always outwardly apparent. "A man who has been in the whirl of New York or in any of the brand new cities of the great West coming into Charleston might easily enough come to the conclusion that the old city was in a sad state of decadence—but our own people who have been accustomed to its quiet way of doing business, if they have their eyes open (or hearts open would perhaps be the better expression) could not fail to see manifest improvement—progress even, if you like the word better."

As the movement proceeded from introspection, the very genius of "Real Reconstruction" was self-help. It took courage to begin, but confidence rallied about every sign of genuine performance. Thus it was said that "Every true South Carolinian must rejoice at the . . . energy exhibited by the citizens of Columbia in their management of the Cotton-Mill Campaign. For years they have appeared to depend on somebody else to help them. The Legislature made liberal concessions. No effort was spared to interest Northern capitalists in the splendid water power. . . . But nothing was done. Tired of waiting a number of business men in Columbia

---

Broadus Mitchell, *The Rise of the Cotton Mills in the South* (Baltimore: Johns Hopkins Press, 1921), 81ff.

took up the matter themselves. They soon found that the citizens generally would sustain them. . . . The city is full of life again. A handsome sum of money has been subscribed already to the capital stock of the Cotton Mill Company. . . . It will be a happy day for the whole State when the hum of a myriad spindles is heard on the banks of the historic Canal." . . .

Understanding the straits of the South at the opening of the cotton mill era, the readiness of Southern men to realize and assume responsibility in public matters, and the spirit of social service which characterized the awakening to a program of "Real Reconstruction," one accepts as natural the fact that cotton manufactories were frequently motivated by the desire to help a community to its feet. Often this wish was joined, and very properly so, with usual commercial promptings, but sometimes it controlled alone. . . .

No undertaking was born more emphatically in the impulse to furnish work than the Salisbury Cotton Mills. All the circumstances of the founding of this factory was singularly in keeping with the philanthropic promptings. The town of Salisbury, North Carolina, in 1887 had done nothing to recover from the war. It was full of saloons, wretched, unkempt. It happened that an evangelistic campaign was conducted; Mr. Pearson, remembered as a lean, intense Tennessean, preached powerfully. A tabernacle was erected for the meeting, which lasted a month and, being undenominational, drew from the whole town and countryside. The evangelist declared that the great morality in Salisbury was to go to work, and that corruption, idleness and misery could not be dispelled until the poor people were given an opportunity to become productive. The establishment of a cotton mill would be the most Christian act his hearers could perform. "He gave Salisbury a moral dredging which made the people feel their responsibilities as they had not before, and made them do something for these folks. There had been little talk of manufacturing before Pearson came; there had been some tobacco factories in the town, but they had failed. The Salisbury Cotton Mills grew out of a moral movement to help the lower classes, largely inspired by this campaign. Without the moral issue, the financial interest would have come out in the long run, but the moral considerations brought the matter to a focus."

4. Labor Organizer Mother Jones Compares Southern Mill Life to Serfdom, 1901

The Rope Factory

I visited the factory in Tuscaloosa, Ala., at 10 o'clock at night. The superintendent, not knowing my mission, gave me the entire freedom of the factory and I made good use of it. Standing by a siding that contained 155 spindles were two little girls. I asked a man standing near if the children were his, and he replied that they were. "How old are they?" I asked. "This one is 9, the other 10," he replied. "How many hours do they work?" "Twelve," was the answer. "How much do they get a night?" "We all three together get 60 cents. They get 10 cents each and I 40."

I watched them as they left their slave-pen in the morning and saw them gather their rags around their frail forms to hide them from the wintry blast. Half-fed,

Mother Jones, "Civilization in Southern Mills," *International Socialist Review,* I (March 1901) 539–541.

half-clothed, half-housed, they toil on, while the poodle dogs of their masters are petted and coddled and sleep on pillows of down, and the capitalistic judges jail the agitators that would dare to help these helpless ones to better their condition.

Gibson is another of those little sections of hell with which the South is covered. The weaving of gingham is the principal work. The town is owned by a banker who possesses both people and mills. One of his slaves told me she had received one dollar for her labor for one year. Every weekly pay day her employer gave her a dollar. On Monday she deposited that dollar in the "pluck-me" store to secure food enough to last until the next pay day, and so on week after week.

There was once a law on the statute books of Alabama prohibiting the employment of children under twelve years of age more than eight hours each day. The Gadston Company would not build their mill until they were promised that this law should be repealed.

When the repeal came up for the final reading I find by an examination of the records of the House that there were sixty members present. Of these fifty-seven voted for the repeal and but three against. . . .

I asked one member of the House why he voted to murder the children, and he replied that he did not think they could earn enough to support themselves if they only worked eight hours. These are the kind of tools the intelligent workingmen put in office. . . .

Almost every one of my shop-mates in these mills was a victim of some disease or other. All are worked to the limit of existence. The weavers are expected to weave so many yards of cloth each working day. To come short of this estimate jeopardizes their job. The factory operator loses all energy either of body or of mind. The brain is so crushed as to be incapable of thinking, and one who mingles with these people soon discovers that their minds like their bodies are wrecked. Loss of sleep and loss of rest gives rise to abnormal appetites, indigestion, shrinkage of stature, bent backs and aching hearts.

Such a factory system is one of torture and murder as dreadful as a long-drawn-out Turkish massacre, and is a disgrace to any race or age. As the picture rises before me I shudder for the future of a nation that is building up a moneyed aristocracy out of the life-blood of the children of the proletariat. It seems as if our flag is a funeral bandage splotched with blood. The whole picture is one of the most horrible avarice, selfishness and cruelty and is fraught with present horror and promise of future degeneration. The mother over-worked and under-fed, gives birth to tired and worn-out human beings.

5. Frederick Douglass Describes a Legacy of Race Hatred, 1883

Born on American soil in common with yourselves, deriving our bodies and our minds from its dust, centuries having passed away since our ancestors were torn from the shores of Africa, we, like yourselves, hold ourselves to be in every sense Americans, and that we may, therefore, venture to speak to you in a tone not lower

"Address to the Louisville Convention," in Frederick Douglass, *Three Addresses on the Relations Between White and Colored People of the United States* (Washington, D.C. 1886), 3–23.

than that which becomes earnest men and American citizens. Having watered your soil with our tears, enriched it with our blood, performed its roughest labor in time of peace, defended it against enemies in time of war, and at all times been loyal and true to its best interests, we deem it no arrogance or presumption to manifest now a common concern with you for its welfare, prosperity, honor and glory. . . .

It is our lot to live among a people whose laws, traditions, and prejudices have been against us for centuries, and from these they are not yet free. To assume that they are free from these evils simply because they have changed their laws is to assume what is utterly unreasonable and contrary to facts. Large bodies move slowly. Individuals may be converted on the instant and change their whole course of life. Nations never. Time and events are required for the conversion of nations. Not even the character of a great political organization can be changed by a new platform. It will be the same old snake though in a new skin. Though we have had war, reconstruction and abolition as a nation, we still linger in the shadow and blight of an extinct institution. Though the colored man is no longer subject to be bought and sold, he is still surrounded by an adverse sentiment which fetters all his movements. In his downward course he meets with no resistance, but his course upward is resented and resisted at every step of his progress. If he comes in ignorance, rags, and wretchedness, he conforms to the popular belief of his character, and in that character he is welcome. But if he shall come as a gentleman, a scholar, and a statesman, he is hailed as a contradiction to the national faith concerning his race, and his coming is resented as impudence. In the one case he may provoke contempt and derision, but in the other he is an affront to pride, and provokes malice. Let him do what he will, there is at present, therefore, no escape for him. The color line meets him everywhere, and in a measure shuts him out from all respectable and profitable trades and callings. In spite of all your religion and laws he is a rejected man.

He is rejected by trade unions, of every trade, and refused work while he lives, and burial when he dies, and yet he is asked to forget his color, and forget that which everybody else remembers. If he offers himself to a builder as a mechanic, to a client as a lawyer, to a patient as a physician, to a college as a professor, to a firm as a clerk, to a Government Department as an agent, or an officer, he is sternly met on the color line, and his claim to consideration in some way is disputed on the ground of color.

Not even our churches, whose members profess to follow the despised Nazarene, whose home, when on earth, was among the lowly and despised, have yet conquered this feeling of color madness, and what is true of our churches is also true of our courts of law. Neither is free from this all-pervading atmosphere of color hate. The one describes the Deity as impartial, no respecter of persons, and the other the Goddess of Justice as blindfolded, with sword by her side and scales in her hand held evenly between high and low, rich and low, white and black, but both are the images of American imagination, rather than American practices.

Taking advantage of the general disposition in this country to impute crime to color, white men *color* their faces to commit crime and wash off the hated color to escape punishment. In many places where the commission of crime is alleged against one of our color, the ordinary processes of law are set aside as too slow for the impetuous justice of the infuriated populace. They take the law into their own bloody hands and proceed to whip, stab, shoot, hang, or burn the alleged culprit, without the intervention of courts, counsel, judges, juries, or witnesses. . . . Every one knows that what is called Lynch law is peculiarly the law for colored people and for nobody else. If there were no other grievance than this horrible and barbarous Lynch law custom, we should be justified in assembling, as we have now done, to expose and denounce it. But this is not all. Even now, after twenty years of so called emancipation, we are subject to lawless raids of midnight riders, who, with black-ened faces, invade our homes and perpetrate the foulest of crimes upon us and our families. This condition of things is too flagrant and notorious to require specifica-tions or proof. Thus in all the relations of life and death we are met by the color line. We cannot ignore it if we would, and ought not if we could. It hunts us at midnight, it denies us accommodation in hotels and justice in the courts; excludes our children from schools, refuses our sons the chance to learn trades, and compels us to pursue only such labor as will bring the least reward. While we recognize the color line as a hurtful force, a mountain barrier to our progress, wounding our bleeding feet with its flinty rocks at every step, we do not despair. We are a hopeful people.

6. A Teacher and Two Pupils Outline the Problems of a "Colored" School, 1883

OPELIKA, ALA., *November* 22, 1883.

C. S. GIDDENS sworn and examined.

By the CHAIRMAN:

Question. You teach this colored school? *Answer.* Yes, sir.

Q. How many scholars do you have? *A.* There are one hundred and sixty-five enrolled in this school.

Q. How long have you taught this school? *A.* Six years, right along, all the time.

Q. Are you hired by the parents of the children, or are you paid by the State? *A.* Just now I am paid by the State. I am paid by the State for about seven months every year, and the balance of the time by the parents.

Q. What wages do you get, or do teachers generally get? *A.* I get in this school $40 a month.

Q. Is there any other colored school in Opelika? *A.* Yes, sir; there is school No. 2. This is school No. 1.

Q. This, I suppose, is a larger and more advanced school? *A.* Yes, sir.

Q. About how many scholars have you present this morning? *A.* There are about twenty-nine present this morning.

Q. I suppose there will be more in during the day? *A.* Yes, sir.

Q. How do your schools compare with the white schools in the town? *A.* The board of trustees think they compare very well.

Relations Between Labor and Capital, IV (Washington, D.C.: Government Printing Office, 1885), 650–653.

Q. Are the members of the board white men? *A.* They are all white.

Q. There are no white teachers of colored schools in this part of the country, I suppose? *A.* No, sir.

Q. And no colored teachers of white schools? *A.* No, sir.

Q. You think that your colored scholars do you as much credit as the white scholars do their teachers? *A.* Yes, sir; I think so. . . .

Q. If the Government would allow you to have some money for your schools that would be a good thing, wouldn't it? *A.* Oh, yes.

Q. I suppose you colored people do not pay much attention to politics now? *A.* No, sir; we do not pay much attention to those things now.

Q. You are trying to make money and let politics alone? *A.* Yes, sir.

Q. I suppose the colored people have talked that over among themselves, and have come to the conclusion that they had better turn their attention to making money and let politics go for one or two generations? *A.* Yes, sir.

Q. Is that so generally? *A.* No, sir. In Montgomery County the colored people take an active part, and also down in Coffee and Dale, they take an active part, because they are more able.

Q. I think it is the best way for you colored people to stick right to work and to try to get some education and to get some property, and that you say is the general idea of the colored people? *A.* Yes, sir; I think so. I took a census of the town and sent it to the superintendent of education, so that he should know how to make appropriations for the children, and I find that we have here about seven hundred children of the legal school age, from seven to twenty-one. That is in this district. We call this the Opelika district. Between the two schools No. 1 and No. 2, we would have about three hundred scholars.

Q. How old are those three women that I see over there studying their lessons? *A.* All of those three are married ladies.

Q. About what age do you take the oldest to be? *A.* About forty-seven or forty-eight.

Q. Have they children? *A.* Only one of them.

Q. Are they learning to read? *A.* Yes, sir; very well.

Q. Which is the oldest one? *A.* The one sitting on the left.

Q. What is their object in learning to read at their age? *A.* Well, their object is just to learn to read and write, so that they can act for themselves.

Q. How long have they attended school here? *A.* About seven months.

Q. How much longer will they attend? *A.* They will attend probably three or four months longer. . . .

Bonney Drake, one of the pupils, was questioned as follows:

By the Chairman:

Q. How old are you? *A.* I am ten years old.

Q. How long have you been at school? *A.* I do not know.

Q. Let us hear you read. (The boy read a few sentences from an elementary reader.)

Q. What State is this? *A.* Opelika.

Q. Which is the larger, a State or a town? *A.* A State.

Q. Do you know the name of this State? (No answer.)

Q. Do any of these little people know the name of this State? *A.* (By one of the girls.) Alabama.

Q. Which is larger, Opelika or Alabama? *A.* Alabama.

Q. Did you ever hear of Montgomery? *A.* Yes, sir.

Q. What is Montgomery? *A.* Alabama.

Q. Montgomery is in Alabama, just as Opelika is; but what is Montgomery? *A.* A town.

Q. Yes; Montgomery is a city, and a good many people live there. You have never been there, have you? *A.* Yes, sir.

Q. It is a good deal larger place than this, is it not? *A.* Yes sir.

Q. They call it the capital, don't they? *A.* Yes, sir.

Q. It is the place where the people live who govern the State, is it not? *A.* Yes, sir.

(The three adult pupils referred to in the testimony of the teacher were questioned by the Chairman. As they gave no names, they are here designated as Nos. 1, 2, and 3.)

No. 1 was questioned, and answered as follows:

Question. What is your age? *Answer.* I am thirty-six years old.

Q. Why are you at school? *A.* I taken a notion I want to learn, after waitin' so long. I been workin' a good deal and lost my health, and I thought I would learn to read and write, and may be it would be more intelligence to me and fetch on to other business to make a livin'.

Q. You are a married lady? *A.* Yes, sir.

No. 2 was questioned as follows:

Question. How old are you? *Answer.* Thirty-five.

Q. How long have you been attending school? *A.* Not quite three weeks.

Q. What success do you have in learning? *A.* Well, not much.

Q. Nobody learns much in three weeks. You must stick to it. Some of the greatest men in the history of the world did not begin certain studies until they were sixty or seventy or eighty years old. You are not discouraged, are you? *A.* No, sir. I hope I will improve.

The following is the examination of No. 3:

Question. How old are you? *Answer.* Thirty-eight.

Q. Are you a married lady? *A.* Yes, sir.

Q. Have you any family? *A.* One child.

Q. How long have you been learning to read? *A.* A month or more.

Q. You are going to stick to it until you learn to read, I suppose? *A.* Yes, sir; that is my aim.

Q. What do you want to learn to read and write for? *A.* I find there is a great advantage in readin' and writin'.

Q. You find that people who can read and write get on best? *A.* Yes, sir.

Q. Are most of the colored people taking pains to teach their children? *A.* Yes, sir.

🌉 *E S S A Y S*

In the following essays, two distinguished historians contrast the myths with the realities of the New South. In the first, University of Virginia Professor Edward L. Ayers examines three defining new industries of the Old South region: phosphate mining, iron and steel, and textiles. In both, he documents a story of exaggerated promise of economic returns, combined with a harsh, exploitative work regime for the new labor force. In the second selection, Jacqueline Jones of Brandeis University sensitively explores the dynamic of black rural life under the impact of the sharecropping contract. In emphasizing the relative equality of economic function between African American men and women, Jones takes pains to disentangle the myth of southern rural "laziness" from the complex realities of a distinctly unfavorable economic position.

Mill and Mine

EDWARD L. AYERS

To many people, Southern industry seemed more of a charade than an actuality. After enduring twenty years of exaggerated claims in the *Manufacturer's Record,* even a Southern trade paper could stand the puffery no longer: "If all the saw mills, cotton mills, tobacco factories, new towns, and other enterprises and undertakings which it has heralded to its advertisers and 'subscribers' as having been started up in the various states of the South, had really been erected and put into operation," the *Southern Lumberman* sneered in 1908, "there wouldn't be surface room for them to stand on, water enough under the earth to supply their boilers, nor room enough in the sky for the smoke from their chimneys." Reality looked nothing like this.

Federal banking policy, railroad freight rates, absentee ownership, reliance on outside expertise, high interest rates, cautious state governments, lack of industrial experience—all these hindered the growth of Southern industry. New Southern enterprises had to compete with long-established Northern counterparts for capital, a share of the market, and skilled technicians. In these ways, much of the broad economic development that industrial growth brought to the North in the nineteenth century did not occur in the South.

Southerners recognized their disadvantages. "The shops north owe their success largely to the mechanics in their employ," a businessman complained, but "down here anybody who can pull a monkey wrench and pound his machine with a hammer and cuss the builder for making such a machine is called a mechanic." Industrial experience on the part of management was in short supply as well. Because "every city, town, and village wanted a cotton mill," a prominent mill owner recalled, it was often impossible to find an experienced textile executive and so "recourse was had to 'leading citizens' to head ventures. Sometimes a 'leading' citizen was a banker, a lawyer, a doctor, or a business man who had demonstrated that he could make a success of his private business. In most instances, however, they possessed no knowledge of manufacturing." This commentator built his own chain

---

of mills by buying such enterprises, which had soon floundered and become available at a fraction of their worth.

Southern critics of the new order were not difficult to find, especially as the
passing years bore witness to its hidden costs. The Southerner "performs the labor,
gets the tuberculosis, reaps the desolation and hardships, while the Northern or
Eastern capitalist gets the profits, and returns the same with a philanthropic strut in
an occasion donation to a negro school or maybe a library building," Corra Harris,
a white novelist, fumed. "And the blame of this arrangement rests no less upon the
devilishly enterprising capitalists than it does upon the shiftless, short-visioned
Southerners who not only permit but seek this method of destroying themselves."
The capitalists might be "ethical rogues trained in the conscienceless school of
finance," but the Southerners were "merely simple-hearted fools with an avarice
for nickels instead of dollars."

Southern manufacturing did not fit what we recognize as the general pattern of
industrial development that transformed other Western countries in the nineteenth
century. While the cigarette, furniture, and textile industries made impressive
strides in the New South, most Southern industrial workers labored in forests and
mines rather than in factories. Those extractive industries became increasingly
dominant throughout the New South era, outstripping the growth of more heavily
mechanized enterprises. Southern industry created relatively few salaried clerks
and other officials and failed to fuel the widespread economic development of the
sort experienced in the Midwest at the same time.

Given these very real limitations, many contemporaries and subsequent scholars
have seen the Southern economy as essentially "colonial," producing new products
for distant markets where the profitable finishing and use of the products took place.
Some have ascribed the South's colonial position to the actions of the federal government, to the unfair policies of major corporations, to the selling-out of the region
by its own political and business leaders, to the machinations of Northern capitalists, to the resistance of powerful planters. These critics stress, with good reason,
the conscious decisions that shaped the industrial experience of the South and look
for those to blame for the region's lack of long-term development.

It is misleading, though, to stop there. Whether or not Southern industry in
the aggregate measured up to standards achieved elsewhere under more favorable
circumstances, it touched the lives of a million people. Whether or not Southern
industry measured up to the claims of the region's boosters—and it did not—it
shaped the histories of hundreds of counties. The impact of industry in the New
South needs to be measured in people's experience, not merely in numbers, not
merely by debunking inflated rhetoric. . . .

The New South had more than enough stories of great expectations followed by
great disappointment, stories of boom and bust, stories of simple stagnation. One
of these stories involved what must have seemed like a sure bet: the mining of
phosphates on the coast of South Carolina, only a short distance by rail from the
major market for such fertilizers, the older plantation districts of the Southeast.
"Almost the whole country adjacent to the railroads in the South Atlantic States, is
pervaded by the pungent fragrance of phosphates and other fertilizers," a reporter
for the *Atlantic Monthly* wrote in 1882. "Travelers in the Pullman night coaches

say they know when they are approaching a station by the potent odors which they encounter. Whole freight trains are laden with these substances, and hundreds of tons in sacks fill the freight platforms at all the stations."

The mining of phosphates began in the coastal areas around Charleston in the 1860s, flourished through the depression of the 1870s, and by the early 1880s was paying large dividends to the investors in the city. The amount of capital invested in the district's phosphate mining rose from $3.5 million in 1880 to $5.5 million in 1892, while the number of employees grew from 3,155 to 5,242. Nevertheless, those workers, almost all black men, performed distinctly old-fashioned back-breaking labor. For one kind of rock, they used a pick and shovel to dig pits from which the phosphate was extracted; for another, they simply waded into the rivers and used crowbars, picks, or oyster tongs to pry the phosphate loose; others dove for the rock in deeper water.

The black men in the phosphate mines, like others along the Carolina coast, refused to work in gangs. They insisted, instead, on working by the task, on getting paid for performing a certain amount of labor rather than for a set amount of time: they were more interested in controlling the pace of work and their daily wage than in making the maximum amount of money. Such preferences had characterized the Afro-American population of the coastal region for generations and had been the way they worked on the rice plantations before the phosphate boom began. The employers had to permit this labor arrangement if they were to get workers at all, for most of the laborers apparently preferred to work as independent farmers. Only steady wages, housing provided by the mine owners, health care, and credit (with its attendant indebtedness) could keep a labor force in the phosphate mines. When the industry went into decline in the 1890s, the black workers resumed the ways of making a living they had pursued before the mines opened.

Just as the labor force sought to conserve the ways of the past, so did the investors. The planters, cotton factors, and merchants who ran the mines used them mainly as a source of revenue to help maintain their accustomed way of life, not to create a New South. Charleston continued to pride itself on its conservatism, its aversion to the allure of progress. As a result of the city's resistance to new men and new money, in fact, businessmen and their capital fled Charleston. "The flower of Charleston's youth" left the city for the better chances of the textile mills in the up-country or the stores and factories of Birmingham or Atlanta. When the phosphate magnates died, their wills showed that their money had not remained in their ancestral city with them. Iron foundries in Alabama, street cars in newer cities, mills in raw textile villages—those were the distant beneficiaries of the phosphate profits.

South Carolina's phosphate boom proved short-lived. A series of terrible storms wrecked the Carolina industry in the early 1890s, just when strong competition from Florida began. "Compare that little speck in South Carolina with the broad flowing band that sweeps through Florida—and then think of the millions of tons—yes probably billions of tons—of phosphate that has been mined and shipped in Charleston," a Tallahassee paper exulted soon after the discovery of phosphate in Florida in 1890. "Think of the millions of money it's brought into South Carolina and your knees will grow weak in attempting to calculate how many trillions of money the Florida phosphate beds will bring into our beloved and flower decked state."

Whereas the older Carolina mines had operated in an environment where generations of blacks and whites had evolved traditional ways of doing things and where men with capital remained quite conservative, the phosphate boom of Florida unleashed the far more typical New South feeding frenzy. "Trains were filled with prospecting parties armed with spades, chemicals, and camping apparatus, Thousands came by horseback, by wagon, and on foot," the industry's historian has written. "The open woods were tracked everywhere by buggy wheels and punctured like a sieve" by the twenty-foot-long steel sounding rods that prospectors used to locate phosphate beds. The few nearby hotels filled to overflowing, and livery stables raked in money renting out horses by the day, "Companies were formed hourly," one observer noted, and "gilt-edged stock" flooded the state.

All through the early 1890s, even through the depression, the boom continued. By 1891, two counties alone could claim eighteen mining companies worth $5 million; within another year, the state saw more than 215 companies in operation; by 1896 over 400 companies had arisen. A familiar pattern set in, though: harder times caused the smaller operations to fail, and larger companies consolidated or replaced them. By 1900, only 50 companies mined phosphate in Florida. The big companies brought in centrifugal pumps, driven by steam engines on dredge boats, that sucked the phosphate pebbles from the beds and dumped them on a revolving screen to separate them from the sand and clay. After the phosphate dried on the wood fires and was screened another time, it was ready to be sold for fertilizer. The mines used prodigious amounts of wood to dry the phosphate—often five hundred cords per day—and local whites cut cord wood by contract. The phosphate boom echoed deep into Florida, Georgia, and Alabama, as the mining companies recruited thousands of black laborers.

The promise of mineral wealth brought capitalists and workers to other places in the South. In the 1870s the transition to coke as a fuel to make pig iron allowed Chattanooga to surge ahead in the industry, and by 1885 the small Tennessee city claimed nine furnaces and seventeen foundries and machine shops. The iron industry was growing just as fast in Virginia and Alabama: the 205,000 tons of pig iron produced in the Southern mineral belt in 1880 had grown to 1,568,000 in 1892. Throughout the 1870s, Birmingham had been merely one of a host of towns between southwest Virginia and north Alabama trying to cash in on the bonanza. In the mid-1880s, though, the Tennessee Coal Iron and Railway Company threw its money and power behind Birmingham and that city rapidly left its Southern competitors behind. As the nation's and the region's cities installed miles of cast-iron pipe for their new utilities, most of it came out of Birmingham; in 1889, even Andrew Carnegie had come to believe that "the South is Pennsylvania's most formidable industrial enemy."

Indeed, Birmingham pig iron was beating Northern competition in Chicago and Cincinnati, in Philadelphia and New York, even in Britain. In one sense, Alabama succeeded too well, for the state's iron makers poured their capital and their energy into pig iron while most American iron producers converted to steel. The merchants and investors laboring to create new iron towns often held on to familiar and successful technologies rather than experimenting with expensive methods that had not yet been proven in the South.

Even the South's greatest drawing card for every industry—cheap and plentiful labor—hurt the iron and steel industry in the long run, delaying the adoption of new techniques. With plenty of black workers rushing into Birmingham to work in the mills at rates far below Northern wages, the mills had little incentive to adopt labor-saving machinery. Even when a mill superintendent invented an important machine in Birmingham in the mid-nineties, only advanced Northern mills bothered to install it; forty years passed before Southern mills adopted the advance. As a result, the South steadily fell behind in productivity.

Ironically, too, the natural attributes that so excited Alabama boosters proved to be deficient in the century of steel: the underground (rather than pit) mines, the erratic seams and topography, and the low iron and high phosphorous content of the ore made the switch to steel far more difficult in Alabama than in the North. Characteristics of the larger regional situation also worked against Alabama steel. The Southern iron industry's late start, its reliance on outside technical expertise, its need for vast sums of capital that could be acquired only outside the South, the relatively small and slowly growing Southern market for steel, and the neglect of the Southern industry by its Northern-oriented parent company, U.S. Steel—all these conspired to keep Birmingham from attaining what had seemed so close at hand in the early 1890s.

Even as iron and steel failed to live up to expectations, Southern cotton textile mills prospered. Although textiles, like iron, involved competition with mature international rivals and required sophisticated technology, they displayed important—and critical—differences from the metals industry. Textile mills could be built anywhere that there was power to run the machinery, and the Piedmont from Virginia through Alabama offered dozens of rivers and streams with an adequate flow of water. After the 1890s, when the production of the Southern coal fields made steam power feasible, textile mills could be located over a much broader area. Moreover, a textile mill required far less capitalization than an iron or steel mill, and most labor in a textile factory required little experience and little physical strength; even children would do for some jobs. Finally, the competition with other regions and countries was less harsh in textiles than in iron and steel, because mills could specialize in particular weaves or grades that other mills were not producing.

While the Southern iron and steel industry became concentrated in the Birmingham district after 1880, the Southern textile industry steadily spread over a large area. The 10,000 textile hands in the South of 1870 (the same number as in 1850 and 1860) grew to 17,000 by 1880, 36,000 by 1890, and 98,000 by 1900. In 1870, the South held only 8 percent of the nation's textile workers; by 1900, 32 percent. Although Georgia claimed twice as many textile operatives as any other Southern state in the 1870s—a continuation of its antebellum domination—in the 1880s both of the Carolinas closed the gap and in the 1890s raced ahead even as Georgia nearly doubled its own labor force. Of the nearly 100,000 people who labored in Southern mills by the turn of the century, a third worked in South Carolina, another third in North Carolina, and a fifth in Georgia; the rest were distributed throughout Alabama, Virginia, Tennessee, Mississippi, and Kentucky. Over a thousand textile workers appeared in Arkansas, Louisiana, and West Virginia, states not usually associated with the industry. The mills varied widely in size: in 1900, the average mill in South Carolina employed 377 workers, in Georgia 270, and in North Carolina 171; the regional average was 243. The larger mills tended to be located in or near cities and large towns, not in isolated enclaves.

The South's textile mills boasted the latest and most sophisticated machinery. While steam drove only 17 percent of Southern mills in 1880, the proportion increased to 47 percent in 1890 and to more than 60 percent by 1900; electricity powered a rapidly growing share of its own. By the 1890s electric lights illuminated some mills during the night shifts, and automatic sprinklers and humidifiers appeared in the more advanced factories. Southern manufacturers were among the first to adopt the latest in manufacturing equipment as well, including a new revolving card in the 1880s and an automatic loom in the 1890s. Of the 222,000 looms installed in American factories around the turn of the century, the South claimed 153,000. The most important innovation, the ring spindle—easily run and repaired, and doubling the output per spinner—operated in 90 percent of Southern mills in the 1890s but in only 70 percent of New England mills.

This rapid proliferation of up-to-date textile mills inspired much of the South's boosterism. Here was evidence, in county after county, state after state, that factories could prosper in the South. Here was an industry that used expensive and sophisticated machinery to manufacture products that could hold their own with those produced in Great Britain or Massachusetts. Here were products sought in China, India, and Latin America, for the South supplied 60 percent of all the American cloth sent abroad at the turn of the century. Here were factories that paid a profit early on and kept on paying for decades. Here were factories that tapped the South's great cotton crop at the source, that saved the expense of transporting the bulky fiber thousands of miles. Here were factories that prospered even during the depression of the 1890s, while virtually every other business in the country— including New England textile factories—suffered.

Perhaps most important for the South's perception of itself, the textile mills were built with local capital and employed local people. Until after the turn of the century, Northern capital played only a small role in building the Southern factories. The Northern capital that did arrive came through the companies that also supplied the machinery and marketing of the Southern crop—not, as in the case of Birmingham, from the owners and managers of competing firms in the North. Every property holder in and around the towns that built textile mills could reasonably expect to profit from the mill's arrival. "Impress this fact upon your merchants," an Atlanta man wrote to an associate in the small Georgia town of Ellijay trying to boost a mill, "a cotton factory means an increase in population with more money in circulation weekly, and means a high price paid farmers for the cotton, with an enlarged market for their produce. Factory operatives being unable to attend gardens buy their produce."

People caught in the excitement of mill-building spoke often of the benefits the mills' working people would enjoy. The argument took different shapes depending on the context. Sometimes the mills were healthy because they would employ "white women and children who could find no other work equally well-adapted to their strength, and producing as large a return for their labor"; sometimes the mill village seemed wholesome because it brought isolated rural folk "together in groups, where they are subject to elevating social influences, encourages them to seek education, and improves them in every conceivable respect, as future husbands and wives, sons and daughters, parents and children." The town people saw the operatives from the very beginning as people unlike themselves, as helpless women, benighted rustics, or failed farmers. For some, that perception of the workers fed a desire to minister to them, to help bring them into the fold of the progressive New South; for others, perhaps most, that sense of otherness bred only pity or contempt.

Near the turn of the century a writer for the *Outlook* visited a mill town near Augusta. He asked several mill families why they had come there. "The reasons given for leaving their rural homes were widely various: 'because we lost our "plantation"'; 'because my wife was lonely'; 'because the darkeys came in.'" The pervasive decline of Southern rural life created a sense of dissatisfaction and desperation among white farming families that made it easier for mill operators to find a work force. The demographic pressure on the land, the decline of cotton prices, the growing proportion of women to men in the older regions, the mobility of blacks, the disaffection of the young for rural life—all these dislocations made it easier to undergo the powerful dislocation of leaving home to work in a textile mill. Instead of leaving his new wife behind to seek work on a railroad or logging crew, one young east Tennessee man told his skeptical father, he would go with his new wife to a mill town. "Well, if I had to go to public works"—the phrase Southerners at the turn of the century used to describe wage labor—"why not move to them [mills] where it would be in my family?"

Some people were obviously more willing to leave than others. Widows with children found the mills a place where they could keep their families together and live without dependence on others; in 1880, early in the mill-building period, almost half of all the mill households in Augusta were headed by women, virtually all widowed. Any family with several young daughters at home might find the mills attractive, for the labor of those daughters was worth far more in a factory than in the countryside. Single young men, on the other hand, found opportunities that paid about as well as the textile mills; at least until the turn of the century, a farm hand made as much as a spinner in a mill and a hard worker could make considerably more money cutting logs or working on a railroad. Those young men who stayed on at a mill through their mid-twenties, however, often remained for the rest of their working lives and rose in the company hierarchy. Women, who moved in and out of the mill as they had children, generally stayed in the lower-paying jobs.

While some parents would do anything to keep the children out of the mills and in school, others saw nothing wrong with children learning to work early on in life, contributing to the family income and being where they could be watched. Employers differed as well; some were anxious to have the cheap labor of children, while others would have happily replaced them with other, more dependable and less controversial workers. In any case, a quarter of all male mill workers at the turn of the century were fifteen or under, and over a third of females were that young; most workers of both genders were in their late teens or early twenties.

This profile of the laboring force was unique among Southern industries, both within the Piedmont and within the South as a whole. While women represented about 15 percent of all manufacturing workers in the Piedmont, the average for the rest of the region was only 4 percent. While youths under sixteen years of age represented about 13 percent of the Piedmont's workers, the regional average was only 3 percent. The textile labor force was also unique in its racial composition. Whereas the workers in virtually every other major industry in the South were nearly balanced between the races, the machine rooms of the cotton mills rapidly became the preserve of whites only. Mill owners would not allow blacks to work alongside the white women and girls who made up the bulk of the work force. Black men were permitted to work only at outside loading and unloading and in the suffocating rooms where they opened bales for processing. Black women found no work at all. . . .

This labor force held many attractions to mill management. By employing the entire family, the employer received not only inexpensive labor but also considerable sway over that labor. Unlike a single man, a family had a difficult time leaving; while workers who moved from mill to mill during those frequent times when there was not enough labor to go around inflated turnover figures, most mills enjoyed a stable core of families. The famous "mill village" setting increased that stability, for the company provided the school, the church, the recreation, and the store as well as the work. At the turn of the century, 92 percent of Southern textile workers lived in such settlements. The villages initially arose because employers had no choice but to provide housing and services for mills located on remote streams, where most of the early mills were built. They persisted because they gave the operatives things they came to expect—houses, schools, churches, stores—and because they gave employers effective means of keeping a steady and sober labor force. Born of necessity, the mill villages quickly became a resilient tradition.

These villages exhibited a broad range of conditions and elicited a broad range of reactions. The workers' evaluation of the results of their move from the countryside varied just as widely as the reasons they had left in the first place: "Some declared they had improved their conditions; others that they had ruined what good fortunes they had had." At first, one mill owner commented, workers seemed "supremely happy and contented" as they enjoyed the water pumps and nearby churches and schools unavailable in most farm communities. Yet "by and by the novelty wears away. Things once longed for and regarded as unattainable become commonplace." As one mill worker put it, "They's more money at the mill, but a better livin' on the farm. Unless a man's mighty sorry he can raise good somethin' t'eat on the land, while he has more spendin' money in the mill—and he spends it too. All he does at either one is jus' about break even."

The typical village combined urban crowding with the kerosene lamps, hand pumps, meddlesome livestock, flies, and mud of the countryside. The factory itself, filled with choking fibers and loud machines, was little better. The typical mill looked something like the one described in a novel of the time: "a low, one-story structure of half-burnt bricks" next to "a squatty low-browed engine room" with a "black, soggy exhaust-pipe stuck out of a hole in its side."

A rare contemporary view of a mill town from a worker's point of view appeared in a letter from J. W. Mehaffry of Concord, North Carolina, to Senator Zebulon Vance. Mehaffry was furious at conditions in the mill and the town. The local cotton mill owners, J. M. Odell and Son, "work their employees, women and children from 6 A.M. to 7 P.M. with a half hour for dinner." Worse, the Odells held back the workers' pay for a month, and used the money to buy cotton for the mill. "Although the owner and his son are *zealous Methodists,*" they are "our slave drivers. J. M. Odell has built a $5000 mausoleum to entomb *his* dead, but the poor women and children can be buried in the Potters field." The workers' houses were piled next to one another, creating a terrible sewage problem and contributing to the deaths of 47 adults and children in the last six months. The letter charged that Southern politicians, despite all their rhetoric, were no help: "We curse the northern people, when to do justice *all* our cursing should be expended on home monsters like J. M. and W. R. Odell." In the 1880s and 1890s, mill owners managed their affairs with little interference from politicians or reformers.

Because not enough families or young women were willing to work in the textile factories, owners experienced recurring labor shortages, especially in the years around the turn of the century. During those times, a steady stream of transient workers flowed into and out of the mill villages, moving to find higher wages, a better house, or merely a new setting. "This mill will be o.k. if we ever get enough weavers to run everything without depending on floating 'bum' labor," a manager for a North Carolina mill wrote his mother in 1897. "Whenever I see a strong, robust country girl, I am almost on my knees in my effort to try to get her to go to the mill to learn to weave." While the mills of the 1880s and 1890s managed to get most of their workers from nearby rural areas, by 1900 mill recruiters often had to search 250 miles afield. Some ran trains into the mountains to persuade families to come to the mill villages. Other mills sent agents into their competitors' towns to entice experienced hands to move, partly by "getting them dissatisfied" with their present lot.

The mill villages, while often separated from neighboring towns by different school systems and churches, were not self-contained paternalistic enclaves. Not only did "floaters" move from village to village, but even the long-term workers seldom had a personal relationship, positive or negative, with the mill owner. The kind of men who had the money to invest in mills had no interest in living in mill villages. "I was so impressed with the uninviting surroundings, lack of educational facilities and civilized society, etc.," one South Carolina man who was considering buying a small mill remarked, "that I decided that I would not move my family down there for the whole outfit as a gift." Groups of investors owned most mills and merely paid a superintendent to keep an eye on things. Those superintendents lived in the villages themselves and sent their children to school with the operative children. Chosen for their character and the respect they held among the workers as well as for their ability to keep things in order and to turn a profit, the superintendents often found themselves caught between employer and employee. Of the worker's class and background, but acting as the agent of absentee owners, the superintendent "only demanded of the operatives what the president demanded of him," a mill pastor pointed out. In turn, "the president demanded what the directors demanded of him; the directors demanded what the stockholders demanded of them. The stockholders demanded large dividends and there is where the driving began and there is where the responsibility rests." As in so much of the South, distant forces seemed to power the machinery, while people struggled in their face-to-face encounters to make the best of hard situations.

The mill people were part of the unstable and rapidly evolving world of the New South, and we should not allow the images conjured up by the phrase "mill village" to obscure the connections between the mill operatives and the world beyond. New and larger mills appeared near towns and cities of considerable size; mill towns ringed cities such as Charlotte or Burlington. Company stores became less common as the years passed; only a third of the mill villages had such a store at the turn of the century, and that proportion declined as competing private stores grew up near the mills. Complex divisions developed among the mill workers, as those who owned their homes in a mill town distanced themselves from the more transient workers renting houses from the company.

Mill workers found it easy to visit nearby saloons or brothels as well as friends back on the farm or in town; mill families saw sons and daughters leave for work elsewhere or to establish families outside the mill village; many mill families took in boarders, kin and strangers; considerable numbers of mill workers farmed nearby, some of them owning land. Even after the mills became firmly established at the turn of the century, high cotton prices enticed enough workers back to the land to try farming again that employers complained of labor shortages. All these trends quickened with the accelerating growth of the industry in the nineties and after, although people then and ever since have tended to envision the villages as they were for a few years in the early 1880s: the embodiments of personal concern or personal domination. Instead, they were part of the much larger transformation of the South, a transformation that soon eroded any lingering paternalistic style. The mills were based on industrial work, on dependence upon friends and allies among one's own class, not a longing for a lost plantation ideal.

The workers' dependence on one another was tested in the years between 1898 and 1902, when strikes shook the Piedmont. Some workers had joined the Knights of Labor in the early 1880s, but unions made little headway in the textile mills through all the boom years. In 1898 and 1899, though, faced with wage reductions, workers quickly organized in the National Union of Textile Workers and launched dozens of strikes against the mill owners. Those most likely to join the union and strike were those who labored in the big urban mills—in Columbus, Augusta, and Atlanta—where skilled workers congregated and from where there was little chance to turn to farming for a season. The supremely confident owners locked the workers out of the mills, coordinating their efforts so that workers would have nowhere to turn. Despite help from Northern unions, the owners crushed the strikes and broke the unions in August in 1902. Organized labor did not reappear in the textile mills for more than a decade.

Bent Backs in the Rural South

JACQUELINE JONES

Late nineteenth-century middle-class white women derived their status from that of their husbands. Unproductive in the context of a money-oriented, industrializing economy, and formally unable to take part in the nation's political process, they enjoyed financial security only insofar as their spouses were steady and reliable providers. In contrast, black working women in the South had a more equal

Jaqueline Jones, *Labor of Love, Labor of Sorrow* (New York: Basic Books, 1985), 99–109. Reprinted by permission of Basic Books, a member of Perseus Books, LLC.

relationship with their husbands in the sense that the two partners were not separated by extremes of economic power or political rights; black men and women lacked both. Oppression shaped these unions in another way. The overlapping of economic and domestic functions combined with the pressures imposed by a surrounding, hostile white society meant that black working women were not so dramatically dependent upon their husbands as were middle-class white wives. Within black families and communities, then, public-private, male-female distinctions were less tightly drawn than among middle-class whites. Together, black women and men participated in a rural folk culture based upon group cooperation rather than male competition and the accumulation of goods. The ways in which this culture both resembled and diverged from that of poor whites in the South helps to illuminate the interaction between class and racial factors in shaping the roles of women.

Referring to the world view of Alabama sharecropper Hayes Shaw, Theodore Rosengarten (the biographer-interviewer of Shaw's son Nate) observed that "righteousness consisted in not having so much that it hurt to lose it." Nate himself remembered that his father as a young man had passed up promising opportunities to buy land because "he was blindfolded; he didn't look to the future." Ruled by "them old slavery thoughts," Hayes Shaw knew that

> whenever the colored man prospered too fast in this country under the old rulins, they worked every figure to cut you down, cut your britches off you. So, it . . . weren't no use in climbin too fast; weren't no use in climbin slow, neither, if they was going to take everything you worked for when you got too high.

Rural black communities that abided by this philosophy sought to achieve self-determination within a limited sphere of action. In this way they insulated themselves from whites and from the disappointment that often accompanied individual self-seeking. They lived like Nate's brother Peter; he "made up his mind that he weren't goin to have anything and after that, why nothin could hurt him."

Northern scholars and journalists, as well as southern planters, charged that rural blacks valued freedom of movement, "furious religious revivals," and community holidays—"none of which brings them profit of any sort." A Georgia landowner characterized in this way the philosophy of his tenants, who tended to "dismiss further thought of economy" once they had fulfilled their financial obligations to him: "*dum vivimus vivamus*" ("while we are living let us live"). Some white observers seized upon this theme and warned of its ramifications for the future of American society. Within a growing economy based upon the production of consumer goods, black people's apparent willingness to make do with the little they had represented not so much a moral transgression as a threat to employee discipline on the one hand and incentives to buy on the other. Why should a black husband and father work hard if he was "content with a log cabin and a fireplace, and with corn, bacon, and molasses as articles of food"? How would he profit southern or national economic development if he was satisfied with "merely enough to keep soul and body together"? . . .

Black settlements in remote areas—especially those that remained relatively self-sufficient through hunting and fishing—experienced the mixed blessings of semiautonomy. These communities existed almost wholly outside the larger regional and national economic system. For example, the people of the Sea Islands who "labor only for the fulfillment of the petition, 'Give us this day our daily bread,' and literally 'take no thought for the morrow,' working only when their necessities compel them," revealed the dilemma of a premodern subculture located within an industrial nation. As independent, self-respecting farmers (a proportion-ately large number owned their own land), the Sea Islanders remained relatively unmolested by whites and managed to preserve African traditions and folkways to a remarkable degree. Their diet, consisting of fowl, fish, shellfish, and fresh vege-tables, was nutritionally superior to that of Cotton Belt sharecroppers. Yet these people lacked proper medical care and the most basic household conveniences. (Water-toting women hailed the installation of a water pump in the early twentieth century as "a most spectacular innovation in domestic economy. . . .") Floods and other natural disasters periodically wrought havoc on their way of life, and pushed young people off the islands and into nearby cities, leaving behind primarily the elderly and the blind.

Even rural communities that lacked the almost total isolation of the Sea Islands possessed a strong commitment to corporatism and a concomitant scorn for the hoarding of private possessions. As government researcher J. Bradford Laws wrote disapprovingly of the sugar workers he studied in 1902, "They have an unfortunate notion of generosity, which enables the more worthless to borrow fuel, food, and what not on all hands from the more thrifty." It is clear that these patterns of be-havior were determined as much by economic necessity as by cultural "choice." if black household members pooled their energies to make a good crop, and if com-munities collectively provided for their own welfare, then poverty and oppression ruled out most of the alternative strategies. Individualism was a luxury that share-croppers simply could not afford.

Rural folk relied on one another to help celebrate the wedding of a young couple, rejoice in a preacher's fervent exhortation, mark the annual closing of the local school, minister to the ill, and bury the dead. Women participated in all these rites and communal events. In addition, they had their own gender-based activities, as well as societies that contributed to the general good of the community. On the Sea Islands, young women would "often take Saturday afternoon as a time for cleaning the yard or the parlor, for ironing their clothes, or for preparing their hair." (Their brothers gathered at a favorite meeting place or organized a "cornfield base-ball game.") Quilting brought young and old women together for a daylong festival of sewing, chatting, and feasting. Supported by the modest dues of their members, female voluntary beneficial societies met vital social-welfare needs that individual families could not always afford; these groups helped their members to pay for life insurance, medical care, and burial services. Even the poorest women managed to contribute a few pennies a month and to attend weekly meetings. In turn-of-the-century Alabama, "The woman who is not a member of one of these is pitied and considered rather out of date."

The impulse for mutual solace and support among rural Afro-Americans culmi-nated in their religious institutions and worship services. At monthly meetings women and men met to reaffirm their unique spiritual heritage, to seek comfort, and to comfort one another. Black women found a "psychological center" in religious belief, and the church provided strength for those overcome by the day-to-day busi-ness of living. For many weary sharecroppers' wives and mothers, worship services allowed for physical and spiritual release and offered a means of transcending earthly cares in the company of one's friends and family. Faith created "a private world inside the self, sustained by religious sentiment and religious symbolism . . . fashioned to contain the world without." "Spiritual mothers" served as the "main pillars" of Methodist and Baptist churches, but they also exercised religious leadership outside formal institutional boundaries; elderly women in particular commanded respect as the standard-bearers of tradition and as the younger generation's link with its ancestors.

Of course, life in "places behind God's back" was shaped as much by racial prejudice as by black solidarity, and the "ethos of mutuality" that pervaded rural communities did not preclude physical violence or overt conflict between individuals. At times a Saturday night "frolic" ended in a bloody confrontation between two men who sought courage from a whiskey bottle and self-esteem through hand-to-hand conflict. Similarly, oppression could bind a family tightly together, but it could also heighten tensions among people who had few outlets for their rage and frustration. Patterns of domestic conflict reflected both historical injustices and daily family pressures. These forces affected black women and men in different ways.

On a superficial level, the roots of domestic violence are not difficult to recognize or understand. Cramped living quarters and unexpected setbacks provoked the most even-tempered of household heads. Like their slave parents, mothers and fathers often used harsh disciplinary techniques on children, not only to prepare them for life in a white-dominated world where all blacks had to act cautiously, but also to exert rigid control over this one vital facet of domestic life. If whites attempted to cut "the britches off" black fathers and husbands, then these men would try to assert their authority over their households with even greater determination. At times that determination was manifested in violence and brutality.

Hayes Shaw epitomized the sharecropping father who lorded over his wives (he married three times) and children. More than once the Shaw children watched helplessly as their father beat their mother, and they too were "whipped . . . up scandalous" for the slightest infraction. Hayes divided his time between his "outside woman"—an unmarried laundress in the neighborhood—and his "regular" family, and he made no effort to conceal the fact. The Shaw womenfolk were hired out or sent to the fields like children, without daring to protest, while Hayes spent his days in a characteristically masculine fashion—alone, away from the house, hunting. . . .

Hayes Shaw was undoubtedly an extreme example of a domestic tyrant, but he and other husbands like him inspired white and black women community leaders, educators, and social workers to formulate a critique of Afro-American family life in the late nineteenth century. Sensitive to the economic problems confronted by black marriage partners, these observers charged that black men enjoyed certain male prerogatives without the corresponding striving and ambition that those prerogatives were meant to reward. Juxtaposed with this "irresponsible" man was his wife—no doubt a "real drudge," but certainly "the greatest sufferer from the stress and strain attendant upon the economic conditions" faced by all Afro-Americans. The chief problem seemed to stem from the fact that black women played a prominent role in supporting the family in addition to performing their domestic responsibilities. In the eyes of their critics, black men as a group were not particularly concerned about "getting ahead" in the world and thus fell short of their wives' spirit of industry and self-sacrifice.

White teacher-social workers like Rossa Cooley and Georgia Washington and black writers and educators like Anna J. Cooper, Katherine Davis Tillman, Frances Harper, and Fannie Barrier Williams focused on the domestic achievements of poor women and with varying degrees of subtlety condemned their "worthless" husbands. Their critique of black womanhood marked the emergence of the "black matriarchy thesis," for they suggested that the main problem in Afro-American family life was an "irresponsible" father who took advantage of his "faithful, hard-working womenfolks." By the mid-twentieth century sociologists had shifted public attention to the "irresponsible" father's *absence;* the relatively large number of single, working mothers in the nation's urban ghettos seemed to lend additional credence to an argument that originally purported to deal with the problems of rural women. Thus the image of the strong, overburdened black mother persisted through the years, and it was usually accompanied by the implicit assumption that women wielded authority over men and children in Afro-American families.

Yet Hayes Shaw's household was never a "matriarchy." Recent historians who have labeled the postemancipation rural black family "patriarchal" hardly help to clarify the issue. The difficulty in conceptualizing black male-female roles derives from the fact that most observers (whether writing in the nineteenth or twentieth century) have used as their basis for comparison the white middle-class model of family life. Black men headed the vast majority of southern rural families, and they self-consciously ruled their wives and children; hence the use of the term patriarchy to describe family relationships. But these households deviated from the traditional sexual division of labor in the sense that wives worked to supplement the family income, and fathers often lacked the incentive to try to earn money so that they could purchase property or goods and thus advance the family's status. These men worked hard—they had to, in order to survive the ruthlessly exploitative sharecropping system—but most realized that even harder work would not necessarily enable them to escape poverty. Those who confronted this dilemma hardly deserved the epithet "worthless manhood." Still, for the two sexes, relative equality of economic function did not imply equality of domestic authority.

Although a husband and wife each made an essential contribution to the welfare of the household, they were compensated in different ways for their labor. This reward differential reflected their contrasting household responsibilities and produced contrasting attitudes toward work and its personal and social value. As a participant in a staple-crop economy, a black father assumed responsibility for a crop that would be exchanged in the marketplace at the end of the year. He supposedly toiled for future compensation in the form of cash. However, not only did his physical exertion gain him little in the way of immediate reward, in fact he tilled the ground only to repay one debt and to ensure that he would have another in the coming year. Under such conditions, most men took pride in their farming abilities, but worked no more strenuously than was absolutely necessary to satisfy white creditors and keep their own families alive in the process.

Their wives, on the other hand, remained relatively insulated from the inevitable frustrations linked to a future-oriented, market economy. For example, women daily performed discreet tasks that yielded tangible results upon completion. Meal preparation, laundering, egg gathering—these chores had finite boundaries in the course of a day. Childcare was a special case, but it had its own special joys. It was an ongoing responsibility that began when a woman had her first baby and ended only years later when her youngest child left home. On a more mundane level, childcare was a constant preoccupation of mothers during their waking hours, and infants' needs often invaded their sleep. Yet a woman's exclusive authority in this area of domestic life earned her emotional gratification. Her husband hardly derived a similar sense of gratification from his responsibility for the cotton crop; he "earned" only what a white man was willing to pay him. Hence the distinction between work patterns simplistically labeled by some contemporary writers as male "laziness" and female "self-sacrifice" actually represented a complex phenomenon shaped by the different demands made upon black men and women and the degree of personal satisfaction resulting from the fulfillment of those demands.

Poor whites in the late nineteenth-century South were also stigmatized by charges of laziness and lethargy; together black and white sharecroppers and tenants endured a form of opprobrium traditionally directed at working people by their employers and social "betters." Like their black counterparts, propertyless whites valued self-sufficiency over cash-crop tenancy, and they too confronted new class relationships established after the war—relationships that turned on mortgages, credit, and crop liens as much as on race and kinship. By 1900 over one-third of all whites employed in agriculture were tenants, and even small landowners remained perched precariously on the brink of financial disaster, only a drought or a boll weevil plague away from indebtedness. . . . Thus all landless farmers, white and black, confronted uncertainties in a period of declining agricultural prices and general economic hardship. It seems likely then that southern poor people as a group deviated from the predominant (that is, white middle-class northern-industrial) culture, a way of life shaped by the powerful ideology of ambition and personal gain.

A comparison of the experiences of poor white and black women in the rural South suggests that to a great extent, class and gender conjoined to determine what all sharecroppers' wives did and how they did it. For example, data on black and white households in the Cotton South for 1880 and 1900 indicate some striking similarities between the family structures characteristic of the two races. For instance, both types of "average" households possessed a male head, and a male head accompanied by his spouse, in the same proportions. Black and white wives shared the same age patterns relative to their husbands. Though slightly larger, white households had a similar configuration compared to black ones and lived near at least some of their kin to the same extent. . . .

. . . Like black women, poor white farm wives bore the domestic burdens that were endemic to the economic system of southern staple-crop agriculture. They married in their late teens and had an average of six children (although large households of twelve or thirteen were not uncommon). Because the family was constantly in debt to a local merchant, family members felt glad if they broke even at the end of the year. Most women made do with very little cash in piecing together the family's subsistence. They performed all the household chores of washing, sewing, cleaning, cooking, and churning, often with the assistance of their eldest daughter, but a majority also helped out in the cotton or tobacco fields during the busy seasons. . . . These wives often added to the family income with the proceeds they earned from selling eggs, vegetables, or milk. In the Deep South, some couples experienced periodic separations when the wives went off to work temporarily in factories, or when their men folk found jobs on the levees in the off-season.

In terms of earthly comforts, life offered little more to white tenant-farm wives than it did to blacks; white women too lived in sparsely furnished two- or three-room cabins that lacked running water, and their Cotton Belt families tended to move every three years or so. Mothers were attended by a midwife during child-birth. Predictably, they knew nothing about modern contraceptive techniques, and although they took pride in their child-rearing abilities, they suffered from the consequent drain on their emotional and physical resources. Dreams and fortune-tellers explained the past and predicted the future for many of these illiterate women, but they seemed to lack the religious devotion and denominational loyalties exhibited by black wives and mothers. Undernourished and overworked, they had to remind themselves of the biblical dictate, "Be content with your lot."

In a rural society that honored a code of neighborliness and mutual coopera-tion, black and white women had few opportunities for interracial contact on any level. Husbands and fathers of both races and all classes observed the ritualized etiquette of southern race relations in the public arena—in town, at the post office, court house, or supply store—but their wives were largely excluded from these encounters. Middle-class white women acted out their own presumptions of racial superiority in their dealings with black servants and laundresses. Tenant-farm wives of course could not afford to employ black women for any length of time or exploit them in a direct way. A few women of the two races did come together in situations that held the promise of enhancing mutual respect and appreciation—for example, when they participated in the Southern Farmers Alliance in the 1880s and 1890s, or when black "grannies" attended white women during childbirth. Yet these opportunities were rare, and for the most part women lacked a formal voice in the politics of interracial protest.

In the end, the fact that the labor of white sharecroppers' wives was so similar to that of their black counterparts is less significant than the social environment in which that work took place. For the outcast group, the preservation of family integrity served as a political statement to the white South. To nurse a child, send a daughter to school, feed a hungry family after a long day at work in the fields, or patch a shirt by the light of a flickering fire—these simple acts of domesticity acquired special significance when performed for a people so beleaguered by human as well as natural forces. If white women also had to make soup out of scraps, at least they and their families remained secure from "bulldosers" (mobs) and Judge Lynch. Finally, and perhaps most important, women of the two races had different things to teach their children about the "southern way of life," its freedoms and its dangers.

Despite the transition in labor organization from slavery to sharecropping, the work of black women in the rural South continued to respond to the same human and seasonal rhythms over the generations. By the early twentieth century, they still structured their labor around household chores and childcare, field and wage work, and community welfare activities. Moreover, emancipation hardly lessened the demands made upon females of all ages; young girls worked alongside their mothers, and elderly women had to provide for themselves and their families as long as they were physically able. Although the specific tasks performed by women reflected constantly changing priorities (determined by the cotton-growing cycle and the size and maturity of individual households), the need for a woman to labor rarely abated in the course of a day, a year, or her lifetime.

In its functional response to unique historical circumstances, the rural black household necessarily differed from the late nineteenth-century middle-class ideal, which assumed that men would engage in individual self aggrandizement. Furthermore, according to this ideal, women were to remain isolated at home, only indirectly sharing in the larger social values of wealth and power accumulation. In contrast, rural black women labored in harmony with the priorities of cooperation and sharing established by their own communities, even as their husbands were prevented from participating in the cash economy in a way that would answer to white-defined notions of masculinity.

Despite the hard, never-ending work performed by rural women—who, ironically, were labeled part of a "lazy" culture by contemporaries and recent historians alike—they could not entirely compensate for the loss of both a husband (through death or another form of permanent separation) and older sons or male relatives who established households on their own. The sharecropping family strove to maintain a delicate balance between its labor resources and its economic needs, and men, as both negotiators in the public sphere and as field workers, were crucial to that balance. Therefore, during the latter part of the nineteenth century, when the natural selection process endemic to commercial crop agriculture weeded out "unfit" households, it forced single mothers, widows, and unmarried daughters to look cityward. Many of them would discover that while the southern countryside continued to mirror the slave past, in the towns that past was refracted into new shapes and images.

F U R T H E R   R E A D I N G

Edward Ayers, *Southern Crossing: A History of the American South, 1877–1906* (1995)
David Carlton, *Mill and Town in South Carolina, 1880–1920* (1982)
Wilbur J. Cash, *The Mind of the South* (1941)
Don H. Doyle, *New Men, New Cities, New South: Atlanta, Nashville, Charleston, Mobile, 1860–1910* (1989)
Grace Elizabeth Hale, *Making Whiteness: The Culture of Segregation in the South, 1890–1940* (1998)
Jacquelyn D. Hall et al., *Like a Family: The Making of a Southern Cotton Mill World* (1987)
Jacqueline Jones, *Labor of Love, Labor of Sorrow* (1985)
Leon Litwack, *Trouble in Mind: Black Southerners in the Age of Jim Crow* (1998)
Peter Rachleff, *Black Labor in the South* (1984)

Roger L. Ransom and Richard Sutch, *One Kind of Freedom: The Economic Consequences of Emancipation* (1977)

Altina Waller, *Feud: Hatfields, McCoys, and Social Change in Appalachia, 1860–1900* (1988)

C. Vann Woodward, *Origins of the New South, 1877–1913* (1951)

Gavin Wright, *Old South, New South: Revolutions in the Southern Economy Since the Civil War* (1986)

George C. Wright, *Life Behind a Veil: Blacks in Louisville, Kentucky, 1865–1930* (1985)

CHAPTER
5

Rise of the
Industrial City:
New Places, New Peoples

The industrial revolution, as we have seen, reached into the frontier West and the agrarian South, but the classic site of nineteenth-century economic development was the industrial city. Indeed, America's rise to industrial preeminence—from fourth-largest (in dollar value) producer of manufactured goods in 1860 to world leader by 1894—was intimately linked to the massing of labor resources in the cities. In 1860, only 13 percent of the population lived in urban areas; by 1900, the figure had jumped to 40 percent, and by 1920 cities and towns were home to a majority of Americans. In the 1880s alone, when manufacturing overtook agricultural production in value, one hundred cities more than doubled their size, and the manufacturing centers of New York, Philadelphia, and Chicago all topped 1 million in population. American cities and their laboring populations, it is fair to say, supplanted England in this period as the "workshop of the world."

The workforce for this urban-industrial transformation was drawn overwhelmingly from outside the country's borders, as the years 1880–1920 witnessed a massive, unprecedented tide of immigration. Attracted by both the promise of economic opportunity and, for many, anticipated relief from religious and political persecution, the "New Immigrants" effectively redrew the demographic map of American cities and basic industries. At the high-water mark, 1900–1910, the 8.8 million immigrants constituted more than 40 percent of urban newcomers, doubling the natural increase by childbirth of the established population. Representing a shift in the incoming stream from the northern and western rim of Europe to the southern and eastern European heartland, the New Immigrants— Italians, Hungarians, Russians, Slavs, Greeks, Jews, and others (including regionally significant concentrations from Asia and Mexico)—came overwhelmingly from peasant or working-class backgrounds and spoke in strikingly different accents, both literally and figuratively, from the native-born population of the United States.

116

After the turn of the century, the foreign-born stream into the cities was enhanced by another important demographic shift. Drawn cityward by the labor needs of the war industries, beginning in 1915, as well as by dreams of escaping the misery of the southern countryside, more than three hundred thousand blacks had migrated to northern cities by 1920. Although this development, in the long run, would energize both individual artistic creation and collective political power, in the short run the new black urban migrants encountered only a more furtive, less official face of the same discriminatory system they were leaving in the South.

The nature of immigrant integration into American society raised serious questions both inside and outside the immigrant communities. For a nation culturally suspended between dreams of social progress and worries about the loss of older virtues, the new urban population roused both nativist and defensive racist fears of mongrelization and anarchistic insurrection. Even those who welcomed the immigrants' labor power coded their receptivity with an insistence on "Americanization" or the rapid inculcation of "acceptable" attitudes and behavior. For the immigrants themselves, the issues surrounding Americanization were usually different but no less complicated. The problem of how to "succeed" in material terms, while maintaining values rooted in a distinct national and religious culture, confronted every arriving group. This issue placed the greatest strain on the basic unit of immigrant survival, the family.

 D O C U M E N T S

The following selections at once highlight the remarkable physical transformation of urban-industrial life and accent the social and cultural conflicts engendered thereby. The two census-derived graphs in Documents 1 and 2 reveal, respectively, the dramatic rise in urban population by region and the equally dramatic imprint of new European migration on the demographic composition of America's industrial cities. In Document 3, Englishman Rudyard Kipling's encounter with Chicago translates dry statistics into an emotional response—in this case, repulsion. A more sympathetic, although no less gritty, view of the city emerges in Document 4 in Carl Sandburg's famous ode to the City of the Big Shoulders. Document 5 reflects the racialist nature of nativist (i.e., anti-immigrant) backlash of the era in which no ethnic group was more vilified than the Chinese, as exemplified here in an 1892 congressional report on immigration, reflecting the paranoia of white workers, which singles out Chinese immigrant labor as a threat to the American way of life. Both the hurt and unfairness of such discrimination is revealed in Document 6, a poem by Chinese writer Huang Zunxiang. Another blemish on the quality of life in American cities was the system of racial discrimination—as clearly evident in Philadelphia in 1899 as in any southern town—revealed here (Document 7) by African American sociologist W. E. B. Du Bois. Finally, we turn to the day-to-day transactions of immigrants making a life for themselves in a challenging new culture. In Document 8, readers of the advice column of the Yiddish-language *Jewish Daily Forward* seek guidance in negotiating some of the most poignant moments of cultural dissonance.

1. Population Growth in Select U.S. Cities, 1870–1920

	1870	1880	1890	1900	1910	1920
New England						
Boston	250,526	362,839	448,477	560,892	670,585	748,060
Lowell	40,928	59,475	77,696	94,969	106,294	112,759
Providence	68,904	104,857	132,146	175,597	224,326	237,595
New Haven	50,840	62,882	86,045	108,027	133,605	162,537
Worcester	41,105	58,291	84,655	118,421	145,986	179,754
Middle Atlantic						
New York	942,292	1,164,673	1,441,216	3,437,202	4,766,883	5,620,048
Brooklyn	419,921	599,495	838,547	In N.Y.C.	In N.Y.C.	In N.Y.C.
Rochester	62,386	89,366	133,896	162,608	218,149	295,750
Buffalo	117,714	155,134	255,664	352,387	423,715	506,775
Newark	105,059	136,508	181,830	246,070	347,469	414,524
Jersey City	82,546	120,722	163,003	206,433	267,779	298,103
Philadelphia	674,022	847,170	1,046,964	1,293,697	1,549,008	1,823,779
Pittsburgh	139,256	235,071	343,904	451,512	533,905	588,343
South Atlantic						
Baltimore	267,354	332,313	434,439	508,957	558,485	733,826
Washington	109,199	147,293	188,932	278,718	331,069	437,571
Richmond	51,038	63,600	81,388	85,050	127,628	171,667
Durham, N.C.	—	2,041	5,485	6,679	18,241	21,719
Charlotte, N.C.	4,473	7,094	11,557	18,091	34,014	46,338
Charleston	48,956	49,984	54,955	55,807	58,833	67,957
Savannah	28,235	30,709	43,189	54,244	65,064	83,252
Atlanta	21,789	37,409	65,533	89,872	154,839	200,616

North Central						
Cincinnati	216,239	255,139	296,908	325,902	363,591	401,247
Cleveland	92,829	160,146	261,353	381,768	560,663	796,841
Detroit	79,577	116,340	205,876	285,704	465,766	993,678
Milwaukee	71,440	115,587	204,468	285,315	373,857	457,147
Chicago	298,977	503,185	1,099,850	1,698,575	2,185,283	2,701,705
St. Louis	310,864	350,518	451,770	575,238	687,029	772,897
Kansas City, Mo.	32,260	55,785	132,716	163,752	248,381	324,410
Wichita, Kans.	—	4,911	23,853	24,671	52,450	72,217
Omaha	16,083	30,518	140,452	102,555	124,096	191,601
Minneapolis	13,066	46,887	164,738	202,718	310,408	380,582
South Central						
Mobile	32,034	29,132	31,076	38,469	51,521	60,777
Birmingham	—	3,086	26,178	38,415	132,685	178,806
New Orleans	191,418	216,090	243,039	287,104	335,075	387,219
Memphis	40,226	33,592	64,495	102,320	131,105	162,351
Nashville	25,865	43,350	76,168	80,865	110,364	118,342
Louisville	100,753	123,758	161,129	204,731	223,928	234,891
Houston	9,382	16,513	27,557	44,633	78,800	138,276
Dallas	—	10,358	38,067	42,638	92,104	158,976
Mountain						
Denver	4,759	35,629	106,713	133,859	213,381	256,491
Salt Lake City	12,854	20,768	44,843	53,531	92,777	118,110
Pacific						
Los Angeles	5,728	11,183	50,395	102,479	319,198	576,673
San Francisco	149,473	233,959	298,997	342,782	416,912	506,676
Portland, Ore.	8,293	17,577	46,385	90,426	207,214	258,288
Seattle	1,107	3,533	42,837	80,671	237,194	315,312

Bayrd Still, *Urban America: A History with Documents* (Boston: Little Brown, 1974), pp. 210–211. Reprinted by permission of Little, Brown and Company.

2. Immigrant Distribution in Six Cities, 1870–1920

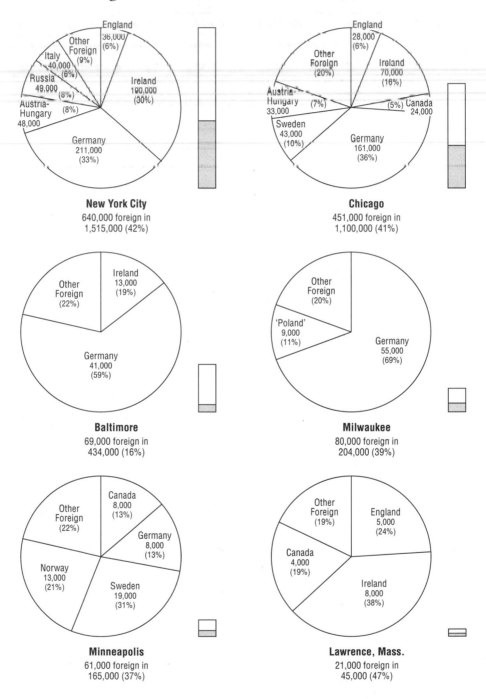

New York City
640,000 foreign in
1,515,000 (42%)

Chicago
451,000 foreign in
1,100,000 (41%)

Baltimore
69,000 foreign in
434,000 (16%)

Milwaukee
80,000 foreign in
204,000 (39%)

Minneapolis
61,000 foreign in
165,000 (37%)

Lawrence, Mass.
21,000 foreign in
45,000 (47%)

3. A Visiting Rudyard Kipling Returns, Unimpressed, from Chicago, 1899

I have struck a city,—a real city,—and they call it Chicago. The other places do not count. San Francisco was a pleasure resort as well as a city, and Salt Lake City was a phenomenon. This place is the first American city I have encountered. It holds rather more than a million people with bodies, and stands on the same sort of soil as Calcutta. Having seen it, I urgently desire never to see it again. It is inhabited by savages. Its water is the water of the Hugli, and its air is dirt. Also it says that it is the 'boss' town of America.

I do not believe that it has anything to do with this country. They told me to go to the Palmer House, which is a gilded and mirrored rabbit-warren, and there I found a huge hall of tessellated marble, crammed with people talking about money and spitting about everywhere. Other barbarians charged in and out of this inferno with letters and telegrams in their hands, and yet others shouted at each other. A man who had drunk quite as much as was good for him told me that this was 'the finest hotel in the finest city on God Almighty's earth.' By the way, when an American wishes to indicate the next county or State he says, 'God A'mighty's earth.' This prevents discussion and flatters his vanity.

Then I went out into the streets, which are long and flat and without end. And verily it is not a good thing to live in the East for any length of time. Your ideas grow to clash with those held by every right-thinking white man. I looked down interminable vistas flanked with nine-, ten-, and fifteen-storeyed houses, and crowded with men and women, and the show impressed me with a great horror. Except in London—and I have forgotten what London is like—I had never seen so many white people together, and never such a collection of miserables. There was no colour in the street and no beauty—only a maze of wire ropes overhead and dirty stone flagging underfoot. A cab-driver volunteered to show me the glory of the town for so much an hour, and with him I wandered far. He conceived that all this turmoil and squash was a thing to be reverently admired; that it was good to huddle men together in fifteen layers, one atop of the other, and to dig holes in the ground for offices. He said that Chicago was a live town, and that all the creatures hurrying by me were engaged in business. That is to say, they were trying to make some money, that they might not die through lack of food to put into their bellies. He took me to canals, black as ink, and filled with untold abominations, and bade me watch the stream of traffic across the bridges. He then took me into a saloon, and, while I drank, made me note that the floor was covered with coins sunk into cement. A Hottentot would not have been guilty of this sort of barbarism. The coins made an effect pretty enough, but the man who put then there had no thought to beauty, and therefore he was a savage. Then my cab-driver showed me business-blocks, gay with signs and studded with fantastic and absurd advertisements of goods, and looking down the long street so adorned it was as though each vendor stood at his door howling: 'For the sake of money, employ or buy of me and me

Rudyard Kipling, "Chicago Barbarism," In *From Sea to Sea; Letters of Travel* (New York: Doubleday & McClure, 1899), II, 126–130.

only!' Have you ever seen a crowd at our famine-relief distributions? You know then how men leap into the air, stretching out their arms above the crowd in the hope of being seen; while the women dolorously slap the stomachs of their children and whimper. I had sooner watch famine-relief than the white man engaged in what he calls legitimate competition. The one I understand. The other makes me ill. And the cabman said that these things were the proof of progress; and by that I knew he had been reading his newspaper, as every intelligent American should. The papers tell their readers in language fitted to their comprehension that the snarling together of telegraph wires, the heaving up of houses, and the making of money is progress.

I spent ten hours in that huge wilderness, wandering through scores of miles of these terrible streets, and jostling some few hundred thousand of these terrible people who talked money through their noses. The cabman left me: but after a while I picked up another man who was full of figures, and into my ears he poured them as occasion required or the big blank factories suggested. Here they turned out so many hundred thousand dollars' worth of such-and-such an article; there so many million other things; this house was worth so many million dollars; that one so many million more or less. It was like listening to a child babbling of its hoard of shells. It was like watching a fool playing with buttons. But I was expected to do more than listen or watch. He demanded that I should admire; and the utmost that I could say was: 'Are these things so? Then I am very sorry for you.' That made him angry, and he said that insular envy made me unresponsive. So you see I could not make him understand.

4. Poet Carl Sandburg Extols the City of the Big Shoulders, 1916

Chicago

Hog Butcher for the World,
Tool Maker, Stacker of Wheat,
Player with Railroads and the Nation's Freight Handler;
Stormy, husky, brawling,
City of the Big Shoulders:

They tell me you are wicked and I believe them, for I
    have seen your painted women under the gas lamps
    luring the farm boys.
And they tell me you are crooked and I answer: Yes, it
    is true I have seen the gunman kill and go free to
    kill again.
And they tell me you are brutal and my reply is: On the
    faces of women and children I have seen the marks
    of wanton hunger.

"Chicago" (1916) in Carl Sandburg, *Chicago Poems* (New York: Henry Holt, 1916), 3–4.

And having answered so I turn once more to those who
    sneer at this my city, and I give them back the sneer
    and say to them:
Come and show me another city with lifted head singing
    so proud to be alive and coarse and strong and
    cunning.
Flinging magnetic curses amid the toil of piling job on
    job, here is a tall bold slugger set vivid against the
    little soft cities;
Fierce as a dog with tongue lapping for action, cunning
    as a savage pitted against the wilderness,
        Bareheaded,
        Shoveling,
        Wrecking,
        Planning,
        Building, breaking, rebuilding,
Under the smoke, dust all over his mouth, laughing with
    white teeth,
Under the terrible burden of destiny laughing as a young
    man laughs,
Laughing even as an ignorant fighter laughs who has
    never lost a battle,
Bragging and laughing that under his wrist is the pulse,
    and under his ribs the heart of the people,
        Laughing!
Laughing the stormy, husky, brawling laughter of
    Youth, half-naked, sweating, proud to be Hog
    Butcher, Tool Maker, Stacker of Wheat, Player with
    Railroads and Freight Handler to the Nation.

5. Congress Takes Aim at the "Chinese Menace," 1892

There is urgent necessity for prompt legislation on the subject of Chinese immigration. The exclusion act approved May 6, 1882, and its supplement expires by limitation of time on May 6, 1892, and after that time there will be no law to prevent the Chinese hordes from invading our country in number so vast, as soon to outnumber the present population of our flourishing States on the Pacific slope. . . .

The popular demand for legislation excluding the Chinese from this country is urgent and imperative and almost universal. Their presence here is inimical to our institutions and is deemed injurious and a source of danger. They are a distinct race, saving from their earnings a few hundred dollars and returning to China. This they succeed in doing in from five to ten years by living in the most miserable manner, when in cities and towns in crowded tenement houses, surrounded by dirt, filth, corruption, pollution and prostitution; and gambling houses and opium joints abound. When used as cooks, farm-hands, servants, and gardeners, they are more cleanly in habits and manners. They, as a rule, have no families here; all are men,

---

"The Chinese Menace," Congressional Report on Immigration, U.S. Congress, House of Representatives, Report No. 255, Feb. 10, 1892.

save a few women, usually prostitutes. They have no attachment to our country, its laws or its institutions, nor are they interested in its prosperity. They never assimilate with our people, our manners, tastes, religion, or ideas. With us they have nothing in common.

Living on the cheapest diet (mostly vegetable), wearing the poorest clothing, with no family to support, they enter the field of labor in competition with the American workman. In San Francisco, and in fact throughout the whole Pacific slope, we learn from the testimony heretofore alluded to, that the Chinamen have invaded almost every branch of industry; manufacturers of cigars, cigar boxes, brooms, tailors, laundrymen, cooks, servants, farmhands, fishermen, miners and all departments of manual labor, for wages and prices at which white men and women could not support themselves and those dependent upon them. Recently this was a new country, and the Chinese may have been a necessity at one time, but now our own people are fast filling up and developing this rich and highly favored land, and American citizens will not and can not afford to stand idly by and see this undesirable race carry away the fruits of the labor which justly belongs to them. A war of races would soon be inaugurated; several times it has broken out, and bloodshed was followed. The town of Tacoma, in 1887, banished some 3,000 Chinamen on twenty-four hours' notice, and no Chinaman has ever been permitted to return.

Our people are willing, however, that those now here may remain, protected by the laws which they do not appreciate or obey, provided strong provision be made that no more shall be allowed to come, and that the smuggling of Chinese across the frontiers be scrupulously guarded against, so that gradually, by voluntary departures, death by sickness, accident, or old age, this race may be eliminated from this country, and the white race fill their places without inconvenience to our own people or to the Chinese, and thus a desirable change be happily and peacefully accomplished. It was thought that the exclusion act of 1882 would bring about this result; but it now appears that although at San Francisco the departures largely exceed the arrivals, yet the business of smuggling Chinese persons across the lines from the British Possessions and Mexico has so greatly increased that the number of arrivals now exceed the departures. This must be effectually stopped.

6. Huang Zunxian Expresses the Chinese Perspective in Poetry, c. 1884

Expulsion of the Immigrants

Alas! What crime have our people committed,
That they suffer this calamity in our nation's fortunes?
Five thousand years since the Yellow Emperor,
Our country today is exceedingly weak.
Demons and ghouls are hard to fathom;

Even worse than the woodland and monsters.
Who can say our fellow men have not met an inhuman fate,
In the end oppressed by another race?
Within the vastness of the six directions,
Where can our people find asylum?

When the Chinese first crossed the ocean,
They were the same as pioneers.
They lived in straw hovels, cramped as snail shells;
For protecting gradually built bamboo fences.
Dressed in tatters, they cleared mountain forests;
Wilderness and waste turned into towns and villages.
Mountains of gold towered on high,
Which men could grab with their hands left and right.
Eureka! They return with a load full of gold,
And bragging this land is paradise.
They beckon and beg their families to come;
Legs in the rear file behind legs in the front.
Wearing short coats, they braid their queues;
Men carry bamboo rainhats, wear straw sandals.
Bartenders lead along cooks;
Some hold tailors' needles, others workmen's axes.
They clap with excitement, traveling overseas;
Everyone surnamed Wong creates confusion. . . .

Gradually the natives turned jealous.
Time to time spreading false rumors,
They say these Chinese paupers
Only wish to fill their money bags.
Soon as their feet touch the ground,
All the gold leaps out of the earth.
They hand ten thousand cash on their waists,
And catch the next boat back to China.
Which of them is willing to loosen his queue,
And do some hard labor for us?
Some say the Chinese are shiftless; . . .
Others say the Chinese are a bunch of hoodlums,
By nature all filthy and unclean.
Their houses are as dirty as dogs';
Their food even worse than pigs'.
All they need is a dollar a day;
Who is as scrawny as they are?
If we allow this cheap labor of theirs,
Then all of us are finished.
We see our own brothers being injured;
Who can stand these venomous vermin? . . .

From now on they set up a strict ban,
Establishing customs posts everywhere.
They have sealed all the gates tightly,
Door after door with guards beating alarms.

Chinese who leave are like magpies circling a tree,
Those staying like swallows nesting on curtains. . . .

Those who do not carry passports
Are arrested as soon as they arrive.
Anyone with a yellow-colored face
Is beaten even if guiltless.
I sadly recollect George Washington,
Who had the makings of a great ruler.
He proclaimed that in America,
There is a broad land to the west of the desert.
All kinds of foreigners and immigrants,
Are allowed to settle in these new lands.
The yellow, white, red, and black races
Are all equal with our native people.
Not even a hundred years till today,
But they are not ashamed to eat his words. . . .
The land of the red man is vast and remote;
I know you are eager to settle and open it.
The American eagle strides the heavens soaring,
With half of the globe clutched in his claw.

7. W. E. B. Du Bois Denounces Racial Prejudice in Philadelphia, 1899

Incidentally throughout this study the prejudice against the Negro has been again and again mentioned. It is time now to reduce this somewhat indefinite term to something tangible. Everybody speaks of the matter, everybody knows that it exists, but in just what form it shows itself or how influential it is few agree. In the Negro's mind, color prejudice in Philadelphia is that widespread feeling of dislike for his blood, which keeps him and his children out of decent employment, from certain public conveniences and amusements, from hiring houses in many sections, and in general, from being recognized as a man. Negroes regard this prejudice as the chief cause of their present unfortunate condition. On the other hand most white people are quite unconscious of any such powerful and vindictive feeling; they regard color prejudice as the easily explicable feeling that intimate social inter-course with a lower race is not only undesirable but impracticable if our present standards of culture are to be maintained; and although they are aware that some people feel the aversion more intensely than others, they cannot see how such a feeling has much influence on the real situation, or alters the social condition of the mass of Negroes.

As a matter of fact, color prejudice in this city is something between these two extreme views: it is not to-day responsible for all, or perhaps the greater part of the Negro problems, or of the disabilities under which the race labors; on the other

W. E. B. Du Bois, *The Philadelphia Negro* (Philadelphia: University of Pennsylvania, 1899), 322–325, 353–355.

hand it is a far more powerful social force than most Philadelphians realize. The practical results of the attitude of most of the inhabitants of Philadelphia toward persons of Negro descent are as follows:

1. As to getting work:

No matter how well trained a Negro may be, or how fitted for work of any kind, he cannot in the ordinary course of competition hope to be much more than a menial servant.

He cannot get clerical or supervisory work to do save in exceptional cases.

He cannot teach save in a few of the remaining Negro schools.

He cannot become a mechanic except for small transient jobs, and cannot join a trades union.

A Negro woman has but three careers open to her in this city: domestic service, sewing, or married life.

2. As to keeping work:

The Negro suffers in competition more severely than white men.

Change in fashion is causing him to be replaced by whites in the better paid positions of domestic service.

Whim and accident will cause him to lose a hard-earned place more quickly than the same things would affect a white man.

Being few in number compared with the whites the crime or carelessness of a few of his race is easily imputed to all, and the reputation of the good, industrious and reliable suffer thereby.

Because Negro workmen may not often work side by side with white workmen, the individual black workman is rated not by his own efficiency, but by the efficiency of a whole group of black fellow workmen which may often be low.

Because of these difficulties which virtually increase competition in his case, he is forced to take lower wages for the same work than white workmen.

3. As to entering new lines of work:

Men are used to seeing Negroes in inferior positions; when, therefore, by any chance a Negro gets in a better position, most men immediately conclude that he is not fitted for it, even before he has a chance to show his fitness.

If, therefore, he set up a store, men will not patronize him.

If he is put into public position men will complain.

If he gain a position in the commercial world, men will quietly secure his dismissal or see that a white man succeeds him.

4. As to his expenditure:

The comparative smallness of the patronage of the Negro, and the dislike of other customers makes it usual to increase the charges or difficulties in certain directions in which a Negro must spend money.

He must pay more house-rent for worse houses than most white people pay.

He is sometimes liable to insult or reluctant service in some restaurants, hotels and stores, at public resorts, theatres and places of recreation; and at nearly all barber-shops.

5. As to his children:

The Negro finds it extremely difficult to rear children in such an atmosphere and not have them either cringing or impudent: if he impresses upon them patience with their lot, they may grow up satisfied with their condition; if he inspires them with ambition to rise, they may grow to despise their own people, hate the whites and become embittered with the world.

His children are discriminated against, often in public schools.

They are advised when seeking employment to become waiters and maids.

They are liable to species of insult and temptation peculiarly trying to children.

6. As to social intercourse:

In all walks of life the Negro is liable to meet some objection to his presence or some discourteous treatment; and the ties of friendship or memory seldom are strong enough to hold across the color line.

If an invitation is issued to the public for any occasion, the Negro can never know whether he would be welcomed or not; if he goes he is liable to have his feelings hurt and get into unpleasant altercation; if he stays away, he is blamed for indifference.

If he meet a lifelong white friend on the street, he is in a dilemma; if he does not greet the friend he is put down as boorish and impolite; if he does greet the friend he is liable to be flatly snubbed.

If by chance he is introduced to a white woman or man, he expects to be ignored on the next meeting, and usually is.

White friends may call on him, but he is scarcely expected to call on them, save for strictly business matters.

If he gain the affections of a white woman and marry her he may invariably expect that slurs will be thrown on her reputation and on his, and that both his and her race will shun their company.

When he dies he cannot be buried beside white corpses.

7. The result:

Any one of these things happening now and then would not be remarkable or call for especial comment: but when one group of people suffer all these little differences of treatment and discriminations and insults continually, the result is either discouragement, or bitterness, or over-sensitiveness, or recklessness. And a people feeling thus cannot do their best.

8. An Advice Column for Jewish Immigrants, 1906, 1907

Worthy Editor,

We are a small family who recently came to the "Golden Land." My husband, my boy and I are together, and our daughter lives in another city.

I had opened a grocery store here, but soon lost all my money. In Europe we were in business; we had people working for us and paid them well. In short, there we made a good living but here we are badly off.

My husband became a peddler. The "pleasure" of knocking on doors and ringing bells cannot be known by anyone but a peddler. If anybody does buy anything "on time," a lot of the money is lost, because there are some people who never intend to

Excerpt from the *Jewish Daily Forward* can be found in Isaac Metzker, *A Bintel Brief* (New York: Doubleday, 1971), 42–44, 54–55, 63–64, 101–102.

pay. In addition, my husband has trouble because he has a beard, and because of the beard he gets beaten up by the hoodlums.

Also we have problems with our boy, who throws money around. He works every day till late at night in a grocery for three dollars a week. I watch over him and give him the best because I'm sorry that he has to work so hard. But he costs me plenty and he borrows money from everybody. He has many friends and owes them all money. I get more and more worried as he takes here and borrows there. All my talking doesn't help. I am afraid to chase him away from home because he might get worse among strangers. I want to point out that he is well versed in Russian and Hebrew and he is not a child any more, but his behavior is not that of an intelligent adult.

I don't know what to do. My husband argues that he doesn't want to continue peddling. He doesn't want to shave off his beard, and it's not fitting for such a man to do so. The boy wants to go to his sister, but that's a twenty-five-dollar fare. What can I do? I beg you for a suggestion.

Your constant reader,

F.L.

Answer: Since her husband doesn't earn a living anyway, it would be advisable for all three of them to move to the city where the daughter is living. As for the beard, we feel that if the man is religious and the beard is dear to him because the Jewish law does not allow him to shave it off, it's up to him to decide. But if he is not religious, and the beard interferes with his earnings, it should be sacrificed.

Dear Editor,

For a long time I worked in a shop with a Gentile girl, and we began to go out together and fell in love. We agreed that I would remain a Jew and she a Christian. But after we had been married for a year, I realized that it would not work.

I began to notice that whenever one of my Jewish friends comes to the house, she is displeased. Worse yet, when she sees me reading a Jewish newspaper her face changes color. She says nothing, but I can see that she has changed. I feel that she is very unhappy with me, though I know she loves me. She will soon become a mother, and she is more dependent on me than ever.

She used to be quite liberal, but lately she is being drawn back to the Christian religion. She gets up early Sunday mornings, runs to church and comes home with eyes swollen from crying. When we pass a church now and then, she trembles.

Dear Editor, advise me what to do now. I could never convert, and there's no hope for me to keep her from going to church. What can we do now?

Thankfully,

A Reader

Answer: Unfortunately, we often hear of such tragedies, which stem from marriages between people of different worlds. It's possible that if this couple were to move to a Jewish neighborhood, the young man might have more influence on his wife.

Dear Editor,

I, too, want to take advantage of this opportunity to tell about my troubles, and I ask you to answer me.

Eight months ago I brought my girlfriend from Russia to the States. We had been in love for seven years and were married shortly after her arrival. We were very happy together until my wife became ill. She was pregnant and the doctors said her condition was poor. She was taken to the hospital, but after a few days was sent home. At home, she became worse, and there was no one to tend her.

You can hardly imagine our bitter lot. I had to work all day in the shop and my sick wife lay alone at home. Once as I opened the door when I came home at dinner-time, I heard my wife singing with a changed, hoarse voice. I was terror-stricken, and when I ran to her I saw she was out of her head with fever.

Imagine how I felt. My wife was so ill and I was supposed to run back to the shop because the last whistle was about to blow. Everybody was rushing back to work, but I couldn't leave. I knew that my boss would fire me. He had warned me the day before that if I came late again he wouldn't let me in. But how could I think of work now, when my wife was so ill? Yet without the job what would happen? There would not be a penny coming into the house. I stayed at my wife's bedside and didn't move till four o'clock.

Suddenly I jumped up and began to run around the room, in despair. My wife's singing and talking drove me insane. Like a madman I ran to the door and locked it. I leaped to the gas jet, opened the valve, then lay down in the bed near my wife and embraced her. In a few minutes I was nearer death than she.

Suddenly my wife cried out, "Water! water!" I dragged myself from the bed. With my last ounce of strength I crept to the door and opened it, closed the gas valve, and when I came to, gave her milk instead of water. She finished a glassful and wanted more, but there wasn't any more so I brought her some seltzer. I revived myself with water, and both of us slowly recovered.

The next morning they took my wife to the hospital, and after a stay of fourteen days she got well. Now I am happy that we are alive, but I keep thinking of what almost happened to us. Until now I never told anyone about it, but it bothers me. I have no secrets from my wife, and I want to know whether I should now tell her all, or not mention it. I beg you to answer me.

The Newborn

Answer: This letter depicting the sad life of the worker is more powerful than any protest against the inequality between rich and poor. The advice to the writer is that he should not tell his wife that he almost ended both their lives. This secret may be withheld from his beloved wife, since it is clear he keeps it from her out of love.

Worthy Editor,

I am eighteen years old and a machinist by trade. During the past year I suffered a great deal, just because I am a Jew.

It is common knowledge that my trade is run mainly by the Gentiles and, working among the Gentiles, I have seen things that cast a dark shadow on the American labor scene. Just listen:

I worked in a shop in a small town in New Jersey, with twenty Gentiles. There was one other Jew besides me, and both of us endured the greatest hardships. That we were insulted goes without saying. At times we were even beaten up. We work in an area where there are many factories, and once, when we were leaving the shop, a group of workers fell on us like hoodlums and beat us. To top it off, we and one of our attackers were arrested. The hoodlum was let out on bail, but we, beaten and bleeding, had to stay in jail. At the trial, they fined the hoodlum eight dollars and let him go free.

After that I went to work on a job in Brooklyn. As soon as they found out that I was a Jew they began to torment me so that I had to leave the place. I have already worked at many places, and I either have to leave, voluntarily, or they fire me because I am a Jew.

Till now, I was alone and didn't care. At this trade you can make good wages, and I had enough. But now I've brought my parents over, and of course I have to support them.

Lately I've been working on one job for three months and I would be satisfied, but the worm of anti-Semitism is beginning to eat at my bones again. I go to work in the morning as to Gehenna, and I run away at night as from a fire. It's impossible to talk to them because they are common boors, so-called "American sports." I have already tried in various ways, but the only way to deal with them is with a strong fist. But I am too weak and they are too many.

Perhaps you can help me in this matter. I know it is not an easy problem.

Your reader,

E.H.

Answer: In the answer, the Jewish machinist is advised to appeal to the United Hebrew Trades and ask them to intercede for him and bring up charges before the Machinists Union about this persecution. His attention is also drawn to the fact that there are Gentile factories where Jews and Gentiles work together and get along well with each other.

Finally it is noted that people will have to work long and hard before this senseless racial hatred can be completely uprooted.

 *E S S A Y S*

Urban America was subject to both material and cultural design. It is to the multiple— and sometimes ironic or conflicting—agents in both these spheres that we turn in this chapter's essays. In the first selection, historians Maury Klein of the University of Rhode Island and Harvey A. Kantor of New York University suggest an interlocking pattern of problem solution and problem creation at the heart of urban technological innovation. In the second essay, historian John Bodnar of Indiana University demonstrates how immigrant adaptation was based on family and community patterns. Old World habits and ties, he suggests, were not so much "uprooted" (as historians once assumed) but "transplanted" in sometimes revised forms. In the final essay, George J. Sanchez of the University of Southern California explores the often frustrated attempts of social workers in Los Angeles to press "American" standards on Mexican American home life through the State Commission of Immigration and Housing.

Technology and the Treadmill of Urban Progress

MAURY KLEIN AND HARVEY A. KANTOR

To the modern urbanite the industrial city seems a quaint, almost primitive place. Its sights and smells bear a strong flavor of nostalgia: streets lit by gas lamps and filled with carriages, drays, and streetcars; sidewalks bustling with gentlemen in tall hats or derbies, wearing high, starched collars; ladies in long dresses with parasols resting on their shoulders; workmen dressed in cheap drab shirts and pants, brightened by gaudy bandanas tied about their neck or head; messenger boys dashing from one office building to another; deliverymen straining beneath their blocks of ice, kegs of beer, or racks of clothing; sidestreets filled with peddlers' carts loaded with wares of every kind, their cries intermingling in a cacophony of confusion; sidewalk markets bulging with fresh fruit and produce, tiers of fish or slabs of meat, all picked over by swarms of shoppers; strolling policemen with bright brass buttons and fat nightsticks; and ragged newsboys trumpeting the day's headlines above the din of the street traffic.

The wishful flavor of this scene is deceptive. While its pace and tumult may appear tame to people in a high-speed, computerized, automated society, contemporaries regarded the city as an engine of progress in which everything seemed constantly on the move. In this feeling, that generation was no less correct than our own; the difference lay largely in the level of technology achieved by each era. To an amazing degree advances in technology shaped the growth, appearance, and pace of the industrial city. Then as now, cities could expand only by discovering new techniques for moving people, goods, and information. New machines, materials, and designs revamped the city's face and accelerated its inner rhythms. Urban growth was therefore both a function of technology and a reflection of its pervasive influence.

Yet technology, even in its most imaginative forms, did not solve problems so much as recast them. Rapid growth strained the city's ability to perform such elementary functions as transporting, feeding, and housing people, protecting them from fire and crime, educating their children, and providing a healthy, attractive environment in which to live. It complicated every aspect of urban life and fragmented urban society. Almost every industrial city endured a phase of madcap expansion during which its distended social system threatened to collapse beneath the weight of increased demands for services and accumulated social tensions.

To solve the physical problems created by rapid growth, most cities resorted to sophisticated technology and techniques. But every "solution" unmasked a tangle of new problems which in turn called for still more sophisticated hardware. Thus the electric trolley and elevated railway moved more people at greater speed than the omnibus, but both presented problems unforeseen in the heyday of the horse and buggy. The result was a vicious circle, a kind of "Catch-22" in which every new stage of technological advance proved less a gateway into some new golden age than a harbinger of fresh difficulties.

Nor was this all. The vicious circle traced by the interaction between technology and growth uncovered a deeper contradiction in the American notion of progress. Americans had always tended to equate progress with growth. During the industrial era, progress came increasingly to be defined in material and mechanical terms. This faith in the notion that "bigger is better" assumed that quantitative growth would improve the quality of life. Since technology was a primary instrument in quantitative growth, Americans logically turned to it as a means for resolving the perplexities of industrial society.

Urban growth especially fed upon advances in technology. In quantitative terms, that growth proceeded at breakneck pace and reached gigantic proportions. But the industrial city turned out to be something less than the promised land. For all the splendors of its swelling statistics, it never became a pleasant or even decent place in which to live for a majority of its inhabitants. Too late city-dwellers discovered that their faith in technology had been misplaced; that mere quantitative growth did not automatically bring qualitative improvement. In their quest for a better life, urbanites had created not a road to utopia but a treadmill which they labeled "progress."

Just as the railroad affected the locations and functions of cities on a national scale, the street railway shaped their internal growth. From its crude beginnings with horse-drawn omnibuses to steam-power trolleys and later the electrified lines, mass transit moved urbanites faster and more efficiently. Every advance in transportation technology quickly outmoded its predecessor only to create new problems in construction, congestion, and pollution.

The most important effect of mass transit was its expanding the physical limits of the city. The street railway destroyed the compact "walking city" of colonial and preindustrial towns. Prior to about 1850 most towns were still intimate locales where street congestion involved nothing more than people on foot, on horseback, or in carriages. Most people lived near their place of work and could reach nearly any spot in the city in a thirty-minute walk. Few towns extended farther than two miles from their core, which usually nestled against some waterway.

During the 1820s the omnibus emerged as the first urban passenger carrier. Initially little more than enlarged hackney coaches, these wagons later resembled boxes on wheels with two lengthwise seats holding twelve to twenty people. They appeared first in the larger cities—New York, Boston, Philadelphia, New Orleans, Washington. . . .

. . . Even though the fare was too steep for the masses, omnibuses drew heavy patronage from small businessmen and clerks, many of whom still went home for lunch. By the 1840s Boston had eighteen omnibus lines, of which twelve extended to outlying suburban communities. Despite its limitations, the omnibus speeded up the tempo of life, regularized transportation patterns, and launched the outward migration of wealthier people from the center of the city to the suburbs.

The era of the omnibus lasted scarcely a generation before the horse railway surpassed it in the 1850s. The horse railway, too, resembled a stagecoach, but utilized flanged wheels operating on iron tracks. . . . By the 1850s [New York,] Boston, Philadelphia, Chicago, Baltimore, St. Louis, Cincinnati, Newark, and Pittsburgh all had laid horsecar tracks and were extending their boundaries. Iron rails allowed horsecars to reach speeds of six to eight miles per hour, about one-third more than the omnibus could muster. Reduced friction did more than add speed. It provided a smoother ride and increased the number of passengers that could be hauled.

Iron rails also increased costs. Inevitably the horsecar companies required a greater capital investment than the omnibus lines. As expenses mounted, financing became more feasible through incorporation rather than individual ownership. . . . Ownership of transit facilities fell increasingly into the hands of outside entrepreneurs who neither knew the local scene nor cared about how cities developed. Each phase of technological innovation made urban transportation a bigger business than it had been. By the end of the nineteenth century, transit or "traction" enterprises held the nexus of political and economic power in most major cities. . . .

The horsecar had another unsavory effect upon the urban landscape: it added to the piles of horse manure littering the streets. Lest we forget that pollution comes in many forms, it is well to heed Joel Tarr's reminder that the automobile was once hailed as the savior of the city from animal waste. "In a city like Milwaukee in 1907," he wrote, ". . . with a human population of 350,000 and a horse population of 12,500, this meant 133 tons of manure a day, for a daily average of nearly three-quarters of a pound of manure for each resident." For New York and Brooklyn in the 1880s, with a total horse population of around 150,000, the problem was much worse. Carcasses of dead horses sprawled in the streets added to the sanitation nightmare.

This contemporary image of mass transit as a crowded, unsafe, unpleasant, and polluting form of transportation sounds hauntingly familiar to the modern ear. Moreover, the horsecar had inherent limitations as a form of transportation: it could go no faster than the horse pulling it and could not increase its passenger load without adding more horses, which posed other difficulties. To growing cities, these became intolerable drawbacks. The obvious solution was to devise a transit system that utilized mechanical rather than muscle power. By the 1860s the search for alternatives was well underway. Louis Ransom of Akron, Ohio, advocated adopting his Ransom Steamer to iron rails. George Clark of Cincinnati promoted a system of compressed-air cars, while a New Orleans firm experimented with a car propelled by ammonia gas. . . .

No innovation in urban mass transit rivaled the application of electircal power. Oddly enough, the pioneer projects developed in the least urbanized area of the nation. James A. Gaboury, the owner of an animal traction line in Montgomery, Alabama, witnessed a demonstration of an electrical car at the Toronto Agricultural Fair in 1885 and determined to adopt the method to his system. In 1886 Montgomery's Court Street line became the first in the country to offer a citywide system of electric transportation. Several years later, Frank J. Sprague, a naval engineer who had worked for Thomas Edison, formed his own company and secured a contract to build a line in Richmond, Virginia. The success of his project spurred the construction of electrical transit lines elsewhere.

The electric cars moved along iron tracks in the streets, drawing current from a central power source passed to the trains through overhead wires. The effect of a wire leading a car resembled that of a "troller"; soon the corruption of the word became universal and the new vehicles were dubbed "trolleys." Trolleys displaced horses so rapidly that by 1900 only 2 percent of the lines were horse-drawn, compared to 70 percent a decade earlier. By 1895, 850 lines embraced over 10,000 miles of electrified track. The new trolleys speeded up travel service to about twelve miles per hour and more in less congested areas. Their overhead wires cluttered the streetscapes of American cities and wreaked havoc during high winds and storms.

Frank Sprague made a second major contribution to transportation systems. He designed an electrical multiple-unit control system which allowed each car to be independently powered, lighted, heated, and braked. These cars did not require a locomotive since they possessed their own power source; yet they could be controlled by a master switch located in any one of them. At one stroke Sprague removed the major obstacles to constructing underground railways. Automated electric cars could operate without the accumulation of smoke, gas, and dirt discharged by steam-powered cars. Between 1895 and 1897 Boston built a mile-and-a-half subway at a cost of $4,000,000. Immediately after the turn of the century, New York constructed a route from downtown City Hall to 145th Street. . . . The popularity of the subway, coupled with the city's extreme congestion, led New York to take the lead in the underground transportation. Moreover, its hard-rock geological formation could support the construction of tall buildings above ground and tunnels below.

All these achievements in the technology of transportation affected the physical growth of cities. The rural ideal retained its hold upon Americans even in the city, where its influence drove people toward the suburbs. Prior to the advent of mass transit lines, however, only the wealthy could maintain houses on the outskirts of the city. Once the pedestrian confines were broken in the 1850s, an outward migration commenced. [Samuel Bass] Warner has painstakingly traced the development of Roxbury, West Roxbury, and Dorchester as bedroom satellites of Boston. Every stage of suburban development expanded the physical limits of Boston to house wealthy, middle-class, and lower middle-class expatriates from the city. Since all of the transit lines were privately built, the new suburbs alongside their tracks were the product of individual decision-making rather than coordinated social policy. . . .

Traction entrepreneurs enthusiastically promoted the flight to the suburbs. They found support among those who regarded the exodus as a boon for relieving congestion in the city's inner core. Adna Weber, the leading student of American cities in the nineteenth century, stated flatly, "it is clear that we are now in the sight of a solution of the problem of concentration of population." Weber advocated the extension of electrified transit lines and cheap fares because he saw in the rise of the suburbs "the solid basis of a hope that the evils of city life, so far as they result from overcrowding, may be in large part removed."

Unhappily, things did not work out that way. While upper- and middle-class urbanites left for greener pastures, the poor remained packed together in the central city, where they shared space with businesses and industries. Mass transit promoted this pattern of segregation within the city. More than any other factor, it transformed the diversified walking city into a central urban core of poor people and businesses surrounded by successive rings of suburban neighborhoods.

In fact, mass transit failed even to relieve population congestion. Transit lines did not scatter people about so much as cluster them in dense communities wherever transportation was available. New housing developments pursued every new construction or extension and quickly overflowed its service. As one alert observer wrote in an 1896 *Harper's Weekly,* "the trolleys seem to have created a new patronage of their own. Travel has been stimulated rather than diverted." Instead of thinning out settlement, mass transit created corridors of dense groupings alongside their lines. This magnetic pull pleased the traction promoters immensely. It was great for business; its effect upon the city's already strained social structure was quite another matter,

Technology extended the city's boundaries in another important way. Innovations in bridge-building made it possible for the first time to span the widest rivers. The implications of this breakthrough for urban growth were enormous: waterways ceased to be an obstacle to physical expansion. More important, it allowed traffic to flow in and out of the city with ease. Just as railroads dissolved limitations upon land travel, so the new bridges banished the fickle vagaries of waterways. Small wonder that to many Americans the Brooklyn Bridge and other mighty spans became the supreme symbol of American civilization. . . .

As mass transit and great bridges expanded the city's outer limits, innovations in building forms lifted its inner face. Like bridge-building, the new age of construction dawned with the shift from wood to iron and steel. Preindustrial cities were filled with two- or three-story buildings, shops, warehouses, and row houses made of timber. Government buildings, merchant exchanges, and athenaeums comprised the major public buildings; the church spire still dominated the skyline.

The industrial city presented a radically different scene. Multi-story buildings filled with corporate and professional offices stretched high into the sky. Cast-iron and sash-steel factories housed long ranks of machines whose operators lived in tall brick tenements. New kinds of buildings—railroad terminals, department stores, theaters, apartments—ornamented the urban landscape. The transition from church spire to skyscraper signified a revolution in construction techniques and in the way city-dwellers identified with their surroundings.

Great movements often hinge upon small details. In construction it was the lowly nail that boomed residential building and urban expansion. Prior to the 1820s home-building in America copied the English method of using heavy beams shaped at the ends to fit into slots in adjoining beams. If there was tension on the two beams, a hole was augured and a wooden peg fitted into place to hold the stress. This mortise-and-tenon method required skilled craftsmen. Houses built in this manner were sturdy but expensive.

The mass production of iron nails in the 1820s liberated builders from the English method. With these inexpensive joining devices, houses could be built in the skeleton form still common today. The "balloon frame," as it was called, consisted of thin plates and studs (usually 2" × 4") "nailed together in such a way that every strain went in the direction of the wood (i.e., against the grain)." The first balloon-frame building appeared in Chicago, where in 1833 a carpenter named Augustine Deodat Taylor built the city's first Catholic church in three months at a cost of only $400.

With that simple edifice, Chicago commenced its long career as a pioneer in urban design. Balloon-frame structures sprang up all over the city, and the popularity of skeleton construction survived even the Great Fire of 1871. Other young western towns like San Francisco, Denver, and Seattle adopted the balloon-frame form, as did the more established cities of the East. Although attacked by contemporaries as shoddy and tasteless, the balloon frame proved irresistible to the urban market with its insatiable appetite for cheap housing. Once transit lines made commuting feasible, developers and speculators bought large tracts of farmland adjacent to the city, carved them into lots, and threw up whole neighborhoods of houses modeled upon a common design.

Like another simple innovation, Eli Whitney's cotton gin, the balloon frame energized an entire industry. It put single-unit dwellings within the reach of many people once unable to afford such a luxury. Home construction soared in every major industrial city and fueled the exodus to the suburbs. Once this pattern of settlement emerged, most cities hastened to annex the new subdivisions that dotted their perimeters. Urban boundaries marched steadily into the surrounding countryside in random fashion, and new towns sprang up everywhere. As Carl W. Condit noted, "Within a generation the balloon frame dominated the West. . . . Without it the towns of the prairies could never have been built in the short time that saw the establishment of rural and urban society in the region."

Commercial buildings underwent no less drastic changes in design and construction techniques. Preindustrial cities utilized wood or bulky masonry for all their buildings. In downtown areas, where buildings were packed closely together, the inhabitants lived in constant fear of fire. The search for stronger, less inflammable materials began as early as the 1820s when two American architects—John Haviland and William Strickland—experimented with iron supports on some of their buildings. . . .

[In the 1850s] James Bogardus, an imaginative mechanic and inventor, . . . constructed the first wholly cast-iron building in New York at the corner of Centre and Duane Streets. The cast-iron design . . . eliminated the thick, space-consuming masonry columns in the interiors, thereby offering more room to economy-minded occupants. Iron buildings went up quickly and could be disassembled quickly if the need arose. For two decades cast iron dominated the construction of warehouses, department stores, and office buildings in American cities. . . . The ability of cast iron to reproduce elaborate details as decorations at low cost gave five- or six-story buildings a unique flavor of elegance in the 1850s and 1860s.

Yet cast iron's primacy lasted only two decades before steel replaced it as the leading construction material. Steel was more durable and stronger for both tension and compression and, unlike cast iron, did not melt when fire reached it. It allowed architects and engineers to raise their structures higher, a compelling feature at a time when downtown land values were soaring. By the 1890s steel framing had converted most major architects through its ability to provide added height and more flexible interior space. The mass production of plate glass gave architects a material for large windows strong enough to withstand wind and stress at high altitudes. This combination of steel framing and plate glass laid the foundation for skyscraper construction in the twentieth century. . . .

The skyscraper mania was not without its detractors. In 1896 the New York Chamber of Commerce declared that tall buildings were "not consistent with public health and that the interests of the majority of our citizens require that the height should be limited." That same year *The New York Times* warned that "the time is evidently near when it will be necessary to proceed in the public interest against the excess of selfishness." The major complaints were that the tall buildings exacerbated the already crowded conditions of most downtown areas, cut off sunlight to adjacent structures and sidewalks, and were basically unsafe. Completion of the Woolworth Building sparked the drive to limit building heights. In 1916 New York City adopted its comprehensive zoning law which included a restriction on height. But architects deftly circumvented the provision by utilizing the "wedding cake" design and skyscrapers continued their upward spiral.* . . .

The physical strain wrought by urban growth involved more than land and buildings. Expanding populations required not only housing but water, gas, electricity, and sewer lines. Better and wider streets were needed to handle the city's heavier traffic. Small cities suddenly grown large found themselves called upon to provide more utilities and services than ever before. Once again municipalities sought refuge in new technology and techniques, and once again every solution gave rise to new problems. As with mass transit, "progress" brought fewer benefits to the public than to the corporate interests that owned the utilities and charged exorbitant rates for their services. Utility franchises, paving contracts, street cleaning, garbage hauling, and maintenance work all reaped financial windfalls for the contractors and politicians in charge of dispensing contracts or fulfilling them.

The importance of streets to urban growth and commerce is so obvious that it needs no elaboration. Yet the history of their construction and care is a dismal chapter in the conflict between public and private interest. Streets in most American cities took a terrific pounding and most were in wretched condition. Any city-dweller who ventured beyond his front door understood that fact only too well. When civic-minded individuals complained about the scandalous condition of their town's thoroughfares, the lament usually fell upon deaf ears. A first-rate street system required a large capital investment, which meant higher taxes. Many other services were also clamoring for more funds even while urbanites protested against more taxes. The result was a pattern of benign neglect in which streets got a relatively low priority in the municipal budget. On one hand, few cities allocated sufficient funds for street construction and care; on the other, graft, inefficiency, and lack of planning sapped the effectiveness of the funds that were allocated.

When it came to paving, for example, most city governments agreed to it only as a last resort, and then tried to do the job as cheaply as possible. Streets were extended long before money was available to pave them. When they were finally paved, the contractor concentrated on the surface rather than the foundation. As a result, few streets enjoyed a long or happy life. Repair were frequent and recurring. . . . But if this "pound-foolish" economy did not serve the public well, it proved a boon to politicians and their friends who discovered that paving contracts were lucrative plums for "friendly" contractors. . . .

---

*The "wedding cake" design involved setting each five or ten stories back from those beneath it. The effect resembled the layers of a wedding cake. . . .

The erratic surfaces of most American streets provoked much consternation as traffic increased. In the 1880s Washington, Buffalo, and Philadelphia adopted the European practice of paving with asphalt. Although it refracted the heat and tended to be slippery, asphalt did provide a quiet surface. Usually it was laid in the suburbs and new sections of town. For the central business district, which required a stronger material, bricks became common in the 1880s, particularly in cities like Philadelphia, Des Moines, Columbus, and Cleveland, which manufactured them.

But American streets did not improve appreciably until builders got beneath the surface of the problem. A substantial and well-drained foundation reduced the amount of surface material used and provided a longer-lasting road. Once cities and their contractors took the trouble to prepare the roadbed, macadam soared in popularity. Cheap stones crushed and mixed with oil, then placed in a well-laid foundation, became the standard paving practice in many cities during the 1880s and 1890s. . . .

Most cities in the 1870s and 1880s constructed major waterworks but the inability to keep up with spiraling demand caused many places to experience "water famines." And the water that did come was virtually untreated. In 1870 no city had a filtration system, and by 1900 only 6 percent of the urban population received filtered water. Pittsburgh, which deposited its industrial waste into and drew its drinking water from the Allegheny River, waited until its death rate from typhoid fever reached four times the national average before constructing a filter system. Between 1908 and 1914, the city installed pumping stations along the Allegheny to filter the water through sediment, whereupon the death rate promptly dropped. Yet even after the improvements, the city's typhoid death rate, although only about half the American average, remained twice that of major European centers.

By 1920 a majority of large American cities possessed filtration and treatment plants. Jersey City pioneered in chemical treatment with a plant built in 1908. But everywhere the surge of population growth pressed hard upon the ingenuity of engineers and resources of municipal governments. The passing decades have brought no solution to the water dilemma; on the contrary, it has reached crisis proportions in many modern cities. Even a century ago it often seemed that in the complex urban environment the most basic needs were the hardest to fulfill satisfactorily.

Technology had another curious effect upon the urban environment: it transformed innovations into necessities of life. The advent of electric energy illustrates the process by which technological breakthroughs generate on a colossal scale demands which had never before existed. Electricity touched every aspect of the city's life—it powered machinery, ran trains, lifted elevators, and lighted streets and homes. To some extent, electricity merely replaced other sources of power and performed old functions in a new way. But once its versatility was recognized, new inventions utilized it for an incredible variety of purposes which urbanites by 1920 accepted as indispensable to their life-style. No one grasped the impact of the dynamo, the means for converting mechanical energy into electric energy, more surely than Henry Adams. "Among the thousand symbols of ultimate energy," he concluded, "the dynamo was not so human as some, but it was the most expressive.". . . .

Even more than gas lamps, electric lighting transformed the city into a twenty-four-hour place. The pace of urban activities livened as nightlife entertainment was extended, people were able to get around more freely and safely, and the evening hours began to attract rather than discourage walkers. Merchants extended their hours, and some industrialists kept their factories running longer. New lighting inspired aesthetic adornments for the city like well-designed lampposts and illuminated monuments, statues, and fountains. The whole atmosphere of city streets seemed cleaner and whiter, a bit like the "Great White City" of the Chicago Fair which had impressed visitors so deeply. It was as if someone, by turning on these electric wonders, had caused urbanites to take a closer look at their cities, and to extract from the shadows a new sense of the degree to which the magic of technology had altered their lives.

As new inventions changed the outward appearance of the industrial city, so did they improve its inner efficiency, . . .

Edison's mimeograph machine (1876), along with the cash register (1876), the stenotype (1876), the adding machine (1888), and the spring-weighing scale (1895), combined with the telephone and typewriter to indicate how far business operations had come from the quill pen, letter book, musty ledger, messenger boy, and hand copyist of an earlier era. Yet none of these equaled another instrument as the supreme symbol of the industrial order: the mass-produced watch.

The hand watch embodied both the genius of American inventiveness and the spirit of the age of mechanization. Fittingly enough, machine watchmaking developed during the 1850s, the same decade in which the preindustrial walking city was giving way to the industrial city. Aaron Dennison's factory in Roxbury, Massachusetts, was the first to manufacture a watch with interchangeable parts in large quantities. Dennison removed his factory to Waltham, Massachusetts, and with Edward Howard formed the American Watch Company which anticipated Henry Ford's assembly line production by fifty years.

Waltham quickly emerged as the center of America's watchmaking industry. By 1900 the factories there averaged 250 watches a year per worker, while Swiss watchmakers could manage only 40. . . . By the late 1870s watchmakers in Waterbury, Connecticut, were producing timepieces at a price the masses could afford. In 1900 a mass-produced watch, complete with a year's guarantee, sold for a dollar. The dollar watch offered tangible benefits and some intangible liabilities. On one hand, the workingman owned a fine timepiece to slide in and out of his pocket; on the other hand, he could no longer plead ignorance or poverty as an excuse for being late to work. . . .

. . . The clock vastly transcended its immediate function of telling time. It symbolized the concerted attempt to harness the raw material of labor to the iron regimen of American work habits. Workmen predictably resisted the efforts as best they could, but the odds turned against them. As immigration swelled the labor force, it created a surplus which heightened the competition for jobs, especially in hard times. However distasteful the factory routine, it was preferable—even inviting—when starvation seemed the only alternative. [Herbert] Gutman cites a verse by Yiddish poet Morris Rosenfeld which vividly portrays the clock as oppressor:

> The Clock in the workshop,—it rests not a moment;
> It points on, and ticks on: eternity—time;
> Once someone told me the clock had a meaning,—
> In pointing and ticking had reason and rhyme. . . .
> At times, when I listen, I hear the clock plainly;—

The reason of old—the old meaning—is gone!
The maddening pendulum urges me forward
To labor and still labor on,
The tick of the clock is the boss in his anger.
The face of the clock has the eyes of the foe.
The clock—I shudder—Dost hear how it draws me?
It calls me "Machine" and it cries [to] me "Sew"!

As urban man grew more apart from his rural cousin with every passing year, nothing separated them more than the clock. While the farmer measured his life by the organic rhythms of seasonal change, of sunrise and sunset, the urbanite chained himself to the "tyranny of time." Trains ran on schedule and were expected to be "on time"; work proceeded with "clockwork efficiency"; mechanical processes were geared "according to the clock"; novels gave way to "periodicals"; and when electricity was mated with the clock in plants, workers had to "clock in." . . .

Technology powered the city, expanded it upward and outward, provided its water, lighted it, carried its wastes, and organized its work patterns. It did much of this crudely, inefficiently, and at great human sacrifice, but Americans had always been slow to reckon the social cost of "progress." More important, it fixed the destiny of the industrial city. Future change or improvement would center upon more sophisticated technology, more prudently applied. No amount of daydreaming or wishful thinking could banish or reverse the technological presence.

The industrial revolution changed the physical city into a larger, more congested, more polluted place. But it had done so under man's guidance. Blind faith in mechanical progress as human progress and the unfettered power of the profit system left little room for pondering the larger ramifications of success. By World War I the industrial city was the dominant urban form which the legacy of unbridled technology willed to the twentieth century.

Families Enter America

JOHN BODNAR

Networks of Migration

Throughout the immigrants' homelands families were forced to select emigration as one possible option in confronting the new order of capitalism. But a multitude of practical problems remained once the decision to move was made. How would information of specific jobs be found? Where could living accommodations be located? How in general did individuals enter sprawling new factories and expanding cities? The answers to these pressing issues emerged not from any long and tedious thought process but largely from familiar patterns cultivated over years of dealing with the vagaries of economic systems, social relationships, and human desires. Work, shelter, and order would be secured in industrial America—as they had been in the pre-industrial and proto-industrial homeland—through an intricate web of kin and communal associations. The immigrant would not enter America

John Bodnar, *The Transplanted: A History of Immigrants in Urban America* (Bloomington: Indiana University Press, 1985), 57–66, 68–84. Reprinted by permission of Indiana University Press.

alone. The intrusion of capitalism in the premigration lands may have raised the alternative of emigration, but it had not destroyed the essential relationship between family and work that most emigrants, regardless of ethnic background, had nurtured. It was a relationship which would enjoy a rejuvenation in the mills and neighborhoods of American industrial cities.

Because families and friends were in close contact even when separated by wide oceans, immigrants seldom left their homelands without knowing exactly where they wanted to go and how to get there. Relatives and friends constantly sent information back regarding locations to live and potential places of employment. Thousands of Poles were brought from Gdansk to Polish Hill in Pittsburgh by aunts, uncles, brothers, and sisters who sent them passage money and instructions of what to bring and where to make steamship and railroad connections. By 1915, as a result of such patterns, investigators could find heavy clusters of families in city neighborhoods. About three-fourths of the Italians and one-half of the Jews who owned property in Providence, Rhode Island, lived in a building with kin at the same address. One Jewish immigrant explained that her father had bought a three-family house with his cousins. Her family lived downstairs, one cousin on the second floor, and another cousin on the top floor. An Italian working for the Scovill Company in Connecticut brought friends who were "big and strong" from Italy. Women brought their sisters or friends into domestic jobs or gave them references of where to go. Chicanos followed each other along railroad lines into Los Angeles and from there throughout southern California. In the early 1920s Chicanos like José Anquiano were arriving in the Chicago area after hearing about openings at the Inland Steel Company and then sending for friends and kin in Texas and in their home villages in Mexico. In fact, relatives and friends were often responsible for movement to second and third locations in America when employment became slack in areas of first settlement. Thus, Italians from southern Illinois moved to the Italian "hill" in St. Louis when coal mining operations were reduced in the 1920s, and Slavs from mines in western Pennsylvania and northern Michigan moved to Detroit's expanding car industry in the same decade.

It was not unheard of for "middlemen" or labor agents to direct large flows of immigrant workers to particular industries or cities in return for modest fees. Such individuals usually shared a common ancestry and language with newcomers and could effectively gather them for shipment to a waiting industry. Oriental workers were channeled in such a fashion into western railroads for a time. . . . Italian "padrones" funneled their fellow countrymen to railroads and public works projects and into labor turmoil as strike-breakers. Ethnic "bankers," such as Luigi Spizziri, advanced passage to individuals in Italy and then found them work in Chicago. . . . In nearly all instances, however, intermediaries functioned only in the early stages of a migration stream. Inevitably the continual and enduring movement of all groups into industrial America would rest on ties and links established in the old world.

Immigrants did not need middlemen in the long run because they received a steady stream of information on labor market conditions and wages from friends and relatives, which allowed them to make reasonably well-informed decisions about where to go and what types of work they could expect to find. Immigrant letters were frequently filled with information on employment prospects, wages, and even the manner in which workers were treated. . . . A Polish steelworker in

Pittsburgh wrote to his family in Poland not to keep his younger brother in school much longer; an extended education would be unnecessary for the toil required in the Pittsburgh mills.

Comparative analysis of Italians migrating to Argentina and New York City further revealed the specificity of the information immigrants used to make the decisions to move. In Argentina Italians formed a sizable portion of the economic structure and had access to numerous opportunities to own business and industrial establishments. At the turn of the century 57 percent of the owners of industrial establishments in Buenos Aires were Italian. The New York labor market offered considerably different opportunities for Italians. In the American metropolis they formed a much smaller percentage of the population and were unable to dominate any important economic sector. Because Italians were generally knowledgeable about the divergent opportunity structures in the two cities, different groups selected different destinations. Those from northern Italy, usually more literate, who intended to remain abroad permanently, went to Buenos Aires. Southern Italians, less literate and with less capital, who hoped to return to Italy, tended to move to New York, where they could easily find unskilled, temporary jobs. Indeed, some indications exist that over time, Italians in Argentina when compared to their American counterparts, invested more in business and their children's education than in housing, because they saw a greater chance for success in the future. . . .

Wages alone, however, did not attract immigrants to specific locations. They were frequently concerned about the type of work they would encounter. Italians often sought outdoor employment and were heavily represented in railroad and other forms of outdoor construction in many American cities. In Chicago they shunned meat-packing because they had heard of the intense cold of refrigerated compartments and the sweltering heat and offensive odors of the killing floors. . . . St. Paul, Minnesota, proved attractive to Irish and German women as a second stop in America because of numerous opportunities for domestic work awaiting them. . . . East European Jews moved into garment trades run by German Jews because they found them easier to work with than Gentile employers.

While immigrants clearly had preferences for work and some advance knowledge of wages and opportunities, however, they were not completely free to move into the industrial economy on an individual basis. Throughout the first century of American industrial expansion both workers and employers experimented with techniques of recruitment and job placement, and no method appeared to be as pervasive or as effective as that of informal familial and ethnic networks. The workplace of early industrial capitalism was a relatively accessible place especially during the six or seven decades after 1850, and kinship ties functioned effectively to provide labor, train new members, and effectively offer status and consolation. Poles, relying on relatives and friends, established occupational beachheads in Pittsburgh at the Jones and Laughlin steel plant. . . . As one newcomer recalled, "The only way you got a job was through somebody at work who got you in." . . . Frequently fathers and uncles taught sons and nephews the operation of industrial equipment. At the Amoskeag textile mills in New Hampshire, French-Canadians brought relatives to work, assisted in their placement in the mills, taught them specific work tasks, substituted for them when they were ill, and informally established production quotas. . . . In one New England textile plant nepotism became so wide-spread in securing employment that workers with familial connections within the plant were actually held in higher esteem than "unattached" employees who were presumed to be more transient.

Kinship not only facilitated the entry of immigrant males into the industrial economy but females as well. A 1930 study of 2,000 foreign-born women revealed that most had secured their initial jobs through relatives and friends. All had worked in either cigar or textile factories, and less than 10 percent had acquired relevant skills for those jobs prior to migrating. Surveys of full-fashioned, hosiery loopers discovered that the majority obtained their positions through acquaintances. . . . A 1924 investigation of Italian females in New York City reported that 75 percent acquired their first jobs through friends or relatives and that these women were "ashamed" to seek employment alone and would quit a job if friends or kin left as well. . . .

The central dynamic, which gradually allowed the industrial workplace to be filled informally by clusters of unskilled immigrants who were usually related, was the quest for greater production. Capitalism in its steady drive toward larger profits and lower costs demanded that goods be produced as quickly and as efficiently as possible. Invariably this imperative required that newer forms of production and technology replace skilled workers. This would not only allow for a faster pace of production but would diminish the influence that skilled workers had exerted over a particular workplace and put more control in the hands of managers and owners. . . .

The most striking result of the decline in skilled jobs was the growing number of immigrant clusters in the nineteenth and twentieth centuries. Nearly one-half of the Philadelphia Irish in 1850 were in unskilled labor, for instance, while 67 percent of the Germans were artisans. In Buffalo, Germans dominated crafts such as masonry, cooperage, and shoemaking while the Irish worked largely as unskilled laborers, domestics, ship carpenters, and teamsters. This early bunching resulted directly from the possession or lack of premigration skills, and newer immigrants after 1880, generally with less skills than the Germans, intensified the pattern of clustering. By 1911 a study of seven urban areas revealed that nearly one-third of all South Italians were categorized as "general laborers" in contrast to only 9 percent of the Poles and 7 percent of the Germans. Fully 65 percent of the Poles were in manufacturing and mechanical pursuits compared to only 28.8 percent of the South Italians. . . . Groups such as the Swedes, Jews, and Germans were considerably underrepresented in "unspecified labor" positions. . . .

Much of this bunching of immigrant workers could be attributed directly to the alteration of skill levels of American workers. As early as the 1840s textile mills in Lowell, Massachusetts, were attempting to improve their productive capacity by switching to spinning mules which could perform more than twice as much work as the older throstle spinners and implement the stretch-out on the assigning of additional looms or spindles to each worker at reduced piece rates. These changes eliminated the homogeneity of the workforce, which was largely native-born, and led directly to an increase in the proportion of immigrants. At one mill, for instance, the foreign-born proportion of the labor force rose from 3.7 percent in 1836 to 61.8 percent by 1860. Thousands of Irish immigrants entered the mills including many women and children who needed the wages and were willing to accept speed-ups and stretch-outs, in part because they were not familiar with an earlier, slower pace. . . .

. . . The substitution of unskilled for skilled labor proceeded rapidly during the final quarter of the nineteenth century. Employers intensified the drive to establish more efficient worker training programs by reducing skill requirements for incoming laborers. Expansion of child, female, and unskilled, foreign-born labor and the decline of apprenticeship programs and of highly skilled operatives underscored the trend. During the early decades of the twentieth century, the number of blacksmiths, machinists, and glassblowers declined substantially. Apprenticeships among brick and stone machinists fell from 39,463 in 1920 to 13,606 a decade later. . . .

The diminution of crafts and skills accelerated after 1900 and had a negative impact upon the older immigrant stocks from northern and western Europe. Germans in nineteenth-century Philadelphia predominated in skilled butchering, tailoring, and shoemaking positions. As these occupations declined, Germans were frequently dislocated and found it more difficult to transfer jobs to their sons. . . .

The blurring of skill distinctions among workers and the implementation of new efficiency schemes were accelerated during the period of the "new immigration." With proletarian protest growing in the late nineteenth century and larger concentrations of workers emerging in urban areas, industrial managers began to impose a bureaucratic structure upon the work force with hierarchical gradations of unskilled and semiskilled operations. This restructuring of work itself resulted in something of a segmentation of the labor market, . . . which created an infinite number of "entry-level" jobs and intensified the process of clustering, while making it extremely unlikely that newcomers could implement any previously acquired skills. The promise of industrial America to immigrant workers was not so much that one could rise as that one could gain access at any number of points of entry. Opportunity was not vertical but horizontal, a fact which tended to blunt any rhetoric of social mobility immediately upon arrival.

If skills were no longer crucial to obtaining work in the expanding sectors of the economy, something else would have to take their place. The alternative would be a random entry of thousands of immigrant workers into the industrial complex. But the widespread existence of clusters suggests that a sense of order in joining newcomers and occupations was operative. In even the most cursory survey of immigrant job acquisition, kinship and ethnic ties invariably emerge as the vital link. . . .

While most newcomers arrived in friendly groups, they were not allowed to function as independently as they might have thought. The industrial economy was certainly accessible but not at every particular point. Frequently, networks of families and relatives could function only where prospective employers allowed them to do so. Owners and managers had distinct impressions regarding the abilities of particular groups, a fact which encouraged group rather than individual movement, and took steps to encourage the hiring of one group at the expense of another. . . . On the Boston and Lowell Railroad in the mid-nineteenth century, only Irishmen were hired as firemen, since it was believed, unlike Yankees, they would not want further promotions. In early Milwaukee, Germans were considered "thrifty, frugal, and industrious" by employers and Poles more industrious than Italians and Greeks. . . . Jewish garment owners sometimes hired only Italians because they were felt to be less amenable to unionization than Jews. On other occasions the

owners hired only fellow Jews, hoping that "fraternal instincts" with employers
might keep them from unionizing. . . . Scandinavian women were strongly preferred in American homes as domestics, in part because they were Protestants
while Irish girls were Catholics. This view caused Finnish women to be in heavy
demand in large cities such as New York. The overall preference for western rather
than eastern Europeans for better paying jobs, it has been estimated, cost the "new
immigrants" on the average of $1.07 per week in wages.

In the case of Chicanos, employer recruitment and attitude were almost solely
responsible for determining where their kinship networks would function. The first
significant movement of Mexican workers into the southwest was due to the agitation of agricultural, mining, and railroad companies in the southwest. Restrictions
of the 1917 Immigration Law were even waived during World War I. Chicanos
could not move into Santa Barbara until the 1880s after inexpensive Chinese labor
had been curtailed, and even then they were confined to work in laundries, domestic
work, and railroad section gangs. . . . A general assumption existed in the southwest that [Mexicans] were interested in working only a short while and then returning to Mexico, although increasing numbers were settling permanently north
of the border after 1880. At El Paso, railroad recruiters considered them "docile,
patient, orderly in camp, fairly intelligent under competent supervision, obedient
and cheap." . . .

The Rise of a Family Economy

While it is apparent that immigrants were not free to move into the industrial economy wherever they desired, they were able to remain within the confines of small
groups and networks, which assisted them tremendously. Such groups could mass
around links of friends, villages, or regions but were mostly held together by ties of
blood. Kinship formed the stable core of immigrant groups as they flowed into the
openings available to them in particular times and places. . . .

The world the immigrant left had exhibited numerous examples of family, in
one form or another, as a central focus of organizing life itself. Families were responsible for socialization patterns, the distribution of land and other resources,
and even served as a forum to resolve the question of who should emigrate and
why. Because they also performed valuable functions in industrial America meant
they were not as much cultural baggage as they were institutions which continued
to find a relevant role to play in both societies. Family economies were as much a
product of industrial capitalism as they were of subsistence agriculture, for in both
systems a mediating institution was necessary to stand between economy and society
in order to reconcile individual and group demands.

The manner in which the immigrant family remained functional in two
economies was its central and enduring attachment to the value of cooperation.
Family members were continually instructed in the necessity of sharing and notions
of reciprocity were constantly reinforced. Parents, children, boarders, and others
who shared particular households were all assigned a series of duties and obligations. By working together, pooling limited resources, and muting individual inclinations, families attempted to assemble the resources sufficient for economic
survival and, occasionally, for an improvement in their standard of living. But the

first goal was always the most immediate: cooperate and survive. French-Canadian children in New England recalled how all contributed their savings to their parents. One who was raised in a large family claimed that it stood to reason that everyone was "gonna start working and pitch in." . . .

Another immigrant elaborated on the reciprocal nature of immigrant life. He recalled.

> When you work, you understand, you used to bring your pay home and give it to your parents. And whatever they feel they want to give you, they decide. There was no disagreement. That was their style. And don't you dare talk about paying board, especially in dad's house. If you want to pay board you have to go somewhere else. "This is no boardinghouse. This is a family," my father would say. He said to us to bring our pay home and whatever it was, we would make do.

It was not until the era of postindustrialism after 1940, when kinship ties to the workplace were gradually weakened and success was equated with an individual quest, that the underlying system of familial cooperation would be threatened.

Essentially, family goals came to supersede individual goals, and parents and children both worked vigorously to contribute to familial welfare. Immigrant parents were often able to direct the career paths of their progeny because of the leverage they derived from being able to provide access to industrial jobs or housing in crowded cities. Boys and girls were frequently asked to leave school early and start work either in a mill or in a family business. Girls were often kept at home caring for younger brothers and sisters or performing household chores. Females who wanted to study music were told it was more practical to stay at home and learn cooking, canning, and sewing. One girl wept when forced by her father to leave school after the sixth grade because he felt a woman did not need schooling "to change diapers." Boys were urged to learn a job skill or a business rather than pursue a formal education, as families responded to the nature of the economy during the first century of American capitalism. Often they received such training on the job from fathers or other kin. Interviews with Poles in the Lawrenceville section of Pittsburgh revealed that during the 1920s and 1930s boys worked alongside their fathers in neighborhood foundries and meat-packing plants.

The family economy was not a product of natural evolution, and the effort to insure that children participated directly in the mustering of resources for familial survival was not accomplished without turmoil and tension. . . . Siblings often complained bitterly if one were allowed to stay in school longer than another. And a few resisted parental attempts to send them to work early. Individual plans and dreams were often formulated but reluctantly put aside for family need. Interviews with immigrant children found careers in electrical engineering, bookkeeping, the priesthood, and business relinquished at the insistence of parents. Studies conducted among Polish immigrant girls in the Chicago stockyard areas revealed that many complained if enough of their wages were not "returned" to them by their parents. . . . Not surprisingly, some immigrant children left home, for they saw their parents as obstacles to happiness.

But parents endured difficult tensions as well. In one study of northern New England textile mills, Steven Dubnoff found that Irish fathers lost some influence in the household as their children began to earn more of their own income. . . .

It is not entirely surprising that the cooperative ideal pervaded most immigrant families. These newcomers were not coming from widely disparate sectors of their homeland social structures but from the ranks of middle-class farm owners and tradesmen and the mass of marginal farmers and landless laborers just below them. A sense of hierarchy existed within the total group but all resided somewhere in the middle of society and experienced neither the hopelessness of extreme poverty nor the self-assurance of power and wealth. Surviving together was a constant preoccupation. . . .

Steeped heavily in a tradition of household and familial cooperation as a vehicle for achieving economic stability and finding an economic system in America which frequently encouraged a good deal of group assistance, immigrants who wished to remain found it relatively easy to establish households of their own. Indeed, the decision to do so represented not only a major commitment to remain in industrial society but suggested the means by which economic and emotional stability would be achieved in new circumstances. The creation of a new family often eased the pain of severing familial ties in the premigration society, especially for women who saw motherhood as a means of adjusting to a new life. Financial considerations also prompted many men to seek a companion who would cook, clean, and care for them for no wages at all. Many immigrants were anxious to reunite with wives and children out of fear that continued separation would ultimately lead to complete family disintegration. One scholar has found that southern Italians were quicker to send for their wives than northern Italians because they were sexually jealous and less culturally prepared to establish strong social relations outside the nuclear family.

If no wife existed in the homeland, immigrant males quickly took whatever steps were necessary to find women of similar linguistic and cultural backgrounds with whom they could establish a household. Marriage patterns remained largely within the ethnic group during the first and much of the second generation. Japanese men sought "picture brides" from Japan and initiated unions which stressed the importance of duty and obligation over love and romance. About one of every four Italians who moved to San Francisco actually returned to their native village just for a marriage. Whether they returned to the homeland or found a wife in America the chances were great she would be from the same region or village, a fact which reinforced notions about the manner in which families and households should function. Thus, it is not surprising to learn that among Germans in Wisconsin 86 percent of the first generation and 80 percent of the second married other Germans. Similar high rates were exhibited by Poles and Russians in the state. . . .

But it would be erroneous to assume that the cooperative family economy grew inevitably out of premigration traditions of collective enterprise or the regional and cultural homogeneity of immigrant streams. Both of these factors . . . would have been insufficient . . . in themselves without the accompanying reality of an industrial workplace which encouraged mutual aid and especially the widespread existence of wages insufficient for even modest standards of living. American industrial wages may have looked attractive to the residents of rural regions undergoing transition, but the available information suggests that the families of most immigrants in this country could not survive on the income of one wage earner. Among Irish millhands in Lowell, Massachusetts, in the 1860s, most fathers could earn only about 54 percent of what was needed to support a family at a minimum level of subsistence. Among packinghouse workers in Chicago in the decade after 1910, the average individual wage earner could earn 38 percent of the minimum needed for a family of four; he could still earn only 48 percent in 1922.... Clearly, family income had to be supplemented in some way.

The economic margin of an immigrant family did not usually improve until children reached working age, about fourteen, and began to contribute to family income. In Philadelphia, to illustrate a case, the children of immigrant Irish and German families entered the labor market to a greater degree than did the children from native-born households. . . . Irish children contribut [ed] between 38 and 46 percent of total family labor. . . . The most "vulnerable" economically were those with small children who could not work and who prevented a mother from work-ing. At Amoskeag about 38 percent of all households had members working other than the head or the wife, but for immigrant households the figure was 50 percent. In fact, textile towns, because they offered employment to teenagers, tended to at-tract families with children of employment age. . . . Families in Chicago's packing-house district even sent wives and daughters into the packinghouses, a move which ironically helped to keep overall wages low. . . .

While opportunities were sought for adolescent employment, immigrant women, like other women, usually terminated toil outside the household with mar-riage and focused attention on the roles of wife, mother, and homemaker. By 1920 in urban America, married women accounted for only 21 percent of the female work force. It is true that the percentage of wage earners among foreign-born adult females over the age of sixteen was one-third higher than the percentage for all white women, but this could be attributed to the heavier reliance of the immigrant family on the earnings of their unmarried daughters. Even for immigrant wives the general plan was not leave home for work after marriage. . . . In Chicago in 1900 less than 2 percent of a sample of Polish, Italian, Jewish, German, and Irish wives left the household to toil, while between 52 and 74 percent of the unmarried females over the age of fifteen in these groups left each day for work.

Strong imperatives existed in many immigrant families to prevent [married] women [from leaving] their homes in search of employment. Traditional perspec-tives on the domestic roles of mothers and wives persisted but were insufficient to account for the pattern by themselves, especially when it was not uncommon for married women to work in the fields of the rural world. Married women also had to raise children, manage the household, and care for boarders because they really had fewer employment opportunities than adult men and adolescents. Restricted opportunity in this case was continually supported by a myriad of cultural prefer-ences. Irish immigrants strongly believed that married women should not work at all. This view was rooted not only in the model family of Irish Catholicism but in a social belief that a working married woman diminished the status of her husband. In Ireland female subservience had reached the point in the 1840s that married women had a shorter life expectancy than fathers and sons because the males were to receive the most nutritious food. . . . Greek families actually considered it a disgrace for a wife, and sometimes a sister, to work outside the house. Whatever the reason for keeping married women at home, the pattern of working-class domesticity was established prior to its celebration by middle-class reformers in urban America. Culture did not simply flow downward from social superiors. . . .

Conclusion

The predisposition toward doing whatever was necessary to sustain a family-based household was nothing new. It had pervaded the immigrant homelands and received additional support ironically from the new system of industrial capitalism which restructured its labor market in a manner which facilitated the entry of groups of untrained toilers who were often related or at least acquainted with each other. Kin and friends were free to assist each other in entering America by providing access to jobs and homes and supplying important information of labor market conditions. New arrivals were adept at determining where they might enter a very large economy. The immigrant family economy survived and flourished among most newcomers in industrial America because new economic structures actually reinforced traditional ways of ordering life and, consequently, contributed to a supportive "external environment" for capitalism to proceed. In this system, individual inclinations were muted and the household, managed effectively by immigrant females, superseded all other goals and objectives. In the face of a sprawling and complex urban industrial structure, newcomers forged a relatively simple device for establishing order and purpose in their lives. This system would remain predominant among working-class families until the labor market was reshaped again after World War II and credentials and skills regained importance in entering new professional sectors of work. It was a system which would be challenged by outside institutions and values as the stay in America became more permanent.

Finally, it could be argued that not all immigrant families functioned alike and that significant differences existed in religion, cultural background, and particular family strategies. Certainly, this was true. But it was also true that such differences coexisted with a fundamental similarity. Families and households were the predominant form in which all immigrants entered the industrial-urban economy and ordered their lives. Members of nearly all groups received indoctrination in the need to remain loyal to the familial and household unit. The goals of individual households could differ as a result of cultural background or positioning within the economy, and these divergences would come into play over time as separate paths of education, occupation, and mobility were taken. But in the movement to a capitalist world and in the initial decades of settlement, familial and communal networks abounded.

Americanization of the Mexican Immigrant

GEORGE J. SANCHEZ

The mechanism by which Mexican immigrant women were to be reached was already in place in the infrastructure of the Commission's activities. In 1915, the California state legislature passed the Home Teacher Act, a law which allowed school districts to employ teachers "to work in the homes of the pupils, instructing children and adults in matters relating to school attendance . . . in sanitation, in the

---

English language, in household duties . . . and in the fundamental principles of the American system of government and the rights and duties of citizenship." After World War I, the home teacher program was expanded, professionalized, and located within the public school system. From 1915 to 1929, the home teacher—usually a single, middle-class, Anglo woman—was the linchpin of Americanization efforts aimed at the Mexican family.

Mexican immigrant women were targeted for a variety of reasons. First, they were assumed to be the individuals primarily responsible for the transmission of values in the home. According to reformer's strategy, if the female adopted American values, the rest of her family would follow suit. Pearl Ellis, who worked with young Mexican women in southern California throughout the 1920s, stressed the important "influence of the home" in creating an employee who is "more dependable and less revolutionary in his tendencies . . . The homekeeper creates the atmosphere, whether it be one of harmony and cooperation or of dissatisfaction and revolt."

Americanization advocates were interested in the contribution Mexican women could make in transforming their families' habits from those of a rural, pre-industrial lifestyle to a modern American one. . . . Because the Southwest lagged behind the rest of the nation in industrialization, local reformers were anxious to introduce Mexican women and men as rapidly as possible to the temperament of industrial society and inculcate Mexican families with the "Protestant work ethic." Targeting mothers was crucial to the overall strategy of Americanization.

Motherhood, in fact, was the Mexican immigrant woman's most highly valued role in Americanization schemes. By focusing on the strategic position of the mother in the Mexican family, Americanizers hoped to have an impact on the second generation, even if the immigrant generation itself turned out to be less malleable than expected. Undeniably, Americanization ideology was infused with the traditional American belief in the exalted role of the mother in shaping the citizenry of the Republic. . . .

Although Americans had debated for almost three decades the conflicts between women's private family responsibilities and their public roles as workers, Americanization programs demonstrated no such concern when addressing the ideal future of the Mexican American woman. With regard to immigrant women, Americanization advocates were readily capable of blurring the public and private spheres. Teaching the Mexican mother proper American homemaking skills was meant to solve two problems at once: a happy and efficient mother would create an environment suitable for molding workers to the industrial order, and her new-found homemaking skills could be utilized in the cheap labor market outside the home. In 1908, a U.S. Bureau of Labor inspector had regretfully noted that Mexican "immigrant women have so little conception of domestic arrangements in the United States that the task of training them would be too heavy for American housewives." However, black and European immigrant women had not migrated to southern California in large enough numbers to fill the growing demand for domestic labor. Consequently, Americanization teachers targeted Mexican women to help alleviate the shortage of housemaids, seamstresses, laundresses, and service workers in the Southwest. By the 1920s, Americanization programs were busy training Mexican women to perform these tasks.

The most potent weapon used to imbue the foreigner with American values was the English language. All social reformers cited the ability to speak English as a fundamental skill necessary for assimilation. During and after World War I, however, English instruction was intended to provide the immigrant with much more than facility with the spoken language of the United States. In 1917, California's Commission of Immigration and Housing recommended "that employers of immigrants be shown the relation between a unified working force, speaking a common language, and industrial prosperity." In 1918, Mrs. Amanda Matthews Chase, a home teacher with twelve years' experience teaching in Mexico City, was hired by the Daughters of the American Revolution and developed a primer to teach English. Home teachers were instructed to associate their lessons "with the pupils' own lives and affairs." Thus, for example, they used the following song (sung to the tune, "Tramp, Tramp, Tramp, the Boys are Marching") to instruct female pupils about women's work as they learned twenty-seven new English words:

> We are working every day,
> So our boys and girls can play.
>   We are working for our homes and country, too;
> We like to wash, to sew, to cook,
> We like to write, or read a book,
>   We are working, working, working every day.
> Work, work, work,
> We are always working,
>   Working for our boys and girls,
> Working for our boys and girls,
> For our homes and country, too—
>   We are working, working, working every day.

Yet despite the attention of reformers, Mexican women continued to lag behind men in learning the English language. A study of 1,081 Mexican families in Los Angeles conducted in 1921 found that while 55 percent of the men were unable to speak English, an overwhelming 74 percent of the women could not speak the language. Similar gaps existed in English reading and writing.

Advocates of Americanization blamed the patriarchal nature of the Mexican family for this discrepancy. "The married Mexican laborer does not allow his wife, as a rule, to attend evening classes," reported USC's Emory Bogardus. Americanization teachers consistently criticized as traditional and unprogressive the alleged limitations placed upon the Mexican wife by her husband. According to one Americanization instructor, if left in the home, the Mexican woman's "intellectual ability is stimulated only by her husband and if he be of the average peon type, the stimulation is not very great." The Mexican home, she concluded, "being a sacred institution, is guarded by all the stolid tradition of centuries." If the Mexican home remained such a fortress, Americanization specialists would not be able to accomplish their mission.

Getting the Mexican woman out of her home, therefore, became a priority for Americanization programs because reformers saw this not only as the only avenue available for her intellectual progress, but as the only method by which they could succeed in altering her values. Home teachers visited each individual Mexican family in their district to gain the trust of members and encourage the husband to allow his wife to attend classes. The scheduling of alternative sessions in the afternoon for wives and mothers facilitated this progress.

Americanization programs, however, did not mean to undermine entirely the traditional Mexican family structure. Ironically, they counted on the cohesiveness of the Mexican family to achieve their assimilationist goals. Home teachers, even when they did get Mexican women out of the house and into classes, encouraged the acquisition of traditionally feminine household skills. In the ditty, "The Day's Work," for example, home teachers utilized the following sequence of phrases both to teach the English language and to instruct women about the proper organization of the family economy in American society.

> In the morning the women get breakfast.
> Their husbands go to work.
> Their children go to school.
> Then the women get their houses in good order.
> They give the baby its bath.
> They wash, or iron, or cook.
> They get the dinner.
> After dinner they wash the dishes.
> Then they sew, or rest, or visit their friends, or go to school.

Americanization programs sought to maintain the structure of family life while transforming familial habits, especially those concerning diet and health. Reformers encouraged Mexican women to give up their penchant for fried foods, their too frequent consumption of rice and beans, and their custom of serving all members of the family—from infants to grandparents—the same meal. According to proponents of Americanization, the modern Mexican woman should replace tortillas with bread, serve lettuce instead of beans, and broil instead of fry. Malnourishment in Mexican families was not blamed on lack of food or resources, but rather on "not having the right varieties of foods containing constituents favorable to growth and development."

Women in the American reform movement were certainly conversant with the turn-of-the-century domestic science movement—a movement which associated scientific homemaking with moral regeneration. Within the rubric of Americanization efforts, food and diet management became yet another tool in a system of social control intended to construct a well-behaved, productive citizenry. In the eyes of reformers, the typical noon lunch of the Mexican child, thought to consist of "a folded tortilla with no filling," could easily be the first step to a lifetime of crime. With "no milk or fruit to whet the appetite" the child could become lazy as well as hungry and might subsequently "take food from the lunch boxes of more fortunate children. Thus, the initial step in a life of thieving is taken." Teaching immigrant women proper food values became a route to keeping the head of the family out of jail and the rest of the family off charity.

Health and cleanliness represented additional catchwords for Americanization programs. One of the primary functions of home teachers was to impress upon the minds of Mexican mothers and mothers-to-be "that a clean body and clean mind are the attributes of a good citizen." . . . Reformers blamed Mexicans' slovenliness for their poor state of health. Such labeling reinforced the stereotype of the "dirty Mexican" and expanded its usage among Anglo urban dwellers. One eminent sociologist working with Americanization programs noted that Anglo Americans objected to the presence of Mexican children in the public schools for fear that their own children would catch a contagious disease.

Pressing "American" standards of diet, health, and cleanliness upon Mexican women was not the only component essential in creating a healthy home environment. None of the potential gains made by these programs could be considered noteworthy if the Mexican female continued to bear too many children. Americanization advocates worried that unless she learned to limit family size, the Mexican mother would be unable to train adequately each individual member of her household.

Limiting the growth of the immigrant population was a long-standing concern of both Progressives and nativists. Americans first noticed that immigrant groups had a higher birthrate than native-born Americans at the end of the nineteenth century, and fears of "race suicide" had existed in the Anglo American mind ever since. When this fear rose in relation to the Mexican immigrant, both nativists and proponents of Americanization became alarmed: nativists wished to stave off an "invasion," while Americanization advocates viewed all unrestricted population growth as a vestige of Old World ways that must be abandoned in a modern industrial setting.

Americanizers held Mexican women responsible for family planning. They also saw her hampered in these efforts by a number of factors. Traditional early marriage and the "inherent sentimentality" of the Mexican female promoted, they believed, a primitive sexuality and reinforced sexual ignorance. In addition, Catholicism discouraged birth control. Despite these barriers, Americanization teachers reported that Mexican mothers were beginning to exhibit dismay with their large families, and occasionally inquired about birth control measures. Some even warned others to delay marriage on the grounds of "much work, too much children."

Americanists viewed such evidence of changing attitudes as a hopeful sign, because limited reproduction opened up new opportunities for Mexican women within and outside the home. As proper household managers, Mexican women could devote more time to raising fewer and more productive children. But family limitation also created new possibilities for female employment by freeing Mexican women from the demands of continual childrearing. Traditionally, Mexican women's family obligations had barred them from wage labor outside the home. When a Mexican immigrant woman worked, it was almost always in her late adolescent or early adult years before marriage.

As industrialization in the American southwestern economy developed, so too did demands for cheap labor performing tasks that had traditionally been performed by women inside the home. While the garment, laundering, domestic service, and food preparation industries gradually relied more on "women's work" in the marketplace, employers in the region had fewer workers because of the restrictions placed upon Asian and European immigration, and because black migration to the Southwest was still quite low. Moreover, demands of the Anglo middle class for these services increased, exacerbating further the labor supply problems. Despite all the traditional objections to Mexican women working outside the home, Americanization programs actively promoted Mexican immigrant women for entrance into these sex-segregated occupations. . . .

Given the dual role reformers envisioned that the Mexican woman would play within and outside the home, every newly learned skill supposedly benefited American society doubly. When Americanists stressed the ability to set a table and to serve food properly, they were encouraging Mexican women not only to arrange home meals by American standards but also to learn that "sloppy appearance and uncleanliness of person would not be tolerated in a waitress." In addition, the burden on a private citizen employing a Mexican woman as a domestic servant would be considerably lightened if the employee had already been adequately trained through their programs. . . .

Encouraging Mexican women to engage in hard work was also viewed as an important step toward "curing" the habits of the stereotypical "lazy Mexican." According to one Americanization teacher, "'*Quien sabe*?' (who knows?) was the philosophy of all of Mexico, and the inability of Mexicans to connect the things that are valued as worthwhile to the effort necessary to obtain them made Mexican laborers inefficient." Another felt that "the laziness of Mexicans was due to climate conditions and inherited tendencies" which only hard work could root out. Consequently, putting Mexican women to work would have the effect of promoting discipline in them, which in turn would encourage them to pass on a similar level of self-control to their children.

Eventually, as national attention increasingly turned toward restricting future immigration from Mexico, Americanization advocates found themselves caught in the middle of the controversy, with little concrete evidence to prove that their efforts had effectively resolved the "Mexican problem." One of the few quantifiable means by which to measure success or failure in Americanization was the rate of naturalization, and in this area Mexican immigrants displayed little progress. Statistics from the period simply did not suggest that Americanization had affected the rate of naturalization. In fact, among the Mexican immigrant population in California, which already had the lowest rate of naturalization of any immigrant group in the state in 1920, the ratio of naturalized citizens to the total foreign-born Mexican population declined during the 1920s. Given this trend, and the long-standing ambivalence of reformers toward the immigrant, Americanizers shifted their focus. In 1927, the Commission of Immigration and Housing sided with restrictionists, calling for an end to unlimited immigration from Mexico, and blaming immigrants for "causing an immense social problem in our charities, schools and health departments."

Moreover, the efforts to alter the immigrant generation itself were abandoned in favor of school-based programs which sought to teach American-born children a culture different from that of their immigrant parents. In the schools, socialization in American values and language skills were even more emphatically combined with the goal of social stability. The increase application of I.Q. testing, always administered in English, invariably segregated Mexican children in special classes for the mentally inferior or mentally retarded. . . . By the late 1920s, the promoters of Americanization put their hopes for the future in vocational education and classes in citizenry directed at American-born Mexican children.

The efforts directed at children, like those aimed earlier at their parents, promoted above all the habits of thrift and time discipline. In southern California, business interests ardently favored Americanization programs that advocated promptness and diligence at work. Businessmen learned to cooperate both with the

Protestant reformers interested in fostering internal controls over morality and economy and with the social feminists hoping to upgrade women's position within the Mexican family. They understood full well that despite the range of motivations behind Americanization, the price of acceptance for Mexicans into American society via their programs was predicated on the abandonment of a culture they perceived as inherently inferior.

Rather than provide Mexican immigrants with an attainable picture of assimilation, Americanization programs could offer these immigrants only idealized versions of American values. In reality what was presented turned out to be little more than second-class citizenship. The most progressive assumptions behind Americanization programs were never fully shared by the government or business interests involved, and thus they could never be fully implemented. One Americanization teacher who spent the decade working with Mexican immigrants noted with disappointment in 1923 that the newly elected governor of California had eliminated financial provisions for the Americanization program in the public schools from his budget. At least one historian has concluded that the "love affair between the progressive and the businessman" in California inevitably led, in the 1920s, to a blunting of "the cutting edge of progressive social reform."

The halfhearted effort of administrators of Americanization programs limited available personnel and resources and ensured that the programs would never be able to cope with the volume of the Mexican migration. The barrios expanded so quickly in the 1920s that any single Americanization teacher found it impossible to keep abreast of the number of new Mexican families in her district who needed a resumption of her program from scratch. Newer areas of Mexican settlement were usually beyond the reach of established Americanization programs entirely. Furthermore, Mexicans experienced a high degree of geographic mobility in this period that easily wiped out whatever progress had been made by these programs in a given community. According to historian Ricardo Romo, fewer than one-third of Mexicans present in Los Angeles in 1917–18 were present in the city one decade later. Americanization teacher Amanda Chase acknowledged the extent of this problem when dealing with Mexican women: "I have had in my class record book this year the names of about half as many Mexican women as there are Mexican families in the district. But a third of them moved to other districts." Mexican immigrants could not hope to develop allegiances to the United States when the economic condition of their families forced them to migrate consistently in search of an economic livelihood.

In the end, Americanization programs never had the time to develop sufficiently even to approach a solution to the problem of Mexican immigrants in the United States. With the stock market crash of 1929 and the subsequent Great Depression of the 1930s, all attempts to Americanize Mexican immigrants came to an abrupt end. Rather than search for ways to assimilate these newcomers, American society looked for methods to be rid of them altogether. About 500,000 Mexicans left the United States during the 1930s under strong pressure from the government and up to one-tenth of these individuals had resided in Los Angeles. Americanists joined in these efforts to repatriate Mexican residents; their commitment to improving the conditions of the Mexican had no place in an economically depressed America.

Instead, Americanization programs are an important window for looking at the assumptions made about both Mexican and American culture by progressive Californians during the 1920s. Mexican culture was seen as malleable, but required intense education in "American values" to fit into a modern, industrialized society. These efforts also made clear, however, that Mexicans were intended only to assimilate into the bottom segment of the American work force as low-paid, yet loyal, workers. As we shall see, Mexican immigrants generated their own version of Americanism without abandoning Mexican culture. What they would create would be quite a different product indeed.

 # F U R T H E R   R E A D I N G

Gunther Barth, *City People* (1980)

John Bodnar, *The Transplanted: A History of Immigrants in Urban America* (1985)

Charles W. Cheape, *Moving the Masses* (1980)

Elizabeth Ewen, *Immigrant Women in the Land of Dollars* (1985)

Donna R. Gabaccia, *Militants and Migrants: Rural Sicilians Become American Workers* (1988)

John Higham, *Strangers in the Land: Patterns of American Nativism, 1860–1925* (1971)

Hartmut Keil, ed., *German Workers in Industrial Chicago, 1850–1920* (1988)

Maury Klein and Harvey A. Kantor, *Prisoners of Progress: American Industrial Cities, 1850–1920* (1976)

Alan M. Kraut, *The Huddled Masses: The Immigrant in American Society, 1860–1921* (1982)

Stephen Meyer, *The Five Dollar Day: Labor Management and Social Control in the Ford Motor Company, 1908–1921* (1981)

Joanne J. Meyerowitz, *Women Adrift: Independent Wage Earners in Chicago, 1880–1930* (1988)

Raymond A. Mohl, *The New City: Urban America in the Industrial Age, 1860–1920* (1985)

Gilbert Osofsky, *Harlem* (1971)

Harold L. Platt, *The Electric City: Energy and the Growth of the Chicago Area* (1991)

George J. Sanchez, *Becoming Mexican-American: Ethnicity, Culture, and Identity in Chicano Los Angeles, 1900–1945* (1993)

Alexander P. Saxton, *The Indispensable Enemy: Labor and the Anti-Chinese Movement in California* (1971)

Judith E. Smith, *Family Connections: A History of Jewish and Italian Immigrant Lives in Providence, Rhode Island, 1900–1940* (1985)

Jon C. Teaford, *The Unheralded Triumph: City Government in America, 1870–1900* (1984)

Judy Yung, *Unbound Feet: A Social History of Chinese Women in San Francisco* (1995)

Politics in the Gilded Age:

Mainstream and Periphery

Of all the elements of late-nineteenth-century America, perhaps the most colorfully notorious has been the political order. How did the nation's public institutions respond to the era's cascade of new wealth, explosive growth, and unprecedented challenges? Not too well, most twentieth-century analysts have concluded. In fact, the national political arena was undergoing a wrenching, and fascinating, period of transition in the 1880s and 1890s as it moved from the popular, if ritualistic, politics of the past toward the more bureaucratic organizational models of the future. As organized through the two major parties, electoral turnout reached a record 77 percent, an astonishing level by today's standards. But to latterday eyes, the fierce partisanship of the major political contests, often playing on older ethno-geographic divisions in the populace, appeared to ignore the country's substantive social changes.

Beneath the surface of electoral results, however, one sees a host of new issues and political constituencies invading the traditional political turf. Especially evident in politicized groups of workers and farmers (see Chapters 2 and 7) and among women's rights and temperance advocates, these issue-oriented social movements pressed hard against the old parties with new demands and even alternative electoral formations. Yet if the frontal assault on the status quo was turned back, the restructuring issues raised in the Gilded Age would return with renewed vigor in the Progressive Era (see Chapters 13 and 14).

DOCUMENTS

The following selections offer a good sampling of Gilded Age political fervor. We begin with the partisan political culture of the dominant two-party system, as reflected at once in contemporary political cartoons (Document 1) and electioneering bombast. In the first cartoon, Thomas Nast attacks the Democrats in 1880 as the party of Tammany Hall and the Confederacy. In the same year, Nast's late-century rival, the Austrian-born Joseph Keppler, ridicules the idea of a third term for scandal-plagued Republican President Ulysses S. Grant. In the third example, amateur caricaturist

Watson Heston targets both major parties and their corporate patrons in the proto-populist *American Non-Conformist and Kansas Industrial Liberator* in 1888. Document 2 offers a stellar rhetorical example of a Republican "waving the bloody shirt" of Civil War loyalties, as excerpted from an address by the celebrated orator and free-thinker Robert G. Ingersoll. Swayed by the orator's combination of gushing sentimentality and piercing sarcasm, Ingersoll's listeners, according to one witness, "cheered till they seemed hypnotized by their own voices." We end with three appeals on behalf of women's rights—the first from a black Virginia activist in 1880, the others from suffrage matriarch Elizabeth Cady Stanton, who at once appealed for basic citizenship rights for women and attacked traditional religious doctrine as the chief cultural agent standing in the way of female progress.

In each case, specific political demands are tinged with passionate regard for the larger morality of the nation's public life. As manifested in this group of documents, what are the main conflicts among contemporary political contestants? What qualities connect, or disconnect, their political culture to or from our own?

1. Three Cartoonists Interpret the Political Scene, 1880, 1888

Thomas Nast Attacks the Democrats, 1880

AS SOLID AND DEFIANT AS EVER

In this vintage example of "waving the bloody shirt," German-born staunch Republican cartoonist Thomas Nast invokes powerful symbols of good and evil to elevate the significance of late-nineteenth-century partisanship. With what counter-imagery might the Democrats have responded?

Thomas Nast cartoon from *Harper's Weekly,* Oct. 2, 1880. Reprinted in J. Chad Vinson, *Thomas Nast: Political Cartoonist* (Athens: University of Georgia Press, 1967), illustration no. 125.

Joseph Keppler Ridicules the Third-Term Aspirations of President Grant, 1880

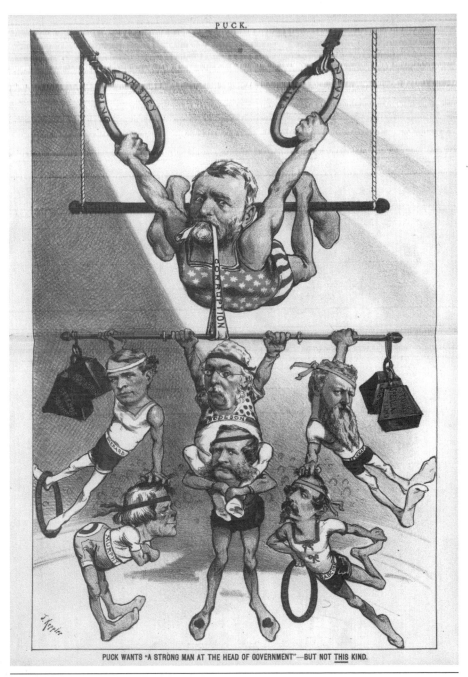

PUCK WANTS "A STRONG MAN AT THE HEAD OF GOVERNMENT"—BUT NOT THIS KIND.

Keppler, a less partisan but worthy successor to Nast as the nation's leading cartoonist, visually documents the influence peddling that had accompanied the first two Grant administrations. Given this record of scandal, why do you suppose Grant was even considered by party leaders for a third term?

Joseph Keppler cartoon from *Puck* (New York: Puck Publishing Company), Feb. 4, 1880.

Watson Heston Lampoons Parties and Their Corporate Patrons, 1888

How the Voting Cattle Obey the Will of the "Powers that Be."--(*Will show the "Powers That Be" in our Next.*)

Heston's critique of the two-party system reflected a common viewpoint among the economically and politically disaffected in the late 1880s and early 1890s. Who might be so alienated and why? What options did they have?

Watson Heston cartoon from *American Non-Conformist and Kansas Industrial Liberator,* March 8, 1888.

2. Free-Thinker Robert G. Ingersoll Waves the Bloody Shirt, c. 1880

Why I Am a Republican

That party has thrown every safeguard around the ballot-box in every State in the Union where any safeguard has been thrown. That party has always been in favor of registration; the Democratic party has always opposed it. That party—the Republican party—has done all it could possibly do to secure an honest expression of the great will of the people. Every man here who is in favor of an honest ballot-box ought to vote the Republican ticket; every man here in favor of free speech ought to vote the Republican ticket. Free speech is the brain of this Republic, and an honest vote is its life-blood. (Applause.) There are two reasons, then, why I am a Republican: First, I believe in free speech; secondly, I want an honest vote.

A crust that the worms had eaten before was a democrat; every man who shot down our men when they happened to step an inch beyond the dead line, every one was a Democrat; and when some poor, emaciated Union patriot, driven to insanity by famine, saw at home in his innocent dreams the face of his mother, and she seemed to beckon him to come to her, and he, following that dream, stepped one inch beyond the dead line, the wretch who put a bullet through his throbbing, loving heart was a Democrat.

We should never forget these things. (A voice, "That's so.") Every man who wept over the corpse of slavery; every man who was sorry when the chains fell from four millions of people; every man who regretted to see the shackles drop from women and children, every one was a Democrat. In the House of Representatives and in the Senate the resolution was submitted to amend the Constitution so that every man treading the soil of the Republic should be forever free, and every man who voted against it was a Democrat. Every man who swore that greenbacks never would be worth any more than withered leaves, every man who swore that he would never pay, our bonds, every man who slandered our credit and prophesied defeat, was a Democrat. Now, recollect it. Do not forget it. And if there is any young man here who is this fall to cast his first vote, I beg of him, I beseech him, not to join that party whose history for the last twenty years has been a disgrace to this country.

3. Virginia Activist Live Pryor Seeks Help for Her Downtrodden Black Sisters, 1880

A Letter to Susan B. Anthony

[I read] Your Call for all woman of These United States to sign a petition . . . to be sent to you, from Your Mass Meeting to be sent to the Republican Presidential Convention asking them to extend to us Woman some recognition of our rights. We are your Sister though Colored still we feel in our Bosom and want of Faternal love

Wit, Wisdom and Eloquence of Col. R. G. Ingersoll (Chicago: Rhodes and McClure, 1894), 126–127.

Chicago Historical Society, National Woman Suffrage Association Correspondence Volume. Reprinted in Ellen Carol DuBois, ed., *Elizabeth Cady Stanton and Susan B. Anthony: Correspondence, Writings, Speeches* (New York: Schocken, 1981), 205–206.

from our White Sister of the Country. Our White men of this State of Virginia, who rule us with a rod of iron, and show themselves on every occasion the same Crule Task Master, as ever, have introduce on the Statute books right to wipp woman for any poor Discretion, that she might be guilt of. During the early part of febuary a poor weak colored Woman who was in the Extremes wants, stole a Over skirt Value fifty Cent, for which the presiding Magistrate Named J. J. Gruchfield, Did order the poor creature 72 lashes to be well laid on. 36 lashes at the time the Other 36 in a week time and the man or, brute, went himself and saw the whipping was exe cuted. Captain Scott a Col man became indignant went to the jail to see the poor Creature, was refused admission at first but succeed at Last. O My God, what a sight he then saw. the poor Woman Breast Cut wide open by the lash, her poor back cut to pieces I call some woman together went to the Governor and stated the Case. he forbid the further lashing of the poor woman because the Dr. Beal said she could not live to receive further whipping. Yet the woman still have to remain in jail 12 months for stealing one over skirt Value fifty Cent and have since then been enable to enroll quite a number of Woman to gather form a Club. Our Object is to petition Lecture and to do all things wich shall so soffen the heart of Mankind that they will see and must grant and respect our rights. Would and pray that the Mass Meeting may endorse or demand of the Republican Convention to be Held in Chicigo the rights of Woman to put an Amendment to the Constitution a Cumpulsory Educa-tion of Every state of this Union.

Pardon me for this long letter i must i feel let my feeling go out, so to you Dear Madam have i address you on Behalf of your Down Trodden Colored Sisters of Virginia.

> LIVE PRYOR, Richmond, Virginia
> President, Ladies Enterprise Club

If you have any papers or book that is of no use to you our society would feel grate-ful to receive them as we wish to form a library.

4. Elizabeth Cady Stanton Demands Suffrage as the Protection of Selfhood, 1892

The point I wished plainly to bring before you on this occasion is the individuality of each human soul—our Protestant idea, the right of individual conscience and judgment—our republican idea, individual citizenship. In discussing the rights of woman, we are to consider, first, what belongs to her as an individual, in a world of her own, the arbiter of her own destiny, an imaginary Robinson Crusoe with her woman Friday on a solitary island. Her rights under such circumstances are to use all her faculties for her own safety and happiness. . . .

The isolation of every human soul and the necessity of self-dependence must give each individual the right to choose his own surroundings. The strongest reason for giving woman all the opportunities for higher education, for the full development

The Woman's Column, Jan. 1892, pp. 2–3. This document can be found in Ellen Carol DuBois, ed., *Elizabeth Cady Stanton and Susan B. Anthony Reader* (Boston: Northeastern University Press, 1992), 247–254.

of her faculties, her forces of mind and body; for giving her the most enlarged freedom of thought and action; a complete <u>emancipation</u> from all forms of bondage, of custom, dependence, superstition; from all the crippling influences of fear is the solitude and personal responsibility of her own individual life. The strongest reason why we ask for woman a voice in the government under which she lives; in the religion she is asked to believe; equality in social life, where she is the chief factor; a place in the trades and professions, where she may earn her bread, is because of her birthright to self-sovereignty; because, as an individual, she must rely on herself. . . .

To throw obstacles in the way of a complete education is like putting out the eyes; to deny the rights of property is like cutting off the hands. To refuse political equality is to rob the ostracized of all self-respect, of credit in the market place, of recompense in the world of work, of a voice in choosing those who make and administer the law, a choice in the jury before whom they are tried, and in the judge who decides their punishment. Shakespeare's play of Titus and Andronicus contains a terrible satire on woman's position in the nineteenth century—"Rude men seized the king's daughter, cut out her tongue, cut off her hands, and then bade her go call for water and wash her hands." What a picture of woman's position! Robbed of her natural rights, handicapped by law and custom at every turn, yet compelled to fight her own battles, and in the emergencies of life to fall back on herself for protection. . . .

How the little courtesies of life on the surface of society, deemed so important from man towards woman, fade into utter insignificance in view of the deeper tragedies in which she must play her part alone, where no human aid is possible! . . .

Is it, then, consistent to hold the developed woman of this day within the same narrow political limits as the dame with the spinning wheel and knitting needle occupied in the past? No, no! Machinery has taken the labors of woman as well as man on its tireless shoulders; the loom and the spinning wheel are but dreams of the past; the pen, the brush, the easel, the chisel, have taken their places, while the hopes and ambitions of women are essentially changed.

We see reason sufficient in the outer conditions of human beings for individual liberty and development, but when we consider the self-dependence of every human soul, we see the need of courage, judgment and the exercise of every faculty of mind and body, strengthened and developed by use, in woman as well as man.

5. Elizabeth Cady Stanton Justifies the Woman's Bible, 1895

From the inauguration of the movement for woman's emancipation the Bible has been used to hold her in the "divinely ordained sphere," prescribed in the Old and New Testaments.

The canon and civil law; church and state; priests and legislators; all political parties and religious denominations have alike taught that woman was made after

Elizabeth Cady Stanton, *The Woman's Bible* (New York: European Publishing Co., 1895), 7–9.

man, of man, and for man, an inferior being, subject to man. Creeds, codes, Scriptures and statutes, are all based on this idea. The fashions, forms, ceremonies and
customs of society, church ordinances and discipline all grow out of this idea. . . .

The Bible teaches that woman brought sin and death into the world, that she
precipitated the fall of the race, that she was arraigned before the judgment seat of
Heaven, tried, condemned and sentenced. Marriage for her was to be a condition
of bondage, maternity a period of suffering and anguish, and in silence and subjection, she was to play the role of a dependent on man's bounty for all her material
wants, and for all the information she might desire on the vital questions of the
hour, she was commanded to ask her husband, at home. Here is the Bible position
of woman briefly summed up. . . .

These familiar texts are quoted by clergymen in their pulpits, by statesmen in
the halls of legislation, by lawyers in the courts, and are echoed by the press of all
civilized nations, and accepted by woman herself as "The Word of God." So perverted is the religious element in her nature, that with faith and works she is the
chief support of the church and clergy; the very powers that make her emancipation impossible. When, in the early part of the Nineteenth Century, women began
to protest against their civil and political degradation, they were referred to the Bible
for an answer. When they protested against their unequal position in the church,
they were referred to the Bible for an answer.

This led to a general and critical study of the Scriptures. Some, having made a
fetish of these books and believing them to be the veritable "Word of God," with
liberal translations, interpretations, allegories and symbols, glossed over the most
objectionable features of the various books and clung to them as divinely inspired.
Others, seeing the family resemblance between the Mosaic code, the canon law,
and the old English common law, came to the conclusion that all alike emanated
from the same source; wholly human in their origin and inspired by the natural
love of domination in the historians. Others, bewildered with their doubts and
fears, came to no conclusion. While their clergymen told them on the one hand,
that they owed all the blessings and freedom they enjoyed to the Bible, on the other,
they said it clearly marked out their circumscribed sphere of action: that the demands for political and civil rights were irreligious, dangerous to the stability of
the home, the state and the church. Clerical appeals were circulated from time to
time conjuring members of their churches to take no part in the anti-slavery or
woman suffrage movements, as they were infidel in their tendencies, undermining
the very foundations of society. No wonder the majority of women stood still, and
with bowed heads, accepted the situation.

E S S A Y S

The following essays combine a synthetic overview of the organization of electoral
politics in the Gilded Age with a selective focus on the advocates of the single largest
group of unenfranchised citizens—American women. In the first essay, Professor
Charles W. Calhoun of East Carolina University rescues national political leaders
of the era from the abiding condescension of contemporary critics and subsequent

historians alike. According to Calhoun, real differences of emphasis separated the parties, and the limitations of legislation in these years were less the result of personal weakness on the part of politicians than doubt among the voters themselves about the proper role for the federal government in their lives. In the second essay, Ellen Carol DuBois of the University of California at Los Angeles explores a crucial ideological and strategic dilemma facing leading suffrage advocate Elizabeth Cady Stanton before the turn of the century. Was Christianity a source of women's bondage or a refuge to which women could usefully turn in a male-defined world of competitive individualism?

The Political Culture: Public Life and the Conduct of Politics

CHARLES W. CALHOUN

The last third of the nineteenth century is the most misunderstood and disparaged period in the political history of the United States. For the better part of the twentieth century, historians painted the era in the darkest hues imaginable, arguing that spoilsmen and corruptionists ruled its political life and that obtaining office for its own sake was the primary motivation for politicians more devoted to partisan advantage than the public good. According to this interpretation, issues and principles counted for little in political contention, and few real differences existed between the Republicans and the Democrats, who dominated elections and office-holding. Over the years scholars sought to outdo one another in censuring the Gilded Age in the most derogatory terms; it was, they said, an age of "negation," "cynicism," and "excess"—a "huge barbecue" for politicos and robber barons that excluded poor farmers and laborers. . . .

What caused traditional historians and some modern scholars to take such a dim view of Gilded Age politics? To a considerable degree, this negative assessment originated in the jaundiced observations of late nineteenth-century critics who were outside the political system. In trying to explain the period, many historians have paid closer attention to these commentators' biting criticisms than to the words and accomplishments of politicians themselves. The very name that scholars assign to the period, the Gilded Age, derives from an 1873 novel of that title by Mark Twain and Charles Dudley Warner, which satirized politics as rife with corruption and fraud committed by self-seeking politicians. Historians have also been fond of quoting Henry Adams, whose insufferable arrogance doomed his own quest for a political career. Late in life Adams used his autobiography to strike back at the system that overlooked him, charging that "one might search the whole list of Congress, Judiciary, and Executive during the twenty-five years 1870 to 1895, and find little but damaged reputation." He could have added that his own prejudiced diatribes had done much to damage the reputations of others.

One of the most influential critics was the Englishman James Bryce, whose 1880s trip to the United States, resulting in his two-volume study, *The American Commonwealth,* led some Americans to label him the Gilded Age Alexis de Tocqueville. Bryce alleged that neither the Republican nor the Democratic party "has anything definite to say on . . . issues; neither party has any principles, any distinctive tenets . . . . All has been lost, except office or the hope of it." In reaching these conclusions, however, Bryce had come under the sway of Edwin L. Godkin, editor of the Mugwump journal *The Nation,* whose disdain for his contemporaries in politics was boundless and not altogether rational. Taking their cue from Adams, Bryce, Godkin, and other hostile contemporaries, many twentieth-century historians looked back with distaste at the politics of the last three decades of the nineteenth century.

Other historical sources, such as newspapers, have contributed to slanted interpretations. Most Gilded Age dailies and weeklies were intensely loyal partisans of one party and had nothing good to say about the politicians of the other. Their "news" pages as well as their editorial columns served up mixtures of vituperation, trumped-up charges of fraud and corruption, and downright falsehoods about the opposing party. Ohio Governor Joseph B. Foraker exaggerated only somewhat when he complained in 1885 that for some newspapers it was a "common thing to call the man with whom they do not happen to agree, a liar, a thief, a villain, a scoundrel, a Yahoo, a marplot, a traitor, a beast, anything and everything they may be able to command in the way of an epithet." One study shows that a movement for "independent" journalism in the 1870s led zealous reporters to produce stories about politicians that were often scurrilous and sometimes wholly imaginary. Scholars' later reliance on these biased journals as sources contributed to their overall negative impression of politics in the period.

Investigations in Congress had a similar effect. At times the party in control of the House or the Senate used committee hearings or other legislative reports to discredit actions or doctrines of the opposing party. As an American diplomat in Paris wrote home to a senator in 1876, "The fury of 'investigation' in Washington has reached such a stage that it is something like the days of the French Revolution when it was enough to cry 'suspect' and the man was ruined." Often rooted more in partisanship than reality, these inquiries seemed to lend an official authentication to charges that, when taken together, have led historians to see the period's politics in the worst possible light.

This problem of skewed sources has been compounded by the tendency of some scholars to read back into the period modern values concerning government activism. In the words of Geoffrey Blodgett, such historians exhibit "a profound impatience with the Gilded Age for having not yet discovered the Welfare State." Today the idea that the government is responsible for the nation's economic growth and the citizens' well-being is widely accepted, but in the late nineteenth century most people clung to the traditional notion that good government meant limited government. Its main purpose was to maintain order and protect persons and property. Most citizens would have resisted the redistributive tendency of many twentieth-century economic policies as a perversion of governmental power. Moreover, allegations of corrupt purposes by government officials, whether true or not, evoked calls for retrenchment and aroused suspicion of government in general that inhibited the espousal, let alone the enactment, of positive programs. The cry of "Job!" greeted many legitimate and worthwhile proposals, particularly those involving subsidies or other expenditures of money. The resulting climate of distrust reinforced among voters a small-government notion that restrained leaders who might have taken more aggressive action but who also wished to win elections. As one congressman who lost reelection in 1868 stated, "My opponent is . . . a popular because a negative man." In 1890 the Republican majority in Congress passed an extraordinary number of important laws, with the result that the party lost overwhelmingly in the congressional elections that year. Lack of achievement is one of the principal failings that scholars have alleged about Gilded Age governance. In reality, leaders accomplished more than historians used to give them credit for, but they often did so in spite of the limitations placed on them by an essentially conservative electorate.

Divided control of the national government also slowed the formulation and adoption of policy. Between 1875 and 1897 each major party held the presidency and a clear majority in both houses of Congress for only a single two-year period, the Republicans in 1889–1891 and the Democrats in 1893–1895. During most of this era, Congress was divided, the Democrats more often than not controlling the House of Representatives and the Republicans usually holding a majority in the Senate. These divisions made the passage of legislation difficult. Each of the seven Congresses between 1875 and 1889, on the average, enacted only 317 public laws. But in the 51st Congress (1889–1891), when Republican President Benjamin Harrison worked with a Republican majority in both the House and the Senate, the number of laws passed shot up to 531, representing an unprecedented level of legislative accomplishment unequalled until Theodore Roosevelt's second term.

The balance between the parties in Congress mirrored an equilibrium between Republicans and Democrats in the national electorate. Except for Democrat Grover Cleveland's two terms, Republicans typically sat in the White House, but in four of the five presidential elections from 1876 to 1892 the Democratic nominee wound up with more popular votes than his Republican opponent. In 1880 defeated Democrat Winfield Scott Hancock trailed Republican James A. Garfield by less than half of 1 percent. A considerable portion of the Democratic votes came from former slave states which, after the end of Reconstruction, witnessed a widespread suppression of voting by African Americans, who nearly unanimously supported the Republican party. To take the two most egregious examples, in Louisiana the black population grew by 33 percent between 1870 and 1880, but from the presidential election of 1872 to that of 1880 the number of Republican votes decreased by 47 percent. In Mississippi the black population growth was 46 percent, and the Republican vote decline was 59 percent. Because of this denial of the suffrage, by 1880 the conservative, white Solid South had emerged, assuring the Democrats of a large bloc of electoral votes that year and in future presidential elections.

To counterbalance the South the Republicans could depend almost as surely on winning several states in the Northeast and the upper Midwest, but neither of these two blocs of sure states by itself held enough electoral votes to win the presidency. Hence, election results usually turned on the outcome in a half-dozen swing or "doubtful" states, the most important of which were New York and Indiana. During campaigns, party leaders and committees focused their efforts in these

states, enlisting the aid of the party's best speakers and expending the largest proportion of campaign funds. In addition, the parties often chose residents from
doubtful states for their national tickets. Between 1876 and 1892 the two major
parties selected twenty nominees for president and vice president; eight were from
New York and five from Indiana.

One of the criticisms traditional historians leveled against Gilded Age politics
was that no real substantive differences divided Republicans from Democrats.
Here again, the equilibrium in party strength offers some explanation. With the
outcome of elections in doubt, party leaders and spokesmen saw the need to exercise caution in articulating party positions and were wary of getting too far ahead
of public opinion. Taking too strong a stand, even on a minor issue, might offend
just enough members of some group to bring defeat at the next election. In 1884,
for instance, the Republicans lost the presidential election after trailing in pivotal
New York by about one thousand votes out of one million. Contemporaries and historians alike could cite many factors, both ideological and organizational, any one
of which could have tipped the balance.

When scholars charge that Gilded Age Republicans and Democrats were
largely indistinguishable, they tend to apply an inappropriate standard. Historically,
American political parties have not been like those of European countries, with
starkly differentiated groupings of left and right. Instead, largely because victory
in the electoral college requires a majority rather than a plurality, major parties in
the United States seek broad consensus and try to make their appeals as wide as
possible, with the result that a considerable area of agreement often exists between
them. In the Gilded Age the even balance between Republicans and Democrats
simply reinforced their perceived need to avoid the fringes of political assertion.

Despite this need for caution, the major parties were not like Tweedledum and
Tweedledee, as some traditional historians have alleged. As several of the revision-
ists scholars have shown, important ideological distinctions existed between Republicans and Democrats. Certainly, each party had its internal disagreements and
inconsistencies, but overall they espoused philosophies and policies that clashed in
significant ways and offered voters real choices at the polls. Generally speaking,
Republicans placed greater stress on government activism, especially at the national
level, with the primary aim of fostering economic development. They welcomed
the nation's burgeoning industrialization and believed the federal government
should assist the process. In the words of Senator John P. Jones, "One of the highest
duties of Government is the adoption of such economic policy as may encourage
and develop every industry to which the soil and climate of the country are adapted."
As the period progressed, the protective tariff emerged as the centerpiece of the
Republicans' economic program. Democrats, on the other hand, tended to cling to
their party's traditional belief in small government and states' rights. They criticized elements in the Republicans' program as favoring special interests. With its
low-tariff wing from the agrarian, largely preindustrial South still looming large,
the Democratic party continued its decades-old opposition to tariff protectionism.
In pursuit of their goals Republicans read the Constitution broadly to find sanction
for national government action; Democrats' interpretation viewed federal power as
more restricted. In the past generation modern scholars have begun to recognize the
differences between parties that Gilded Age politicians knew instinctively. As the

Maine statesman James G. Blaine put it (in a somewhat partisan fashion) in his book *Twenty Years of Congress,* late nineteenth-century Democrats and Republicans displayed the same "enduring and persistent line[s] of division between the two parties which in a generic sense have always existed in the United States;—the party of strict construction and the party of liberal construction, the party of State Rights and the party of National Supremacy, the party of stinted revenue and restricted expenditure and the party of generous income with its wise application to public improvement."

At the state and local levels Republicans again were more willing to resort to government action for what they perceived to be the good of society. They were more likely than Democrats to advocate restrictions on the consumption of alcohol, although many Republicans approached the question warily, fearful of repelling blocs of voters, such as German Americans or Irish Americans, who resented such interference in their personal lives. Similarly, Republicans were more inclined to favor measures to hasten the assimilation of immigrants, such as requiring the use of the English language in parochial schools. Again, Democrats tended to oppose such paternalism. In the past few decades several historians, using quantitative methods to measure voter reaction to such issues, have argued that ethnic and religious distinctions lay at the root of party affiliation. In this view, voters from pietistic, evangelical Protestant denominations tended to favor the moralistic stewardship associated with the Republicans, while liturgical, ritualistic sects, especially Roman Catholics, found comfort in the Democrats' defense of individuals' private lives.

Not all citizens felt well-served by either of the two major parties, and the period witnessed occasional third-party campaigns. In 1872 a group of Republicans, primarily well-educated, economically independent professionals and businessmen, bolted their party. Disenchanted with the policies and administrative style of President Ulysses S. Grant, these self-proclaimed Liberal Republicans mounted an effort to block his reelection. Their nominee, Horace Greeley, won endorsement by the Democrats, but he met the fate of most third-party candidates, a crushing defeat. The Prohibitionists, another group drawn mostly from Republican ranks, fielded presidential tickets every year starting in 1880. They reached their high-water mark in 1888 with just under 2.2 percent of the popular vote. The Greenback-Labor or National party, whose chief policy objective was the inflation of the currency, ran nominees for president from 1876 to 1884. They garnered their largest vote in 1880 with 3.36 percent of the total. They did manage to elect a few congressmen, their greatest success coming in 1878 with fifteen members of the House out of a total of 293. Occasionally these third parties were able to upset the calculations of major party leaders, especially in closely contested states. As Senator Benjamin Harrison noted in 1885, "I have little hope of making Indiana a Republican state with 4,000 Republican Prohibitionists and 8,000 Republican Greenbackers voting separate tickets." Even so, the possibility of such parties achieving power themselves remained virtually non-existent, and fringe groups, such as the Socialists, had even less chance.

The third party that came closest to moving into major party status was the People's party, or the Populists, in the 1890s. Historians disagree over the degree to which economic distress or other causes moved farmers to become Populists, but the party's rhetoric was heavily freighted with economic issues. Farmers found themselves increasingly caught up in a world market structure with volatile prices for farm commodities. A general downward trend in prices magnified the debt burden of farmers, many of whom had overextended themselves into regions of dubious agricultural productivity. Blaming their troubles on a variety of scapegoats, including railroads, manufacturing trusts, bankers, and the monetary system, many farmers were disappointed when the two-party system seemed unwilling to adopt their various proposals for relief. In 1892 the Populist presidential candidate, James B. Weaver, won over one million popular votes (out of twelve million cast) and twenty-two electoral votes. The Populists elected some members of Congress and achieved momentary success in some individual states and parts of states. In the nation as a whole, however, most voters, even in many farming regions, stuck with the two major parties.

Indeed, throughout the late nineteenth century the vast majority of voters stood by the Republicans or the Democrats, in congressional and state elections as well as in presidential contests. Moreover, whatever their motivation, party supporters went to the polls in huge numbers. In presidential election years over 75 percent of eligible voters typically cast ballots, a turnout rate far in excess of twentieth-century averages. In this sense the active political community in the Gilded Age was much broader than its modern-day counterpart. In another sense, however, the political community was narrower, for virtually everywhere women were denied the ballot, and in the South, after the end of Reconstruction, conservative white Democrats employed a variety of means to block voting by African Americans. But even with these egregious exclusions from the suffrage, politics remained a consuming interest to people throughout the nation, engaging the enthusiastic participation of millions of citizens.

What kind of leader emerged in this popular political culture? Among the most enduring stereotypes from the period is that of small-minded, grasping politicians who used public office mostly to serve their own interests, and often for their own financial gain, with little real concern for matters of policy or the public good. Recent research reveals a strikingly different portrait of the people who lead the two major parties, especially at the national level. Certainly, the idea of conflict of interest was underdeveloped and some politicians took bribes or otherwise engaged in corrupt practices, but in all likelihood no higher percentage did so than during most other times in the nation's history. Indeed, the zealous partisan quest for scandalous material about political opponents probably resulted in allegations of questionable conduct regarding behavior that in other eras might have been winked at or overlooked.

In reality many men who rose to be party leaders considered politics much more a financial burden than a boon. The pay of a congressman or cabinet member, for instance, while considerably above the wages of the average American, fell far short of what most such men could earn in private life. Moreover, the expenses that accompanied politics and government service diminished their finances still further. Typically, a congressman discovered that campaign costs ate up a year's worth of his salary. . . .

. . . The result too frequently was that only men of independent means or substantial wealth could afford or would accept such service. If, by the end of the century, Americans complained that the Senate had become a "millionaires' club," to some degree they had themselves to blame.

One compensation for congressional service was supposed to be the patronage power, the privilege of placing one's political friends and supporters in subordinate offices. Typically, senators and representatives from the party in power sent the president and other executive-branch officers recommendations of people to fill federal offices in their own states and in Washington. As a personnel program for the federal bureaucracy with its one hundred thousand-plus positions, this so-called spoils system was not without its own internal logic. With respect to governance, the system's defenders maintained that the president's policy aims would best be served by employees recruited from his own party and that he should gladly take the advice of senators and representatives who better knew the qualifications of applicants from their localities. On the political level, they argued, elections were won through the interested labor of a committed cadre of party workers, and rewarding such labor by the bestowal of appointive office was essential to the recruitment and maintenance of these cadres.

To many political leaders, however, dealing with patronage seemed more a punishment than a power. Yes, one might build a loyal core of backers from those who received appointments, but for each office, ranging from postal clerk to cabinet officer, a dozen or more applicants might press their claims, and as Senator John Sherman noted, "however wise may be the selection there will be many disappointments." Disappointing an office seeker might be politically damaging, but it could also be personally wrenching. As one Interior Department official wrote during the depression of the 1890s, "I have hungry men and women by the score coming to see me in the hope and belief that I can give them employment, and this has made my office here a burden. I cannot refuse to see them, and my inability to help them has come to be a kind of torture." On top of it all, politicians who recommended or who made appointments found themselves severely denounced by a growing civil service reform lobby that called for merit considerations over partisanship in the selection and promotion of government employees. . . .

National political leaders faced other vexations, not least of which was the sheer physical discomfort of working in Washington much of the year. "It is so terribly hot here that we can hardly live," one congressman wrote his wife in 1870. During the summer the mercury inside the House of Representatives frequently topped ninety degrees, even after sundown. In September 1888, Spooner described the poorly ventilated Senate chamber as "a box within a box." "I have been pretty nearly laid up with a headache for a week or ten days," he complained. "Hardly a man in the Senate feels well." Moreover, although committee chairmen had the use of their committee rooms as quasi-offices, most members of Congress received no office space beyond their small desks in the crowded chamber. They were thus forced to rent offices at their own expense or do most of their work in their living quarters. Similarly, a committee chairman enjoyed the assistance of the committee's clerk, but the typical member had no staff unless he hired and paid a clerk out of his own pocket.

Even with the help of a clerk, a member frequently felt overwhelmed by the work. In addition to the patronage burden, constituent correspondence was often heavy, and a member could delay answers to letters only at his political peril. Citizens expected their representative or senator to serve as their agent whenever they had business before the government, with the result that congressmen spent much time prowling the executive departments tracking down veterans' pensions, pushing claims, or otherwise advocating constituents' causes. Furthermore, with rare exceptions, members of Congress researched and wrote their own speeches, sometimes several hours in length. The work did not stop once a speech was given; a congressman who delivered a major speech or extended remarks during a day's session might stay up until two or three o'clock the next morning correcting the text for the *Congressional Record.* "It is up hill work all of it," one wrote to his wife in 1872, "and last night when I came home I could hardly draw one foot after another."

Over in the executive branch conditions were hardly better. In 1891 the second in command of the Post Office Department begged for another assistant, telling Congress, "I average at my desk—without a moment's absence from the building—more than ten hours a day, besides night work." Two months after leaving the White House, Harrison confessed, "There is nothing further from my mind or thought or wish than the resumption of public office. I was thoroughly tired and worn out." Possibilities for achievement by politicians did, of course, exist, and many posted creditable records. "But," as Senator George F. Edmunds noted, "whether their own lives have been the happier for such labor, with such inevitable trials and exposures, may be greatly doubted."

Grueling work, pay unequal to the labor, uncertainty of tenure—who would want such a job? Why would men pursue careers in national politics? Explaining the mystery of ambition lies perhaps more with the psychologist than the historian, but it seems clear that, like most successful politicians, men who attained positions of leadership in the late nineteenth century simply took immense satisfaction from being at the center of action and power. Garfield, a man of intellect with wide interests, frequently thought of leaving politics but could never quite bring himself to do it. After reading poet Ralph Waldo Emerson's book *Society and Solitude,* the Ohio congressman mused that "the calm spirit which [Emerson] breathes around him, makes me desire greatly to get up and out of the smoke and dust and noise of politics into the serene air of literature. Still," he confessed, "I suppose, if I were there, I should grow weary of the silence." In the words of Senator Spooner, "There is in public life . . . much that is burdensome and distasteful to a man of sensibility," and yet, "with it all there is a fascination about public life which I hardly know how to define but the existence of which is unmistakable." . . .

For most Gilded Age political leaders, their commitment to principle, as well as their personal ambition, was inextricably linked to devotion to party. They could not achieve their goals unless they gained power, which they could not do except through the agency of one of the two major parties. Leaders high and low, and many voters as well, displayed a dedication to party that bordered on zealotry. Even so level-headed a politician as Treasury Secretary John Sherman once confessed to a friend that the idea of the opposing party coming to power "haunts me like a nightmare."

Parties were nearly as old as the Republic. The emergence of mass politics earlier in the nineteenth century had led to the creation of partisan structures and methods that were well established by the beginning of the Gilded Age. In a general sense, party organizations served as the essential link between leaders, who formulated policy and governed, and the voters, who, with their own beliefs and notions, sought guidance and inspiration. In an age when politicians had no independent means for reaching masses of voters (such as television in the late twentieth century), the party constituted the essential vehicle for communicating with the electorate.

The traditional interpretation of Gilded Age politics held that in conducting their campaigns, politicians relied mostly on organizational techniques and machine management to win elections. Indeed, one important study labeled the era's political culture as "the triumph of organizational politics." Certainly, party managers perfected remarkably accurate advance polling schemes and created elaborate get-out-the-vote mechanisms, but close examination of politicians' behavior reveals that, in fact, they also placed great stress on the discussion of issues. The late nineteenth century saw a decline in the significance of parades, picnics, bonfires, rallies, and similar devices to ignite the emotions of the party faithful. More and more, political leaders turned to what they called the "campaign of education," appealing to voters on questions of government policy, especially those that affected citizens' economic well-being in an industrializing society. In the words of one campaign official in 1868, who was sending out tens of thousands of pamphlets to voters each day. "The people are intelligent and want something different from 'horrible caricatures and sensational trash.'"

Successful politicians came to realize that winning or retaining power rested largely on the flow of information to the electorate. Because communications technology had advanced little beyond the telegraph, they could reach voters only through public speeches or in print. Hence, in the months before elections, hundreds of state and national party leaders took to the hustings, speaking to audiences day after day for weeks on end, laying out their party's doctrines and appealing for support. For these men, the campaign season was a punishing time, filled with poorly ventilated halls or huge outdoor crowds, endless miles in jostling, dirty railroad cars, sleep deprivation, and indigestion. One campaigner reported to the Republican national committee in 1872 that "breathing railroad dust every day and speaking in the open air every night has played havoc with my voice. I am very hoarse and must lay up a day or two for repairs." By midcampaign that year the seemingly tireless James G. Blaine confessed that eight weeks of speechmaking had left him "completely worn out." Still, he and others returned to the task year after year, because they were convinced of the continuing need to appeal to what Blaine called the "will of the Sovereign People."

The closeness of elections heightened the possibility that vote buying or other forms of corruption could influence the outcome. It was a rare election that did not bring a barrage of allegations of fraud leveled by the two major parties against each other or by self-styled reformers and third-party losers against one or both major parties. Substantiating the myriad charges is difficult, however, and modern scholars disagree about the amount or the impact of election corruption in the period. According to one study, citizens who took money for their votes were relatively few in number and selected candidates from their own party anyway; those who sold their vote to the party that paid them more for it were an even smaller minority of purchased voters. Of course, in a close election even a small number of purchased "floating" votes could contribute to the result, but it is equally true that all the unpurchased votes—usually the vast majority—influenced the result as well. "The majority of voters," this study asserts, "were not bribed but, rather, voted for their party out of deep and long-standing loyalty."

Much more than bribery, legitimate campaign outlays represented a consistent and pervasive drain on party resources. Such expenses included the salaries of paid party officials and workers, travel expenses for campaigners, polling, outfitting headquarters rooms and public lecture halls, advertising, office supplies, postage, printing and distributing documents and textbooks, financial support for party newspapers, and on and on. In 1888, *Irish World* editor Patrick Ford itemized his expenses for organizing the Irish-American voters in New York City for the Republican party. Most of the funds went for salaries (district organizers, assistant directors, clerks, messenger boys, and so forth), but his list also included "Fitting Up 30 Ward Rooms" with such items as three thousand chairs at 35 cents each, banners and signs for each room at $25.00, and gaslight for each room at $3.00 per week for fourteen weeks. The total came to $73,465, and this was for only one portion of the population in a city usually carried by the opposing party. . . .

As the period progressed, parties looked increasingly to other sources of revenue, including economic interests that stood to benefit from the enactment of party policies. Traditional historians have referred to this sort of fund-raising as "frying the fat" from large capitalists who, in turn, expected subservience from the politicians, especially on issues affecting their businesses. In reality, the relationship was more complex. For one thing, there was no certainty that such contributions would be forthcoming. After narrowly losing his race for the presidency in 1884, Blaine complained, "I was beaten in New York simply for the lack of $25,000 which I tried in vain to raise in New York in the last week of the campaign. With all the immense interests of the tariff at stake, I don't think a single manufacturer gave $20,000. I doubt if one gave $10,000." . . .

Raising funds from business sources thus met with erratic success, and even when the party received such contributions, they did not automatically lead to businessmen getting what they wanted. James M. Swank, general manager of the American Iron and Steel Association, a strong backer of the protective tariff and always a big contributor to the Republican party, complained about the party's poor performance in the passage of the Tariff of 1883. "It is unfortunate," he wrote the chairman of the Senate Finance Committee, "that your Committee, in considering the Tariff Commission's schedules, did not invite a few leading representatives of the most important industries of the country to appear before it. The new tariff does not give satisfaction in many quarters." Swank and the iron and steel interests had to wait seven years, until the McKinley Act, for a tariff they found fully satisfactory.

Swank had been on hand in Washington for the hectic final days of congressional debate on the 1883 tariff, only to return home to Philadelphia disappointed and suffering from a severe cold and "physical prostration." His experience was not unusual and belies the stereotype of the overbearing lobbyist whipping politicians into line. The negative reputation of lobbyists notwithstanding, there was nothing inherently corrupt or even unreasonable in a legislator's listening to the recommendations of constituents and others affected by legislation. It was not unusual for a congressman to turn to such individuals as the only available source of information about a particular industry or interest. Moreover, politicians and business lobbyists frequently subscribed to the same basic views anyway. Senate Finance Committee leaders such as Justin Morrill, John Sherman, and Nelson Aldrich did not need Swank to convince them of the importance of tariff protection to further the nation's industrial development, although circumstances did not always permit them to enact their ideas.

More problematic were those instances in which congressmen came under pressure from conflicting interests. What was a senator to do, for instance, when woolen manufacturers urged a decrease in import duties on raw wool and sheep farmers demanded an increase? Consider the case of New York Senator William M. Evarts who, while Congress was considering the Interstate Commerce Act, received pleas from a Buffalo coal wholesaler "to render all the aid you possibly can to the passage of the Reagan Bill," and from a Seneca Falls pump manufacturer to "use your very best endeavors in killing this suicidal bill." American business interests, or "capitalists," were not a monolith, and a congressman obviously could not have a "sweetheart relationship" with both sides of diametrically opposed interests. . . .

In assessing the Gilded Age political universe as a whole, one might well ask: Was it wrong for citizens to have faith in their leaders? If not, why did not government accomplish more, especially at the federal level? In one sense, Americans got the government they asked for. With the major-party electorate evenly divided between Republicans and Democrats—leading to divided party control of the national government—stalemate often resulted. Yet, it would be wrong to dismiss the era as a whole as one of little accomplishment. The decades after the Civil War saw a shift in political concern away from the dominance of sectional issues toward questions of economic policymaking, with important implications for the evolution of government's role in the following century. When Gilded Age politicians tried to cope with the vexing and divisive currency issue, for example, they implicitly recognized that the government had a part to play in determining the country's money supply and, hence, the level of economic activity, a role that would be the essence of twentieth-century fiscal and monetary policy. The tariff issue had the power to touch people all across economic lines, and Congress's grappling with it was at its core a debate over what the government should do to promote prosperity— a question that continues to dominate policy debate to this day. Subsidies to railroads or other enterprises, often criticized as the quintessence of Gilded Age misfeasance, could be seen as an innovative approach to government/business cooperation in creating and modernizing the infrastructure of an industrializing nation. The late nineteenth century also witnessed the beginning of serious government regulation of business with the foundations laid down by the Interstate Commerce Act and the Sherman Antitrust Act, and the government began to police itself with the Pendleton Civil Service Act. Some scholars even see the government's pension program for Union veterans as an important antecedent for twentieth-century welfare policies.

Among the most important developments in the late nineteenth century was the growing strength and importance of the office of president. Having recovered from the blows struck by the attempted impeachment of Andrew Jackson and the scandals of the Grant administration, the presidency, by the end of the century, had become the center of the national political system. Historically, policymaking had been the province of Congress, but, more and more, presidents went beyond their traditional administrative role to act as legislative leaders on behalf of their policy objectives. By the end of the century, much legislation was being originally drafted in the executive branch. As with much else in American life, the 1890s brought an extraordinary transformation in presidential activism. At the beginning of the decade, Harrison employed a variety of means to achieve his ends: veto threats to influence the shape of legislation, well-timed messages and public statements to garner support, and informal dinners and other consultations with congressmen at the White House to push them in the right direction. Harrison's successor, Grover Cleveland, was in many ways a strong executive, but his ham-handed efforts to pressure Democrats in Congress frequently backfired and left him isolated from much of his party. McKinley picked up where Harrison left off. As a smoother, more skillful politician who saw the importance of cultivating good press relations, McKinley proved so effective as an administrator and legislative leader that recent scholars consider him the first modern president.

A strong national executive, with the president voicing citizens' concerns from the "bully pulpit," emerged as a defining feature of the Progressive Era that followed. In other ways as well the Gilded Age foreshadowed the Progressive Era, including the increasing emphasis on government activism to address economic problems and other issues and in the impulse toward reform. Progressivism was not merely the discovery of new purposes for government; it also represented the release of government activism from the restraining effect of the previous era's two decades of political equilibrium. One of the main reasons the Progressive Era started when it did was that the stalemate had been broken. Because the Republicans had established themselves as the majority party in the mid-1890s, President Theodore Roosevelt was freer than his predecessors of worries about perpetuating his party in power. Less fearful of frustration at the hands of historically obstructionist Democrats (many of whom were now taking on progressive ways of thinking), Roosevelt could move toward governing much more boldly.

The late nineteenth century witnessed profound changes in the United States. Scholars once treated its political life almost as an historical embarrassment, in Henry Adam's words, "poor in purpose and barren in result." Most historians now realize how inadequate that judgment was to describe this complex and portentous time, bridging the age of Abraham Lincoln and that of Theodore Roosevelt. In a rapidly evolving society, political leaders confronted problems of unprecedented intricacy and scope. That they were locked in partisan stalemate much of the time and frequently hamstrung by one of the major parties, the Democrats, who believed that Americans wanted less government, not more, often prevented vigorous action. Yet, they were able to post some modest success in reaching solutions to the society's problems. More important, leaders of a more activist inclination, including Republicans such as John Sherman, Benjamin Harrison, and William McKinley, glimpsed, if they did not fully appreciate, the broader possibilities for energetic government. In important ways they helped lay the groundwork for the twentieth-century American polity.

The Limitations of Sisterhood

ELLEN CAROL DUBOIS

In the 1850s and 1860s, divisive political conflict characterized most efforts of American feminists, but by the mid-1870s and on through the end of the century, these conflicts had lessened. During the Gilded Age, politically active women made a strong commitment to consolidation. Ideologically, women emphasized their similarities rather than their differences; organizationally, they emphasized unity over division. Women of the period tended to create multi-issue, all-inclusive, and non-ideological organizations that, at least theoretically, embraced all women and united them in a sisterhood dedicated to the elevation of their sex. The consolidation of women's reform efforts might be said to have begun with Frances Willard's assumption of the presidency of the Woman's Christian Temperance Union (WCTU) in 1879 and to have reached maturity with the formation of the National Council of Women and the General Federation of Women's Clubs, both in the late 1880s. By this time, suffragists participated enthusiastically in the move to unite women politically, consolidate them organizationally, and harmonize them ideologically. In 1890 the suffrage movement, which had divided in 1869, reunified into a single organization that foreswore all political distinctions among proponents of woman suffrage and welcomed all women, whatever their differences, to work for "the Cause." Even Susan B. Anthony, who had always gloried in a good factional fight, embraced this strategy. She displayed an excessive reverence for harmony in fighting for the suffrage and avoided any issue that would split the unity she was intent on building around the demand for the vote.

How real in fact was the harmony and consensus that seemed to predominate in late nineteenth-century feminism? Under the calm surface feminists presented to the world, there is evidence of a considerable amount of conflict, which their belief in the overriding importance of unity and dedication to the principle of sisterhood led them to obscure in the historical record. Here I wish to examine the ideas and experiences of the leading feminist dissident of the late nineteenth century, Elizabeth Cady Stanton. The quality of Stanton's thought is so extraordinary, so original and thought-provoking, that it is always profitable to examine her ideas closely. Moreover, in a situation in which she had to fight against a stifling ideological consensus to get a hearing, her insights and criticism were considerably sharpened. The issues that divided the late nineteenth-century women's movement—religion, sex, and family, and the role of the state in women's liberation—are critical for an understanding of the development of feminism. We can gain a perspective on our own situation by considering how feminists differed over these matters and how the relation of these issues to women's liberation has changed over the last eighty years.

Central to the conflict between Stanton and other leaders of the late nineteenth-century feminist movement were differences over the role of religion, especially

Christianity, in the oppression of women. Stanton had been a militant anticleric since she was a teenager, when exposure to secular and rationalist ideas helped her to recover her emotional balance after an evangelical revival. Politically, she was much more influenced by secular than by evangelical radicalism. Encouraged by Lucretia Mott, she read Frances Wright, Mary Wollstonecraft, and Tom Paine. In the 1840s she knew of and was influenced by the two leading secular feminists in the United States, Robert Dale Owen and Ernestine Rose. In the early phases of her career, she advocated reforms for women that these two had championed and that were generally associated with secular radicalism—the liberalization of divorce law and property rights for married women. Even Stanton's role in developing the demand for the vote, and the emphasis she placed on politics, is most comprehensible when we recognize the militantly secular and anti evangelical character of her approach to change, and her preference, throughout her career as a leader of American feminism, for political as opposed to moral reform.

In the 1860s and early 1870s, Stanton's interest in religion temporarily abated—perhaps because she concerned herself more with other reforms, perhaps because the clergy were less uniform in their opposition to women's rights, perhaps because women of orthodox religious belief were drawing closer to feminism. In 1878 Stanton's friend and political comrade, Isabella Beecher Hooker, held a prayer meeting in connection with the National Woman Suffrage Association convention and introduced pro-Christian resolutions at its proceedings. "I did not attend," Stanton wrote to Anthony, " . . . as Jehovah has never taken a very active part in the suffrage movement, I thought I would stay at home and get ready to implore the [congressional] committee, having more faith in their power to render us the desired aid."

In the early 1880s, however, she became convinced once again that religion held the key to women's oppression. What led to this reawakening of her interest in religion, and how did it differ from her pre–Civil War anticlericalism? Social developments in the United States, particularly the revival of crusading Protestantism, helped to alert her to the continuing hold religion had on women's consciousness. Postwar Christianity spoke less of hellfire than of divine love and, in part because of the growth of the women's rights movement itself, women were especially active in its spread. Indeed, one of the major avenues for the growth both of revivalism and feminism in the late nineteenth century was the Woman's Christian Temperance Union.

Stanton was also affected by political developments in England, where she went in 1882 to be with her daughter and lived, on and off, for the next decade. In England Stanton was involved with and influenced by many political movements— Fabian socialism, the movement to repeal the Contagious Diseases Act, the suffrage movement, and above all, British secularism. The continued existence in England of an established church meant that the secularist demand for separation of church and state remained a powerful political issue. Non-Christians still could not sit in Parliament, and blasphemy, which included antigovernment remarks, remained a civil crime. Stanton's diary in this period is filled with remarks about religion. Soon after she arrived in London, she gave a speech on the religious dimension of women's subordination to the progressive congregation of her old friend, Moncure Conway. "I never enjoyed speaking more than on that occasion," she wrote in her autobiography, "for I had been so long oppressed with the degradation of woman under canon law and church discipline, that I had a sense of relief in pouring out my indignation."

Stanton was especially impressed with Annie Besant, one of the foremost leaders of British secularism. Besant was a feminist and a sexual radical as well as a militant secularist. In 1878 she was arrested, along with Charles Bradlaugh, for distribution of a pamphlet advocating birth control. While the more moderate wing of the secularist movement held to ideas about gender and sexuality that were too genteel for Stanton's taste, Besant combined militant secularism with sexual radicalism and the kind of uncompromising individualism that had always been so important to Stanton's feminism. Stanton wrote of Besant, "I consider her the greatest woman in England." As a result of Stanton's experiences in England, as well as the impact on her of the American Protestant revival, her approach to religion in the 1880s was closely linked to her ideas about sexuality and to new questions she began to form about social coercion and state interference with individual development and personal freedom.

Stanton contributed to late nineteenth-century secularism by examining the impact religion had on women. She believed that all organized religions degraded women and that women's religious sentiments had been used to keep them in bondage. However, she concentrated her fire on Christianity, and on refuting the assertion, made in its defense, that Christianity had elevated woman's status by purifying marriage, spreading social justice, and insisting on the spiritual equality of men and women. On the basis of considerable historical scholarship, she demonstrated that the status of women in pre-Christian societies had been high, and conversely, that the impact of Christianity had been to debase and degrade the position of women. She also argued that historically the church had tolerated prostitution, polygamy, and other practices associated with the slavery of women. Christianity, she charged, excluded women from the priesthood and identified the deity solely with the male element. Finally, she argued that, with the Reformation, Christianity had abandoned what little respect it had retained for women, in particular the cult of the Virgin Mary and the existence of the religious sisterhoods. Given the confidence with which late nineteenth-century Protestants believed their faith represented the absolute height of human civilization, we can imagine that they found Stanton's assertion that Catholicism treated women with more respect than Protestantism especially infuriating.

Stanton's criticisms of Christianity's spiritual claims were closely related to her challenge to its sexual morality. She suspected that part of the explanation for Christianity's hold over women was the fact that it denied the power of female sexuality, while at the same time drawing on it in the form of religious passion. To her daughter she suggested that "the love of Jesus, among women in general, all grows out of sexual attraction." Stanton was particularly critical of the doctrine of original sin, which identified sex with evil and both with the carnal nature of women. This fear of female sexuality permeated Pauline doctrine, which treated marriage primarily as an institution to permit men to satisfy their sexual cravings without having to resort to sin. Stanton dissented from the idea, at the center of late nineteenth-century Christian morality, that the "civilized" approach to human sexuality was the establishment of a single, absolute standard of sexual behavior, a morality to which all individuals should be held. Stanton had always been suspicious of official standards of sexual conduct, but the debates of the 1880s and 1890s clarified her position and made her profoundly skeptical of the idea that a universal standard of sexual morality could be ascertained. Of one thing she was sure: sexual purity did not prevail under nineteenth-century Christianity. "There never has been any true standard of social morality and none exists today," she insisted. "The true relation of the sexes is still an unsolved problem that has differed in all latitudes and in all periods from the savage to the civilized man. What constitutes chastity changes with time and latitude; its definition would be as varied as is public opinion on other subjects."

On the basis of her interest in Christianity and its role in the oppression of women, Stanton began as early as 1886 to plan an ambitious feminist analysis of the Bible. She wanted to avoid treating the book as a "fetish," but to assess what it had to say about women's position "as one would any book of human origin." General developments in Biblical criticism, the publication in 1881 of a new revised version of the Bible, and the growing tendency of Biblical scholars to treat the Bible historically rather than metaphysically no doubt inspired her. Stanton's own opinion was that the Bible taught "the subjection and degradation of women." She realized, however, that other feminists interpreted its teachings more positively, and she genuinely sought to stir debate on the nature of the Bible's ethical teachings about women. Years before she had read Voltaire's *Commentary* on the Bible, which was organized in the form of selected Biblical passages at the head of the page, followed by Voltaire's own "arch skeptical" analyses. Stanton adopted this form, but proposed that the commentaries be written by several women of different opinions. The editors would then "add a few sentences, making some criticisms of our inconsistencies." "Our differences would make our readers think," Stanton wrote enthusiastically," and teach them to respect the right of individual opinion."

Stanton was genuinely surprised when most of the feminists to whom she wrote refused to join the *Woman's Bible* project. She had invited women with a wide range of opinions, including those "belonging to orthodox churches," and at first some of them showed interest in the idea. Ultimately, almost all refused to participate. The reasons they gave varied. Harriot Hanson Robinson and her daughter Harriet Shattuck, close political allies of Stanton for several years, claimed that they did not see why the project was important and doubted their ability to make any contribution of significance. Frances Willard and her friend Lady Henry Somerset withdrew their support because the project did not include enough "women of conservative opinion" and therefore could not "find acceptance with the women for whom we work." Even Anthony refused to cooperate on the grounds that a battle over religion would divert attention from the fight for suffrage. "I don't want my name on that Bible Committee," she wrote Stanton. "I get my share of criticism. . . . Read and burn this letter." Mary Livermore, who shared Stanton's goal of bringing the masses of women to more liberal religious ideas, also feared that any effort to which "the mad dog cry of atheist, infidel, and reviler of holy things" could be attached would do more harm than good. In part, what was at work here were different ideas about how to build and develop a social movement. Livermore thought that leaders should move their followers' ideas gradually, carefully, by persuasion and reassurance, always seeking to preserve ideological consensus. Stanton believed in the value of debate and conflict, in sharpening differences rather than muting them.

This leaves us with the question of why religion should be the source of such deep differences among late nineteenth-century feminists. What did Christianity signify, especially for those who revered the Bible and found Stanton's ideas objectionable? In the context of late nineteenth-century capitalism, surrounded by intensely competitive individualism, many reformers were drawn to Christian values as an alternative to the ideology of laissez-faire. Christianity represented to them a set of beliefs about loving and selfless conduct toward others that, if universally followed, would eliminate tyranny and injustice. "Wherever we find an institution for the care and comfort of the dependent and defective classes," Frances Willard explained, "there the spirit of Christianity is at work." Even to feminists, women were among the dependent classes, placed there by their maternity and the economic relation it put them in with respect to men. "That woman is handicapped by peculiarities of physical structure seems evident," wrote Ednah Dow Cheney, another feminist who objected to the *Woman's Bible,* "but it is only by making her limitations her powers"—her motherhood her glory—"that the balance can be restored." Thus, the most important Christian institution for the care of dependent classes was the family, and women were at its center—dedicated to the care of dependent children, while themselves relying on the protection and goodwill of men. Women's inescapable dependence is what made Christian morality so important to feminists: a common belief in Christian ethics was the only thing that would ensure that men treated women with respect and that the family functioned to protect women and children rather than permit their abuse. "The gospel of Christ has mellowed the hearts of men until they become willing to do women justice," wrote Frances Willard, the most impassioned preacher of feminist Christianity. "To me the Bible is the dear and sacred home book which makes a hallowed motherhood possible because it raises woman up."

While Stanton agreed with some of the elements of this argument—for instance, the practice of appealing to woman's position as mother of the race—at the most basic level she disagreed with this approach to women's emancipation. She believed that the task of the women's movement was not to assume women's vulnerability and to protect them from its consequences, but to so transform women and the condition in which they lived that they would no longer need protection, but would be fully independent. Even, while recognizing that the structures of inequality were very strong, she held to the classical feminist goal of equality and continued to emphasize the necessity of achieving it with respect to the sexes. Her most powerful assertion of these ideas can be found in "The Solitude of Self," her 1892 meditation on the relative importance to women's liberation of protection versus freedom, differences between the sexes versus similarities, and community morality and Christian ethics versus individual autonomy and self-determination. Christianity's message was "to bear ye one another's burdens," and Stanton granted that humanity would be better off if we did, but the point of her speech was "how few the burdens that one soul can bear for another." "No matter how much women prefer to lean, to be protected and supported, nor how much men desire them to do so," she explained, "they must make the voyage of life alone, and for safety's sake . . .

should know something of the laws of navigation." Stanton believed that the idea of safe dependence was an illusion for women for several reasons: because no matter how secure one's home life, how kindly the husband, emergencies arose and women had to be prepared to care for themselves; because each life was different, each woman had her "individual necessities" with which no one else could grapple but herself; above all, because the philosophical truth of human existence was the same for women as for men, "that in the tragedies and triumphs of human experience, each mortal stands alone." "The talk of sheltering woman from the fierce storms of life is the sheerest mockery," Stanton argued, "for they beat on her just as they do on man, and with more fatal results, for he has been trained to protect himself." Faced with these truths, the only security for women, as for men, was in full self-development. As a positive vision of women's liberation, Stanton stressed women's emancipation into the "infinite diversity in human character," the human condition that simultaneously distinguished each of us from the other, and is common to all of us, men and women alike.

These philosophical differences became political differences, and debates over religion became debates over government, as Christian reformers worked to introduce religious values into law and religious feminists sought to marshal the power of the government behind their idea of the family. By the end of the century, the idea that government should enforce Christian morality was becoming popular with reformers, as were proposals for Bible education in the public schools, legal enforcement of Sunday closings, a wide variety of sexual morals legislation, and—most hauntingly—a constitutional amendment recognizing the Christian basis of the American political system. The 1888 platform of the Prohibition party, for instance, called for Sunday closing laws and restrictive divorce legislation, as well as for antimonopoly and prolabor measures. Feminists played an important role in this Christian political movement. Their special concern was sexual morality legislation: social purity laws to raise the age of consent, strengthen the bonds of marriage, limit the number of divorces, censor obscene literature, and eliminate prostitution. Feminists involved in social purity politics included Mary Livermore, Julia Ward Howe, Anna Garlin Spencer, Frances Harper, and all of the Blackwells. The WCTU was especially active in social purity politics. Under the leadership of Frances Willard, it allied with Anthony Comstock, formed its own department for repressing impure literature, endorsed a constitutional amendment recognizing Christianity, and formed a department of "Christian citizenship."

Although Christian morality and social purity ideology dominated the late nineteenth-century feminist movement, these ideas did not go unchallenged. A minority of feminists—Matilda Gage, Josephine Henry, Clara Colby, and Olympia Brown, to name a few—tried to halt the interpenetration of feminism and Christian reform in the 1890s. Stanton provided secular feminists with leadership. Despite Anthony's urgings to keep conflict out of the women's movement, Stanton insisted on raising the level of debate and bringing feminists' differences into the open. At the 1890 suffrage unity convention, where pressure to present a united face to the world was great, Stanton's keynote speech challenged feminists' efforts to introduce Christian morality into civil law. "As women are taking an active part in pressing on the consideration of Congress many narrow sectarian measures," she declared, ". . . I hope this convention will declare that the Woman Suffrage Association is

opposed to all Union of Church and State and pledges itself . . . to maintain the secular nature of our government." She was particularly incensed over efforts to suppress all nonreligious activities on Sunday, especially the upcoming Chicago
World's Fair. She also opposed Christian reformers' attempts to make divorce laws
more conservative and divorces harder to get. She criticized both measures on the
grounds that they were destructive of individual liberty, especially for women. She
particularly objected to the suppression of individual choice when it came to divorce,
because women as yet enjoyed so little self-determination in matters of marriage
and sexuality. In contrast to her social purity opponents, she argued that liberal divorce laws were in women's interests, that more and more women were initiating
divorce, and that the obligation of the women's movement was to encourage this
development, not to repress it. "The rapidly increasing number of divorces, far
from showing a lower state of morals, proves exactly the reverse," she contended.
"Woman is in a transition period from slavery to freedom, and she will not accept
the conditions in married life that she has heretofore meekly endured."

Underlying Stanton's objections to the coercive character of social purity legislation was a growing concern over the uses of state power in general. Most late
nineteenth-century reformers, including most feminists, relied on a unified community faith, backed by the power of the government, for the creation of a just social
order. One has only to think of Edward Bellamy's *Looking Backward,* with its vision of a state-run utopia, where national government organized all aspects of social
life and met—one might say anticipated—all one's personal needs. While many reformers embraced this vision, there were those who saw problems with it. "The
spring of the [Bellamy nationalist] movement is the very best cooperation in the
place of the deadly competition of our so-called Christian civilization," William F.
Channing wrote Stanton. "But the spring is made to drive the wheels of a state socialism more arbitrary than the government of the czar or the Emperor William."
Stanton was of the same opinion. "All this special legislation about faith, Sabbath,
drinking, etc. is the entering wedge of a general government interference," she wrote
in 1888, "which would eventually subject us to espionage, which would become
tyrannical in the extreme." Stanton's concerns about the impact of Christian ideology on American reform politics are worth considering. The explicitly religious
dimension of this approach to reform soon faded, but its coercive and paternalistic
aspects remained and formed the basis of the most disturbing, undemocratic elements of twentieth-century Progressivism.

Stanton's ideas about religion and sex were not very popular in the late
nineteenth-century women's movement. In 1890 she was narrowly elected president of the National American Woman Suffrage Association (NAWSA), and two
years later she resigned, frustrated at the opposition she consistently encountered.
In 1895 she finally published the *Woman's Bible,* which only heightened the opposition to her leadership. At the 1896 suffrage convention, Rachel Foster Avery, corresponding secretary of NAWSA and one of Anthony's protégés, criticized the
Woman's Bible as "a volume with a pretentious title . . . without either scholarship
or literary merit, set forth in a spirit which is neither that of reverence or inquiry."
Avery recommended that the suffrage association "take some action to show that it
was not responsible for the individual actions of its officers"—Stanton was no
longer an officer—and moved that NAWSA disavow any connection with the

Woman's Bible. There was considerable debate: Charlotte Perkins Gilman, at her first suffrage convention, defended Stanton eloquently, but the resolution of censure passed, 53 to 41. The censorship left Stanton bitter. "Much as I desire the suffrage," she wrote in 1896, "I would rather never vote than to see the policy of our government at the mercy of the religious bigotry of such women. My heart's desire is to lift women out of all these dangerous and degrading superstitions and to this end will I labor my remaining days on earth." The low regard in which suffrage leaders held Stanton at the end of her life was carried after her death in 1902 into the historical record of the movement, through organizational histories and autobiographies, so that her historical contribution and her conception of the emancipation of women continued to be undervalued in the feminist tradition. There was not even a full-length biography of Stanton until 1940, in contrast to several written about Anthony within years of her death.

As a modern feminist, I find myself a good deal closer to Stanton's ideas about women's liberation, her focus on independence and egalitarianism, her emphasis on freedom rather than protection, than I feel to her social purity opponents. When I read "Solitude of Self" and ask myself what I think of it, I truly believe that Stanton's description of the dangerous, unpredictable, necessarily "solitary" nature of life describes what it means for women to leave the sheltered world of home and sexually stereotyped social role, each individual to find a way of life and a sense of self appropriate to her. It is interesting that the arguments of Stanton's feminist opponents—that religious values, a strengthened family, and a more uniform social morality offer women the best protection—are no longer put forward primarily by feminists. Although we can hear echoes of such ideals in some aspects of cultural feminism, Christian reform arguments are now primarily the province of the anti-feminist movement—the Moral Majority, the right-to-lifers, Phyllis Schlafly, and STOP-ERA. What are we to make of this curious development? On the one hand, the similarities between feminist arguments of the past and antifeminist arguments of the present should give feminists pause and make us think more carefully about just how precisely feminists represent all women's aspirations. Profamily politicians, for all their conservatism, are addressing aspects of women's discontent and offering visions of family and social reform that are attractive, at least to some women. There is no one solution to women's oppression; there may not even be one "women's oppression," and the history of women's efforts to reform their social position, to give voice to their discontent, is as complex a phenomenon as American reform in general, and as contradictory in its development.

At the same time, the appropriation of protectionist arguments by modern antifeminists is also a reason for optimism, a development on which feminists can pin historical faith. Nineteenth-century Christian feminists focused on women's weaknesses and vulnerability, and on the creation of safe environments and external power to protect them from exploitation and abuse. Given the position of the masses of women in the nineteenth century—economically dependent, unable to support themselves or their children, absolutely deprived of personal freedom, either sexual or reproductive—even the feminist movement could aspire to little more than this defensive and protectionist program on women's behalf. This no longer need be the case. Women's lives are no longer so completely circumscribed, at least no longer circumscribed in precisely the same ways. Modern feminist programs are much less protectionist as a result, women's goals much more libertarian and egalitarian. Once we understand that as the conditions of women's lives change, so do their visions of freedom, our approach to the history of feminism changes. We must study feminism's byways as well as its mainstreams, its dissidents as well as its representative voices; we must understand that our heritage is complex, so that we uncover the whole range of precedents on which we can draw.

 # FURTHER   READING

Paula Baker, *The Moral Frameworks of Public Life: Gender, Politics, and the State in Rural New York, 1870–1930* (1991)

Lois Banner, *Elizabeth Cady Stanton, A Radical for Woman's Rights* (1980)

John M. Dobson, *Politics in the Gilded Age: A New Perspective on Reform* (1972)

Ray Ginger, *Altgeld's America* (1973)

Richard Hofstadter, *The American Political Tradition* (1973)

Morton Keller, *Affairs of State: Public Life in Nineteenth Century America* (1977)

Aileen S. Kraditor, *The Ideas of the Women's Suffrage Movement, 1890–1915* (1963)

Don Lawson, *Famous Presidential Scandals* (1990)

Robert D. Marcus, *Grand Old Party: Political Structure in the Gilded Age* (1971)

Michael E. McGerr, *The Decline of Popular Politics: The American North, 1865–1928* (1986)

Mary Ryan, *Women in Public: Between Banners and Ballots, 1825–1880* (1990)

Lynn Sherr, *Failure Is Impossible: Susan B. Anthony in Her Own Words* (1995)

John G. Sproat, *The Best Men: Liberal Reformers in the Gilded Age* (1968)

Sally Wagner, *A Time of Protest: Suffragists Challenge the Republic, 1870–1887* (1988)

Richard E. Welch, *The Presidencies of Grover Cleveland* (1988)

CHAPTER
7

The 1890s:
Economic Depression
and Political Crisis

Beginning in May 1893, a financial panic touched off by rising farm foreclosures and railroad bankruptcies plunged the nation into serious economic depression; by the end of the year, seventy-four railroads and some six hundred banks had gone bust. During the four years of hard times of the Depression of 1893–1897, unemployment reached nearly 25 percent of the industrial workforce, and the figure of the "tramp"—a shaggy immigrant man riding freight trains from city to city seeking work—played upon public fears of disorder. Economic hard times led to wage cutting and other belt-tightening moves by employers, and this, in turn, touched off labor unrest. In 1892 the country's strongest trade union, the Amalgamated Association of Iron, Steel, and Tin Workers, fought and lost an epic battle against the Carnegie steel interest at Homestead, Pennsylvania, and Eugene V. Debs' fledgling industrial union of railroad workers, the American Railway Union, similarly went down to bitter defeat in the Pullman strike and boycott of 1894. In both cases, the workers' cause was crushed by naked government power in the form of troops and legal prosecution of strike leaders. Social tensions were likewise evident when public works advocate Jacob Coxey organized a march of the unemployed from across the country on Washington in March 1894. When a few hundred of Coxey's "army" reached the Capitol grounds, President Grover Cleveland had the leaders arrested and the ranks dispersed.

At the political level, the economic crisis gave renewed impetus to the Populist movement, a farmer-based cooperative and antimonopoly crusade, which had already established a strong organization base in the cotton South and among wheat farmers of the Plains and western states in the 1880s. The high point of political insurgency came in the formation of the People's Party in 1892. Demanding access to cheap credit for farmers through government granaries, nationalization of the railroads, an eight-hour day for workers, as well as the parity of silver with gold coin (or "free silver"), the third party secured an electoral base stretching from Texas to North Dakota and from Oregon to Kansas to North Carolina. The Populist challenge crested in the presidential election of 1896 with the crushing defeat of the fusion Populist-Democratic ticket led by William Jennings Bryan at the hands of Republican William McKinley. Yet if the frontal assault on the status quo was turned back, the restructuring issues raised in the Gilded Age would return with renewed vigor in the Progressive Era.

 D O C U M E N T S

The following documents neatly capture the polarization of social sentiments in the 1890s. Document 1 reports the experience of a Pinkerton guard who had been summoned to Homestead to protect the steel works in 1892 only to face the armed rage of well-prepared strikers. In Document 2, jailed ARU leader, Eugene V. Debs, analyzes the forces of the opposition to the workers' Pullman boycott, a joining of private and governmental power that would shortly turn Debs into the nation's best-known socialist advocate. Turning to the political wars of the period, Document 3 presents the Omaha platform of the People's Party of 1892, surely one of the most radical agendas of any political party seriously contending for power at the national level in U.S. history. Document 4, Bryan's "Cross of Gold" address, the most famous speech of perhaps the nation's greatest orator of all time, was delivered at the Democratic national convention in Chicago on July 9, 1896, in support of a free-silver plank in the party platform. In the Republican Party platform of the same year (Document 5), an effective counter-response to the populist message is laid out in an appeal to sound money, protectionist tariff policy, and a vigorous assertion of American trading rights abroad. In Documents 6 and 7 two cartoons from the commercial press offer further clues to the Republicans' effective demonization of Bryan's "Popocrat" alternative and recentering of public focus on their preferred issue of economic growth.

1. John W. Holway, a Pinkerton Guard, Views the Battle of Homestead, 1892

JOHN W. HOLWAY sworn and examined.

By the CHAIRMAN:

Q. Please state your name, age, residence, and occupation.—*A.* John W. Holway; 23½ years old; 1008 Twelfth street, Chicago; occupation, chiefly that of student. . . .

Q. Were you a member of the company that was sent by the Pinkertons to Homestead during the recent strike?—*A.* Yes, sir.

Q. What kind of a contract did you enter into at that time?—*A.* The contract was stated about this way, that in case we were injured we would not sue the company for damages, and that in case we deserted their employ at any time without asking their leave we would forfeit the wages which were then due us.

U.S. Congress, Senate, Report No. 1280. 52d Session (Washington, D.C.: Government Printing Office, 1893), 68–73.

Q. And on the other hand, what were they to do for you; what rate of wages was to be paid?—*A.* We were to be paid $15 a week and expenses.

Q. How many men accompanied you from Chicago to Homestead?—*A.* I judge there was 125. . . .

Q. Did you understand, when you left here, that you were to bear arms when you reached your destination?—*A.* No, sir.

Q. Did you anticipate it? *A.* From nothing that they had told us. I read the newspapers, and I formed that private opinion, but we received no such information from them.

Q. Were you given any arms of any kind when you left here? *A.* No, sir.

Q. Were you transported rather quietly and secretly from this point to Homestead?—*A.* The trip was rather a quiet one, and very quickly and secretly planned.

Q. Describe it, and give us the route you took?—*A.* We started out from the office on Fifth avenue and we went along the street to the Lake Shore depot, where we entered the rear entrance on the platform. Instead of going up to the regular passenger entrance we took the one the employés take, so we went into the rear cars of the train very quickly. Directly we entered the rear of the cars, men who seemed to be detectives and not patrolmen, stationed themselves at the doors, and they prevented our exit, and they prevented the entrance of any outside parties who might wish to enter. We then, on this regular midnight train, went to Toledo, reaching there about 9 o'clock next morning. At Toledo a special engine was hitched on to our three special cars, and we went by way of Sandusky, not through Elyria, and around to Cleveland. We did what was called "running wild." We ran rather slowly—it was not a scheduled train—on to Cleveland, and there they gave us some lunches, and we went as fast as 40 or 50 miles an hour through Painesville, down to Ashtabula. There we waited for an hour. . . . We then, the whole train, went rapidly on through Jefferson County to Youngstown, and from Youngstown to Bellview, where we landed rapidly. We were told to prepare to land—to leave the cars. During our trip we were not allowed to leave the cars at all, we were kind of prisoners. We did not have any rights. That might have been because they were afraid of union men, perhaps spies, who would telegraph ahead to Homestead. They wanted to get inside the works without bloodshed, but we had no rights whatever. Then we entered the boats, some 300 of us. There was two covered barges, like these Mississippi covered boats. One was fitted up with bunks that reached to the ceiling on the sides. I entered that and we supposed that we would be allowed to sleep, but we did not sleep for twenty-four hours, but Capt. Nordrum, the man in charge, told us to leave the boat with bunks in and go to the other boat, and we did so. We were told to fall in, and the roll of our names was called, and we were told to secure our uniforms, which consisted of coat, hat, vest, and pair of trowsers. When we had secured our uniforms we were some distance down the river, and we were told to keep quiet, and the lights were turned out, and everything kept very quiet until we were given orders softly to arise. I was lying down about an hour when the order was sent around the boat for all the men to get ready to land. Then the captain called out for men who could handle rifles. I did not want to handle a rifle, and then he said we want two or three men here to guard the door with clubs, so I said I would do that, and I got over the table and got a club like a policeman's club to guard the side door—that was to prevent men from coming in boats and jumping on to our barge from the river. I stayed there while the men who could handle rifles were marched down to the open end of the boat, and I did not see anything more of them until the firing commenced.

Q. Tell what further occurred as a matter of knowledge on your part?—*A.* I had a curiosity to see what was going on on the bank. I was stationed inside the boat at the side door, and as there were three or four other men afraid to carry rifles, they took upon themselves the duty of watching the door, and so I was told to go down to the other end of the boat to see what was going on, and I saw what appeared to be a lot of young men and boys on the bank, swearing and cursing and having large sticks. I did not see a gun or anything. They were swearing at our men. I did not see any more, but came back and resumed my position at the door. I had not been back more than two minutes when I heard a sharp pistol shot, and then there were 30, 40, or 100 of them, and our men came running and stampeding back as fast as they could and they got in the shelter of the door, and then they turned around and blazed away. It was so dark I could see the flames from the rifles easily. They fired about 50 shots—I was surprised to see them stand up, because the strikers were shooting also, but they did not seem to be afraid of being hit. They had some shelter from the door. They fired in rather a professional manner I thought. The men inside the Chicago boat were rather afraid at hearing the rifles, and we all jumped for rifles that were laying on a table ready, and some one, I think a sergeant, opened a box of revolvers, and said, "all get revolvers," so I had now a Winchester rifle and a revolver. I called out to see if anybody had been hurt, and I saw a man there apparently strangling. He had been shot through the head and he died sometime afterwards, I think. His name was Kline, I believe. Of course it rather made us incensed to be shot at that way, but I kept out of danger as much as possible.

I was standing there when Nordrum came up, and he said to follow him, and I crossed over to the New York boat, where there were 40 men with rifles standing on the edge of the boat watching what was going on on shore. Nordrum spoke to the men on shore. He spoke in rather a loud manner—say a commanding manner. He said: "We are coming up that hill anyway, and we don't want any more trouble from you men." The men were in the mill windows. The mill is ironclad. There were a few boys in sight, but the men were under shelter, all of them. I supposed I should have to go up the hill, and I didn't like the idea very well, because it was pretty nearly certain death, as I supposed. I thought it over in what little time I had, and I thought I would have to go anyway. While I was standing there, waiting for Nordrum to charge up the hill and we follow him, he went away, and he was gone quite a few minutes. I took advantage of that to look around the New York men's boat to see what was going on, and I saw about 150 of the New York men hiding in the aisle furthest from the shore. It was divided into bunks. They were hiding in the bunks—they were hiding under the mattresses; they didn't want to be told to shoulder a rifle and charge up the hill; they were naturally afraid of it. They were watchmen, and not detectives. Now the men who had the rifles were mostly detectives. There were 40 of the detectives, who I afterwards learned were regular employés of Pinkerton, but these other men were simply watchmen, and hired as watchmen, and told so, and nothing else. Seeing these men so afraid and cowering rather dispirited the rest of us, and those who had rifles—I noticed there seemed to be a fear among them all. I went to the end of the boat, and there I saw crowds on the bank, waving their hands, and all looking at the boat and appearing to be very frantic.

I judged we were going to have trouble and went back to the end where I had been placed and waited for Nordrum to come, but he did not turn up, and after I stood there about half an hour I concluded, as there was no one there to order us to do anything and as it was stated that the steam tug had pulled out, taking all those who had charge of us—I concluded I would look out for my life, and if anything was said about my leaving and not staying there I would say I did not intend to work for them any more; so I returned to the door I was told to guard, and in that place I stayed for the remainder of the day, during all the shooting and firing. I concluded if the boat was burned—we expected a thousand men would charge down the embankment and put us to massacre; that was what we expected all throughout the day—I concluded if the boat was burned I would defend my life with the other men. . . .

At about 3 o'clock we heard something; we thought was a cannon, but it was dynamite. Afterwards I learned it was worse than a cannon; sounded like a very large cannon. It partially wrecked the other boat. A stick of it fell near me. It broke open the door of the aisles, and it smashed open the door, and the sharpshooters were firing directly at any man in sight. That was about 3 o'clock. Most of the men were for surrender at this time, but the old detectives held out and said, "If you surrender you will be shot down like dogs; the best thing is to stay here." We could not cut our barges loose because there was a fall below, where we would be sunk. We were deserted by our captains and by our tug, and left there to be shot. We felt as though we had been betrayed and we did not understand it, and we did not know why the tug had pulled off and didn't know it had come back. About 4 o'clock some one or other authorized a surrender, effected by means of a medical student, who studies at the eclectic college over here, the most intelligent man on board for that matter, a Freemason. He secured a surrender. I don't know how he secured it— by waving a flag. We secured a surrender. What he wanted was that our steam tug pull us away, but instead of that the strikers held that we should depart by way of the depot.

That surrender was effected, and I started up the embankment with the men who went out, and we were glad to get away and did not expect trouble; but I looked up the hill and there were our men being struck as they went up, and it looked rather disheartening. . . . I ran down a side street and ran through a yard. I ran about half a mile I suppose, but was rather weak and had had nothing to eat or drink and my legs gave out, could not run any further, and some man got hold of me by the back of my coat, and about 20 or 30 men came up and kicked me and pounded me with stones. I had no control of myself then. I thought I was about going and commenced to scream, and there were 2 or 3 strikers with rifles rushed up then and kept off the crowd and rushed me forward to a theater, and I was put in the theater and found about 150 of the Pinkerton men there, and that was the last violence offered me.

2. Eugene V. Debs Denounces the Role of Corporations and the Courts in the Pullman Strike, 1895

Proclamation to American Railway Union*

TERRE HAUTE, IND., June 1, 1895.

Sirs and Brothers—A cruel wrong against our great order, perpetrated by Wm. A. Woods, United States Circuit Judge, has been approved by the United States Supreme Court, and from under its shadow I address this communication to you; but though prison walls frown upon myself and others whom you chose as officials, I assure you that neither despondency nor despair has taken the place of the courage which has characterized our order since the storms of persecution first began to beat upon us. Hope has not deserted us. Our faith in the future of our great order is as strong as when our banners waved triumphantly over the Great Northern from St. Paul to the coast. Our order is still the undaunted friend of the toiling masses and our battle-cry now, as ever, is the emancipation of labor from degrading, starving and enslaving conditions. We have not lost faith in the ultimate triumph of truth over perjury, of justice over wrong, however exalted may be the stations of those who perpetrate the outrages.

The Storm and the Battle

I need not remind you, comrades of the American Railway Union, that our order in the pursuit of the right was confronted with a storm of opposition such as never beat upon a labor organization in all time. Its brilliant victory on the Great Northern and its gallant championship of the unorganized employes of the Union Pacific had aroused the opposition of every railroad corporation in the land.

To crush the American Railway Union was the one tie that united them all in the bonds of vengeance; it solidified the enemies of labor into one great association, one organization which, by its fabulous wealth, enabled it to bring into action resources aggregating billions of money and every appliance that money could purchase. But in this supreme hour the American Railway Union, undaunted, put forth its efforts to rescue Pullman's famine-cursed wage slaves from the grasp of an employer as heartless as a stone, as remorseless as a savage and as unpitying as an incarnate fiend. The battle fought in the interest of starving men, women and children stands forth in the history of Labor's struggles as the great "Pullman Strike." It was a battle on the part of the American Railway Union fought for a cause as holy as ever aroused the courage of brave men; it was a battle in which upon one side were men thrice armed because their cause was just, but they fought against the combined power of corporations which by the use of money could debauch justice, and, by playing the part of incendiary, bring to their aid the military power of the government, and this solidified mass of venality, venom and vengeance constituted the foe against which the American Railway Union fought Labor's greatest battle for humanity.

---

*Issued when Debs' jail sentence for having participated in the Pullman strike was affirmed by the Supreme Court of the United States.

Writings and Speeches of Eugene V. Debs (New York: Hermitage Press, 1948), 1–2.

3. Populist Principles: The Omaha Platform, 1892

Assembled upon the 116th anniversary of the Declaration of Independence, the People's Party of America, in their first national convention, invoking upon their action the blessing of Almighty God, puts forth, in the name and on behalf of the people of this country, the following preamble and declaration of principles:—

The conditions which surround us best justify our cooperation: we meet in the midst of a nation brought to the verge of moral, political, and material ruin. Corruption dominates the ballot-box, the legislatures, the Congress, and touches even the ermine of the bench. The people are demoralized; most of the States have been compelled to isolate the voters at the polling-places to prevent universal intimidation or bribery. The newspapers are largely subsidized or muzzled; public opinion silenced; business prostrated; our homes covered with mortgages; labor impoverished; and the land concentrating in the hands of the capitalists. The urban workmen are denied the right of organization for self-protection; imported pauperized labor beats down their wages; a hireling standing army, unrecognized by our laws, is established to shoot them down, and they are rapidly degenerating into European conditions. The fruits of the toil of millions are boldly stolen to build up colossal fortunes for a few, unprecedented in the history of mankind; and the possessors of these, in turn, despise the republic and endanger liberty. From the same prolific womb of governmental injustice we breed the two great classes—tramps and millionaires.

The national power to create money is appropriated to enrich bondholders; a vast public debt, payable in legal tender currency, has been funded into gold-bearing bonds, thereby adding millions to the burdens of the people. Silver, which has been accepted as coin since the dawn of history, has been demonetized to add to the purchasing power of gold by decreasing the value of all forms of property as well as human labor; and the supply of currency is purposely abridged to fatten usurers, bankrupt enterprise, and enslave industry. A vast conspiracy against mankind has been organized on two continents, and it is rapidly taking possession of the world. If not met and overthrown at once, it forebodes terrible social convulsions, the destruction of civilization, or the establishment of an absolute despotism.

We have witnessed for more than a quarter of a century the struggles of the two great political parties for power and plunder, while grievous wrongs have been inflicted upon the suffering people. We charge that the controlling influences dominating both these parties have permitted the existing dreadful conditions to develop without serious effort to prevent or restrain them. Neither do they now promise us any substantial reform. They have agreed together to ignore in the coming campaign every issue but one. They propose to drown the outcries of a plundered people with the uproar of a sham battle over the tariff, so that capitalists, corporations, national banks, rings, trusts, watered stock, the demonetization of silver, and the oppressions of the usurers may all be lost sight of. They propose to sacrifice our homes, lives and children on the altar of mammon; to destroy the multitude in order to secure corruption funds from the millionaires.

Edward A. Stanwood, *History of the Presidency,* Vol. I (Boston: Houghton Mifflin, 1928), 509–513.

Assembled on the anniversary of the birthday of the nation, and filled with the spirit of the grand general and chieftain who established our independence, we seek to restore the government of the Republic to the hands of "the plain people," with whose class it originated. We assert our purposes to be identical with the purposes of the National Constitution, "to form a more perfect union and establish justice, insure domestic tranquillity, provide for the common defence, promote the general welfare, and secure the blessings of liberty for ourselves and our posterity." We declare that this republic can only endure as a free government while built upon the love of the whole people for each other and for the nation; that it cannot be pinned together by bayonets; that the civil war is over, and that every passion and resentment which grew out of it must die with it; and that we must be in fact, as we are in name, one united brotherhood of freemen.

Our country finds itself confronted by conditions for which there is no precedent in the history of the world; our annual agricultural productions amount to billions of dollars in value, which must, within a few weeks or months, be exchanged for billions of dollars of commodities consumed in their production; the existing currency supply is wholly inadequate to make this exchange; the results are falling prices, the formation of combines and rings, the impoverishment of the producing class. We pledge ourselves, if given power, we will labor to correct these evils by wise and reasonable legislation, in accordance with the terms of our platform. We believe that the powers of government—in other words, of the people—should be expanded (as in the case of the postal service) as rapidly and as far as the good sense of an intelligent people and the teachings of experience shall justify, to the end that oppression, injustice, and poverty shall eventually cease in the land.

While our sympathies as a party of reform are naturally upon the side of every proposition which will tend to make men intelligent, virtuous, and temperate, we nevertheless regard these questions—important as they are—as secondary to the great issues now pressing for solution, and upon which not only our individual prosperity but the very existence of free institutions depends; and we ask all men to first help us to determine whether we are to have a republic to administer before we differ as to the conditions upon which it is to be administered; believing that the forces of reform this day organized will never cease to move forward until every wrong is remedied, and equal rights and equal privileges securely established for all the men and women of this country.

We declare, therefore,—

First. That the union of the labor forces of the United States this day consummated shall be permanent and perpetual; may its spirit enter all hearts for the salvation of the republic and the uplifting of mankind!

Second. Wealth belongs to him who creates it, and every dollar taken from industry without an equivalent is robbery. "If any will not work, neither shall he eat." The interests of rural and civic labor are the same; their enemies are identical.

Third. We believe that the time has come when the railroad corporations will either own the people or the people must own the railroads; and, should the government enter upon the work of owning and managing all railroads, we should favor an amendment to the Constitution by which all persons engaged in the government service shall be placed under a civil service regulation of the most rigid character, so as to prevent the increase of the power of the national administration by the use of such additional government employees.

First, *Money.* We demand a national currency, safe, sound, and flexible, issued by the general government only, a full legal tender for all debts, public and private, and that, without the use of banking corporations, a just, equitable, and efficient means of distribution direct to the people, at a tax not to exceed two per cent per annum, to be provided as set forth in the sub-treasury plan of the Farmers' Alliance, or a better system; also, by payments in discharge of its obligations for public improvements.

(a) We demand free and unlimited coinage of silver and gold at the present legal ratio of sixteen to one.

(b) We demand that the amount of circulating medium be speedily increased to not less than fifty dollars per capita.

(c) We demand a graduated income tax.

(d) We believe that the money of the country should be kept as much as possible in the hands of the people, and hence we demand that all state and national revenues shall be limited to the necessary expenses of the government economically and honestly administered.

(e) We demand that postal savings banks be established by the government for the safe deposit of the earnings of the people and to facilitate exchange.

Second, *Transportation.* Transportation being a means of exchange and a public necessity, the government should own and operate the railroads in the interest of the people.

(a) The telegraph and telephone, like the post-office system, being a necessity for the transmission of news, should be owned and operated by the government in the interest of the people.

Third, *Land.* The land, including all the natural sources of wealth, is the heritage of the people, and should not be monopolized for speculative purposes, and alien ownership of land should be prohibited. All land now held by railroads and other corporations in excess of their actual needs, and all lands now owned by aliens, should be reclaimed by the government and held for actual settlers only. . . .

4. William Jennings Bryan Scorns Advocates of the Gold Standard: The "Cross of Gold" Speech, 1896

And now, my friends, let me come to the paramount issue. If they ask us why it is that we say more on the money question than we say upon the tariff question, I reply that, if protection has slain its thousands, the gold standard has slain its tens of thousands. If they ask us why we do not employ in our platform all the things that we believe in, we reply that when we have restored the money of the Constitution all other necessary reforms will be possible; but that until this is done there is no other reform that can be accomplished.

Why is it that within three months such a change has come over the country? Three months ago, when it was confidently asserted that those who believe in the

W. J. Bryan, *The First Battle: A Story of the Campaign of 1896* (Chicago: W. B. Conkey, 1898), 199ff.

gold standard would frame our platform and nominate our candidates, even the advocates of the gold standard did not think that we could elect a president. And they had good reason for their doubt, because there is scarcely a State here today asking for the gold standard which is not in the absolute control of the Republican party. But note the change. Mr. McKinley was nominated at St. Louis upon a platform which declared for the maintenance of the gold standard until it can be changed into bimetallism by international agreement. Mr. McKinley was the most popular man among the Republicans, and three months ago everybody in the Republican party prophesied his election. How is [it] today? Why, the man who was once pleased to think that he looked like Napoleon—that man shudders today when he remembers that he was nominated on the anniversary of the battle of Waterloo. Not only that, but as he listens he can hear with ever-increasing distinctness the sound of the waves as they beat upon the lonely shores of St. Helena.

Why this change? Ah, my friends, is not the reason for the change evident to any one who will look at the matter? No private character, however pure, no personal popularity, however great, can protect from the avenging wrath of an indignant people a man who will declare that he is in favor of fastening the gold standard upon this country, or who is willing to surrender the right of self-government and place the legislative control of our affairs in the hands of foreign potentates and powers. . . .

Mr. Carlisle said in 1878 that this was a struggle between "the idle holders of idle capital" and "the struggling masses, who produce the wealth and pay the taxes of the country;" and, my friends, the question we are to decide is: Upon which side will the Democratic party fight; upon the side of "the idle holders of idle capital" or upon the side of "the struggling masses?" That is the question which the party must answer first, and then it must be answered by each individual hereafter. The sympathies of the Democratic party, as shown by the platform, are on the side of the struggling masses who have ever been the foundation of the Democratic party. There are two ideas of government. There are those who believe that, if you will only legislate to make the well-to-do prosperous, their prosperity will leak through on those below. The Democratic idea, however, has been that if you legislate to make the masses prosperous, their prosperity will find its way up through every class which rests upon them.

You come to us and tell us that the great cities are in favor of the gold standard; we reply that the great cities rest upon our broad and fertile prairies. Burn down your cities and leave our farms, and your cities will spring up again as if by magic; but destroy our farms and the grass will grown in the streets of every city in the country.

5. The Republican Party Platform, 1896

. . . For the first time since the civil war the American people have witnessed the calamitous consequence of full and unrestricted Democratic control of the government. It has been a record of unparalleled incapacity, dishonor, and disaster. In administrative management it has ruthlessly sacrificed indispensable revenue, entailed an unceasing deficit, eked out ordinary current expenses with borrowed

K. Porter, ed., *National Party Platforms* (New York: Macmillan, 1924), 201ff.

money, piled up the public debt by $262,000,000, in time of peace, forced an adverse balance of trade, kept a perpetual menace hanging over the redemption fund, pawned American credit to alien syndicates and reversed all the measures and results of successful Republican rule. In the broad effect of its policy it has precipitated panic, blighted industry and trade with prolonged depression, closed factories, reduced work and wages, halted enterprise and crippled American production, while stimulating foreign production for the American market. Every consideration of public safety and individual interest demands that the government shall be wrested from the hands of those who have shown themselves incapable of conducting it without disaster at home and dishonor abroad and shall be restored to the party which for thirty years administered it with unequaled success and prosperity. And in this connection, we heartily endorse the wisdom, patriotism and success of the administration of Benjamin Harrison.

We renew and emphasize our allegiance to the policy of protection as the bulwark of American industrial independence and the foundation of American development and prosperity. This true American policy taxes foreign products and encourages home industry. It puts the burden of revenue on foreign goods; it secures the American market for the American producer. It upholds the American standard of wages for the American workingman; it puts the factory by the side of the farm, and makes the American farmer less dependent on foreign demand and price; it diffuses general thrift, and founds the strength of each. In its reasonable application it is just, fair and impartial, equally opposed to foreign control and domestic monopoly, to sectional discrimination and individual favoritism.

We denounce the present tariff as sectional, injurious to the public credit and destructive to business enterprise. We demand such an equitable tariff on foreign imports which come into competition with the American products as will not only furnish adequate revenue for the necessary expense of the Government, but will protect American labor from degradation and the wage level of other lands. We are not pledged to any particular schedules. The question of rates is a practical question, to be governed by the condition of time and of production. The ruling and uncompromising principle is the protection and development of American labor and industries. The country demands a right settlement, and then it wants a rest. . . .

Protection and Reciprocity are twin measures of American policy and go hand in hand. Democratic rule has recklessly struck down both, and both must be re-established. Protection for what we produce; reciprocal agreement of mutual interests, which gain open markets for us in return for our open markets for others. Protection builds up domestic industry and trade and secures our own market for ourselves; reciprocity builds up foreign trade and finds an outlet for our surplus. . . .

The Republican party is unreservedly for sound money. It caused the enactment of a law providing for the resumption of specie payments in 1879. Since then every dollar has been as good as gold. We are unalterably opposed to every measure calculated to debase our currency or impair the credit of our country. We are therefore opposed to the free coinage of silver, except by international agreement with the leading commercial nations of the earth, which agreement we pledge ourselves to promote, and until such agreement can be obtained the existing gold standard must be maintained. All of our silver and paper currency must be maintained at parity with gold, and we favor all measures designated to maintain inviolable the obligations of the United States, of all our money, whether coin or paper, at the present standard, the standard of most enlightened nations of the world

Our foreign policy should be at all times firm, vigorous and dignified, and all our interests in the western hemisphere should be carefully watched and guarded.

The Hawaiian Islands should be controlled by the United States, and no foreign power should be permitted to interfere with them. The Nicaragua Canal should be built, owned and operated by the United States. And, by the purchase of the Danish Islands we should secure a much needed Naval station in the West Indies.

6. *Puck* Assails William Jennings Bryan and the "Popocrats," 1896

IN BATTLE ARRAY, — AND THERE S NOT MUCH DOUBT ABOUT THE RESULT.

To the nation's political establishment, the Populist coalition gathered around Bryan in 1896 represented an unholy conspiracy to undermine the foundations of domestic peace and security. Judging from the symbols invoked by the cartoonist, what was so threatening?

Cartoon from *Puck,* Vol. XL, Sept. 30, 1896.

7. McKinley Takes Credit for New Prosperity, 1900

In this poster, the McKinley reelection campaign linked sound money with jobs for blue-collar workers. By implication, what aspersions does it cast on the Democratic campaign of William Jennings Bryan?

Photo: © Bettmann/Corbis.

E S S A Y S

In the first essay, Professor Nell Irvin Painter of Princeton University neatly connects the various strands of 1890s social distress and political unrest, combining treatment of the Homestead, Pullman, and Coxey's Army confrontations with a focus on congressional monetary policy and the presidential election of 1896. In the second selection Michael Kazin of Georgetown University probes the political-cultural vision behind the Populist movement. Joining a Jacksonian-era antimonopoly critique to a currency radicalism that originated in mid-century by the Greenbackers, the Populists fashioned a moralistic appeal to the "commonwealth of toilers" to move beyond a society riven by class conflicts and interests towards a new social harmony. Kazin examines both the power of this message and its limitations, with special attention to alternative voter loyalties based on race, region, and the established logic of the two-party political system.

The Depression of the 1890s

NELL IRVIN PAINTER

The showpiece of American progress, the American steel industry in the valleys of the Monongahela, Mahoning, and Ohio rivers of western Pennsylvania, northeastern Ohio, and northern West Virginia, was technologically sophisticated and efficient. Millions of tons of steel and steel products—rails, armor for railroad cars and locomotives, machines and the machines that made machines (the crucial capital goods sector of the economy)—poured out of the steel region in quantities that rivaled Europe's total output. For Americans who prized progress, this industry offered a splendid symbol of modernity.

The plants of Andrew Carnegie turned out a quarter of the nation's steel production in the mid-1890s, but the industry was still competitive, divided among three or four large companies and several small ones. But labor conditions in the steel industry were exceedingly harsh. For less than subsistence wages, workers put in twelve-hour days and seven-day weeks. In 1892 wage cuts, the early manifestation of hard times, struck the heart of the steel region. A sensational strike at Homestead, Pennsylvania, in 1892 pitted the nation's largest steel producer against the nation's strongest trade union. The bloody struggle ended in military occupation.

Writer Hamlin Garland found the steel town of Homestead "squalid and unlovely," a place whose people seemed "discouraged and sullen." The hot, onerous, dangerous work of attending the gigantic furnaces of the Carnegie mills struck him as downright inhuman. Once every two weeks steelworkers switched shifts and worked a long shift of twenty-four hours, then had twenty-four hours off. Considering the hours and the extremes of heat and cold, Garland wondered after a tour of the open-hearth works how steelworkers survived.

A factory town on the Monongahela River a few miles upstream from Pittsburgh, Homestead was the site of the most modern steelworks in the country. Andrew

Nell Irvin Painter, *Standing at Armageddon: United States, 1877–1919* (New York: W. W. Norton, 1987), 110–140. Copyright © 1987 by Nell Irvin Painter. Used by permission of W. W. Norton & Company, Inc.

Carnegie—the "star-spangled Scotchman"—had bought the mill from Henry Clay Frick in 1882. Carnegie also owned twelve neighboring plants, at Beaver Falls, Duquesne, Braddock, Pittsburgh, and other nearby locations. The Carnegie Steel Company owned every facet of the business, from ore mining to steel distribution, a vertically integrated trust. Thanks to efficient management and the scope of operations, Carnegie's industrial empire made more than $40,000,000 in profits per year in the early 1890s.

During the 1870s and 1880s Carnegie had written about labor sympathetically, insisting that manufacturers should "meet the men *more than half way*" and that "the right of the workingmen to combine and form trade-unions is not less sacred than the right of the manufacturer to enter into association and conferences with his fellows." He said experience had taught him that in general at least, unions were beneficial to both capital and labor, which were natural allies. An apostle of identity of interest, Carnegie preached that cooperative effort served the interests of capital and labor simultaneously. During strikes in the 1880s he had advised Henry Clay Frick, now his plant manager, to bargain with strikers. But in the 1890s Carnegie strengthened his position in the industry and took a harder line.

Carnegie and Frick's adversary at Homestead was the Amalgamated Association of Iron, Steel, and Tin Workers, formed in 1876. At its largest—in 1891—the Amalgamated Association had more than 24,000 members. The best organized and strongest union in the American Federation of Labor, the Amalgamated Association had won a strike at Homestead in 1889. But in 1892 Frick decided to break the union. According to the Homestead managers, the union undermined efficiency by objecting to workers' being fired when laborsaving equipment was installed and by demanding that workers receive higher wages when productivity increased. The union "placed a tax on improvement," a Carnegie partner concluded, "therefore the Amalgamated had to go."

When the contract between the Amalgamated Association and the Homestead mill expired in June 1892, Carnegie was at his castle in Scotland, and he gave Frick a free hand. Carnegie remained in Europe, while Frick broke the strike and the union, using wage cuts as an entering wedge. Instead of bargaining when the union rejected his terms, Frick locked workers out and erected a fence that was eight feet high and three miles long, surrounding the whole property of the Carnegie mill from the railroad to the river. Topped with barbed wire, the fence had a series of holes in it that appeared to have been designed for sharpshooters. At the ends of the mill buildings, twelve-foot-high platforms supported electric searchlights. As much as the wage cut, Frick's fortifications angered the workers, who interpreted his refusal to bargain as arrogance. They saw his barricading the plant, which they called Fort Frick, as warlike provocation, which it was.

The lockout began on June 28. The workers immediately established an advisory committee and began patrolling the town and the riverfront. On July 2 the company discharged all workers, with the intention of bringing in 300 Pinkerton agents, a private police force, to protect the new, nonunion workers from attack as they came into the plant.

The Pinkerton National Detective Agency had served in similar circumstances since the railroad strike of 1877. For working people, Pinkertons had come to symbolize the tyranny of corporate power and strikebreaking. A mercenary army independent of local police and beyond the reach of local politics, Pinkertons protected strikebreakers (scabs) from strikers, a role in which workers found the agents careless and trigger-happy. In 1890 Pinkertons had killed five people in a railroad strike.

When the Pinkertons appeared the morning of July 6 on two covered barges, the discharged workers understood the plan and stormed down to the river to prevent the Pinkertons from landing at the mill. . . .

Throughout the day Pinkertons traded gunfire with workers, who had hastily erected barricades of pig and scrap iron. Workers fired upon the barges with rifles and a cannon and attempted twice to set the barges afire with a burning barge and a flaming oil-doused handcart. They threw stones, metal, bricks, and lighted dynamite at the barges, injuring several Pinkertons, some fatally. The Pinkertons continued to return the fire. As it became clear that the workers could neither burn up nor kill off the Pinkertons and that the Pinkertons could neither return to Pittsburgh nor land, a committee of union men arranged an armistice. The Pinkertons were allowed to land, but they had to run a 600-yard-long gauntlet of workers, beating and kicking them.

When hostilities ceased, nearly 150 of the 300 Pinkertons were injured; 9 steelworkers and 7 Pinkertons were dead. Most Americans, shocked at the bloodshed and the passion displayed by the workers, blamed the Carnegie management for provocation through wage cuts and the fortification of the mill. But this was not the end of the chaos at Homestead.

Governor William Stone of Pennsylvania sent 8,000 militiamen to the town in the middle of July to maintain order. Thanks to a tightening of discipline after the 1877 railroad strike, the Pennsylvania militia was the best drilled in the country at a time when state militia routinely served to protect strikebreakers and company property in labor disturbances. Once the militia occupied Homestead, new workers began to come to the mill, which resumed operations, department by department, on July 15.

The regular work force, convinced that Frick would not be able to find enough skilled workers to run a nonunion plant, continued to strike. They gained support when workers at the Carnegie plants at Beaver Falls and Pittsburgh struck in sympathy. But the Homestead mill's schedule grew more normal every day. Even an assassination attempt failed to remedy the deterioration of the strikers' position. On July 23 Alexander Berkman, an anarchist. . . , shot Henry Clay Frick, thereby creating the first sympathy for Frick in the whole affair. Berkman was quickly sentenced to twenty-two years' imprisonment, and Frick recovered speedily.

In September affairs in Homestead took a new turn. Scores of striking workers were indicted on 167 counts of murder, rioting, and conspiracy. Some charges were dropped, and workers were acquitted of others; but as soon as the first round of trials ended, thirty-five of the leading union men were charged with treason under a hitherto unused 1860 Pennsylvania law that transformed what has been assaults against an employer into crimes against the state.

Unable to make their bail, the union men languished in jail until the middle of October, when the jury found them all not guilty. By then the Amalgamated leaders had been immobilized and isolated from their men for three weeks while their legal costs mounted. Meanwhile, the leaderless steelworkers of Homestead watched with resentment as new workers, many black, took their jobs. The Amalgamated Association barred blacks, and strikebreaking was one of the few avenues through which black workers could secure what were, for them, well-paid jobs in industry.

The last of the soldiers left Homestead in the middle of October, leaving a legacy of intense bitterness and a demoralized work force. the Homestead tragedy, where sixteen men lost their lives and thousands lost their jobs, was the first of the tremendous labor upheavals of the 1890s, and it showed that a strong employer could break a union that was strong if the company could hire a mercenary police force and could count on the cooperation of the courts. A company wealthy enough to shut down operations for a time could eventually starve its employees back to work on its terms. . . .

. . . [H]ard times scarred every part of the nation. In the fall of 1893, as the depression made jobs scarce, groups of unemployed workers in the Far West who had taken to the road looking for work had organized themselves along military lines, calling themselves industrial armies or industrials. Numbering from 50 to 300 each, these tramp armies overpowered railroad guards and rode about on trains for free. They personified the problem of joblessness as well as their hope that a political democracy would provide economic democracy, which they saw as the chance to get paid for a day's work.

Jacob S. Coxey led the best known of the industrial armies. Coxey's Army, also known as the "Commonweal of Christ," set out from Coxey's hometown of Massillon, Ohio (20 miles south of Akron), on Easter Sunday, March 25, 1894, intending to reach Washington on May Day. Forty years old and by no means unemployed, Coxey was a self-made businessman worth $200,000 who wore costly, hand-tailored suits and bred horses. Despite his prosperous appearance, he had been a currency reformer for years, having left the Democratic party for the Independent-Greenback party and the Greenbackers for the People's party.

Coxey's remedy for unemployment was a pair of bills that he had had introduced in Congress in 1892 and 1894 and that had won AFL backing in 1893. The non-interest-bearing bond bill, recalling the Greenbackers, interconvertible bond of the 1860s and 1870s, never gained congressional support because bonds that paid no interest were a contradiction in terms. Coxey's good roads bill, intended to put the unemployed to work, attracted wider support, particularly from labor, Populists, and the unemployed. According to Coxey's proposal, Congress would issue $500,000,000 in paper currency (greenbacks) at the rate of $20,000,000 per month, which would pay the unemployed $1.50 per day for eight-hour days, building good roads throughout the country, and would provide work for all who applied. To lobby Congress on the good roads bill, Coxey led his Commonweal of Christ to Washington, calling his army "a petition in boots." . . .

The Commonweal of Christ, about 100 strong and led by a young black man carrying an American flag, set out in snow flurries on Easter Sunday. . . . Behind a trumpeter Jacob Coxey, his wife, and baby son—named Legal Tender Coxey—rode in their coach. From time to time the army sang songs such as "Coxey's Army Song," written by Commonweal member George Nixon, to the air of the Union army song "Marching Through Georgia":

Come, we'll tell a story, boys, we'll sing another song,
As we go trudging with sore feet,
    The road to Washington!
We never shall forget this tramp,
    Which sounds the nation's gong.
As we go marching to Congress.

CHORUS
Hurrah, hurrah, we'll sound the jubilee;
Hurrah, hurrah for the flag that makes you free;
    So we'll sing the chorus now,
    Wherever we may be,
While we go marching to Congress.

All along the way the army received generous contributions of food and shelter from working-class settlements hard hit by the depression, a fact that impressed even skeptical observers. In labor and populist strongholds the welcome was especially enthusiastic, and the marchers received assistance from the WCTU at several points. Greeting committees, bands, and hundreds of volunteers met the Commonweal at Homestead and Beaver Falls, Pennsylvania, where workers had confronted the Carnegie Steel Company in 1892. At Homestead the Commonweal reached its greatest strength of 600 men.

When Coxey's Army reached Washington at the end of April, it was only one of several industrial armies converging on the capital from every part of the country except the South. A small but extremely radical army had left Boston on April 22, and several armies had left midwestern cities like St. Louis and Chicago (which contributed a Polish army). The biggest and most troublesome armies for the authorities and the railroads came from the West. . . . Industrial armies left from Los Angeles, Tacoma, Seattle, Spokane, and Portland. But all the western armies faced difficulties securing provisions and crossing the great distances between the West Coast and Washington, D.C. Industrial armies from Montana, Colorado, and Utah commandeered trains and waged pitched battles with sheriffs' deputies, winning the fights but losing volunteers for lack of food. By the time the remnants of these western armies reached Washington, Coxey had long since attempted to present his views.

Coxey's Army had marched through the city, 500 strong, accompanied by Annie L. Diggs, a Populist organizer and lecturer from Kansas. On a splendid white horse Jacob Coxey's seventeen-year-old daughter represented the goddess of peace. . . . Coxey, his wife, and baby Legal Tender rode in their carriage. The parade had stopped at the Capitol, where Coxey had mounted the steps and removed his hat to speak. Before he could begin his address, two policemen had grabbed him. . . . Mayhem broke loose, and police began clubbing spectators. As their supporters had expected, Coxey and his lieutenants were charged with walking on the grass.

Various industrial armies continued to arrive at the Coxey campground during the late spring and summer, swelling the numbers to 800 in mid-May and to more than 1,000 in July. The demonstration ended on August 10, after authorities had broken up all the camps and scattered 1,200 men.

Jacob Coxey died in 1951 at the age of ninety-seven, still believing in his good roads scheme and feeling vindicated by the federal government's adoption of much of his program in the Civilian Conservation Corps and the Works Progress

Administration in the 1930s. By then few remembered Coxey, but in the 1890s his movement had alerted many who belonged to the middle and upper classes to the magnitude of unemployment and the desperation of the jobless. . . .

As catastrophic incidents succeeded one another without pause, the spring of 1894 permitted little leisurely reflection on the larger meaning of recent events for the evolution of industrial society in the United States. No sooner had the Commonweal of Christ marched into Washington than labor unrest flared up in Chicago, throttling rail traffic throughout the central section of the country. The Pullman strike precipitated such chaos that it was called the Debs rebellion, after the Indianan Eugene Debs, who led a union of railroad employees.

The pullman strike in Chicago shared four characteristics with other labor disturbances of the 1890s: A cut in wages during a depression precipitated a strike sharpened by long-standing conflicts; George Pullman and the Pullman company management dealt with workers arrogantly; government entered the struggle on the employers' side; and the strikers and the unemployed attacked railroad property with an angry ferocity. But in this hostile exchange the government in question was not the state of Illinois. The Democratic administration in Washington initiated governmental support of the Pullman company and other railroads in Chicago against the American Railway Union (ARU), led by Eugene V. Debs, who had served his apprenticeship with the Brotherhood of Locomotive Engineers. What began as a strike against one company ended as a war between workers and the combined forces of the U.S. Army and the General [Railroad] Managers' Association.

In the wake of the railroad strike of 1877—which in Chicago had pitted strikers and supporters against police in a four-day battle that killed 13 and injured hundreds—George Pullman had conceived his own remedy for unrest and built a model town for his workers near his Pullman Palace Car Company. Carefully planned, Pullman village was clean, orderly, rationally arranged, carefully maintained, expensive, and dry (no liquor allowed). Pullman's purpose was to inculcate what he called "habits of respectability," and he predicted that housing workers in uplifting surroundings would initiate "a new era for labor" free from strikes and unrest. The town of Pullman epitomized the hierarchical ideal.

But workers rarely remained in Pullman for more than a few years. They preferred living beyond the village limits, where rents were lower and they could do as they pleased, including taking a drink at a favorite saloon, unobserved by informers. Workers complained that foremen pressured them to live in Pullman and that when workers were rehired after layoffs, the residents of Pullman came back first. Resisting such pressures, Pullman workers stayed as briefly as possible in a town in which they constantly felt spied upon.

At the outset of the Panic of 1893 the Pullman company had cut wages an average of 28 percent, without cutting rents in Pullman village. As rents were ordinarily deducted from pay, workers sometimes received pay envelopes containing $1 or $2 for two weeks' work, even less than $1 on occasion. In May 1894 a delegation of Pullman employees had petitioned for the restoration of wages to their 1892 level, but as at Homestead, the company refused to bargain; within a week three members of the committee had been laid off. The Pullman workers called a strike and asked the American Railway Union to represent them. Led by Eugene Debs and organized by industry instead of by craft, the ARU failed to persuade the Pullman workers not to go out during hard times. When the Pullman workers steadfastly refused to call off their strike, the 150,000 ARU members supported them and stopped handling Pullman sleeping cars. The strike began on May 12, 1894. By the end of June rail traffic through Chicago had stopped, shipping was tied up from California to Ohio, and the shortages that resulted sent food prices soaring in Chicago.

The General Managers' Association, formed in 1886 by managers of twenty-four railroads centered or terminating in Chicago, backed the Pullman company fully. However, the association's most powerful ally, Richard Olney, the attorney general of the United States, formerly a railroad officer and lawyer, was not in Chicago. After he had authorized the deputizing of U.S. marshals, railroad companies deputized their own personnel, making company men into law enforcement officers of the United States government. On July 2 Olney obtained a blanket injunction ordering strikers back to work for having blocked the U.S. mails. Strikers denied that they were interfering with the passage of mail and continued the strike.

Seeing Debs as a demagogic leader of the ignorant and lawless and the strike as a prelude to class war, President Cleveland ordered U.S. troops into Chicago on July 3 to disperse the crowds that he contended were obstructing the mails. (They had scrupulously avoided obstructing the passage of mail.) Troops arrived on the Fourth of July, over the strenuous objections of the governor of Illinois, John P. Altgeld. At that point violence began in earnest. Crowds stoned, burned, and wrecked trains and fought in the streets with police, state militia, and the U.S. Army numbering 14,000.

The combined military forces brought the strike to an end on July 8, after it had spread to several states and cost 34 lives. Debs was convicted for contempt of court (ignoring the blanket injunction), and he served six months in a federal penitentiary.

What came to be called the labor injunction made striking, an activity that had not previously been defined as illegal, a crime—contempt of court. The use of labor injunctions triggered a torrent of criticism, not only from Populists and organized labor but also from liberals in the legal field. The injunction served on Debs and the ARU leadership was the best publicized early such response, but it was not the first. During earlier strikes in 1893 judges had enjoined "all persons generally" from striking, notably in Milwaukee in December, on the ground that strikes that threatened to hinder the operations of the corporation in question (a railroad) might damage company property and intimidate strikebreakers. In the Pullman strike the injunction effectively rendered all strike activity illegal. After Pullman, courts used the labor injunction widely to declare strikes conspiracies to interfere with commerce and thereby within the purview of the Sherman Antitrust Act of 1890.

Like the labor injunction, President Cleveland's dispatch of federal troops to Chicago over the governor's protests also proved controversial. On the one hand, college men joined militia companies, sharing the belief of one Harvard alumnus "that it was a necessary police force. Like almost everyone else I was totally in the dark as to the merits of the Pullman strike of 1894 which led me to enlist. I approved President Cleveland's intervention in that strike and for many years considered Governor Altgeld a very dangerous person."

On the other hand, others criticized the President if only for his flagrant overriding of states' rights. Henry George, who had voted for Cleveland in 1888 and had attended the Democratic National Convention in 1892, now sided with Governor

Altgeld. Accusing the General Managers' Association of conspiring to block the mails expressly to bring the federal government into the struggle, George blamed capitalists for seeking to increase the standing army for use against the masses "because the millionaire monopolists are becoming afraid of the armies of poverty-stricken people which their oppressive trusts and combinations are creating."

Eugene Debs saw federal intervention as decisive. The American Railway Union had challenged corporate power as never before, and the union would have won but for the managers' enlistment of federal courts and armies, he said in a speech following his release from the penitentiary. Debs termed this an "exhibition of the debauching power of money," which Americans were seeing more often than ever before.

Quickly realizing that the Pullman strike had effectively destroyed the 150,000-member American Railway Union, Debs concluded, as Terence Powderly had eight years earlier, that strikes were self-defeating. Strikers were economically vulnerable, particularly in the hard times that caused so many strikes, and unions could not control the crowds (many of whom were not union members but people angry at the rich) that furnished a rationale for military intervention. . . .

The 1890s had been a period of hard, hard times, political instability, and popular explosions that seemed to be harbingers of revolution. But as serious as the crises of the nineties had been, power relationships did not change radically. In part this was due to the removal of some of the unemployed who were so volatile a part of the masses. Europeans and Canadians who lacked work—their motive for coming here in the first place—simply went home. And in cases of labor unrest, like the Pullman strike of 1894, the federal government stepped in to undermine the bargaining power of organized labor and thereby curb serious challenges to the economic status quo. The army and courts of the United States attempted with considerable success to control strikes and related disorders through the use of labor injunctions and National Guards.

The Righteous Commonwealth of the Late Nineteenth Century

MICHAEL KAZIN

Jesus was only possible in a barefoot world, and he was crucified by the few who wore shoes.

—Ignatius Donnelly

On Washington's Birthday in 1892, hundreds of grassroots activists from all over the nation came to St. Louis to participate in a four-day Industrial Conference that concluded by launching a new political party.

This was not a unique occurrence. Third parties were common if not entirely respectable features of the frenzied political landscape of the late nineteenth century, which featured lavish pageants and the highest voter participation in American history. For two decades, critics of the Democrats and Republicans had been contesting national, state, and local elections under a diversity of banners: Prohibition, Greenback, Anti-Monopoly, Labor Reform, Union Labor, United Labor, Workingmen, and hundreds of local and state Independent parties whose very name denoted repudiation of the rules of the electoral game. Established politicians had grown accustomed to deploying whatever linguistic and legal weapons were needed—ridicule, repression, co-optation—to swat down these disjointed but persistently fractious challengers.

But the People's Party formed inside St. Louis's Exposition Hall appeared to be, at least potentially, a much broader vehicle than its predecessors, one capable of speaking to and for the millions of Americans who were alienated from the corporate order that had grown to maturity since the Civil War. The base of the party was among debt-ridden small farmers in cotton-growing regions of the old Confederacy and wheat-growing areas of the Great Plains, many of whom were members of the Farmers' Alliance that had begun in Texas in 1877. But Populist organizers reached out, with increasing success, to some of the most visible, active reformers of their time: to the middle-class, anti-saloon crusaders of the Woman's Christian Temperance Union (WCTU) and the Prohibition Party, to the urban workers of the Knights of Labor and the American Federation of Labor (AFL), to the saloon utopians of Edward Bellamy's Nationalist Clubs and the mostly working-class advocates of Henry George's single tax on land, and to Christian Socialists in seminaries and evangelical churches across the land.

To marshal such a grand coalition of outsiders required a meld of the kinds of discourse that were favored by pietists and producers, Catholics as well as Protestants. The central metaphor was salvation from an elite whose power appeared both monstrous and seamless. "There is a party that the people can trust," the journalist Henry Demarest Lloyd told a working-class audience in Chicago during the campaign of 1894, "because in the face of overwhelming odds, without distinguished leaders, money, office, or prestige, it has raised the standard of a principle to save the people." Such rhetoric attempted to bridge divisions bred of class, ethnicity, religious denomination, and prior partisan loyalties. Perhaps, by adhering to principle, the David of Populism would be able to convince enough Americans to join in toppling the Goliath of concentrated wealth and corrupt state power. But failure, warned activists, would guarantee the domination of the "money power" into a dark and distant future.

The reformers who came to St. Louis late in the winter of 1892 represented this hope and this fear. In the grandiose (and, in terms of gender, inaccurate) phrase of a sympathetic reporter for Joseph Pulitzer's *Post-Dispatch,* "Every man who sat in Exposition Hall as a delegate . . . believed in his soul that he sat there as a history-maker."

The meeting concluded with a unifying, inspirational moment to rival any in Gilded Age politics. A 61-year-old Minnesotan named Ignatius Donnelly—novelist, amateur scientist, professional lecturer, Roman Catholic, a man who had, for a generation, fueled the antimonopoly cause with his eloquent if somewhat eccentric energies—read the crowd of 10,000 his preamble to the conference platform. The document of twelve short paragraphs, as altered slightly for the party's first nominating convention in Omaha that July, was the pithiest—and soon became the most widely circulated—statement of the Populist credo.

"The conditions which surround us best justify our co-operation," began this "Declaration of Union and Industrial Independence." "We meet in the midst of a nation brought to the verge of moral, political, and material ruin." With the practiced modulation and cadence of a veteran (and sometime professional) orator, Donnelly made the indictment: "Corruption dominates the ballot-box . . . The people are demoralized . . . The newspapers are subsidized or muzzled . . . The urban workmen are denied the right of organization for self-protection . . . A vast conspiracy against mankind has been organized on two continents and is rapidly taking possession of the world." And what were the Democrats and Republicans doing to alleviate these "dreadful conditions"? They were ignoring them, to debate, yet again, about tariff rates, "a sham battle" that only demonstrated their venality and utter neglect of America's needs.

Having reminded the delegates of the urgency of their task, Donnelly turned to the solution. As befit the tone of republican jeremiad that he had established, he pointed toward the virtues of the past. The Populists would bring the nation back to its roots of egalitarian principle and the harmony of all social classes. Donnelly vowed, "we seek to restore the Government of the Republic to the hands of the 'plain people' with whom it originated. Our doors are open to all points of the compass. We ask all honest men to join with and help us." Then he quoted, almost verbatim, the preamble to the U.S. Constitution.

Finally, Donnelly underlined the moral and political basis for the Populists' proposals, a collection of demands he and other reformers had promoted for decades: a graduated income tax, the unlimited coinage of both silver and gold, government ownership of the railroads, and more. "Wealth belongs to him who creates it," Donnelly intoned. Putting the same principle in harsher, biblical terms, he quoted St. Paul: "If any will not work neither shall he eat." And, to fuse rhetorically the two halves of the potential new majority, he asserted: "The interests of rural and urban labor are the same; their enemies are identical." Then he sat down.

It was a remarkable performance. Donnelly had summarized both the deepest fears and the most profound hopes of his audience. He had represented their cause as both radical and conservative: they would expand the power of the state only in order to restore the glories of an earlier day. They would challenge the power of the corporate, upper class and its political handmaidens only in order to expose the multiple evils of class rule itself, an incubus that was defiling the American dream.

Following Donnelly, Hugh Kavanaugh, chairman of the platform committee, read out the short list of demands. When he finished, the huge crowd exploded. According to a sympathetic journalist in attendance, "Hats, papers, handkerchiefs, etc. were thrown into the air; wraps, umbrellas and parasols waved; cheer after cheer thundered and reverberated through the vast hall, reaching the outside of the building where thousands had been waiting [*sic*] the outcome, joined in the applause till for blocks in every direction the exultation made the din indescribable." No Populist candidate, no symbol in flesh of the reform upsurge of the 1890s ever had or ever would receive such an ovation. Cherishing principles over leaders, the men and women who had gathered in St. Louis set out to realize their mission.

The road to St. Louis had not been an easy one. The nascent producer coalition upon which the Populists based their hopes was an unstable amalgam of social groups and political organizations with clashing priorities. Small farmers anxious about their debts wanted to inflate the money supply; while urban workers feared a hike in the prices they paid for food and rent. Prohibitionists and currency reformers both opposed the big money but differed over which of its sins was primary—the peddling of drink or the constriction of credit. And socialist voices in all their variety—Christian, Marxian, and Bellamyite—were at odds with most unionists and agrarian rebels, who affirmed their faith in private property and the malleability of the class structure. Factionalism was a perennial feature of reform politics in these years; not until 1892 did most groups cease pitching their panaceas long enough to unite behind the same third-party ticket.

But, over the preceding two decades, these disparate bands agreed about two vital matters: what had gone wrong in America since Lee's surrender at Appomattox and why; and the urgent need for a messianic awakening to bring about the sweeping changes required. These commonalities made a grand coalition seem possible.

Ignatius Donnelly was speaking to every segment of the dissident throng when he evoked the misery of working Americans and blamed it on immoral men at the top. . . . The unprecedented size, market dominance, union-busting and price-gouging behavior of such corporations as Standard Oil, Carnegie Steel, and Southern Pacific Railroad led many late-nineteenth-century reformers to question the laissez-faire views which had previously seemed the best assurance that hard work would receive its just reward. Power was no longer married to principle.

All the movements that rose after the Civil War used a similar vocabulary of self-defense, of urgent fortification against elitist foes. Their different constituencies and programs aside, Greenbackers and Knights of Labor, Prohibitionists and Socialists, members of the Farmers' Alliance, and disciples of Bellamy and Henry George agreed that a national crisis was at hand, comparable to the one that had led to the Civil War. Their beloved America had been wrenched from the path of righteousness and the control of the majority. Only the courageous, strenuous action of ordinary citizens could win it back. . . .

The sharp disillusionment that followed the war bred a bumper crop of anger. . . . Reform activists typically believed that they, or at least their parents, had fought a ruinous war to repel an assault on their freedom and way of life. But the war had solved nothing. Worse, in its aftermath, a new group of oppressors had captured power—armed with wealth, technology, and foreign allies far more extensive than those the antebellum lords of either lash or loom had been able to muster.

In their wrath, Gilded Age insurgents made no mean contribution to the era's reputation for extravagant rhetoric. Erstwhile Republicans, whose old party had led the nation when the betrayal began, were particularly immoderate. Ignatius Donnelly came to Washington during the war as a Radical Republican congressman but left several years later, denouncing "the waste, extravagance, idleness and corruption" of the federal government and observing that "the great men of the nation dwindle into pygmies as you draw near them." The suffragist Elizabeth Cady Stanton, the prohibitionist Frances Willard, the financial reformer James Weaver, and the labor journalist Andrew C. Cameron had also been dedicated Republicans. They broke with the party of Lincoln because they believed it had deserted its founding principles of free labor and moral government in the rush to court wealthy industrialists—in Donnelly's words, "the cruelest of all aristocracies, a

moneyed aristocracy." These reformers dedicated (or, in Stanton's case, rededi-
cated) themselves to causes that required the same missionary zeal and certainty
that a momentous choice was at hand that had earlier motivated their actions as
abolitionists and/or Radical Republicans. In contrast, former Democrats . . . were
restrained and ironic; they had never expected the party of Northern factory owners
to serve the public interest.

For all grassroots reformers, the contemporary enemy bore many of the same
names Jacksonians had employed—especially "the money power" and "monopoly."
To these was added "plutocrat," a neologism all but unknown in the antebellum era.
By any name, central banks and investment houses were still the main culprits. But
now they were perceived as intertwined with large manufacturing concerns; men
like J. P. Morgan and Andrew Carnegie had . . . assembled a malignant force of unprecedented strength and unity of purpose. . . . The "money power" now signified a
nonproductive, immeasurably wealthy octopus whose long, slimy tentacles reached
from private firms on both sides of the Atlantic to grasp every household, business,
and seat of government. "The money monopoly is the parent of all monopolies—the
very root and essence of slavery," asserted labor's Andrew Cameron, underlining a
dread of bondage older than the republic itself.

It was the unsung Greenbackers, who, starting in the late 1860s, first made
elaborate arguments about the links between plutocrats and the low wages and lost
chances of many Americans. Then, amid the severe depression of the mid-1870s,
"the money power" trope was sprinkled generously throughout the speeches, articles,
and letters of millions of people who were seeking a way to stigmatize the unseen,
faraway forces that had such influence over their lives. When the term *capitalist*
was used, it normally referred to the men who controlled investment markets rather
than, as in the Marxist sense, to the employers of wage labor.

Curiously, such attacks never explained why "the money power" had shifted
from the advocacy of paper currency that had drawn Old Hickory's fire to a "hard
money" position that sanctified the gold standard. Clearly, what mattered, in each
case, was the monster's theft of honest labor and hard-won property, not the particular brand of financial fire it spouted.

The continuity from the age of Jackson is obvious. Like that earlier generation of rhetorical democrats, Gilded Age reformers could disagree about which
particular elite represented the greatest evil but were in accord on the immorality
of parasitic wealth itself and the need to educate all citizens to its dangers. Neither
Henry George's speculative landlords, the WCTU's liquor traffickers, nor Terence
Powderly's "industrial oligarchs" had amassed their fortunes through honest toil—
unless conspiracies to corner a market, to buy cheap and sell dear, or to debauch
tired laborers were to be considered honest.

This attack on the most successful men in American society could be crude, as
in Greenback oratory about "thieves" and "frauds," or brilliant, as in *Progress and
Poverty* (1879), Henry George's clear, passionate dissection of the woeful intri-
cacies of land tenure and industrial development. In fact, long, learned arguments
like George's against reigning economic orthodoxy were surprisingly popular.
Progress and Poverty sold well over a million copies. The traveling lecturers and
local editors of the Populist crusade delivered briefer but similar messages to audiences of small farmers and wage earners across the South and West. These political

circuit rides assumed "the plain people" would comprehend their sermons, which were larded with metaphors drawn from European history and ancient philosophy as well as the Bible, simply because it was in their self-interest to do so.

At the same time, insurgents often predicted that deliverance would have to come from a higher Power than the people themselves. "Revolution of some sort is not far off," warned Reverend George Herron, a Christian socialist, in 1895, "Either a religious movement, producing a revival such as the prophets dimly or never dreamed of, or blood such as never flowed will remit the sins of the existing order." In a plainer style, Jacob Coxey told his band of angry, unemployed followers before they set out on their small but well-publicized 1894 march on Washington, "This movement will either mark the second coming of Christ or be a total failure."

Christian language was ubiquitous among those who tried to knit together an insurgent coalition. Secular arguments alone could neither evoke the scale of the problem nor incite the upheaval needed to set it right. A new surge of Christian revivalism—the third Great Awakening in American history—provided the context. In the 1870s and 1880s, hundreds of thousands of Americans flocked to tent meetings featuring the enormously popular sermons of Dwight L. Moody and the music of Ira Sankey; missionary societies sprouted from nearly every Protestant denomination. A growing number of urban ministers argued that the Lord's Prayer and the life of Jesus taught the collective nature of sin; these social gospelers—whose most prolific figures included Washington Gladden, Walter Rauschenbusch, and George Herron—aimed to create a new community of altruistic souls and rejected the conservative image of the individual miscreant left alone to face divine wrath. Mass movements had the potential to realize a solidarity that would turn America away from the worship of Mammon. Purifying society mattered more than did personal piety. . . .

. . . Most insurgents used a Christian vocabulary because it was the only way they knew to speak with great emotion about ultimate social concerns. Few activists called bluntly for the "application of Christian principles to politics," as did the Prohibition Party of Maine. But the contrast with prominent elite thinkers at the time is striking. In the late nineteenth century, appeals to "science" and "reason" came far more frequently from social Darwinist intellectuals like William Graham Sumner than from the ranks of trade unionists, discontented farmers, and temperance advocates.

Thus, Gilded Age insurgents wailed that Mammon and hypocrisy reigned over God, man, and principle in every major institution from the church to the factory to the once hallowed places where laws were debated and passed. Their prescription for change was, in a sense, a reactionary one. Edward Bellamy, the railroad union leader Eugene Debs, and the journalist Henry Demarest Lloyd all called for a "counterrevolution of the people" to dismantle this alarmingly radical new system that had fastened on the American republic.

But defining "the people" created something of a problem. It was not enough to say that the majority of Americans belonged to what a Greenback propagandist called "the wealth-producing classes" and leave it at that. . . . [B]y the late nineteenth century, the nation's social demography had become fearfully complex.

Freed slaves and new immigrants from Eastern and Southern Europe and East Asia competed in the cities and on the land for work, property, and profits with those who had come earlier. How would the emerging producer coalition bridge gaps that were as much cultural as economic?

The path taken was a contradictory one, viable for a few election campaigns but ill suited to a movement seeking a long term constituency and a secure niche in the political landscape. On the one hand, activists tended to inflate their definitions of producer and labor into a grand abstraction that ignored most differences of income and occupation. In so doing, they negated, ironically, their own impassioned charge that a yawning social gulf had made America resemble the "two nations" that had always existed in places like Britain, France, and Russia. Insurgents denounced the misery caused by unemployment, low wages, and tight money. But the humanitarian impulse led few to criticize employers or property owners as a class. To envision a political force parallel to that which Jackson or Lincoln had once commanded, it was necessary to deny that unequal economic rewards for various "producers" might hinder the search for a just, permanent solution to America's troubles.

Therefore, the most compelling definition of class standing became one's politics. Any sincere fighter against monopoly and plutocracy, regardless of occupation or social status, was, in effect, a producer. Among the "platforms of labor societies" printed in a widely circulated 1886 book about grassroots activism were statements from a variety of third parties, organizations of self-employed farmers, and groups composed mainly of wage earners. Nearly every platform—whether from the Knights of Labor, Agricultural Wheel, or Anti-Monopoly Party—hailed the "industrial masses" or "working classes" of both field and factory and cursed their "plundering" enemies.

Under construction here was a moral community of self-governing citizens, not a conflict of economic classes. In fact, sympathetic local businessmen and professionals joined many local organizations of producers and sometimes served as their spokesmen. The Knights of Labor rarely allowed people other than wage earners to lead their local assemblies. But the Knights underlined the ethical core of their identity by barring only five groups from membership: bankers, land speculators, lawyers, liquor dealers, and gamblers. Such men (the gender was assumed) either preyed on human weaknesses or made a lucrative income without having to work very hard for it. Certainly, no sweat begrimed their well-fed countenances.

Divisions on moral rather than class lines did inspire short-lived displays of social unity against "monopolistic" foes. The entire towns that rose up against railroad corporations during the mass strike of 1877, the explosive creation of independent parties in the 1880s, and the regional successes of the People's Party in the early 1890s all demonstrated the potential that support for a class-inclusive producer ethic had to throw a scare into local and national elites.

However, there was a danger in such an appeal that had not been evident upon its creation earlier in the nineteenth century. First, its fuzziness and hortatory style were fairly simple to imitate; Democratic and Republican competitors—who shared ideological roots and ancestral icons with the reformers—could and did co-opt it, plucking the chords of antimonopoly while rejecting enforceable measures to break up or discipline big corporations. The very suppleness of their rhetoric prevented Gilded Age reformers from blocking the political competitors who wanted to put them out of business.

Second, the romance of producerism had a cultural blind spot; it left unchallenged strong prejudices toward not just African-Americans but also toward recent immigrants who had not learned or would not employ the language and rituals of this variant of the civic religion. Many insurgents who lauded the producer also stated or hinted that certain groups of people lacked the capacity to take on the monopolists in a sustained, ideologically stalwart way. This belief was clearest among unionists who asserted that "Slavs and 'Tally Annes' . . . Hungarians and Chinamen" were ignorant "black sheep" whom industrialists could easily manipulate and use to break strikes. "The republic cannot afford to have such ignorant animals within its borders," wrote one labor editor from Pittsburgh. . . .

. . . By the 1880s, sharp, derogatory references to "Asiatics" and "Mongolians" were commonplace in the literature of the Knights of Labor and Farmers' Alliances, which aimed to attract working-class support. *Breaking the Chains,* a serialized 1887 novel by T. Fulton Gantt that championed the Knights, featured one Chinese character, the clever and unscrupulous cook for an opium-smoking land speculator and army officer. "He was among the most intelligent of the Chinamen immigrating to this country when Asia first turned loose upon us her horde of filthy, festering degradation," wrote Gantt. "He was a slave Coolie. . . . Upon getting his freedom he determined to seek employment as a body servant to the wealthiest debauchee he could find."

That image of the scheming, amoral "Chinaman" starkly outlined the cultural limits of Gilded Age producerism. The regular performance of manual work was not enough to qualify one as a member of the laboring classes. As in Jackson's time, one also had to demonstrate a manly self-reliance, a refusal to defer to unjust authorities that was considered to be at the heart of Christian and American principles. Even a "most intelligent" immigrant from East Asia was still judged to be thinking and acting like a slave.

African-Americans recently freed from bondage could conceivably meet the test. But they had to eschew black nationalist sentiments, join white-dominated movements of workers and farmers, and avoid demanding a halt to the brutal regimen of Jim Crow instituted in the wake of Reconstruction. It also helped if blacks echoed the view that "Chinamen" naturally preferred submission to freedom, thus shifting the onus of dependency away from themselves. In 1879, a black coal miner wrote to a Greenback-Labor paper about "how divided the miners on the North and South railroad of Alabama are as regards a uniform price for mining coal. One would suppose that all emigrated from China or some other heathen country, to see the way they conduct themselves."

For two decades before the founding of the People's Party, then, insurgents were nurturing a language of bitterness and betrayal. Sentimental about the mythic, lost world of smallholders and artisans, they demanded that elites cease their financial manipulation and political corruption and allow the people to rule once again. Millions of Americans were drawn to this critique—as the great popularity of *Progress and Poverty* and *Looking Backward* testified.

As politics, however, it fell woefully short. In no national election from 1872 to 1888 did the combined votes of all alternative parties top 4 percent of the total. The People's Party offered the best and perhaps the last chance to convert antimonopoly sentiment into a winning strategy.

Leading Populists understood that collective anger, no matter how well articulated, was not enough. To transcend despair, champions of the producing classes had to appeal to the majority of citizens whose interests they were so fond of invoking. Social differences had to be submerged, controversial moral issues played down, and regional divisions overcome in order to build a truly national organization.

A concept of Americanism unsullied by Civil War rancor could help. Opening the 1892 St. Louis conference, Benjamin Terrell of Texas counseled delegates that "the eyes of the toiling masses are upon you and they are expecting a second declaration of independence." Leonidas Polk of North Carolina, a favorite for the new party's presidential nomination, received a standing ovation when he declared: "This meeting represents those men who are loyal to duty and loyal to country." And Polk, a former Confederate colonel (but never an apologist for slavery) took part in a ceremony that symbolically healed the sectional wound. Before the entire assemblage, he clasped hands with former Union Navy Commodore Van De Voort of Nebraska. A group of delegates then unfurled a huge American flag and waved it as the crowd cheered. Similar ceremonies of reconciliation were taking place elsewhere in the country as the nineteenth century neared its end—just as racial segregation was, not coincidentally, being written into law.

Also needed was a broad definition of "the people" that did not dull the term's producerist edge. Polk called on "the great Northwest, great South, and great West" to take over the government and right the economic balance upset by the financial powers of the Northeast. Orator after orator hailed "the toilers," "the industrial classes," and "farmers and laborers of the entire country" in a manner simultaneously vague and imbued with a muscular pride in manual production that men who worked for a living and were accustomed to voting for one of the two major parties could appreciate.

There were occasional hints of a more restrictive meaning. Terence Powderly of the Knights of Labor, himself an Irish Catholic, scorned new immigrants as "unfortunate" creatures whom good Americans "must educate year after year to prevent them from using bombs instead of ballots." But this narrowing of "the people" to earlier arrivals and the American-born apparently brought no protest. Few Populists were flagrant nativists. But all could applaud Powderly's implication that they were defending vital national interests "plutocrats" and their pawns in government were betraying. . . .

The Populists put forth a platform intended to satisfy a range of constituencies, only a few of which were already safely inside its fold. For debt-ridden agrarians, they promised an increase in the money supply, a ban on alien land ownership, and a state takeover of the railroads that so often made small farmers pay whatever they could bear. For wage earners, they endorsed the ongoing push for a shorter working day, called for the abolition of the strike-breaking Pinkerton Agency, and declared that "the interests of rural and civil labor are the same." For currency reformers and residents of Western mining states, they demanded the unlimited coinage of both silver and gold. Appended to the platform were such "supplementary resolutions" as a "pledge" to continue the healthy pensions already being granted to Union veterans and support for a boycott of a Rochester clothing manufacturer being struck by the Knights of Labor.

Except for the pensions (a Republican standby), this was an agenda neither of the major parties would support. But it clearly showed a desire to move away from the monistic nostrums that had gripped the competing battalions of reform for a generation. The defeat of planks for prohibition and woman suffrage at the St. Louis conference signaled there would be no open attack on cultural attitudes that separated Northern men from Southern men, and most Catholics from most Protestants. The Populists didn't just want to be heard, they wanted to win. Through a network of over 150 local newspapers (most in the South and West) and scores of skilled itinerant lecturers attached to the movement, the Populists articulated a shrewd synthesis of beliefs grassroots reformers and radicals had been writing, orating, and praying about for the past twenty years.

They first attempted to reconcile the contradictory truths inherited from antebellum and more recent champions of the common man. To keep faith with a proud (and consensual) lineage, Populist writers and orators repeatedly quoted one or more of the deceased icons of democracy. Perhaps the best practitioner of this was the popular Texas lecturer James "Cyclone" Davis. As he spoke around the nation, Davis kept the complete works of Thomas Jefferson—"the sainted sire of American liberty"—close to him on the podium. He often searched through them, as if they were scripture, for answers to audience questions about such issues as free silver and government ownership of the railroads. In a few Southern states, reformers called their new political organization Jeffersonian Democrats before adhering to the People's Party; similarly, in Kansas, the Abraham Lincoln Republicans provided one route out of the GOP. In such ways did insurgents express their hope that, with God's assistance, "the simplicity, the purity and the prosperity of the early days" might return.

To this end, classical liberal cries for individual freedom and against "artificial" restraints on economic competition were combined with a classical republican emphasis on the need to enhance public virtue and oppose corporate assaults on industrious communities. The interests of the self-aggrandizing property owner could thus coexist, rhetorically, with a nostalgic evocation of a past in which champions of the people had ruled for the good of the vast majority. As one perceptive historian comments, the Populists "tried to make use of their heritage without allowing themselves to be limited by it, to recreate with new policies a society of equal right for all and special privileges to none."

While not mentioned in the Omaha Platform, the traditional Protestant concern with upright behavior was woven throughout the language of most committed Populists. A party based among evangelical, rural churchgoers could not help speaking about vanquishing all agents of corruption—saloon keepers as well as plutocrats, secular urban sophisticates as well as dishonest public officials, and occasionally "English Jew bankers" as well as more generic financiers at home and abroad—on the way to the promised commonwealth. "The party was known as the party of righteousness, and such groups as the Germans feared for their Sunday cards and beer," writes one scholar.

Opponents of Populism were quick to criticize this tendency. Republican Senator John Ingalls of Kansas complained, baroquely, to a New York reporter: "The decalogue and the Golden Rule have no place in a political camp. . . . This modern cant about the corruption of politics is fatiguing in the extreme. It proceeds from the tea-custard and syllabub dilettantism of the frivolous and desultory sentimentalism of epicenes." But the fact that this interview helped the new party make Ingalls one of its first electoral victims testifies to the power of Christian moralism to motivate critics of an unethical status quo.

The senator's charge of effeminancy also indicated something more than his view (common among major-party stalwarts) that politics was just another form of war. Women played a role in Populism far beyond the incidental status accorded them in Democratic or Republican circles, before or after the Civil War. They organized revivalistic camp meetings on the prairies, spoke in public and wrote articles for movement newspapers, and extended female networks already established in the WCTU and local farmers' alliances. Most Populist women spoke of their actions as extensions of the domestic ideology and evangelical fervor that had propelled them and other female activists through decades of collective struggles since the 1820s. Swore one woman: "I am going to work for prohibition, the Alliance, and for Jesus as long as I live." A male journalist from the North Carolina Farmers' Alliance viewed that stance as a political necessity: "The ladies are and always have been the great moral element in society; therefore *it is impossible to succeed without calling to our aid the greatest moral element in the country.*" To battle the manifest corruption of the old parties, the tough, manly aspect of the producer ethic was thus temporarily suspended.

Morality, for Populists, meant the tacit (if not active) encouragement of state temperance legislation and even the eventual abolition of the "liquor traffic." It meant forcing nominally Christian candidates and officeholders to stop compromising with big business and urban machines and to stand up for policies that favored the meek and the exploited. The notion that a democratic politics must concern itself with the enforcement of ethical standards, both public and private, was integral to the appeal of Populism. Near the end of another century, we know how explosive that conviction can be, how difficult to confine its targets to one end of the ideological spectrum.

Unlike the call for a new moral order, the issue of race posed an acute dilemma for white Populists, particularly those in the powerful detachments of the cotton-growing South. Black farmers and tenants, over 90 percent of whom lived in Dixie, shared many of the economic grievances of white yeomen and suffered to a greater degree from mounting debts to furnishing merchants and landlords. It would have been foolish for the People's Party to neglect black voters, many of whom were unhappy with a Republican Party that no longer said or did much about racial inequity. Yet, the Populists had no chance to win statewide contests or presidential electors unless they also won over a plurality of white Democrats. And not a few of the latter, the majority constituency, would certainly have agreed with the sentiments of the upcountry Alabama farmer depicted in a later novel, who grumbled: "Them black bastards is takin' the food out 'n our mouths. . . . They're down there sharin' the good things with the rich while good white folks in the hills have to starve."

That almost all white Populists (Northern and Southern) shared the era's dogma about the desirability of Caucasian supremacy made the dilemma even more agonizing. How could they promise blacks enough to get their votes without unleashing fears of "nigger equality" that would send whites fleeing back to the "party of the fathers"?

The Southern Populists' solution was to appeal to blacks exclusively on matters of shared economic concern while assuring fellow whites that nothing resembling a biracial order was being contemplated. Thus, the segregated Colored Farmers' Alliance, led by the white Baptist minister Richard Manning Humphrey, grew when it attacked the crop-lien system but fell apart in 1891 after some of its members who were tenants waged an unsuccessful strike against white landowners, some of whom were Populists (which did not stop the lynching of fifteen strikers). Thus, Tom Watson risked the ire of Democratic mobs when he shared speaking platforms with black Populists and derided his opponents' manipulation of race: "The argument against the independent political movement in the South may be boiled down into one word—NIGGER!" But Watson also opposed any federal intervention to protect black voters, endorsed the Jim Crow laws that Populist and Democratic legislators alike were then passing in Georgia and other states, and hotly denied allegations that he had broken bread with a black ally.

Certainly, as many historians have argued, even a limited, tactical alliance with black Southerners was a dangerous, even heroic step at the time. But such an alliance did not represent a break with white Americans' racial beliefs or the social hierarchy they justified. By themselves, the Populists could not have transformed the color consciousness of the Southern electorate even if that had been one of their primary aims—which it never was. Black farmers and laborers, for their party, had to be extremely courageous to join a rebellion against the Bourbon Democrats who controlled the land, businesses, and local governments on which the very survival of African-Americans depended. But the Populists continued to assume, as had their Jeffersonian and Jacksonian forebears, that "the plain people" meant those with white skin and a tradition of owning property on the land or in a craft. Not surprisingly, most blacks did not accept the Populists' circumscribed offer and instead cast their ballots, where they were still allowed to do so, either for the party of Lincoln or for that of their ancestral overlords.

Of course, Populist speakers in every region devoted most of their energy to waging a zealous and skillful assault on corporate wealth. "Old-party debaters," wrote the historian John Hicks, "did not tackle their Populist antagonists lightly, for as frequently as not the bewhiskered rustic, turned orator, could present, in support of his arguments, an array of carefully sorted information that left his better-groomed opponent in a daze." Movement publicists were pioneers of the investigative morality plays Theodore Roosevelt would later disparage as muckraking. They gathered thousands of damning details, large and small, about trusts that secretly conspired to bilk the public and bribe politicians. In the mode of alternative economists like Henry George, Populist writers educated their audiences about securities and commodities markets, business organization, and international trade while never neglecting to draw a taut battle line. "The most distressing feature of this war of the Trusts," wrote the antimonopoly reformer James B. Weaver, in a 1892 tract entitled *A Call to Action,* "is the fact that they control the articles which the plain people consume in their daily life. It cuts off their accumulations and deprives them of the staff upon which they fain would lean in their old age."

As a counterbalance, the Populists argued that a stronger state could, if the electoral ground shifted their way, be the plain people's best ally—an enhancer of democracy instead of the servant of plutocracy. Weaver advocated "stringent penal statutes" against corporations that broke the law and a tax of up to 40 percent on any business controlled by a trust. The Omaha Platform called for "the powers of government" to "be expanded" and, in a revealing aside, named the postal service as a model because of its tradition of cheap, efficient, and absolutely egalitarian delivery. Party activists made clear they were not advocating socialism. In fact, they maintained that their reforms would improve not lower the status of the millions of Americans who owned small amounts of property.

At the same time, the Populists remained ambivalent about a more powerful state. The American icons the Populists worshiped had left no clear guidance on the limits of federal power. Jefferson and Jackson preached the virtues of a small, nonintrusive government and insisted on a literal interpretation of the Constitution. Yet the Louisiana Purchase and the Cherokee Removal demonstrated how elastic such pronouncements could be. Even Lincoln, who vastly expanded the federal purview to defeat the Confederacy, had never advocated a nationalized rail system or laws to end land speculation.

The Populists resolved their doubts in a pragmatic way. They spoke about the state as the creation and property of people like themselves. Greedy, tyrannical men had usurped that birthright; government power itself was not the problem. Everything depended on what kind of men with what ideas and ethics sat in the statehouse, the Capitol, and the White House.

In the elections of 1892 and 1894, the Populists thrust their well-crafted message into the cauldron of national politics. At first glance, the results seemed encouraging. In 1892, the presidential nominee James Weaver, a former Union officer from Iowa (Leonidas Polk, the Southern favorite, had died that June) gained over a million votes, 8.5 percent of the total. Weaver . . . won a majority in three states (Colorado, Idaho, and Nevada) and pluralities in two others (North Dakota and Kansas). Two Populist governors were also elected. In 1894, the party did even better. Its candidates won over 1.5 million votes; seven nominees for the House and six for the Senate were victorious, along with hundreds of state legislators. At the state level, the insurgents were not averse to tactical alliances; some of their victories were the result of a fusion with the weaker of the major parties—Republicans in the South, Democrats in the North. Nevertheless, the "producing classes" seemed, at last, to have found their national voice and to be striding forward to reshape American society.

But the image of mounting strength was an illusion. The People's Party scored all its wins in two underdeveloped regions—the Deep South and the trans-Mississippi West—whose white residents had long nursed an anger against the urban, moneyed East. Aside from knots of radical unionists in such cities as Chicago and San Francisco, the Populists had failed to reach the craft and industrial workers they hoped would be responsive to their message of producer redemption. Pleasing words alone could not bridge the gap between rural evangelicals and American-born city dwellers, a great many of whom were neither American born nor Protestant.

Agrarian "organizers looked at urban workers and simply did not know what to say to them—other than to repeat the language of the Omaha Platform," observes the historian Lawrence Goodwyn. Only radical workers who thought in strategic terms were willing to ignore the cultural gap, and they had little more success with the Populist standard than with earlier alternative tickets.

To break out of their electoral confinement, the Populists took a fatal leap into compromise. After the 1894 campaign, a large faction in the party began to downplay the more radical planks in the Omaha Platform (like state-run railroads) and to emphasize the inflationary demand for the free coinage of silver, which appealed to underemployed and indebted citizens in several regions of the country. Meanwhile, national Democrats, severely weakened by a serious depression that began in 1893, were reborn as Jacksonian scourges of "parasites" and "privilege." In 1896, the flagging party came out for free silver and nominated for president William Jennings Bryan, a former Nebraska congressman who had built his short political career on the foundation of monetary reform and cooperation with local Populists (Republicans being the majority party in his state).

In their own national convention that year, the Populists argued long and heatedly about whether to support Bryan or to keep to the independent road. But the outcome was never really in doubt. A majority of delegates chose the hope of partnership in a governing coalition of producers over the fear that their party was being seduced and destroyed. They asked only that the Democrats accept Tom Watson as their candidate for vice president instead of Arthur Sewall, the Maine shipping magnate who'd already been nominated. The request was curtly declined.

During the presidential campaign, the major parties fought, more pointedly than ever before, to control the symbols and definitions of patriotism. The Republicans . . . distributed millions of American flags, many of them at "flag days" organized to honor nominee William McKinley as the nation's protector of order and, amid a depression, its "advance agent of prosperity." The fusion ticket was likened to a Confederacy controlled by Socialists. As in 1861, traitors were gathering strength, "plotting a social revolution and the subversion of the American Republic," in Theodore Roosevelt's overwrought opinion. In the Midwest, where the election would be close, Union Army veterans, calling themselves "Patriotic Heroes," perched on a flatcar filled with battlefield regalia and rode against the rebellion one last time. "So pervasive was the Republican campaign," writes Lawrence Goodwyn, "that frustrated Democrats found it difficult to show proper respect for the national emblem without participating in some kind of public endorsement of McKinley." The most expensive campaign ever waged to that date was undertaken to save the nation from those who would destroy it in the name of reform.

Against this onslaught, the only response the underfinanced effort led by William Jennings Bryan could make was to protest that the Republicans did not represent the *real* America of farms and workshops. But the message had to be conveyed almost entirely through the spoken word; almost every urban newspaper outside the South backed McKinley. And Democratic cartoons displaying the flag with a field of moneybags instead of stars only confirmed that the opposition was setting the terms of the iconographic debate.

Bryan, with the help of a few Populist surrogates like the stalwart Tom Watson, did his best to redefine the electoral contest. It *was* a struggle to defend America, he said. But the assault was not coming from a half-crazed rabble but from the wealthiest men in the land—"goldbugs," "the idle rich," and the lawyers and politicians who did their bidding. Campaign buttons proclaiming free silver to be, unlike the Anglophiles' gold standard, "American Money for Americans" played a nativist variation on the same class-conscious theme.

The most radical Populists never supported Bryan; they correctly, if futilely, argued that fusion for free silver would condemn the third party's broad platform to irrelevance. "The Democracy raped our convention while our own leaders held the struggling victim," Ignatius Donnelly contended in characteristically, purple language. Yet even he could not miss the brilliant way the 36-year-old Bryan gathered under the rhetorical umbrella of the money issue both the Populists' cherished ideals and their favorite modes of expressing them: evangelical fervor; a broad, moralistic definition of producerism; continuity with the icons of democracy; the equation of Americanism with the interests of the common people; and the need for a popular uprising to cleanse the nation.

That synthetic skill is what made the "Cross of Gold" speech, first given at the Democratic nominating convention and paraphrased by Bryan hundreds of times in his 18,000 miles of barnstorming that summer and fall, such a powerful document— inspiring to many yet threatening to more. "Bryan . . . said nothing new," one historian points out; "he had made no profound argument which men would remember and cite later. He had said, however, what hundreds of delegates, inarticulate and mute, felt and believed."

Bryan's great speech framed the campaign in pietistic terms ("With a zeal approaching the zeal which inspired the Crusaders who followed Peter the Hermit" and with his final, unforgettable crucifixion image itself). He challenged the Republican claim to being the party of business—proclaiming that "the farmer who goes forth in the morning and toils all day" and "the miners who go down a thousand feet into the earth" were "businessmen" equal to "the few financial magnates who, in a back room, corner the money of the world." He declared, echoing Jefferson, that agrarian pursuits were more vital than urban ones: "Burn down your cities and leave our farms, and your cities will spring up again as if by magic; but destroy our farms and the grass will grow in the streets of every city in the country." He cited Jackson and Jefferson on the right of the people, through the government, to regulate the currency; and flayed those who allowed "foreign potentates and powers" to violate American sovereignty. Speaking to and for loyal citizens who once believed in the system, Bryan raged: "We have petitioned, and our petitions have been scorned; we have entreated, and our entreaties have been disregarded; we have begged, and they have mocked when our calamity came. We beg no longer; we entreat no more; we petition no more. We defy them!"

The barrier such eloquence could never surmount was that Bryan was, despite his leadership of the nation's oldest political party, a protest candidate. Voters who did not agree that America was gripped by crisis (or who defined "crisis" as the breakdown of social and political norms) tended to view the fusionists as advocates of an unpredictable, perhaps dangerous future, in which those who had organized Coxey's Army, waged the 1894 national railway strike, and talked, like Kansas Populist Mary Lease, about "raising less corn and more hell" might actually run the government. Moreover, Bryan's pietistic rigor and his criticisms of urban life chilled many Catholic workers and other city dwellers in the East and Midwest who usually voted Democratic. Thousands heard the Republicans promise not to disturb the nation's ethnic and religious heterogeneity and marked their ballots for McKinley. Bryan drew more votes than any Populist could have, but he had cast his lot on the same side of the cultural divide.

So the man who became known as the Great Commoner went down to the first of three national defeats, and the People's Party rapidly shrank from the spearhead of a social movement into an insignificant sect (before expiring in 1908). In the decades to come, many Bryan supporters—and their scholarly defenders—would speak of the election of 1896 as a negative millennium. It was, they believed, the pivotal defeat for the grand coalition of the industrial classes and a decisive victory for corporate America, an event that had never been revenged or redeemed.

In 1896, Vachel Lindsay was a teenager living in rural Illinois. In 1919, after the disillusioning struggle of World War I, he wrote "Bryan, Bryan, Bryan, Bryan," a long (and once widely read) poem that captures the blend of cultural resentment, regional pique, and producer antagonism that helped stoke the Populist revolt. Lindsay, chanted, in part:

> Election night at midnight:
> Boy Bryan's defeat.
> Defeat of western silver.
> Defeat of the wheat.
> Victory of letterfiles
> And plutocrats in miles
> With dollar signs upon their coats,
> Diamond watchchains on their vests
> And spats on their feet.
> Victory of custodians,
> Plymouth Rock,
> And all that inbred landlord stock.
> Victory of the neat.
> Defeat of the aspen groves of Colorado valleys,
> The blue bells of the Rockies,
> And blue bonnets of old Texas,
> By the Pittsburg alleys.
> Defeat of the alfalfa and the Mariposa lily.
> Defeat of the Pacific and the long Mississippi.
> Defeat of the young by the old and silly.
> Defeat of tornadoes by the poison vats supreme.
> Defeat of my boyhood, defeat of my dream.

Lindsay was not wrong to eulogize the insurgent agrarians whose spirit he had imbibed at the end of the nineteenth century. Small farmers would never again possess the numbers, the confidence, or the leadership to mount a national crusade capable of drawing in reform-minded Americans from other classes and fusing with a major party. But the significance of the People's Party transcended its own demographic and electoral fate. Through Populism coursed a rich, sometimes contradictory amalgam of dreams, demands, and prejudices whose expression, since the founding of the United States, had been indispensable to the making of democratic politics.

The People's Party stood at a point of transition for that language. On the one hand, it spoke out in pride and anger for the lost commonwealth of agrarians and artisans, the moral center of a society that had spun away from its once noble orbit. Wordsmiths like Ignatius Donnelly, Tom Watson, and Frances Willard may have been looking backward in order to vault ahead. But one cannot escape their yearning for a social harmony that could be glimpsed again only in Heaven. On the other hand, the Populists were forerunners of a more pragmatic style of expressing discontent. Blending the many hues of reform and radicalism into a single national organization, however short-lived, and maneuvering, however fatally, to take advantage of an opening at the political top demonstrated the zeal of missionaries armed with a sensible method. In the Populists' wake, activists from narrower but more durable movements would deny there was any contradiction between a faith in social progress and a defense of the hardworking people.

FURTHER READING

Robert A. Cherny, *A Righteous Cause: The Life of William Jennings Bryan* (1985)

Lawrence Goodwyn, *The Populist Movement: A Short History of the Agrarian Revolt in America* (1978)

Stephen Hahn, *The Roots of Southern Populism* (1983)

Michael Kazin, *Populist Persuasion: An American History* (1995)

Robert C. McMath, *American Populism* (1993)

Scott G. McNall, *The Road to Rebellion: Class Formation and Kansas Populism, 1865–1900* (1988)

Nell Painter, *Standing at Armageddon: United States, 1877–1919* (1987)

Norman Pollack, *The Just Polity: Populism, Law, and Human Welfare* (1987)

Nick Salvatore, *Eugene V. Debs: Citizen and Socialist* (1982)

Carol A. Schwantes, *Coxey's Army: An American Odyssey* (1985)

William Serrin, *Homestead: The Glory and Tragedy of an American Steel Town* (1992)

Barton Shaw, *The Wool-Hat Boys: Georgia's Populist Party* (1984)

Carol Smith, *Urban Disorder and the Shape of Belief: The Great Chicago Fire, the Haymarket Bomb, and the Model Town of Pullman* (1995)

Professionalism and the
Uses of New Knowledge

From 1870 to 1910, the number of university and college students rose four times
as fast as the country's population. The change was especially dramatic at the post-
graduate level. The number of graduate students increased from fewer than 50 in
1870 to nearly 6,000 by 1900. Together, these figures marked the expansion not only
of a new professional or "knowledge" class but of a new role altogether for accredited
expertise in American business and cultural life. The world of commerce, in particular, quickly became wedded to scientifically based invention and innovation to fulfill its promise of ever-greater satisfactions and material progress. In the careers of
inventors Alexander Graham Bell and Thomas Alva Edison—whom one historian
has called "the only authentic heroes" of the Gilded Age—the rewards were clear for
experimentation and applicaton of the scientific method to industrial process.

But to be sure, the professions, like the world of politics and industry they sought
to influence, remained a distinctly gendered arena. On the one hand, the numbers
of women enrolled in both women's colleges and coeducational institutions had
mounted rapidly in the late nineteenth century, far more, for example, than in any
European country. By 1880, some 40,000 women constituted a third of all college
students. Yet their numbers in the higher levels of graduate training were generally
small and highly selective. Only five women, for example, had received a Ph.D. in
economics by 1900. Tellingly, by 1910, while women constituted a mere 1 percent of
lawyers and 6 percent of physicians, they represented 93 percent of nurses and 52
percent of social workers.

But the province of the "new knowledge" was nearly ubiquitous. In industry
itself, not only the new technology but the recruitment and training of the (usually
immigrant) workforce came under the influence of a new professional managerial-
ism or "scientific management." Likewise, public discussion of enduring social problems like poverty and inequality was guided by those who presumed to apply to
society the scientific theory gleaned from their own higher learning. Perhaps the most
momentous body of scientific thought bequeathed to the late nineteenth century
stemmed from the evolutionary theory of Charles Darwin whose Origins of Species
had appeared in 1859. Drawing on Darwin, the British philosopher Herbert Spencer
developed an analysis of how human society had evolved through competition and

"survival of the fittest." This version of Social Darwinism, as Spencer's ideas be-
came known, was promulgated in America by the Yale sociology professor William
Graham Sumner, who effectively turned Darwinism into a justification for laissez-
faire (or non-interventionist) government economic policy. But critics of laissez-faire
also turned to evolutionary theory, in a form that came to be called Reform Darwin-
ism, to legitimate their political position. Interestingly enough, within the arena of
contemporary social thought, the semiautonomous realm of female social settlement
workers, which substituted direct, practical contact between the social classes for the
formal tradition of graduate school training, may have offered the clearest alternative
to the "scientistic" tendencies of academic learning. Outside of business and politics,
even religious faith bent noticeably before the winds of scientific authority. By the
1890s, most Protestant and Catholic theologians had creatively assimilated evolution-
ary theory into their accounts of the Creation; it was only later (from the tensions
arising out of the Great War and a new revolt against Modernism gathering force in
the 1920s) that a powerful wave of antievolutionary Fundamentalism would arise.

 D O C U M E N T S

The following documents offer examples of the assimilation of "scientific" knowledge
into various pathways of American life. In Document 1, Harvard-educated lecturer
John Fiske attempts to resolve the conflict between biblical Christianity and evolutionary science by spiritualizing the doctrines of philosopher Herbert Spencer. Delivered
at a grand banquet in honor of Spencer's visit to New York in 1882, the lecture demonstrated the broad acceptance of Darwinist thinking in genteel Protestant circles. In Document 2, sociologist William Graham Sumner, in a classic account of Social Darwinism,
assimilates evolutionary doctrine to conservative social ends. Another sociologist,
Lester Frank Ward, offers an alternative interpretation in Document 3. With a selection
from the diary of Thomas Alva Edison, Document 4 captures the "Wizard of Menlo
Park" in one of his lighter moments but one that nevertheless shows the methodical and
prodding method behind the inventive genius of the man who perfected the light bulb,
the phonograph, mimeograph machine, microphone, and the motion-picture camera
and film. Based on her Chicago Hull House experience, Jane Addams's explanation of
the necessity of the social settlement (Document 5) also bespeaks a female-centered,
practice-oriented, "interpretive sociology" at odds with often arid, intellectual theorizing
predominating in the academy. Finally (in Document 6), industrial engineer Frederick
Winslow Taylor, using the tools of what he called "scientific management," aims to
rationalize the recruitment and efficiency of hired labor.

1. John Fiske Reconciles Evolutionism and
Christian Doctrine (1882), 1902

All religions agree in the two following assertions, one of which is of speculative
and one of which is of ethical importance. One of them serves to sustain and
harmonize our thoughts about the world we live in, and our place in that world;

John Fiske, *Essays, Historical and Literary,* Vol. 2. (New York: Macmillan, 1902), 227–237.

the other serves to uphold us in our efforts to do each what we can to make human life more sweet, more full of goodness and beauty, than we find it. The first of these assertions is the proposition that the things and events of the world do not exist or occur blindly or irrelevantly, but that all, from the beginning to the end of time, and throughout the furthest sweep of illimitable space, are connected together as the orderly manifestations of a divine Power, and that this divine Power is something outside of ourselves, and upon it our own existence from moment to moment depends. The second of these assertions is the proposition that men ought to do certain things, and ought to refrain from doing certain other things; and that the reason why some things are wrong to do and other things are right to do is in some mysterious, but very real, way connected with the existence and nature of this divine Power, which reveals itself in every great and every tiny thing, without which not a star courses in its mighty orbit, and not a sparrow falls to the ground. . . .

Having thus seen what is meant by the essential truths of religion, it is very easy to see what the attitude of the doctrine of evolution is toward these essential truths. It asserts and reiterates them both; and it asserts them not as dogmas handed down to use by priestly tradition, not as mysterious intuitive convictions of which we can render no account to ourselves, but as scientific truths concerning the innermost constitution of the universe—truths that have been disclosed by observation and reflection, like other scientific truths, and that accordingly harmonize naturally and easily with the whole body of our knowledge. The doctrine of evolution asserts, as the widest and deepest truth which the study of nature can disclose to us, that there exists a power to which no limit in time or space is conceivable, and that all the phenomena of the universe, whether they be what we call material or what we call spiritual phenomena, are manifestations of this infinite and eternal Power. Now this assertion, which Mr. Spencer has so elaborately set forth as a scientific truth—nay, as the ultimate truth of science, as the truth upon which the whole structure of human knowledge philosophically rests—this assertion is identical with the assertion of an eternal Power, not ourselves, that forms the speculative basis of all religions. When Carlyle* speaks of the universe as in very truth the star-domed city of God, and reminds us that through every crystal and through every grass blade, but most through every living soul, the glory of a present God still beams, he means pretty much the same thing that Mr. Spencer means, save that he speaks with the language of poetry, with language coloured by emotion, and not with the precise, formal, and colourless language of science. By many critics who forget that names are but the counters rather than the hard money of thought, objections have been raised to the use of such a phrase as the Unknowable, whereby to describe the power that is manifest in every event of the universe. Yet, when the Hebrew prophet declared that "by him were laid the foundations of the deep," but reminded us "Who by searching can find him out?" he

---

*Thomas Carlyle (1795–1881) was a Scots essayist and man of letters, extremely popular in both Great Britain and the United States.

meant pretty much what Mr. Spencer means when he speaks of a power that is inscrutable in itself, yet is revealed from moment to moment in every throb of the mighty rhythmic life of the universe.

And this brings me to the last and most important point of all. What says the doctrine of evolution with regard to the ethical side of this twofold assertion that lies at the bottom of all religion? Though we cannot fathom the nature of the inscrutable Power that animates the world, we know, nevertheless, a great many things that it does. Does this eternal Power, then, work for righteousness? Is there a divine sanction for holiness and a divine condemnation for sin? Are the principles of right living really connected with the intimate constitution of the universe? If the answer of science to these questions be affirmative, then the agreement with religion is complete, both on the speculative and on the practical side; and that phantom which has been the abiding terror of timid and superficial minds—that phantom of the hostility between religion and science—is exorcised now and forever. Now, science began to return a decisively affirmative answer to such questions as these when it began, with Mr. Spencer, to explain moral beliefs and moral sentiments as products of evolution. For clearly, when you say of a moral belief or a moral sentiment, that it is a product of evolution, you imply that it is something which the universe through untold ages has been labouring to bring forth, and you ascribe to it a value proportionate to the enormous effort it has cost to produce it. Still more, when with Mr. Spencer we study the principles of right living as part and parcel of the whole doctrine of the development of life upon the earth; when we see that in an ultimate analysis that is right which tends to enhance fulness of life, and that is wrong which tends to detract from fulness of life—we then see that the distinction between right and wrong is rooted in the deepest foundations of the universe; we see that the very same forces, subtle, and exquisite, and profound, which brought upon the scene the primal germs of life and caused them to unfold, which through countless ages of struggle and death have cherished the life that could live more perfectly and destroyed the life that could only live less perfectly, until humanity, with all its hopes, and fears, and aspirations, has come into being as the crown of all this stupendous work—we see that these very same subtle and exquisite forces have wrought into the very fibres of the universe those principles of right living which it is man's highest function to put into practice. The theoretical sanction thus given to right living is incomparably the most powerful that has ever been assigned in any philosophy of ethics. Human responsibility is made more strict and solemn than ever, when the eternal Power that lives in every event of the universe is thus seen to be in the deepest possible sense the author of the moral law that should guide our lives, and in obedience to which lies our only guarantee of the happiness which is incorruptible—which neither inevitable misfortune nor unmerited obloquy can ever take away. I have but barely touched upon a rich and suggestive topic. When this subject shall once have been expounded and illustrated with due thoroughness—as I earnestly hope it will be within the next few years—then I am sure it will be generally acknowledged that our great teacher's services to religion have been no less signal than his services to science unparalleled as these have been in all the history of the world.

2. William Graham Sumner Elaborates the Principles of Social Darwinism, 1885

The competition of life has taken the form, historically, of a struggle for the possession of the soil. In the simpler states of society the possession of the soil is tribal, and the struggles take place between groups, producing the wars and feuds which constitute almost the whole of daily history. On the agricultural stage the tribal or communal possession of land exists as a survival, but it gives way to private property in land whenever the community advances and the institutions are free to model themselves. The agricultural stage breaks up tribal relations and encourages individualization. This is one of the reasons why it is such an immeasurable advance over the lower forms of civilization. It sets free individual energy, and while the social bond gains in scope and variety, it also gains in elasticity, for the solidarity of the group is broken up and the individual may work out his own ends by his own means, subject only to the social ties which lie in the natural conditions of human life. It is only on the agricultural stage that liberty as civilized men understand it exists at all. The poets and sentimentalists, untaught to recognize the grand and world-wide cooperation which is secured by the free play of individual energy under the great laws of the social order, bewail the decay of early communal relations and exalt the liberty of the primitive stages of civilization. These notions all perish at the first touch of actual investigation. The whole retrospect of human history runs downwards towards beast-like misery and slavery to the destructive forces of nature. The whole history has been one series of toilsome, painful, and bloody struggles, first to find out where we were and what were the conditions of greater ease, and then to devise means to get relief. Most of the way the motives of advance have been experience of suffering and instinct. It is only in the most recent years that science has undertaken to teach without and in advance of suffering, and as yet science has to fight so hard against tradition that its authority is only slowly winning recognition. The institutions whose growth constitutes the advance of civilization have their guarantee in the very fact that they grew and became established. They suited man's purpose better than what went before. They are all imperfect, and all carry with them incidental ills, but each came to be because it was better than what went before, and each of which has perished, perished because a better one supplanted it.

It follows once and for all that to turn back to any defunct institution or organization because existing institutions are imperfect is to turn away from advance and is to retrograde. The path of improvement lies forwards. Private property in land, for instance, is an institution which has been developed in the most direct and legitimate manner. It may give way at a future time to some other institution which will grow up by imperceptible stages out of the efforts of men to contend successfully with existing evils, but the grounds for private property in land are easily perceived, and it is safe to say that no *a priori* scheme of state ownership or other tenure invented *en bloc* by any

Albert Galloway Keller, ed., *War and Other Essays by William Graham Sumner* (New Haven: Yale University Press, 1911), 167–192.

philosopher and adopted by legislative act will ever supplant it. To talk of any such thing is to manifest a total misconception of the facts and laws which it is the province of sociology to investigate. The case is less in magnitude but scarcely less out of joint with all correct principle when it is proposed to adopt a unique tax on land, in a country where the rent of land is so low that any important tax on land exceeds it, and therefore becomes indirect, and where also political power is in the hands of small landowners, who hold, without ever having formulated it, a doctrine of absolute property in the soil such as is not held by any other landowners in the world. . . .

We have seen that if we should try by any measures of arbitrary interference and assistance to relieve the victims of social pressure from the calamity of their position we should only offer premiums to folly and vice and extend them further. We have also seen that we must go forward and meet our problems. We cannot escape them by running away. If then it be asked what the wit and effort of man can do to struggle with the problems offered by social pressure, the answer is that he can do only what his instinct has correctly and surely led him to do without any artificial social organization of any kind, and that is, by improvements in the arts, in science, in morals, in political institutions, to widen and strengthen the power of man over nature. The task of dealing with social ills is not a new task. People set about it and discuss it as if the human race had hitherto neglected it, and as if the solution of the problem was to be something new in form and substance, different from the solution of all problems which have hitherto engaged human effort. In truth, the human race has never done anything else but struggle with the problem of social welfare. That struggle constitutes history, or the life of the human race on earth. That struggle embraces all minor problems which occupy attention here, save those of religion, which reaches beyond this world and finds its objects beyond this life. Every successful effort to widen the power of man over nature is a real victory over poverty, vice, and misery, taking things in general and in the long run. It would be hard to find a single instance of a direct assault by positive effort upon poverty, vice, and misery which has not either failed or, if it has not failed directly and entirely, has not entailed other evils greater than the one which it removed. The only two things which really tell on the welfare of man on earth are hard work and self-denial (in technical language, labor and capital), and these tell most when they are brought to bear directly upon the effort to earn an honest living, to accumulate capital, and to bring up a family of children to be industrious and self-denying in their turn. I repeat that this is the way to work for the welfare of man on earth; and what I mean to say is that the common notion that when we are going to work for the social welfare of man we must adopt a great dogma, organize for the realization of some great scheme, have before us an abstract ideal, or otherwise do anything but live honest and industrious lives, is a great mistake. From the standpoint of the sociologist pessimism and optimism are alike impertinent. To be an optimist one must forget the frightful sanctions which are attached to the laws of right living. To be a pessimist one must overlook the education and growth which are the product of effort and self-denial. In either case one is passing judgment on what is inevitably fixed, and on which the approval or condemnation of man can produce no effect. The facts and laws are, once and for all, so, and for us men that is the end of the matter. The only persons for whom there would be any sense in the question whether life is worth living are primarily the yet unborn children, and secondarily the persons who are proposing to found families. For these latter the question would take a somewhat modified form: Will life be worth living for children born of me? This question is, unfortunately, not put to themselves by the appropriate persons as it would be if they had been taught sociology. The sociologist is often asked if he wants to kill off certain classes of troublesome and burdensome persons. No such inference follows from any sound sociological doctrine, but it is allowed to infer, as to a great many persons and classes, that it would have been better for society, and would have involved no pain to them, if they had never been born.

3. Lester Frank Ward Attacks Laissez Faire in the Name of Reform Darwinism, 1884

When a well-clothed philosopher on a bitter winter's night sits in a warm room well lighted for his purpose and writes on paper with pen and ink in the arbitrary characters of a highly developed language the statement that civilisation is the result of natural laws, and that man's duty is to let nature alone so that untrammeled it may work out a higher civilisation, he simply ignores every circumstance of his existence and deliberately closes his eyes to every fact within the range of his faculties. If man had acted upon his theory there would have been no civilisation, and our philosopher would have remained a troglodyte.

But how shall we distinguish this human, or anthropic, method from the method of nature? Simply by reversing all the definitions. Art is the antithesis of nature. If we call one the natural method we must call the other the artificial method. If nature's process is rightly named natural selection, man's process is artificial selection. The survival of the fittest is simply the survival of the strong, which implies, and might as well be called, the destruction of the weak. And if nature progresses through the destruction of the weak, man progresses through the *protection* of the weak. This is the essential distinction.

In human society the psychic power has operated to secure the protection of the weak in two distinct ways: first, by increasing the supply of the necessities of life, and, secondly, by preventing the destruction of life through the enemies of man. The immediate instrumentality through which the first of these processes is carried on is art, the product of invention. The second process takes place through the establishment of positive institutions.

It is difficult to say which of these agencies has been most effective. Both were always indispensable, and therefore all comparison is unprofitable.

Art operates to protect the weak against adverse surroundings. It is directed against natural forces, chiefly physical. By thus defeating the destructive influences of the elements and hostile forms of life, and by forcing nature to yield an unnatural supply of man's necessities, many who would have succumbed from inability to resist these adverse agencies—the feebler members of society—were able to survive, and population increased and expanded. While no one openly denies this, there is a

Lester Frank Ward, *Glimpses of the Cosmos* (3 vols.: New York: G. P. Putnam's Sons, 1913), Vol. III, 361–377. This document can also be found in R. Jackson Wilson, *Darwinism and the American Intellectual, An Anthology* (Chicago: The Dorsey Press, 1989), 124–132.

tendency either to ignore it in politico-economic discussions, or to deny its application to them as an answer to naturalistic arguments.

If, on the other hand, we inquire into the nature of human institutions, we shall
perceive that they are of three kinds, tending to protect the weak in three ways, or
ascending degrees. These three successively higher means through which this end
is attained are, first, Justice, second, Morality, and third, Charity. These forms of
action have been reached through the development, respectively, of the three corresponding sentiments: Equity, Beneficence, and Benevolence.

All of these altruistic sentiments are wholly unknown, or known only in the
merest embryo, to all animals below man, and therefore no such means of protection exist among them. They are strictly human, or anthropic. Many evolutionists
fail to recognise this. Some sociologists refuse to admit it. They look about and see
so much injustice, immorality and rapacity that they are led to suppose that only
natural methods are in operation in society. This is a great mistake. In point of fact,
the keener the sense of justice the more conspicuous the diminishing number of
violations of it come to appear, and conversely, the obviousness of injustice proves
the general prevalence of justice. It is the same with morality and philanthropy.

If we consider the effect of these three codes of human conduct in the direction
of enabling the weaker ones to survive we shall see that it has been immense. Out of
the first has arisen government, the chief value and function of which has always
been and still is such protection. Great systems of jurisprudence have been elaborated, engrossing the attention of a large portion of the population of enlightened
as well as of barbaric states. To say that these have been failures because often
weighted with grave defects is to misinterpret history and misunderstand society.
No one could probably be found to gainsay that the moral law of society has exerted
a salutary influence, yet its aim is strictly altruistic, opposed to the law of the survival
of the fittest, and wholly in the direction of enabling those to survive who would
not survive without its protection. Finally, the last sentiment to be developed, and
doubtless the highest, is so universally recognised as peculiar to man that his very
name has been given to it—the sentiment of *humanity.* Yet the mode of protecting
the weak arising out of this sentiment is the one that has been most seriously called
in question by the naturalistic school. It must be admitted that humanitarian institutions have done far less good than either juridical or ethical institutions. The sentiment itself is of recent origin, the product only of highly developed and greatly
refined mental organisation. It exists to an appreciable degree only in a minute
fraction of the most enlightened populations. It is rarely directed with judgment;
no fixed, self-enforcing code of conduct, as in the other cases, having had time to
take shape. The institutions established to enforce it are for the most part poorly
supported, badly managed, and often founded on a total misconception of human
nature and of the true mode of attaining the end in view. Hence they are specially
open to attack. But if ever humanitarian sentiments become diffused throughout
the body politic, become the object of deep study, as have those of justice and right,
it may be confidently predicted that society will prove itself capable of caring for
the most unfortunate of its members in a manner that shall not work demoralisation.

In all these ways man, through his intelligence, has laboured successfully to
resist the law of nature. His success is conclusively demonstrated by a comparison
of his condition with that of other species of animals. No other cause can be assigned

for his superiority. How can the naturalistic philosophers shut their eyes to such obvious facts? Yet, what is their attitude? They condemn all attempts to protect the weak, whether by private or public methods. They claim that it deteriorates the race by enabling the unfit to survive and transmit their inferiority. This is true only in certain cases of hereditary diseases or mental deficiencies, which should be taken account of by man because they are not by nature. Nothing is easier than to show that the unrestricted competition of nature does not secure the survival of the fittest possible, but only of the actually fittest, and in every attempt man makes to obtain something fitter than this actual fittest he succeeds, as witness improved breeds of animals and grafts of fruits. Now, the human method of protecting the weak deals in some such way with men. It not only increases the number but improves the quality.

But "government," at least, must *laisser faire*. It must not "meddle" with natural laws. The laws of trade, business, social intercourse, are natural laws, immutable and indestructible. All interference with them is vain. The fallacy here is a *non sequitur.* It may be readily granted that these laws are immutable and indestructible. Were this not the case it would certainly be hopeless to interfere with their action. But every mechanical invention proves that nothing is easier than to interfere successfully with the operation of these uniform natural forces. They have only to be first thoroughly understood and then they are easily *controlled*. To *destroy* a force is one thing, to control its action is quite another. Those who talk in this way involve themselves in the most palpable inconsistency. They must not be allowed to stop where they do. They must go on and carry their strictures to a logical conclusion. They must deny to government the right to protect its citizens from injustice. This is a clear interference with the natural laws of society. They must deny to society the right to enforce its code of morals. Nothing is more unnatural. They must suppress the healing art which keeps the sick from dying as they do among animals. Nor is this all. They must condemn all interference with physical laws and natural forces. To dam a stream must be characterised as a "vain" attempt to overcome a natural law. The wind must be left free to blow where it will, and not be forced against the fan of a wind-mill. The vapour of heated water must be allowed to float off naturally into the air and not be pent up in a steam-boiler and thence conducted into the cylinder of a steam-engine. All these things and every other device of inventive man are so many attempts to "violate" the laws of nature, which is declared impossible.

What then remains of the *laissez faire* doctrine? Nothing but this: That it is useless, and may be dangerous, to attempt to control natural forces until their character is first well understood. This is a proposition which is true for every department of force, and does not involve the surrender of the whole domain of sociology after it has been demonstrated that society is a threatre of forces.

The truth thus comes forth from a rational study of nature and human society that social progress has been due only in very slight degree to natural evolution as accomplished through the survival of the fittest, and its chief success has resulted from the reduction of competition in the struggle for existence and the protection of the weaker members. Such competition, in so far as it has been permitted to operate, has tended to lower the standard of the fittest and to check advancement. It is not, of course, claimed that the natural method has ever been fully overcome. It has always operated, and still operates, powerfully in many ways. It has been chiefly in the simpler departments of physical and mechanical phenomena that the psychic, or anthropic, method has superseded it. The inventive arts have been the result. Vital forces have yielded to some extent to the influence of mind in bringing about improved stocks of animals and vegetables, and even certain social laws have come under rational control through the establishment of institutions. Still, every step in this progress has been contested. It was not enough that the intellect was feeble and ill-fitted to grapple with such problems. It was not enough that ignorance of nature's laws should cause unnumbered failures. A still stronger barrier was presented by the intellect itself in the form of positive error embodied in philosophy. As already remarked, philosophy has always been negative and nihilistic, and has steadily antagonised the common sense of mankind. It is only quite recently that there has come into existence anything like a truly *positive* philosophy, i.e., a philosophy of *action*. . . .

4. A Day in the Life of Thomas Alva Edison, 1885

Menlo Park, N.J.
Sunday, July 12, 1885

Awakened at 5:15 A.M. My eyes were embarrassed by the sunbeams—turned my back to them and tried to take another dip into oblivion—succeeded—awakened at 7 A.M. Thought of Mina,* Daisy, and Mamma G—. Put all 3 in my mental kaleidoscope to obtain a new combination à la Galton. Took Mina as a basis, tried to improve her beauty by discarding and adding certain features borrowed from Daisy and Mamma G. A sort of Raphaelized beauty, got into it too deep, mind flew away and I went to sleep again.

Awakened at 8:15 A.M. Powerful itching of my head, lots of white dry dandruff— what is this d—mnable material. Perhaps it's the dust from the dry literary matter I've crowded into my noodle lately. It's nomadic. Gets all over my coat; must read about it in the Encyclopedia.

Smoking too much makes me nervous—must lasso my natural tendency to acquire such habits—holding heavy cigar constantly in my mouth has deformed my upper lip, it has a sort of Havana curl.

Arose at 9 o'clock; came downstairs expecting 'twas too late for breakfast— 'twasn't. Couldn't eat much, nerves of stomach too nicotinny. The root of tobacco plants must go clear through to hell. Satan's principal agent Dyspepsia must have charge of this branch of the vegetable kingdom. It has just occurred to me that the brain may digest certain portions of food, say the etherial part, as well as the stomach—perhaps dandruff is the excreta of the mind—the quantity of this material being directly proportional to the amount of reading one indulges in. . . .

Dot just read to me outlines of her proposed novel. The basis seems to be a marriage under duress. I told her that in case of a marriage to put in bucketfuls of misery. This would make it realistic. Speaking of realism in painting, etc., Steele

---

*Mina Miller, daughter of Lewis Miller of Akron, Ohio. She and Mr. Edison were married Feb. 24, 1886. Mamma G. was wife of Ezra Gilliland (nicknamed Damon), who was Edison's friend from his days as telegrapher and was at this time working with him on a form of wireless telegraph.

Dagobert D. Runes, ed., *The Diary and Sundry Observations of Thomas Alva Edison* (Westport, Conn.: Greenwood Press, 1968), 3–4.

Mackaye, at a dinner given to H. H. Porter, Wm. Winter and myself, told us of a definition of modern realism given by some Frenchman whose name I have forgotten. "Realism is a dirty long-haired painter sitting on the head of a bust of Shakespeare painting a pair of old boots covered with dung."

The bell rings for supper. Igoe sardines the principal attraction. On seeing them was attacked by a stroke of vivid memory of some sardines I ate last winter that caused a rebellion in the labyrinth of my stomach. Could scarcely swallow them today. They nearly did the "return ball" act.

After supper Dot pitched a ball to me several dozen times—first I ever tried to catch. It was as hard as Nero's heart—nearly broke my baby-finger. Gave it up. Taught Dot and Maggie how to play "Duck on the rock." They both thought it great fun. And this is Sunday. My conscience seems to be oblivious of Sunday. It must be incrusted with a sort of irreligious tartar. If I was not so deaf I might go to church and get it taken off or at least loosened. Eccavi! I will read the new version of the bible.

Holzer is going to use the old laboratory for the purpose of hatching chickens artificially by an electric incubator. He is very enthusiastic. Gave me full details. He is a very patient and careful experimenter. Think he will succeed. Everything succeeded in that old laboratory.

Just think electricity employed to cheat a poor hen out of the pleasures of maternity. Machine-born chickens! What is home without a mother?

I suggested to H that he vaccinate his hens with chicken-pox virus. Then the eggs would have their embryo hereditarily inoculated and none of the chickens would have the disease. For economy's sake he could start with one hen and rooster. He being a scientific man with no farm experience, I explained the necessity of having a rooster. He saw the force of this suggestion at once.

The sun has left us on time. Am going to read from the Encyclopedia Brittanica to steady my nerves, and go to bed early. I will shut my eyes and imagine a terraced abyss, each terrace occupied by a beautiful maiden. To the first I will deliver my mind and they will pass it down to the uttermost depths of silence and oblivion. Went to bed. Worked my imagination for a supply of maidens. Only saw Mina, Daisy and Mamma. Scheme busted—sleep.

5. Jane Addams Explains the Need for Social Settlements, 1892

In a thousand voices singing the Hallelujah Chorus in Handel's "Messiah," it is possible to distinguish the leading voices, but the differences of training and cultivation between them and the voices of the chorus, are lost in the unity of purpose and in the fact that they are all human voices lifted by a high motive. This is a weak illustration of what a Settlement attempts to do. It aims, in a measure, to develop whatever of social life its neighborhood may afford, to focus and give form to that life, to bring to bear upon it the results of cultivation and training; but it receives in exchange for the music of isolated voices the volume and strength of the chorus. It is

"The Subjective Necessity for Social Settlements," in Jane Addams, *Twenty Years at Hull House* (New York: Macmillan, 1910), 97–100.

quite impossible for me to say in what proportion or degree the subjective necessity which led to the opening of Hull-House combined the three trends: first, the desire to interpret democracy in social terms; secondly, the impulse beating at the very source of our lives, urging us to aid in the race progress; and, thirdly, the Christian movement toward humanitarianism. It is difficult to analyze a living thing; the analysis is at best imperfect. Many more motives may blend with the three trends; possibly the desire for a new form of social success due to the nicety of imagination, which refuses worldly pleasures unmixed with the joys of self-sacrifice; possibly a love of approbation, so vast that it is not content with the treble clapping of delicate hands, but wishes also to hear the bass notes from toughened palms, may mingle with these.

The Settlement, then, is an experimental effort to aid in the solution of the social and industrial problems which are engendered by the modern conditions of life in a great city. It insists that these problems are not confined to any one portion of a city. It is an attempt to relieve, at the same time, the overaccumulation at one end of society and the destitution at the other; but it assumes that this overaccumulation and destitution is most sorely felt in the things that pertain to social and educational advantages. From its very nature it can stand for no political or social propaganda. It must, in a sense, give the warm welcome of an inn to all such propaganda, if perchance one of them be found an angel. The one thing to be dreaded in the Settlement is that it lose its flexibility, its power of quick adaptation, its readiness to change its methods as its environment may demand. It must be open to conviction and must have a deep and abiding sense of tolerance. It must be hospitable and ready for experiment. It should demand from its residents a scientific patience in the accumulation of facts and the steady holding of their sympathies as one of the best instruments for that accumulation. It must be grounded in a philosophy whose foundation is on the solidarity of the human race, a philosophy which will not waver when the race happens to be represented by a drunken woman or an idiot boy. Its residents must be emptied of all conceit of opinion and all self-assertion, and ready to arouse and interpret the public opinion of their neighborhood. They must be content to live quietly side by side with their neighbors, until they grow into a sense of relationship and mutual interests. Their neighbors are held apart by differences of race and language which the residents can more easily overcome. They are bound to see the needs of their neighborhood as a whole, to furnish data for legislation, and to use their influence to secure it. In short, residents are pledged to devote themselves to the duties of good citizenship and to the arousing of the social energies which too largely lie dormant in every neighborhood given over to industrialism. They are bound to regard the entire life of their city as organic, to make an effort to unify it, and to protest against its over-differentiation.

It is always easy to make all philosophy point one particular moral and all history adorn one particular tale; but I may be forgiven the reminder that the best speculative philosophy sets forth the solidarity of the human race; that the highest moralists have taught that without the advance and improvement of the whole, no man can hope for any lasting improvement in his own moral or material individual condition; and that the subjective necessity for Social Settlements is therefore identical with that necessity, which urges us on toward social and individual salvation.

6. F. W. Taylor Recruits the Ideal Worker with the Principles of Scientific Management, 1910

Our first step was the scientific selection of the workman. In dealing with workmen under this type of management, it is an inflexible rule to talk to and deal with only one man at a time, since each workman has his own special abilities and limitations, and since we are not dealing with men in masses, but are trying to develop each individual man to his highest state of efficiency and prosperity. Our first step was to find the proper workman to begin with. We therefore carefully watched and studied these 75 men for three or four days, at the end of which time we had picked out four men who appeared to be physically able to handle pig iron at the rate of 47 tons [as opposed to the customary 12½ tons] per day. A careful study was then made of each of these men. We looked up their history as far back as practicable and thorough inquiries were made as to the character, habits, and the ambition of each of them. Finally we selected one from among the four as the most likely man to start with. He was a little Pennsylvania Dutchman who had been observed to trot back home for a mile or so after his work in the evening about as fresh as he was when he came trotting down to work in the morning. We found that upon wages of $1.15 a day he had succeeded in buying a small plot of ground, and that he was engaged in putting up the walls of a little house for himself in the morning before starting to work and at night after leaving. He also had the reputation of being exceedingly "close," that is, of placing a very high value on a dollar. As one man whom we talked to about him said, "A penny looks about the size of a cart wheel to him." This man we will call Schmidt.

The task before us, then, narrowed itself down to getting Schmidt to handle 47 tons of pig iron per day and making him glad to do it. This was done as follows. Schmidt was called out from among the gang of pig-iron handlers and talked to somewhat in this way:

"Schmidt, are you a high-priced man?"

"Vell, I don't know vat you mean."

"Oh yes, you do. What I want to know is whether you are a high-priced man or not."

"Vell, I don't know vat you mean."

"Oh, come now, you answer my questions. What I want to find out is whether you are a high-priced man or one of these cheap fellows here. What I want to find out is whether you want to earn $1.85 a day or whether you are satisfied with $1.15, just the same as all those cheap fellows are getting."

"Did I vant $1.85 a day? Vas dot a high-priced man? Vell, yes, I vas a high-priced man."

"Oh, you're aggravating me. Of course you want $1.85 a day—every one wants it! You know perfectly well that that has very little to do with your being a high-priced man. For goodness' sake answer my questions, and don't waste any more of my time. Now come over here. You see that pile of pig iron?"

F. W. Taylor, "Principles of Scientific Management," in *Scientific Management* (New York: Harper & Brothers, 1910), 5–8, 39–45.

"Yes."

"You see that car?"

"Yes."

"Well, if you are a high-priced man, you will load that pig iron on that car to-morrow for $1.85. Now do wake up and answer my question. Tell me whether you are a high-priced man or not."

"Vell—did I got $1.85 for loading dot pig iron on dot car to-morrow?"

"Yes, of course you do, and you get $1.85 for loading a pile like that every day right through the year. That is what a high-priced man does, and you know it just as well as I do."

"Vell, dot's all right. I could load dot pig iron on the car to-morrow for $1.85, and get it every day, don't I?"

"Certainly you do—certainly you do."

"Vell, den, I vas a high-priced man."

"Now, hold on, hold on. You know just as well as I do that a high-priced man has to do exactly as he's told from morning till night. You have seen this man here before, haven't you?"

"No, I never saw him."

"Well, if you are a high-priced man, you will do exactly as this man tells you to-morrow, from morning till night. When he tells you to pick up a pig and walk, you pick it up and you walk, and when he tells you to sit down and rest, you sit down. You do that right straight through the day. And what's more, no back talk. Now a high-priced man does just what he's told to do, and no back talk. Do you understand that? When this man tells you to walk, you walk; when he tells you to sit down, you sit down, and you don't talk back at him. Now you come on to work here to-morrow morning and I'll know before night whether you are really a high-priced man or not."

This seems to be rather rough talk. And indeed it would be if applied to an educated mechanic, or even an intelligent laborer. With a man of the mentally sluggish type of Schmidt it is appropriate and not unkind, since it is effective in fixing his attention on the high wages which he wants and away from what, if it were called to his attention, he probably would consider impossibly hard work. . . .

Schmidt started to work, and all day long, and at regular intervals, was told by the man who stood over him with a watch, "Now pick up a pig and walk. Now sit down and rest. Now walk–now rest," etc. He worked when he was told to work, and rested when he was told to rest, and at half-past five in the afternoon had his 47½ tons loaded on the car. And he practically never failed to work at this pace and do the task that was set him during the three years that the writer was at Bethlehem. And throughout this time he averaged a little more than $1.85 per day, whereas before he had never received over $1.15 per day, which was the ruling rate of wages at that time in Bethlehem. That is, he received 60 percent higher wages than were paid to other men who were not working on task work. One man after another was picked out and trained to handle pig iron at the rate of 47½ tons per day until all of the pig iron was handled at this rate, and the men were receiving 60 percent more wages than other workmen around them.

The writer has given above a brief description of three of the four elements which constitute the essence of scientific management: first, the careful selection

of the workman, and, second and third, the method of first inducing and then training and helping the workman to work according to the scientific method. Nothing
has as yet been said about the science of handling pig iron. The writer trusts, however, that before leaving this illustration the reader will be thoroughly convinced
that there is a science of handling pig iron, and further that this science amounts to
so much that the man who is suited to handle pig iron cannot possibly understand
it, nor even work in accordance with the laws of this science, without the help of
those who are over him.

E S S A Y S

The following selections emphasize the encompassing reach of the professionalizing
wave in the late nineteenth century, its peculiarly gendered quality, and the impact of
professionalized expertise as measured in one arena in which new, scientific knowledge
was brought to bear on social problems. In the first essay, Burton J. Bledstein of the
University of Illinois at Chicago delimits both the structure and characteristic habits of
mind of the expanding world of middle-class professionalism, circa 1890. Among other
factors, he stresses the role of higher education in establishing a visible framework of
credentialing in a remarkably wide range of endeavors. Professor Robyn Muncy of the
University of Maryland at College Park uses the example of Jane Addams's Hull House
to describe an emergent subcategory of professional careers: the "female dominion"
of the social settlement houses that would become a powerful new force for urban political reform as well as an alternative center of institutionalized social knowledge. In the
third essay Edward Caudill, professor of journalism at the University of Tennessee at
Knoxville, offers a nuanced intellectual portrait of the two doyens of Social Darwinism,
Professors Herbert Spencer and William Graham Sumner.

The Culture of Professionalism

BURTON J. BLEDSTEIN

A Radical Idea

[T]he professionalization of American lives manifested itself everywhere, in popular culture, the academy, and spectator sports, indeed in the ordinary habits of a
middle-class life as an individual learned the hygienic way to bathe, eat, work, relax,
and even have sexual intercourse. The middle class in America matured as the Mid-
Victorians perfected their cultural control over the release of personal and social
energies. And the professions as we know them today were the original achievement
of Mid-Victorians who sought the highest form in which the middle class could pursue its primary goals of earning a good living, elevating both the moral and intellectual tone of society, and emulating the status of those above one on the social ladder.
Americans after 1870, but beginning after 1840, committed themselves to a culture
of professionalism which over the years has established the thoughts, habits, and

Burton J. Bledstein, *The Culture of Professionalism: The Middle Class and the Development of Higher
Education in America* (New York: Norton, 1976), 81–101. Reprinted by permission of the author.

responses most modern Americans have taken for granted, a culture which has admirably served individuals who aspire to think very well of themselves.

In the 1870s and 1880s, examples of professional trends were already numerous. At the level of popular culture, the mass distribution of books by subscription both rationalized marketing procedures and created a vast new audience. Grant's *Personal Memoirs* (1885), for instance, was a publishing bonanza, earning the family a fortune in royalties. In 1868, James Redpath began eliminating the confusion, duplication, and waste in the lecture rooms of the American lyceum by organizing a national lecturing bureau—Redpath Lyceum Bureau—which now became responsive to particular and local needs. Founded in 1874, the Chautauqua movement began drawing renowned scholars inside its brown canvas tents, first with its national program in adult education and then with its university extension.

Spectator sports quickly displayed tendencies toward professionalization. The first Kentucky Derby was run at Churchill Downs in 1875. Baseball became the country's most popular late-nineteenth century pastime, and Cincinnati organized the first professional club in 1869, the Red Stockings. Professional recognition required distinctive forms of dress with which the public was familiar, and the Red Stockings became the first team to wear the traditional baseball uniform, designed by a local dressmaker. . . .

In more traditional fields of specialization, the outline of professional structures emerged boldly. The law established its first national professional association in 1878, librarianship in 1876, and social work in 1874. Dentistry founded its first university school (in contrast to a training school) in 1867, architecture and pharmacy in 1868, schoolteaching and veterinary medicine in 1879, and accounting in 1881. The Wharton School of Finance and Economy was founded in 1881, a prelude to the declaration that business was a profession. The first state license law for dentistry appeared in 1868, for pharmacy in 1874, for veterinary medicine in 1886, for accounting in 1896, and for architecture in 1897. By 1894, twenty-one states had established an examination system for medical doctors, and fourteen others permitted only graduates from accredited medical schools to practice.

The number of professional schools and students, and the standards for graduation, rose quickly in the last quarter of the century. . . . By 1899, the majority of law schools taught a three-year course of studies; by contrast only one school had in 1875. By 1899, nearly all the medical-school programs were four years in length, whereas most had been two years in 1875, and none had been four.

By 1880, medical specialization so dominated the profession, especially in urban areas, that one physician warned, "there is now danger lest, all being specialists, none shall be general practitioners." It was generally acknowledged that the specialist's work was easier, his hours more manageable, his prestige greater, and his fees higher than the general practitioner's. Specialists were determining the direction of American medicine, and they identified their professional interests with the exclusive national speciality medical societies. . . . "In the brief period of less than fifty years," N. S. Davis, president of the American Medical Association, told his colleagues in 1883, "we have specialities for almost every part or region of the human body." But Davis also implied more. Specialists were consolidating their considerable status as they moved to monopolize the presidency of the AMA, control the faculties of medical colleges, pressure for the creation of speciality hospitals, dominate the staffs of general hospitals and dispensaries, and establish a clientele among persons with means and power.

Mid-Victorians appreciated the value to a career of membership in professional associations with "distinguished" titles. In the 1870s and 1880s, at least two hundred learned societies were formed, in addition to teachers' groups. . . .

. . . [I]n the 1880s, historians (1884), church historians (1888), economists (1885), political scientists (1889), modern-language scholars and teachers (1883), and folklorists (1888) all established their associations, which stepped beyond the American Social Science Association, originally founded in 1865. Nearly every group included "American" in its title, a symbol that served to emphasize the scope of both its membership and its professional interest.

What was the meaning of this professional interest? As commonly understood, a profession was a full-time occupation in which a person earned the principal source of an income. During a fairly difficult and time-consuming process, a person mastered an esoteric but useful body of systematic knowledge, completed theoretical training before entering a practice or apprenticeship, and received a degree or license from a recognized institution. A professional person in the role of a practitioner insisted upon technical competence, superior skill, and a high quality of performance. Moreover, a professional embraced an ethic of service which taught that dedication to a client's interest took precedence over personal profit, when the two happened to come into conflict.

Yet, in the mind of the Mid-Victorian, professionalism meant more than all this. Professionalism was also a culture which embodied a more radical idea of democracy than even the Jacksonian had dared to dream. The culture of professionalism emancipated the active ego of a sovereign person as he performed organized activities within comprehensive spaces. The culture of professionalism incarnated the radical idea of the independent democrat, a liberated person seeking to free the power of nature within every worldly sphere, a self-governing individual exercising his trained judgment in an open society. The Mid-Victorian as professional person strove to achieve a level of autonomous individualism, a position of unchallenged authority heretofore unknown in American life.

In contrast to the tradesman and the craftsman, the professional person defined the unique quality of a subject, its special basis in an exclusive and independent circle of natural experiences. The craftsman traditionally handled a series of individual objects, according to the custom of his work, varying his own specific practices by trial and error. The professional excavated nature for its principles, its theoretical rules, thus transcending mechanical procedures, individual cases, miscellaneous facts, technical information, and instrumental applications. Frederick Jackson Turner, for instance, isolated the unique nature of American history, and Oliver Wendell Holmes, Jr., the unique nature of the law in America; G. Stanley Hall isolated the distinctive characteristics of "adolescence," and Jane Addams the professional woman social worker's special, natural sensitivity to injustice. The intellectual pretensions of these persons were specific in aim and definite in purpose. As professionals, they attempted to define a total coherent system of necessary knowledge within a precise territory, to control the intrinsic relationships of their subject by making it a scholarly as well as an applied science, to root social existence in the inner needs and possibilities of documentable worldly processes.

In contrast to the empiricists, the professional person grasped the concept behind a functional activity, allowing him both to perceive and to predict those inconspicuous or unseen variables which determined an entire system of developments. The professional penetrated beyond the rich confusion of ordinary experience, as he isolated and controlled the factors, hidden to the untrained eye, which made an elaborate system workable or impracticable, successful or unattainable: for instance, a deep-level mining operation for low-grade ore, a suspension bridge or a skyscraper with its network of internal stresses, a commercial farm in the West, with its delicate ecological balance, producing cereals for export. Before submitting a report, to take the first instance, the mining engineer surveyed the ground, studied the geology, assayed a representative sample of ore, estimated its tonnage, determined the cost of extraction and marketing, and evaluated the dangers of production both to financial investment and to human life within the context of the rugged circumstances. Normally the risks were high in writing these reports, but in addition the educated ability of the consultant to sample accurately and estimate tonnage could never be taken for granted, and miscalculation ruined many reputations. The experienced engineer with a solid record of professional achievement was literally worth his weight in precious metal.

Utilizing his trained capacity, the professional person interpreted the special lines along which such complex phenomena as a physical disease, a point of law, a stage of human psychological growth, or the identity of an historical society developed in time and space. The professional did not vend a commodity, or exclusively pursue a self-interest. He did not sell a service by a contract which called for specific results in a specific time or restitution for errors. Rather, through a special understanding of a segment of the universe, the professional person released nature's potential and rearranged reality on grounds which were neither artificial, arbitrary, faddish, convenient, nor at the mercy of popular whim. Such was the august basis for the authority of the professional.

The jurisdictional claim of that authority derived from a special power over worldly experience, a command over the profundities of a discipline. Such masterful command was designed to establish confidence in the mind of the helpless client. The professional person possessed esoteric knowledge about the universe which if withheld from society could cause positive harm. In the cases of the doctor, the lawyer, the engineer, and the chemist, the consequences could be lethal. No less, however, did society require the minister to recite knowingly at the grave, the teacher to instruct intelligently in the classroom, the national historian to discover a meaning that related the present to the past. Laymen were neither prepared to comprehend the mystery of the tasks which professionals performed, nor—more ominously—were they equipped to pass judgment upon special skills and technical competence. Hence, the culture of professionalism required amateurs to "trust" in the integrity of trained persons to respect the moral authority of those whose claim to power lay in the sphere of the sacred and the charismatic. Professionals controlled the magic circle of scientific knowledge which only the few, specialized by training and indoctrination, were privileged to enter, but which all in the name of nature's universality were obligated to appreciate.

For middle-class Americans, the culture of professionalism provided an orderly explanation of basic natural processes that democratic societies, with their historical need to reject traditional authority, required. Science as a source for professional authority transcended the favoritism of politics, the corruption of personality, and the exclusiveness of partisanship. And science as an attitude for professional discipline required inner control and an individual respect for rules, proven experience, and a system of hygienic laws concerned with such personal habits as diet, bathing, sex, dress, work, and recreation. Typically, middle-class Americans with professional pretensions translated the moral cause of temperance into a scientific truth for successful living. In the same way they transformed masturbation into a legitimate medical "disease," an abnormality of nature with its set of related signs and symptoms. Medical doctors made it possible for the deviant afflicted by masturbation to control his or her unnatural excitement by prescribing such radical treatments as vasectomy, clitoridectomy, castration, electrodes inserted into the bladder and rectum, and the cauterization of the prostatic urethra.

The person who mastered professional discipline and control emerged as an emulated example of leadership in American society. He was self-reliant, independent, ambitious, and mentally organized. He structured a life and a career around noble aims and purposes, including the ideal of moral obligation. But most importantly, the professional person absolutely protected his precious autonomy against all assailants, not in the name of an irrational egotism but in the name of a special grasp of the universe and a special place in it. In the service of mankind—the highest ideal—the professional resisted all corporate encroachments and regulations upon his independence, whether from government bureaucrats, university trustees, business administrators, public laymen, or even his own professional associations. The culture of professionalism released the creative energies of the free person who was usually accountable only to himself and his personal interpretation of the ethical standards of his profession. . . .

The conservative consequences of professional behavior were many and commonplace, especially after an individual completed years of training followed by lifetime membership affiliation. By means of ceremonies and rituals, for instance, the professions cultivated the inner aristocratic or elitist social instincts often found in the democrat. The autonomy of a professional person derived from a claim upon powers existing beyond the reach or understanding of ordinary humans. Special rituals, including many of the activities formalized in a graduate school, reinforced the mysteriousness of those powers and enhanced the jurisdictional claim. Specifically, comprehensive examinations for higher degrees, such as the Bar examination or medical boards, tested the larger resources of a candidate, not only the individual's superior intellectual accomplishments but superior emotional control under duress. Moreover, the Ph.D. dissertation was an exercise not only in scholarly method, but in the human endurance and delayed gratification necessary to make an "original contribution to knowledge." Internships, professional oaths, ordination, association meetings, scholarly papers, awards, prizes, recognition of a priesthood of elders: all served ceremonial functions that both indoctrinated the select participants and transmitted general information to the client public. Mid-Victorians favored formidable, enduring, massive displays of their legitimacy and influence. Professional structures provided an excellent forum. . . .

Symbols of professional authority—including the number of technical aids in an office, the number of articles and books on a vita, the income and life style of a successful practitioner—reinforced the public's consciousness of its dependence. Indeed, the pattern of dependence was the most striking conservative consequence of the culture of professionalism. Practitioners succeeded by playing on the weaknesses of the client, his vulnerability, helplessness, and general anxiety. The client's imagination easily did the rest.

Professionals tended to confide the worst, often evoking images of disaster and even a horrible death. The physician might hint at the possibility of an undetected cancer, leaving the patient to his own thoughts. The lawyer might threaten the client with high bail, a long trial, and visions of being locked up and sexually abused in jail. The professor might intimidate the student with failure in his studies, which might permanently obstruct the pursuit of a promising career. The policeman might menace the average citizen with pictures of meaningless, catastrophic, and racial violence in the streets, especially at the hands of a mugger or a psychopath. The minister might vividly portray for the juvenile the hideous ruin of the inebriated and the oversexed. The insurance man might warn the client of sudden destitution and moral irresponsibility toward one's family. The accountant might confront his client with the discovery of fraud and financial disgrace.

By pointing to and even describing a potential disaster, the professional often reduced the client to a state of desperation in which the victim would pay generously, cooperate fully and express undying loyalty to the knowledgeable patron who might save him from a threatening universe. The culture of professionalism tended to cultivate an atmosphere of constant crisis—emergency—in which practitioners both created work for themselves and reinforced their authority by intimidating clients.

The Female Dominion of Professional Service

ROBYN MUNCY

"There's power in me, and will to dominate which I must exercise," wrote Jane Addams in 1889, "they hurt me else." In late-nineteenth-century America, frustrated ambition was injuring other college-educated women as well. Consequently, when Addams eased her own pain by founding a social settlement in Chicago, her venture attracted a group of women similarly bruised by constraints on their aspirations and ready to unfetter their capacities for personal independence and public authority. The desire to unlock the shackles that would have bound them to obscure, private lives provided Addams and her followers with a motive for creating a female dominion within the larger empire of policymaking; their experiences at Hull House supplied the values and strategies that made their creation possible. . . .

Such aspirations burned in the souls of Jane Addams and Ellen Gates Starr, two women who met in 1877 at Rockford Female Seminary in Rockford, Illinois. Addams, destined to become the better known, had been born in 1860 to Cedarville, Illinois's wealthiest family. At his daughter's birth, John Huy Addams had already served as a Republican state senator for six years and would represent

Robyn Muncy, *Creating a Female Dominion in American Reform, 1890–1935* (New York: Oxford University Press, 1991), 3–22. Copyright © by Robyn Muncy. Used by permission of Oxford University Press.

his district for another decade. He owned saw and grist mills in addition to substantial parcels of land. In 1864, he would become president of the Second National Bank of Freeport and would eventually leave an estate worth $250,000. Perhaps because her mother died when Jane was only two, she idolized her father, cherished her time with him, and strove for his approval. Fortunately for Jane, her father supported female education, but unfortunately he made no parallel commitment to a daughter's independent decisionmaking: despite Jane's longing to attend Smith College her father sent her to nearby Rockford Female Seminary.

At the Seminary, Jane Addams blossomed. She achieved popularity with faculty and students and excelled in virtually everything she undertook. Here, too, she began developing her ideas about new roles for women. Of a collegiate woman, Addams wrote in 1880: "She wished not to be a man, not like a man, but she claims the same right to independent thought and action." And the action that Addams alluded to subsisted especially in service to the world which she argued had always been woman's duty: "So we [collegiate women] have planned to be 'Bread-givers' throughout our lives; believing that in labor alone is happiness, and that the only true and honorable life is one filled with good works and honest toil, we have planned to idealize our labor, and thus happily fulfill Woman's Noblest Mission." With this reasoning, Addams was attempting to reconcile her ambition for independence with conventional female roles. The necessity for this reconciliation would continue to mold Addams's thought, self-presentation, and career.

As a student, Addams revealed other traits that would also follow her through life. Her popularity, for instance, seemed to result from her considerable intellect, a zestful enthusiasm for learning, and genuine engagement with every project, but she lacked warmth in personal relationships. In these, she seemed always to hold something back, to be detached, careful, deliberate. Addams wanted to control situations, and she seemed to believe that control required that she play her cards close to the chest. Even in letters to close friends, the seminarian refused to disclose too much of herself. In one such missive, she apologized for "how shallow my religion is"; and then suggested that she and her friend not discuss religion any more. Later she would open a paragraph, "I will not write of myself . . . ," which might well have been her motto. Too profound a self-revelation apparently threatened Addams's sense of independence and control, neither of which she was willing to relinquish.

In these ways, Addams could not have been more different from her closest college friend, Ellen Gates Starr. Born in 1859 to an Illinois farmer and small businessman, Ellen Starr craved intimacy and surrendered herself unself-consciously to passionate attachments. During her first year at Rockford, she opened herself to Addams, and, when a financial shortfall prevented her return thereafter, she continued her self-disclosures through the mail.

Though she would have much preferred to remain at Rockford, Starr bravely accepted the family's need for her labor. Of the break in her formal education she wrote to Addams: "I do not say I am not sorry, but I do this voluntarily . . . for when duty calls and bread and butter . . . it behooves me to respond." In 1878, she took up school teaching and the next year received an offer to teach in Chicago at Miss Kirkland's School for Girls, an offer she felt she could not refuse. One of the enticements to the midwestern capital was proximity to her unmarried Aunt Eliza Allen Starr, who had made a reputation writing books on Christian art.

At first, Starr was happy in Chicago. She enjoyed her teaching, her aunt, a group of close friends, and preparation for Harvard's entrance exam. Especially dear to her was the friendship of Mary Runyon, whom Starr described thus: "She is so *beautiful.* The first handsome friend I ever had." In mid-1882, however, Runyon had to leave Chicago, and her departure occasioned Starr's expression of intense romantic communion with her friend: "The first real *pain* I had in parting, came with separation from her. I began to think myself incapable of that kind of feeling, finding that I am not is worth much more than the price." She went on to confide: "I don't speak of it [this feeling], because people don't understand it. . . . 'People' would understand if it were a man." Starr's love for Runyon was one example of an ardent relationship between women that, though perhaps incomprehensible to the world at large, seemed perfectly acceptable in the world of middle class women. Jane Addams certainly accepted Starr's profession of love for Runyon, as did other of Starr's female friends.

Just as Mary Runyon's departure from Chicago signaled a deterioration in the quality of Starr's life, graduation from Rockford in 1881 sent Addams on a downward spiral. Though in February before her graduation, she reported that her "former vague dream to study medicine for a year in Edinburgh is growing into a settled passion," by the following year, her father's sudden death and her own illnesses combined to thwart Addams's attempts to continue her education. Now, she settled into the family fold, where for a decade she managed her late father's estate, helped to rear her nieces and nephews, and accompanied her stepmother on extended visits to Baltimore and Europe.

Both Addams and Starr originally tried to enter professions through the same doors that admitted men, and both failed. Illness and family obligations blocked Addams's approach to medical school. Harvard's discriminatory rules obstructed Starr: when she arrived to take the entrance exam in Chicago, proctors told Starr that women could take the test only in Cambridge, New York, and Cincinnati, even though women took precisely the same exam as male applicants. Robbed of a specific object for her ambition, Starr grew weary with grading "huge piles of worthless compositions," and Addams showed even deeper dejection when she warned: "I will not write of myself or how purposeless and without ambition I am, only prepare yourself so you won't be too disappointed in me when you come." Two years later, Addams complained that she remained "low in mind."

Supposing a change of scenery might at least lift their spirits, the two women set out for a European tour with a mutual friend—Sara Anderson—in December 1887. Both Starr and Anderson were in large part Addams's guests on this trip, and the three women spent some time together, some time separated. Several months into their tour, when Addams was off on her own, Starr revealed that she had developed the same fierce passion for Addams that she had earlier felt for Mary Runyon. Addams did not reciprocate. Referring to the big double bed that she and Anderson were sharing in Pompeii, Starr wrote to Addams: "I wonder if I am wicked to wish that you were on one edge of it, & I in the middle, comme toujours. I didn't know I was going to miss you so much." Starr continued in a characteristically passionate passage: "I knew well enough in Munich that I was going to sacrifice our old relations & never get it back. . . . but I'm too old now to say that I will never love anybody again as much as I can. It's about all there is worth doing, & if it pulls you to pieces a good deal when you have to give up what you've had & got dependent on—why let it!" It is impossible to know how Starr sacrificed her previous relationship with Addams, but it is clear that the pair successfully reformed their understanding probably in accordance with Addams's less ardent desires. Their friendship remained strong and central for several years yet, and they would never make a final break with each other.

Indeed, during their European trip, the couple lighted on a joint project that would cement their relationship as it suggested a way around the roadblocks in their careers. While in London, they visited the first settlement house in the world. Toynbee Hall, founded by Samuel A. Barnett in 1884, invited university men to live in the midst of a working-class neighborhood. The purpose of the settlement was to bridge the gap between London's educated and laboring classes, to promote understanding between those groups, and especially to provide education and culture to working people. Though Addams and Starr had surely witnessed similar poverty in American cities, the very unfamiliarity of London permitted them to see the suffering of working-class life with new eyes. So impressed were the two women by both the living conditions of working-class London and the settlement's response to those conditions that they determined to open their own settlement in Chicago.

Addams and Starr were not the first American women to be intrigued by the settlement idea. Also inspired by trips to Toynbee Hall, a group of graduates from Smith College founded the Settlement Association in 1887. Chapters of the Association formed at Vassar, Smith, Wellesley, Bryn Mawr, and Harvard Annex. Opening its first settlement on Rivington Street in New York City, the Association began with seven female residents, and received over eighty applications for residence by the end of the first year.

Relocating in working-class neighborhoods attracted educated women in America because it offered them wholly new opportunities in public life that could be justified as an extension of accepted female activities. On the conventional side, settlements appeared simply to extend female philanthropic activities. After all, the cult of true womanhood had slated women for leadership in charitable service, and because settlements required women to surrender themselves to the needs of others, they seemed to fulfill the imperative to female self-sacrifice. On the innovative side, settlements promised women independence from their families, unique possibilities for employment, and the sort of communal living arrangement they had cherished in college.

More radical still, life in the American settlements would turn gender relationships upside down: women on top; men on the bottom. Because men had alternative routes to independence, they did not flock to the settlement movement in the numbers that women did. Indeed, by 1911, the first year for which a measure of male and female participation was available, 53 percent of the 215 settlements reporting to investigators housed women only; less than 2 percent only men. The rest accommodated both sexes. . . .

Female dominance at Hull House matched the blueprint that Addams and Starr had drafted for their project. Intending to create a predominantly female community, they recruited volunteers through Chicago's female organizations and philanthropic societies. They found the Chicago Woman's Club especially receptive. In 1889, the settlement project spoke directly to the emerging interests of such groups because they were in the process of shifting focus from literary and charitable pursuits to increasingly political activities. As these organizations enlisted college-educated members already well read and dissatisfied with their post-collegiate lives, the clubs themselves began to participate in a search for innovative female roles in American society. In 1890, isolated, local clubs gave their search a nation-wide base by uniting in the national General Federation of Woman's Clubs. Very much a part of this national trend, the Chicago Woman's Club saw the settlement as potentially broadening women's opportunities.

This warm reception confirmed Addams's and Starr's suspicion that other women shared their discontent. Indeed, by May 1889, Addams could easily support her contention that the settlement idea had become "a fashionable fad" among Chicago's leading ladies: an activist in the Chicago Woman's Club had invited thirty young women to hear Addams expound on her plan, and on the spot, several had offered to take up residence at the settlement and others to volunteer in its programs. Furthermore, an article in one of Chicago's newspapers announced that the plan had won the support of "several rich ladies," and on first hearing the scheme, a male supporter insisted that he knew at least three young women who would jump at the chance to join Addams because they were "dying from inaction and restlessness."

Addams later identified that female "inaction" as a subjective motive for the settlement movement in America. In her famous essay, "The Subjective Necessity for Social Settlements," Addams argued that America's middle-class women were "taught to be self-forgetting and self-sacrificing, to consider the good of the whole before the good of the ego." But "when the daughter comes back from college and begins to recognize her social claim . . . the family claim is strenuously asserted. . . ." As a result, according to Addams, "the girl loses something vital out of her life to which she is entitled. She is restricted and unhappy; her elders, meanwhile, are unconscious of the situation and we have all the elements of tragedy." Settlement life offered a worthy vocation for these tragic figures, who otherwise languished in a society that had little use for them. The success of the settlement movement at the turn of the century thus represented the middle-class female quest for a new place in American life.

In addition to the subjective necessity for settlements, Addams identified an objective need: the great chasm that separated America's working and middle classes. In fact, Addams defined a settlement as "an experimental effort to aid in the solution of the social and industrial problems which are engendered by the modern conditions of life in a great city." . . .

Thus, driven by their own need for meaningful work and drawn by the social problems they might solve, Addams and Starr opened their settlement at 335 South Halsted Street on September 18, 1889. Located in an immigrant neighborhood on the southwest side of Chicago, the mansion of the late Charles Hull provided enough space for a start and promised more room in the future. The women originally rented only part of the house because several businesses operated out of the ground floor. Dilapidated houses and commercial strips suggested that Halsted Street was a perfect place to begin what one columnist called an "interesting departure in humanitarian work."

When Addams and Starr first settled into the Hull mansion, their plans were vague. No one knew exactly how the women intended to bridge the gulf between classes or provide a "people's parlor." Addams herself referred to the first year as "experimental," a time during which she and Starr would get to know their neighbors' needs. Until familiarized with the neighborhood, the women followed Toynbee Hall's example: they organized social clubs for the young according to age and sex; parties for all according to nationality; lecture series for adults; concerts and exhibits. From the beginning, the settlement housed a kindergarten and sponsored a visiting nurse.

During the next few years, the settlement proved a remarkably flexible institution, devoted especially to serving women and children. As Addams and Starr acquainted themselves with immigrants from southern and eastern Europe, who constituted the bulk of their neighbors, they witnessed the problems encountered by these newest groups of America's working class. When the women became aware of a specific problem, they endeavored as best they could to solve it. Having discovered by 1891, for instance, that mothers in these families often worked outside the home, Addams and Starr opened a day nursery. By then familiar with the vagaries of wage-paying employment, they started a free labor bureau for men and women. Remembering with nostalgia the fresh air and wide-open spaces of their rural childhoods, the women opened Chicago's first public playground. Growing concerned about the horrid working conditions and low pay suffered by working-class women, Addams began to invite female labor unions to meet at the settlement, and she raised funds to build a cooperative living club for working women just down the street from Hull House. Grateful residents named it the Jane Club. In addition, the settlement experimented with a public kitchen to offer cheap meals to working parents and a cooperative coal association for the neighborhood. In those early years, the residents also sought in individual cases to support deserted women, widows, and injured workers. . . .

Where there were not existing organizations to support a resident's work, Addams sought individual patrons. At first Addams had drawn from her own independent income to pay the salaries of a few workers, but as the settlement grew, she began to ask wealthy friends to help finance the work of individual residents. By 1895, Addams had ordered the process. Whenever she identified a need in the community and found a woman ready to meet the need, Addams went in search of an individual donor to pay the worker's monthly salary. This Addams called the fellowship system. While soliciting a fellowship for Anne Withington, Addams described the system to Anita McCormick Blaine. Anne, she said, "is obliged to be self-supporting, and could not possibly give her time for less than $50.00 a month. It would cost her about $25.00 a month to live at the house, and as her mother is particularly dependent upon her, she could not possibly come for less. Several people—Miss Coonley, Mrs. Wilmarth, Miss Mary Rozet Smith, and Miss Colvin—pay sums of $50.00 a month, which are known as fellowships. The person receiving these sums devotes herself to a special sort of work and reports to me, of course, but [also] directly to the persons giving the money."

Individual donors thus supported many of the budding professionals at Hull House. Ellen Starr herself was paid by fellowship. The four women who directed the settlement's day nursery received fellowships, as did the women who ran the labor bureau. Art, music, and gym teachers were usually beholden to a specific patron. When the settlement opened a model lodging house for dependent women, a fellowship paid the director, and even women who read to sick children in their homes earned fellowship money.

The fellowship system allowed women to experiment with and to begin defining new professions. Many of the services provided by fellowships were supplied previously by volunteers in charitable organizations or not at all. Before 1890, no one could have earned her living by reading to sick children or minding the neighbors' kids. Schools did not yet hire teachers specifically to offer music or art lessons or to exercise their students. Unemployment did not earlier provoke the intervention of a professional devoted to nothing else save finding one a job, and few homeless women could have sought shelter in a lodging home whose director received a salary. Often, after a period of definition and testing, women convinced established institutions to incorporate these services into their regular programs. During the early twentieth century, public schools, for instance, began to hire kindergarten teachers, art teachers, and gym teachers as part of their permanent educational staffs. Municipalities and state governments established employment bureaus, and even charitable organizations replaced volunteers with salary-earning professionals.

In other areas, too, this process allowed women to create altogether new professions for themselves. Originating outside of Hull House in the 1890s, a group of women in Chicago united to agitate for the establishment of a Juvenile Court. These women had been indignant to learn that young legal offenders were routinely locked up in the same jails and tried by the same procedures that shuffled adults in and out of the justice system. In keeping with a new view of childhood and adolescence as distinct stages in individual development, the women insisted that the justice system should treat juvenile offenders in ways appropriate to their age. Because the young remained impressionable, their mode of detention and their court itself should simulate the home, nurturing the youthful charges toward a responsible and respectable adulthood. In 1899, the women won the country's first Juvenile Court. To their dismay, however, the law called for clerks and probation officers but allocated no funds for salaries. Determined that women who filled these positions should not be volunteers but self-supporting professionals, the women who had lobbied for the court raised funds to pay the court's probation officers and clerks. The president of the committee resided at Hull House, and the group moved its meetings to the settlement. The first probation officer hired by the committee was also a resident of Hull House, and the fundraisers met with the clerks and officers regularly to discuss their mutual responsibilities and performance. Not until eight years later did the committee convince the county government to pay these officials from the public coffers.

Visiting nurses had the same sort of help from non-professional women. In the 1880s and 1890s, wealthy women in American cities formed Visiting Nurses Associations. The purpose was primarily charitable: to provide nursing care to those who could not otherwise afford it. As with kindergarten teachers and probation officers, however, the nurses themselves were equally beneficiaries of this charity. Paid by generous women, nurses demonstrated the value of their services. After the turn of the century, nurses and their benefactors convinced schools, municipalities, counties, and even states to hire women to conduct public health programs.

In New York City, Lillian Wald founded a settlement for visiting nurses. Born in 1867, Wald graduated from the nursing school at New York Hospital in 1891. After practicing for a year at the Juvenile Asylum in New York, Wald entered the city's Women's Medical College, where she was asked to go to a Sabbath School on the Lower East Side to teach a mothers' class on hygiene. Stunned by the poverty she found during her visit to the immigrant neighborhood, Wald determined to quit medical school and to live among those who seemed to need her special nursing skills. To finance her move, she approached Mrs. Solomon Loeb, who had funded the health lessons at the Sabbath School. Wald, with another nurse in tow, stayed at the College Settlement on Rivington Street while looking for an apartment among Russian and Rumanian immigrants on the Lower East Side. She and her friend began immediately to build a practice among patients who could not pay them. Overwhelmed by the need, the women recruited two more nurses, moved into a larger place, and by 1900 housed fifteen nurses and several other residents who staffed the Nurses' Settlement, soon made famous as the Henry Street Settlement. Lillian Wald was later credited with creating the first independent public health nursing service, establishing the independence of nurses from doctors, and defining nursing as a dignified profession for American women. Without the salaries paid by other interested women, however, Wald could never have defined public health nursing for female professionals.

This process, whereby elite women funded the professionalization process for other women, was widespread and would continue through the early twentieth century. Historian Margaret Rossiter has identified what she called "creative philanthropy" as a strategy that women used to open educational opportunities in the sciences. Groups of fundraising women involved in these schemes slid their opportunity-seeking sisters into all-male educational programs on scholarships, bequests, and post-doctoral teaching fellowships specified for women only. Moreover, wealthy women like Josephine Shaw Lowell in the late nineteenth century and Lucy Sprague Mitchell in the twentieth financed the careers of other women in philanthropic work, educational administration, pre-school education, and child development.

In the 1890s, women were thus creating a professional culture different from that of the older, male professions. One reason for the difference was that women entered the professional world most successfully when they carved out wholly new areas of expertise in which they did not compete with men for jobs or training. Their successes increased when they could justify their professional ambitions as fulfillments of the Victorian imperative for women to serve children and the poor. Because this clientele could not afford to pay for services, female professionals looked to wealthy women for financial support. The income of female professionals, unlike those of men in law, medicine, or business, consequently came not from a fee-paying client but from wealthy benefactors who vicariously fulfilled their own missions through the professionals they supported. This peculiar position required professionals to draw non-professional women into their work and to convince both client and patron that their services were important. Under these circumstances, the female professions could not develop the exclusivity of the older male professions. At precisely the time when those traditional male professions were seeking to increase their fees and status by emphasizing their esoteric knowledge, women were creating professions that depended on the cooperation of lay people. Though specialization and specific training increasingly characterized those female professions, the women who claimed expertise had continually to interpret that knowledge to their lay sisters. They had to be popularizers as well as professionals.

These relationships provided a socio-economic motive for the peculiarities of the new female professions emerging in the early twentieth century. But there were other motives as well. Recent research has shown that even before the late nineteenth century, women in America often performed the task of popularizing scientific knowledge in their voluntary organizations and women's magazines. Moreover, female doctors in the nineteenth and early twentieth centuries saw as their special mission the dissemination of medical knowledge. Thus, women in older, male-dominated professions and female amateurs, as well as women in the newer, female-dominated professions, were inclined toward this position as a bridge between the producers/practitioners of scientific knowledge and the utterly naive laity. The persistence of this inclination suggests that the educating role suited Victorian ideals of womanhood. The cult of true womanhood had envisioned women as the healers of divisions in communities. By popularizing technical knowledge, women were fulfilling their obligation to pull groups together, to heal the divisions between the educated and uneducated, between professionals and potential clients, between elite and mass. Thus, cultural constructions of femininity and the socio-economic location of aspiring women in the late nineteenth century provided the motives for the relative inclusiveness of new female professions and their propensity for popularizing.

Popularization was not, however, an exclusively female element of professions at the turn of the century. Simultaneous with the creation of female professions, men were shaping new service professions, many of which also aimed to ameliorate problems coughed up by industrialization and urbanization. Men were elbow-deep in the clay they were using to sculpt, for instance, innovative forms of engineering, social scientific research, city planning, journalism, and scientific management. Many of these new male professions—especially journalism—committed themselves to popularizing expert knowledge. Popularizing, then, was not a quintessential female characteristic of professions at the turn of the century, but new female professions were nonetheless quintessentially popularizing. Furthermore, the *sources* of the popularizing element in the female professions were peculiar to women: the specific socio-economic and cultural position of women in the 1890s encouraged them to embrace popularization as a defining characteristic of the professions they were creating. Men drew the same commitment from different sources, and in both cases the refusal to hoard esoteric knowledge lowered the prestige of the new professions relative to the older male professions.

In addition to popularizing scientific knowledge, the emerging female professional ethos valued self-sacrificing service. Whether in male- or female-dominated professions, women could not escape the cultural imperative to submerge their egos in service to others. While male professionals were also expected to serve, their professional culture did not define service as self-sacrificing. One historian has written: "The professional concept of service essentially required no more than competent performance; its altruism was general and abstract, a vague commitment to a disembodied, 'public interest.'" This definition of service held true for professional men at the turn of the century. But for women, service continued to imply self-abnegation.

This peculiar element in the female professional ethos arose not only from turn-of-the-century constructions of femininity but also from the social positions of women creating professions. In order to maintain the sponsorship of their benefactors—those wealthy women funding the professionalization process—

professional women had to direct their individual ambitions toward service. After all, the true object of the patronage of elite women was to aid the downtrodden—not to subsidize individual careers. Only by justifying an occupation in terms of service to the dispossessed could professional women solicit such support. In some sense, these professionals were conduits of charity. their labor was the charitable contribution of one class to another, and this position required an erasure of self on the part of women defining new careers.

Social Darwinism: Adapting Evolution to Society

EDWARD CAUDILL

For a concept that seems so familiar to so many historians, the meaning of the term "social Darwinism" is strangely elusive. Despite the familiarity of the term, it is a misnomer. That social Darwinism could be derived from *On the Origin of Species* is obvious, but it is debatable whether Darwin supported the idea. Although he never endorsed the idea, Darwin did not protest the application of his biological theory to society, and passages from his writings even suggest that Darwin himself made such applications. For example, in his *Descent of Man,* Darwin wrote:

> The wonderful progress of the United States, as well as the character of the people, are [*sic*] the results of natural selection; for the more energetic, restless, and courageous men from all parts of Europe have emigrated , , , and have there succeeded best.
>
> With savages, the weak in body or mind are soon eliminated; and those that survive commonly exhibit a vigorous state of health. We civilized men, on the other hand, do our utmost to check the process of elimination; we build asylums for the imbecile, the maimed, and the sick; we institute poor-laws; and our medical men exert their utmost skill to save the life of everyone to the last moment. . . . Thus, the weak members of civilized societies propagate their kind. No one who has attended to the breeding of domestic animals will doubt that this must be highly injurious to the race of man.

Nevertheless, social Darwinism's relationship to Darwin himself is problematic for several reasons. First, the philosophy was attributed to the wrong person. Second, it was a *social* philosophy, based on the writings of the English philosopher Herbert Spencer, rather than a scientific theory. This distinction often was lost in popular accounts and, in later decades, in the work of eugenicists. Third, the ideas that eventually grew up around it, particularly in the field of eugenics, went far beyond even Spencerian ideas about evolution and human society.

Darwin responded to Spencer with a lack of enthusiasm, his remarks about the philosopher ranging from snide to befuddled. Darwin wrote to [botanist Joseph] Hooker that he was sorry pangenesis, Darwin's theory of heredity, perplexed Hooker, confessing "that it is abominably wildly horridly speculative (worthy even of Herbert Spencer)." On another occasion, Darwin admitted that he enjoyed his talk with Spencer, "though he does use awesomely long words." Darwin, with his habits of observation and inductive reasoning, confessed his exasperation in reading Spencer: "I am quite delighted with what you [Hooker] say about Herbert Spencer's

Edward Caudill, *Darwinian Myths: The Legends and Misuses of a Theory* (Knoxville: University of Tennessee Press, 1997), 64–68, 71–78. Copyright © 1997. Used with permission of the University of Tennessee Press.

book; when I finish each number I say to myself what an awfully clever fellow he is, but when I ask myself what I have learnt, it is just nothing."

Social Darwinism was not merely the adaptation of Darwinism to economics. Originally it was a social philosophy that applied evolution to human society. In this respect, the philosophy coincided with Darwin's insistence on seeking material and not supernatural explanations of phenomena. Social Darwinism gained its "tooth-and-claw" reputation because, too often, people explained competition in Darwinian terms but forgot about the role of cooperation in his theory of natural selection. In its popular origins, social Darwinism was not a rationale for eliminating the weak. For example, many social Darwinists noted the inevitability of suffering in society. This was not, however, a proclamation of the necessity of suffering; it was an empirical observation about the state of society. Social Darwinism also pushed evolution far beyond the evidence presented by Darwin, who worked largely in natural science rather than in the emerging social sciences. For the two individuals who are the focus of this reassessment of social Darwinism, improving society was the goal, not eradicating unfit people. Those two were the most prominent social Darwinists of America in the late nineteenth and early twentieth centuries: Spencer, the philosopher of evolution, and William Graham Sumner, a Yale professor of sociology. Spencer enjoyed greater fame and notoriety in America than in his native England, and his concept of survival of the fittest in society was the primary inspiration for Sumner's social philosophy. . . .

Social Darwinism and the Problem of Definition

Social Darwinism seems a very straightforward proposition: applying natural selection, Darwin's explanation of how evolution works, to human society. However, defining the idea has been difficult. It has been used to defend both socialism and capitalism, to explain the need for cooperation and for competition, and to justify both social harmony and conflict. The rise of eugenics in the early twentieth century added another layer of meaning to the term, incorporating Mendel's theories of heredity and Francis Galton's genetics. The ultimate consequence of eugenics—Nazi Germany's attempt to purify the "Aryan" race in the 1930s—gave social Darwinism an especially evil cast and destroyed whatever intellectual integrity it may have had.

Social Darwinism has encompassed concepts that are broadly evolutionary, as well as those that apply to society only the narrower theory of natural selection. A number of scholars in the twentieth century have written about the subject, with Hofstadter remaining the one cited most frequently. However, Hofstadter's very broad definition of the term blurs distinctions among important thinkers, especially between Darwin and Spencer, and is so expansive that just about anyone can be classified as a social Darwinist, merely by accepting the idea that life has evolved. Barzun, in *Darwin, Marx, Wagner,* notes the confusion surrounding the idea. Darwin's *Descent of Man,* Barzun says, "wobbled between keeping man under the regime of natural selection and putting him under the modified regime of cooperation, reason, and love." That work also wobbled between asserting the primacy of the individual and reserving primacy for the group. Was the fittest individual to survive, or the fittest group?

In addition, there has been debate over the extent of the influence of the movement. Hofstadter, Curti, and others assign it great power, while Wyllie and Russett believe that it was appropriated by the few, not the many. LaVergata points out that social Darwinism has been used to defend capitalism, socialism, and even anarchism. Interpretation, he says, ranges from seeing the idea as a merely reactionary phenomenon to seeing it as part of a larger movement of "biologism." Bannister, studying the "myth" of social Darwinism, does an excellent job of exploring this definitional morass, stating that social Darwinism "consistently derived its sting from the implication that the struggle and selection of the animal realm were also agents of change (and progress) in human society—the governing assumption being that men shared natural laws with the rest of Creation." So social Darwinism has been many things, including contradictory.

Spencer and Sumner: The Heart of Social Darwinism

Spencer, not Darwin, was the original and foremost social Darwinist. And in America, Sumner was the most eminent, visible, and vocale disciple of Spencer. Part of the strength of the idea of social Darwinism lay in its "scientific" foundation, which was extremely important to both Spencer and Sumner and greatly affected the meaning they attached to the concept. Spencer was a self-taught Englishman with an ambition to explain everything in the universe. Over the course of a dozen volumes of philosophy, he argued for an evolutionary philosophy of the universe, encompassing the inorganic and organic worlds, including human society.

Spencer was a social determinist who believed that society gradually would move toward its potential in a uniform manner. The progress of society would be accelerated by favorable conditions or slowed by neglecting or impeding those conditions, although social evolution could not be diverted from its general direction. He was a defender of free enterprise and was extremely critical of government intervention in the economy. Free competition, he argued, was a natural law of economics and the best guarantor of a community's well-being. Government interference with the natural law of competition would hinder social progress and ultimately would result in economic misfortune. From the end of the Civil War through the 1880s, Spencer influenced thinkers in virtually all intellectual fields and had a particularly strong impact upon the founders of American sociology. One of those founders was Sumner.

Sumner, who was most prominent in the 1880s and 1890s, always was oriented toward the practical consequences of his work. He taught the first sociology course in the United States (perhaps in the world) and offered the first methodology course in the subject. Sumner believed that state interference in any economic matter betrayed the individualism that was so highly valued in the nation and so firmly fixed in the laws of nature. For Sumner, competition was as much a natural law as gravity, and regulation of competition ultimately was as futile as attempting to regulate gravity. Sumner used Spencer's social determinism to battle reformers, who he believed were operating under the illusions that there were no natural laws of society and that society could be remade with legislation. Sumner attacked socialists, sentimentalists, and metaphysicians as well, as he advocated free trade and laissez-faire economic policies. He believed that Spencer's science would explode socialist and reformer fantasies. . . .

Spencer's "Survival of the Fittest"

It was Spencer, not Darwin, who coined the term "survival of the fittest," but Darwin incorporated it into later editions of *On the Origin of Species*. Spencer was not pleased with Darwin's preeminence in evolutionary thought. On several occasions, Spencer criticized Darwin and pointed out that he had preceded Darwin in publishing work on evolution. It did not escape Spencer, as it sometimes did other writers in popular periodicals, that Darwin's chief contribution was the idea not of evolution, but of natural selection, the mechanism by which evolution worked. A bit of jealousy was in the air at times, as Spencer and other writers for *Popular Science Monthly* found it necessary to show readers that Spencer had been publishing books and essays on evolution well before Darwin published *The Origin* in 1859.

Spencer's and his allies' struggles to establish his primacy in evolutionary thinking reveals a problem in studying social Darwinism—Spencer's criticism of Darwin. Struggling to differentiate himself from Darwin, Spencer said that the concept of natural selection was an "untenable hypothesis," basically because of what he called the assumption that it could "pick out and select any small advantageous trait; while it can, in fact, pick out no traits, but can only further the development of traits which, *in marked ways,* [emphasis in original] increase the general fitness for the conditions of existence." Spencer argued that it was not shown how the slight variations posited by Darwin actually were providing an advantage. Spencer subtly rejected an important part of Darwin's argument, and at the same time assimilated parts of Darwin's thinking into his system of synthetic philosophy. In discussing the evolution of society, Spencer said that it was "impossible for artificial molding to do that which natural molding does," apparently denying the relevance of Darwin's argument from artificial selection in domesticated animals. But, he stated, "in the absence of variety, life would never have evolved at all." Variation was, of course, a critical part of Darwin's explanation of evolution.

Spencer's attempts to distinguish himself from Darwin often were labored and his points unclear. Both men clearly saw "survival of the fittest" as being cooperative as well as competitive, but they differed on the significance of natural selection as an explanation of biological evolution. This latter point was the problem for Spencer because Darwin increasingly became preeminent in the realm of biological evolution, so much so that he appeared to be gaining credit in the public mind for all of evolutionary thinking. Darwin was a scientist, Spencer a philosopher. The theory of natural selection was of limited use to a philosopher but invaluable to a biologist.

Popular Science Monthly correctly considered Spencer a philosopher first and a scientist second. The philosopher's social Darwinism was far more complex than economic survival of the fittest, as Spencer attempted to embrace physical and intellectual vitality, along with individual and social progress. Most significant for Spencer and the popular concept of "survival of the fittest," however, is the fact that he was not endorsing a vicious, tooth-and-claw social order. Subsequent interpretations of social Darwinism often ignored the role of cooperation in evolution and dwelled upon competition, particularly when it was manifested as conflict. Spencer's brand of social evolution allowed for "sentiments and institutions both relaxing" from a predatory atmosphere. He attacked government welfare and embraced private charity.

Like Darwin, Spencer accommodated cooperation as well as competition in evolution. He did not want the less fit, "the feeble, the unhealthy, the deformed, the stupid" to be eradicated, but he suggested some "private industrial institution" to discourage their marriage and breeding. He conceded that suffering might be necessary to decrease government welfare, which encouraged a stratum of "worthless people." However, he believed that the movement from "state-beneficence to a healthy condition of self-help and private beneficence, must be like the transition from an opium-eating life to a normal life—painful but remedial."

Spencer opposed government but not private help. He believed that programs to aid the poor should promote self-help, in order that the poor might elevate themselves. His endorsement of self-help revealed a positive side of Spencer's social Darwinism. He was a critic of what he called the "pleasure-hunting life," which he believed would result in an unfit individual and, ultimately, an unfit society. Self-assertion and self-preservation, he said, benefited society by keeping the divisions of society strong, or "more fit." In numerous instances, Spencer's survival of the fittest was rather benign, notably lacking in tooth-and-claw logic. Spencer denied that he wished the principle to operate identically among people as among "brutes": "The survival of the fittest, as I construe it in its social applications, is the survival of the industrially superior and those who are fittest for the requirements of social life. . . . aggression of every kind is hateful to me; . . . I have urged the change of all laws which either inflict injustice or fail to remedy injustice."

Spencer explained that two "sets of conditions" were necessary in order for people living together to achieve the greatest happiness: justice and generosity. The closest that *Popular Science Monthly* came to espousing a brutal kind of social Darwinism was in an editor's column that criticized socialism's condemnation of economic competition. The problem, the editor said, was not "survival of the fittest," but human nature: "We have only to think for one moment of what the world would be in the complete absence of competition—in other words, in the absence of all means for selecting the fit and rejecting the unfit or the less fit—in order to see that competition in itself is not and cannot be evil. That evils attach themselves to it signifies nothing more than that human society is as yet imperfect." Most of the article was devoted to the "golden rule": Do unto others as you would have them do unto you. The editor argued that competition served that rule by promoting the general welfare of society via orderly and *fair* competition.

Spencer, in the pages of *Popular Science Monthly,* fit evolution to society. Contrary to popular interpretations, however, Spencer was not a Darwinian, and he actually disavowed natural selection. Riding the crest of popular interest that *The Origin* generated, Spencer agreed with Darwin that both competition and cooperation were critical to social, as well as biologic, evolution. This point was lost on later eugenicists.

Sumner: Putting Spencer into Practice

Sumner was a prolific writer and lecturer, but in some respects he contrasted strongly with Spencer. The latter man outlined fairly early in his career a twenty-year agenda for completing the multitude of volumes that would comprise his synthetic philosophy. He then set about writing the intellectually weighty tomes. Sumner, who praised Spencer as the man "who has opened the way" to sociology, was not so disciplined in publishing or so subservient to an agenda as his mentor. Much of his writing has survived as lecture notes, drafts of chapters, and essays that were never published, as well as in the form of wide-ranging articles for, and letters to, various newspapers and magazines. From 1869 to 1896, he wrote approximately 125 articles and letters for popular publications, including daily newspapers in New York and Chicago, and magazines such as *Collier's Harper's Monthly, Cosmopolitan, London Economist,* and *The Independent.* The specialty publications for which he wrote included the *New York Mercantile Journal,* the *Northwestern Lumberman, Rand McNally's Banker's Monthly,* and the *Bond Review.* His debates, too, were public matters. In 1883, in New York and New Haven newspapers, nearly twenty letters were exchanged, with Sumner opposing protective tariffs and a local linen manufacturer strongly favoring them.

Both Sumner and Spencer tended to publish in the upscale literary magazines most likely to have an educated audience interested in social, economic, and political issues. In *Collier's,* for example, one would find a literary orientation that attempted to rival *Harper's. Collier's,* founded in 1888, published the work of such writers as Rudyard Kipling and Frank Norris, the poetry of James Whitcomb Riley, and Henry James's serialized *The Turn of the Screw.* The magazine's content was a bit lighter than that of *Harper's,* which was viewed as both a model and a competitor, but the circulation of *Collier's* rose to three hundred thousand shortly after the turn of the century. Similarly, *Cosmopolitan,* founded in 1886, was a general literary magazine, not quite on the level of *Harper's* or the *Atlantic,* but comparing favorably to them. It was oriented more toward public affairs and by the 1890s was one of the leading illustrated magazines in the nation, noted for its coverage of current events as well as its fiction, which included work by William Dean Howells and Jack London. Compared to its competitors, *Cosmopolitan* carried more features on economic, political, and social issues, and here Sumner's writing fit very well.

Like Spencer's, Sumner's popular writings were concerned with large social issues, and "survival of the fittest" constituted only a part of his arguments. A character sketch in *Popular Science Monthly* very accurately and succinctly provided the context for studying Sumner, to whom the magazine attributed a philosophy that "denies anything arbitrary or accidental in social phenomena, or that there is any field in them for the arbitrary intervention of man. He therefore allows but very limited field for legislation. He holds that men must do with social laws what they do with physical laws—learn them, obey them, and conform to them." Sumner followed Spencer's thinking in believing that society, like nature, was subject to laws, and people were obligated to follow them, and should not attempt to tamper with them. The basic law, of course, was evolution. Furthering this philosophy was a major theme in Sumner's popular writing. For Sumner, the role of government was narrow. He stated, in his widely read *What Social Classes Owe to Each Other,* that government had to deal only with two primary things: "They are the property of men and honor of women. These it has to defend against crime."

Folkways (1907) was the book upon which Sumner's reputation came to rest. Sociologist Charles Horton Cooley compared *Folkways,* which was the first book to become a sociological classic in America, to *The Origin* in significance. Sumner's primary contribution to sociology was the introduction of general concepts that were based upon methodical observation and collection of evidence. His sociology was descriptive and based on facts, in contrast to Spencer's abstract philosophizing.

Sumner and "Natural Law"

Sumner paralleled Darwin in relying upon natural law, not metaphysics or theology, for answers to questions about the workings of the world. But where Darwin disciplined himself to stay within the confines of empirical science, Sumner did not, putting his energy into economic policy, immigration, tariffs, and any number of legislative initiatives that he saw as naïvely defying the law of evolution. This was Sumner's distortion of Darwinian evolutionary theory, as well as the way in which he applied the Spencerian philosophy to everyday political and social issues.

Sumner's intellectual relationship to Spencer is most apparent in the idea of an "organic" society. Like Spencer, Sumner declared that customs, including laws and regulations, had to evolve slowly in order to be effective: "Legislation and state action are stiff, rigid, inelastic, incapable of adaptation to cases. . . . Hence, the higher the organization of society, the more mischievous legislative regulation is sure to be." In the same essay, Sumner asserted that people were limited in their power and by their antecedents. The answer was "in ourselves," and there was no escaping the "struggle for existence."

Sumner believed that legislative meddling in the economy usually started with legislators and their backers, who worked in ignorance of the nature of society and economics. Typically they only made matters worse by attempting to change natural law. For example, he cautioned that regulating railroads should begin with knowledge gained by "experience and observation," and he even conceded that a regulatory commission might be a good idea—a concession that would not have been made by one espousing a merely antagonistic survival of the fittest. But Sumner warned that "blundering experiments in legislation cannot be simply abandoned if they do not work well; . . . they leave their effects behind." Sumner extended Spencer's "organic society" concept by making each component of a more complex society, like the organs of more highly evolved life forms, highly sensitive to changes in any other "organ" of the society.

This highlights one of the points of confusion about social Darwinism, as it was presented to the public: the "unit of analysis" problem. What was being studied, society as a whole or the individuals within society? Both Sumner and Spencer compared "organic society" to a biological organism, implying that society was the object of analysis; but they also spoke of individual fitness as being critical to the progress of society, suggesting that the essential concern was with the individual. This ambiguity invited conflicting applications of Darwinism. If the law acted upon society generally, then one easily could interpret it as advocating cooperation and regulation. If, however, the individual was preeminent, then competition and minimal government were the engines of progress.

Sumner drew not only from Darwin and Spencer but also from Malthus, who articulated the idea that a very real law affecting humanity was the ratio of population to available land. Populations would grow geometrically (2, 4, 8, 16), Malthus hypothesized, while resources grew only arithmetically (2, 4, 6, 8). Sumner called this one of the "facts of the social order . . . which control the fate of the human race." Ignoring these laws meant being unable to understand the workings of society. In the laws of nature, he said, "It will be found that men are subject to supply and demand, . . . and that any correct comprehension of the existing industrial system must proceed from supply and demand."

It was in this broader conception of laws that Sumner found a place for the idea of "survival of the fittest" in society. For both Sumner and Spencer, the concept of natural selection, or survival of the fittest, was actually an idea of secondary importance in understanding humanity. Unlike Spencer, who was working out a whole philosophical system, Sumner was dealing only with the sociological impact of Darwin's theory. The struggle for existence was necessary, according to Sumner, because it was dictated by natural law and could not be abolished. But for Sumner, to posit a struggle for existence was not to glorify men grinding one another out in bloody struggle. In fact, he condemned strife: "It is legitimate to think of Nature as a hard mistress against whom we are maintaining the struggle for existence. All our science and art are victories over her, but when we quarrel amongst ourselves we lose the fruits of our victory just as certainly as we should if she were a human opponent. All plunder and robbery squander the fund which has been produced by society for the support of society. It makes no difference whether the plunder and robbery are legal or illegal in form." He did not deny that "weaker" societies had perished at the hands of stronger ones, a pattern that he saw in history when civilized and uncivilized societies clashed, with the former usually emerging as victors. Europeans dominated the world, he believed, because they had been the most enterprising people in the fifteenth and sixteenth centuries.

Economic competition was, for Sumner, a law that forced individuals to develop "all powers that exist according to their measure and degree. . . . Liberty of development and equality of result are therefore diametrically opposed to each other." Individuals varied according to inherited powers, advantages of training, and personal attributes such as courage and perseverance; the results of their efforts varied accordingly. Millionaires, he said, "are a product of natural selection, acting on the whole body of men to pick out those who can meet the requirement of certain work to be done." Society benefited by imposing discipline on the economic system, as competitors studied the victor's winning ways, and by insuring that those talented in special areas eventually would find their way to those areas. In this fashion he reconciled a "ceaseless war of interests" with the betterment of the whole society.

The struggle for existence, Sumner said, was a struggle with nature. Moreover, "Competition . . . is a law of nature." He abhorred socialism, which he saw as a system making some people pay for the self-indulgence, idleness, and ignorance of others: "We shall favor the survival of the unfittest, and we shall accomplish this by destroying liberty. Let it be understood that we cannot go outside of this alternative: liberty, inequality, survival of the fittest; not-liberty, equality, survival of the unfittest. The former carries society forward and favors all its best members; the latter carries society downward and favors all its worst members." Socialism was mere sentimentalism that ignored the reality of society's fixed laws, "precisely analogous to those [laws] of the physical order." The socialist or philanthropist who saved victims of poverty was accused of "only cultivating the distress which he pretends to cure." Sumner believed that hardships were the products of thousands of years of evolution of human society and that poverty was part of the whole system. "This is a world in which the rule is, 'Root, hog, or die,' . . . It is the popular experience which has formulated these sayings. How can we make them untrue?"

Socialism's antithesis was individualism. Sumner called socialism a scheme to defraud an individual of liberty, "robbing him of his best chance of improving his position." The complaint against socialism was the same as the complaint against undue state interference in the economy—it would impede the natural progress of society by stifling the advancement of the fittest members. The "observation of facts will show that men are unequal through a very wide range of variation," he asserted, setting up the proposition that survival of the fittest was a scientific concept based upon observable fact. Even the idea that monopolies should be controlled by the state was a "sort of current dogma" that had not been adequately studied with attention to observable facts. Sumner's disdain for sentimental socialism, misguided reformers, and whimsical regulation was based upon his insistence on the necessity of looking at the "facts," of treating the study of society like a physical science, with observation, analysis, and verification at the core of the search for knowledge. Any other path, he believed, was mere speculation.

Sumner was willing to peel back the assumptions (which he felt commonly were paraded as facts) of human existence to a core of discomforting propositions: "Our assumption is that we should all be here, under any circumstances whatever, and that the provision for us here is, or ought to be, somewhere on hand. Unfortunately none of these ideas can be verified by an examination of the facts. We are not needed here at all; the world existed no one knows how long without any men on it."

Natural Law, Natural Selection

Sumner and Spencer stressed the results of a long evolutionary process on society. They offered social reality as evidence—the existence of the poor, the existence of weaker and stronger nations, and the economic progress of the U.S. under capitalism—and in doing so borrowed the prestige of Darwin and of science. They used the language of Darwin—employing such terms as "selection" and "organism"— but not his painstaking, tedious attention to collecting data in support of a theory.

As popularizers, . . . Spencer and Sumner were prominent at a time when science and social science were increasingly important in the academy and for the public. Social Darwinism justified a number of Victorian ideals: the divisions of society, the rewards of industry, the goal of "the good life," the virtues of civility and civilization. Hofstadter depicts social Darwinism as basically a defense of unregulated capitalism, a system of ideas that fit easily into the American mythology of the rugged individualist. Hofstadter recognizes the contradictory applications of social Darwinism, such as defending both socialism and capitalism, but he asserts that the American middle class's ideology of achievement made tooth-and-claw Darwinism the accepted version of the philosophy's many permutations. However, Spencer's and Sumner's writing in periodicals, which were aimed at middle- and upper-class audiences, reveal far greater complexity in the tenets of the movement. Although the robber barons might seize upon social Darwinism, such an application was only one act in the grander mission of uplifting all of society. This use of social Darwinism may have reached its zenith in Andrew Carnegie's 1889 article of social Darwinism, in which the author linked individualism, social divisions, and economic competition. But Sumner and Spencer reached a conclusion unlike Carnegie's, because their goal was to elaborate a coherent world view which might both explain society and establish an agenda for further sociological inquiry. Carnegie, as well as others who eschewed his simplistic view, were only defending the status quo.

Social Darwinism itself was well suited to popularization. Its core idea was rather simple: the survival of the fittest in human society. Although it had its complexities and contradictions, its essence was, and is, quite easy to convey in non-technical language. The idea gained power and attention because it offered a good explanation of social problems, such as poverty and disease. At the same time, it provided a good defense of one's relative wealth and health. Thus, inequality could be seen not as a political or social problem but merely as the working out of natural law.

However, an incongruity arose in the association of Darwin with nonbiological social Darwinism. The nonbiological nature of the ideas espoused by Sumner and Spencer is shown in their attempts to divorce themselves from, and at times to criticize, the central tenet of Darwinism—natural selection. The social Darwinists could not divorce themselves from the Darwin name, nor would they have wanted to lose the credibility that association with his empirical science entailed. To the chagrin of Spencer, Darwin's name became a vehicle for popularizing an evolutionary philosophy. Through its association with Darwin and natural selection, the philosophy took on the aura of a science. For both Sumner and Spencer, so-called "social Darwinism" (neither of them used the term) was a secondary idea, not a primary one. Both derived their social laws from the broader concept of natural law, to which humanity, as well as the rest of the universe, was subject. Both Spencer and Sumner gave minimal credit to Darwin but were strongly identified with him. Charles Darwin was not central to the philosophy of social Darwinism in its popular origins.

FURTHER READING

Robert C. Bannister, *Social Darwinism: Science and Myth in Anglo-American Social Thought* (1989)
———. *Sociology and Scientism: The American Quest for Objectivity, 1880–1940* (1987)
Robert V. Bruce, *Alexander Graham Bell and the Conquest of Solitude* (1973)
Alfred Chandler, Jr., *The Visible Hand: The Managerial Revolution in American Business* (1977)
Peter Conn, *The Divided Mind; Ideology and Imagination in America 1898–1917* (1983)
George Cotken, *Reluctant Modernism: American Thought and Culture, 1880–1900* (1992)
Ellen F. Fitzpatrick, *Endless Crusade: Women Social Scientists and Progressive Reform* (1900)
Mary O. Furner, *Advocacy & Objectivity: A Crisis in the Professionalization of American Social Science, 1865–1905* (1975)
Thomas L. Haskell, *The Emergence of Professional Social Science* (1977)
David Kohn, ed., *The Darwinian Heritage* (1985)
T. J. Jackson Lears, *No Place of Grace: Anti-modernism and the Transformation of American Culture, 1880–1920* (1982)
Henry F. May, *The End of American Innocence* (1959)
Mark Pittenger, *American Socialists and Evolutionary Thought* (1993)
Gary Scott Smith, *The Seeds of Secularization: Calvinism, Culture, and Pluralism in America, 1870–1915* (1985)
R. Jackson Wilson, *In Quest of Community: Social Philosophy in the United States 1860–1920* (1985)

CHAPTER
9

The Language of Empire

In the final decade of the nineteenth century, American policy and public opinion foresook their traditional isolationism and adopted an increasingly assertive stance toward the rest of the world. Together, depression-related fears of economic overproduction, anxieties over the closing of the frontier (see Frederick Jackson Turner, Chapter 3), Social Darwinian concern with survival of the white (Anglo-American) race, and a desire to match the nation's industrial might with commensurate strength in the world's trading lanes fueled an expansionist fever. Reflecting diverse origins, the language of empire was marked by different accents. In practice, America's early international muscle flexing, focusing on Cuba, Central America, the Philippines, and island steppingstones to China, was a comparatively restricted affair. Indeed, the inflated rhetoric and great expectations attached to international adventures indirectly addressed domestic tensions—over race, immigration, and even the renewal of manhood—while explicitly treating matters of substantive foreign engagement.

DOCUMENTS

The following selections feature some of the most influential voices in the debate over American expansionism. Captain Alfred T. Mahan of the Naval War College, in *The Influence of Sea Power upon History* (1890), from which Document 1 is taken, was one of the first to link the need for a bigger navy with an analysis of the growth of overseas trade. Document 2, Rough Rider Theodore Roosevelt, in an address to a Chicago men's club in 1899, connects the application of American firmness abroad to the quality of moral fiber at home. In Documents 3 and 4, Democratic standard-bearer and anti-imperialist William Jennings Bryan matches arguments in 1890 with pro-imperialist Republican Senator Albert J. Beveridge of Indiana over U.S. policy in the Philippines. Finally, Document 5 presents the famous Roosevelt Corollary to the Monroe Doctrine, issued by way of a presidential message in 1904, in which President Roosevelt establishes the official justification for U.S. intervention in Latin America.

1. Alfred T. Mahan Proclaims the Importance of Sea Power, 1890

To turn now from the particular lessons drawn from the history of the past to the general question of the influence of government upon the sea career of its people, it is seen that that influence can work in two distinct but closely related ways.

First, in peace: The government by its policy can favor the natural growth of a people's industries and its tendencies to seek adventure and gain by way of the sea; or it can try to develop such industries and such sea-going bent, when they do not naturally exist; or, on the other hand, the government may, by mistaken action check and fetter the progress which the people left to themselves would make. In any one of these ways the influence of the government will be felt, making or marring the sea power of the country in the matter of peaceful commerce; upon which alone, it cannot be too often insisted, a thoroughly strong navy can be based.

Secondly, for war: The influence of the government will be felt in its most legitimate manner in maintaining an armed navy, of a size commensurate with the growth of its shipping and the importance of the interests connected with it. More important even than the size of the navy is the question of its institutions, favoring a healthful spirit and activity, and providing for rapid development in time of war by an adequate reserve of men and of ships and by measures for drawing out that general reserve power which has before been pointed to, when considering the character and pursuits of the people. Undoubtedly under this second head of war-like preparation must come the maintenance of suitable naval stations, in those distant parts of the world to which the armed shipping must follow the peaceful vessels of commerce. The protection of such stations must depend either upon direct military force, as do Gibraltar and Malta, or upon a surrounding friendly population, such as the American colonists once were to England, and, it may be presumed, the Australian colonists now are. Such friendly surroundings and backing, joined to a reasonable military provision, are the best of defences, and when combined with decided preponderance at sea, make a scattered and extensive empire, like that of England, secure; for while it is true that an unexpected attack may cause disaster in some one quarter, the actual superiority of naval power prevents such disaster from being general or irremediable. History has sufficiently proved this. England's naval bases have been in all parts of the world; and her fleets have at once protected them, kept open the communications between them, and relied upon them for shelter.

Colonies attached to the mother-country afford, therefore, the surest means of supporting abroad the sea power of a country. In peace, the influence of the government should be felt in promoting by all means a warmth of attachment and a unity of interest which will make the welfare of one the welfare of all, and the quarrel of one the quarrel of all; and in war, or rather for war, by inducing such measures of organization and defence as shall be felt by all to be a fair distribution of a burden of which each reaps the benefit.

Alfred Mahan, *The Influence of Sea Power upon History, 1660–1783* (Boston: Little, Brown, 1893), 81–87.

Such colonies the United States has not and is not likely to have. As regards purely military naval stations, the feeling of her people was probably accurately expressed by an historian of the English navy a hundred years ago, speaking then of Gibraltar and Port Mahon. "Military governments," said he, "agree so little with the industry of a trading people, and are in themselves so repugnant to the genius of the British people, that I do not wonder that men of good sense and of all parties have inclined to give up these, as Tangiers was given up." Having therefore no foreign establishments, either colonial or military, the ships of war of the United States, in war, will be like land birds, unable to fly far from their own shores. To provide resting-places for them, where they can coal and repair, would be one of the first duties of a government proposing to itself the development of the power of the nation at sea. . . .

The question is eminently one in which the influence of the government should make itself felt, to build up for the nation a navy which, if not capable of reaching distant countries, shall at least be able to keep clear the chief approaches to its own. The eyes of the country have for a quarter of a century been turned from the sea; the results of such a policy and of its opposite will be shown in the instance of France and of England. Without asserting a narrow parallelism between the case of the United States and either of these, it may safely be said that it is essential to the welfare of the whole country that the conditions of trade and commerce should remain, as far as possible, unaffected by an external war. In order to do this, the enemy must be kept not only out of our ports, but far away from our coasts.

2. Theodore Roosevelt Links War in the Philippines to the Ideal of the Strenuous Life, 1899

In speaking to you, men of the greatest city of the West, men of the State which gave to the country Lincoln and Grant, men who preëminently and distinctly embody all that is most American in the American character, I wish to preach, not the doctrine of ignoble ease, but the doctrine of the strenuous life, the life of toil and effort, of labor and strife; to preach that highest form of success which comes, not to the man who desires mere easy peace, but to the man who does not shrink from danger, from hardship, or from bitter toil, and who out of these wins the splendid ultimate triumph.

A life of slothful ease, a life of that peace which springs merely from lack either of desire or of power to strive after great things, is as little worthy of a nation as of an individual. I ask only that what every self-respecting American demands from himself and from his sons shall be demanded of the American nation as a whole. Who among you would teach your boys that ease, that peace, is to be the first consideration in their eyes—to be the ultimate goal after which they strive? You men of Chicago have made this city great, you men of Illinois have done your share, and more than your share, in making America great, because you neither preach nor practise such a doctrine. You work yourselves, and you bring up your sons to work.

Theodore Roosevelt, *The Strenuous Life: Essays and Addresses* (New York: Century Co., 1902), 1–9, 16–21.

If you are rich and are worth your salt, you will teach your sons that though they may have leisure, it is not to be spent in idleness; for wisely used leisure merely means that those who possess it, being free from the necessity of working for their livelihood, are all the more bound to carry on some kind of nonremunerative work in science, in letters, in art, in exploration, in historical research—work of the type we most need in this country, the successful carrying out of which reflects most honor upon the nation, We do not admire the man of timid peace. We admire the man who embodies victorious effort; the man who never wrongs his neighbor, who is prompt to help a friend, but who has those virile qualities necessary to win in the stern strife of actual life. It is hard to fail, but it is worse never to have tried to succeed. In this life we get nothing save by effort. Freedom from effort in the present merely means that there has been stored up effort in the past. A man can be freed from the necessity of work only by the fact that he or his fathers before him have worked to good purpose. If the freedom thus purchased is used aright, and the man still does actual work, though of a different kind, whether as a writer or a general, whether in the field of politics or in the field of exploration and adventure, he shows he deserves his good fortune. But if he treats this period of freedom from the need of actual labor as a period, not of preparation, but of mere enjoyment, even though perhaps not of vicious enjoyment, he shows that he is simply a cumberer of the earth's surface, and he surely unfits himself to hold his own with his fellows if the need to do so should again arise. A mere life of ease is not in the end a very satisfactory life, and, above all, it is a life which ultimately unfits those who follow it for serious work in the world.

In the last analysis a healthy state can exist only when the men and women who make it up lead clean, vigorous, healthy lives; when the children are so trained that they shall endeavor, not to shirk difficulties, but to overcome them; not to seek ease, but to know how to wrest triumph from toil and risk. The man must be glad to do a man's work, to dare and endure and to labor; to keep himself, and to keep those dependent upon him. The woman must be the housewife, the helpmeet of the homemaker, the wise and fearless mother of many healthy children. In one of Daudet's powerful and melancholy books he speaks of "the fear of maternity, the haunting terror of the young wife of the present day." When such words can be truthfully written of a nation, that nation is rotten to the heart's core. When men fear work or fear righteous war, when women fear motherhood, they tremble on the brink of doom; and well it is that they should vanish from the earth, where they are fit subjects for the scorn of all men and women who are themselves strong and brave and high-minded.

As it is with the individual, so it is with the nation. . . .

If we are to be a really great people, we must strive in good faith to play a great part in the world. We cannot avoid meeting great issues. All that we can determine for ourselves is whether we shall meet them well or ill. In 1898 we could not help being brought face to face with the problem of war with Spain. All we could decide was whether we should shrink like cowards from the contest, or enter into it as beseemed a brave and high-spirited people; and, once in, whether failure or success should crown our banners. So it is now. We cannot avoid the responsibilities that confront us in Hawaii, Cuba, Porto [*sic*] Rico and the Philippines. . . . The timid man, the lazy man, the man who distrusts his country, the over-civilized man, who has lost the great fighting, masterful virtues, the ignorant man, and the man of dull mind, whose soul is incapable of feeling the mighty life that thrills "stern men with empires in their brains"—all these, of course, shrink from seeing the nation undertake its new duties; shrink from seeing us build a navy and an army adequate to our needs; shrink from seeing us do our share of the world's work, by bringing order out of chaos in the great, fair tropic islands from which the valor of our soldiers and sailors has driven the Spanish flag. These are the men who fear the strenuous life, who fear the only national life which is really worth leading. . . .

I preach to you, then, my countrymen, that our country calls not for the life of ease but for the life of strenuous endeavor. The twentieth century looms before us big with the fate of many nations. If we stand idly by, if we seek merely swollen, slothful ease and ignoble peace, if we shrink from the hard contests where men must win at hazard of their lives and at the risk of all they hold dear, then the bolder and stronger peoples will pass us by, and will win for themselves the domination of the world. Let us therefore boldly face the life of strife, resolute to do our duty well and manfully; resolute to uphold righteousness by deed and by word; resolute to be both honest and brave, to serve high ideals, yet to use practical methods. Above all, let us shrink from no strife, moral or physical, within or without the nation, provided we are certain that the strife is justified, for it is only through strife, through hard and dangerous endeavor, that we shall ultimately win the goal of true national greatness.

3. William Jennings Bryan Opposes U.S. Occupation of the Philippines, 1900

The young man upon reaching his majority can do what he pleases. He can disregard the teaching of his parents; he can trample upon all that he has been taught to consider sacred; he can disobey the laws of the State, the laws of society and the laws of God. He can stamp failure upon his life and make his very existence a curse to his fellow men, and he can bring his father and mother in sorrow to the grave; but he cannot annul the sentence, "The wages of sin is death."

And so with the nation. It is of age and it can do what it pleases; it can spurn the traditions of the past; it can repudiate the principles upon which the nation rests; it can employ force instead of reason; it can substitute might for right; it can conquer weaker people; it can exploit their lands, appropriate their property and kill their people; but it cannot repeal the moral law or escape the punishment decreed for the violation of human rights. . . .

Some argue that American rule in the Philippine Islands will result in the better education of Filipinos. Be not deceived. If we expect to maintain a colonial policy, we shall not find it to our advantage to educate the people. The educated Filipinos are now in revolt against us, and the most ignorant ones have made the least resistance to our domination. If we are to govern them without their consent and give

William Jennings Bryan's speech at the Indianapolis Democratic Convention, August 8, 1900, *Speeches* (New York: Funk and Wagnalls Co., 1909), 39–44, 46–47.

them no voice in determining the taxes which they must pay, we dare not educate them, lest they learn to read the Declaration of Independence and Constitution of the United States and mock us for our inconsistency.

The principle arguments, . . . , advanced by those who enter upon a defense of imperialism are:

First—That we must improve the present opportunity to become a world power and enter into international politics.

Second—That our commercial interests in the Philippine Islands and in the Orient make it necessary for us to hold the islands permanently.

Third—That the spread of the Christian religion will be facilitated by a colonial policy.

Fourth—That there is no honorable retreat from the position which the nation has taken.

The first argument is addrest to the nation's pride and the second to the nation's pocket-book. The third is intended for the church member and the fourth for the partisan.

It is sufficient answer to the first argument to say that for more than a century this nation has been a world power. For ten decades it has been the most potent influence in the world. Not only has it been a world power, but it has done more to shape the politics of the human race than all the other nations of the world combined. Because our Declaration of Independence was promulgated others have been promulgated. Because the patriots of 1776 fought for liberty others have fought for it. Because our Constitution was adopted other constitutions have been adopted.

The growth of the principle of self-government, planted on American soil, has been the overshadowing political fact of the nineteenth century. It has made this nation conspicuous among the nations and given it a place in history such as no other nation has ever enjoyed. Nothing has been able to check the onward march of this idea. I am not willing that this nation shall cast aside the omnipotent weapon of truth to seize again the weapons of physical warfare. I would not exchange the glory of this Republic for the glory of all the empires that have risen and fallen since time began. . . .

A war of conquest is as unwise as it is unrighteous. A harbor and coaling station in the Philippines would answer every trade and military necessity and such a concession could have been secured at any time without difficulty.

It is not necessary to own people in order to trade with them. We carry on trade today with every part of the world, and our commerce has expanded more rapidly than the commerce of any European empire. We do not own Japan or China, but we trade with their people. We have not absorbed the republics of Central and South America, but we trade with them. It has not been necessary to have any political connection with Canada or the nations of Europe in order to trade with them. Trade cannot be permanently profitable unless it is voluntary.

When trade is secured by force, the cost of securing it and retaining it must be taken out of the profits, and the profits are never large enough to cover the expense. Such a system would never be defended but for the fact that the expense is borne by all the people, while the profits are enjoyed by a few.

Imperialism would be profitable to the army contractors; it would be profitable to the ship owners, who would carry live soldiers to the Philippines and bring dead soldiers back; it would be profitable to those who would seize upon the franchises, and it would be profitable to the officials whose salaries would be fixt here and paid over there; but to the farmer, to the laboring man and to the vast majority of those engaged in other occupations it would bring expenditure without return and risk without reward.

Farmers and laboring men have, as a rule, small incomes and under systems which place the tax upon consumption pay much more than their fair share of the expenses of government. Thus the very people who receive least benefit from imperialism will be injured most by the military burdens which accompany it.

In addition the evils which he and the farmer share in common, the laboring man will be the first to suffer if oriental subjects seek work in the United States; the first to suffer if American capital leaves our shores to employ oriental labor in the Philippines to supply the trade of China and Japan; the first to suffer from the violence which the military spirit arouses and the first to suffer when the methods of imperialism are applied to our own Government. . . .

The religious argument varies in positiveness from a passive belief that Providence delivered the Filipinos into our hands, for their good and our glory, to the exultation of the minister who said that we ought to "thrash the natives (Filipinos) until they understand who we are," and that "every bullet sent, every cannon shot and every flag waved means righteousness."

We cannot approve of this doctrine in one place unless we are willing to apply it everywhere. If there is poison in the blood of the hand it will ultimately reach the heart. It is equally true that forcible Christianity, if planted under the American flag in the far-away Orient, will sooner or later be transplanted upon American soil.

If true Christianity consists of carrying out in our daily lives the teachings of Christ, who will say that we are commanded to civilize with dynamite and proselyte with the sword? . . .

There is an easy, honest, honorable solution of the Philippine question. It is set forth in the Democratic platform and it is submitted with confidence to the American people. This plan I unreservedly indorse. If elected, I will convene Congress in extraordinary session as soon as inaugurated and recommend an immediate declaration of the nation's purpose, first, to establish a stable form of government in the Philippine Islands, just as we are now establishing a stable form of government in Cuba; second, to give independence to the Filipinos as we have promised to give independence to the Cubans; third, to protect the Filipinos from outside interference while they work out their destiny, just as we have protected the republics of Central and South America, and are, by the Monroe doctrine, pledged to protect Cuba.

A European protectorate often results in the plundering of the ward by the guardian. An American protectorate gives to the nation protected the advantage of our strength, without making it the victim of our greed. For three-quarters of a century the Monroe doctrine has been a shield to neighboring republics and yet it has imposed no pecuniary burden upon us. After the Filipinos had aided us in the war against Spain, we could not honorably turn them over to their former masters; we could not leave them to be the victims of the ambitious designs of European nations, and since we do not desire to make them a part of us or to hold them as subjects, we propose the only alternative, namely, to give them independence and guard them against molestation from without.

When our opponents are unable to defend their position by argument they fall back upon the assertion that it is destiny, and insist that we must submit to it, no matter how much it violates our moral precepts and our principles of government. This is a complacent philosophy. It obliterates the distinction between right and wrong and makes individuals and nations the helpless victims of circumstance.

Destiny is the subterfuge of the invertebrate, who, lacking the courage to oppose error, seeks some plausible excuse for supporting it. Washington said that the destiny of the republican form of government was deeply, if not finally, staked on the experiment entrusted to the American people. How different Washington's definition of destiny from the Republican definition!

4. Albert Beveridge Defends U.S. Imperialism, 1900

Mr. President, the times call for candor. The Philippines are ours forever, "territory belonging to the United States," as the Constitution calls them. And just beyond the Philippines are China's illimitable markets. We will not retreat from either. We will not repudiate our duty in the archipelago. We will not abandon our opportunity in the Orient. We will not renounce our part in the mission of our race, trustee, under God, of the civilization of the world. And we will move forward to our work, not howling out regrets like slaves whipped to their burdens, but with gratitude for a task worthy of our strength, and thanksgiving to Almighty God that He has marked us as His chosen people, henceforth to lead in the regeneration of the world.

This island empire is the last land left in all the oceans. If it should prove a mistake to abandon it, the blunder once made would be irretrievable. If it proves a mistake to hold it, the error can be corrected when we will. Every other progressive nation stands ready to relieve us.

But to hold it will be no mistake. Our largest trade henceforth must be with Asia. The Pacific is our ocean. More and more Europe will manufacture the most it needs, secure from its colonies the most it consumes. Where shall we turn for consumers of our surplus? Geography answers the question. China is our natural customer. She is nearer to us than to England, Germany, or Russia, the commercial powers of the present and the future. They have moved nearer to China by securing permanent bases on her borders. The Philippines give us a base at the door of all the East.

Lines of navigation from our ports to the Orient and Australia; from the Isthmian Canal to Asia; from the Oriental ports to Australia, converge at and separate from the Philippines. They are a self-supporting, dividend-paying fleet, permanently anchored at a spot selected by the strategy of Providence, commanding the Pacific. And the Pacific is the ocean of the commerce of the future. Most future wars will be conflicts for commerce. The power that rules the Pacific, therefore, is the power that rules the world. And, with the Philippines, that power is and will forever be the American Republic. . . .

Nothing is so natural as trade with one's neighbors. The Philippines make us the nearest neighbors of all the East. Nothing is more natural than to trade with those you know. This is the philosophy of all advertising. The Philippines bring us permanently

Congressional Record, 56th Cong., 1st Sess., 704–712.

face to face with the most sought-for customers of the world. National prestige, national propinquity, these and commercial activity are the elements of commercial success. The Philippines give the first; the character of the American people supply the last. It is a providential conjunction of all the elements of trade, of duty, and of power. If we are willing to go to war rather than let England have a few feet of frozen Alaska, which affords no market and commands none, what should we not do rather than let England, Germany, Russia, or Japan have all the Philippines? And no man on the spot can fail to see that this would be their fate if we retired. . . .

Here, then, Senators, is the situation. Two years ago there was no land in all the world which we could occupy for any purpose. Our commerce was daily turning toward the Orient, and geography and trade developments made necessary our commercial empire over the Pacific. And in that ocean we had no commercial, naval, or military base. To-day we have one of the three great ocean possessions of the globe, located at the most commanding commercial, naval, and military points in the eastern seas, within hail of India, shoulder to shoulder with China, richer in its own resources than any equal body of land on the entire globe, and peopled by a race which civilization demands shall be improved. Shall we abandon it? That man little knows the common people of the Republic, little understands the instincts of our race, who thinks we will not hold it fast and hold it forever, administering just government by simplest methods. . . .

But, Senators, it would be better to abandon this combined garden and Gibraltar of the Pacific, and count our blood and treasure already spent a profitable loss, than to apply any academic arrangement of self-government to these children. They are not capable of self-government. How could they be? They are not of a self-governing race. They are Orientals, Malays, instructed by Spaniards in the latter's worst estate.

They know nothing of practical government except as they have witnessed the weak, corrupt, cruel, and capricious rule of Spain. What magic will anyone employ to dissolve in their minds and characters those impressions of governors and governed which three centuries of misrule has created? What alchemy will change the oriental quality of their blood and set the self-governing currents of the American pouring through their Malay veins? How shall they, in the twinkling of an eye, be exalted to the heights of self-governing peoples which required a thousand years for us to reach, Anglo-Saxon though we are? . . .

The three best educators on the island at different times made to me the same comparison, that the common people in their stupidity are like their caribou bulls. They are not even good agriculturists. Their waste of cane is inexcusable. Their destruction of hemp fiber is childish. They are incurably indolent. They have no continuity or thoroughness of industry. They will quit work without notice and amuse themselves until the money they have earned is spent. They are like children playing at men's work.

No one need fear their competition with our labor. No reward could beguile, no force compel, these children of indolence to leave their trifling lives for the fierce and fervid industry of high-wrought America. The very reverse is the fact. One great problem is the necessary labor to develop these islands—to build the roads, open the mines, clear the wilderness, drain the swamps, dredge the harbors. The natives will not supply it. A lingering prejudice against the Chinese may prevent us from letting them supply it. Ultimately, when the real truth of the climate and human conditions is known, it is barely possible that our labor will go there. Even now young men with the right moral fiber and a little capital can make fortunes there as planters. . . .

The Declaration of Independence does not forbid us to do our part in the regeneration of the world. If it did, the Declaration would be wrong, just as the Articles of Confederation, drafted by the very same men who signed the Declaration, was found to be wrong. The Declaration has no application to the present situation. It was written by self-governing men for self-governing men. . . .

Senators in opposition are estopped from denying our constitutional power to govern the Philippines as circumstances may demand, for such power is admitted in the case of Florida, Louisiana, Alaska. How, then, is it denied in the Philippines? Is there a geographical interpretation to the Constitution? Do degrees of longitude fix constitutional limitations? Does a thousand miles of ocean diminish constitutional power more than a thousand miles of land? . . .

Mr. President, this question is deeper than any question of party politics; deeper than any question of the isolated policy of our country even; deeper even than any question of constitutional power. It is elemental. It is racial. God has not been preparing the English-speaking and Teutonic peoples for a thousand years for nothing but vain and idle self-contemplation and self-admiration. No! He has made us the master organizers of the world to establish system where chaos reigns. He has given us the spirit of progress to overwhelm the forces of reaction throughout the earth. He has made us adept in government that we may administer government among savage and senile peoples. Were it not for such a force as this the world would relapse into barbarism and night. And of all our race He has marked the American people as His chosen nation to finally lead in the regeneration of the world. This is the divine mission of America, and it holds for us all the profit, all the glory, all the happiness possible to man. We are trustees of the world's progress, guardians of its righteous peace. The judgment of the Master is upon us: "Ye have been faithful over a few things; I will make you ruler over many things."

5. The Roosevelt Corollary to the Monroe Doctrine, 1904

It is not true that the United States feels any land hunger or entertains any projects as regards the other nations of the Western Hemisphere save such as are for their welfare. All that this country desires is to see the neighboring countries stable, orderly, and prosperous. Any country whose people conduct themselves well can count upon our hearty friendship. If a nation shows that it knows how to act with reasonable efficiency and decency in social and political matters, if it keeps order and pays its obligations, it need fear no interference from the United States. Chronic wrongdoing, or an impotence which results in a general loosening of the ties of civilized society, may in America, as elsewhere, ultimately require intervention by some civilized nation, and in the Western Hemisphere the adherence of the United States to the Monroe Doctrine may force the United States, however reluctantly, in

James D. Richardson, ed., *Messages and Papers of the Presidents,* Vol. XIV (Washington, D.C.: Government Printing Office, 1896–99), 6923 ff.

flagrant cases of such wrongdoing or impotence, to the exercise of an international police power. If every country washed by the Caribbean Sea would show the progress in stable and just civilization which with the aid of the Platt amendment Cuba has shown since our troops left the island, and which so many of the republics in both Americas are constantly and brilliantly showing, all question of interference by this Nation with their affairs would be at an end. Our interests and those of our southern neighbors are in reality identical. They have great natural riches, and if within their borders the reign of law and justice obtains, prosperity is sure to come to them. While they thus obey the primary laws of civilized society they may rest assured that they will be treated by us in a spirit of cordial and helpful sympathy. We would interfere with them only in the last resort, and then only if it became evident that their inability or unwillingness to do justice at home and abroad had violated the rights of the United States or had invited foreign aggression to the detriment of the entire body of American nations. It is a mere truism to say that every nation, whether in America or anywhere else, which desires to maintain its freedom, its independence, must ultimately realize that the right of such independence can not be separated from the responsibility of making good use of it.

 *E S S A Y S*

The following essays probe the political assumptions and projections of American leaders as they set out to reorder the wider world. In the opening selection, historian Paul Kennedy of Yale University succinctly analyzes the connections between the national economy and foreign affairs as the United States emerged as a world power, between 1890 and 1940. Next, Louis A. Perez of the University of North Carolina at Chapel Hill places the catalytic event of the Spanish-American War—the sinking of the battleship *Maine*—in the more extended context of U.S.–Cuban relations. The popular imagery of U.S. heroism and sacrifice surrounding the *Maine,* Perez argues, both hid and blunted the more extended fight for independence waged by the Cubans themselves. In the third selection, Gail Bederman of the University of Notre Dame connects the imperialist impulse among American policymakers at the turn of the century to internal domestic tensions, including, most notably, a perceived crisis of American manhood.

The United States as New Kid on the Block, 1890–1940

PAUL KENNEDY

Of all the changes which were taking place in the global power balances during the late nineteenth and early twentieth centuries, there can be no doubt that the most decisive one for the future was the growth of the United States. With the Civil War over, the United States was able to exploit . . . many advantages . . . rich agricultural land, vast raw materials, and the marvelously convenient evolution of modern technology (railways, the steam engine, mining equipment) to develop such resources;

the lack of social and geographical constraints; the absence of significant foreign dangers; the flow of foreign and, increasingly, domestic investment capital—to transform itself at a stunning pace. Between the ending of the Civil War in 1865 and the outbreak of the Spanish-American War in 1898, for example, American wheat production increased by 256 percent, corn by 222 percent, refined sugar by 460 percent, coal by 800 percent, steel rails by 523 percent, and the miles of railway track in operation by over 567 percent. "In newer industries the growth, starting from near zero, was so great as to make percentages meaningless. Thus the production of crude petroleum rose from about 3,000,000 barrels in 1865 to over 55,000,000 barrels in 1898 and that of steel ingots and castings from less than 20,000 long tons to nearly 9,000,000 long tons." This was not a growth which stopped with the war against Spain; on the contrary, it rose upward at the same meteoric pace throughout the early twentieth century. Indeed, given the advantages listed above, there was a virtual inevitability to the whole process. That is to say, only persistent human ineptitude, or near-constant civil war, or a climatic disaster could have checked this expansion—or deterred the millions of immigrants who flowed across the Atlantic to get their share of the pot of gold and to swell the productive labor force.

The United States seemed to have *all* the economic advantages which *some* of the other powers possessed *in part,* but *none* of their disadvantages. It was immense, but the vast distances were shortened by some 250,000 miles of railway in 1914 (compared with Russia's 46,000 miles, spread over an area two and a half times as large). Its agricultural yields per acre were always superior to Russia's; and if they were never as large as those of the intensively farmed regions of western Europe, the sheer size of the area under cultivation, the efficiency of its farm machinery, and the decreasing costs of transport (because of railways and steamships) made American wheat, corn, pork, beef, and other products cheaper than any in Europe. Technologically, leading American firms like International Harvester, Singer, Du Pont, Bell, Colt, and Standard Oil were equal to, or often better than, any in the world; and they enjoyed an enormous domestic market and economies of scale, which their German, British, and Swiss rivals did not. "Gigantism" in Russia was not a good indicator of industrial efficiency; in the United States, it usually was. For example, "Andrew Carnegie was producing more steel than the whole of England put together when he sold out in 1901 to J. P. Morgan's colossal organization, the United States Steel Corporation." When the famous British warship designer Sir William White made a tour of the United States in 1904, he was shaken to discover fourteen battleships and thirteen armored cruisers being built simultaneously in American yards (although, curiously, the U.S. merchant marine remained small). In industry *and* agriculture *and* communications, there was both efficiency and size. It was therefore not surprising that U.S. national income, in absolute figures and per capita, was so far above everybody else's by 1914.

The consequences of this rapid expansion are reflected in Table 1, and in the pertinent comparative statistics. In 1914, the United States was producing 455 million tons of coal, well ahead of Britain's 292 million and Germany's 277 million. It was the largest oil producer in the world, and the greatest consumer of copper. Its pig-iron production was larger than those of the next three countries (Germany, Britain, France) combined, and its steel production almost equal to the next four

Table 1   National Income, Population, and per Capita Income of the Powers in 1914

	NATIONAL INCOME	POPULATION	PER CAPITA INCOME
United States	$37 billion	98 million	$377
Britain	11	45	244
France	6	39	153
Japan	2	55	36
Germany	12	65	184
Italy	4	37	108
Russia	7	171	41
Austria-Hungary	3	52	57

countries (Germany, Britain, Russia, and France). Its energy consumption from modern fuels in 1913 was equal to that of Britain, Germany, France, Russia, and Austria-Hungary together. It produced, and possessed, more motor vehicles than the rest of the world together. It was, in fact an entire rival continent and growing so fast that it was coming close to the point of overtaking all of Europe. According to one calculation, indeed, had these growth rates continued and a world war been avoided, the United States would have overtaken Europe as the region possessing the greatest economic output in the world by 1925. What the First World War did, through the economic losses and dislocations suffered by the older Great Powers, was to bring that time forward, by six years, to 1919. The "Vasco da Gama era"— the four centuries of European dominance in the world—was coming to an end even before the cataclysm of 1914.

The role of foreign trade in the United States' economic growth was small indeed (around 8 percent of its GNP derived from foreign trade in 1913, compared with Britain's 26 percent), but its economic impact upon other countries was considerable. Traditionally, the United States had exported raw materials (especially cotton), imported finished manufactures, and made up the usual deficit in "visible" trade by the export of gold. But the post–Civil War boom in industrialization quite transformed that pattern. Swiftly becoming the world's largest producer of manufactures, the United States began to pour its farm machinery, iron and steel wares, machine tools, electrical equipment, and other products onto the world market. At the same time, the Northern industrialists' lobby was so powerful that it ensured that foreign products would be kept out of the home market by higher and higher tariffs; raw materials, by contrast, or specialized goods (like German dyestuffs) were imported in ever-larger quantities to supply American industry. But while the surge in the country's industrial exports was the most significant change, the "transportation revolution" also boosted American farm exports. With the cost of carrying a bushel of wheat from Chicago to London plummeting from 40 cents to 10 cents in the half-century before 1900, American agricultural produce streamed across the Atlantic. Corn exports peaked in 1897 at 212 million bushels, wheat exports in 1901 at 239 million bushels; this tidal wave also included grain and flour, meat and meat products.

The consequences of this commercial transformation were, of course, chiefly economic, but they also began to affect international relations. The hyperproductivity of American factories and farms caused a widespread fear that even its enormous domestic market might soon be unable to absorb these goods, and led powerful interest groups (midwestern farmers as well as Pittsburgh steel producers) to press the government to give all sorts of aid to opening up, or at least keeping open, markets overseas. The agitation to preserve an "open door" in China and the massive interest shown in making the United States the dominant economic force in Latin America were only two of the manifestations of this concern to expand the country's share of world trade. Between 1860 and 1914 the United States increased its exports more than sevenfold (from $334 million to $2.365 billion), yet because it was so protective of its own market, imports increased only fivefold (from $356 million to $1.896 billion). Faced with this avalanche of cheap American food, continental European farmers agitated for higher tariffs—which they usually got; in Britain, which had already sacrificed its grain farmers for the cause of free trade, it was the flood of American machines, and iron and steel, which produced alarm. While the journalist W. T. Stead wrote luridly of "the Americanization of the world"—the phrase was the title of his book of 1902—Kaiser Wilhelm and other European leaders hinted at the need to combine against the "unfair" American trading colossus.

Perhaps even more destabilizing, although less well understood, was the impact of the United States upon the world's financial system and monetary flows. Because it had such a vast surplus in its trade with Europe, the latter's deficit had to be met by capital transfers—joining the enormous stream of direct European investments into U.S. industry, utilities, and services (which totaled around $7 billion by 1914). Although some of this westward flow of bullion was reversed by the returns on European investments and by American payments for services such as shopping and insurance, the drain was a large one, and constantly growing larger; and it was exacerbated by the U.S. Treasury's policy of accumulating (and then just sitting on) nearly one-third of the world's gold stock. Moreover, although the United States had by now become an integral part of a complete global trading system—running a deficit with raw-materials-supplying countries, and a vast surplus with Europe—its own financial structure was underdeveloped. Most of its foreign trade was done in sterling, for example, and London acted as the lender of last resort for gold. With no central bank able to control the financial markets, with a stupendous seasonal outflow and inflow of funds between New York and the prairie states conditioned solely by the grain harvest and that by a volatile climate, and with speculators able to derange not merely the domestic monetary system but also the frequent calls upon gold in London, the United States in the years before 1914 was already becoming a vast but unpredictable bellows, fanning but also on occasions dramatically cooling the world's trading system. The American banking crisis of 1907 (originally provoked by an attempt by speculators to corner the market in copper), with consequent impacts on London, Amsterdam, and Hamburg, was merely one example of the way the United States was impinging upon the economic life of the other Great Powers, even before the First World War.

This growth of American industrial power and overseas trade was accompanied, perhaps inevitably, by a more assertive diplomacy and by an American-style rhetoric of *Weltpolitik*. Claims to a special moral endowment among the peoples of the earth which made American foreign policy superior to those of the Old World were intermingled with Social Darwinistic and racial arguments, and with the urging of industrial and agricultural pressure groups for secure overseas markets. The traditional, if always exaggerated, alarm about threats to the Monroe Doctrine was accompanied by calls for the United States to fulfill its "Manifest Destiny" across the Pacific. While entangling alliances still had to be avoided, the United States was now being urged by many groups at home into a much more activist diplomacy which, under the administrations of McKinley and (espe cially) Theodore Roosevelt, was exactly what took place. The 1895 quarrel with Britain over the Venezuelan border dispute—justified in terms of the Monroe Doctrine was followed three years later by the much more dramatic war with Spain over the Cuban issue. Washington's demand to have sole control of an isthmian canal (instead of the older fifty-fifty arrangement with Britain), the re-definition of the Alaskan border despite Canadian protests, and the 1902–1903 battle-fleet preparations in the Caribbean following the German actions against Venezuela were all indications of U.S. determination to be unchallenged by any other Great Power in the western hemisphere. As a "corollary" of this, however, American administrations showed themselves willing to intervene by diplomatic pressure *and* military means in Latin American countries such as Nicaragua, Haiti, Mexico, and the Dominican Republic when their behavior did not accord with United States norms.

But the really novel features of American external policy in this period were its interventions and participation in events *outside* the western hemisphere. Its at-tendance at the Berlin West Africa Conference in 1884–1885 had been anomalous and confused: after grandiose speeches by the U.S. delegation in favor of free trade and open doors, the subsequent treaty was never ratified. Even as late as 1892 the *New York Herald* was proposing the abolition of the State Department, since it had so little business to conduct overseas. The war with Spain in 1898 changed all that, not only by giving the United States a position in the western Pacific (the Philip-pines) which made it, too, a sort of Asiatic colonial power, but also by boosting the political fortunes of those who had favored an assertive policy. Secretary of State Hay's "Open Door," note in the following year was an early indication that the United States wished to have a say in China, as was the commitment of 2,500 American troops to the international army sent to restore order in China in 1900. Roosevelt showed an even greater willingness to engage in *grosse Politik,* acting as mediator in the talks which brought an end to the Russo-Japanese War, insisting upon American participation in the 1906 conference over Morocco, and negotiat-ing with Japan and the other Powers in an attempt to maintain the "Open Door" in China. Much of this has been seen by later scholars less as being based upon a sober calculation of the country's real interests in the world than as reflecting an immaturity of foreign-policy style, an ethnocentric naiveté, and a wish to impress audiences both at home and abroad—traits which would complicate a "realistic" American foreign policy in the future; but even if that is true, the United States was hardly alone in this age of imperialist bombast and nationalist pride. In any case, ex-cept in Chinese affairs, such diplomatic activism was not maintained by Roosevelt's successors, who preferred to keep the United States free from international events occurring outside the western hemisphere.

Along with these diplomatic actions went increases in arms expenditures. Of the two services, the navy got the most, since it was the front line of the nation's defenses in the event of a foreign attack (or a challenge to the Monroe Doctrine) and also the most useful instrument to support American diplomacy and commerce in Latin America, the Pacific, and elsewhere. Already in the late 1880s, the rebuilding of the fleet had commenced, but the greatest boost came at the time of the Spanish-American War. Since the easy naval victories in that conflict seemed to justify the arguments of Admiral Mahan and the "big navy" lobby, and since the strategists worried about the possibility of a war with Britain and then, from 1898 onward, with Germany, the battle fleet was steadily built up. The acquisition of bases in Hawaii, Samoa, the Philippines, and the Caribbean, the use of naval vessels to act as "policemen" in Latin America, and Roosevelt's dramatic gesture of sending his "great white fleet" around the world in 1907 all seemed to emphasize the importance of sea power.

Consequently, while the naval expenditures of $22 million in 1890 represented only 6.9 percent of total federal spending, the $139 million allocated to the navy by 1914 represented 19 percent. Not all of this was well spent—there were too many home fleet bases (the result of local political pressures) and too few escort vessels—but the result was still impressive. Although considerably smaller than the Royal Navy, and with fewer *Dreadnought*-type battleships than Germany, the U.S. Navy was the third largest in the world in 1914. Even the construction of a U.S.-controlled Panama Canal did not stop American planners from agonizing over the strategical dilemma of dividing the fleet, or leaving one of the country's coastlines exposed; and the records of some officers in these years reveal a somewhat paranoid suspicion of foreign powers. In fact, given its turn-of-the-century *rapprochement* with Great Britain, the United States was immensely secure, and even if it feared the rise of German sea power, it really had far less to worry about than any of the other major powers.

The small size of the U.S. military was in many ways a reflection of that state of security. The army, too, had been boosted by the war with Spain, at least to the extent that the public realized how minuscule it actually was, how disorganized the National Guard was, and how close to disaster the early campaigning in Cuba had come. But the tripling of the size of the regular army after 1900 and the additional garrisoning tasks it acquired in the Philippines and elsewhere still left the service looking insignificant compared with that of even a middle-sized European country like Serbia or Bulgaria. Even more than Britain, the United States clung to a laissez-faire dislike of mass standing armies and avoided fixed military obligations to allies. Less than 1 percent of its GNP went to defense. Despite its imperialist activities in the period 1898–1914, therefore, it remained what the sociologist Herbert Spencer termed an "industrial" society rather than a "military" society like Russia. Since many historians have suggested that "the rise of the superpowers" began in this period, it is worth noting the staggering *differences* between Russia and the United States by the eve of the First World War. The former possessed a front-line army about ten times as large as the latter's; but the United States produced six times as much steel, consumed ten times as much energy, and was four times larger in total industrial output (in per capita terms, it was six times more productive). No doubt Russia seemed the more powerful to all those European general staffs thinking of swiftly fought wars involving masses of available troops; but by all other criteria, the United States was strong and Russia weak.

The United States had definitely become a Great Power. But it was not part of the Great Power system. Not only did the division of powers between the presidency and the Congress make an active alliance policy virtually impossible, but it was also clear that no one was in favor of abandoning the existing state of very comfortable isolation. Separated from other strong nations by thousands of miles of ocean, possessing a negligible army, content to have achieved hemispheric dominance and, at least after Roosevelt's departure, less eager to engage in worldwide diplomacy, the United States in 1913 still stood on the edges of the Great Power system. And since most of the other countries after 1906 were turning their attention from Asia and Africa to developments in the Balkans and North Sea, it was perhaps not surprising that they tended to see the United States as less a factor in the international power balances than had been the case around the turn of the century. That was yet another of the common pre-1914 assumptions which the Great War itself would prove wrong.

1898: The Meaning of the *Maine*

LOUIS A. PEREZ

Remember the Maine*!*
To hell with Spain!
—Popular refrain (1898)

On the evening of February 15, 1898, the battleship *Maine* exploded in Havana harbor. The explosion occurred in the forward part of the vessel, near the port side, almost directly under the enlisted men's quarters. The loss of life was staggering: out of a total complement of 354 officers and men, 266 perished in the explosion.

The destruction of the *Maine* had immediate repercussions and lasting implications. Relations between the United States and Spain, already strained by mutual suspicions and mounting tensions, deteriorated rapidly thereafter. American impatience with Spain's conduct of the war in Cuba was increasing. So was popular support for Cuba Libre. For almost three years public officials and public opinion acted upon one another in such a fashion as to make the insurrection in Cuba an unsettling intrusion in domestic politics. These conditions were exacerbated by the excesses of "yellow journalism," in which sensational new stories about the Cuban war had become the stock-in-trade of the circulation rivalry between William Randolph Hearst's *New York Journal* and Joseph Pulitzer's *New York World*. Anti-Spanish sentiment was on the rise. Only one week before the destruction of the *Maine,* ill will toward Spain had flared over the publication of the de Lôme letter.

But the impact of the *Maine* was not only a matter of timing. The explosion was also a question of circumstances. That a U.S. warship exploded in Havana harbor, waters nominally under Spanish jurisdiction, invited immediate and obvious conclusions. "The *Maine* was sunk by an act of dirty treachery on the part of the Spaniards," Theodore Roosevelt concluded the day after the tragedy—a suspicion that gained currency in many quarters.

Events moved quickly after February 15. On the following day President McKinley convened a naval court of inquiry to investigate the cause of the explosion. Two weeks later Congress appropriated $50 million for war preparations. On March 25 the naval court completed its investigation and three days later released its findings. Two explosions were responsible for the destruction of the *Maine,* the naval inquiry concluded. An initial external explosion—one that "could have been produced only by the explosion of a mine situated under the bottom of the ship"— detonated a second internal blast in "two or more of the forward magazines." The court of inquiry declined to fix responsibility for the disaster, but the determination that the first explosion originated externally, attributed explicitly to a submarine mine, could mean only one of two things: the explosion was either the result of criminal negligence or the work of malicious intent. In either case, the implication was clear: Spain was responsible.

The destruction of the *Maine* developed almost immediately into one of the dominant narrative vehicles for the explanation of 1898. The mysterious coincidence and unforeseen consequences, matters of chance and circumstance, combined intriguingly to provide more than ample material with which to contemplate the imponderables of 1898: a presumed random casus belli of unverifiable if not unknown origins, apparently a case of bad timing at a bad place, and of such far-reaching consequences. These have been some of the subplots that have made the *Maine* the object of such enduring appeal: a wholly fortuitous event to which is attributed the cause of a war that altered the course of U.S. history. . . .

The persistence of the *Maine* as a dominant explanatory element underscores some of the more enduring characteristics of the historical literature. Historiographical advances have been conspicuously few; indeed, the principal conceptual formulations of 1898 have remained largely unchanged. . . . The importance of the *Maine* has been presumed self-evident and self-explanatory, derived more from a reworking of the historical literature than from a reexamination of historical evidence.

If there has been general agreement about the causal role of the *Maine,* there has been no comparable consensus about specifically how the *Maine* acted to cause the war. Central to the explanatory functions of the *Maine* have been derivative arguments about the role of public opinion. In fact, public opinion has served as the historiographical device of choice and has played an important part in making explanatory formulations "work." The relationship of public opinion to the coming of the war has undergone repeated presentations and representations in the course of one hundred years of historical writing. So, too, have the ways public opinion has been measured. Whatever else may separate the varieties of usages of the notion of "public opinion," however, the historical literature has been all but unanimous in the conclusion that popular sentiment figured prominently in propelling the United States to war.

The historiography has long pointed to the destruction of the *Maine* as a source of public wrath, whereupon a climate of opinion developed in which war became an acceptable if not inevitable course of action. This proposition has appeared in a variety of narrative formulations but over time has remained substantially constant. The historiographical consensus has indeed been striking. "The disaster to the *Maine* was but a match touched to the powder of public sentiment," stated Charles Morris a year after the war ended: "an unparalleled wave of horror and indignation swept over the United States," Russell H. Fitzgibbon agreed Thomas Bailey similarly insisted that "the explosion of the *Maine* was matched by an explosion of public opinion." George Kennan wrote that "the American public was profoundly shocked and outraged to hear that the battleship *Maine* had been sunk," and Daniel Smith noted that "the sinking of the *Maine* aroused the public to a fighting temper."

The electorate was thus depicted as having entered directly into the decision-making process, transforming an issue of foreign policy into a concern of domestic politics. The public did not merely resign itself to the possibility of hostilities; on the contrary, it demanded the prosecution of war. Implicit in this argument was the proposition that once public opinion began to influence the course of events, the drift to war became irreversible. . . . Dexter Perkins stated the argument succinctly: "Never was there a clearer case of a war brought about by public opinion."

The role attributed to public opinion, from which a number of corollary generalizations have been derived, serves several functions—some conceptual, some theoretical, some methodological. Public opinion provides a plausible causal factor without the necessity of explanation or evidence. Accordingly, the onset of the war in 1898 was portrayed as a function of an aroused public opinion that, as commonly acknowledged, did not need to be rational and therefore required no explanation. The inference was inescapable: the United States was propelled to war by an agitated citizenry, overcome by stirred passions and at the brink of mass hysteria. Represented as a powerful undercurrent, public opinion was thus depicted as an unseen, relentless force that, once aroused, assumed an inexorable logic of its own, one that could be calmed by nothing less than war. Responsibility for war was attributed to the aroused masses, who, it was suggested, had taken collective leave of their senses.

The literature is rich with such characterizations: "an ungovernable burst of popular emotion"; "war hysteria swept the country"; "public opinion outran . . . sober judgment"; the "lid was now off" as a result of "the unthinking American masses"; "the nation had gone mad" . . . "the people, acting out of powerful irrational impulses, dictated the decision of April 1898." . . .

The linkage between the *Maine* and public opinion, on one hand, and war, on the other, is not, however, without historiographical anomalies. The contradictions have not been simply a matter of conflicting interpretations, although at times differences in interpretation have been sufficiently great to raise larger questions about attention to accuracy and use of evidence. There are, in fact, at least two substantially different and irreconcilable accounts of the timing and character of public reaction, both of which appear to share a congenial and untroubled coexistence in the historiography. In one version, public opinion is depicted as having been aroused immediately after and in direct response to the explosion, that is, immediately after February 15. This formulation is best represented by Foster Rhea Dulles: "When it mysteriously blew up . . . an already worked-up public went wild. There were occasional cautionary voices urging that judgment should be withheld until an official investigation could determine the cause of the *Maine*'s destruction, but they were scarcely heard in the noisy clamor demanding immediate retaliation against Spain as without question being responsible for the disaster." . . .

A second version, however, describes a public reaction substantially different in chronology and character. In this account the citizenry is represented as having remained calm during the days and weeks following February 15, and not until March 28, when the naval court of inquiry implicated Spain in the explosion, did public wrath erupt. Henry Watterson wrote in 1898 that citizens "awaited patiently the report of their commission. No more than the President did they wish to perpetuate any injustice against Spain." "There was no violent demand for vengeance," Harry Peck maintained. "The gravity of the situation gave steadiness and poise to public opinion. The nation displayed a universal willingness to suspend judgment until a full and vigorous inquiry should be made. The tone of the press through the country was admirable." Roscoe Lewis Ashley insisted that "for five weeks, with rare self-control, the nation waited." Thomas Bailey wrote that it was "to the credit of the American people that on the whole they were inclined to suspend judgment. . . . This fact is all the more remarkable when one considers the surcharged atmosphere." But, Bailey added, "following the official report on the *Maine,* the masses were on fire for war." "When the court of inquiry reported that the explosion was caused by a mine," wrote John Holladay Latané, "the American people, who had displayed great self-control, threw aside all restraint and the country witnessed an outburst of patriotic fervor such as had not been seen since 1861." . . .

Discrepancies of this type suggest ambiguities of other kinds. The linkage of public opinion to the coming of the war, a causal formulation long associated with explanations of 1898, stands as one of the more problematical constructs of the historical literature and, indeed, sets in sharp relief the degree to which interpretations of 1898 have often tended to operate independently of the requirements for evidence. Public opinion arguments derive plausibility more from normatively derived democratic theory than from a body of assembled evidence. A vast literature has formed around arguments for which adequate verification is either incomplete or unavailable, or both. Explanations have relied freely if implicitly on the theoretical functions of public opinion in a political democracy: the electorate, from which emanates political legitimacy and to which elected officials are presumed responsible, is represented as dictating the pace of events and the course of policy. . . .

The role attributed to public opinion makes for an appealing causal construct on several counts. It provides a plausible explanation for a war that many scholars have judged harshly or otherwise represented as having lacked both clear reason and compelling purpose. A war depicted often as senseless and irrational—described variously in the historiography as "unfortunate," . . . "foolish and unnecessary," . . . and "needless"—is thus rendered comprehensible. George Kennan made the point explicitly, insisting that the United States "resorted to war for subjective and emotional reasons" and at another point describing the war "as an example of superficiality in concept as well as the power of chauvinistic rhetoric and war hysteria." Robert E. Riegel and David F. Long characterized the conflict as the "strangest war in American history," one of "sheer military aggression against a hopelessly outclassed and conciliatory adversary." In this way, the explanation of acts that fail to conform to preconceived and generally implicit norms of political rationality can be attributed to the recklessness of the public. It was not the leaders who failed, or their policies that fell short, but the body politic that was derelict.

Attributing the war to the demands of aroused public opinion suggests a subtext of another kind. The proposition of war by design, deliberate and intentional, is thus by implication rendered inadmissible. Political leaders are presumed innocent of willing war and thereby absolved of responsibility for it. They are overtaken by events, or they are weak or incompetent. But they are not represented as willing war in the defense of national interests. . . .

Historiographical formulations of public opinion, aided and aroused by yellow journalism, as the explanation for 1898 have not, however, always been convincing or conclusive. Certainly not all narratives accord the same prominence to the press. Lewis Gould argued quite the opposite, insisting that the press "reflected what the public wanted, rather than shaping it." John Offner similarly insisted that "there is no evidence" to indicate that the "sensational press" influenced McKinley's policy, suggesting that "its impact on changing public opinion may have been limited."

But even if it were possible to demonstrate the relationship between policy and public opinion, the larger and perhaps more important question involves precisely the character of popular opinion. What, in short, was the opinion of the public that was said to have moved political leaders toward a specific course of action? On this question there does exist scattered if admittedly anecdotal evidence. In fact, "public opinion" by all accounts had arrayed fully in support of Cuban independence. As early as September 1895, Secretary of State Richard Olney prepared an internal memorandum on the Cuban insurrection, submitted for "the careful consideration of the Executive," warning about "public opinion." Olney wrote: "The contest [is] attracting the attention of all our people as well as enlisting their sympathies, if for no other reason, than because the insurgents are apparently the weaker party— politicians of all stripes, including congressmen, either already setting their sails or preparing to set them so as to catch the popular breeze—it being not merely probable but almost certain that next winter Washington will swarm with emissaries of the insurgents demanding at least recognition of their belligerency." Years later Senator Foraker reflected on his support for recognizing the insurgent provisional government: "In entertaining the opinion by which I was governed that the Government known as the Republic of Cuba was entitled to recognition, I was but in harmony . . . with the majority of my colleagues, and an overwhelming majority of the American people."

If, indeed, public opinion in a democracy acted in such a decisive fashion to determine the course and conduct of policy, the steadfast opposition of both the Cleveland and McKinley administrations to Cuban independence in the face of "public opinion" poses an apparent problem. In fact, public pressure in behalf of Cuba Libre, including the call for the recognition of the Cuban provisional government and granting belligerency status, was rejected at every turn. Cleveland and McKinley were unabashed in their resistance to "public opinion." On the contrary, opposition to popular clamor was celebrated at the time as evidence of courageous presidential leadership. Occasionally this point is acknowledged in the historical literature. James MacGregor Burns took note of the "popular sympathy for the Cuban revolution" but stressed that the Cleveland administration "had resisted these pressures." . . . [A]t the time President McKinley was congratulated for standing up against public opinion. The *Philadelphia Inquirer* praised McKinley for resisting popular support of the Cuban cause: "The President was wise when he fought valiantly against the recognition of a Cuban republic." The *Hartford Post,* published by McKinley's private secretary, John Addison Porter, was openly exultant. "President McKinley" the *Post* editorialized, "was right when with all his power he successfully resisted the demand of Congress and of a large section of people that these cowardly, good-for-nothing insurgents be recognized as an independent government." . . .

Public opinion further implicated the actions of President McKinley. The representation of the wars has often been personalized and linked to the character of the president, his temperament and disposition. Formulation of policy has often been eclipsed by formation of personality; questions of the national interest are overshadowed by individual idiosyncrasies. In one view, McKinley is depicted as standing up courageously against mounting pressure from an aroused public and a bellicose Congress. The White House is a bastion of reason during a time of irrationality, but eventually is obliged to capitulate to the will of the people and the demands of their elected representatives. James Henretta et al. argued that "President McKinley did not seek war. He had no stomach for the martial spirit sweeping the country. . . . But, in the end, McKinley had no choice." . . .

Not all observers agree, however. Other interpretations of 1898 question the inevitability of the war and reject the proposition that McKinley was without choices. That he capitulated to public pressure, the inflammatory press, and jingoes in Congress, some have argued, says more about the character of the president than the constraints on his options. The logic of the school of thought that represents the war as unnecessary often leads directly to the president, to whom the inexplicable war is attributed. McKinley was incompetent and ineffective, and thus the war was his fault. By implication, war became possible because of a weak president who, at a decisive moment of a deepening political crisis, failed to assert executive leadership. "Possibly a strong President might have headed off the rush to war by openly denouncing the clamor for intervention," speculated T. Harry Williams, Richard Current, and Frank Freidel, "but McKinley was not a strong executive." The *Maine* so emboldened jingoes, Wayne Cole suggested, that it "would have required a stronger President than McKinley to resist their war-making influence." McKinley "had not the nerve and power to resist the pressure for war," argued James Ford Rhodes, and Frederick Merk observed that "moral courage . . . was not part of the kindly make-up of this President." . . .

In still another explanation of 1898, the relationship between the *Maine* and public opinion, on one hand, and Congress, the president, and the coming of the war, on the other, have been modified and transformed into a proposition from which significantly different causal hierarchies have been arranged. With a slight change of sequence and a shift of emphasis, the *Maine* was represented as the occasion contrived as a pretext for war rather than a chance precipitant. The incident was thus exploited by expansionist politicians to mobilize public opinion in behalf of a policy of territorial expansion. It was not an aroused public that pressured unwilling politicians into war but, on the contrary, unscrupulous politicians who manipulated the unsuspecting public into war. The *Maine* simply played into the hands of expansionist elements in Congress and the administration. "Our government," wrote Horace Edgar

Flack, "had practically decided on war . . . the *Maine* question was considered the best thing to arouse popular enthusiasm." "The shocking disaster was a stroke of good fortune for America's interventionists," insisted Walter Karp, "a stroke of good fortune" that "drastically shortened the road to war." . . . D. A. Graber described the *Maine* as one of the incidents "used by the yellow press and by expansionist Ameri cans such as Senator [Henry Cabot] Lodge and Assistant Secretary of the Navy Theodore Roosevelt to inflame public opinion." William Appleman Williams similarly argued that the *Maine* incident "significantly increased the tension and did encourage those, like Roosevelt, who had been 'hoping and working ardently to bring about our interference in Cuba.'" . . . In a careful study of policy and public opinion, Robert C. Hildebrand concluded that as early as 1897, President McKinley had formulated a Cuban policy that could only lead to war. Public support was "made certain" by the destruction of the *Maine* and "rendered superfluous any efforts of [McKinley] to prepare the public for war." Hildebrand concluded: "The president could . . . predict the direction of the public's drift, and he saw little reason to guide a public opinion that was moving—parallel to his own diplomacy—inexorably toward war."

This interpretation produced a substantially different assessment of McKinley. No longer characterized as weak and ineffectual, buffeted by forces he neither controlled nor comprehended, McKinley was portrayed as an expansionist, calculating and clever, steadfastly pursuing clear objectives and skillfully exploiting a fortuitous event to embark on an expansionist policy. With the naval court report completed, Karp wrote, "McKinley's difficulties were at an end." It was now only necessary to "bring his diplomacy with Spain to a crisis—never very difficult in dealing with a fifth-rate power." Karp concluded: "Had McKinley been seeking a peaceful solution, the Spanish concessions certainly provided the basis for one. Instead, McKinley rejected the offer. . . . With the official release of the *Maine* report on March 28, he now had overwhelming popular support for armed intervention."

Conspicuously absent from most accounts of 1898 has been the possibility of U.S. intervention as a response to the imminence of a Cuban triumph. Some of the conflicting and otherwise contradictory explanations of U.S. policy acquire far greater coherence when set against the prospects of an insurgent victory. Julius Pratt argued that the war would have been avoided "if McKinley had been resolute enough to exercise a little more patience with Spain and defy Congress." No doubt, too, James Ford Rhodes was correct in suggesting that had McKinley not succumbed to public pressure and "abandoned his policy and went over to the war party," Spain "might have been led to grant independence to Cuba." But that was precisely the one eventuality McKinley was seeking to foreclose. Thus, on one hand, a rebellious Congress responded to public pressure to intervene in behalf of Cuban independence and, on the other, rebellious Cubans within a measurable distance of military victory defined the necessary policy course in defense of U.S. interests. Henry Bamford Parkes came slightly closer to the mark by noting that Spanish capitulation to the March 27 ultimatum "would probably have led to the liberation of Cuba without war; but a peaceful settlement would not have . . . enabled the United States to acquire bases overseas."

Perhaps the most persistent criticism of McKinley has centered on his decision to proceed with war despite Spanish acquiescence to the U.S. ultimatum of March 27. Without an acknowledgment of the Cuban role in these events, U.S. historians have been left to improvise an explanation to account for McKinley's actions. One line of argument has maintained that the Spanish concessions were, in fact, suspect, and that McKinley lacked confidence in Spain's commitment to peace. "Spanish evasion and delay had destroyed confidence in the good faith of the Spanish government," was the way that William MacDonald saw it. W. E. Woodward speculated that McKinley "may have thought the Spaniards were insincere and playing for time." Nelson Blake and Oscar Barck suggested that McKinley "could thus shrug off the Spanish concession . . . as insincere and worthless." Richard Leopold indicated that Spanish concessions were rejected by "contemporaries who had grown weary of broken promises and the inevitable Spanish *mañana*." It was Thomas Bailey's belief that Spanish acquiescence did not matter, for Spain "had pursued such a tortuous course that McKinley had little faith in her promises, or in her ability to carry them out." According to Arthur M. Schlesinger, McKinley "doubted Spain's good faith in complying," and John Bassett argued that the administration believed that last-minute concessions "would be evaded, as in the past."

Various types of weaknesses have been attributed to McKinley: weakness of character, or of courage, or of conviction were all offered as explanations of why he proceeded to war even after Spain had apparently capitulated to his demands. "Any President with a backbone would have seized this opportunity for an honorable solution," pronounced Samuel Eliot Morison. Randolph Greenfield Adams arrived at a similar conclusion: "left alone, McKinley would probably have avoided a war, as he was a peaceful and gentle man." . . .

In fact, the problem McKinley confronted had less to do with Spain than with Cubans, who, in refusing to observe the cease-fire and suspend military operations, seemed poised to overrun Spanish positions. Indeed, intervention was as much against the expanding Cuban claim of sovereignty as the declining Spanish claim. McKinley could not have accepted Spanish acquiescence to the March 27 ultimatum without Cuban participation, and Cuban participation was predicated entirely on the proposition of independence.

Thus, the war arrived in the early spring of 1898 and its origins have continued to be debated in terms established one hundred years ago. The *Maine* propelled the nation to war, a denouement that was inexorable in the face of an aroused public and timid public officials. In the process, an "unnecessary" war became known an "inevitable" one.

Theodore Roosevelt and the Strenuous Life

GAIL BEDERMAN

In 1882, a newly elected young state assemblyman arrived in Albany. Theodore Roosevelt, assuming his first elective office, was brimming with self-importance and ambition. He was only twenty-three—the youngest man in the legislature—and he looked forward to a promising career of wielding real political power. Yet Roosevelt

Gail Bederman, *Manliness and Civilization: A Cultural History of Gender and Race in the United States, 1880–1917* (Chicago: University of Chicago Press, 1995), 170–171, 187–196. Copyright © 1995, reprinted by permission of the University of Chicago Press.

was chagrined to discover that despite his intelligence, competence, and real legislative successes, no one took him seriously. The more strenuously he labored to play "a man's part" in politics, the more his opponents derided his manhood.

Daily newspapers lampooned Roosevelt as the quintessence of effeminacy. They nicknamed him "weakling," "Jane-Dandy," "Punkin-Lily," and "the exquisite Mr. Roosevelt." They ridiculed his high voice, tight pants, and fancy clothing. Several began referring to him by the name of the well-known homosexual Oscar Wilde, and one actually alleged (in a less-than-veiled phallic allusion) that Roosevelt was "given to sucking the knob of an ivory cane." While TR might consider himself a manly man, it was becoming humiliatingly clear that others considered him effeminate.

Above all other things, Roosevelt desired power. An intuitive master of public relations, he knew that his effeminate image could destroy any chances for his political future. Nearly forty years before women got the vote, electoral politics was part of a male-only subculture, fraught with symbols of manhood. Besides, Roosevelt, who considered himself a man's man, detested having his virility impugned. Although normally restrained, when he discovered a Tammany legislator plotting to toss him in a blanket, TR marched up to him and swore, "By God! if you try anything like that, I'll kick you, I'll bite you, I'll kick you in the balls, I'll do anything to you—you'd better leave me alone!" Clearly, the effeminate "dude" image would have to go.

And go it did. Roosevelt soon came to embody powerful American manhood. Within five years, he was running for mayor of New York as the "Cowboy of the Dakotas." Instead of ridiculing him as "Oscar Wilde," newspapers were praising his virile zest for fighting and his "blizzard-seasoned constitution." In 1898, after a brief but highly publicized stint as leader of a regiment of volunteers in the Spanish American War, he became known as Colonel Roosevelt, the manly advocate of a virile imperialism. Never again would Roosevelt's name be linked to effeminacy. Even today, historians invoke Roosevelt as the quintessential symbol of turn-of-the-century masculinity.

Roosevelt's great success in masculinizing his image was due, in large part, to his masterful use of the discourse of civilization. As a mature politician, he would bring his claim to political power on his claim to manhood. Skillfully, Roosevelt constructed a virile political persona for himself as a strong but civilized white man.

Yet Roosevelt's use of the discourse of civilization went beyond mere public relations: Roosevelt drew on "civilization" to help formulate his larger politics as an advocate of both nationalism and imperialism. As he saw it, the United States was engaged in a millennial drama of manly racial advancement, in which American men enacted their superior manhood by asserting imperialistic control over races of inferior manhood. To prove their virility, as a race and a nation, American men needed to take up the "strenuous life" and strive to advance civilization—through imperialistic warfare and racial violence if necessary.

Thus, TR framed his political mission in terms of race and manhood, nationalism and civilization. Like G. Stanley Hall and Charlotte Perkins Gilman, Roosevelt longed to lead evolution's chosen race toward a perfect millennial future. Yet Roosevelt harbored larger ambitions than either Hall or Gilman. Hall merely wanted to develop a pedagogy that would produce the "super-man." Gilman only wanted to revolutionize society by civilizing women. Roosevelt, on the other hand, yearned

to be the virile leader of a manly race and to inspire his race to wage an international battle for racial supremacy. He hoped that, through this imperialistic evolutionary struggle, he could advance his race toward the most perfect possible
civilization. This, for Roosevelt, was the ultimate power of manhood. . . .

Imperialism: The Masterful Duty of the Manly Race

From 1894 until he became president in 1901, Roosevelt wrote and lectured widely
on the importance of taking up what Rudyard Kipling, in 1899, would dub "the
White Man's burden." Kipling coined this term in a poem written to exhort American men to conquer and rule the Philippines. "The white man" . . . simultaneously
meant the white race, civilization itself, and white males as a group. In "The
White's Man's Burden," Kipling used the term in all the senses to urge white males
to take up the racial burden of civilization's advancement. "Take up the White
Man's burden," he wrote, capitalizing the essential term, and speaking to the manly
civilized on behalf of civilization. "Send forth the best ye breed"—quality breeding was essential, because evolutionary development (breeding) was what gave
"the White Man" the right and duty to conquer uncivilized races.

> Go bind your sons to exile
>   To serve your captives' need;
> To wait in heavy harness,
>   on fluttered folk and wild—
> Your new-caught, sullen peoples,
>   Half-devil and half-child.

. . . [M]anly men had the duty of taking unselfish care of those weaker than
themselves—to "wait in heavy harness" and "serve their captives' need." And by
calling the Filipinos "half-devil and half-child," Kipling underlined the essential
fact that whatever these races were, there were not *men*.

Roosevelt called Kipling's poem "poor poetry but good sense from the expansionist standpoint." Although Roosevelt did not use the term "the white man's burden" in his writings on imperialism, he drew on the same sorts of race and gender
linkages which Kipling deployed in his poem. TR's speeches of this period frequently conflate manhood and racial power, and draw extended analogies between
the individual American man and the virile American race.

For example, "National Duties," one of TR's most famous speeches, represents
both American men and the American race as civilized entities with strong virile
characters—in popular parlance, both were "the white man." Roosevelt begins by
outlining this racial manhood, which he calls "the essential manliness of the American character." Part of this manliness centered around individual and racial duties to
the home. On the one hand, individual men must work to provide for the domestic
needs of themselves and their families. On the other hand, the men of the race must
work to provide for their collective racial home, their nation. Men who shirked
these manly homemaking duties were despicably unsexed; or, as TR put it, "the
willfully idle man" was as bad as "the willfully barren woman."

Yet laboring only for his own hearth and nation was not enough to satisfy a
real man. Virile manhood also required the manly American nation to take up

imperialistic labors outside its borders, just as manhood demanded individual men to labor outside the home: "Exactly as each man, while doing first his duty to his wife and the children within his home, must yet, if he hopes to amount to much, strive mightily in the world outside his home, so our nation, while first of all seeing to its own domestic well-being, must not shrink from playing its part among the great nations without." It would be as unmanly for the American race to refuse its imperialist destiny as it would be for a cowardly man to spend all his time loafing at home with his wife. Imperialist control over primitive races thus becomes a matter of manhood—part of a male-only public sphere, which TR sets in contradistinction to the home.

After setting up imperialism as a manly duty for both man and race, Roosevelt outlines the imperialist's appropriate masculine behavior—or, should we say, his appropriate masculine appendage? Roosevelt immediately brings up the "big stick." It may be a cheap shot to stress the phallic implications of TR's imagery, yet Roosevelt himself explained the meaning of the "big stick" in terms of manhood and the proper way to assert the power of a man: "A good many of you are probably acquainted with the old proverb: 'Speak softly and carry a big stick—you will go far.' If a man continually blusters, if he lacks civility, a big stick will not save him from trouble; and neither will speaking softy avail, if back of the softness there does not lie strength, power." Just as a manly man avoided bluster, relying instead on his self-evident masculine strength and power, so virile American men should build a powerful navy and army, so that when they took up the white man's burden in primitive lands, they would receive the respect due to a masterful, manly race.

This imperialistic manliness underlay the virile power of both man and race; yet it was not self-seeking. It was intended only for the advancement of civilization. Therefore, Roosevelt insisted, Americans never directed their virile expansionism against any civilized race. "No nation capable of self-government and of developing by its own efforts a sane and orderly civilization, no matter how small it may be, has anything to fear from us." Only barbarous nations incapable of developing "a sane and orderly civilization"—for example, the Hawaiians and the Filipinos—required the correction of the manly American race.

Unfortunately, Roosevelt conceded, this unselfish civilizing duty might well become bloody and violent. Civilized men had a manly duty to "destroy and uplift" lesser, primitive men, for their own good and the good of civilization: "It is our duty toward the people living in barbarism to see that they are freed from their chains, and we can free them only by destroying barbarism itself. The missionary, the merchant, and the soldier may each have to play a part in this destruction and in the consequent uplifting of the people." Yet this unselfish racial uplift would be worth the bloodshed, even for the destroyed barbarians themselves. Both Indians on the Great Plains and the Tagalogs in the Philippines—at least, those who still survived—would be far happier after the white man had conquered them, according to Roosevelt.

Roosevelt closed his speech by reiterating his analogy between the manful race and the race's men. By conquering and civilizing primitive races, the American nation was simply girding up its racial loins to be "men" of the world, just as they had long been "men" at home in the United States: "We gird up our loins as a nation, with the stern purpose to play our part manfully in winning the ultimate triumph;

and therefore . . . with unfaltering steps [we] tread the rough road of endeavor, smiting down the wrong and battling for the right, as Greatheart smote and battled in Bunyan's immortal story." In its imperialist glory, the virile American race would embody a warlike manliness, smiting down and battling its unmanly foes in the primitive Philippines. Were American men to be frightened from this work, they would show themselves, as TR put it, "weaklings."

Roosevelt always considered imperialism a question of both racial and individual manhood. Privately, he scorned anti-imperialists as "beings whose cult is non-virility." Publicly, he derided men who refused to take up the white man's burden as decadent, effeminate, and enemies of civilization. . . .

An unmanly, anti-imperialist race was as despicable as an unmanly anti-imperialist man. As TR saw it, overly peaceful races were like unsexed decadents who refused to breed, whereas expansive races left heirs, just as fathers left sons. "Nations that expand and nations that do not expand may both ultimately go down, but the one leaves heirs and a glorious memory, and the other leaves neither." As TR saw it, the only way to avoid effete, unmanly decadence—on the part of either race or man—was to embrace virile imperialism.

In short, racial health and civilized advancement implied both manhood and imperialism. An effeminate race was a decadent race; and a decadent race was too weak to advance civilization. Only by embracing virile racial expansionism could a civilization achieve its true manhood. This, as TR saw it, was the ultimate meaning of imperialism.

The Rough Rider: The War Hero Models the Power of a Manly Race

Roosevelt was not content merely to make speeches about the need for violent, imperialistic manhood. He always needed to embody his philosophy. The sickly boy had remade himself into an adventure-book hunter-naturalist; the dude politician had remade himself into a heroic Western rancher. The 1898 outbreak of the Spanish-American war—for which he had agitated long and hard—let Roosevelt remake himself into Colonel Roosevelt, the fearless Rough Rider.

Reinventing himself as a charismatic war hero allowed Roosevelt to model the manful imperialism about which he had been writing for four years. TR became a walking advertisement for the imperialistic manhood he desired for the American race. Indeed, from the moment of his enlistment until his mustering out four months later, Roosevelt self-consciously publicized himself as a model of strenuous, imperialistic manhood. In late April 1898, against all advice, Roosevelt resigned as assistant secretary of the navy and enlisted to fight in the just-declared war on Spain. Aged thirty-nine, with an important subcabinet post, a sick wife, and six young children, no one but Roosevelt himself imagined he ought to see active service. Roosevelt's decision to enlist was avidly followed by newspapers all over the country. Several editorialized against his enlistment, saying he would do more good for the war effort as assistant secretary of the navy. Roosevelt enlisted nonetheless and lost no opportunity to publicize his reasons to friendly newspapers. As he explained to the *New York Sun,* it would be unmanly—hypocritical—to allow other men to take his place on the front lines after he had agitated so strenuously for war. "I want to go because I wouldn't feel that I had been entirely true to my beliefs and convictions, and to the ideal I had set for myself if I didn't go." Embracing the glare of publicity, TR demonstrated to all that when a member of the manly American race took up the white man's burden, he risked his life willingly and joyously, for the good of civilization.

Roosevelt, commissioned at the rank of lieutenant colonel, raised a volunteer cavalry regiment which he described as "peculiarly American." It was designed to reflect Americans' masculine racial power as well as their civilized manly advancement. TR accepted only a fraction of the host of men who tried to enlist in his well-publicized regiment. Most of those he accepted were Westerners—rough cowboys and frontiersmen, the heirs and descendants of the masculine Indian fighters who had been forged into the American race on the Western frontier. But, to emphasize the American race's civilized superiority to the Spanish enemy, TR also enlisted several dozen young Ivy League college graduates, many of them athletes. These Harvard and Yale men, presumably the beneficiaries of the race's most advanced moral and intellectual evolution, represented the ever-advancing heights of civilization to which the manly American race could aspire. The regiment's combination of primitive Western masculinity and advanced civilized manliness dramatized the superior manhood of the American race. They would undoubtedly whip the pants off the inferior Latin Spaniards, and show Americans the glories of imperialistic manhood.

The press, fascinated by the undertaking, christened the regiment "Roosevelt's Rough Riders." Roosevelt's heroic frontiersman identity thus came full circle, as he no doubt intended. As Richard Slotkin has pointed out, the term "Rough Riders" had long been used in adventure novels to describe Western horsemen. Thus, by nicknaming his regiment the "Rough Riders," the nation showed it understood the historical connections Roosevelt always drew between Indian wars in the American West and virile imperialism in Cuba and the Philippines.

But lest anyone miss the connections he was trying to draw between continued manhood and racial expansion, Roosevelt made certain the press, and thus the public, remained fully informed about the Rough Riders' doings. He encouraged several journalists to attach themselves to the regiment throughout its sojourn in Cuba and even rounded up an interested motion-picture crew. The public avidly followed the newspaper reports of the Rough Riders' masculine cowboy heroics, manly collegiate athleticism, and overall wartime heroics.

Roosevelt, himself, was the core of the Rough Riders' popularity—he embodied the whole manly, imperialistic enterprise. Like his Western recruits, Roosevelt was both a masculine cowboy-hero and (by reputation and association, although not in reality) an Indian fighter. But TR was also a civilized Harvard man, manfully sacrificing his life of ease and privilege to take up the white man's burden and do his duty by the downtrodden brown Cubans. His widely reported, dashing exploits, including the heroic charge up "San Juan" Hill, proved the American race's violent masculinity had lost none of its potency since the bygone days of the Western frontier. According to Edmund Morris, when Roosevelt returned from the war he was "the most famous man in America."

After his mustering out, TR the politician continued to play the role of virile Rough Rider for all he was worth. In November, he was elected governor of New York, campaigning as a war hero and employing ex-Rough Riders to warm up the election crowds. By January 1899, his thrilling memoir, *The Rough Riders,* was appearing serially in *Scribner's Magazine.* And in 1900 his virile popularity convinced Republican party leaders that Roosevelt could counter Bryan's populism better than any other vice-presidential candidate. Roosevelt had constructed himself and the Rough Riders as the epitome of civilized, imperialistic manhood, a model for the American race to follow. His success in modeling that imperialistic manhood exceeded even his own expectations and ultimately paved the way for his presidency.

"The Strenuous Life"

On April 10, 1899, Colonel Roosevelt stood before the men of Chicago's elite, all-male, Hamilton Club and preached the doctrine of "The Strenuous Life." As governor of New York and a fabulously popular ex-Rough Rider, he knew the national press would be in attendance; and though he spoke *at* the Hamilton Club, he spoke *to* men across America. With the cooperation of the press and at the risk of his life, TR had made himself into a national hero—the embodiment of manly virtue, masculine violence, and white American racial supremacy—and the antithesis of overcivilized decadence. Now he urged the men of the American race to live the sort of life he had modeled for them: to be virile, vigorous, and manly, and to reject overcivilized decadence by supporting a strenuously imperialistic foreign policy. When contemporaries ultimately adopted his phrase "the strenuous life" as a synonym for the vigorous, vehement manhood Roosevelt modeled, they showed they correctly understood that his strenuous manhood was inextricably linked to his nationalism, imperialism, and racism.

Ostensibly, "The Strenuous Life" preached the virtues of military preparedness and imperialism, but contemporaries understood it as a speech about manhood. The practical import of the speech was to urge the nation to build up its army, to maintain its strong navy, and to take control of Puerto Rico, Cuba, and the Philippines. But underlying these immediate objectives lay the message that American manhood—both the manly race and individual white men—must retain the strength of their Indian-fighter ancestors, or another race would prove itself more manly and overtake America in the Darwinian struggle to be the world's most dominant race.

Roosevelt began by demanding manliness in both the American nation and American men. Slothful men who lacked the "desire and power" to strive in the world were despicable and unmanly. "We do not admire the man of timid peace. We admire the man who embodies victorious effort." If America and its men were not man enough to fight, they would not only lose their place among "the great nations of the world," they would become a decadent and effeminate race. Roosevelt held up the Chinese, whom he despised as the most decadent and unmanly of races, as a cautionary lesson: If we "play the part of China, and be content to rot by inches in ignoble ease within our borders," we will "go down before other nations which have not lost the manly and adventurous qualities." If American men lacked the manly fortitude to go bravely and willingly to a foreign war, the race would decay, preached TR, the virile war hero.

In stirring tones, the Rough Rider of San Juan Hill ridiculed the overcivilized anti-imperialists who had lost the "great fighting, masterful virtues." Lacking the masculine impulse toward racial aggression and unmoved by virile visions of empire, these men had been sapped of all manhood. . . . Like "cloistered" monkish celibates these "over-civilized" men "shrink, shrink, shrink" from carrying the "big stick." Dishonorably, they refused to do their manly duty by the childish Filipinos. Had the United States followed these anti-imperialists' counsel and refused to undertake "one of the great tasks set modern civilization," Americans would have shown themselves not only unmanly but also racially inferior. "Some stronger, manlier power would have to step in and do the work, and we would have shown ourselves weaklings, unable to carry to successful completion the labors that great and high-spirited nations are eager to undertake." As TR saw it, the man, the race, and the nation were one in their need to possess virile, imperialist manhood.

Then TR got down to brass tacks, dwelling at length on Congress' responsibility to build up the armed forces. After again raising the specter of Chinese decadence, which American men faced if they refused to strengthen their army and navy, Roosevelt stressed America's duty to take up the white man's burden in Cuba, Puerto Rico, and the Philippines. If the American race was "too weak, too selfish, or too foolish" to take on that task, it would be completed by "some stronger and more manful race." He ridiculed anti-imperialists as cowards who "make a pretense of humanitarianism to hide and cover their timidity" and to "excuse themselves for their unwillingness to play the part of men."

"The Strenuous Life" culminates with a Darwinian vision of strife between races for the "dominion of the world," which only the most manful race could win.

> I preach to you then, my countrymen, that our country calls not for the life of ease but for the life of strenuous endeavor. . . . If we stand idly by . . . then the bolder and stronger peoples will pass us by, and will win for themselves the domination of the world. Let us therefore boldly face the life of strife, resolute to do our duty well and manfully.

American men must embrace their manly mission to be the race which dominates the world. Struggle for racial supremacy was inevitable, but the most manful race— the American race—would triumph, if it made the attempt. Its masculine strength was proven by military victories over barbarous brown races. Its manly virtue was evident in its civilized superiority to the primitive childish races it uplifted. White American men must claim their place as the world's most perfect men, the fittest race for the evolutionary struggle toward a perfect civilization. This was the meaning of "The Strenuous Life."

We can now answer the question, "How did the title of an essay calling for American dominance over the brown races become a catchphrase to describe virile masculinity?" Roosevelt's desire for imperial dominance had been, from the first, intrinsically related to his views about male power. As he saw it, the manhood of the American race had been forged in the crucible of frontier race war; and to abandon the virile power of that violence would be to backslide toward effeminate racial mediocrity. Roosevelt wanted American men to be the ultimate in human evolution, the world's most powerful and civilized race. He believed that their victory over the Indians on the frontier proved that the American race possessed the racial superiority and masculine power to overcome any savage race; and he saw a glorious future for the race in the twentieth century, as it pressed on toward international dominance and the perfection of civilization. The only danger which Roosevelt saw menacing this millennial triumph of manly American civilization came from within. Only by surrendering to overcivilized decadence—by embracing unmanly racial sloth instead of virile imperialism—could American men fail. Thus, American men must work strenuously to uphold their civilization. They must refuse a life of ease, embrace their manly task, and take up the white man's burden. Only by living that "strenuous life" could American men prove themselves to be what Roosevelt had no doubt they were—the apex of civilization, evolution's most favored race, masterful men fit to command the barbarous races and the world's "waste spaces"—in short, the most virile and manly of men.

In later years, as Americans came to take international involvement for granted and as imperialism came to seem less controversial the phrase "the strenuous life" underwent a subtle change of meaning. Always associated with Roosevelt, it came to connote the virile manhood which he modeled for the nation as imperialistic Western hero and Rough Rider—the peculiar combination of moral manliness and aggressive masculinity which he was able to synthesize so well. As Roosevelt's presidency wore on, Americans grew accustomed to taking up the white man's burden, not only in the Philippines, but also in Cuba, Panama, and the Dominican Republic. The "strenuous life" came to be associated with any virile, manly effort to accomplish great work, whether imperialistic or not. Yet on a basic level, "the strenuous life" retained TR's original associations with the evolutionary struggle of the American race on behalf of civilization. "The strenuous life," as it came to be used, meant the opposite of "overcivilized effeminacy." Or, as Roosevelt summed it up himself in his *Autobiography,* the man who lives the strenuous life regards his life "as a pawn to be promptly hazarded whenever the hazard is warranted by the larger interests of the great game in which we are all engaged." That great game, for Roosevelt, was always the millennial struggle for Americans to perfect civilization by becoming the most manly, civilized, and powerful race in the world.

 F U R T H E R   R E A D I N G

Howard K. Beale, *Theodore Roosevelt and the Rise of America to World Power* (1956)
Robert L. Beisner, *From the Old Diplomacy to the New, 1865–1900,* 2nd ed. (1986)
W. B. Gatewood, Jr., *Black Americans and the White Man's Burden* (1975)
Amy Kaplan and Donald Pease, eds., *Cultures of United States Imperialism* (1993)
Michael Hunt, *Ideology and U.S. Foreign Policy* (1987)
———, *The Making of a Special Relationship: The United States and China to 1914*
     (1983)
Lester D. Langley, *The United States and the Caribbean in the Twentieth Century* (1982)
Walter LeFeber, *The American Search for Opportunity, 1865–1913* (1993)
Catherine Lutz and Jane Collins, *Reading National Geographic* (1993)
Thomas G. Paterson, *Major Problems in American Foreign Policy* (1989)
David Spurr, *The Rhetoric of Empire* (1993)
James C. Thomson, Jr., Peter W. Stanley, and John C. Perry, *Sentimental Imperialists*
     (1981)
Marilyn Blatt Young, *The Rhetoric of Empire* (1968)

Race and Power
Under Jim Crow

*Although high hopes and faith in an ever-expanding order of progress marked
most Americans at the turn of the century, the situation was different in the
black community, in the North as well as in the South. In the eyes of many post-
slavery historians, this period represented the nadir of African American influence in U.S. public life. In the South, the de facto reinstatement of one-party
white rule was accompanied by a sharp rise in lynchings of blacks, the general
exclusion of African Americans from active citizenship via disfranchisement
statutes, and the erection of a virtual caste system of institutional segregation,
called Jim Crow after the name of an old blackfaced vaudeville character. By
1900, the principle of segregation extended into every area of southern life,
including street railways, hotels, hospitals, restaurants, recreational facilities,
and the workplace. Discrimination was the norm in the North as well, but there
it was enforced less by specific legislation than by restrictive real-estate zoning,
employment practices (on the part of both employers and many trade unions),
and popular racism. The very density of such ghettoized northern black neighborhoods as Harlem in New York and Chicago's Back o' the Yards, however, offered
a creative, self-governing cultural space, which by the 1920s suggested new
possibilities for a mass politics.*

*Even the black educated elite found early twentieth-century America a
tough world to negotiate, since the strategic maneuvering room for black advancement as a whole was severely limited. Nevertheless, the realities of Jim Crow
elicited a wide range of responses. The conservative strategy, associated most
closely with Booker T. Washington at Tuskegee, Alabama, recognized the impos-
sibility of frontal resistance to white racial norms and opted instead for politically
inoffensive self-improvement efforts that might win not only white acceptance
but even financial endowment. The more radical course, advocated by sociologist
W. E. B. Du Bois and a tiny minority of northern professionals, counseled a direct
challenge to the legal, political, and ideological props of Jim Crow. Most contemporary black leaders fell somewhere between these two poles, struggling to gain a
foothold amidst an outrushing tide.*

DOCUMENTS

In Document 1, from *Plessy* v. *Ferguson,* a case involving the forced separation of the races on railroad cars, the U.S. Supreme Court set an important precedent on behalf of legalized segregation. Equally significant, the lone dissent of Justice John Harlan of Kentucky foreshadowed the wisdom of a later age. If the court, in *Plessy,* chose to defend segregation laws on rather narrow and technical grounds, the more assertive, unapologetic voice of Jim Crow is reflected in Document 2, in the political oratory of Congressman Frank Clark of Florida, supporting an amendment introduced by Congressman J. Thomas Heflin of Alabama to segregate streetcars in Washington, D.C.

Contemporary African American political opinion is in turn represented in the next three selections. In Document 3, Booker T. Washington offers a classic version of his collective self-help philosophy before an admiring white audience at the Atlantic Exposition in 1895. W. E. B. Du Bois, who shortly thereafter led the Niagara group of black intellectuals into the National Association for the Advancement of Colored People (NAACP), answers Washington (Document 4) with bitter sarcasm. In Document 5, Mary Church Terrell, an Oberlin graduate and the cofounder of the Colored Women's League Clubs, gives voice to the uplift ideology prevalent among the "respectable" black middle class as they sought to socialize the ranks of their poor, uneducated rural cousins.

1. The U.S Supreme Court Upholds Segregation:
Plessy v. *Ferguson,* 1896

Justice Brown The constitutionality of this act is attacked upon the ground that it conflicts both with the 13th Amendment of the Constitution, abolishing slavery, and the 14th Amendment, which prohibits certain restrictive legislation on the part of the states.

1. That it does not conflict with the 13th Amendment, which abolished slavery and involuntary servitude, except as a punishment for crime, is too clear for argument. . . .

A statute which implies merely a legal distinction between the white and colored races—a distinction which is founded in the color of the two races, and which must always exist so long as white men are distinguished from the other race by color—has no tendency to destroy the legal equality of the two races, or re-establish a state of involuntary servitude. . . .

The object of the [14th] amendment was undoubtedly to enforce the absolute equality of the two races before the law, but in the nature of things it could not have been intended to abolish distinctions based upon color, or to enforce social, as distinguished from political, equality, or a commingling of the two races upon terms unsatisfactory to either. Laws permitting, and even requiring their separation in places where they are liable to be brought into contact do not necessarily imply the inferiority of either race to the other, and have been generally, if not universally, recognized as within the competency of the state legislatures in the exercise of their police power. The most common instance of this is connected with the establishment of

---

Plessy v. *Ferguson,* 1896," 163 U.S. 537 (1896).

separate schools for white and colored children, which have been held to be a valid exercise of the legislative power even by courts of states where the political rights of the colored race have been longest and most earnestly enforced. . . .

So far, then, as a conflict with the 14th Amendment is concerned, the case reduces itself to the question whether the statute of Louisiana is a reasonable regulation, and with respect to this there must necessarily be a large discretion on the part of the legislature. In determining the question of reasonableness it is at liberty to act with reference to the established usages, customs, and traditions of the people, and with a view to the promotion of their comfort, and the preservation of the public peace and good order. Gauged by this standard, we cannot say that a law which authorizes or even requires the separation of the two races in public conveyances is unreasonable or more obnoxious to the 14th Amendment than the acts of Congress requiring separate schools for colored children in the District of Columbia, the constitutionality of which does not seem to have been questioned, or the corresponding acts of state legislatures.

We consider the underlying fallacy of the plaintiff's argument to consist in the assumption that the enforced separation of the two races stamps the colored race with a badge of inferiority. If this be so, it is not by reason of anything found in the act, but solely because the colored race chooses to put that construction upon it. The argument necessarily assumes that if, as has been more than once the case, and is not unlikely to be so again, the colored race should become the dominant power in the state legislature, and should enact a law in precisely similar terms, it would thereby relegate the white race to an inferior position. We imagine that the white race, at least, would not acquiesce in this assumption. The argument also assumes that social prejudice may be overcome by legislation, and that equal rights cannot be secured to the Negro except by an enforced commingling of the two races. We cannot accept this proposition. If the two races are to meet on terms of social equality, it must be the result of natural affinities, a mutual appreciation of each other's merits and a voluntary consent of individuals. . . . Legislation is powerless to eradicate racial instincts or to abolish distinctions based upon physical differences, and the attempt to do so can only result in accentuating the difficulties of the present situation. If the civil and political right of both races be equal, one cannot be inferior . . . to the other civilly or politically. If one race be inferior to the other socially, the Constitution of the United States cannot put them upon the same plane.

Justice Harlan, dissenting. . . . In respect of civil rights, common to all citizens, the Constitution of the United States does not, I think, permit any public authority to know the race of those entitled to be protected in the enjoyment of such rights. Every true man has pride of race, and under appropriate circumstances, when the rights of others, his equals before the law, are not to be affected, it is his privilege to express such pride and to take such action based upon it as to him seems proper. But I deny that any legislative body or judicial tribunal may have regard to the race of citizens when the civil rights of those citizens are involved. Indeed such legislation as that here in question is inconsistent, not only with that equality of rights which pertains to citizenship, national and state, but with the personal liberty enjoyed by every one within the United States. . . .

In my opinion, the judgment this day rendered will, in time, prove to be quite as pernicious as the decision made by this tribunal in the *Dred Scott* Case. It was adjudged in that case that the descendants of Africans who were imported into this country and sold as slaves were not included nor intended to be included under the word "citizens" in the Constitution, and could not claim any of the rights and privileges which that instrument provided for and secured to citizens of the United States; that at the time of the adoption of the Constitution they were "considered as a subordinate and inferior class of beings, who had been subjugated by the dominant race, and, whether emancipated or not, yet remained subject to their authority, and had no rights or privileges but such as those who held the power and the government might choose to grant them." The recent amendments of the Constitution, it was supposed, had eradicated these principles from our institutions. But it seems that we have yet, in some of the states, a dominant race, a superior class of citizens, which assumes to regulate the enjoyment of civil rights, common to all citizens, upon the basis of race. The present decision, it may well be apprehended, will not only stimulate aggressions, more or less brutal and irritating, upon the admitted rights of colored citizens, but will encourage the belief that it is possible, by means of state enactments, to defeat the beneficent purposes which the people of the United States had in view when they adopted the recent amendments of the Constitution, by one of which the blacks of this country were made citizens of the United States and of the states in which they respectively reside and whose privileges and immunities, as citizens, the states are forbidden to abridge. Sixty millions of whites are in no danger from the presence here of eight millions of blacks. The destinies of the two races in this country are indissolubly linked together, and the interests of both require that the common government of all shall not permit the seeds of race hate to be planted under the sanction of law. What can more certainly arouse race hate, what more certainly create and perpetuate a feeling of distrust between these races, than state enactments which in fact proceed on the ground that colored citizens are so inferior and degraded that they cannot be allowed to sit in public coaches occupied by white citizens? That, as all will admit, is the real meaning of such legislation as was enacted in Louisiana. . . .

If evils will result from the commingling of the two races upon public highways established for the benefit of all, they will be infinitely less than those that will surely come from state legislation regulating the enjoyment of civil rights upon the basis of race. We boast of the freedom enjoyed by our people above all other peoples. But it is difficult to reconcile that boast with a state of the law which, practically, puts the brand of servitude and degradation upon a large class of our fellow citizens, our equals before the law. The thin disguise of "equal" accommodations for passengers in railroad coaches will not mislead anyone, or atone for the wrong this day done. . . .

I am of opinion that the statute of Louisiana is inconsistent with the personal liberty of citizens, white and black, in that state, and hostile to both the spirit and letter of the Constitution of the United States. If laws of like character should be enacted in the several states of the Union, the effect would be in the highest degree mischievous. Slavery as an institution tolerated by law would, it is true, have disappeared from our country, but there would remain a power in the states, by sinister legislation, to interfere with the full enjoyment of the blessings of freedom; to regulate civil rights, common to all citizens, upon the basis of race; and to place in a condition of legal inferiority a large body of American citizens, now constituting a part of the political community, called the people of the United States, for whom and by whom, through representatives, our government is administered. Such a system is inconsistent with the guarantee given by the Constitution to each state of a republican form of government, and may be stricken down by Congressional action, or by the courts in the discharge of their solemn duty to maintain the supreme law of the land, anything in the Constitution or laws of any state to the contrary notwithstanding.

For the reasons stated, I am constrained to withhold my assent from the opinion and judgment of the majority.

2. Congressman Frank Clark Praises Segregation, 1908

On last Sunday afternoon an old negro man living in this city came to my office and spent the afternoon with my wife and myself, and I have not spent a more pleasant afternoon for years. [Applause] He belonged to my father, and he was the first human being that ever carried me out in the yard after my birth. [Applause on the Democratic side.] . . . I love that old negro man [applause], and . . . in a contest between him and others, in a physical contest, I would be found by his side protecting and defending him. [Renewed applause.] . . .

Mr. Chairman, the question raised by the amendment [to segregate street cars in Washington, D.C.] offered by the gentleman from Alabama [Cong. Heflin] is purely a question of disposing of a situation in such manner as will lessen the friction between the races. The adoption of that amendment will not discriminate against the negro race, nor will it inure to the advantage of the white race alone. It will inure to the benefit of both races. It is not intended by the gentleman from Alabama as an attack upon the negro, nor is it an attempt by that gentleman, or by any of us who support it, to deprive the negro of a single right which he has under the law of the land. On its very face it provides equal accommodation for both races on the street cars in the Capital City of this Republic. . . . It is idle to call this amendment a discrimination against the negro. Wherein is the discrimination? The amendment itself contains no discrimination. The language used contains no hint of discrimination, yet gentlemen seize upon it as an excuse to arraign the people of an entire section of this country for alleged wrongs to the negro race. Is this fair? Do gentlemen imagine that even the negro, who has been the willing dupe of the Republican party for all these long years, can be longer deceived by these loud quadrennial protestations of affectionate regard for him? . . .

While on this phase of the subject, Mr. Speaker, I desire to refer to the unsupported, bald declarations of gentlemen that negroes are not supplied with accommodations equal to those furnished to white people upon railroads in the South. Why gentlemen will persist in these statements I can not understand. Let me suggest something here that in all probability these gentlemen have never thought of. On our Florida railroads—and I presume it is the same in other Southern States—

Congressional Record, 60th Cong., 1st sess. (February 22, 1908), appendix, 38–40. This document can also be found in I. A. Newby, ed., *The Development of Segregationist Thought* (Homewood, Ill.: Dorsey Press, 1968), 91–97.

the cars furnished for negro passengers are just as good as those furnished for white passengers. I am free to admit, however, that they do not long remain as good, as comfortable, and as clean as do those set apart for white passengers. You will not have to search long for the reason of this change. The average negro is perfectly happy when he finds himself eating a watermelon or going on a railroad excursion. The railroad companies in the South cater to this weakness of the negro for riding on trains, and scarcely a week passes in the summer time that a negro excursion is not "pulled off" in every neighborhood. They flock to these excursion trains by thousands and of course the cars set apart for the negroes on the regular passenger trains are used for negro excursions.

Imagine a nice, new passenger coach, packed with dirty, greasy, filthy negroes, down South, in midsummer, and you can readily understand why that car does not long remain as good, as clean, and as desirable as a similar car occupied exclusively by white travelers. It is said of Sam Jones, the great Georgia revivalist, that on one occasion a certain Northern gentleman asked him if there was very much difference in the instincts of a "nigger" and a white man. Sam replied that he didn't know as to that, but of one thing he was absolutely sure, and that was that there was a vast difference in the *"out stinks"* of the two.

For more than forty years, Mr. Chairman, the white people of the South have been taxing themselves to educate negro children, have been building churches for them, and in every conceivable way, with a patience and forbearance never excelled in any age, have struggled along with the stupendous task of elevating and fitting for the duties of citizenship this black mass of ignorant, vicious, and incapable freedmen. I am not wise enough to foretell the end of the problem confronting us. Mr. Lincoln said that this nation could not exist "half slave and half free." I think it is equally true that this nation can not exist *half white* and *half black.* I am very sure that no country having within its borders two distinct races, alien to each other in every essential respect, can long exist with any degree of harmony between the two upon the beautiful theory of perfect equality of all before the law.

The position which we of the South occupy on this question is not one of hostility to the negro. It is one of patriotic love for our own race. We would not destroy the negro, but we would preserve the Caucasian. We will do the black man no harm, and we will not allow him to harm the white man. Members of Congress who are dependent upon a few negro votes in order to retain their seats in this body, a few long-haired negrophilists in various sections of the country, and a lot of short-haired white women who disgrace both their race and sex, may rant of injustice and wrong to the end of time, but they had as well realize now as at any other time that, no matter what the cost or how great the sacrifice, we shall under any and all circumstances maintain the integrity of our race and preserve our civilization.

If God Almighty had intended these two races to be equal, He would have so created them. He made the Caucasian of handsome figure, straight hair, regular features, high brow, and superior intellect. He created the negro, giving him a black skin, kinky hair, thick lips, flat nose, low brow, low order of intelligence, and repulsive features. I do not believe that these differences were the result of either accident or mistake on the part of the Creator. I believe He knew what He was doing, and I believe He did just what He wanted to do.

We believe in God, and we are willing to accept His work just as it fell from His hands. But these people who profess to believe that "a white man may be as good as a negro if the white man behaves himself" are not satisfied with God's work in this regard. They are quite sure that they can make a better job of it than did the Creator, hence we find them attempting to remove the black man from the menial sphere for which he was created, and where he may be useful, to a higher circle for which he is entirely unfitted and where he is perfectly useless. . . .

The gentleman from New York [Congressman Driscoll] says that we have been allowed to have our own way down South with this question for so long that we have grown "bold" enough to come on the floor of this House and make demands for this kind of legislation. The gentleman uses that word "bold" as though he thought we did not have the right to come here and make demands. We do demand, and we have the right to demand. The blood of the "heroes of the Revolution" flows through our veins; from the Revolution to the present day no foreign foe has ever engaged this Republic in battle that Southern blood has not consecrated every place of conflict; in all our history no foreign foe has ever threatened the flag that we did not rally to its defense. In these emergencies we volunteer, and do not have to be drafted. Yes; we have the right to demand. This is our country, as it was the country of our fathers. The country of the white man, not the home of the mongrel. It will always be the white man's country. If the black man and the yellow man each desire to remain with us, occupying the sphere in life for which God Almighty intended each, let them do so. If not content with that, then let them go elsewhere.

3. Booker T. Washington Advocates Self-Help, 1895

A ship lost at sea for many days suddenly sighted a friendly vessel. From the mast of the unfortunate vessel was seen a signal, "Water, water; we die of thirst!" The answer from the friendly vessel at once came back, "Cast down your bucket where you are." A second time the signal, "Water, water; send us water!" ran up from the distressed vessel, and was answered, "Cast down your bucket where you are." And a third and fourth signal for water was answered, "Cast down your bucket where you are." The captain of the distressed vessel, at last heeding the injunction, cast down his bucket, and it came up full of fresh, sparkling water from the mouth of the Amazon River. To those of my race who depend on bettering their condition in a foreign land or who underestimate the importance of cultivating friendly relations with the Southern white man, who is their next-door neighbor, I would say: "Cast down your bucket where you are"—cast it down in making friends in every manly way of the people of all races by whom we are surrounded.

Cast it down in agriculture, mechanics, in commerce, in domestic service, and in the professions. And in this connection it is well to bear in mind that whatever other sins the South may be called to bear, when it comes to business, pure and simple, it is in the South that the Negro is given a man's chance in the commercial world, and in nothing is this Exposition more eloquent than in emphasizing this

Booker T. Washington, *Up from Slavery: An Autobiography of Booker T. Washington* (New York: Doubleday, 1901), 114–117.

chance. Our greatest danger is that in the great leap from slavery to freedom we may overlook the fact that the masses of us are to live by the productions of our hands, and fail to keep in mind that we shall prosper in proportion as we learn to dignify and glorify common labour and put brains and skill into the common occupations of life; shall prosper in proportion as we learn to draw the line between the superficial and the substantial, the ornamental gewgaws of life and the useful. No race can prosper till it learns that there is as much dignity in tilling a field as in writing a poem. It is at the bottom of life we must begin, and not at the top. Nor should we permit our grievances to overshadow our opportunities.

To those of the white race who look to the incoming of those of foreign birth and strange tongue and habits for the prosperity of the South, were I permitted I would repeat what I say to my own race, "Cast down your bucket where you are." Cast it down among the eight millions of Negroes whose habits you know, whose fidelity and love you have tested in days when to have proved treacherous meant the ruin of your firesides. Cast down your bucket among these people who have, without strikes and labour wars, tilled your fields, cleared your forests, builded your railroads and cities, and brought forth treasures from the bowels of the earth, and helped make possible this magnificent representation of the progress of the South. Casting down your bucket among my people, helping and encouraging them as you are doing on these grounds, and to education of head, hand, and heart, you will find that they will buy your surplus land, make blossom the waste places in your fields, and run your factories. While doing this, you can be sure in the future, as in the past, that you and your families will be surrounded by the most patient, faithful, law-abiding, and unresentful people that the world has seen. As we have proved our loyalty to you in the past, in nursing your children, watching by the sick-bed of your mothers and fathers, and often following them with tear-dimmed eyes to their graves, so in the future, in our humble way, we shall stand by you with a devotion that no foreigner can approach, ready to lay down our lives, if need be, in defence of yours, interlacing our industrial, commercial, civil, and religious life with yours in a way that shall make the interests of both races one. In all things that are purely social we can be as separate as the fingers, yet one as the hand in all things essential to mutual progress. . . .

The wisest among my race understand that the agitation of questions of social equality is the extremest folly, and that progress in the enjoyment of all the privileges that will come to us must be the result of severe and constant struggle rather than of artificial forcing. No race that has anything to contribute to the markets of the world is long in any degree ostracized. It is important and right that all privileges of the law be ours, but it is vastly more important that we be prepared for the exercises of these privileges. The opportunity to earn a dollar in a factory just now is worth infinitely more than the opportunity to spend a dollar in an opera-house.

In conclusion, may I repeat that nothing in thirty years has given us more hope and encouragement, and drawn us so near to you of the white race, as this opportunity [to participate in] the Exposition; and here bending, as it were, over the altar that represents the results of the struggles of your race and mine, both starting practically empty-handed three decades ago, I pledge that in your effort to work out the great and intricate problem which God has laid at the doors of the South, you shall have at all times the patient, sympathetic help of my race; only let this be constantly in mind, that, while from representations in these buildings of the product of field, of forest, of mine, of factory, letters, and art, much good will come, yet far above and beyond material benefits will be that higher good, that, let us pray God, will come, in a blotting out of sectional differences and racial animosities and suspicions, in a determination to administer absolute justice, in a willing obedience among all classes to the mandates of law. This, this, coupled with our material prosperity, will bring into our beloved South a new heaven and a new earth.

4. W. E. B. Du Bois Rejects Washington's Strategy of Accommodation, 1903

Mr. Washington represents in Negro thought the old attitude of adjustment and submission; but adjustment at such a peculiar time as to make his programme unique. This is an age of unusual economic development, and Mr. Washington's programme naturally takes an economic cast, becoming a gospel of Work and Money to such an extent as apparently almost completely to overshadow the higher aims of life. Moreover, this is an age when the more advanced races are coming in closer contact with the less developed races, and the race-feeling is therefore intensified; and Mr. Washington's programme practically accepts the alleged inferiority of the Negro races. Again, in our own land, the reaction from the sentiment of war time has given impetus to race-prejudice against Negroes, and Mr. Washington withdraws many of the high demands of Negroes as men and American citizens. In other periods of intensified prejudice all the Negro's tendency to self-assertion has been called forth; at this period a policy of submission is advocated. In the history of nearly all other races and peoples the doctrine preached at such crises has been that manly self-respect is worth more than lands and houses, and that a people who voluntarily surrender such respect, or cease striving for it, are not worth civilizing.

In answer to this, it has been claimed that the Negro can survive only through submission. Mr. Washington distinctly asks that black people give up, at least for the present, three things,—

    First, political power,

    Second, insistence on civil rights,

    Third, higher education of Negro youth,—

and concentrate all their energies on industrial education, the accumulation of wealth, and the conciliation of the South. This policy has been courageously and insistently advocated for over fifteen years, and has been triumphant for perhaps ten years. As a result of this tender of the palm-branch, what has been the return? In these years there have occurred:

1. The disfranchisement of the Negro.
2. The legal creation of a distinct status of civil inferiority for the Negro.
3. The steady withdrawal of aid from institutions for the higher training of the Negro.

W. E. B. Du Bois, *The Souls of Black Folk* (Chicago: A. C. McClurg, 1903), 153–156, 47–59.

These movements are not, to be sure, direct results of Mr. Washington's teachings; but his propaganda has, without a shadow of doubt, helped their speedier accomplishment. The question then comes: Is it possible, and probable, that nine millions of men can make effective progress in economic lines if they are deprived of political rights, made a servile caste, and allowed only the most meagre chance for developing their exceptional men? If history and reason give any distinct answer to these questions, it is an emphatic *No*, And Mr. Washington thus faces the triple paradox of his career:

1. He is striving nobly to make Negro artisans business men and property-owners; but it is utterly impossible, under modern competitive methods, for workingmen and property-owners to defend their rights and exist without the right of suffrage.

2. He insists on thrift and self-respect, but at the same time counsels a silent submission to civic inferiority such as is bound to sap the manhood of any race in the long run.

3. He advocates common-school and industrial training, and depreciates institutions of higher learning; but neither the Negro common-schools, nor Tuskegee itself, could remain open a day were it not for teachers trained in Negro colleges, or trained by their graduates. . . .

[Critics of Washington] do not expect that the free right to vote, to enjoy civic rights, and to be educated, will come in a moment; they do not expect to see the bias and prejudices of years disappear at the blast of a trumpet; but they are absolutely certain that the way for a people to gain their reasonable rights is not by voluntarily throwing them away and insisting that they do not want them; that the way for a people to gain respect is not by continually belittling and ridiculing themselves; that, on the contrary, Negroes must insist continually, in season and out of season, that voting is necessary to modern manhood, that color discrimination is barbarism, and that black boys need education as well as white boys. . . .

. . . On the whole the distinct impression left by Mr. Washington's propaganda is, first, that the South is justified in its present attitude toward the Negro because of the Negro's degradation; secondly, that the prime cause of the Negro's failure to rise more quickly is his wrong education in the past; and, thirdly, that his future rise depends primarily on his own efforts. Each of these propositions is a dangerous half-truth. The supplementary truths must never be lost sight of: first, slavery and race-prejudice are potent if not sufficient causes of the Negro's position; second, industrial and common-school training were necessarily slow in planting because they had to await the black teachers trained by higher institutions, . . . and, third, while it is a great truth to say that the Negro must strive and strive mightily to help himself, it is equally true that unless his striving be not simply seconded, but rather aroused and encouraged, by the initiative of the richer and wiser environing group, he cannot hope for great success.

In his failure to realize and impress this last point, Mr. Washington is especially to be criticised. His doctrine has tended to make the whites, North and South, shift the burden of the Negro problem to the Negro's shoulders and stand aside as critical and rather pessimistic spectators; when in fact the burden belongs to the nation. . . .

The South ought to be led, by candid and honest criticism, to assert her better self and do her full duty to the race she has cruelly wronged and is still wronging.

Victimization of blacks — [handwritten margin note]

The North—her co-partner in guilt—cannot salve her conscience by plastering it with gold. We cannot settle this problem by diplomacy and suaveness, by "policy" alone, If worse come to worst, can the moral fibre of this country survive the slow throttling and murder of nine millions of men?

The black men of America have a duty to perform, a duty stern and delicate,—a forward movement to oppose a part of the work of their greatest leader. So far as Mr. Washington preaches Thrift, Patience, and Industrial Training for the masses, we must hold up his hands and strive with him, rejoicing in his honors and glorying in the strength of this Joshua called of God and of man to lead the headless host. But so far as Mr. Washington apologizes for injustice, North or South, does not rightly value the privilege and duty of voting, belittles the emasculating effects of caste distinctions, and opposes the higher training and ambition of our brighter minds,—so far as he, the South, or the Nation, does this,—we must unceasingly and firmly oppose them. By every civilized and peaceful method we must strive for the rights which the world accords to men, clinging unwaveringly to those great words which the sons of the Fathers would fain forget: "We hold these truths to be self-evident: That all men are created equal; that they are endowed by their Creator with certain unalienable rights; that among these are life, liberty, and the pursuit of happiness."

invoke Constitution [handwritten margin note]

5. Mary Church Terrell Praises the Club Work of Colored Women, 1901

Should anyone ask me what special phase of the Negro's development makes me most hopeful of his ultimate triumph over present obstacles, I should answer unhesitatingly, it is the magnificent work the women are doing to regenerate and uplift the race. Though there are many things in the Negro's present condition to discourage him, he has some blessings for which to be thankful: not the least of these is the progress of our women in everything which makes for the culture of the individual and the elevation of the race.

For years, either banding themselves into small companies or struggling alone, colored women have worked with might and main to improve the condition of their people. The necessity of systematizing their efforts and working on a larger scale became apparent not many years ago, and they decided to unite their forces. Thus it happened that in the summer of 1896 the National Association of Colored Women was formed by the union of two large organizations, from which the advantage of concerted action had been learned. From its birth till the present time its growth has been steady. Interest in the purposes and plans of the National Association has spread so rapidly that it has already been represented in twenty-six states. Handicapped though its members have been, because they lacked both money and experience, their efforts have for the most part been crowned with success.

Kindergarten have been established by some of its organizations, from which encouraging reports have come. A sanitarium with a training school for nurses has

Essay by Mary Church Terrell. As edited in Mary Beth Norton and Ruth M. Alexander, eds., *Major Problems in American Women's History: Documents and Essays* (Lexington, Mass.: D. C. Heath, 1996), 254–256. Reprinted by permission of Houghton Mifflin Company.

been set on such a firm foundation by the Phyllis Wheatley Club of New Orleans, Louisiana, and has proved itself to be such a blessing to the entire community, that the municipal government of that Southern city has voted it an annual appropriation of several hundred dollars. By the members of the Tuskegee branch of the association the work of bringing the light of knowledge and the gospel of cleanliness to their poor benighted sisters on the plantations in Alabama has been conducted with signal success. Their efforts have thus far been confined to four estates, comprising thousands of acres of land, on which live hundreds of colored people yet in the darkness of ignorance and in the grip of sin, and living miles away from churches and schools.

Plans for aiding the indigent orphaned and aged have been projected, and in some instances have been carried into successful execution. One club in Memphis, Tenn., has purchased a large tract of land on which it intends to erect an Old Folks' Home, part of the money for which has already been raised. Splendid service has been rendered by the Illinois Federation of Colored Women's Clubs, through whose instrumentality schools have been visited, truant children looked after, parents and teachers urged to cooperate with each other, rescue and reform work engaged in, so as to reclaim unfortunate women and tempted girls, public institutions investigated, and garments cut, made and distributed to the needy poor.

Questions affecting our legal status as a race are sometimes agitated by our women. In Tennessee and Louisiana colored women have several times petitioned the legislature of their respective states to repeal the obnoxious Jim Crow car laws. . . .

Homes, more homes, better homes, purer homes, is the text upon which our sermons have been and will be preached. There has been a determined effort to have heart-to-heart talks with our women, that we may strike at the root of evils, many of which lie at the fireside. If the women of the dominant race, with all the centuries of education, culture and refinement back of them, with all the wealth of opportunity ever present with them, feel the need of a Mothers' Congress, that they may be enlightened upon the best methods of rearing their children and conducting their homes, how much more do our women, from whom shackles were stricken but yesterday, need information on the same vital subjects! And so the Association is working vigorously to establish mothers' congresses on a small scale, wherever our women can be reached.

From this brief and meagre account of the work which has been and is still being accomplished by colored women through the medium of clubs, it is easy to observe how earnest and effective have been our efforts to elevate the race. No people need ever despair whose women are fully aroused to the duties which rest upon them, and are willing to shoulder responsibilities which they alone can successfully assume. The scope of our endeavors is constantly widening. Into the various channels of generosity and beneficence the National Association is entering more and more every day.

Some of our women are urging their clubs to establish day nurseries, a charity of which there is an imperative need. The infants of wage-earning mothers are frequently locked alone in a room from the time the mother leaves in the morning until she returns at night. Not long ago I read in a Southern newspaper that an infant thus locked alone in the room all day had cried itself to death. When one reflects on the slaughter of the innocents which is occurring with pitiless persistency every day, and thinks of the multitudes who are maimed for life or are rendered imbecile, because of the treatment received during their helpless infancy, it is evident that by establishing day nurseries colored women will render one of the greatest services possible to humanity and to the race. . . .

Nothing lies nearer the heart of colored women than the cause of the children. We feel keenly the need of kindergartens, and are putting forth earnest efforts to honeycomb this country with them from one extreme to the other. The more unfavorable the environments of children the more necessary is it that steps be taken to counteract baleful influences upon innocent victims. How imperative is it then, that, as colored women, we inculcate correct principles and set good examples for our own youth, whose little feet will have so many thorny paths of prejudice, temptation and injustice to tread. . . .

And so, lifting as we climb, onward and upward we go, struggling, striving and hoping that the buds and blossoms of our desires will burst into glorious fruition ere long. With courage born of success achieved in the past, we look forward to a future large with promise and hope. Seeking no favors because of our color, nor patronage because of our needs, we knock at the bar of Justice and ask for an equal chance.

 *E S S A Y S*

In the first essay, Yale University historian Glenda Elizabeth Gilmore offers a psychosocial explanation of black disfranchisement as played out particularly in North Carolina in the 1890s. Drawing on a new language of white supremacy, fashioned in part by the rise of an American empire and the masculinist ethic that this empire embraced (as discussed in Chapter 9), southern middle-class men challenged themselves and their peers to take back control of public life and thus finally eradicate the "stain" of Reconstruction. As Gilmore indicates, the sudden aggressiveness on the part of "New White Men" posed a grave challenge to the leadership of the black community, male and female, which was simultaneously engaged in its own struggle to impose a standard of respectability on an unruly laboring class. In the second selection, Kevin K. Gaines of the University of Texas at Austin elaborates on the specific dilemmas and limited strategic options facing the black elite under Jim Crow. As he demonstrates, various forms of "uplift ideology" united black leaders from Booker T. Washington to W. E. B. Du Bois, even as political and philosophical differences, exacerbated by different regional experiences, drove a wedge between them.

Whiteness and Manhood

GLENDA ELIZABETH GILMORE

Rudyard Kipling thought he knew a man when he saw one. From his post in colonial India, he worked feverishly to explain why Indian men needed ruling and why the British were the men for the job. In the end, it all came down to self-control in the service of moderation. Unlike the darker races of the world, the Anglo-Saxon peoples had evolved far enough to bear up to adversity without crumbling; at the same

Glenda Elizabeth Gilmore, *Gender and Jim Crow: Women and the Politics of White Supremacy in North Carolina, 1896–1920* (Chapel Hill: University of North Carolina Press, 1996), 61–76. Copyright © 1996 by the University of North Carolina Press. Used by permission of the publisher.

time, they could handle success without resorting to excess. Darker people too often feel victim to their emotions; they were at best childlike and at worst animalistic, like Kipling's character Mowgli in *The Jungle Book*. In his instantly successful 1899 poem, "The White Man's Burden," Kipling described nonwhites as "fluttered folk and wild / . . . Half devil and half child."

Halfway around the world, in North Carolina, white men and boys read Kipling's poetry as an endorsement of their own ideas of manhood and racial order. No one, they thought, had borne the "white man's burden" longer or more stoically than they. Suddenly the world was turning to their way of thinking. In the 1890s, southern middle-class white men embraced the racialization of manhood—so international, so scientific, so modern—and put it to work in their own backyards. As one Charlottean, calling himself "Anglo-Saxon," put it, "Why should any man think that North Carolina is destined to prove an exception to Herbert Spencer's law of the 'Survival of the Fittest.' . . . It is all tommy-rot . . . to charge that prejudice, on account of color, is the foundation upon which is predicated white men's objections to negro domination." To "Anglo-Saxon," white supremacy was more than skin deep. Race was not simply much ado about a silly thing like color; the order of the universe depended on race, and "white" and "black" were outward manifestations of inner constitution.

Thirty years earlier, during Reconstruction, the fathers of the men now reading Kipling and Spencer had faced the exigencies of organizing a biracial society in the wake of defeat. Black enfranchisement and federal scrutiny had forced the men of that generation to reckon with black political power, even as they tried to limit it through violence, fraud, gerrymandering, and poll taxes. Along with those pernicious methods, however, they grudgingly employed a meritorious concept—the ideology of the Best Man—to reduce the number of black voters and officeholders. According to this paradigm, only the Best Men should hold office, the men who, by faith and by works, exhibited benevolence, fair-mindedness, and gentility. Southern white men's belief in their own superiority gave them confidence that they could effectively manipulate the Best Man criteria to exclude most African Americans from officeholding, and the threat of federal oversight limited their choices in any event. Although it was inevitable that a few black men would be elected, the Best Man ideal could be used to hold them to the strictest of standards. Of course, not all white men who held office lived up to the model. The Best Man was not real but a theoretical device that worked to limit democracy by invoking the language of merit.

Although African Americans most often reasoned from a political ideology of natural rights, they seized upon the Best Man figure because it offered their only path to power. At the same time, it resonated with many educated African Americans' own religious beliefs and ideas of merit. The Best Man pursued higher education, married a pious woman, and fathered accomplished children. He participated in religious activities, embraced prohibition, and extended benevolence to the less fortunate. He could collaborate on social issues across racial lines, as the women of the WCTU did. He could hold a modest number of political offices. Edward Dudley certainly qualified as Best Man in the eyes of African Americans, and his political career attests to the way in which the ideology could successfully be put into practice with a lifetime of careful calculation. Such a steep path to power might prove arduous, but it constituted the only way African Americans could hope to gain a political hearing from whites.

Black Best Men believed that in order to continue to enjoy "manhood's rights," as they referred to the franchise and officeholding, they must conform to middle-class whites' definitions of manhood. African Americans recognized the exclusiveness of the Best Man definition and its dependence on whites' inclinations to privilege class status over racial lines. Reliance on the Best Man ideal meant that African Americans constantly had to prove their manhood in order to maintain civil rights, even if they could never prove it to whites' satisfaction. If a certain black man led an exemplary life, whites still held him accountable for the conduct of his entire race. His Best Man status was measured not just by his own behavior but also by that of any random stranger who happened to be African American.

To the young white men whose fathers had forged the Best Man compromise, two events in the last decade of the nineteenth century underscored its current un-desirability. First, an interracial coalition of Populists and Republicans gained control of the state legislature and moved to return many local offices to a popular vote. As a result, the number of black officeholders and appointees increased dramatically. Then, the Spanish-American/Cuban War forced ideologies of imperialism, race, and manhood to stand out in sharp relief as Afro-Cubans took the lead in their country's revolution. Black men rushed to prove their manhood and patriotism by enlisting in the Third North Carolina Regiment, the first in U.S. history commanded entirely by black officers.

As young white Democrats searched for ways to exclude African Americans from politics and power once and for all, international circumstances produced rhetoric that offered them a fresh rationale for white supremacy at the same time that it licensed their actions. After the Spanish-American/Cuban War, empire presented democracy with vexing representational problems. The closing of the frontier, a growing mass of impoverished wage workers, and increasing immigration shook many Americans' confidence in the broad extension of the franchise. Evolutionary theories exported wholesale from biology to society convinced many that progress was inevitable, though hard-won. Races, governments, and economies all moved forward in orderly, unavoidable "stages." It was up to those at the top to guide those below. These events and ideas gave rise to a new social language that implicitly authorized white supremacy in the South, while a modern international image of self-restrained, yet virile, white manhood lent urgency to the white supremacists' task.

Seizing upon the language of empire, a new generation of white men—educated, urban, and bourgeois—used it in their effort to eclipse the possibility of the rise of a black Best Man. They plotted to replace the white Democrats of their fathers' generation within the party structure and to recapture power from the Populist/Republican coalition. Then the young white men would clean up the urban disorderliness and racial confusion in the state, chaos that demonstrated the need for firmer male control. They openly disavowed the lip service their fathers had paid to black political participation and argued that only one kind of man was fit for politics, the New White Man. The South's New White Man stated bluntly that the prerogatives of manhood—voting, sexual choice, freedom of public space—should be reserved for him alone. To claim his proper place, he must toss out black men completely and nudge his father aside.

Thus, as North Carolina's New White Men read Kipling, they fancied that they saw themselves between the lines. If they liked Kipling's description of darker men, they loved his model of manhood illustrating ideals of self-restraint for a new generation of southern white men. Kipling's poem "If" serves as an example:

> If you can keep your head when all about you
> Are losing theirs and blaming it on you,
>
> . . . .
>
> If you can talk with crowds and keep your virtue
> Or walk with Kings—nor lose the common touch,
> If neither foes nor loving friends can hurt you,
> If all men count with you, but none too much;
> If you can fill the unforgiving minute
> With sixty seconds' worth of distance run,
> Yours is the Earth and everything that's in it,
> And—which is more—you'll be a Man, my son!

Evolution rendered black men "half devil and half child" and inscribed on white men alone a tendency toward the "golden mean." This biological balance meant that because of their constitutional forbearance only white men were capable of political participation and governance. Obviously, they must regain control of politics and then disfranchise black men for their own good and everyone else's. . . .

These supremely self-conscious young white men believed that the white-bearded Redeemers who controlled the state's Democratic Party spent most of their days in a catatonic stupor, growing progressively deaf to the cries of down-wardly mobile whites. Convinced that the state would never attract industry under such leadership, they banded together in 1883 to form Raleigh's Watauga Club. At that precipitate moment in their lives—no man in the club was over thirty years old—the precocious Wataugans foreshadowed the methods of New White Men who would mature fifteen years later. They chose "Watauga," a name of Native American origins, because it sounded wholesome and rural and disguised the group's true purpose: to industrialize the state. . . .

The New White Man's carefully cultivated modernity sprang mainly from his economic aspirations, but his disappointment in his father and his bitterness about his mother's stunted life contributed to his rage for change. Although he would never have said so straightforwardly, when the New White Man cataloged his region's ills, he recognized his father's failings. New White Men could blame their fathers for losing the Civil War, retarding industry, neglecting public education, tolerating African Americans in politics, and creating a bottleneck in the Democratic Party. They had ample evidence that the older generation of men had mistreated white women by failing to provide for them after the Civil War. Charles Aycock remembered that his mother ran the farm while his father dabbled in politics. Even though she managed the family's affairs, Serena Aycock signed legal papers with an "X." Her son Charles vowed to build a better public school system to educate the state's poor white women. Josephus Daniels's father died during the war, and his mother's life was no tale of moonlight and magnolias. She worked as the post-mistress in Wilson, serving a biracial public from her front parlor. Wataugan Thomas Dixon, Jr., nursed a grievance over his mother's treatment at his father's hands that drove him to write and rewrite the New White Man's (auto)biography.

Walter Hines Page's company published Dixon's *The Leopard's Spots: A Romance of the White Man's Burden, 1865–1900* and his sequel, *The Clansman: An Historical Romance of the Ku Klux Klan,* which became the film, *The Birth of a Nation.* Northern and southern readers believed Dixon's accounts to be the inside— and true—story of Reconstruction and Thomas Dixon to be the ideal southern man. Dixon saw himself as the latest link in the evolution of a superman who, because of his personal racial purity, his experience in managing African Americans, and his triumph of will, could unify the nation.

Born in 1864 nine miles north of Shelby, Dixon watched his parents give up on farming and move to town to wring a living out of operating a general store while his father preached at several poor Baptist churches. At sixteen, Dixon left home for Wake Forest College. In the fall of 1883, he entered graduate school at Johns Hopkins University to study political science and history. Alongside classmate Woodrow Wilson, Dixon studied under Herbert Baxter Adams, whom he recalled as a "genius of the highest order." Professor Adams combined the latest in evolutionary science with Victorian romanticism to construct his Teutonic germ theory. Adams believed that democracy sprang from the intellectual equivalent of a gene that made its way from German forests to Britain and then to colonial America. Moving only through pure bloodlines, it predisposed some men for self-government. Adams's theory crested around the time Dixon entered Johns Hopkins. The Teutonic germ theory lent Dixon an explanatory system that anointed the Reconstruction racism of his youth with scientific balm: because African Americans lacked the Teutonic germ, their voting and officeholding amounted to a cruel hoax. The earlier generation of white men should have limited African Americans' political participation more strictly.

Dixon's preoccupation with interracial sex demonstrates how closely the personal and political were linked for southern white men of his generation. For Dixon, the fathers' racial sins ran deep, even into the blood. In *The Crucible of Race,* historian Joel Williamson constructed an intricate analysis of Dixon's sensationalization of miscegenation. Building a new understanding of Dixon's family life, Williamson notes that Dixon's mother married when she was thirteen and thus became "a curiosity." Dixon's internal personal struggle, according to Williamson, centered around his inability to come to grips with white women's sexuality, especially that of his mother. Dixon projected his own insecurity about the sexual penetration of the impenetrable southern white woman onto black men, whom he routinely portrayed as rapists. At the same time, Dixon never overtly resented his father, whom he portrays in his autobiography, *Southern Horizons,* as a tower of strength. . . .

. . . After the publication of *The Leopard's Spots,* a biracial man who lived in New York City began to claim publicly and often that he was Thomas Dixon's half brother, the son of Baptist preacher Thomas Dixon, Sr. When confronted with this allegation, Thomas, Jr., replied, "Yes I know that darky, he is always getting himself into trouble and I have helped him a number of times. His mother was a cook in our family in N.C." Although African Americans circulated accounts of Dixon's purported half brother, whites buried the information. Whites' treatment of the claim reflects the conspiracy of silence that obscured biracial people of the time from their white contemporaries and from the historical record. Biracial children were almost always the progeny of white men and black women. Yet in the 1890s, respectable whites would admit no such thing. Miscegenation presented an acute problem for

the generation that came of age amid Darwinian science and the rhetoric of imperialism. Dixon filled a real cultural need for whites when he emphasized the menace
of black men raping white women and predicted that a "mongrel breed" threatened
the social order. Through this fiction, he explained away the biracial people abound-
ing in the South and erased from historical memory white men's sexual liaisons
with and rape of black women. Whether in so doing he also deleted his personal
memory of an intimate relationship between his father and the family cook will
probably never be known. . . .

Intimate interracial relationships, tolerated through the 1880s, became intolerable to New White Men because interracial sex violated evolutionary principles and
demonstrated an appalling lack of self-control among white men that could ultimately jeopardize political power. No longer was a white man who slept with a
black women demonstrating his strength; instead, he was proving his weakness.
Such liaisons resulted in mixed-race progeny who slipped back and forth across the
color line and defied social control. Thomas Dixon put this speech in the mouth of a
leading character in *The Leopard's Spots:* "The future American must be an Anglo-
Saxon or a Mulatto! We are now deciding which it shall be. . . . This Republic can
have no future if racial lines are broken, and its proud citizenship sinks to the level
of a mongrel breed."

If New White Men wanted to regulate whiteness in public and private social
relations, they would have to put force behind their haphazard efforts to police
poor white women's sexuality. White men had always excluded black women from
definitions of purity and spoke in rapturous terms of southern white women, generally ignoring "unruly" poor white women. Now, however, New White Men set out
to naturalize white women's purity, just as they naturalized black men's impurity.
White women should now be chaste, regardless of their class, manners, or living
conditions. The assumption of purity must be implicit, essential to all white
women. Such purity was central to Aycock's definition of progress: "I would have
all our people believe in the possibilities of North Carolina; in the strength of her
men and the purity of her women."

Eventually, the assumption of poor white women's purity would constitute
more than just a tool for racial solidarity; it would become an integral part of an exchange for poor men's votes. If their men put race over class at the polling place,
the Democrats promised, poor white women could be boosted up to the pedestal.
At the same time, assuming white women's purity made it easy to draw clear lines
in rape cases involving black men and white women. Henceforth, there could be no
consensual interracial sex between white women and black men. White women
would be incapable of it.

Despite the urgency of their task, New White Men had chosen an inauspicious
moment to insist on poor white women's purity. Poverty, rapid urbanization, and
industrialization exposed working women to new social codes and opportunities,
broke the ties of patriarchal authority, and made poor white women more visible
than ever before. Southern towns had always harbored white prostitutes, but they
had long remained out of sight and unspoken of by whites. . . .

As North Carolina's towns grew, however, it became more difficult to overlook the white prostitutes, wayward girls, and drunken women who elbowed their
way down the sidewalks beside the dignified white maidens and matrons. . . .

The difficulty of patrolling white women's sexuality in public went hand in glove with other urban problems. Not only had the white fathers failed to uphold racial purity in their personal lives, but also they had tolerated racial impurity and social chaos in public life. In the 1890s, questions of racial segregation remained unsettled in North Carolina's towns. Although New Bern residents sometimes observed the color line, it wavered in certain places: the station waiting room, the post office, and the revenue department, for example. Moreover, racial boundaries faded at periodic public attractions ranging from circuses to church services. Black and white New Bernians congregated to see Mille Christine, billed as "the two headed girl" but actually cojoined African American twins. When Nora Clarette Avery, the "colored girl preacher," came to Sarah Dudley Pettey's church, whites sat on the right and blacks on the left, and the white section stayed packed throughout her revival. Just as whites attended functions hosted by African Americans, African Americans joined whites at citywide functions. A photograph of the 1897 New Bern Fish, Oyster, and Game Fair reveals a knot of white women chatting with each other, while a few feet away, a black teenager stares at the camera in wonder. Nearby, Charles Pettey, in a silk top hat, stands beside his carriage.

Increasingly in the 1890s, the growing commercial class of white men took such urban disorder to indicate a failure of manhood, and they worried about how such chaos looked to investors. When a Baltimore lawyer and a Swedish industrialist toured the state, looking to invest and relocate, what they saw appalled them. In Weldon, they sniffed "something rotten under the surface" and thought the town seemed "20 years behind the times." The problem, it seemed, was "Negro rule." The "old darkey" who served their dinner served as well on the city council. The train ride to Wilmington revealed a land "desolate" and "lying idle"; a "great desert with a few scrubby pines" just waiting for good Teutons—"thrifty German and Scandinavian families"—to transform it into a Garden of Eden. Finally, in Wilmington, they saw a plethora of black policemen and listened to whites bemoaning disorder in the streets. Alas, the visitors' "dream of a Florida at the mouth of the Cape Fear" must be deferred as long as "negroes guid[e] your Legislature and municipal bodies." The idea of losing a "Florida at the mouth of the Cape Fear" must have been unbearable for the state's New White Men.

Such interracial proximity meant that social relations had to be negotiated and renegotiated each time a person walked down the street. Since Reconstruction, African Americans had strongly contested any attempt to limit their claims to manhood and womanhood in public. In 1882, when who would count as a man or woman in Charlotte was anyone's guess, two African American teenagers, Laura Lomax and her suitor, Jim Harris, set out on a stroll. A cultured and educated young woman, the daughter of an AME Zion bishop, Laura was her brothers' pride. On a narrow sidewalk, the couple brushed past old Doc Jones, a white herb doctor. Jones turned back and "insulted and struck" Laura Lomax. Jim Harris ran into a nearby barber shop, borrowed a gun, and pistol-whipped the offending white man. Despite the fact that Jones claimed the incident resulted from his affliction with "St. Vitus' dance," that night, a dozen young black men, including two of Laura Lomax's brothers, broke into Doc Jones's house and beat him up a second time. In their eagerness to avenge the insult, the men made no attempt to disguise their identities. Quickly police hauled Harris and Jones before a magistrate. Harris paid a twenty-five dollar fine for carrying a gun, but the magistrate made no ruling on the assault. The Lomax brothers stood trial and went free for payment of court costs. Even though her boyfriend and brothers had by now thoroughly pulverized Doc Jones, Laura Lomax pressed the issue and ultimately won a verdict against him for assault.

In addition to the free-flowing urban turbulence this tale reveals, it points up the fact that some African Americans, those who saw themselves as Best Men and Best Women, demanded that class serve as a marker of manhood and womanhood. When the editor of a white newspaper referred to Laura Lomax as Harris's "sweetheart" and "a colored girl," the editor of the black newspaper was quick to take exception: "We will remind [the white editor] that she is a respectable young lady, whose family is more prominent and wealthy than his." Then he invoked the Best Man bargain: " We want our ladies respected. . . . White men make us respect white ladies, and they must make white men respect ours. . . . They must not look upon us *all* as boys and wenches." This threat, not so thinly veiled, depends on class recognition across racial lines. A translation: if you want us to use our influence on the "boys and wenches" among our race to protect *your* ladies, then you'd better use your influence on the crackers among your race to protect *our* ladies.

Many black Best Men who lived in those rowdy towns and cities watched the growing disorder around them with great concern. An integral piece of the Best Man compromise was the requirement that leading African Americans influence for the better the behavior of poor blacks. For that reason, and because of their own embrace of Victorian manners and morals, middle-class black men and women worried constantly about poor black people's public activities. Urban avenues provided a stage upon which African Americans acted out the rituals of courtship while exercising the freedom and enjoying the relative anonymity that city life conferred. African American leaders of both sexes fretted, despaired, and condemned the unfolding tableau. Fifteen years after the Lomax affair, an African American in Charlotte glanced out of his office window to see a group of black men and women flirting, laughing, and eating ice cream on the corner. He castigated the men, calling them "corner-loafers and suckers who strut like a peacock, assume the air of a turkey gobbler, have the cunning of a fox, the grin of a possum, the cowardice of a cat, and are the boss liars of town."

Black women's behavior gave race leaders pause as well. The novelty of urban amusements lured black women away from home and church and into danger, sometimes in interracial settings. In addition to generating negative images that middle-class black women and men wanted to keep out of whites' sight, these rambunctious women jeopardized racial politics when they put themselves beyond male protection. One black man condemned the "thousands of young girls and women who are daily going down to degradation . . . in peanut galleries in theatres." The man who commented on the "boss liars" meted out strong words to the women on the corner as well. Only "soft women" stood around eating ice cream, he scolded, and "giddy-head girls" who gave their "money to these street dudes in order to have them keep their company" would earn only sorrow as interest on their investment. Two weeks later, he fumed at seeing "a young mulatto woman and two white women . . . smoking cigars on the streets." "What next?" he gasped.

Middle-class African Americans worried not just about poor people but also about young people, many of them educated and from good homes, who seemed deliberately to tweak Victorian sensibilities. "Puck," a young African American man in Charlotte, offered a rare view of his teenage peers' style. He comically described the "masher," who "hangs about on street corners," the "vapid" young man "who parts his hair in the middle and cultivates about fifteen hairs on his upper lip," and the "boaster." Most often, in youthful cultural signification, the provocateur does not completely understand the implications of the provocation, but black elders thought *they* did, and they did not like what they saw. Getting a clear view of these young people from the distance of a century is extremely difficult, partly because the black middle class controlled the African American press and wanted to present a united front of purpose and dignity, and partly because what grated on adults was youths' "attitude," a quality rarely recovered in archives. One place to look for "attitude" is in white complaints about blacks, which rose to a crescendo in the 1890s. "The Negro," whites sighed, is not what he or she used to be. These observations complemented explanations of racial degeneracy that contributed to the re definition of manhood as white.

What whites were seeing, of course, was not biological degeneracy but a rising African American youth culture that proffered a competing image of manhood. The black "community"—even the African American middle class—was not monolithic. A new assertive generation of middle-class African Americans believed that the only way to guarantee rights was to exercise them in daily actions. Some in the rising generation demanded instantly the same level of respect that the Best Men had so carefully earned over a lifetime. While black Best Men screened their private lives behind lace curtains, young African Americans were public men: "corner-loafers" and "street dudes." Whites would have to take them into account if only because they loomed so large. Black middle-class elders wanted to sweep away this masculine counterimage because they believed such men wildly miscalculated the power dynamic. To black Best Men, the vote was the wellspring of all possibility. Exercising the franchise carefully would bring about a time when African American manhood would no longer have to prove itself.

Uplift and the Decline of Black Politics

KEVIN K. GAINES

In the post-Reconstruction era, egalitarian assumptions were . . . eroded as theories of racial hierarchy extended their authority within U.S. political culture. These theories provided the intellectual and ideological foundations of racial uplift ideology. Despite political and tactical differences among black politicians and intellectuals, they all shared roots in the missionary culture of evangelical reform, and in its rhetoric conflating moral and social uplift. Elite blacks' vision of self-help regarded bourgeois values of self-control and Victorian sexual morality as a crucial part of the race's education and progress. Through these efforts, black leaders and intellectuals sought to demonstrate to potential white sympathizers African Americans' capacity for assimilation and citizenship. By the turn of the century, theories of racial hierarchy were understood in evolutionary terms, and African Americans argued along these civilizationist lines for the race's development and potential. . . . For those who remained innocent of, or silent on, or unabashedly approving of the brutality in their midst . . . the concept of civilization represented progressive, humanitarian thinking on race questions. Moreover, it was deemed by black elites a significant advance over the view that blacks were biologically inferior and unassimilable. Given the objections of southern extremists that black education was a futile, if not risky, endeavor, education of the freedpeople was often tied to moral evolution and industrial training rather than citizenship and political independence. In a period in which many elite blacks, including those supposed antagonists W. E. B. Du Bois and Booker T. Washington, were largely in agreement on endorsing restrictions on citizenship, education was a hotly contested issue among black leadership.

The sociopolitical impact of racial hierarchies inscribed in evolutionary theory kept pace with their widespread appeal. . . . [B]lacks faced a tradition of prejudice in the courts that distinguished political equality from social equality. Indeed, it was this narrow, "whites only" view of equality that the abolitionists had opposed. Although the Fourteenth Amendment was widely perceived by the courts not to pertain to social segregation, in 1887, Ida B. Wells castigated blacks for retreating from principles of full equality. By taking segregated excursions, and accepting segregated public facilities, blacks gave whites further justification for drawing ever more rigid social barriers. "Consciously or unconsciously," Wells argued, "we do as much to widen the breach already existing and to keep prejudice alive as the other race." There seemed to be a class component to Wells's criticism, as black elites in pulpit and press periodically scorned the masses' penchant for segregated excursions. They may also have been objecting to what they perceived as the embarrassing public displays of uninhibited leisure at such occasions, which, to them, were injurious to the race's image. But the central issue of segregated public facilities was particularly urgent for Wells, because three years earlier she had successfully sued a Tennessee railroad company after three of its employees physically tried to remove her to the train's Jim Crow car. To Wells's dismay, the decision was reversed in April of 1887 by the state supreme court. Whatever the accuracy of Wells's claim that acquiescence to the de facto segregation of public facilities in the 1880s made de jure segregation possible, the principle of equality seemed to her to be losing force among the black masses, and black leadership as well.

Evolutionary Alternatives: Domination or Uplift

Amidst national debates over the recent American past, the African American intelligentsia disputed the meaning of slavery and Reconstruction within American culture. At the heart of these conflicting interpretations of recent history, epitomized by the conflicting positions on slavery and Reconstruction taken by Frances Harper and Booker T. Washington, were questions of the capacity of blacks for education, citizenship, and leadership. Black writers' commentaries on the meaning of racial uplift and the role of black leadership in pursuing it were often shaded by social Darwinian conceptions of racial struggle, specifically, the view that two distinct races on the same land mass could never coexist, as the dominant race would inevitably annihilate the subordinated one.

In her 1892 novel set during slavery and emancipation, *Iola Leroy, Or Shadows Uplifted,* Frances Harper described blacks' current plight by portraying social relations between "stronger and weaker races." Her analysis informed by popular Darwinian notions of the "survival of the fittest," Harper posed a choice between two possibilities: domination or uplift. She dramatized this set of options in a debate between Dr. Gresham, a northern white doctor, and Iola, Harper's black (though white in appearance) female protagonist. To Gresham's claim that blacks "learn to struggle, labor and achieve" against a "proud, domineering, aggressive," Anglo-Saxon race "impatient of a rival, and . . . [with] more capacity for dragging down a race than uplifting it," Iola countered that blacks would one day assume a higher level of civilization than that of "you Anglo-Saxons," who "will prove unworthy of your high vantage ground if you only use your superior ability to victimize feebler races and minister to a selfish greed of gold and a love of domination."

By placing the reunion of family members separated by slavery at the center of the novel's action, Harper reinforced her theme of a natural, organic relationship between black elites and masses, figuring the race as a family transcending class, cultural, and color differences. . . . Through her novel, an intervention against reactionary antiblack trends nationwide (including lynching), Harper sought to promote a moral vision of racial uplift ideology that might revive the abolitionist, Radical Republican legacy of the Reconstruction era. Her depiction of slavery's cruelty, remanding Iola into slavery despite her education, refinement, and white appearance and tearing apart black families, debunked the popular plantation legend of the Old South. Harper also meant to strengthen the resolve of educated blacks to devote themselves to service to their race, and to rekindle the sympathies of whites who might have strayed from the cause of blacks. Although the novel ends on an uplifting note of romantic love and marriage, Iola has, on behalf of black women, insisted on her right to economic independence as a clerical worker, a position from which black women were excluded. For Harper and subsequent generations of blacks, uplift would be epitomized by the quest of blacks for literacy, higher education, power, and self-reliance.

As Harper's writing suggests, in addition to its roots in reform traditions, uplift ideology felt the cultural impress of the conservative, social Darwinist thought of the times. The desire among northern and southern industrialists for national reunion led religious and secular guardians of social stability and economic expansion to espouse a Darwinian view of social evolution and economic growth. In addressing problems of class conflict, the writings of influential social theorists such as Herbert Spencer, Benjamin Kidd, and William Graham Sumner ascribed a moral imperative to capitalist accumulation and deemphasized social conflict in favor of a conciliatory, organic notion of social "equilibration." Social reforms were regarded by Spencerian social Darwinists as meddlesome in light of the social principle of "the survival of the fittest," elevating government laissez-faire and business prosperity to the status of moral necessity. In addition, racial separation was said to be embedded in human nature and thus impossible to legislate away. Booker T. Washington, the prominent black educator and spokesman, was adapting uplift ideology along the contours of Gilded Age conservatism when he declared in 1900 that black Americans would receive citizenship "through no process of artificial forcing, but through the natural law of evolution."

The Rise of Booker T. Washington

Reflecting national antiblack trends, Washington appropriated the evangelical reform spirit in a manner that eclipsed the Radical Republican tradition exemplified by Harper. In his popular 1901 autobiography *Up From Slavery,* Washington captured the spirit of uplift ideology, transforming freedmen's education into his program of industrial training. But his was a more conservative version of uplift in tune with the times, one that portrayed enslavement less harshly that did Harper, and one that depended for its content not only on evangelical missionary crusades but also on a none-too-subtle language of empire. Notwithstanding what he called the "cruelty and moral wrong" of enslavement, Washington asserted that American blacks who "went through the school of American slavery" were "materially, intellectually, morally, and religiously" the most advanced "black people in any other portion of the globe." Pressing his point, Washington noted that those assimilated graduates of "the school of slavery are constantly returning to Africa as missionaries to enlighten those who remained in the fatherland." Washington's ideological bid for the status of an agent of civilization had more to do with the status aspirations of African American elites like himself than the material advancement of African Americans. Rooted in assumptions of evolutionary racial hierarchy, Washington's comments contributed to the view that the African American people of the South were incapable of self-government. Such evolutionary thinking lent credibility to the fallacy that peoples of color were culturally undeveloped, rather than at the mercy of political and economic subordination, in the U.S. South as well as in Cuba and the Philippines.

Along with his skillful use of the success myth, Washington manipulated civilizationist ideology and uplift ideals of self-help. He saw no contradiction in his self-help philosophy and his success in monopolizing the philanthropy of the business classes. He portrayed his message as a beacon of enlightenment among benighted southern blacks. Washington pathologized blacks' pursuit of higher education and politics, those false idols of the Reconstruction period, putting these errors down to "generations in slavery, and before that, generations in the darkest heathenism." Throughout *Up From Slavery,* Washington (who as a member of the Knights of Labor had been burned by antilabor repression as a young man) spoke of black opposition—strikes or independent black voting—as the archaic, almost minstrel-like behavior of the undeveloped "Old Negro," who was "largely disappearing" to make way for a more responsible black leadership committed to a vision of uplift that, as Washington would have it, served the interests of all races and classes. Washington carried forward the habit of Tuskegee supporters, philanthropists, and reformers, products of those laissez-faire times, of referring to rights and duties as mutually exclusive categories. Political rights, it was held, were the subject of unproductive agitation when they would more certainly accrue to those who had demonstrated their fitness for them through property ownership and dutiful service to the community through self-help. It is of no small import that such sentiments, embodied by a southern black man and former slave, helped legitimize a settlement that might well have otherwise been regarded as morally suspect.

Much of Washington's popularity and power stemmed from his talent for speaking simultaneously to differently situated audiences. He became, after the death of Frederick Douglass in 1895, the most powerful black leader. A trusted political advisor to President Theodore Roosevelt, the "Wizard" was able to appease the more rabid elements in the white South, secure political patronage for reliable black allies, and drive a wedge in black opposition by skillfully dispensing political favors and punishments. Washington's use of civilizationist rhetoric was as compelling to blacks as it was to whites, because it coincided with an avid missionary interest in Africa among elite black Americans. . . .

. . . Since the antebellum period, the missionary enterprise, with its image of a "pagan" Africa awaiting "regeneration" by its elite progeny, was central to some black Americans' self-image and attempts to demonstrate black progress in a racist society that barred conventional routes to power and professional status. According to a black historian of the 1880s, "A morning star of Hope for the millions in Africa who have yet learned nothing of Christianity, nor taken the first lessons of civilization, shines over the lowly cabins of their brothers in America." By the 1890s, the analogous function posited by elite blacks' responsibility for the uplift of black Americans would serve a similar mission. The imagined uplift of African peoples from their presumed degraded condition offered elite African Americans an affirming sense of purposefulness. It represented an early version of the so-called Progressive Era's modern cultural construction of Western bourgeois identity through an understanding of its relation to "primitive" peoples.

African Americans' interest in Africa, whether missionary or emigrationist in intent, fused evangelical ideals of self-help with the political, nationbuilding aspirations that . . . elites projected onto the "dark continent" in lieu of political influence and social opportunities at home. For Washington had often proclaimed—in tandem with northern white philanthropists, religious and civic leaders, and southern politicians and planter elites—that blacks forsake politics for an indefinite period of time. He discredited the political and educational gains of Reconstruction as "mistakes," their reforms "artificial and forced." Perhaps the gravest of these errors was "the desire to hold office" among blacks; he described his own "temptations to enter political life" as if he had weathered a struggle against sin and damnation. Washington's use of the myths of black political immaturity and corruption within the repressive New South social and economic order of disfranchisement, political terror, debt slavery, and gerrymandering had grave consequences for black leadership and a black population whose only recourse in those days was to leave the South, often at considerable risk from local white elites.

Black spokespersons believed universally in uplift and education. The sticking point of debate was over precisely what sort of education would be made available to blacks. W. E. B. Du Bois's Atlanta University study, *The College-Bred Negro,* defended higher education for blacks. Such a stand had become necessary with Washington's frequent assertions, in print and in platform lectures, that blacks sought the useless "abstract knowledge" of higher education to escape what he, and many white elites perceived, as their true calling as farm workers. While Washington had carried on the Reconstruction tradition of southern black leaders' demands of economic opportunity for the race and had celebrated the freedpeople's thirst for literacy, he broke with tradition by disparaging higher education as unnatural. Washington, a tireless and effective fundraiser for Tuskegee, seldom lost opportunities to recite anecdotes about overeducated ministers working in poverty and squalor because they had been taught useless luxuries like theology and Greek syntax, instead of "the dignity of labor and practical farming." Moreover, Washington believed that "a large proportion took up teaching and preaching as an easy way to make a living," rather than as a means of practical service and uplift. By conjuring the specter of indolent, immoral, urban blacks, Washington exploited and legitimized the racial fears of his time, for like white elites, he realized that educated blacks might threaten the social order. . . . As late as 1912, Washington reassured concerned whites that "we are trying to instill into the Negro mind that if education does not make the Negro humble, simple, and of service to the community, then it will no longer be encouraged."

By portraying educated blacks as suspect, unproductive, and potentially criminal, Washington echoed the general hostility toward black elites and higher education. In suggesting that education for blacks achieved the opposite from its intended purpose of producing a black leadership class, Washington blurred the social distinction that many educated blacks labored to maintain between themselves and the black majority, a distinction crucial to defining and legitimizing their role as race leaders. With the threat of being so ignominiously declassed, cast down into the urban slum underworld, it must have seemed to many educated blacks that they had no alternative, really, but to insist on their moral superiority to the black masses, both urban and rural. . . . "Something must be done," said a participant in the Hampton Negro Conference, referring to the moral shortcomings of the black masses, "or these people will drag us down." Such a view reflected prevailing middle-class anxieties about the poor as a threatening source of moral and social disorder.

Self-Help and Uplift as Critique: Rising above Politics

As Washington's rhetoric indicates, the post-Reconstruction South was notable for its hostility to black involvement in politics and higher education. While black radicals like William Monroe Trotter, Fortune, and Wells denounced disfranchisement, white reformers and philanthropists incessantly advised blacks to forsake politics for the sake of social peace in the South. Following Washington's example (and coerced by rampant violence), many black elites withdrew from political agitation and stressed self-help.

While Washington made much of the view that blacks and politics did not mix, others, noting the hopelessness of the situation, shaped uplift ideology into a critique of racial accommodation, denouncing the venality of politicians who betrayed the race's interests. Corrupt office-seeking politicians gave the occupation—and the race—a bad name. In one of his regular diatribes against such men, John E. Bruce denounced these "perennial office holders and professional Negroes" as "foul niggers" and "white darkies." Color, for Bruce and others like him, symbolized a bitter struggle among blacks for possession of the few opportunities for leadership positions. Among many upwardly mobile blacks shut off from political power or its trappings, those men who managed to secure appointments were "time-serving demagogues" who reaped the unjust benefits of a combination of white ancestry and of political spoils controlled by Washington and his black Republican allies, among them, William Lewis in Boston and Charles Anderson in New York.

For many intellectuals, reformers, and journalists, the alternative to office seeking and influence peddling was a vision of uplift that asserted mutuality of interest between leaders and masses. The black intelligentsia cultivated the disinterested Christian ideals of sacrifice and service against the grasping ambition and material-ism of the times. Intellectual integrity, and a true commitment to social uplift, partic-ularly through higher education, were the core principles of these dissenting views. The writer and educator Anna Julia Cooper denounced what she saw as the selfish opportunism of black "demagogues and politicians" and regarded the race's true leaders to be "men of intellect . . . to whom the elevation of their people means more than personal ambition and sordid gain." Du Bois counseled an assembly of black high school graduates in Washington, D.C., that they would do well to model their lives after St. Francis of Assisi, who renounced wealth and status for a life of service and hardship. In *The Souls of Black Folk,* which contained an attack on Washington, Du Bois noted the betrayal of higher ideals implicit in limiting the training of blacks to industrial education. "In the Black World," he wrote, "the Preacher and Teacher" embodied the race's strivings toward freedom, enlightened religion, and knowledge. Such ideals were endangered by "a question of cash and a lust for gold." . . .

Similarly, in Washington, D.C., black intellectuals of the American Negro Academy believed that Washington's advocacy of manual training threatened higher education for blacks. Alexander Crummell saw civilization as a "primal need," pro-viding the spiritual and idealistic alternative to those men, black and white, who stressed "material ideas . . . as the master need of the race, and as the surest way to success." Rather than from property or money, "the greatness of a people springs from their ability to grasp the grand conceptions of being." Crummell visualized black intellectuals as philosopher-kings, as only "trained and scholarly men," he believed, could sufficiently bring their expertise, knowledge, and culture down to the "crude masses." According to Crummell, . . . true leadership and independent thought were impossible for those mired in the fray of political rivalries, ignoring the fact that his organization had been founded in part as a counteroffensive against Washington's conservatism.

Black women joined the chorus denouncing those who exploited the ideals of uplift for personal power and gain. While they also urged an altruistic vision of up-lift against self-serving black leadership, their remarks on the subject challenged the male authority generally assumed within such uplift institutions as churches, schools, and hospitals. Barred from white women's clubs, socially active black women participated in their own club movement partly out of the conviction that their contributions were also not respected by black male elites. To Anna Julia Cooper, the emphasis on individual achievement in the professions and politics as evidence of the race's progress was a fallacy. It obscured the vital role of black women, who were "the fundamental agency under God in the regeneration, the re-training of the race," and the "starting point of its progress upward." Cooper also criticized what she regarded as black male leaders' reluctance to speak out boldly against racism. Liberal whites such as Albion Tourgee, in her opinion, were more forthright. "Not many colored men," she observed, "would have attempted Tourgee's brave defense of Reconstruction" or "would have dared, fearlessly as he did," to seek reparations for blacks for their unpaid labor as slaves.

Cooper was hardly alone in such views. The Chicago clubwoman Fannie Barrier Williams hailed the antilynching efforts of Ida B. Wells, which were supported by the National Association of Colored Women. She remarked that "at the very time when race interest seems at such a low ebb, when our race leaders seem tongue-tied and stupidly inactive in the presence of unchecked lawlessness and violent re-sistance to Negro advancement, it is especially fortunate and reassuring to see and feel the rallying spirit of our women." Sharing the era's belief in woman's moral superiority, Williams regarded the unholy machinations of politics as particularly inappropriate within the clubwomen's movement, which claimed to serve the highest ideals of uplift. . . .

The barrier to politics was absolute for educated, ambitious black women, leaving a void for a wide range of literary, journalistic, protest, and social reform activities, including the temperance movement for northern black women like Harper and Wells. Yet however much black elites disclaimed politics for the self-help, social purity activities of uplift, it would be inaccurate to see their views and actions as inhabiting a realm altogether distinct from politics. On the contrary, the range of uplift endeavors provided the context for hotly contested debates over black politics, the role of the federal government, the quality of leadership, gender roles, and the true meaning of progress—of uplift itself.

Black Leadership in the North

There was a regional cast to the political and ideological factions of black leader-ship, which, along with personal and gendered differences and divisions, placed the phantom of a unified black middle-class male subject imagined by racial uplift ideology even further out of reach. Yet as we have seen, racial uplift ideals might provide the terms for political dissent among black elites, who challenged Booker T. Washington's legitimacy as "the Moses of his race." Nowhere was this the case more than among northern blacks, who enjoyed a relative measure of freedom and political power through the suffrage, and who certainly enjoyed more freedom of expression than leaders in the South. This is not to say, however, that northern blacks knew nothing of economic discrimination and segregation, as they were de-nied white collar jobs and equal access to hotels, restaurants, and theaters. Then again, they, too, labored under the same popular journalistic attacks on their morals and aspirations to bourgeois selfhood. In an attempt to counter the biases of the white press on matters of sexual morality, one black muckraker from Philadelphia published a luridly detailed exposé of news accounts of white rape, incest, and gang rape in the North, seeking to affirm that white men were the worst offenders when it came to "the unmentionable crime." This approach would have been dan-gerous in the South. Members of the small, relatively prosperous black profes-sional class, which included the Boston journalist Trotter, the physician Nathan Mossell of Philadelphia, and the antilynching crusader Wells, from Chicago, op-posed Washington's leadership. Northern blacks were freer to criticize the deplor-able conditions in the South. On one notable occasion, they forcefully did so in Washington's presence. In 1903, Trotter, a man devoted to the principle of equal rights but possessed of the discretion of a runaway locomotive, was jailed briefly for his role in what became known as the "Boston riot," after he and several others, including the Yale-educated intellectual William Ferris, disrupted a Washington lecture in that city.

Northerners shared with southern black elites a bitter awareness of the diffi-culty of making a decent living through work commensurate with their education and status aspirations. Pauline Hopkins, the Boston-based journalist and author of several novels that addressed politics and uplift at the turn of the century, observed in her best known work, *Contending Forces*, that educated black women were barred from office work in Boston. Drawing on her own experience as a stenographer, Hopkins noted the tension between apparent freedom and restricted economic op-portunities: "Here in the North we are allowed every privilege. There seems to be no prejudice until we seek employment; then every door is closed against us." Along with the unpredictability of discrimination or hostility, northern blacks were excluded from skilled trades, and their traditional hold on such service jobs as caterers, barbers, and headwaiters was slipping. The northern press shared the common contempt for the higher aspirations of black Americans. "Let the Negro learn," the *New York Times* admonished in 1900 in the wake of a race riot in that city in which blacks were assaulted for two days by white mobs and police, "to clean stables, care for horses, feed and harness and drive them, run lawn mowers, and also keep engagements."

When it became impossible to ignore the challenge posed by northern blacks, conservative blacks wielded self-help as a weapon against protest. An editorial in the Tuskegee-controlled *Colored American Magazine* attacked the Niagara move-ment, which demanded civil and political rights for blacks. "It is much easier to make an abusive speech 'cussing out' [presidents] Roosevelt and Taft, than it is to go South and teach a school or pastor a church, or give a lecture that will be uplifting and helpful to our people in that section who need help." In rural southern districts, where public schooling was neglected by the state, it had become common for black student teachers to fill the void during their summers away from college. These teachers were compensated, housed, and fed by the black community, prac-ticing the best ideals of self-help. Such criticism, however, reflected a tendency among conservative black leaders to condemn dissenters—a kill-the-messenger mentality that fetishized the pragmatism of self-help (or, at least, paid lip service to self-help ideals) over insisting on equal rights. During the nadir, such pronounce-ments were hardly persuasive to those many blacks, including Du Bois, Charles Chesnutt, Ida B. Wells, and many others, who had already worked in the South as teachers or had fled repression and a lack of opportunities there.

FURTHER READING

Bess Beatty, *A Revolution Gone Backward: The Black Response to National Politics, 1876–1896* (1987)

Elizabeth Rauh Bethel, *Promiseland: A Century of Life in a Negro Community* (1981)

Kevin K. Gaines, *Uplifting the Race: Black Leadership, Politics, and Culture in the Twentieth Century* (1996)

Raymond Gavins, *"The Meaning of Freedom: Black North Carolinians in the Nadir,
    1880–1900"* in Jeffrey J. Crow et al., eds., *Race, Class, and Politics in Southern
    History* (1989)
Paula Giddings, *When and Where I Enter: The Impact of Black Women on Race and Sex in
    America* (1984)
Glenda Gilmore, *Gender and Jim Crow: Women and the Politics of White Supremacy in
    North Carolina, 1896–1920* (1996)
Louis R. Harlan, *Booker T. Washington: Wizard of Tuskegee, 1901–1915* (1983)
Evelyn Higginbotham, *The Women's Movement in the Black Baptist Church, 1880–1920*
    (1984)
Neil R. McMillen, *Dark Journey: Black Mississippians in the Age of Jim Crow* (1989)
Cynthia Neverdon-Morton, *Afro-American Women of the South and the Advancement of the
    Race, 1895–1925* (1989)
Theodore Rosengarten, *All God's Dangers: The Life of Nate Shaw* (1984)
Herbert Shapiro, *Black Violence and White Response* (1988)
William M. Tuttle, Jr., *Race Riot* (1972)
Joel R. Williamson, *A Rage for Order* (1986)
C. Vann Woodward, *The Strange Career of Jim Crow* (1974)

Consumer Culture and

Commercialized Leisure

The industrial revolution associated with mass production methods and new work habits of the factory system also depended on a system of mass consumption and new play habits—in effect, an entire reorganization of Americans' leisure time. Whereas work and communal socializing had once been intertwined in agrarian activities like barn raisings and quilting bees, the pace and noise of the factory set a new barrier between the two. Now more than ever, people worked in order to "live," not vice versa, even as workers demanded—and gradually received—-a shortened working day. Even as immediate control of work, or its product, became a distant memory to millions of toiling Americans, a new realm of immediate satisfaction beckoned— albeit in a highly gendered way—in the self-transformations, at once real and fantasized, available through the acquisition of new goods and services.

Increasingly absorbed in a new consumer culture, what Americans, especially city dwellers, did with their "time off" changed drastically. The very marketplace that replaced the artisan with the factory worker also created the professional athlete and the athletic spectator, the shopper, a national movie-going audience, and cabaret and dance hall patrons. Instead of localized, neighborhood-based, and informally organized recreational pursuits, Americans by 1920 were fully enmeshed in a commercialized leisure and entertainment network. Collapsing older social divisions based on region, ethnicity, class, and sex, the new mass leisure and communication empires exercised a powerful nationalizing force within the culture. Among sports that captured the national imagination, two—baseball and boxing—may be said to have fully matured as professional mass spectacles by the time of World War I. Baseball, in particular, suggested the opposite tuggings on the popular psyche toward a pastoral idealism on the one hand and a modern, competitive, rulebound world on the other.

D O C U M E N T S

The five documents that follow testify to the encompassing diversity as well as the inner texture of consumer culture and commercialized leisure pursuits. In Document 1, taken from his novel *Sister Carrie*, the American exemplar of hard social realism, or "naturalism," Theodore Dreiser, provides an immortal portrait of a poor country girl's confrontation with the lure of the department store. As if to provide the theoretical backdrop to Carrie's state, feminist Charlotte Perkins Gilman in Document 2 takes women's centrality in consumer roles as a chief indicator of their subordinate status as citizens. In Document 3, an excerpt from *Everybody's Magazine*, Coney Island's master amusement park promoter Frederic Thompson explains the secret of his success. Document 4, a 1910 article from New York's lively *Independent* magazine, speculates on the advantages of the motion picture over the traditional stage production. Document 5 is drawn from the contemporary saga of professional baseball. In an engaging spoof appearing as a serial in the *Saturday Evening Post*, humorist Ring Lardner's Jack Keefe, "the busher," presents himself and his fellow players as a "childish and stupid and not a little mean-spirited"—but still lovable—collection of ordinary human beings.

1. Theodore Dreiser's Carrie Discovers the Department Store, 1900

At that time the department store was in its earliest form of successful operation, and there were not many. The first three in the United States, established about 1884, were in Chicago. Carrie was familiar with the names of several through the advertisements in the "Daily News," and now proceeded to seek them. The words of Mr. McManus had somehow managed to restore her courage, which had fallen low, and she dared to hope that this new line [of department store work] would offer her something. Some time she spent in wandering up and down, thinking to encounter the buildings by chance, so readily is the mind, bent upon prosecuting a hard but needful errand, eased by that self-deception which the semblance of search, without the reality, gives. At last she inquired of a police officer, and was directed to proceed "Two blocks up," where she would find "The Fair."

The nature of these vast retail combinations, should they ever permanently disappear, will form an interesting chapter in the commercial history of our nation. Such a flowering out of a modest trade principle the world had never witnessed up to that time. They were along the line of the most effective retail organisation, with hundreds of stores coordinated into one and laid out upon the most imposing and economic basis. They were handsome, bustling, successful affairs, with a host of clerks and a swarm of patrons. Carrie passed along the busy aisles, much affected by the remarkable displays of trinkets, dress goods, stationery, and jewelry. Each separate counter was a show place of dazzling interest and attraction. She could not help feeling the claim of each trinket and valuable upon her personally, and yet she did not stop. There was nothing there which she could not have used—nothing which she did not long to own. The dainty slippers and stockings, the delicately frilled skirts and petticoats, the laces, ribbons, hair-combs, purses, all touched her with individual desire, and she felt keenly the fact that not any of these things were in the range of her purchase. She was a work-seeker, an outcast without employment, one whom the average employee could tell at a glance was poor and in need of a situation.

Theodore Dreiser, *Sister Carrie* (New York: Harper, 1912), 23–25.

It must not be thought that any one could have mistaken her for a nervous, sensitive, high-strung nature, cast unduly upon a cold, calculating, and unpoetic world. Such certainly she was not. But women are peculiarly sensitive to their adornment.

Not only did Carrie feel the drag of desire for all which was new and pleasing in apparel for women, but she noticed too, with a touch at the heart, the fine ladies who elbowed and ignored her, brushing past in utter disregard of her presence, themselves eagerly enlisted in the materials which the store contained. Carrie was not familiar with the appearance of her more fortunate sisters of the city. Neither had she before known the nature and appearance of the shop girls with whom she now compared poorly. They were pretty in the main, some even handsome, with an air of independence and indifference which added, in the case of the more favoured, a certain piquancy. Their clothes were neat, in many instances fine, and wherever she encountered the eye of one it was only to recognize in it a keen analysis of her own position—her individual shortcomings of dress and that shadow of *manner* which she thought must hang about her and make clear to all who and what she was. A flame of envy lighted in her heart. She realized in a dim way how much the city held—wealth, fashion, ease—every adornment for women, and she longed for dress and beauty with a whole heart.

2. Charlotte Perkins Gilman Seeks to Extricate Women from the Trap of Consumption, 1899

For the woman there is, first, no free production allowed; and, second, no relation maintained between what she does produce and what she consumes. She is forbidden to make, but encouraged to take. Her industry is not the natural output of creative energy, not the work she does because she has the inner power and strength to do it; nor is her industry even the measure of her gain. She has, of course, the natural desire to consume; and to that is set no bar save the capacity or the will of her husband.

Thus we have painfully and laboriously evolved and carefully maintain among us an enormous class of non-productive consumers,—a class which is half the world, and mother of the other half. We have built into the constitution of the human race the habit and desire of taking, as divorced from its natural precursor and concomitant of making. We have made for ourselves this endless array of "horse-leech's daughters, crying, Give! give!" To consume food, to consume clothes, to consume houses and furniture and decorations and ornaments and amusements, to take and take and take forever,—from one man if they are virtuous, from many if they are vicious, but always to take and never to think of giving anything in return except their womanhood,—this is the enforced condition of the mothers of the race. What wonder that their sons go into business "for what there is in it"! What wonder that the world is full of the desire to get as much as possible and to give as little as possible! What wonder, either, that the glory and sweetness of love are but a name among us, with here and there a strange and beautiful exception, of which our admiration proves the rarity!

Charlotte Perkins Gilman, *Women and Economics: A Study of the Economic Relationship Between Men and Women as a Factor of Social Evolution* (Boston: Small, Maynard and Company, 1899), 118–121.

Between the brutal ferocity of excessive male energy struggling in the marketplace as in a battlefield and the unnatural greed generated by the perverted condition of female energy, it is not remarkable that the industrial evolution of humanity has shown peculiar symptoms. One of the minor effects of this last condition—this limiting of female industry to close personal necessities, and this tendency of her over-developed sex-nature to overestimate the so-called "duties of her position"—has been to produce an elaborate devotion to individuals and their personal needs,—not to the understanding and developing of their higher natures, but to the intensification of their bodily tastes and pleasure. The wife and mother, pouring the rising tide of racial power into the same old channels that were allowed her primitive ancestors, constantly ministers to the physical needs of her family with a ceaseless and concentrated intensity. They like it, of course. But it maintains in the individuals of the race an exaggerated sense of the importance of food and clothes and orna ments to themselves, without at all including a knowledge of their right use and value to us all. It developes personal selfishness.

Again, the consuming female, debarred from any free production, unable to estimate the labor involved in the making of what she so lightly destroys, and her consumption limited mainly to those things which minister to physical pleasure, creates a market for sensuous decoration and personal ornament, for all that is luxurious and enervating, and for a false and capricious variety in such supplies, which operates as a most deadly check to true industry and true art. As the priestess of the temple of consumption, as the limitless demander of things to use up, her economic influence is reactionary and injurious. Much, very much, of the current of useless production in which our economic energies run waste—man's strength poured out like water on the sand—depends on the creation and careful maintenance of this false market, this sink into which human labor vanishes with no return. Woman, in her false economic position, reacts injuriously upon industry, upon art, upon science, discovery, and progress. The sexuo-economic relation in its effect on the constitution of the individual keeps alive in us the instincts of savage individualism which we should otherwise have well outgrown. It sexualizes our industrial relation and commercializes our sex-relation. And, in the external effect upon the market, the over-sexed woman, in her unintelligent and ceaseless demands, hinders and perverts the economic development of the world.

3. Amusement Park Promoter Frederic Thompson Creates the Carnival Spirit, 1908

The difference between the theatre and the big amusement park is the difference between the Sunday-school and the Sunday-school picnic. The people are the same; the spirit and the environment are wholly different. It is harder to make the picnic successful than successfully to conduct a session of the school; and it is harder to make a success of a big amusement park than of a theatre. There isn't any irreverence in this comparison with the Sunday-school, for if the amusement park doesn't attract people who are interested in the Sunday-school, it isn't going to succeed. . . .

Frederic Thompson, "Amusing the Millions," *Everybody's Magazine,* September 19, 1908.

In the theatre and in the Sunday-school conventional standards of behavior are accepted as a matter of course. The picnic and the open-air part are designed to give the natural, bubbling animal spirits of the human being full play, to give people something fresh and new and unusual, to afford them respite from the dull routine of their daily lives.

The one thing that makes a picnic or an amusement park a success—it doesn't make any difference whether the picnic is made up of ten people or ten thousand, whether the park is a little one or a great international exposition—the one thing absolutely necessary is the carnival spirit. Without that no show in the open, nothing that has to do with people in the mass, can hope to succeed. Whenever any enterprise that is intended to appeal to the million fails, the failure can always be traced to the lack of carnival enthusiasm.

This spirit of gaiety, the carnival spirit, is not spontaneous, except on extraordinary occasions, and usually its cause can be easily traced. Almost always it is manufactured. Take a big political meeting, for instance. Ninety-nine times out of a hundred the steps that culminate in a great outburst are carefully planned. There are men who make it a business to insure the success of great mass meetings. When you get right down to it, the fundamentals are the same, whether the application is to a church picnic, a political meeting, a circus, or a big exposition. . . .

In the year 1901 I had a show called "A Trip to the Moon" on the Midway at the Pan-American Exposition in Buffalo. Architecturally and from an educational standpoint this exposition was one of the most remarkable in all the history of world's fairs. It was beautiful; it was tremendous; but it wasn't paying. After several months I went to the executive committee and to the president and told them why their outlay of millions of dollars was attracting only thirty thousand people a day. I told them they were failing miserably because there wasn't a regular showman in the lot. I told them about the carnival spirit, and they came back by telling me about the educational value of the exposition.

"But what's the use of a college if there are not students?" I asked. "Before we talk of educational benefits let's get in the crowd to educate."

They didn't take kindly to my notions at first. Then I suggested that they turn over the show to me for one day, which would be sufficient to test what the executive gentlemen were pleased to call my theories. President Milburn was with me, and I finally won the point. The exposition was to be mine for August 3, and I told them that it would be known as "Midway Day."

Within six hours after the final interview I had four printing-houses at work getting out the paper with which I was going to plaster the country. I and my side-show associates sent ten advance men on the road to herald the coming of the big day, and within a week a large part of the eastern half of the United States was screaming: "August third! Midway Day at the Pan-American! Don't miss it!"

They didn't. On the night of August 2 a crowd of would-be excursionists was left on every railway station within twenty-four hours' ride of Buffalo, and when the gates of the exposition were thrown open, the police reserves had to be summoned to stop a panic. They arrived too late to prevent ten thousand people from forcing their way in without paying. There were more than enough left to make the gate receipts satisfactory. . . .

How was it done? By paying no attention to Machinery Hall, the architectural beauty of the State Building, or the interesting exhibits of Trade and Industry; and by smearing the sign-boards of forty-five states with the carnival spirit. Instead of advertising an organ concert in Music Hall we yelled ourselves hoarse about high diving, greased poles, parades, and every other crazy thing we could think of. I instructed all bands to play marching and to go to the band-stands only when they wished to rest. To the Stadium, which had never held a quarter of its capacity, I drew 23,000 people to see a race contested by an ostrich, a camel, an elephant, a man on a bicycle, another on a horse, an automobile, and a zebra. I had a man sliding by his teeth from the top of the sky-scraping electric tower to the esplanade below. True, he had never before traveled more than thirty feet in that fashion, but we tied him on, so there was no danger. The illusion was great, and the stunt made a sensation.

In every part of the grounds something extraordinary was going on all the time. There were speed, light, gaiety, color, excitement. The crowd entered into it. They didn't sit on the benches and admire the sculptural work with the aid of official guides—not a bit of it. They joined in the spirit of the occasion—they caught the carnival spirit—and the Pan-American was "made," as far as any exposition could be made at such a late day.

To create a carnival spirit a showman may use other means than ballyhoos—which means the sample shows on the outside, with the patter of the barkers—bands, freak shows, and free circuses. I use architecture. It's all right to copy the capitol at Washington in making a state building at an exposition, and there is no objection to constructing Machinery Hall and the House of Manufactures with an outward indication of the staid and serious exhibits within—if the heads of the exposition are philanthropists. But if they are trying to have their enterprise make both ends meet it is suicidal. The scenery of a comic opera suggests the spirit and the environment of the piece, and the scenery of an exposition or an amusement park must do the same if the place is to score what in theatrical parlance is known as a "hit." Straight lines are necessarily severe and dead. They have no right in the place of honor of a great outdoor show. The very architecture must be in keeping with the spirit of carnival. It must be active, mobile, free, graceful, and attractive. It must be arranged so that visitors will say, "What is this?" and "Why is that?" . . .

One result is Luna Park, the sky-line of which is utterly unlike anything else of its kind in the two Americas. The architecture of Luna Park helps rather than hinders the spirit of carnival. Luna Park has been, and is, tremendously successful. There are other amusement parks in its vicinity that are chastely beautiful from an artistic standpoint, but that so far as dollars and cents are concerned are utter failures. Visitors admire the buildings—and don't go near the shows. I have built their sort of buildings, too, but not for a Luna Park. They don't pay. An exposition is a form of festivity, and serious architecture should not enter into it if it will interfere with the carnival spirit.

In amusing the million there are other essential elements besides gaiety. One is decency—the absolutely necessary quality in every line of the world's business. There is nothing that pays so well. . . .

The first rowdy I caught in Luna Park was soundly thrashed, and before he was thrown out of the grounds I told him the place was not run for him, but for his mother and sister. I think that did him more good than the punishment. For several seasons I advertised the park as "the place for your mother, your sister, and your sweetheart." If I hadn't believed it was that I wouldn't have spent upward of a hundred thousand dollars in impressing the fact upon the public.

Courtesy on the part of the employee is as necessary as decency on the part of the visitor. If I hear of one of my employees resenting an insult offered by a visitor, I dismiss him. I tell him that so long as he wears my uniform he is representing me, and that I am the only person who can be insulted inside the gates.

An amusement park is a condensed Broadway, if that is understood to represent metropolitan theatreland. In a park the best things of a theatrical nature must be presented in capsule form. The shows must be diversified because the appeal must be universal. The whole gamut of the theatre must be run, and no show can last more than twenty minutes. If you have a two-hour show, it should be boiled down to a quarter of an hour. It is foolish to make people serious or to point a moral, for you are dealing with a moral people. Nor is it worth while to try to educate the amusement-seeking public. It is better to take it for granted that they are educated, and if you start out to amuse them, to stick to that.

People are just boys and girls grown tall. Elaborated child's play is what they want on a holiday. Sliding down cellar doors and the make-believes of youngsters are the most effective amusements for grown-ups. An appreciation of that fact made "The Trip to the Moon" possible, and "The Trip to the Moon" made for me and my partner, Dundy, half a million dollars. "The Tickler," "Bump the Bumps," and "The Virginia Reel" are nothing more than improved cellar doors. "The Trip to the Moon," "Night and Morning," "The Witching Waves," and "The Lost Girl" are only elaborations of the doll-house stunts of childhood, and they are successful largely for that reason. But they must be short and decisive. I would rather have a good show that lasts three minutes than a better one that runs an hour. And I prefer one that is over in a minute but enables the spectator to become a part of it to one that runs three minutes and never permits him to become more than an onlooker.

Speed is almost as important a factor in amusing the millions as is the carnival spirit, decency, or a correct recollection of school days. Speed has become an inborn American trait. We as a nation are always moving, we are always in a hurry, we are never without momentum. "Helter Skelters," "Scenic Railways," "Shoot the Chutes," "The Dragon's Gorge," the thousand and one varieties of roller-coasters are popular for the same reason that we like best the fastest trains, the speediest horses, the highest powered motor-cars, and the swiftest sprinters.

Not only must some rides be speedy and all shows be short, but the employees must work fast visibly, thereby promoting by suggestion speed in the mind, heart, and steps of the most laggard visitors. Throughout Luna Park and all exposition grounds there are benches for the weary. I want the benches there, but I don't want people to sit on them. Whenever, on my frequent tours of the grounds, I find men and women seated watching the lights or the crowds or the free shows, I order out a band, make the musicians march about playing the liveliest tunes, and inject into the very atmosphere such excitement, gaiety, and speed that the resters get up and again take an interest in things. I have never seen this ruse fail.

To keep up the carnival spirit everybody and everything must be on the "go." There can be no carnival without speed. The moment a crowd of folk who are slowly meandering around catch this spirit they walk faster, they laugh, they spend money, they have a good time. I instruct my "talkers" to be always on the alert and to interest people while they are approaching. "Mills won't grind with water that's past" is an old motto, but a good one. It applies to the business of amusing the millions perhaps more than to any other kind of activity.

4. Democracy at the Movies, 1910

The cinematograph is doing for the drama what the printing press did for literature, bringing another form of art into the daily life of the people. Plays are now within the reach, literally, of the poorest, as are good books and good pictures. The secret of cheapness in art as in other things is mechanical multiplication. So long as a play required for each presentation the active co-operation of a considerable number of more or less talented persons it could never be cheap, and in its better forms it was necessarily accessible to a comparatively small part of the population. But once on a celluloid film a spectacle can be reproduced indefinitely, the good as cheaply as the poor, and superiority is no longer handicapped. The same effect is shown in the field of literature. Among the dollar and a half books published every year there is a large proportion of trash or worse, but the volumes sold for fifty cents or less comprise the world's best literature.

The moving picture shows are in general superior, both artistically and morally, to the vaudeville and melodrama that they have driven out of business. It is a mistake to suppose that their amazing popularity is due altogether to their low price of admission. On the contrary the cinematograph has some advantages, not only over the cheap shows which it at first rivaled, but over any previous form of dramatic art. The most conspicuous of these advantages is spaciousness, distance. The stage is at the best but a narrow platform. The characters must dodge out of the wings or pop out of a door at the back. They have their exits and their entrances, but all both necessarily sudden, more "dramatic" than lifelike.

But the moving picture show has a third dimension. The characters have a gradual approach and recession. The railroad train rushes out toward the spectator; the horseman rides off thru the woods or across the plain until he disappears in the distance. . . .

The abolition of the painted scenery of the backdrop gives to the drama a sense of reality, a solidity, that it never had before. The mountains and clouds do not now show spots of threadbare canvas. The tumbling waves do not throw up a dust. The rocks and trees do not shiver at the touch of the actors. The sunshine is such as never came from calcium or carbon, and the wind that blows about loose hair and garments is not that of the electric fan. . . .

On the ordinary stage there is no good way of showing what is being written or read, however essential this may be to the plot. The actor has to read aloud his letter as he writes it as tho he was not sure of its grammar. This device is no longer necessary. The incriminating note, the long lost will, the visiting card, the portrait, and the newspaper paragraph are shown to us directly and we do not have to hear of them at second hand. We see instantly what the hero sees when he puts the spyglass

"The Drama of the People," *Independent* September 29, 1910. This document can also be found in Gerald Mast, ed., *The Movies in Our Midst: Documents in the Cultural History of Film in America* (Chicago: University of Chicago Press, 1982), 56–58.

to his eye, and what the housemaid is looking at thru the keyhole. Ghosts, visions, and transformation scenes are accomplished in a manner truly magical, without the aid of the old stage contrivances, the steam curtain, the trap and the *deus ex machina.* Flying is as easy as walking. Acrobatic feats are unlimited All miracles are possible, even that most marvelous of miracles, the reversal of the course of life. . . .

The disadvantages of the cinematograph in comparison with the ordinary drama cannot well be discussed at present because we do not know which of them are inherent and which remediable. The flickering and jerky action, now often so disagreeable, can be obviated by more rapid exposures and better adjustment of apparatus. The cinematograph drama is still pantomime as was all drama everywhere in its primitive form. But the phonograph is losing its metallic twang and may soon be satisfactorily synchronized with the running film. The problem of photography in natural colors may be regarded as solved altho it cannot in its present stage stand the quick exposure and great enlargement necessary for moving pictures. If once the cinematograph drama can be made vocal and given lifelike color, the only thing further required for a perfect illusion of reality is a real perspective. It can be done by giving our two eyes different pictures and this is not impossible. It has been accomplished for small stationary pictures by means of red and blue spectacles and other contrivances. How it can be managed we do not know. If we did we would not be engaged in writing editorials for a living. But we expect to see some time a stereoscopic colored speaking moving picture drama and it will be well worth seeing. It will be a new form of fine art not unworthy to rank with the elder arts.

5. Ring Lardner's Baseball "Busher" Writes Home, 1914

TERRE HAUTE, INDIANA, September 6

FRIEND AL: Well, Al old pal I suppose you seen in the paper where I been sold to the White Sox. Believe me Al it comes as a surprise to me and I bet it did to all you good old pals down home. You could of knocked me over with a feather when the old man come up to me and says Jack I've sold you to the Chicago Americans.

I didn't have no idea that anything like that was coming off. For five minutes I was just dum and couldn't say a word.

He says We aren't getting what you are worth but I want you to go up to that big league and show those birds that there is a Central League on the map. He says Go and pitch the ball you been pitching down here and there won't be nothing to it. He says All you need is the nerve and Walsh or no one else won't have nothing on you.

So I says I would do the best I could and I thanked him for the treatment I got in Terre Haute. They always was good to me here and though I did more than my share I always felt that my work was appresiated. We are finishing second and I done most of it. I can't help but be proud of my first year's record in professional baseball and you know I am not boasting when I say that Al.

Well Al it will seem funny to be up there in the big show when I never was really in a big city before. But I guess I seen enough of life not to be scared of the high buildings eh Al?

Ring W. Lardner, *You Know Me Al* (New York: Scribner, 1925), 21–22, 25–28.

I will just give them what I got and if they don't like it they can send me back to the old Central and I will be perfectly satisfied.

I didn't know anybody was looking me over, but one of the boys told me that Jack Doyle the White Sox scout was down here looking at me when Grand Rapids was here. I beat them twice in that serious. You know Grand Rapids never had a chance with me when I was right. I shut them out in the first game and they got one run in the second on account of Flynn misjudging that fly ball. Anyway Doyle liked my work and he wired Comiskey to buy me. Comiskey come back with an offer and they excepted it. I don't know how much they got but anyway I am sold to the big league and believe me Al I will make good.

Well Al I will be home in a few days and we will have some of the good old times. Regards to all the boys and tell them I am still their pal and not all swelled up over this big league business.

Your pal,

Jack

PASO ROBLES, CALIFORNIA, March 2

OLD PAL AL: Well Al we been in this little berg now a couple of days and its bright and warm all the time just like June. Seems funny to have it so warm this early in March but I guess this California climate is all they said about it and then some.

It would take me a week to tell you about our trip out here. We came on a Special Train De Lukes and it was some train. Every place we stopped there was crowds down to the station to see us go through and all the people looked me over like I was a actor or something. I guess my hight and shoulders attracted their attention. Well Al we finally got to Oakland which is across part of the ocean from Frisco. We will be back there later on for practice games.

We stayed in Oakland a few hours and then took a train for here. It was another night in a sleeper and believe me I was tired of sleepers before we got here. I have road one night at a time but this was four straight nights. You know Al I am not built right for a sleeping car birth.

The hotel here is a great big place and got good eats. We got in at breakfast time and I made a B line for the dining room. Kid Gleason who is a kind of asst. manager to Callahan come in and sat down with me. He says Leave something for the rest of the boys because they will be just as hungry as you. He says Ain't you afraid you will cut your throat with that knife. He says There ain't no extra charge for using the forks. He says You shouldn't ought to eat so much because you're overweight now. I says You may think I am fat, but it's all solid bone and muscle. He says Yes I suppose it's all solid bone from the neck up. I guess he thought I would get sore but I will let them kid me now because they will take off their hats to me when they see me work.

Manager Callahan called us all to his room after breakfast and give us a lecture. He says there would be no work for us the first day but that we must all take a long walk over the hills. He also says we must not take the training trip as a joke. Then the colored trainer give us our suits and I went to my room and tried mine on. I ain't a bad looking guy in the White Sox uniform Al. I will have my picture taken and send you boys some.

My roommate is Allen a lefthander from the Coast League. He don't look nothing like a pitcher but you can't never tell about them dam left handers. Well I didn't go on the long walk because I was tired out. Walsh stayed at the hotel too and when he seen me he says Why didn't you go with the bunch? I says I was too tired. He says Well when Callahan comes back you better keep out of sight or tell him you are sick. I says I don't care nothing for Callahan. He says No but Callahan is crazy about you. He says You better obey orders and you will git along better. I guess Walsh thinks I am some rube.

When the bunch come back Callahan never said a word to me but Gleason come up and says Where was you? I told him I was too tired to go walking. He says Well I will borrow a wheel-barrow some place and push you round. He says Do you sit down when you pitch? I let him kid me because he has not saw my stuff yet.

Next morning half the bunch mostly vetrans went to the ball park which isn't no better than the one we got at home. Most of them was vetrans as I say but I was in the bunch. That makes things look pretty good for me don't it Al? We tossed the ball round and hit fungos and run round and then Callahan asks Scott and Russell and I to warm up easy and pitch a few to the batters. It was warm and I felt pretty good so I warmed up pretty good. Scott pitched to them first and kept laying them right over with nothing on them. I don't believe a man gets any batting practice that way. So I went in and after I lobbed a few over I cut loose my fast one. Lord was to bat and he ducked out of the way and then throwed his bat to the bench. Callahan says What's the matter Harry? Lord says I forgot to pay up my life insurance. He says I ain't ready for Walter Johnson's July stuff.

Well Al I will make them think I am Walter Johnson before I get through with them. But Callahan come out to me and says What are you trying to do kill somebody? He says Save your smoke because you're going to need it later on. He says Go easy with the boys at first or I won't have no batters. But he was laughing and I guess he was pleased to see the stuff I had.

There is a dance in the hotel to-night and I am up in my room writing this in my underwear while I get my suit pressed. I got it all mussed up coming out here. I don't know what shoes to wear. I asked Gleason and he says Wear your baseball shoes and if any of the girls gets fresh with you spike them. I guess he was kidding me.

Write and tell me all the news about home.

Yours truly,

JACK

 *E S S A Y S*

The interaction between leisure-time recreation and a changing society is the focus of the following essays. In the first selection, historian Gunther Barth of the University of California at Berkeley speculates that baseball's soothing answers to a worried public in an industrial age had much to do with its emergence as the national pastime. Then Lewis A. Erenberg of Loyola University of Chicago examines the pre–World War I dance craze as a white appropriation of African American musical forms as well as a revolution in sexual relations among a youthful generation of men and women.

Baseball and the Values of Industrial America

GUNTHER BARTH

Old men, young men, and small boys, usually "confined in offices, shops, and factories," packed the Polo Grounds on May 30, 1888, for a baseball game between
New York and Pittsburgh, "and saw the popular sport to their hearts' content." . . .
The spectators yelled, "jumped like colts, clapped their hands, threw their hats into
the air, slapped their companions on the back, winked knowingly at each other, and
. . . enjoyed themselves hugely." On that afternoon, according to the account of a
New York *Times* reporter, 13,333 "anxious sightseers" experienced in the ball park
the quintessence of urban leisure: watching others do things.

The scene, barely a few years old, seemed timeless to the spectators. Engulfed
by the surging city, . . . the baseball field exposed within its boundaries the remnants of a ravaged countryside in the form of scarred ravines protected by their ugli-
ness from building construction. Here, with weathered wooden grandstands and
solid clapboard fences as dikes, a lake of grass contrasted with the surrounding
shades of brown. Its green faded away around the bases, where the intense play had
turned the grass to dirt, a baseball diamond without a diamond's glitter. Oblivious
of this, however, thousands of spectators looked only for the sparkle of perfection
in the play on the field. To them going to the ball park meant surrender to the spell
of baseball and to the motions of the players. . . .

In addition to the excitement, a visit to the ball park provided men with a new
perspective on life in the modern city. . . .

Thousands and thousands of men, frequently mystified by the operation of the
economic sphere or the actions of their fellowmen in public office, saw in the ball
park how rules affected one sector of modern city life, the athletic contest. In ways
they could perceive, the spectacle demonstrated the regulation of one of their elementary drives—competition. When their knowledge of the rules of baseball put
them in a position to detect how at times some players tried to win by getting away
with infractions, city people came to an understanding of how regulations operated
in the free-for-all of the modern world. A quick assessment of the swift action on
the diamond revealed that restraints curbed the struggle for success, ordinarily pursued obtrusively by reckless men or obscured by the hustle of daily life. This insight reassured the spectators that elements of order permeated the turmoil of the
modern city. . . .

The practice of conducting an entire game according to established rules signaled the arrival of spectator sports as big business in the nineteenth century. Apart
from their basic function of distinguishing one sport from another, rules made a
game a socially acceptable outlet for emotions. By regularizing procedures, they
fostered interest, shaped the sport to the liking of spectators, and provided the
framework for a sequence of related events leading to a championship. The use of
rules set the big-city spectacle apart from impromptu play, which is attractive

because it is freely improvised, utilizes make-believe instead of rules, and provides the pleasure of assuming roles. Rules also heightened enormously the popularity of a contest because they facilitated betting on the results. . . .

Although the fans paid admissions to sports spectacles and thus influenced their development, general social and cultural trends also affected the divisions of nineteenth-century urbanites. The disintegration of traditional society that accompanied the rise of the modern city undermined forms of popular recreation that were rooted in a predominantly agrarian social system. The newly emerging leisure culture was molded according to the requirements of capitalist society and industrial production. Unlike their ancestors in pre-industrial societies, relieved from incessant labor by climatic vicissitudes and rewarded for prolonged toil by seasonal feast days, in general the residents of the modern city learned to be satisfied with brief but more frequent opportunities to enjoy themselves.

This formula suited their working hours, which could stretch through day and night, with some workers idle while others toiled if factory shifts required several sets of men. In consequence, the sporting events which attracted the most attention came to be reduced in length. However, the number of contests and of competitors increased and provided a steady stream of excitement that fitted most people's schedules and directed the use of leisure time toward relaxation rather than rest. . . .

Popular sports, connecting the urban population with a rising sports industry, shared a potential for educating as well as entertaining crowds of spectators. Among these spectacles, baseball occupied a special position as the most popular and most organized of all spectator sports in the last decades of the nineteenth century. It was the most convenient way for city people to enjoy themselves and also to demonstrate a commitment to standards of excellence in a leisure-time activity. Within a generation the game had made the transition from a pastime for gentlemen to a social institution illuminating the inner workings of new patterns of urban life.

Baseball conquered the United States in the decades between 1840 and 1870, which saw the standardization of the diamonds, the organization of teams, the refinement of rules, the establishment of game schedules, and the first grand tour by a professional baseball team. . . .

Historical evidence links baseball, as we know it, with the modern city. In the early 1840's a group of New York gentlemen who on sunny days enjoyed playing ball games in a lot at the corner of Madison Avenue and Twenty-Seventh Street formed the first association and in 1845 adopted the first set of modern rules. These merchants, brokers, and physicians enjoyed dining and playing together. In 1846 their Knickerbocker Baseball Club played its first match against another team of gentlemen, the New York Nine, in a popular summer resort across the Hudson River. The New York *Clipper* considered that contest the beginning of baseball "as now played" in its preview of the Centennial Year season of 1876. Social as well as athletic exclusiveness distinguished these early gatherings. More often than not, formal challenges initiated the contests and social events concluded them. Soon uniforms— white shirts, blue trousers, and straw hats in the case of the Knickerbockers—added another stylish note.

Despite several efforts to create a uniform game, there were no generally accepted rules regulating strikes and balls until the Civil War. The time the play consumed was still of little consequence, and games often dragged on, endlessly it appeared, because the man at bat, the "striker," waited for the pitch that suited him or hoped to tire out the pitcher. Often, local circumstances dictated the number of passes as well as the layout of the field, the distance between bases, the size of the diamond, and the position of the umpire.

The aristocratic setting of the game vanished during the 1850's when new clubs sprang up in New York, Brooklyn, Philadelphia, Baltimore, and Boston. Fascinated with baseball, laborers, mechanics, and clerks put onto diamonds teams that rejected the assumption that the Knickerbockers arbitrated the game simply because they had organized it first. . . . In 1858, the search for more order brought together delegates from twenty-two clubs who established the National Association of Base Ball Players. Although a far cry from a national unit, the Association placed all clubs on an equal basis by forming a rules committee, establishing procedures for new clubs to join the group, and regulating players, umpires, and scorers. Following the time-honored American practice demonstrated by churches, political parties, labor unions, and charity groups, it grew from the local level to a state, regional, and ultimately a national organization. . . .

The Civil War . . . hasten[ed] the emergence of baseball as a game that was played everywhere in the same way. The young men liked to throw, hit, and catch, and when they met on a field as strangers they needed a standard game so that they could enjoy a contest without prolonged arguments. Whether bored by army life, ordered by officers to attend games, or fascinated by baseball, soldier spectators contributed to the emergence of a standard game because they needed to know not only what went on but also what to anticipate in order to enjoy themselves. Far from home, they watched strangers, and their interest centered more on the play as a whole than on an individual player in the field. When these captive audiences vanished with the end of the war, the systematic baseball reports in the sports press and the metropolitan newspapers sealed the uniform character of the game and contributed to the emergence of professional baseball as the great urban spectator sport.

The reports, tables, and statistics that the leading American sports journalists compiled in the 1860's and 1870's enabled thousands of spectators who flocked into the ball parks of the big cities after the Civil War to follow both teams and games methodically. An English immigrant, Henry Chadwick, saw himself in his old age as the "head gardener" who had raised the "now giant oak of the American game of baseball." . . . He considered it "important and necessary" to give "the full record of each season," and his readers' responses reinforced his view. The accuracy of his scientifically oriented approach underpinned the emotional support given the game during the 1850's by William Trotter Porter in the New York *Spirit of the Times*. This editor, also credited with publishing the first box scores, had put emphasis on "inside" human interest stories and called baseball "our National Game." . . .

The writings of Henry Chadwick and his colleagues gave baseball an identity and helped popularize game and players. They upheld faith in baseball as a noble and clean game when the fans' enthusiasm lagged in the face of reports about fixed games, gambling scandals, warring leagues, and protracted infighting between owners and players for shares in the new sports bonanza. . . .

In the 1880's, Chicago reporters expressing the raw energies of the wildly growing city added slang and frivolity, metaphor and simile to baseball reports and turned them into news that at times qualified as lead stories. In 1913, the Charleston

News and Courier called the resulting style "a distinctive and peculiar tongue, . . . not English, . . . not precisely slang, . . . full of idiomatic eccentricities, rich in catch-phrases and technical terms, wonderfully expressive and in the highest degree flexible." This novel approach gave such a remarkable importance to baseball that in the same year the *Nation* slyly wondered why the baseball language "should so far outdo the feats of the players who it glorifies." It also affected general reporting.

In 1896 a Chicago newspaper editor sent one of his baseball reporters to help cover the Democratic National Convention and to write a follow-up on the reception of William Jennings Bryan's "Cross of Gold" speech. The language of the sportswriter's story on the front page of the Chicago *Daily News* on July 9, 1896, documents one aspect of the impact of baseball on modern city culture. It enlivened what had been the rather staid and dull form of political reporting in an attempt to describe the "almost indescribable":

HOW BRYAN SWAYED THE CROWD

SCENE AFTER HIS REMARKABLE ORATION WAS ALMOST INDESCRIBABLE

When Bryan's words: "You shall not crucify mankind upon the cross of gold" rang out over the throng there was a pause, a break of the smallest fraction of a second. The orator turned and made ready to leave the stand.

Then from the rearmost wall to the speaker's stand, from end to end of the gigantic hall, came like one great burst of artillery the answer of the convention: "You shall not crucify mankind upon the cross of gold." Roar upon roar, crash upon crash of fierce, delirious applause.

The people, men and women, were upon their chairs, their hats were in the air, their handkerchiefs tossing like whitecaps on the winter sea. Flags were flying, waving, streaming; the broad stripes of old glory were intermixed with the banners of states and territories and the pennons of the candidates.

Far down in the rear of the hall a woman was on her chair waving her cloak, blue with red lining, and the alternate flashes of red and blue blazed more conspicuous than any other banner in the hall.

People sprung upon Bryan as he struggled toward his chair. They leaped at him like hungry wolves and hugged him and crushed him in their strong arms. Old men, white with age and with the frenzy of the hour, tottered to him to grasp his hand.

Young men stood on the seats and strove to strike approving hands upon his shoulders as he passed by. His progress to his seat was such as never any Roman coming home to triumph had—the orator was literally whirled off his feet and borne on by the struggling masses of frantic friends.

Then some one in a western delegation uprooted the blue guidon that marked the place of his colleagues. In a second twenty other guidons were twisted from their sockets, and the men who tore them free were crowding toward the spot, where Bryan bewildered, half frightened, panting, yet proud and satisfied, was fighting off the caresses, the adoration of his myriad friends. Over the head of the Nebraska man the blue guidons were clustered. More and more the group grew in numbers every second.

As each blue guide post was added to the throng the crowd simply joined delirium to its previous frenzy. Round the hall, waving the guidons on high, marched the men of Florida, of Illinois, of Idaho.

Twenty other states followed and there would have been but one man before the public eye could a vote have been taken then. Presently, exhausted, the banner-bearers sought their places—Bryan sunk utterly wearied into his seat—the mightiest demonstration of many a convention year was over.

. . . Joseph Pulitzer's *World* had produced the first sports page in the 1880's, and William Randolph Hearst's interest "in stories of the great American game" led to the development of the modern sports section in his New York *Journal* in the 1890's. . . .

Commercialization and professionalization went hand in hand. Young men quickly spotted baseball as a new road to fortune and fame. The growing demand for good baseball put a premium on good players and induced more and more clubs to offer gifts or money to attract them. The practice violated the Association rule against paying players, so that at times clubs used unrelated salaried jobs to attract athletes who were in effect being paid for playing baseball, thus evading the regulation. Rumors about a player getting money under the table circulated as early as 1860. . . .

In 1868, the National Association of Base Ball Players terminated its futile struggle against the monetary practices that produced professional players. The group accepted a recommendation of its rules committee to recognize two distinct classes of players, amateurs and professionals, in an attempt to straighten out the confusing variety of players.

Similar considerations motivated Henry Chadwick to champion an all-professional team. The New York *Clipper* writer realized that the game could survive as a big spectator sport only if played by professionals. In his preview of the 1868 season he stressed the professional status that distinguished the Cincinnati Red Stockings from the other good teams he discussed: the New York Mutuals, the Brooklyn Athletics, the Troy Haymakers, the Chicago White Stockings, the Philadelphia Athletics, and the Baltimore Marylands. He strongly supported the Cincinnati arrangement, which had each player under contract for the entire season at a negotiated rate of pay ranging from $800 to $1,400.

The new industry experienced dismal years, but open and definite professionalism also made the conduct of the game into something approaching a system. The momentum of money squelched the hopes of small-scale speculators who had dreamed of exploiting the new bonanza by luring players and spectators to their own teams. The big clubs built or took over ball parks and clubhouses and organized a game schedule that glorified inter-urban competition on a national basis. . . .

Although breach of contract and bribery, drinking and gambling tarnished the image of baseball, in Boston Harry Wright and other members of the disbanded Cincinnati super-team maintained discipline and won the Association championship for four consecutive years. In 1875, when the original clubs had shrunk to seven, the first major professional baseball league folded, but the presence of the professional players it had developed and the economic potential of professional baseball brought the National League into existence in the following year.

The modern business structure of big-time American baseball grew around the organizational framework conceived in the 1870's. Attempts to break the monopoly of the National League gave rise to the American Association in 1882. Within two years the rivals were able to agree to end competition over cities and for players. The Association failed in 1890; however, ten years later, another major league formed—the American League. From 1900 on, big-time baseball operated within the context of two league championships, figuratively called the Pennants, and soon added a play-off series between the champions called the World Series.

From its start in 1876, the National League of Professional Baseball Clubs, to give it its full title, meant business. Its owners established themselves as masters of the game. William A. Hulbert, the first League president, engineered the development. In contrast to some of the gentlemen players, political bosses, or gambling operators who had previously dabbled in managing baseball, he was a member of the Chicago Board of Trade who used his managerial experience to lay the foundation for another flourishing business. Hulbert was "a typical Chicago man" in the eyes of Albert G. Spalding, who pitched for him before becoming a successful manufacturer of sporting goods. As booster of his city, Hulbert "never spoke of what *he* would do, or what *his* club would do, but it was always what *Chicago* would do." He set up an oligarchy of club owners who ran the game efficiently. With draconic measures he restored the surface honesty of the sport and the public confidence in its operation that seemed so essential for good business.

The governmental and economic structure of baseball became autocratic, but the atmosphere of the ball park preserved the appearance of freedom. The public, fed up with corrupt practices, largely ignored the undemocratic features of the new regime, which, in turn, struggled to square the owners' business monopoly with democracy and even make baseball its symbol. . . .

Any notion that gentlemen may once have had about the proper conduct of a ball player or the correct form of making a play vanished with the emergence of professionalism. The idea governing the related game of cricket—that some behavior on the field was "not cricket"—never took hold in professional baseball. Its players, Bruce Catton concluded in his reflections on the game, "have borrowed nothing from the 'sportsmanship' of more sedate countries; they believe that when you get into a fight you had better win, and the method by which you win does not matter very much." As soon as the skills of the professionals turned the drama of sport into an exhibition, Lewis Mumford stressed in his assessment of mass sport, the rule became "Success at Any Price" instead of "Fair Play." The disappearance of a tacit understanding about the conduct of the game, as well as the necessity of basing a judgment call on an observation made in a fraction of a second, increased the interaction between player and umpire on the field.

The intense rivalry encouraged the player constantly to seek advantages by bending a rule or trying to get away with an infraction. "Boys, you've heard the new rules read," the captain of the New York Giants would say in beginning his annual talk at the opening of the season during the 1880's; "now the question is: what can we do to beat them?" A generation seasoned by the Civil War began to assume that any behavior, however outrageous, was acceptable in baseball, too, and this feeling may have generated the metaphor that spoke of baseball as war. "Infractions are expected by the crowd, and hence by players, umpires and managers," explained Walter Camp, who almost singlehandedly shaped the rules of American football, in 1910. "In the long run, the people make the law," he added, unwittingly identifying the spectators' influence over the enforcement of the rules with the workings of rules committees eager to attract the largest crowds.

For the people in the ball park, the umpire represented the voice of authority. To the spectators he was a convenient target for their frequent irritations and deep-seated frustrations both within and outside the ball park. The umpire became a personification of the rulers of their lives, who in the workaday world remained hidden behind the whirl of urban life, the faceless corporate structures, the anonymity of technocracy, and the mystery of public affairs. During the strife-ridden 1880's and 1890's, in their urge to identify and challenge a villain in the drama they lived, the crowds ignored any distinction between the rules committee of the league that had made the regulations and the umpire on the field calling a play.

Thus the grandstand crowds had a field day in exploiting to their hearts' content the pressure put on the umpire. Over decades of changing styles of play he was called on to decide the legality of the tricky delivery (a new overhand pitching style), unusual batting tactics, fielding aberrations, and base-running maneuvers. What mattered was that all decisions allowed the spectators to challenge vehemently and vociferously the ruler, clearly identified from the 1880's on by his dark blue coat and cap.

On the surface the umpire appeared to exercise an authority like that of some other powers that regulated life. Like constables and clerks, he also lost his standing as a gentleman. Though he had once been specifically honored because refereeing evidenced his intimate knowledge of the game, the rise of baseball as a spectator sport had made him just another member of the cast of characters in the show—at times a villainous buffoon. Before the introduction of the double umpire system at the beginning of the twentieth century, the single man working behind either the pitcher or the catcher frequently cut a pathetic figure.

Definitely not omnipotent and hardly omnipresent, the umpire was abused or even mobbed on the field by spectators and players, and ridiculed or slandered in the sports papers as "the mortal enemy" of everyone, if "he does not especially favor the local club." Among the many fatuous comments on umpire-baiting, few rivaled the explanation that rowdy fans were merely exercising their democratic right to protest tyranny. Any protection the league might have extended to the umpire, and he received none, would have interfered with his actual role. Shaping the game to maximize attendance was of utmost significance to the club owners, so that they tolerated the rowdy behavior of players, managers, and spectators as long as it enhanced the excitement of the game.

This desire for an exciting spectacle eventually led to new rules speeding up the moments of spectacular action in the game and also to the introduction of protective equipment, because gloves and face masks allowed men to make without injury the rough, fast, and exciting plays of the game, in bursts of speed, that most people waited for. Speed occupied the spectators, who were constantly under pressure to match the hectic tempo of the modern city. The action in the ball park demonstrated to them that it was possible, after all, to keep up with the fleeting moment. . . .

Although the players' concern for protection introduced gloves and catcher's masks into baseball, these innovations escaped being ridiculed as unmanly because the age worshiped the result they produced—memorable moments packed with action. Baseball had been played with bare hands until the glove began appearing in the early 1880's, supposedly after a shortstop had used a crude version to protect his hand. Other players followed his example when they noticed that he did not have to ease off catching the ball, could meet it solidly, and got his throw away faster than the other infielders. The spectators, who liked what they saw, supported the change, and sporting goods firms soon began furnishing gloves to professionals. A few years earlier, the first body shields had permitted the umpire to stand behind the catcher and enforce the strike and ball rules in a way that heightened the game's drama. The introduction of the mask and the fingerless glove with light padding on the palm in 1877 allowed the catcher to become the director of team action on the field, an effective way to coordinate the play.

In addition to the protective devices, the change from the large six-ounce elastic ball to the hard regulation ball hastened the transformation of a pastime into a spectacle. An ironic twist of circumstances accompanied these developments. While the new equipment opened up baseball to everyone it also made the professional game the exclusive domain of specialists. Hundreds of agile, hard-throwing men who had not qualified for old-time baseball because they were not born with hands and arms for barehanded fielding replaced the so-called natural players. They did not have to worry about protecting their hands while catching the ball, and their swift plays quickened the pace of the game. New waves of players, each raising the standards of performance, quickly drove each other out of big-league baseball. They constantly advanced the quality of the game, heightened the level of competition, and increased the expectations of spectators until only a handful of big-league-caliber experts could participate.

Less became more early in professional baseball, but the enthusiastic spectators caught on quickly and watched more carefully. Gloves and masks contributed to the decline of the high scores that characterized mid-nineteenth century baseball by allowing steady improvement in pitching and fielding. This intensified a trend marked by revoking the old straight-arm delivery restriction which had forced pitchers to obtain speed only by an underhand throw or a wristy jerk of the ball. In 1900, Adrian C. ("Cap") Anson, after his retirement as manager and captain of the Chicago club, called the high scores of old-time baseball "performances impossible in these days of great speed and curve pitching." In 1859, in the first inter-collegiate baseball game on record, Amherst beat Williams 73 to 32. When the celebrated Cincinnati Red Stockings ruled in 1869, they trounced an opponent 103 to 8, and that was only about half the largest number of runs ever scored in an old-style game. However, at the turn of the twentieth century big-league teams rarely scored more than 10 runs per game.

By that time only sandlot baseball, with the help of the mitt and, from 1896 on, such literary embellishment of baseball virtues as the feats recorded in *Frank Merriwell* by Gilbert Patten, had acquired some of the free and open features that many people identified with the sport. Boys and men tried to emulate the professionals on empty streets and vacant lots, in parks and on playgrounds. In big cities amateur clubs sometimes attracted more fans than the professionals. Eighty thousand people saw the game between the Telling Strollers and the Hanna Street Cleaners for the Cleveland championship of 1914. One year later, in the same natural amphitheater, more than 100,000 cheered the victory of the Cleveland Indians over the Omaha Luxus for the world amateur championship. In 1917 Frederic L. Paxson saw the rise of sports in the United States as another "safety valve" replacing Frederick Jackson Turner's frontier. Baseball "succeeded as an organized spectator sport," he observed, but it contributed something neither racing nor boxing could "in turning the city lot into a playground and the small boy into an enthusiastic player." . . .

While street baseball reaffirmed the social importance of play in the city, professional baseball followed "the individualistic tendencies of America" that left leisure to commerce, giving everyone who could buy a ticket the choice of watching the kind of sport he or she liked best, without making an effort to persuade a group of people to agree on playing one specific game, as an urban reformer of the age commented. It ignored any urge to participate in the play and, like urban politics, followed representational lines. Professional experts took places on the field which from time to time many men in the grandstands dreamed of occupying themselves. . . .

The hazards of the game opened up baseball to gifted players from major immigrant groups. In addition to the many athletes of English and Irish ancestry who had always been present in major-league baseball, American Indians, Frenchmen, Germans, Jews, Poles, Italians, and Latin Americans entered the game. At the turn of the century some of these players had risen beyond any narrow immigrant identity to become some of the great heroes of the sport. Big Ed Delahanty, Louis Francis "Chief" Sockalexis, Napoleon "Larry" Lajoie, and John Peter "Honus" Wagner represented these giants of the game. However, black players remained barred from major-league teams perpetuating the discrimination officially introduced in 1867 when the rules of the National Association of Base Ball Players barred black players and black clubs from membership. In this respect, too, baseball mirrored life in the modern city. . . .

City people, at the turn of the century, considered the ball park not as a testing ground for the egalitarian promises of their society but as a source of diversion. As with their limited role in urban politics, they were satisfied with being represented on the field by their sports idols.

In the ball park they watched a spectacle that responded to their concerns. The game enriched their dreary urban existence by providing a few leisure hours in the outdoors. In the warmth of the afternoon sun, the spectators transcended temporarily the physical limitations urban life imposed upon them and experienced relief from the tension of their complex surroundings. They saw plays that reduced their bewildering struggle for success to a game of one-thing-at-a-time and to the measurable progress of a successful athlete mastering one obstacle after another. They detected few gray areas in the ball park. The game presented immediate and clear-cut wins and losses and pitted good guys against bad guys.

During a few hours in the ball park, city people saw plays that they could remember afterwards because of the way specific events built up to a memorable moment—the sudden skillful triumph over an adversary. By making intense competition against an opponent its essential feature, baseball seemed to legitimize and extole each spectator's daily struggle for success. Watching the rivalry on the diamond introduced standards of competition into the spectators' lives. The game also reduced their daily tensions because its ups and downs seemed more momentous than their own lives.

The spectators learned to appreciate baseball's demonstrations of efficiency and excellence—qualities many of them took as keys to success in industrial America. They followed the dynamic between individual competition and cooperative triumph. Their involvement in the lessons of the diamond thrived on an appreciation of a faster throw, a better catch, or a longer hit. . . .

Mark Twain, in a "Welcome Home" speech to a team returning from a world tour in 1889, hailed baseball as "the very symbol, the outward and visible expression, of the drive and push and rush and struggle of the raging, tearing, booming nineteenth century." He went on to use baseball as a sign to delineate the "modern world," describing the game as a new, visible equator separating the part that mattered from the remainder of the globe where men did not steal "bases on their bellies." The title "world champion," given to the most successful big-league team, confirmed this new geography. It came to designate the winner of the first seven World Series, played between the champions of the National League and the Association in the 1880's. Later, the title was awarded the victor in the annual World Series between the champions of the National League and the American League—established in the first decade of the twentieth century

With the great expanse of greenery that it required, baseball also appeared to bring the countryside into the metropolis. It radiated the wholesome air of a timeless country sport which, each spring, cleansed anew the foul atmosphere of the modern city. From the 1880's on, a new feature of the baseball year strengthened the effect of conjuring up a bit of countryside. Big-league teams began to go into rural isolation, preferably a fashionable resort in the South, to get over the effects of a winter of loafing with "the hardest five weeks' grind in the world," thus seeming to extend baseball's links with country life and sunshine. Big-time baseball now returned every year to the country, whence many enthusiasts assumed it had come, to recharge its energy.

Baseball's manipulation of reality extended to man-made time, too. Although its spectacular plays were the epitome of swift motion and speedy action, baseball rose above any ordinary concern for an economy of time. If the score was tied after nine innings, the game continued as long as it took to achieve victory. While mechanical time prevailed almost everywhere in the modern city, with the factory whistle and the time clock regulating laborers in factories and clerks in stores, natural time regulated baseball. Only nature itself, requiring postponement on account of rain or termination of play after sundown, could interfere with the course of play.

The game's close ties with nature were used to underscore its virtue. In order to make sure that the tangible blessings of baseball were recognized, apologists extolled those of its features that filled the needs of city people. Untouched by logic or evidence, they stressed that getting out into the fresh air of the ball park promised to open men's eyes to their "business interests" and to protect boys from "immoral association." Despite news stories about dishonest games, umpire baiting, rowdy behavior on and off the field, and shady business deals, the importance of baseball as an inspiration for moral and upright behavior was rarely contested. Nothing was allowed to shatter the mystique of the popular game: upright young men fighting to excel on a green field under a clear sky in the big city. Clergymen of all denominations seemed to agree on the value of the game, and testified to their faith in baseball or used baseball as a testimony of their faith. . . .

Baseball offered a lesson in modern living in an imitation of a pastoral setting. Its features of intense rivalry as well as a limited amount of sportsmanship, general enthusiasm as well as rabid partisanship oriented crowds of people toward an acceptance of competition as a part of daily life, an awareness of a distinct urban vitality, and an appreciation for recreation. Spectators packing grandstands and bleachers intensified the pressure on factories and stores for a half-holiday once a week, lightening the routine of living and working. Seeing others play ball for a living encouraged them to play sandlot baseball or to take up other sports. In the 1890's, the *Nation* called the growing interest in sports "the athletic craze" and likened its intensity to preceding crazes involving greenbacks, silver, and grangers. . . .

The feeling of community that the ball park could evoke among crowds of city people struck a young Harvard graduate writing a newspaper column for a college pal in the late 1880's as incongruous with the diversity of the modern city. Ernest Lawrence Thayer set his baseball ballad, "Casey at the Bat," in Mudville, a rural heaven of shared sentiments. His lines about the luckless batter appeared in the Sunday edition of the San Francisco *Examiner,* next to the column of the avowed cynic Ambrose Bierce. Together with "Casey's Revenge," which followed several weeks later, it might have been lost with the weekend, had it not found a stage larger than the ball park.

A few weeks later, a young vaudeville performer recited the poem, fortuitously clipped by a friend, as entr'acte in a comic opera at the baseball night of a New York theater, when he had to acknowledge the presence among the spectators of members of the New York Giants and the Chicago White Stockings. The audience "shouted its glee," De Wolf Hopper recalled, because it "had expected, as any one does on hearing 'Casey' for the first time, that the mighty batsman would slam the ball out of the lot." With "Casey," baseball reached the stage of the popular theater that provided a setting where people could not only laugh about their own frustrated hopes and the shattered illusions of others but also learn to bridge some of the conflicts inherent in the modern city.

Steppin' Out

LEWIS A. ERENBERG

> *The afternoon was already planned; they were going dancing—*
> *for those were the great days: Maurice was tangoing in "Over the*
> *River," the Castles were doing a stiff-legged walk in the third act*
> *of the "Sunshine Girl"—a walk that gave the modern dance a*
> *social position and brought the nice girl into the café, thus begin-*
> *ning a profound revolution in American life. The great rich empire*
> *was feeling its oats and was out for some not too plebeian, yet not*
> *too artistic fun.*
>
> F. Scott Fitzgerald, "The Perfect Life"

F. Scott Fitzgerald was not alone in estimating the importance of the nationwide dance craze sweeping through the cities from 1912 to 1916 and the central role played in the excitement by such popular ballroom teams as Irene and Vernon Castle and Maurice Mouvet and Florence Walton. "It's about th' on'y thing ye see in the pa-pers," observed Finley Peter Dunne's wizened Mr. Dooley at the height of the hysteria. "People ar-re dancin' that a few years ago wud've as soon thought 'iv lettin' their mothers or their bankers see them on a slippery flure as entrin' an opyum joint." Mayors, vice commissions, and social reformers looked on in horror at what they considered the degeneration of public and private morality, but they were powerless to prevent all types of people from every class level—debutantes, staid businessmen,

Lewis A. Erenberg, *Steppin' Out: New York Nightlife and the Transformation of American Culture, 1890–1930* (Westport, Conn.: Greenwood Press, 1981), 146–158. Reproduced with permission of Greenwood Publishing Group, Inc., Westport, Conn.

housewives, Lower East Side dwellers, and Upper West Side matrons—from feeling the spell cast by the dance and flocking to the dance halls, hotel ballrooms, and cabarets. Jesse Lasky recalled the important role that the renaissance of public dancing played in the growth of the cabaret. In 1911, he observed, "it was still scandalous to dance in a public place. Only a year or two later that prejudice was swept aside, and then nightclubs blossomed like magic."

Having begun with exhibition dancers only, the cabarets by 1912 had almost universally installed dance floors so that patrons might partake of the novel proceedings. After an initial period of reluctance, sedate Fifth Avenue hotels followed suit to meet a demand that fluctuated but did not diminish into the 1920s. Centrally located urban institutions had come to replace the lower-class dance halls, vacation resorts, and amusement-park halls as the major places of public dancing. Dancing was becoming a regular and public urban form of entertainment.

To extend the hours of the dance even into the afternoons, cabarets and then hotels inaugurated tea dances, or as they were known in fashionable circles, *thé dansants,* in 1913. Noting the prevailing trend, the *Craftsmen* exclaimed that "suddenly in the midst of this money-getting machine-made age, we throw all our caution to the wind; we give up some of our business hours, and we do not only dance in the evening, but in the afternoon and in the morning." Two general policies governed the afternoon events. The hotels charged one dollar admission, which included tea or other light refreshments, while the cabarets limited their profits to the sale of tea or liquor rather than charging an entrance fee. Lasting from two or three in the afternoon until six in the evening, *thé dansants* drew all kinds of women to public dance institutions during the formerly sedate tea hour, which was transformed into "merely an excuse for dancing." This tremendous expansion of commercial dance facilities led Troy and Margaret Kinney to wonder in amazement that "there should have been a period of sixty years in which people did not wish to dance every day."

In the cabarets, special bands played for dancing before, during, and after the dinner hour. Patrons needed little encouragement to drop their forks and take a few turns around the floor, exhibiting as they did so the active hand they took in their own entertainment. The dance craze of 1912–1916 helped establish the first stars of the cabaret. Irene and Vernon Castle and Maurice Mouvet and his many partners found success and an aura of glamour in the cafés of New York City. Their relationship to the dance craze was an intimate one, for they exhibited all of the current dances and represented the deeper values desired through dance. Appearing at midnight, Irene and Vernon slipped from their table and glided ever so gracefully out onto the dance floor. The lights dimmed, the spotlights played upon them, and they stepped through a series of dances before the delighted eyes of their bewitched fans. After they had finished, patrons themselves tried to imitate what they had just witnessed. In the years of the dancing mania, the ballroom teams personalized many of the fears and dreams of urban life and offered guides as to how the dances were done and life could be lived; the upper and middle classes performed styles established by the Castles, the premier ballroom and cabaret artists of their day, and looked to them for clues on new relationships between men and women. . . .

Prior to 1910 the well-to-do who desired to dance could do so largely in private and on irregular occasions. Small parties did not necessarily revolve around it. The upper classes valued dancing in their social life, but they generally held their balls during the winter season for a restricted group. In humbler circles a club or an organization hired a hall for a general dance and occasionally the police held a grand ball. The seclusion of dancing reflected a society bent on maintaining privacy against the intrusions of outsiders and the dangerous urban world. Women in particular, as bearers of class and culture, were to inhabit a distinct sphere. To step outside the private social network of balls, teas, and debuts was to abrogate social class and propriety. In this atmosphere, it was difficult to introduce respectable women into public, commercial dance halls associated in the public mind with concert saloons that dispensed liquor and prostitution. The fear of women mixing with all elements of urban life mitigated against widespread public dancing.

Unlike those inaugurated after 1912, the favored dances of the nineteenth century exhibited control, regularity, and patterned movement. Set and figure dances—the german, cotillion, and lancers—were favorites at the exclusive Patriarch balls in New York City in the 1870s and 1880s; these dances emphasized that individual pleasure arose from participation in hierarchy, social interdependence, and group unity. Allen Dodworth, a society dancing master, considered the german "an epitome of all there is in private dancing." Introduced to New York about 1844, the german was an elaborate round dance, perfect for private parties because its frequent partner exchanges during the course of the dance ensured a general acquaintanceship among members of the same social set. Its figure formations also elevated group cohesion over the pleasure of the individual. Dodworth advised fledgling steppers to remember that all "pleasure depends entirely upon the kindly cooperation of others." Each individual had a duty to the larger body, and when all united in a cooperative endeavor, "the pleasure is augmented in proportion to the number engaged." Dances of this kind required practice for some time before a ball to ensure that all parts would work well together. As such, they were the ritualistic height of the evening, and the fact that they were organized and led by a society grande dame served to heighten order, refinement, and social responsibility over tendencies toward privatization between partners.

The waltz, introduced into western Europe in 1812, was also a nineteenth- and early twentieth-century favorite for the upper classes and the rest of society. The first closed couple dance, replacing the open hold of the minuet, the waltz changed the position of the feet from ballet to normal but kept an overall pattern movement. Beginning with a certain step, the dancer had to complete an entire sequence of steps until reaching the original place. . . . The attraction of the waltz lay in the actual steps, which varied little from individual to individual. Both the set and sequence dances, in their group and individual manifestations, required a certain unity in the steps, creating a standardized form of motion.

Initially the source of much consternation, the waltz established the close hold whereby the man held the woman at the waist in semi-embrace. The proper hold, however, established a definite distance of three to four inches at the shoulders, increasing downward. The rapid turns prevented lingering embraces and cheek-to-cheek contact. Each partner looked over the other's shoulder while maintaining an erect posture. The formal distance, the courtly style, and the emphasis on a sequence of steps circumscribed the amount of expression allowed mutual body movement and contact. The waltz perhaps expressed the emphasis on disembodied love in the nineteenth century. It was a more companionate dance to be sure, but the movement of the dance, much like the mobility enshrined in the society, kept the man and woman apart. Given the correct hold, the waltz expressed a look but do not touch approach to one's partner, a distance between sexes under the guise of ideal, bodiless love contained in the face of one's partner. Moreover, the institution of the dance card mitigated against individuals fulfilling their heart's desires, since they had to dance with a number of different people to meet social obligation. Even with the waltz, individuals had to follow group norms. . . .

The challenge to this formalism in the dance began in the 1890s, burst into flower in the 1910s, and continued with a good deal of creativity into the 1920s. In the 1890s, men and women began to do the more active strains of the two-step and the "Washington Post March." John Philip Sousa wrote the "Washington Post March" in 1891, and the music caught on immediately. It had a new kind of military march beat, and the two-step, the dance done to it, was not much more than a double-quick march with a skip in each step, done rapidly as a couple could go forward, backward, and turn. The actual "Washington Post" dance arrived before 1894. In it the man stood behind his partner, slightly to the left, while she raised her hands above her shoulders to take those of the man. Barely perceptible beneath the march rhythms, the dancers of the two-step and the "Washington Post" began expressing themselves to a heightened beat. The Boston waltz, moreover, which reached the height of popularity around 1900, was already moving to the leisurely walk step, as dancers took a full four bars instead of two in their turns.

After 1912 social dancing changed dramatically. Several commentators estimated that "over one hundred new dances found their way, in and out of our fashionable ballrooms" from 1912 to 1914. The vast increase in dances with such exuberantly unpretentious names as the turkey trot, Texas tommy, bunny hug, monkey hug, lame duck, foxtrot, and tango, together with their astonishing rapidity of discovery, gave to this regeneration of social dancing the appearance of a mania. Caught in its spell, New Yorkers picked up these new steps from around the nation and danced in new rhythms in public and private places of amusement. In dance halls, ballrooms, cabarets, and private homes, the rest of the nation was quickly bent on following suit. The dances, like the cabaret itself in the 1910s, were part of a growing social and cultural ferment as men and women turned to greater intimacy in social and sexual relations and a single standard of sexual relations. As an element lying at the core of the body, dancing's regeneration bespoke a society breaking from gentility and discovering new options and forms of behavior between the sexes.

Well-to-do New Yorkers found new forms of the dance to match their impulses in the steps borrowed from black American dance, music, and culture, rather than formal European steps. In borrowing from the more natural shuffle walk-step, in which partners moved about shuffling their feet as if walking, respectable whites sought a greater emphasis on body movement rather than patterned feet movement. In seeking new sources of vitality, respectable whites looked outside the halls of propriety to a people and a culture they had previously considered disreputable. The first attempts by whites to copy black steps for the ballroom occurred in the 1890s and early 1900s. Often in the honky-tonks of this period, an occasional white would perform the Negro cakewalk to vary the waltz and two-steps. The cakewalk soon penetrated even high society. The William K. Vanderbilts found it a unique diversion for one of their balls. The cakewalk, however, was primarily an exhibition rather than a social dance for common usage, and it was not until the 1910s that the rate of influx from lower groups increased and specifically social forms predominated. After the almost nonexistent beginning in the cakewalk, whites turned with ever-increasing frequency to the more primitive steps of black culture. The Texas tommy, turkey trot, fox-trot, charleston, and black bottom, for example, had Negro origins and were originally performed in black communities or in red-light districts. . . . Because of the paucity of sources, it is difficult to tell how old these dances were within the black community, but it is clear that, under the demands of whites, they were beginning to make their way into the larger society during this period.

Ragtime, the music for the new dances, also came from black culture, and it stimulated a host of new steps. Another product of the 1890s, it too started in southern black dives and cabarets as blacks began moving in increasing numbers into the city and coming into contact with each other, minstrel show music, white march and band music, and Negro barrelhouse piano. Irving Berlin brought the music to its widest vogue after the publication of "Alexander's Ragtime Band" in 1911, when Tin Pan Alley joined in the production of the musical form. Previously intended for listening, ragtime now became an important element in the intimate movement of mainstream whites. The music originally permitted blacks to laugh at white culture and behavior through the "ragging" of the host culture's cherished melodies and sentiments. . . . When whites adopted ragtime, it meant that they were beginning to question some of the formal aspects of their culture. In its spirit and rhythm, rag, when combined with the dance, provided the pep that men and women sought in their music.

As purveyors of the new music, black bandsmen found jobs in the Broadway cabarets and restaurants from which they were otherwise excluded. They replaced the gypsy string orchestras intended for listening only, and their opportunities derived from the new demand and the formidable organizing job performed by James R. Europe. He helped form black musicians into the Clef Club, a place where work could be efficiently handed out and where black bands could be contacted. Europe quit the Clef Club in 1914 to play for dancers Irene and Vernon Castle. His star rose with the Castles, reaching a peak when his bands played all along Broadway in 1915, and his own Tempo Club was a mainstay of the dance craze before the war. While whites to a degree could accept happy-go-lucky black music because it fit their image of the Negro, they were reluctant to accept black culture's serious music. They ignored the more complex rag compositions of Scott Joplin, just as did the Negro musicians who were afraid to acknowledge seriously their lower-class musical tradition. Black and white musicians thus wrote and played a light kind of dance music, which the white public was willing to accept. The black dominance of Broadway cabarets did not outlast the war. As whites borrowed the newer musical styles after 1917, they also took over the high-paying jobs.

Along with the more natural shuffle walk-steps of black dancing and their Afro-American and Tin Pan Alley ragtime accompaniment, dancers enjoyed heightened bodily expression and intimacy with their partners. Black music, according to music historian Maud Cuney-Hare, "ignores any division of time that follows the natural pulse of a regular metrical beat," and anticipates or holds over accents beyond their expected time. Emphasizing rhythm and a beat, this complex music encouraged spontaneous movement and undercut the formal conventions about moving the body that had prevailed in social dancing. As Vernon Castle remarked, "When a good orchestra plays a 'rag' one has simply *got* to move." The music emphasized rhythm rather than the vocals, redefining popular music and the music business as an extension of dancing rather than listening. It is no accident that from this period on, Tin Pan Alley decreed that a successful song had to be danceable.

The simplicity of the shuffle walk and the finely accented rhythms of the music encouraged couples to interpret the beat in a wider variety of ways than had occurred previously. One couple, for example, could be dancing one dance, while others did quite another to the very same music. Styles such as the tango and the one-step contained innumerable variations from which a couple could choose the ones that most appealed to them. The new styles freed the dancers from the sequence of steps that had served to prescribe their behavior in the past. . . .

The major attraction of the new dances rested on the rhythm rather than on prescribed steps. By adding body movements to the steps, dancers experienced immediate pleasure in the dance—expression of the body—rather than going in a purposeful direction. A number of commentators observed the boring and monotonous movements of the steps, but what they saw was the box step, which submitted to the external constraints of an urban industrial society but within those constraints subtly elevated the body as an irreducible unit of freedom. Irving Berlin's popular "Everybody's Doin' It Now" of 1911 illustrates the new-style shoulder, arm, and hip movements done to the irregularly accented ragtime beat, describing couples swaying, throwing their shoulders in the air, snapping their fingers, and hunching like bears to the phrase, "It's a bear." Dancing now contained pleasure along the way; it was not just a direction to travel. Instead of using the steps alone to define the dance, women and men moved their bodies in response to the rhythm.

The acceptance of black music and dance paralleled and drew upon a reevaluation of the previous formalism between men and women. The wonderful nomenclature of the dances, taken from the barnyard, added to the general tone of exuberance, unpretentiousness, and informality between the sexes. Doing the turkey trot, grizzly bear, monkey glide, bunny hug, lame duck, or fox-trot, whites did movements that placed them closer to the natural processes of the animal kingdom than to the restrained pinnacle of the genteel hierarchy that they and well-to-do women had occupied in the Victorian era. By turning to the animal world, black culture, and the red-light district for the sources of their cultural regeneration, well-to-do urbanites were searching for a way to liberate some of the repressed wilder elements, the more natural elements, that had been contained by gentility. Their liberation found their way into dance and into social relations. The new dances were part of the rebellion against the older sexual mores.

Indeed the dances fostered an unheard-of casualness between partners, permitted greater options in holds and distances, and symbolized the high value placed on mutual heterosexual intimacy and attraction. Couples often held each other very close, grasping each other firmly about the waist or about the neck as if in a hug. The one-step brought men and women into closer contact than the formal six inches decreed for the waltz. And unlike the waltz, in which couples whirled about so that they nearly lost touch with each other, the one-step, the bunny hug, and the other new dances allowed a lingering close contact. "Certainly their essence is a very close proximity," emphasized Julian Street in *Welcome to Our City.* "Two persons, moving with the music, as one—much more as one than in the old time waltz or two step." Conventions had changed drastically. "The debutantes of five years since would have indignantly refused to dance with the young man who held her as he must needs hold her in the dance of today." To the dismay of moralists, men and women in the tango even brought legs and pelvic regions into intimate contact in the much feared dip portion of the dance, which placed women in a horizontal position reeking of sexual exploration and subjugation. In the new dances, men and women were taking on a sexual cast and bringing their bodies into greater affectionate contact. As one society dance instructor summed it up, "The young dancers simply take advantage of the dances to embrace."

Whether these dances were done in private or public, they reflected an emphasis on the primacy of the intimate couple instead of the group. In the public cabaret, this was even more so, because a man and woman usually came together, and the chances of their dancing with someone they did not know were, if not impossible, at least remote. In the cabaret there were few mechanisms to facilitate the mixing of people who did not know each other. The dance card was not in force, and the idea that one should never dance with the same person twice in succession was forever broken. The customs of the private dance did not apply in the public space, and even cutting in was frowned upon. This left the partners performing their own steps to a common music. Within the public dancing area, the desire for more life, for more fun, for more adventure, was confined to the couple. The couple carried the weight of these and other cultural changes.

The new dances bespeak a reevaluation of women of the prosperous classes and the institution of marriage. By the early twentieth century the institution of marriage among the upper and upper middle classes perhaps began shifting away from the traditional economic and childbearing functions toward more personal factors as the determinants of a relationship. Moreover, the ideal of the family oriented to duty or toward male success was in the process of transformation. What was important were the personal compatibilities of two people, their companionableness, and their mutual sexual attractiveness. The positive value placed on sexual factors extended the institution of dating for the young. They needed a certain amount of free opportunity to explore each other if the personal factors were to be found right. Sexual attractiveness could not be measured merely by talking; it had to be explored in a mutual excitement of each other's bodies. By emphasizing this in the dance and in public places like the cabaret outside the eyes of parents or friends whom one did not want to have watching, young people of well-to-do backgrounds could search for a mate who met their personal definition of a marriage partner.

The renaissance of public dancing, furthermore, provided young men and women a relatively safe place and manner of searching out the sexual factors for marriage and lifelong companionship. Private dances took place in front of such authority figures as parents and social superiors. The cabaret offered a degree of freedom from watchful eyes of people they knew. Yet while there was room to explore in some ways, the cabaret was also a public place, filled with anonymous eyes so that nothing could progress beyond a mildly intimate stage. A woman and a man might proceed by automobile to a secluded place after leaving, but if they were young, they most probably had to be home by a certain time to answer to their parents. Within these constraints, the dances themselves offered a greater realm for exploration of those indefinable qualities associated with the body. Shuffling around the floor, swaying and moving, couples could feel if the person they danced with was compatible for pleasure along the path of life and offered a chance of personal fulfillment.

Although the young made up a large bulk of the dancing crowd, they were not the only ones who danced in the public cabarets. Geared to a new mood of self-expression, the dance craze also drew on the impulses of older people. Prior to 1910 the dance was primarily the recreation of the young, with parents in society circles joining in for an occasional figure or a set dance. As Frederick Lewis Allen noted, "Through the length and breadth of middle class America few people danced after they were married, or had reached the age of twenty-five." . . .

Consequently when married and unmarried couples began to dance regularly in hotels and cabarets, it signaled their adaptation to a more youthful set of social values. While the young developed special peer styles for themselves, older men and women also tried to perpetuate a sense of youthfulness in the marriage institution. . . . Dancing became a way of affirming one's identity as a youthful individual, vital to and in society. It also meant that older people confirmed the activities of adolescents, looking to them to set the styles. The continuation of dancing after marriage also showed that sexual attractiveness was an ongoing theme.

For the older set, having public places to dance meant that dancing recaptured a spontaneity that it had missed when it was regulated by the round of society or occasional ball activities. Whenever a couple who could afford it felt like dancing, all they had to do was step out. The public atmosphere meant that parents could escape their children, and couples could escape their particular social set and concentrate on dancing and each other. The opening up of this public realm afforded greater anonymity and potentially greater personal freedom.

The reevaluation of marriage implied by the dance craze was caught in one of the many short stories that explored the dance craze, Mary Cutting's "Dance-Mad Billy." The story opens with a depiction of a young married couple mired in the genteel family of male duty and female refinement. Working as an architect in a large firm, William Stirling finds that his imagination has dried up, and as a consequence, he turns to dancing and the body as a new realm for his energies. Unfortunately his wife, Tips, insists on abjuring joy and remaining a homebody. She wants Bill to settle down, work hard, and stay away from pleasurable activities that would prevent him from achieving financial success. In her stubborn resistance to the new fashions, she symbolizes the older notion of the home and family as a place of regularity, responsibility, and sobriety. Because of her insistence on the older virtues, Bill goes alone to afternoon dances where he trots with a friend's wife. The conflict in the story derives from whether his dancing will lead his sexual impulses outside the family and thus destroy their home. Cutting resolves the issue by having Tips, through a miraculous change of heart, choose to share joy with her husband. We learn at the end that she refused to accompany him only because he did not make his desires for her presence forcefully known. She was hurt. Her new feelings resolve the dilemma: "I'm sick and tired of being a makeweight, I want— I want—I want—" her voice rises uncontrollably— "to en-*joy* myself too." The story ends as Bill proclaims, with Tips's full agreement, "Let's go out to-night and have a lark!" This story demonstrates that dancing was a way for both sexes to revitalize their marriage and to legitimize joy in marriage as a positive value that both partners should expect. Marriage was to fulfill the personal expectations of both people.

 F U R T H E R   R E A D I N G

Gunther Barth, *City People* (1980)

Susan Porter Benson, *Counter Cultures: Saleswomen, Managers, Customers in American Department Stores, 1890–1940* (1986)

Francis G. Couvares, *The Remaking of Pittsburgh* (1984)

John T. Cumbler, *Working-Class Community in Industrial America* (1979)

Elliot J. Gorn, *The Manly Art: Bare Knuckle Prize Fighting in America* (1986)

Stephen Hardy, *How Boston Played* (1982)

Daniel Horowitz, *The Morality of Spending* (1985)

John F. Kasson, *Amusing the Millions: Coney Island at the Turn of the Century* (1978)

William Leach, *Land of Desire: Merchants, Power, and the Rise of a New American Culture* (1993)

T. Jackson Lears, *Fables of Abundance: A Cultural History of Advertising in America* (1994)

Lawrence Levine, *Black Culture, Black Consciousness* (1977)

Donald J. Mrozek, *Sport and American Mentality, 1880–1910* (1983)

Kathy Peiss, *Cheap Amusements* (1986)

Robert Peterson, *Only the Ball Was White* (1970)

Roy Rosensweig, *Eight Hours for What We Will* (1983)

David Q. Voigt, *American Baseball* (1966)

C H A P T E R

12

Progressivism: Roots of
the Reform Vision

*In the first decade of the twentieth century, a burst of reform activity, deriving
from all social classes but especially notable for initiatives from educated professionals, commonly adopted the adjective* progressive. *Encompassing journalistic
muckrakers, social workers, enlightened businessmen, and child welfare and
labor reformers, as well as issue-oriented political activists, the reform fervor helped
transform public opinion as well as public policy in the years before the Great World
War. Indeed, in 1912, when Theodore Roosevelt's third-party candidacy formally
adopted the Progressive party label, three of the four candidates (Roosevelt, the
Democrat Wilson, and the Socialist Debs) openly appealed to the reform constituency,
and the fourth (the Republican Taft) could also claim an organic connection.*

*Yet for all of its popularity at the time, historiographic debate has swirled ever
since around the pros and cons, and even the basic coherence, of the progressive
vision. On the one hand, progressive thought clearly inherited much of its antimonopoly impetus from the labor-populist impetus of the 1890s, but its urban,
middle-class character also bent the populist message toward a more optimistic
faith in rational, incremental reform and a new emphasis on social efficiency and
the moral rehabilitation of immigrant slums. The issue remains debatable whether
progressivism served, on the whole, to define a necessary agenda for a twentieth-
century welfare state or (perhaps in so doing) established a big-brother role for a
new class of moralizing bureaucrats.*

DOCUMENTS

The selections in this chapter suggest the far-flung nature of contemporary reform
interests and something of their deeper inspiration. In Document 1, University of
Chicago philosopher and educator John Dewey, a radical pragmatist, links pedagogical
changes within the classroom to a larger democratic transformation outside. In Document 2, an excerpt from perhaps the most influential single piece of contemporary
muckraking, *The Shame of the Cities,* Lincoln Steffens in 1904 stresses the connections
between the supposedly respectable world of business and the sordid world of municipal

politics. As a direct response to Steffens and other reformers, Tammany Hall boss George Washington Plunkitt (in conversation with journalist William L. Riordan) openly defends his tried-and-true methods of city government (Document 3). In Document 4, in a manner that illustrates the contested connections between considerations of "efficiency" (drawn from the business world) and social justice, socialist writer and reformer Robert Hunter calculates the social cost of substandard urban housing. Walter Rauschenbusch, a Baptist clergyman whose work among German immigrants in New York City led him to champion the this-worldly doctrines of the social gospel, gives voice in Document 5 to a powerful moral-religious motivation behind the progressive critique of industrial individualism. As a final illustration of the progressive mindset, Document 6 presents two women's suffrage cartoons—at once identifying women as a cleansing agent against urban boss rule and the source of a more nurturing, "maternalist" sensibility in public affairs.

1. John Dewey Advocates a Democratic Schoolroom 1900

Some few years ago I was looking about the school supply stores in the city, trying to find desks and chairs which seemed thoroughly suitable from all points of view—artistic, hygienic, and educational—to the needs of the children. We had a great deal of difficulty in finding what we needed, and finally one dealer, more intelligent than the rest, made this remark: "I am afraid we have not what you want. You want something at which the children may work; these are all for listening." That tells the story of the traditional education. Just as the biologist can take a bone or two and reconstruct the whole animal, so, if we put before the mind's eye the ordinary schoolroom, with its rows of ugly desks placed in geometrical order, crowded together so that there shall be as little moving room as possible, desks almost all of the same size, with just space enough to hold books, pencils, and paper, and add a table, some chairs, the bare walls, and possibly a few pictures, we can reconstruct the only educational activity that can possibly go on in such a place. It is all made "for listening"— because simply studying lessons out of a book is only another kind of listening; it marks the dependency of one mind upon another. The attitude of listening means, comparatively speaking, passivity, absorption; that there are certain ready-made materials which are there, which have been prepared by the school superintendent, the board, the teacher, and of which the child is to take in as much as possible in the least possible time. . . .

Another thing that is suggested by these schoolrooms, with their set desks, is that everything is arranged for handling as large numbers of children as possible; for dealing with children *en masse,* as an aggregate of units; involving, again, that they be treated passively. The moment children act they individualize themselves; they cease to be a mass and become the intensely distinctive beings that we are acquainted with out of school, in the home, the family, on the playground, and in the neighborhood.

John Dewey, "The School and the Life of The Child," in *The School and Society* (Chicago: University of Chicago Press, 1915), 47–73.

On the same basis is explicable the uniformity of method and curriculum. If everything is on a "listening" basis, you can have uniformity of material and method. The ear, and the book which reflects the ear, constitute the medium which is alike for all. There is next to no opportunity for adjustment to varying capacities and demands. There is a certain amount—a fixed quantity—of ready-made results and accomplishments to be acquired by all children alike in a given time. It is in response to this demand that the curriculum has been developed from the elementary school up through the college. There is just so much desirable knowledge, and there are just so many needed technical accomplishments in the world. Then comes the mathematical problem of dividing this by the six, twelve, or sixteen years of school life. Now give the children every year just the proportionate fraction of the total, and by the time they have finished they will have mastered the whole. By covering so much ground during this hour or day or week or year, everything comes out with perfect evenness at the end—provided the children have not forgotten what they have previously learned. The outcome of all this is Matthew Arnold's report of the statement, proudly made to him by an educational authority in France, that so many thousands of children were studying at a given hour, say eleven o'clock, just such a lesson in geography; and in one of our own western cities this proud boast used to be repeated to successive visitors by its superintendent. . . .

The real child, it hardly need be said, lives in the world of imaginative values and ideas which find only imperfect outward embodiment. We hear much nowadays about the cultivation of the child's "imagination." Then we undo much of our own talk and work by a belief that the imagination is some special part of the child that finds its satisfaction in some one particular direction—generally speaking, that of the unreal and make-believe, of the myth and made-up story. Why are we so hard of heart and so slow to believe? The imagination is the medium in which the child lives. To him there is everywhere and in everything which occupies his mind and activity at all a surplusage of value and significance. The question of the relation of the school to the child's life is at bottom simply this: Shall we ignore this native setting and tendency, dealing, not with the living child at all, but with the dead image we have erected, or shall we give it play and satisfaction? If we once believe in life and in the life of the child, then will all the occupations and uses spoken of, then will all history and science, become instruments of appeal and materials of culture to his imagination, and through that to the richness and the orderliness of his life. Where we now see only the outward doing and the outward product, there, behind all visible results, is the readjustment of mental attitude, the enlarged and sympathetic vision, the sense of growing power, and the willing ability to identify both insight and capacity with the interests of the world and man. Unless culture be a superficial polish, a veneering of mahogany over common wood, it surely is this—the growth of the imagination in flexibility, in scope, and in sympathy, till the life which the individual lives is informed with the life of nature and of society. When nature and society can live in the schoolroom, when the forms and tools of learning are subordinated to the substance of experience, then shall there be an opportunity for this identification, and culture shall be the democratic password.

2. Lincoln Steffens Exposes the Corruption of Municipal Politics, 1904

When I set out on my travels, an honest New Yorker told me honestly that I would find that the Irish, the Catholic Irish, were at the bottom of it all everywhere. The first city I went to was St. Louis, a German city. The next was Minneapolis, a Scandinavian city, with a leadership of New Englanders. Then came Pittsburg, Scotch Presbyterian, and that was what my New York friend was. "Ah, but they are all foreign populations," I heard. The next city was Philadelphia, the purest American community of all, and the most hopeless. And after that came Chicago and New York, both mongrel-bred, but the one a triumph of reform, the other the best example of good government that I had seen. The "foreign element" excuse is one of the hypocritical lies that save us from the clear sight of ourselves.

Another such conceit of our egotism is that which deplores our politics and lauds our business. This is the wail of the typical American citizen. Now, the typical American citizen is the business man. The typical business man is a bad citizen; he is busy. If he is a "big business man" and very busy, he does not neglect, he is busy with politics, oh, very busy and very businesslike. I found him buying boodlers in St. Louis, defending grafters in Minneapolis, originating corruption in Pittsburg, sharing with bosses in Philadelphia, deploring reform in Chicago, and beating good government with corruption funds in New York. He is a self-righteous fraud, this big business man. He is the chief source of corruption, and it were a boon if he would neglect politics. But he is not the business man that neglects politics; that worthy is the good citizen, the typical business man. He too is busy, he is the one that has no use and therefore no time for politics. When his neglect has permitted bad government to go so far that he can be stirred to action, he is unhappy, and he looks around for a cure that shall be quick, so that he may hurry back to the shop. Naturally, too, when he talks politics, he talks shop. His patent remedy is quack; it is business.

"Give us a business man," he says ("like me," he means). "Let him introduce business methods into politics and government; then I shall be left alone to attend to my business."

There is hardly an office from United States Senator down to Alderman in any part of the country to which the business man has not been elected; yet politics remains corrupt, government pretty bad, and the selfish citizen has to hold himself in readiness like the old volunteer firemen to rush forth at any hour, in any weather, to prevent the fire; and he goes out sometimes and he puts out the fire (after the damage is done) and he goes back to the shop sighing for the business man in politics. The business man has failed in politics as he has in citizenship. Why?

Because politics is business. That's what's the matter with it. That's what's the matter with everything,—art, literature, religion, journalism, law, medicine,—

Lincoln Steffens, *The Shame of the Cities* (New York: McClure, Phillips, and Co., 1904), 134–141.

they're all business, and all—as you see them. Make politics a sport, as they do in England, or a profession, as they do in Germany, and we'll have—well, something else than we have now,—if we want it, which is another question. . . .

But do the people want good government? Tammany says they don't. Are the people honest? Are the people better than Tammany? Are they better than the merchant and the politician? . . .

No, the contemned methods of our despised politics are the master methods of our braggart business, and the corruption that shocks us in public affairs we practice ourselves in our private concerns. There is no essential difference between the pull that gets your wife into society or for your book a favorable review, and that which gets a heeler into office, a thief out of jail, and a rich man's son on the board of directors of a corporation; none between the corruption of a labor union, a bank, and a political machine; none between a dummy director of a trust and the caucus-bound member of a legislature; none between a labor boss like Sam Parks, a boss of banks like John D. Rockefeller, a boss of railroads like J. P. Morgan, and a political boss like Matthew S. Quay. The boss is not a political, he is an American institution, the product of a freed people that have not the spirit to be free.

And it's all a moral weakness; a weakness right where we think we are strongest. Oh, we are good—on Sunday, and we are "fearfully patriotic" on the Fourth of July. But the bribe we pay to the janitor to prefer our interests to the landlord's, is the little brother of the bribe passed to the alderman to sell a city street, and the father of the air-brake stock assigned to the president of a railroad to have this life-saving invention adopted on his road. And as for graft, railroad passes, saloon and bawdy-house blackmail, and watered stock, all these belong to the same family. We are pathetically proud of our democratic institutions and our republican form of government, of our grand Constitution and our just laws. We are a free and sovereign people, we govern ourselves and the government is ours. But that is the point. We are responsible, not our leaders, since we follow them. We *let* them divert our loyalty from the United States to some "party"; we *let* them boss the party and turn our municipal democracies into autocracies and our republican nation into a plutocracy. We cheat our government and we let our leaders loot it, and we let them wheedle and bribe our sovereignty from us. True, they pass for us strict laws, but we are content to let them pass also bad laws, giving away public property in exchange; and our good, and often impossible, laws we allow to be used for oppression and blackmail. And what can we say? We break our own laws and rob our own government, the lady at the customhouse, the lyncher with his rope, and the captain of industry with his bribe and his rebate. The spirit of graft and of lawlessness is the American spirit. . . .

We Americans may have failed. We may be mercenary and selfish. Democracy with us may be impossible and corruption inevitable, but . . . we can stand the truth; that there is pride in the character of American citizenship; and that this pride may be a power in the land. So this little volume [*The Shame of the Cities*], a record of shame and yet of self-respect, a disgraceful confession, yet a declaration of honor, is dedicated, in all good faith, to the accused—to all the citizens of all the cities in the United States.

3. New York City's Boss Plunkitt
Defends "Honest" Graft, 1905

Everybody is talkin' these days about Tammany men growin' rich on graft, but nobody thinks of drawin' the distinction between honest graft and dishonest graft. There's all the difference in the world between the two. Yes, many of our men have grown rich in politics. I have myself. I've made a big fortune out of the game, and I'm gettin' richer every day, but I've not gone in for dishonest graft—blackmailin' gamblers, saloonkeepers, disorderly people, etc.—and neither has any of the men who have made big fortunes in politics.

There's an honest graft, and I'm an example of how it works. I might sum up the whole thing by sayin': "I seen my opportunities and I took 'em."

Just let me explain by examples. My party's in power in the city, and it's goin' to undertake a lot of public improvements. Well, I'm tipped off, say, that they're going to lay out a new park at a certain place.

I see my opportunity and I take it. I go to that place and I buy up all the land I can in the neighborhood. Then the board of this or that makes its plan public, and there is a rush to get my land, which nobody cared particular for before.

Ain't it perfectly honest to charge a good price and make a profit on my investment and foresight? Of course, it is. Well, that's honest graft.

Or supposin' it's a new bridge they're goin' to build. I get tipped off and I buy as much property as I can that has to be taken for approaches. I sell at my own price later on and drop some more money in the bank.

Wouldn't you? It's just like lookin' ahead in Wall Street or in the coffee or cotton market. It's honest graft, and I'm lookin' for it every day in the year. I will tell you frankly that I've got a good lot of it, too.

I'll tell you of one case. They were goin' to fix up a big park, no matter where. I got on to it, and went lookin' about for land in that neighborhood.

I could get nothin' at a bargain but a big piece of swamp, but I took it fast enough and held on to it. What turned out was just what I counted on. They couldn't make the park complete without Plunkitt's swamp, and they had to pay a good price for it. Anything dishonest in that?

Up in the watershed I made some money, too. I bought up several bits of land there some years ago and made a pretty good guess that they would be bought up for water purposes later by the city.

Somehow, I always guessed about right, and shouldn't I enjoy the profit of my foresight? It was rather amusin' when the condemnation commissioners came along and found piece after piece of the land in the name of George Plunkitt of the Fifteenth Assembly District, New York City. They wondered how I knew just what to buy. The answer is—I seen my opportunity and I took it. I haven't confined myself to land; anything that pays is in my line.

For instance, the city is repavin' a street and has several hundred thousand old granite blocks to sell. I am on hand to buy, and I know just what they are worth.

William L. Riordan, *Plunkitt of Tammany Hall* (New York: McClure, Phillips, 1905), 3–10.

How? Never mind that. I had a sort of monopoly of this business for a while, but once a newspaper tried to do me. It got some outside men to come over from Brooklyn and New Jersey to bid against me.

Was I done? Not much. I went to each of the men and said: "How many of these 250,000 stones do you want?" One said 20,000, and another wanted 15,000, and another wanted 10,000. I said: "All right, let me bid for the lot, and I'll give each of you all you want for nothin'."

They agreed, of course. Then the auctioneer yelled: "How much am I bid for these 250,000 fine pavin' stones?"

"Two dollars and fifty cents," says I.

"Two dollars and fifty cents!" screamed the auctioneer. "Oh, that's a joke! Give me a real bid."

He found the bid was real enough. My rivals stood silent. I got the lot for $2.50 and gave them their share. That's how the attempt to do Plunkitt ended, and that's how all such attempts end.

I've told you how I got rich by honest graft. Now, let me tell you that most politicians who are accused of robbin' the city get rich the same way.

They didn't steal a dollar from the city treasury. They just seen their opportunities and took them. That is why, when a reform administration comes in and spends a half million dollars in tryin' to find the public robberies they talked about in the campaign, they don't find them.

The books are always all right. The money in the city treasury is all right. Everything is all right. All they can show is that the Tammany heads of departments looked after their friends, within the law, and gave them what opportunities they could to make honest graft. Now, let me tell you that's never goin' to hurt Tammany with the people. Every good man looks after his friends, and any man who doesn't isn't likely to be popular. If I have a good thing to hand out in private life, I give it to a friend. Why shouldn't I do the same in public life?

Another kind of honest graft. Tammany has raised a good many salaries. There was an awful howl by the reformers, but don't you know that Tammany gains ten votes for every one it lost by salary raisin'?

The Wall Street banker thinks it shameful to raise a department clerk's salary from $1500 to $1800 a year, but every man who draws a salary himself says: "That's all right. I wish it was me." And he feels very much like votin' the Tammany ticket on election day, just out of sympathy.

Tammany was beat in 1901 because the people were deceived into believin' that it worked dishonest graft. They didn't draw a distinction between dishonest and honest graft, but they saw that some Tammany men grew rich, and supposed they had been robbin' the city treasury or levyin' blackmail on disorderly houses, or workin' in with the gamblers and lawbreakers.

As a matter of policy, if nothing else, why should the Tammany leaders go into such dirty business, when there is so much honest graft lyin' around when they are in power? Did you ever consider that?

Now, in conclusion, I want to say that I don't own a dishonest dollar. If my worst enemy was given the job of writin' my epitaph when I'm gone, he couldn't do more than write:

"George W. Plunkitt. He Seen His Opportunities, and He took 'Em."

4. Socialist Reformer Robert Hunter Decries Murder by Tenement, 1907

Unnecessary disease and death are mainly active in bringing misery to the working classes and especially to those in poverty. The well-to-do classes are relatively free from preventable, disease-producing conditions of work and of living. It is questionable whether, in the long run, the well-to-do classes, who own the tenements, the mines, and the factories, are really adding to their profits by resisting sanitary improvements, and by refusing, whenever possible to remedy conditions which undermine the health and increase the death rate of the working people. To put it upon this criminally low commercial basis, even that is questionable. An increase of population is profitable to the owners of tenements; they see this very clearly when they support, as some of them do, unrestricted immigration. A large immigration means an increasing demand for tenements; but so does a decreased death rate. And yet, for the sake of profits, they often support unrestricted immigration and oppose measures for decreasing the death rate. The cost of sickness, now a loss to both landlord and tenant, might go toward an increased rental for a more sanitary tenement. The financial burden of sickness is considerable even among well-to-do people. The workmen, with their smaller purses, must bear far heavier burdens. But the loss to the world of productive laborers, and the financial loss by sickness, are after all as nothing compared to the crime of unnecessarily and unconcernedly adding to the number of widows and to the number of the fatherless.

The entire matter sums itself up very easily. In the first place, we put property before human life; we unconsciously estimate it more highly and foster it more tenderly; we do it as individuals and we do it collectively. The railroads consider the Block System of signals and automatic couplers unwarranted luxuries because profits are valued more than the lives of the workmen. "The sanitary improvements which this law forces on us will ruin us," the landlords and manufacturers say, when a law is proposed to remedy the insanitary conditions of home and workshop. They will not, of course. Such laws never have, although many of the most important sanitary measures of the last hundred years have been opposed on these grounds. But suppose they did? Must we then withdraw our sanitary measure and continue to sacrifice certain human beings in order that other human beings may make profits? A few years ago I urged that a certain tenement be destroyed because it was vile and insanitary and caused about eight unnecessary deaths every year. An officer answered my complaint in these words: "To demolish this tenement would do a great injury to the widow woman who owns it. It is her only property." Now murder is murder—whether the killing is done by a tenement or carbolic acid, whether in hatred and revenge or in cold blood, for a certain price or for profits, for the benefit of a rich man's purse or for the last crust which a widow may ever hope to have. As I understand it, THOU SHALT NOT KILL admits of no exceptions. It applies to the man who makes profits by the killing as truly as it applies to the hold-up man.

This evil, as indeed most evils, is rooted in the old, old sins and in the old, old crimes. They are merely in new guises. Murder, Adultery, and Thievery have so

---

Robert Hunter, *Poverty* (New York: Macmillan, 1907), 183–187.

disguised themselves that we do not recognize them. No one can help knowing that sickness is caused by vile tenements, by dangerous employments and insanitary workshops; every one must know also that much poverty and misery inevitably result from unnecessary sickness; furthermore, no one can fail to know that an excessive number of deaths occur among the work-people employed in certain industries and living in certain tenements. The cause and effect are clear. Then why does not the owner or employer remedy the cause of the sickness, poverty, and death? "He probably does not know it exists," is the ordinary answer. But it is no answer. Attempt to remedy the evils by legislation, or by enforcement of the laws, and then you begin to realize that you are in a fight, and that, for one reason or another, the landlords and employers are against you. Every movement you make is watched and attacked. Even bribery will be used to defeat sanitary measures; that is to say, measures to save life. Now the conclusion one is forced to draw from an experience of that sort is not a pleasant one, but the logic by which one reaches the conclusion seems clear and certain. These men are murderers.

Mr. Jacob A. Riis says, "You can kill a man with a tenement as easily as you can kill a man with an axe." But in the one case there is no concern. The newspapers do not mention the murder and no one is indicted or sent to prison. In the other case the whole town is more than likely to be in a fever of excitement. By preventing legislation, or by using influence or bribes to prevent enforcement, a man may kill thousands of human beings and still be considered perfectly respectable; he may remain a member of the best uptown clubs, and free to go on repeating his crimes; but Heaven help the man who uses the axe! We are deceived by the use of new methods in killing. One is a social method for the sake of profits; the other the use of individual physical force. It would seem as if we had arrived at the point where a social act may be understood. Almost every important act to-day is a social act and the most important crimes are social crimes.

5. Baptist Clergyman Walter Rauschenbusch Seeks a Social Christianity, 1912

The chief purpose of the Christian Church in the past has been the salvation of individuals. But the most pressing task of the present is not individualistic. Our business is to make over an antiquated and immoral economic system; to get rid of laws, customs, maxims, and philosophies inherited from an evil and despotic past; to create just and brotherly relations between great groups and classes of society; and thus to lay a social foundation on which modern men individually can live and work in a fashion that will not outrage all the better elements in them. Our inherited Christian faith dealt with individuals; our present task deals with society.

The Christian Church in the past has taught us to do our work with our eyes fixed on another world and a life to come. But the business before us is concerned with refashioning this present world, making this earth clean and sweet and habitable. . . .

Walter Rauschenbusch, *Christianizing The Social Order* (New York: Macmillan, 1921), 41–44.

Twenty-five years ago the social wealth of the Bible was almost undiscovered to most of us. We used to plow it six inches deep for crops and never dreamed that mines of anthracite were hidden down below. Even Jesus talked like an individualist in those days and seemed to repudiate the social interest when we interrogated him. He said his kingdom was not of this world; the things of God had nothing to do with the things of Caesar; the poor we would always have with us; and his ministers must not be judges and dividers when Labor argued with Capital about the division of the inheritance. To-day he has resumed the spiritual leadership of social Christianity, of which he was the founder. It is a new tribute to his mastership that the social message of Jesus was the first great possession which social Christianity rediscovered. . . .

With true Christian instinct men have turned to the Christian law of love as the key to the situation. If we all loved our neighbor, we should "treat him right," pay him a living wage, give sixteen ounces to the pound, and not charge so much for beef. But this appeal assumes that we are still living in the simple personal relations of the good old times, and that every man can do the right thing when he wants to do it. But suppose a business man would be glad indeed to pay his young women the $12 a week which they need for a decent living, but all his competitors are paying from $7 down to $5. Shall he love himself into bankruptcy? In a time of industrial depression shall he employ men whom he does not need? And if he does, will his five loaves feed the five thousand unemployed that break his heart with their hungry eyes? If a man owns a hundred shares of stock in a great corporation, how can his love influence its wage scale with that puny stick? The old advice of love breaks down before the hugeness of modern relations. We might as well try to start a stranded ocean liner with the oar which poled our old dory from the mud banks many a time. It is indeed love that we want, but it is socialized love. Blessed be the love that holds the cup of water to thirsty lips. We can never do without the plain affection of man to man. But what we most need today is not the love that will break its back drawing water for a growing factory town from a well that was meant to supply a village, but a love so large and intelligent that it will persuade an ignorant people to build a system of waterworks up in the hills, and that will get after the thoughtless farmers who contaminate the brooks with typhoid bacilli, and after the lumber concern that is denuding the watershed of its forests. We want a new avatar of love.

6. Two Suffrage Cartoons

· "The Corn or the Cob—Which?" 1911

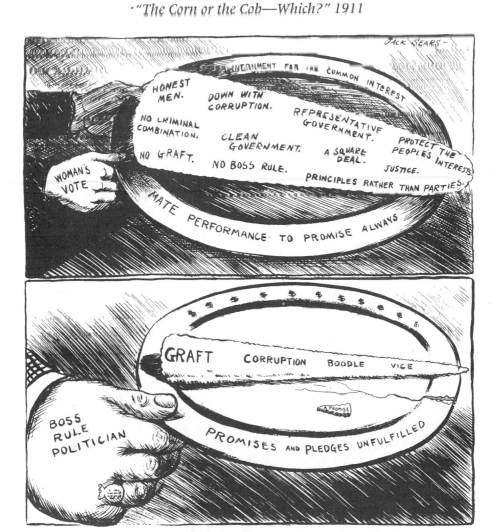

As evidenced in these two cartoons, to what traditional American political and family values did advocates of women's suffrage appeal?

Jack Sears cartoon from *Women Voter,* November 1911. Reprinted in Alice Sheppard, *Cartooning for Suffrage* (Albuquerque: University of New Mexico Press, 1994), 135.

"Double the Power of the Home," 1915

Blanche Ames cartoon from *Woman's Journal,* October 23, 1915. Reprinted in Alice Sheppard, *Cartooning for Suffrage* (Albuquerque: University of New Mexico Press, 1994), 135. Photo: The Schlesinger Library, Radcliffe Institute, Harvard University.

⛩ *E S S A Y S*

From different angles, the following two essays treat the ambivalence (and the inter nal differentiation) of progressive reform. In a sweeping review of progressive histo- riography, historian Richard L. McCormick of the University of Washington reclaims the social-justice side of progressive reformers from recent preoccupation with their coercive, social-control tendencies. In the second essay, along the same lines, Professor Robert Westbrook of Northwestern University, contrasts the ethics of Progressive Era documentary photographer Lewis Hine with those of his more manipulative, and socially condescending, contemporaries.

Evaluating the Progressives

RICHARD L. McCORMICK

Convulsive reform movements swept across the American landscape from the 1890s to 1917. Angry farmers demanded better prices for their products, regulation of the railroads, and the destruction of what they thought was the evil power of bankers, middlemen, and corrupt politicians. Urban residents crusaded for better city services, more efficient municipal government, and, sometimes, the control of social groups whose habits they hated and feared. Members of various professions, such as social workers and doctors, tried to improve the dangerous and unhealthy conditions in which many people lived and worked. Businessmen, too, lobbied in- cessantly for goals which they defined as reform. By around 1910, many of these crusading men and women were calling themselves progressives. Ever since, histo- rians have used the term "progressivism" to describe the reform movements of the early twentieth-century United States.

　　Yet many historians today are no longer very comfortable with the term. David P. Thelen, one of the best scholars working in the field of early twentieth-century reform, recently observed that "progressivism seems basically to have disappeared from historiographical and political discussion." Thelen perhaps exaggerated the point, but this much, at least, is true: there is a malaise among historians about the concept of progressivism and a growing urge to avoid the word itself whenever possible.

　　Three causes account for this situation. For one, the terms "progressive" and "progressivism" commonly have been invoked in a casual way to denote people and changes that are "good" or "enlightened" or "farsighted." These are the connotations which the progressives themselves gave to the words. Historians, being naturally wary of such value-laden terms, tend to seek a more neutral language that is better suited to impartial analysis. Such disinclination to use the word "progressivism" has been strengthened by the now-common judgment that early twentieth-century re- form was not entirely good or enlightened or farsighted.

　　Second, the malaise about progressivism reflects a general discouragement with the liberal reform tradition in American history. I refer not simply to the nation's current political conservatism (for relatively few professional historians share the new mood) but more generally to a widespread sense, both within and without academe, that liberalism historically has been characterized by both insincerity and failure. These are the dual criticisms most frequently leveled against the Great Society programs of the 1960s. They were not genuinely intended to uplift the disadvantaged, but rather to assuage guilty liberal consciences. And the devices upon which they relied, namely, expensive governmental bureaucracies, proved conspicuously unequal to the problems at hand.

The same two complaints, of insincerity and failure, underlie most of the contemporary criticism of the early twentieth-century liberals who called themselves progressives. They are said to have used democratic rhetoric only as a cloak for elitist purposes. And they are berated for placing too much confidence in scientific methods and administrative techniques that turned out to possess few of the magical powers which the reformers attributed to them. Almost every major political figure of the era is said to have supported remedies that were grossly inadequate to the observed problems.

Often these two criticisms are conjoined in the notion that the progressives never intended their reforms to succeed, only to appear successful. Thus Richard Hofstadter explained the progressives' attraction to "ceremonial," rather than far-reaching, solutions by observing the reformers' own deep need to feel better about American society and their own status within it. Other historians, including Gabriel Kolko and James Weinstein, have suggested that even more consciously selfish motives—specifically the drive of business elites to turn government to their own ends—lay behind the failure of progressivism to solve the problems of industrial society.

These alleged evils of progressivism—its dishonest rhetoric and its inadequate methods—bring us to an attribute of liberalism that goes a long way toward explaining the sour reputation it has today. Liberals frequently excel in recognizing—indeed, in dramatizing—the social and economic conflicts of American society, but they quickly cover up those conflicts by declaring them solved through expertise and government. The progressives of the early 1900s did this. Conservatives are at least consistent in affirming that capitalism produces a fundamental "harmony of interests," while radicals, for their part, consider social conflict unremitting and unsolvable, save through revolution. But liberals often seem (and seemed) to occupy the foolish, middle position of alternately recognizing and denying the existence of basic social and economic divisions. I call attention to this pattern because it strikes me as essential to understanding why so many of today's historians appear to have lost respect for progressivism and to avoid the term whenever they can.

The third reason why contemporary historians are dissatisfied with the concept of progressivism is the awful complexity and diversity of early twentieth-century reform. Nothing illustrates this better than the long-standing historiographical debate over the progressives' identity that flourished during the 1950s and 1960s. Farmers, businessmen, professionals, old middle classes, and immigrants all were named by one scholar or another as the key progressives. The historians offering these diverse interpretations were not content with carving out niches within the reform movement for the groups they studied. Rather they tended to claim, at least implicitly, that "their" key progressives placed a distinctive stamp on early twentieth-century reform and to define progressivism narrowly enough to substantiate that claim. We learned a great deal from these studies about how different social and economic groups experienced and responded to the problems of the early 1900s. But obviously all the historians debating the identity question cannot have been right about what progressivism was. For while many groups had a hand in it, none exclusively shaped it.

Of all the answers to the question of who the progressives were, one has exerted an especially pronounced influence upon the field: the so-called "organizational" interpretation. Led by Samuel P. Hays and Robert H. Wiebe, a number of scholars have located the progressive impulse in the drive of newly formed business and professional groups to achieve their goals through cooperation and expertise. Other groups then copied the organizers, whose bureaucratic methods gave progressivism its distinctive character.

Yet while it has influenced dozens of scholars, the organizational model is too limited to encompass much that we know about early twentieth-century reform. Hays's and Wiebe's organized, expert progressives seem too bland, too passionless, and too self-confident to have waged the frantic battles many reformers did. Their interpretations particularly err in downplaying the dramatic events that punctuated the chronology of progressivism, aroused ordinary people, and gave reform its shape and timing: a sensational muckraking article, an amazing political scandal, or a tragic social calamity. Without taking into account how the masses of Americans perceived and responded to such occurrences, progressivism cannot be understood.

More than ten years ago, Peter G. Filene and John D. Buenker published articles recognizing the progressives' diversity and suggesting ways to reorient historical scholarship on the subject. Filene proposed the more drastic response to the complexity of progressivism: abandon the concept of a progressive movement. It had no unity, either of supporters, or purposes, or ideas. Indeed, it "displays a puzzling and irreducible incoherence." Like Filene, Buenker denied there was a unified progressive movement, but he was more optimistic about the meaningfulness of progressivism. Divergent groups, Buenker suggested, came together on one issue and changed alliances on the next. Often, he observed, reformers favored the same measure for different, even opposing, reasons. Only by looking at each reform and the distinctive coalition behind it could progressivism be understood.

Here were two shrewd proposals for coping with the baffling diversity of early twentieth-century reform. Both have been heeded. Filene's pessimism stirred many scholars to abandon the term *progressivism* altogether. Buenker's call for research on individual reforms helped inspire an outpouring of monographic work on discrete aspects of progressivism. Their two responses offer a classic case of the historical profession's effort to cope with the numbing complexity of the past: give up the game or restore coherence through infinite particularizing.

Neither response will do. We cannot avoid the concept of progressivism—or even a progressive movement—because, particularly after 1910, the terms were deeply embedded in the language of reformers and because they considered the words meaningful. We cannot go on merely particularizing because (however valuable many recent monographs have been) it is important to appreciate and understand progressivism as a whole. The "whole" will scarcely turn out to have been unified or simple, but it is unlikely to have been either incoherent or utterly beyond comprehension. The renewed acceptance of the concept of progressivism may have the added benefit of enabling us to regain respect for the reformers—to see why their rhetoric and their true goals sometimes clashed; to understand why they sometimes failed to achieve their purposes: and to grasp how they, like liberals ever since, often were confused over whether the United States was, in the final analysis, a harmonious society or a divided one.

Two lines of analysis seem to me useful in achieving such an understanding of progressivism. The first is to identify the basic characteristics that were common, in varying measure, to many (and probably most) progressive reforms. No one list of progressive characteristics will satisfy every historian, but I think we know enough for a tentative enumeration. The second way to proceed is by distinguishing with care the goals of reform, the reasons publicly given for it, and the actual results. Purposes, rationale, and results are three different things, and the unexamined identification of any one with another is invalid.

Progressivism was characterized, first of all, by a distinctive set of attitudes toward industrialism. By the early 1900s, most Americans seem reluctantly to have accepted the permanence of big business. The progressives shared this attitude. They undertook reforms not to dismantle modern industry and commerce but rather to improve and ameliorate the conditions of industrial life. Yet progressivism was infused with a deep, lingering outrage against many of the worst consequences of industrialism. Outpourings of anger and dismay about corporation wrongdoing and of suspicion for industrial values frequently punctuated the course of reform. Both the acceptance of industrialism and the anger against it were intrinsic to progressivism. This does not mean that the movement was mindless or that it must be considered indefinable. What it suggests is that a powerful irony lay at the heart of progressivism: reforms that gained vitality from a people angry with industrialism ended up by assisting them to accommodate to it.

These ameliorative reforms were distinguished, secondly, by a basic optimism about people's ability to improve their environment through continuous human action. Those hurt by industrialization could be protected and their surroundings made more humane. Progressive intellectuals, as well as popularizers, produced a vast literature denouncing *laissez-faire* and affirming the capacity of men and women to better their conditions. Even reformers with little interest in philosophical questions absorbed the era's optimism and environmentalism. Their reforms reflected this habit of mind.

Improving the environment meant, above all, intervening in people's economic and social affairs to channel natural forces and give them order. This attribute of interventionism, of regulation, and even of coercion, constitutes a third essential characteristic of progressivism, visible in almost every reform of the early 1900s. Intervention could be accomplished through both private and public means. Given a choice, most progressives preferred to work through voluntary associations for non-coercive improvements in economic and social conditions. As time passed, however, more and more of their reforms relied on the hand of government.

Progressive reforms may, then, be characterized as interventions in the environment intended to improve the conditions of industrial life. But such a description says little about the ideals behind progressivism or about its distinctive methods.

These must make up part of any account of the character of early twentieth-century reform. Progressivism took its inspiration, as well as much of its substance and technique, from two bodies of belief and knowledge: evangelical Protestantism and the sciences, both natural and social. Each imparted distinctive qualities to the reforms of the age.

Progressivism visibly bore the imprint of the evangelical ethos. Basic to this mentality was the drive to purge the world of sin—such as the sins of slavery and intemperance, against which nineteenth-century reformers had crusaded. Now the progressives carried the struggle into the modern citadels of sin, the teeming industrial cities of the nation. No one can read their moralistic appeals without realizing how deeply many of them felt a Christian duty to right the wrongs that sprang from industrialism. The reforms that followed from such appeals could be generous in spirit, but they also could be intolerant. Some progressive reforms were frankly intended to perpetuate a Protestant social order. Not every progressive shared the evangelical ethos, much less its intolerance, but few of the era's reforms were untouched by the spirit and the techniques of Protestant revivalism.

Science, too, had a pervasive influence on the contents and methods of progressivism. Many of the leading reformers considered themselves social scientists— that is, members of the newer disciplines of economics, sociology, statistics, and psychology that came into being between 1880 and 1910. Sharing the environmentalist and interventionist assumptions of the day, they believed that rational measures could be devised and applied to improve the human condition. Their methods inspired elements common to nearly every reform of the age: the investigation of facts, the application of social-science knowledge, the entrusting of trained experts to decide what should be done, and the authorization of governmental officials to take the steps that science suggested.

Dispassionate as these methods sound, they actually were compatible with the moralizing tendencies within progressivism. In its earliest days, American social science was infused by ethical concerns. An essential purpose of economics, sociology, and psychology was to improve and uplift people's lives. Progressives blended science and religion into a view of human behavior that was unique to their generation of Americans: people who had grown up in an age of revivals and come to maturity at the birth of social science.

Finally, progressivism was the first (perhaps the only) reform movement to be experienced by the whole American nation. Widely circulated magazines gave people everywhere the shameful facts of corruption and carried the clamor for reform into every town and city of the country. Almost no one in the United States in, say, 1906 could have been unaware that ten-year-old children worked through the night in dangerous factories or that many United States senators served the big business corporations. Progressivism's national reach and mass base vastly exceeded that of Jacksonian reform several generations before. And its dependence on the people for its shape and timing has no comparison in the later executive-dominated New Deal and Great Society. Wars and depressions had previously engaged the whole nation's attention, but never reform.

These half-dozen attributes of progressivism go a long way toward defining the movement as a whole, but they do not tell us much about who was doing what to whom or about what the reforms accomplished. Most progressive crusades shared in the methods and assumptions enumerated above, but they did so in different measure and with different emphases. Some reflected greater acceptance of industrialism, while others expressed more of the outrage against it. Some intervened to improve the environment through private means; others depended on government. Each reform struck a distinctive balance between the claims of Protestant moralism and scientific rationalism.

To move beyond what are essentially a series of continuums along which diverse reforms ranged, we must distinguish goals from rhetoric from results. This is a more difficult task than might be supposed. Older interpretations of progressivism implicitly assumed that the rhetoric explained the goals and that if a reform became law the results fulfilled the intentions behind it. Neither assumption is a good one. Writing in 1964, Samuel P. Hays shrewdly exposed the fallacy of equating the reformers' democratic language with their true purposes. The two may have coincided, but the historian has to show that, not take it for granted. The automatic identification of either intentions or rhetoric with results is also invalid, although it is still a common feature of scholarship on progressivism. Only within the last decade or so have historians begun to examine with care the actual achievements of the reformers. To do so is to observe the ironies, complexities, and disappointments that accompanied progressivism. For the reformers by no means always got what they wanted, or what they said they wanted.

If the two lines of analysis sketched out here were systematically applied to early twentieth-century reform, our comprehension of—and possibly our respect for—progressivism would be substantially enhanced. The existing research and scholarship do not permit that; nor, if they did, is my space here sufficient for it. Instead of being systematic, the following pages are illustrative, taking up, in turn, political reform and social reform. The end in view remains a better understanding of American liberalism and its limits.

Shortly after 1900 many of the basic elements of American politics and government were transformed. New patterns of political participation emerged, while the structure and tasks of government changed, too. Ever since the Jackson period, casting party ballots on election day had formed by far the most important means of political expression and involvement. Sectional, cultural, and historical influences all had contributed to shaping men's party loyalties, and to judge from the available evidence most of them took those loyalties seriously indeed. Only under unusual circumstances did ordinary people turn away from their parties and seek other means of influencing the government, although it is worth observing that nonelectoral methods were the *only* possible avenues of political expression for all women and many blacks. Prior to 1900, however, those nonelectoral avenues were difficult to travel and commonly led to failure.

Beginning in the early twentieth century this older structure of political participation gave way to new patterns. Voter turnout fell, ticket-splitting rose and relatively fewer voters could be counted upon to support the regular party candidates year after year. In the same period, a great variety of interest groups successfully pioneered new ways of influencing the government and its agencies. By organizing their members, raising money, hiring lobbyists, pressuring officials, and inundating the public with their propaganda, the strongest of these groups managed to compel the government to attend to their demands—not just on election day but whenever their interests were vitally affected.

During the same years, the nature and functions of American government also saw significant changes. To a degree unprecedented in the nineteenth century, public officials became widely involved in monitoring and regulating how people lived and worked. In consequence, both the institutions of government and the content of public policy were decisively altered. Legislatures, which had dominated nineteenth-century governments in both the states and the nation, now lost power to increasingly strong executives and, even more importantly, to the recently created boards and agencies that made up a virtually new branch of government. These new agencies, moreover, carried out policies of a sort only rarely seen before. Where nineteenth-century governmental action had mainly concerned discrete groups and locales (to which governments distributed resources and privileges), public authorities now began to recognize and deal with clashing interests throughout the whole society. In-consistently at first—but with increasing determination—American governments assumed the responsibility for mitigating social conflicts by taking on such pre-viously neglected functions as regulation, administration, and even planning.

These political and governmental changes were important in themselves, quite apart from what they tell us about progressivism. One might, indeed, be tempted to study them on their own terms, with only passing reference to an upsurge of re-form. The changes were, after all, products of those all-powerful, ubiquitous forces in modern American history: industrialization, urbanization, and immigration. His-torians accordingly have devoted much of their attention to tracing the twisted pathways leading from economic and social developments to the political and gov-ernmental responses. Without progressivism, however, the shape and timing and, above all, the results of the political transformation are impossible to understand.

For in light of the long-term social and economic forces involved, the new pat-terns of politics and government were established with remarkable speed. In 1900 they were just beginning to make their appearance, but by 1915 they were largely in place. During these years three historic barriers to political and governmental change were significantly weakened: the traditional American devotion to small government, the long-standing unwillingness to enact "class legislation" recog-nizing the competing needs of different groups, and the intense partisan loyalties of the nineteenth-century electorate. These barriers had largely held throughout the class warfare of the 1880s and the political turmoil of the 1890s. Now they gave way, under assault from a nationwide wave of resentment against bosses and businessmen.

The precipitating crisis came in the form of a series of revelations concerning politico-business corruption. During the two years following Theodore Roosevelt's reelection as president in 1904, while muckraking journalists were trumpeting the details of corruption to a nationwide magazine audience, a remarkable number of cities and states went through wrenching discoveries of how local businessmen bribed legislators, conspired with party leaders, and controlled nominations. . . .

In response, innumerable pent-up proposals for political and governmental reform were enacted. Commonly the progressives presented their plans in moralis-tic, democratic language, but often the true purposes of many reformers were more complicated. Often, as well, the actual results of reform surprised some of its proponents. On the whole, the anti-boss, anti-business forces that had inspired the outcries of 1905–06 found it difficult to keep control of the complex political developments that followed.

Many new laws redefined the eligible electorate by excluding certain people from voting and including others. Even electors whose eligibility remained unchanged found that the new laws had altered the rules, and even the purposes, of voting. The progressives defended these reforms—together with related measures of direct democracy, including the initiative, referendum, and recall—as efforts to curtail corruption, weaken party bosses, and restore power to ordinary people. But nearly every election-law reform contained fundamental ambiguities, and most brought results that amazed some of their advocates.

A series of laws directed against the party machines provides a case in point. During the years after 1906, most states enacted the direct primary, placing party nominations in the hands of party voters themselves. In practice, this reform eliminated the most blatant abuses of the machine's control over convention nominations, but it left the party leaders substantially in charge of selecting candidates because voter turnout in primary elections tended to be so low. Other progressive measures established stringent governmental regulation of the parties, but in so doing they embedded parties more firmly in the legal machinery of the elections than they had ever been before. In the cities, antimachine elites supported structural reforms, such as commission government, in order to take power from local politicians. But the commissions frequently succumbed to shrewd bosses who learned the new rules of politics. Commission government became the very basis of Frank Hague's rule of Jersey City for three decades.

Governmental policies of economic regulation also were enacted in the aftermath of the exposures of politico-business corruption. Many states established railroad commissions for the first time, while others strengthened their existing boards. Other industries, too, came under effective supervision, not just from state governments but also from the cities and the nation. Yet considerable irony attended the regulatory laws of the early 1900s. Brought forth amidst progressive cries for restraining corrupt corporations and protecting consumers, the new measures usually were opposed by the businesses to be supervised. When it came to shaping the details of regulation, plural, competing interests took a hand in the process and maneuvered to obtain favorable treatment in the law. In actual practice, the regulated corporations often found benefits in the legislation they had initially opposed, although this was not always the case. Perhaps the most significant result of the regulatory revolution of the Progressive era was one that few had expected: the shifting of economic policymaking from the noisy legislative halls to the quiet offices of little-known administrators. There organized interests found a congenial environment for doing their business with the government.

By the end of the Progressive era, the political and governmental system of the United States looked very different than it had in the late nineteenth century. Political parties had been regulated, and the active electorate had become relatively smaller and less enthusiastic. Interest groups had taken over many of the parties' old functions and achieved recognition as legitimate agencies for influencing the now-expanded government. The legislature was less important than before, and the executive more powerful, but many of the government's new roles fell to independent administrative agencies which performed their tasks of investigation and adjustment well outside the public's eye. These changes were not revolutionary, but considering how stable American politics have commonly been (compared, say, with those of Europe) they were changes of great importance.

It would be hard to say whether the new system was more or less democratic than the old one. Voting had become more difficult for many (especially blacks and new immigrants), but for others new avenues of political participation had opened up. The recently created agencies of administrative government often bent to the will of the rich, but so had legislative government in the nineteenth century. Probably we will never have a fully satisfactory answer to the question of whether early twentieth-century American politics became more "progressive" in the casual sense of the word. We can be certain, however, that no one could have anticipated the actual results of political and governmental reform—not the ordinary people whose resentment of bosses and businessmen gave the era its vitality, nor their enemies either.

Progressive social reform, like economic regulation, was based on the recognition of group conflict and on a willingness to intervene in people's lives to mitigate disharmony. Some reformers, inspired by evangelical Protestantism, acted on the basis of a heartfelt desire to alleviate suffering and bring justice. Others sought the professional prestige that went with providing scientific solutions for social problems. Still others craved the power and satisfaction that came to those who imposed what they considered right forms of behavior on the masses. Few of them failed to employ the moralistic rhetoric of altruism; fewer still neglected the needs of their own group or class in determining how to act.

What distinguished the progressive reformers of the early 1900s was their conviction that men and women were social creatures. People who lived in large cities, where social contacts and conflicts were unrelenting, had little choice but to accept their dependence on each other and seek common solutions to problems. Doctors learned that venereal disease and tuberculosis were indices of social conditions; curing them meant stamping out prostitution and eradicating the insanitary conditions that accompanied poverty. Policemen and lawyers saw that crime was most prevalent in certain social circumstances; stopping it depended on improving the environment and rehabilitating the criminal. Many progressives blamed social ills on the habits and practices of the southern and eastern European immigrants who were crowding into the United States; reform thus meant restricting immigration, prohibiting the use of alcoholic beverages, and encouraging the Anglo-Saxon way of life. It might even necessitate preventing unfit people from having children. Whatever changes they advocated, progressives tended to recognize the need for solutions that were citywide, statewide, or even nationwide in scope. Whether tolerant or culturally imperialistic, they saw that everybody was bound up in a common social system. It mattered to everyone how employers treated their employees. It even mattered who was having sexual intercourse with whom.

As the foregoing examples suggest, the progressives sought reforms that would accomplish at least two analytically distinct goals: the establishment of social justice and the imposition of social control. Many reformers focused their efforts on improving the lives of exploited industrial workers and impoverished city dwellers. The progressive campaigns for the abolition of child labor, shorter hours of work and better wages for women, industrial safety and workmen's compensation, improved housing conditions, and the alleviation of poverty were among the leading reforms of this sort. The settlement-house movement was perhaps the most characteristic progressive endeavor for social justice, and Jane Addams of Hull House was the ideal reformer. Traditional scholarship placed predominant emphasis on these progressive campaigns for social justice.

Recent historical writing makes clear that this is too restricted a view. Numerous social reforms of the early twentieth century expressed the progressives' desire to impose uniform living habits on a culturally diverse population whose behavior sometimes seemed to threaten the morality and health of the community. The campaigns for immigration restriction, racial segregation, sterilization of the mentally defective, and mandatory school attendance demonstrated the reformers' passion for social control. The prohibition of alcoholic beverages was perhaps the prototypical reform of this type.

Weighing the relative gains made by progressives for social justice and social control is a significant problem in historical interpretation. But it is equally important to recognize that most reforms and reformers expressed both goals. There was scarcely any social change that was not advocated, often sincerely, as a means of bringing justice. Yet, in practice, almost every progressive reform gave added control to those who implemented it. . . .

Justice and control scarcely meant the same things to all progressives. The settlement-house workers, the reforming professionals, and the advocates of such coercive measures as immigration restriction and racial segregation each gave distinctive interpretations to these goals and placed different emphases upon them. Some progressive controls entailed relatively benign environmental constraints; others mandated recognized "experts" to set standards of behavior within the areas of their supposed competence; still other social controls were frankly racist and repressive.

Whatever meaning they gave to justice and control and whatever balance they struck (or failed to strike) between them, most social progressives adopted roughly similar methods. In time a pattern of social reform became familiar, variations of which were followed by progressives in almost every area. They typically began by organizing a voluntary association, investigating a problem, gathering mounds of relevant social data, and analyzing it according to the precepts of one of the newer social sciences. From such an analysis, a proposed solution would emerge, be popularized through campaigns of education and moral suasion, and—as often as not, if it seemed to work—be taken over by some level of government as a permanent public function. Usually the details of the law were worked out through bargaining among the competing groups interested in the measure.

Certain assumptions guided those who adopted this approach to reform. One concerned the utility of social science in fostering harmony. Progressives knew full well that different groups in American society had competing interests, and they recognized that conflicting social elements often hurt one another. They were not deluded by a belief in a natural harmony of interests. Yet the social sciences, based as they were on a vision of human interdependence, offered the possibility for devising reforms that regulated and harmonized antagonistic social groups. If the facts were gathered and properly understood, solutions could be found that genuinely benefited everyone. Individual reforms might assist one group against another, but a carefully crafted program of reforms would establish a more perfect harmony of interests than ever appeared in nature.

A related progressive assumption held that government could be trusted to carry out broad social reforms. In social policy, just as in the economic area, nineteenth-century American governments had tended to produce haphazard legislative decisions, each having little connection to the next. What Gerald N. Grob has called "clear policy formation and social planning" were largely absent. Most social progressives did not initially set out to expand the limited scope of government. They placed their confidence first in private organization. As time passed, however, the reformers increasingly looked to public agencies to carry out their programs.

Having methods that were largely untried and assumptions that often approximated mere articles of faith, the progressives not surprisingly failed to achieve many of their social purposes. Often they succeeded, however, and their basic approach to social problems has not yet been repudiated in the United States. The foregoing discussion of progressivism has frequently pointed to the differences between the rhetoric, intentions, and results of reform. In every area there were wide gaps between what the progressives said they were doing, what they actually wanted to do, and what they accomplished. It is important to deal explicitly with the reasons for these seeming inconsistencies and to reflect on what they tell us about progressivism.

The failure of reform to fulfill all of the expectations behind it was not, of course, unique to the Progressive era. Jacksonian reform, Reconstruction, and the New Deal all exhibited ironies and disappointments. In each case, the clash between reformers having divergent purposes, the inability to predict how given methods of reform would work in practice, and the ultimate waning of popular zeal for change all contributed to the disjuncture of rationale, purpose, and achievement. Yet the gap between these things seems more noticeable in the Progressive era. So many movements for reform took place in a relatively brief span of time, accompanied by such resounding rhetoric and by such high expectations for improving the American social and political environment. The effort to change so many things at once and the grandiose claims made for the moral and material betterment that would result meant that disappointments were bound to occur.

Yet even the great number of reforms and the uncommonly high expectations behind them cannot fully account for the consistent gaps between the stated purposes, real intentions, and actual results of progressivism. Several additional factors, intrinsic to the nature of early twentieth-century reform, help explain the ironies and contradictions. One of these factors was the progressives' confident reliance on modern methods of reform. Heirs of recent advances in science and social science, they enthusiastically crafted and applied new techniques for improving American government and society. Often their methods worked, but often progressive programs simply did not prove capable of accomplishing what had been expected of them. This was not necessarily the reformers' fault. Making hopeful use of untried methods, they nonetheless lacked a science of society that was equal to all the great problems they perceived. Worse, the progressives' scientific reforms frequently involved the collection of data, making it possible to know just how far short of success their programs sometimes fell. The evidence of their failures was thus more visible than in any previous era of reform. To the progressives' credit, they usually published that evidence—for contemporaries and historians alike to see.

A second aspect of early twentieth-century reform that helps to account for the gaps between aims and achievements was the progressives' deep ambivalence about industrialism and its consequences. Individual reformers were divided, and so was their movement as a whole. Compared with many reformers of the late 1800s, the progressives fundamentally accepted an industrial society and sought mainly to order and ameliorate it. Even reformers who were intellectually committed to socialist doctrines often acted the part of reformers, not radicals. Yet progressivism was infused and vitalized by people truly angry with an industrial society and its conditions. Few of them wished to tear down the modern institutions of business and commerce, but their anger was real, their moralism genuine, and their passions essential to the era's reforms. Progressivism went forward because of their fervor.

Unfortunately, the reform movement never surmounted this ambivalence about industrialism. Much of its rhetoric and popular passion pointed in one direction, while its leaders and their programs went in another. Often the result was confusion and bitterness. Reforms frequently did not measure up to the popular, anti-business expectations for them—and, indeed, never were expected to measure up by those who designed and implemented them.

Perhaps of most significance, progressivism failed to achieve all its goals because, despite their real efforts to do so, the reformers never fully came to terms with the divisions and conflicts in American society. Again and again, they acknowledged the existence of social disharmony more fully and frankly than had nineteenth-century Americans. Nearly every reform of the era was predicated on the progressives' recognition that diverse cultural and occupational groups had conflicting interests and that the responsibility for mitigating and adjusting those differences lay with the whole society, usually the government. Such recognition formed one of the progressives' greatest achievements. Indeed, it stands as one of the most important accomplishments of liberal reform in all of American history. For by accepting social disharmony, the progressives committed the twentieth-century United States to recognizing—and dealing with—the inevitable conflicts within a heterogeneous, industrial society.

Yet significant as it was, the progressives' recognition of diversity was clouded by the methods and institutions they adopted for coping with conflict. Through scientific data-gathering and analysis, they believed that impartial programs could be devised that genuinely benefited every interest. And through expert, administrative government, those programs could be carried out in fairness to all. But science and administration turned out to be less neutral than the progressives expected. No scientific reform could be any more impartial than the experts who gathered the data or than the bureaucrats who implemented the program. In practice, administrative government often succumbed to the admonition of special interests.

It would be pointless to blame the reformers for the failure of their new methods and agencies to eliminate the divisions within an industrial society. But it is perhaps fair to ask why the progressives adopted measures which tended to disguise and obscure social conflict almost as soon as they had uncovered it. For one thing, they honestly believed in the almost unlimited potential of science and administration. Our late twentieth-century skepticism of these wonders should not blind us to the sincerity with which the progressives embraced them and imbued them with what now seem magical properties. For another, most progressives were reformers, not radicals. It was one thing to recognize social conflict, but quite another to admit that it was permanent. By and large these men and women were personally and ideologically inclined to believe that America was fundamentally a harmonious society and that such conflicts as existed could be resolved. Finally, the leading progressives' own class and cultural backgrounds often made them insensitive to lower-class immigrant Americans and their cultures. Reducing social divisions sometimes came down to imposing middle-class Protestant ways. Together these factors diminished whatever chance the progressives may have had of eliminating social conflict. Seeing the problem more fully than had their predecessors, the reformers of the early twentieth century nonetheless tended to consider conflicts resolved when, in fact, they had only been disguised by the establishment of scientific policies and the creation of governmental agencies.

Thus progressivism fell short of its rhetoric and intentions. Lest that seem an unfairly critical evaluation, it is important to recall how terribly ambitious were the reformers' stated aims and true goals. They missed some of their marks because they sought to do so much. And despite the shortcomings, they accomplished an enormous part of what they intended to achieve.

The problems with which the progressives struggled have, by and large, occupied Americans ever since. And although the assumptions and techniques of progressivism no longer command the confidence which early twentieth-century Americans placed in them, no equally comprehensive body of reforms has ever been adopted in their place. I have criticized the progressives for having too much faith in their untried methods. Yet if this was a failing, it was also a source of strength, now missing from reform in America. For the essence of progressivism lay in the hopefulness and optimism the reformers brought to the tasks of applying science and administration to the high moral purposes in which they believed. The historical record of their aims and achievements leaves no doubt that in the United States in the early 1900s there lived people who were not afraid to confront the problems of a modern industrial society with vigor and imagination. They of course failed to solve all those problems, but no other generation of Americans has done conspicuously better with the political and social conditions it faced.

Lewis Hine and the Two Faces of Progressive Photography

ROBERT WESTBROOK

No one contributed more to the iconography of American industrialization than Lewis Hine; yet Hine died a penniless and unappreciated artist. Even today, despite the widespread familiarity of his photographs, few people are much aware of who Lewis Hine was or of the ways in which his work reflected a consistent moral vision

Robert Westbrook, "Lewis Hine and the Ethics of Progressive Camerawork," *Tikkun* 2 (April/May 1987), 24–29. Reprinted with permission of Tikkun Magazine, a bimonthly Jewish critique of politics, culture, and society based in Oakland, Calif.

and engaged some of the central ethical and political issues posed by progressive reform in the United States between 1890 and 1940. In order to grasp the full significance and power of Hine's photographs, they must be seen not only as evidence documenting the lives of those who populate his images but also as important texts in the cultural history of progressivism, less because they reflect the beliefs Hine shared with those in the mainstream of American reform than because they pose a challenge to the benevolent posture at the heart of progressive ideology.

I

In some important respects, Lewis Hine was a *typical* progressive reformer in that he was committed to what historian Richard Hofstadter termed the "business of exposure." Before I turn to an effort to number Hine among those extraordinary progressives who were attuned to the ethical pitfalls of this business, it is perhaps worth recalling Hine's commitment to this widely shared progressive impulse.

Hine's reform credentials were, of course, impeccable. He began his career as a photographer during a brief stint as a teacher in the Ethical Culture School in New York City, an important center of educational experimentation. After abandoning the classroom for a full-time career as a photographer, he signed on as the photographer for Paul Kellogg's pathbreaking 1907 survey of social conditions in Pittsburgh and began his longtime affiliation with Kellogg's important reform journal, *Survey.* Around the same time, he began to accept the series of assignments from the national Child Labor Committee that over the next decade would provide the occasion for the photographs of working children that are his finest work. Although in the last decade of his life Hine was excluded from the remarkable photographic project of the Farm Security Administration, which set the standards for documentary expression in the 1930s, he did find some work with the Tennessee Valley Authority, the Works Progress Administration, and other New Deal agencies.

As a reform photographer, Hine shared with many other progressives a belief that his first task was that of providing his fellow citizens with a clear view of the sordid realities of American social life that had been obscured by ignorance and unconcern. As Hofstadter observed, reality for these men and women was:

> a series of unspeakable plots, personal iniquities, moral failures, which, in their totality, had come to govern American society only because the citizen had relaxed his moral diligence. The failures of American society were thus no token of the ultimate nature of man, of the human condition, much less the American condition; they were not to be accepted or merely modified, but fought with the utmost strenuosity at every point. First, reality must in its fullness be exposed, and then it must be made the subject of moral exhortation; and then, when individual citizens in sufficient numbers had stiffened in their determination to effect reform, something could be done.

For these men and women, progressive reform was a politics of revelation. Knowledge of the "inside story" of what American society was "really" like would activate the will of its citizenry to clean up its dirty, hitherto hidden corners.

Hine fully shared this commitment to the business of exposure and urged his fellow reformers to recognize the importance of the camera to their cause. In an important lecture to the National Conference of Charities and Correction in 1909 entitled "Social Photography: How the Camera May Help in the Social Uplift," he argued that "the great social peril is darkness and ignorance" and urged social workers to take their byword from Victor Hugo; "Light! Light in floods!" In the crucial task of opening the eyes of the "great public" the camera was an essential tool. "In this campaign for light," he declared, "we have as our advance agent the light writer   the photograph." The picture was a powerful symbol that "brings one immediately into close touch with reality," for it told "a story packed into the most condensed and vital form." Reformers should not hesitate to take advantage of the heightened realism of these pictures and play upon the widespread belief that "the photograph cannot falsify."

Hine's work for the National Child Labor Committee was a paradigm of the progressive business of exposure. As Alan Trachtenberg has observed, Hine opened to view workplaces that were "fast becoming secret and secretive places, buried in dark corners of tenements, hidden behind imposing brick walls of factories. . . . This secrecy, Hine learned, hid shameful sights . . . and he came to define his task as that of showing the world of consumers exactly what the world of makers was like. This task became a ripping aside of the veil that disguised and mystified the brutal system of production."

His work entailed as wide a range of humanitarian espionage as reform ideology recommended. Hine was called upon in many of his investigations to act as a progressive spy, passing himself off as a salesman or a photographer of machinery in order to infiltrate mills, fields, and sweatshops brutally exploiting children. Concealing a note pad in his pocket, he recorded the ages and sizes of the children he encountered, many of whom he measured against the buttons on his coat. Like any secret agent he worked under the constant threat of violence: "I have a number of times been very near getting what has been coming to me from those who do not agree with me on child labor matters."

II

The naive optimism of reformers like Hine has been an easy target of criticism, and such historians as Hofstadter have attacked progressives for their blind faith in the power of knowledge and the efficacy of good will. This is an important criticism, but it does not get at the most troubling feature of the progressive politics of exposure.

A more penetrating criticism is that advanced by historians who have found in progressive ideology a will to power that seeks to rescue the victims of industrialism from the depredations of evil capitalism only to subject them to the cultural hegemony of the reformers themselves. From this perspective, the overriding aim of the progressive in exposing the exploitation of the immigrant working class was to render these unfortunate people the object of paternal bourgeois benevolence. This, in effect, substituted one form of objectification for another. Critical of unscrupulous factory owners who treated immigrant workers merely as a factor of production, middle-class reformers sought to render them little more than passive beneficiaries of the solicitude and culture of their more fortunate neighbors. The language of middle-class benevolence often betrayed in its metaphors this sense of the "urban masses" as inert material upon which reformers might work their will. Addressing an audience of female social workers, for example, one reformer warned that the "Christian worker" who went among the "unchurched masses" must "root up weeds of false teaching, dig out rocks of ignorance and prejudice, break up the fallow ground, and be glad if it is given to her to drop a seed of divine truth here and there."

The critical perspective on this sort of farming for souls has produced an abundant historical literature that treats progressive reform as a species of "social control." This is an argument that is, in many instances, persuasive. What it often overlooks, however, is the presence among progressive reformers of several important figures who were well aware of the troubling ethical implications of paternal benevolence. Lewis Hine, I contend, was among these figures.

Before attempting to support this contention, it is worth considering briefly how this issue was treated in the work of the most important progressive critic of the paternalistic impulse, John Dewey. Although Dewey's own thought and activism,

Lewis Hine, "Young Russian Jewess at Ellis Island"

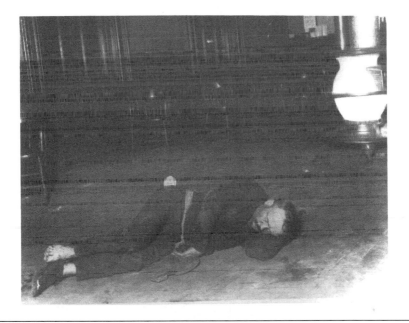

Jacob Riis, "Quarters for the Night"

Lewis Hine, "Boy Miner"

particularly his philosophy of education, has also been targeted (unpersuasively) by the critics of bourgeois hegemony, there is abundant evidence, from the earliest stages of his career forward, of Dewey's deep antipathy to "do-gooders" and to the objectification and antidemocratic consequences of paternalistic benevolence. To cite but one example of this, writing in his *Ethics* (1908), Dewey argued that "regard for the happiness of others means *regard for those conditions and objects which permit others freely to exercise their own powers from their own initiative, reflection, and choice.*" It was precisely in this regard that so many reformers were deficient:

> the vice of the social leader, of the reformer, of the philanthropist and the specialist in every worthy cause of science, or art, of politics, is to seek ends which promote the social welfare in ways which fail to engage the active interest and cooperation of others. The conception of conferring the good upon others, or at least of attaining it for them, which is our inheritance from the aristocratic civilization of the past, is so deeply embodied in religious, political, and charitable institutions and in moral teaching, that it dies hard. Many a man, feeling himself justified by the social character of his ultimate aim (it may be economic, or educational, or political), is genuinely confused or exasperated by the increasing antagonism and resentment which he evokes, because he has not enlisted in his pursuit of the "common" end the freely cooperative activities of others. This cooperation must be the root principle of the morals of democracy.

Surveying the course of reform in his own society, Dewey concluded this cooperative ideal had "as yet made little progress," and "the inherent irony and tragedy of much that passes for a high kind of socialized activity is precisely that it seeks a common good by methods which forbid its being either common or good."

Hine may well have been influenced by Dewey's argument. He studied briefly with the philosopher at the University of Chicago, and they traveled in the same circles in New York after the turn of the century. An even more likely source of Dewey's influence on Hine was Frank Manny, a member of a coterie of undergraduates who gathered around Dewey at the University of Michigan in the 1880s and who were deeply influenced by his moral philosophy. It was Manny who brought Hine to the Ethical Culture School when he became superintendent of that institution in 1901, and the two remained lifelong friends (Hine's only book, *Men at Work,* is dedicated to Manny). In any case, whether or not Dewey's philosophy directly influenced Hine, his camerawork manifested the same sensitivity to the ethical problems of reform.

Perhaps the greatest strength of Hine's work in this regard was its sensitivity to the ways a reform photograph that "exposed" the seamy side of society ran the risk of conveying "knowledge" of its subject as little more than an object of horror or pity. He seems to have perceived the ethical implications in the way reformers *saw* the oppressed and to have recognized that various "ways of seeing" served as a condition of or an obstacle to the development of democratic reform politics that would permit all the members of the society to, as Dewey put it, "exercise the voluntary capacities of a voluntary agent."

In keeping with this Deweyan ethic, Hine approached his subjects with decorum and tact. He rarely took candid shots but rather encouraged eye contact between the camera lens and the subject. As Trachtenberg says, "he learned how to achieve a certain physical distance, corresponding to a psychological distance, that allowed for a free interaction between the eyes of the subject and the camera. . . . he allowed his subjects room for *their* self-expression."

Hine's respectful approach contrasted sharply with that of Jacob Riis, the father of American reform photography, whose expeditions into the dark world, the "other half," were literal attacks on vulnerable working-class targets. Recalling his adventures, Riis remarked that.

> It is not too much to say that our party carried terror wherever it went. The flashlight of those days was contained in cartridges fired from a revolver. The spectacle of half a dozen strange men invading a house in the midnight hour armed with big pistols which they shot off recklessly was hardly reassuring, however sugary our speech . . . and it was not to be wondered at if the tenants bolted through windows and down fire escapes wherever we went. But as no one was murdered, things calmed down after a while, . . . though months after I found the recollection of our visits hanging over a Stanton Street block like a nightmare.

The people Riis fixed with his flashgun were dazed and off-guard. In few of the photographs in his pathbreaking book, *How the Other Half Lives,* do his subjects face the camera on their feet, and many are not only "down" but "out," altogether without consciousness.

Unlike Riis, who regarded the posing of his subjects as a *problem.* Hine welcomed it as an *opportunity* for them to collaborate in their portrait, rendering it less an "exposure" of a life than a revelation and, in part, a self-revelation. Hine's best reform photography is *democratic* in Dewey's sense; it allows its subjects to participate actively in the production of the knowledge others will have of them. His was an ethics of reform camerawork that pointed toward working-class self-portraiture, a conclusion that Hine appears to have recognized. "The greatest advance in social work," he wrote in 1909, "is to be made by the popularizing of camerawork, so that these records can be made by those who are in the thick of the battle." And near the end of his life he wrote a friend that "I have had all along, as you know, a conviction that my demonstration of the value of the photographic appeal can find its real fruition best if it helps the workers realize that they themselves can use it as a lever even though it may not be the mainspring of the works."

As a consequence of his commitment to a democratic ethic and his resistance to benevolent paternalism, Hine's photographs of workers not only opened to view the difficult circumstances of their lives but also revealed their strength and solidarity. The persistent power of Hine's photographs of children also rests, in part, on his refusal to present them simply as one-dimensional victims of industrial capitalism. His children, like his adults, are not thoroughly beaten down into passivity and defeat but retain resources of resistance: They are tough, defiant, and more often than not, they smile. The child labor photographs are moving because we are made aware of the *struggle* that was waged in factories, fields, and sweatshops between the spirit of Hine's children and their exploiters. We face not deadened boys and girls, but are thrust instead into the midst of their deadening, a much more painful prospect. Hine's photographs call upon us not to "do good" for (or to) such children but, as Dewey would say, to establish the conditions that will enable them to actively develop for themselves the powers that peek out from beneath their coal-smudged faces.

⚓ *F U R T H E R   R E A D I N G*

Arthur A. Ekirch, *Progressivism in America* (1974)

Paul Boyer, *Urban Masses and Moral Order in America, 1820–1920* (1978)

John D. Buenker, *Urban Liberalism and Progressive Reform* (1973)

Robert Crunden, *Ministers of Reform: The Progressives' Achievement in American
      Civilization* (1982)

Leon Fink, *Progressive Intellectuals and the Dilemmas of Democratic Commitment* (1998)

Jack Temple Kirby, *Darkness at Dawning: Race and Reform in the Progressive South*
      (1972)

Seth Koven and Sonya Michel, *Mothers of a New World: Maternalist Politics and the
      Origins of the Welfare States* (1993)

Elizabeth Lasch-Quinn, *Black Neighbors: Race and the Limits of Reform in the American
      Settlement House Movement, 1890–1945* (1990)

Richard L. McCormick, *Progressivism* (1983)

Robyn Muncy, *Creating a Female Dominion in American Reform, 1890–1935* (1991)

David W. Noble, *The Progressive Mind, 1890–1917* (1981)

Daniel T. Rodgers, "In Search of Progressivism," *Reviews in American History 10* (1982),
      113–132

Nick Salvatore, *Eugene V. Debs: Citizen and Socialist* (1982)

David E. Shi, *Facing Facts: Realism in American Thought and Culture, 1850–1920* (1995)

Katherine Kish Sklar, "Hull House in the 1890s: A Community of Women Reformers,"
      Signs 10 (Summer 1985), 658–677

Robert B. Westbrook, *John Dewey and American Democracy* (1991)

C H A P T E R
13

Progressivism: Foundations for
a New American State

Progressive reformers made numerous claims on the comparatively underdeveloped
administrative and regulative functions of the federal government. Beginning in
progressive bulwarks like the state of Wisconsin, and later highlighted in the 1912
and 1916 presidential campaigns, political discussion turned increasingly to the construction of a new balance between individual liberties and public responsibilities.
Although advancing legislative initiatives at both the state and federal levels, however, reformers frequently collided with another peculiarly American governing
instrument, the judicial review authority of the U.S. Supreme Court. Despite the
pleas of legal reformers for a more flexible, "sociological" interpretation of constitutional guidelines, the Court, citing the Due Process Clause of the Fourteenth
Amendment, remained throughout this period a major obstacle to expanded public
regulation of the private marketplace. An important exception, nevertheless, emerged
in the acceptance of government "protection" for those groups (especially women and
children) deemed unable to provide for themselves. The result was an ambiguous
legacy: a stream of path-breaking regulations governing the hours and conditions
of work, which effectively shut women out of many trades and factories.

 D O C U M E N T S

The state-building character of progressive action and thought is exemplified in the
following documents. In Document 1, the U.S. Supreme Court, in *Muller* v. *Oregon*
(1908)—impressed with the sociological brief of state counsel Louis Brandeis—sets
important precedent by letting stand an Oregon law that limits the hours of laundresses
and other women factory workers. In Document 2, Wisconsin's legislative librarian,
Charles McCarthy, offers a compendium of a rich harvest of legislation, dating from
1909 to 1911, inspired by the state's progressive commander in chief, Senator Robert
M. La Follette. Documents 3 and 4 present the competing attempts of Theodore
Roosevelt and Woodrow Wilson, respectively, to offer a justification for government
initiatives within a compelling political vision. Roosevelt's "New Nationalist" platform is taken from his famous speech delivered in Osawatomie, Kansas, on August 31,

1910, where he displayed a willingness to create an enhanced set of government-ordered rules for the operation of the private marketplace. Wilson's "New Freedom" inaugural address of 1913 somewhat similarly assails the human price of American economic progress and reaffirms a role for government in ensuring equality of opportunity to all citizens. Document 5, the Clayton Anti-Trust Act of 1914, a Wilsonian measure reflecting the antimonopoly philosophy of advisor Louis Brandeis, is perhaps most notable for its attempt (a failure in practice) in Section 6 to shield labor unions (who overwhelmingly supported the Democratic Wilson) from prosecution for restraint of trade.

1. The Supreme Court Accepts Limits on Working Women's Hours: *Muller* v. *Oregon,* 1908

Justice Brewer. The single question is the constitutionality of the statute under which the defendant was convicted so far as it affects the work of a female in a laundry. . . .

. . . It may not be amiss, in the present case, before examining the constitutional question, to notice the course of legislation as well as expressions of opinion from other than judicial sources. In the brief filed by Mr. Louis D. Brandeis, for the defendant in error, is a very copious collection of all these matters. . . .

The legislation and opinions referred to [in the brief] may not be, technically speaking, authorities, and in them is little or no discussion of the constitutional question presented to us for determination, yet they are significant of a widespread belief that woman's physical structure, and the functions she performs in consequence thereof, justify special legislation restricting or qualifying the conditions under which she should be permitted to toil. . . .

That woman's physical structure and the performance of maternal functions place her at a disadvantage in the struggle for subsistence is obvious. This is especially true when the burdens of motherhood are upon her. Even when they are not, by abundant testimony of the medical fraternity continuance for a long time on her feet at work, repeating this from day to day, tends to injurious effects upon the body, and as healthy mothers are essential to vigorous offspring, the physical well-being of woman becomes an object of public interest and care in order to preserve the strength and vigor of the race. . . .

Differentiated by these matters from the other sex, she is properly placed in a class by herself, and legislation designed for her protection may be sustained, even when like legislation is not necessary for men and could not be sustained. It is impossible to close one's eyes to the fact that she still looks to her brother and depends upon him. Even though all restrictions on political, personal and contractual rights were taken away, and she stood, so far as statutes are concerned, upon an absolutely equal plane with him, it would still be true that she is so constituted that she will rest upon and look to him for protection; that her physical structure and a proper discharge of her maternal functions—having in view not merely her own health, but the well-being of the race—justify legislation to protect her from the

---

Muller v. *Oregon,* 208 U.S. 412 (1908).

greed as well as the passion of man. The limitations which this statute places upon her contractual powers, upon her right to agree with her employer as to the time she shall labor, are not imposed solely for her benefit, but also largely for the benefit of all. Many words cannot make this plainer. The two sexes differ in structure of body, in the functions to be performed by each, in the amount of physical strength, in the capacity for long-continued labor, particularly when done standing, the influence of vigorous health upon the future well-being of the race, the self-reliance which enables one to assert full rights, and in the capacity to maintain the struggle for subsistence. This difference justifies a difference in legislation and upholds that which is designed to compensate for some of the burdens which rest upon her. . . ,

For these reasons, and without questioning in any respect the decision in *Lochner* v. *New York,* we are of the opinion that it cannot be adjudged that the act in question is in conflict with the Federal Constitution, so far as it respects the work of a female in a laundry, and the judgment of the Supreme Court of Oregon is

Affirmed.

2. Charles McCarthy Inventories Wisconsin's La Follette–Era Reforms (1909–1911), 1911

The following proposed amendments to the constitution were adopted this year [1911]:

The initiative, referendum.

Providing that the salaries of members of the legislature shall be $600 per annum, instead of $500 for each biennial session.

Permitting cities to acquire lands for park purposes.

Permitting the state to install a system of insurance against sickness, death, accident and invalidity.

Permitting the state to appropriate for internal improvements—"for the purpose of acquiring, preserving and developing the water power resources and forests of the state"; limiting the appropriation therefore to a $\frac{2}{10}$ of a mill tax on the property of the state.

Empowering the legislature to provide for the recall of any public elective officer, except judges.

Declaring "all lanes, mineral rights, water powers and other natural resources of natural wealth within the state which are now or may thereafter become the property of the state, shall remain forever the property of the state and shall not be alienated"; permitting the state to lease or rent such resources; and providing that all mineral rights hitherto reserved in contracts, deeds or instruments conveying real estate are abolished after Jan. 1, 1920, and are declared to inhere to the state except where they have been developed in full or in part prior to Jan. 1, 1920.

The following constitutional amendments were adopted at the 1909 and also the 1911 session and will be submitted to the people at the general election in 1912:—

Permitting municipalities to acquire land within or outside their limits, for park or other public purposes and to plat or sell any part of such land for the purpose of adding to a fund for the maintenance of parks, playgrounds, etc.

Charles McCarthy, *The Wisconsin Idea* (New York: Macmillan, 1912).

Permitting the state legislature to remove the five percent limit upon the public debt of any city, county, town, village or school district, when the debt is incurred for the purpose of purchasing and improving public parks, etc.

The following under the heading "Public health and welfare," show what was accomplished in this line:

Empowering county boards, with the consent of the state board of control, to erect upon grounds of county insane asylums, hospitals for the care of chronic insane affected by pulmonary tuberculosis.—Chapter 461.

Authorizing the secretary of the state board of health to provide biennially for a state conference of health officers and health commissioners of cities and villages.—Chapter 465.

Empowering county boards of supervisors to purchase sites and establish quarters for the treatment of persons suffering from tuberculosis in advanced or secondary stages.—Chapter 457.

Specifying the manner in which the state shall care for dependent, neglected, and delinquent children.—Chapter 460.

Making pandering a felony and providing a penalty therefor.—Chapter 420.

Empowering the state board of health to abate nuisances caused by the pollution of streams and public water supplies.—Chapter 412.

Making it unlawful to store or exhibit fruits, vegetables, or other food products on any sidewalk or outside any place of business, unless covered by glass, wood or metal cases and providing a penalty therefor.—Chapter 379.

Requiring owners or occupants of public or quasi-public institutions to provide cuspidors and cleanse and disinfect same daily.—Chapter 330.

Making it unlawful to abuse, neglect, or illtreat any person confined in a police station or any other place of confinement, and fixing a penalty therefor.—Chapter 375.

Requiring trained nurses to register with the state board of health.—Chapter 346.

Making it unlawful to manufacture, sell, or transport adulterated or misbranded insecticides or fungicides.—Chapter 325.

Prohibiting the manufacturing and sale of certain kinds of firecrackers and fireworks.—Chapter 313.

Making it unlawful for physicians or surgeons to prescribe intoxicating liquor for any person, when unnecessary for the health of such person, and providing a penalty therefor.—Chapter 290.

Empowering common councils to regulate the emission of dense smoke into the open air within the corporate limits of any city, and within one mile therefrom.—Chapter 314.

Making it unlawful to spit or expectorate in any public place.—Chapter 407.

Empowering health officers to take precautions against the spread of dangerous communicable diseases and prescribing the duties of principals of schools and parents, where such diseases are known to exist.—Chapter 44.

Making it a misdemeanor to sell or have in possession, canned goods containing any artificial coloring matter or bleaching compound and fixing the penalty therefor.—Chapter 46.

Prescribing the manner in which explosives may be manufactured and stored within the state.—Chapter 223.

Prescribing the duties of health officers in determining the diagnosis of contagious or infectious diseases.—Chapter 248.

Extending the police authority of agents and superintendents of certain humane societies.—Chapter 258.

Conservation received some attention also:—

Empowering boards of supervisors to lease swamp lands under certain conditions, and conferring the same powers upon the state board of forestry in certain sections of the state.—Chapter 238

Making it unlawful to waste or maliciously destroy or impair any natural re sources and providing a penalty therefor.—Chapter 143.

Making it unlawful to injure, mutilate, cut down, or destroy any shade tree on any street or highway in villages.—Chapter 459.

Requiring all engines operated in, through or near forest, or brush land to be equipped with screen or wire netting between March 1 and December 1 to protect such forest or brush land from fire.—Chapter 494.

Appropriating $50,000 a year for five years for purchase of lands for reforestation.—Chapter 639.

Labor was not ignored in this session as is shown by the following laws:—

Prohibiting the employment of children between the ages of 14 and 16 years unless there is first obtained from the commissioner of labor, state factory inspector or any assistant factory inspector or from a judge of any county, municipal or juvenile court a written permit.—Chapter 479.

Requiring safety appliances and automatic feeding devices on corn shredders.—Chapter 466.

Empowering the state bureau of labor and industrial statistics to investigate contracts between employers and employees and making an appropriation therefor.—Chapter 453.

Increasing the scope of the state employment office located at Milwaukee.—Chapter 419.

Making it the absolute duty of an employer to guard or protect machines or appliances on all premises used for manufacturing purposes and to maintain same after installation.—Chapter 396.

Making it unlawful to employ labor by false representation and providing a penalty therefor.—Chapter 364.

Requiring owners or occupants of all public or quasi-public institutions and factories to keep exit doors unlocked during working hours and requiring all such exit doors to swing outward.—Chapter 378.

Specifying the manner in which indenture and apprenticeship contracts may be made, and providing a penalty for non-compliance therewith.—Chapter 347.

Requiring safety appliances on dangerous machinery and sanitary conditions in factories.—Chapter 470.

Requiring contractors and owners, when constructing buildings in cities, to take proper precautions for the protection of workmen and specifying what precautions are necessary.—Chapter 49.

Requiring owners of factories and manufacturing establishments to provide proper ventilation for same and prescribing a penalty for non-compliance.—Chapter 170.

Limiting the hours of labor on public buildings to eight hours per day and fixing a penalty for non-compliance.—Chapter 171.

Limiting the hours of labor of women to ten a day or fifty-five a week (Chapter 548); and of children under 16 years of age to eight a day and forty-eight a week (Chapter 479).

3. Theodore Roosevelt Announces the New Nationalism, 1910

In every wise struggle for human betterment one of the main objects, and often the only object, has been to achieve in large measure equality of opportunity. In the struggle for this great end, nations rise from barbarism to civilization, and through it people press forward from one stage of enlightenment to the next. One of the chief factors in progress is the destruction of special privilege. The essence of any struggle for healthy liberty has always been, and must always be, to take from some one man or class of men the right to enjoy power, or wealth, or position, or immunity, which has not been earned by service to his or their fellows. That is what you fought for in the Civil War, and that is what we strive for now.

At many stages in the advance of humanity, this conflict between the men who possess more than they have earned and the men who have earned more than they possess is the central condition of progress. In our day it appears as the struggle of free men to gain and hold the right of self-government as against the special interests, who twist the methods of free government into machinery for defeating the popular will. At every stage, and under all circumstances, the essence of the struggle is to equalize opportunity, destroy privilege, and give to the life and citizenship of every individual the highest possible value both to himself and to the commonwealth. That is nothing new. . . .

I stand for the square deal. But when I say that I am for the square deal, I mean not merely that I stand for fair play under the present rules of the game, but that I stand for having those rules changed so as to work for a more substantial equality of opportunity and of reward for equally good service. . . .

Now, this means that our government, national and state, must be freed from the sinister influence or control of special interests. Exactly as the special interests of cotton and slavery threatened our political integrity before the Civil War, so now the great special business interests too often control and corrupt the men and methods of government for their own profit. We must drive the special interests out of politics. . . .

The true friend of property, the true conservative, is he who insists that property shall be the servant and not the master of the commonwealth; who insists that the creature of man's making shall be the servant and not the master of the man who made it. The citizens of the United States must effectively control the mighty commercial forces which they have themselves called into being. . . .

Combinations in industry are the result of an imperative economic law which cannot be repealed by political legislation. The effort at prohibiting all combination has substantially failed. The way out lies, not in attempting to prevent such combinations, but in completely controlling them in the interest of the public welfare. For that purpose the Federal Bureau of Corporations is an agency of first importance. Its powers, and therefore, its efficiency, as well as that of the Interstate Commerce Commission, should be largely increased. We have a right to expect from the Bureau of Corporations and from the Interstate Commerce Commission a

Theodore Roosevelt, *The New Nationalism* (New York: Outlook Co., 1910), 9–14, 15–16, 24–25, 27–33.

very high grade of public service. We should be as sure of the proper conduct of the interstate railways and the proper management of interstate business as we are now sure of the conduct and management of the national banks, and we should have as effective supervision in one case as in the other. . . .

But I think we may go still further. The right to regulate the use of wealth in the public interest is universally admitted. Let us admit also the right to regulate the terms and conditions of labor, which is the chief element of wealth, directly in the interest of the common good. The fundamental thing to do for every man is to give him a chance to reach a place in which he will make the greatest possible contribution to the public welfare. Understand what I say there. Give him a chance, not push him up if he will not be pushed. Help any man who stumbles; if he lies down, it is a poor job to try to carry him; but if he is a worthy man, try your best to see that he gets a chance to show the worth that is in him. No man can be a good citizen unless he has a wage more than sufficient to cover the bare cost of living, and hours of labor short enough so that after his day's work is done he will have time and energy to bear his share in the management of the community, to help in carrying the general load. We keep countless men from being good citizens by the conditions of life with which we surround them. We need comprehensive work-men's compensation acts, both state and national laws to regulate child labor and work for women, and, especially, we need in our common schools not merely education in book learning, but also practical training for daily life and work.

4. Woodrow Wilson Proclaims the New Freedom, 1913

Nowhere else in the world have noble men and women exhibited in more striking forms the beauty and the energy of sympathy and helpfulness and counsel in their efforts to rectify wrong, alleviate suffering, and set the weak in the way of strength and hope. We have built up, moreover, a great system of government, which has stood through a long age as in many respects a model for those who seek to set liberty upon foundations that will endure against fortuitous change, against storm and accident. Our life contains every great thing, and contains it in rich abundance.

But the evil has come with the good, and much fine gold has been corroded. With riches has come inexcusable waste. We have squandered a great part of what we might have used, and have not stopped to conserve the exceeding bounty of nature, without which our genius for enterprise would have been worthless and impotent, scorning to be careful, shamefully prodigal as well as admirably efficient. We have been proud of our industrial achievements, but we have not hitherto stopped thoughtfully enough to count the human cost, the cost of lives snuffed out, of energies overtaxed and broken, the fearful physical and spiritual cost to the men and women and children upon whom the dead weight and burden of it all has fallen pitilessly the years through. The groans and agony of it all had not yet reached our ears, the solemn, moving undertone of our life, coming up out of the mines and factories and out of every home where the struggle had its intimate and familiar seat. With the great Government went many deep secret things which we too long

Wilson's First Inaugural Address, 63d Cong., special session (March 4, 1913), Senate Doc, I. 3, pp. 3–6.

delayed to look into and scrutinize with candid, fearless eyes. The great Government we loved has too often been made use of for private and selfish purposes, and those who used it had forgotten the people.

At last a vision has been vouchsafed us of our life as a whole. We see the bad with the good, the debased and decadent with the sound and vital. With this vision we approach new affairs. Our duty is to cleanse, to reconsider, to restore, to correct the evil without impairing the good, to purify and humanize every process of our common life without weakening or sentimentalizing it. There has been something crude and heartless and unfeeling in our haste to succeed and be great. Our thought has been "Let every man look out for himself, let every generation look out for itself," while we reared giant machinery which made it impossible that any but those who stood at the levers of control should have a chance to look out for themselves. We had not forgotten our morals. We remembered well enough that we had set up a policy which was meant to serve the humblest as well as the most powerful, with an eye single to the standards of justice and fair play, and remembered it with pride. But we were very heedless and in a hurry to be great.

We have come now to the sober second thought. The scales of heedlessness have fallen from our eyes. We have made up our minds to square every process of our national life again with the standards we so proudly set up at the beginning and have always carried at our hearts. Our work is a work of restoration.

We have itemized with some degree of particularity the things that ought to be altered and here are some of the chief items: A tariff which cuts us off from our proper part in the commerce of the world, violates the just principles of taxation, and makes the Government a facile instrument in the hands of private interests; a banking and currency system based upon the necessity of the Government to sell its bonds fifty years ago and perfectly adapted to concentrating cash and restricting credits; an industrial system which, take it on all its sides, financial as well as administrative, holds capital in leading strings, restricts the liberties and limits the opportunities of labor, and exploits without renewing or conserving the natural resources of the country; a body of agricultural activities never yet given the efficiency of great business undertakings or served as it should be through the instrumentality of science taken directly to the farm, or afforded the facilities of credit best suited to its practical needs; water-courses undeveloped, waste places unreclaimed, forests untended, fast disappearing without plan or prospect of renewal, unregarded waste heaps at every mine. We have studied as perhaps no other nation has the most effective means of production, but we have not studied cost or economy as we should either as organizers of industry, as statesmen, or as individuals.

Nor have we studied and perfected the means by which government may be put at the service of humanity, in safeguarding the health of the Nation, the health of its men and its women and its children, as well as their rights in the struggle for existence. This is no sentimental duty. The firm basis of government is justice, not pity. These are matters of justice. There can be no equality of opportunity, the first essential of justice in the body politic, if men and women and children be not shielded in their lives, their very vitality, from the consequences of great industrial and social processes which they can not alter, control, or singly cope with. Society must see to it that it does not itself crush or weaken or damage its own constituent parts. The first duty of law is to keep sound the society it serves. Sanitary laws, pure food laws, and laws determining conditions of labor which individuals are powerless to determine for themselves are intimate parts of the very business of justice and legal efficiency. . . .

And yet it will be no cool process of mere science. The Nation has been deeply stirred, stirred by solemn passion, stirred by the knowledge of wrong, of ideals lost, of government too often debauched and made an instrument of evil. The feelings with which we face this new age of right and opportunity sweep across our heartstrings like some air out of God's presence, where justice and mercy are reconciled and the judge and the brother are one. We know our task to be no mere task of politics but a task which shall search us through and through, whether we be able to understand our time and the need of our people, whether we be indeed their spokesmen and interpreters, whether we have the pure heart to comprehend and the rectified will to choose our high course of action.

This is not a day of triumph; it is a day of dedication. Here muster, not the forces of party, but the forces of humanity. Men's hearts wait upon us; men's lives hang in the balance; men's hopes call upon us to say what we will do. Who shall live up to the great trust? Who dares fail to try? I summon all honest men, all patriotic, all forward-looking men, to my side. God helping me, I will not fail them, if they will but counsel and sustain me!

5. The Clayton Anti-Trust Act, 1914

. . . SEC. 2. That it shall be unlawful for any person engaged in commerce, in the course of such commerce, either directly or indirectly to discriminate in price between different purchasers of commodities which commodities are sold for use, consumption, or resale within the United States or any . . . other place under the jurisdiction of the United States, where the effect of such discrimination may be to substantially lessen competition or tend to create a monopoly in any line of commerce: . . .

SEC. 3. That it shall be unlawful for any person engaged in commerce, to lease or make a sale of goods, . . . or other commodities, . . . for use, consumption or resale within the United States or . . . other place under the jurisdiction of the United States, or fix a price charged therefor, or discount from, or rebate upon, such price, on the condition, . . . that the lessee or purchaser thereof shall not use or deal in the goods, . . . or other commodities of a competitor or competitors of the lessor or seller, where the effect of such lease, sale, or contract for sale or such condition, agreement, or understanding may be to substantially lessen competition or tend to create a monopoly in any line of commerce. . . .

SEC. 6. That the labor of a human being is not a commodity or article of commerce. Nothing contained in the anti-trust laws shall be construed to forbid the existence and operation of labor, agricultural, or horticultural organizations, instituted for the purposes of mutual help, and not having capital stock or conduced for profit, or to forbid or restrain individual members of such organizations from

---

"Clayton Anti-Trust Act, 1914," in *U.S. Statutes at Large,* Vol. 38, pp. 703ff. This document can also be found in Henry Steele Commager, ed., *Documents of American History,* Vol. II (New York: Meredith Publishing Co., 1963), 99–101.

lawfully carrying out the legitimate objects thereof; nor shall such organizations or the members thereof, be held or construed to be illegal combinations or conspiracies in restraint of trade, under the anti-trust laws.

SEC. 7. That no corporation engaged in commerce shall acquire, directly or indirectly, the whole or any part of the stock or other share capital of another corporation engaged also in commerce, where the effect of such acquisition may be to substantially lessen competition between the corporation whose stock is so acquired and the corporation making the acquisition, or to restrain such commerce in any section or community or tend to create a monopoly of any line of commerce. . . .

This section shall not apply to corporations purchasing such stock solely for investment and not using the same by voting or otherwise to bring about, or in attempting to bring about, the substantial lessening of competition. . . .

SEC. 8. That from and after two years from the date of the approval of this act no person shall at the same time be a director or other officer or employee of more than one bank, banking association or trust company, organized or operating under the laws of the United States, either of which has deposits, capital, surplus, and undivided profits aggregating more than $5,000,000; and no private banker or person who is a director in any bank or trust company, organized and operating under the laws of a State, having deposits, capital, surplus, and undivided profits aggregating more than $5,000,000, shall be eligible to be a director in any bank or banking association organized or operating under the laws of the United States. . . .

That from and after two years from the date of the approval of this Act no person at the same time shall be a director in any two or more corporations, any one of which has capital, surplus, and undivided profits aggregating more than $1,000,000, engaged in whole or in part in commerce, other than banks, banking associations, trust companies and common carriers subject to the Act to regulate commerce, approved February 4th, 1887, if such corporations are or shall have been theretofore, by virtue of their business and location of operation, competitors, so that the elimination of competition by agreement between them would constitute a violation of any of the provisions of any of the anti-trust laws. . . .

SEC. 10. That after two years from the approval of this Act no common carrier engaged in commerce shall have any dealings in securities, supplies, or other articles of commerce, . . . to the amount of more than $50,000, in the aggregate, in any one year, with another corporation, firm, partnership or association when the said common carrier shall have upon its board of directors or as its president, manager, or as its purchasing or selling officer, or agent in the particular transaction, any person who is at the same time a director, manager, or purchasing or selling officer of, or who has any substantial interest in, such other corporation, firm, partnership, or association, unless and except such purchases shall be made from, or such dealings shall be with, the bidder whose bid is the most favorable to such common carrier, to be ascertained by competitive bidding under regulations to be prescribed by rule or otherwise by the Interstate Commerce Commission. . . .

SEC. 20. That no restraining order or injunction shall be granted by any court of the United States, or a judge or the judges thereof, in any case between an employer and employees or between employers and employees, or between employees, or between persons employed and persons seeking employment, involving, or growing out of, a dispute concerning terms or conditions of employment, unless necessary to prevent irreparable injury to property, or to a property right, of the party making the application, for which injury there is no adequate remedy at law, and such property or property right must be described with a particularity in the application, which must be in writing and sworn to by the applicant or by his agent or attorney.

 ## E S S A Y S

The contributions in this section treat the internal complexities of progressive political culture in two distinct areas. In the first essay, Professor Alan Dawley of Trenton State University sets the larger parameters for Progressive Era reform legislation by emphasizing its response to specific social deformities induced by the Industrial Revolution. In the second contribution, distinguished historian Eric Foner of Columbia University finds in the progressive reformers' idea of freedom—that is, an activist, socially conscious state prepared to redress economic injustice—the beginnings of "modern liberalism."

Progressive Statecraft

ALAN DAWLEY

After years of social ferment it seemed to Walter Lippmann, perhaps the most discerning social critic of the day, that American civilization was coming apart at the seams: "the sanctity of property, the patriarchal family, hereditary caste, the dogma of sin, obedience to authority,— the rock of ages, in brief, has been blasted for us." Lippmann's catalogue of disintegration was a clear sign that on the eve of the First World War American culture was breaking free from nineteenth-century orthodoxies. Newspapers rang with popular clamor about predatory practices by the "money trust," landlord abuses in tenement slums, and the cruelties of child labor. Mass meetings convened to hear sexual radicals foretell the dawn of erotic delight and social radicals extol collective ownership of wealth. City streets were exotic, open-air bazaars of Russian Orthodox peasants, Jewish pushcart operators, and Italian anarcho-syndicalists, whose raw energy was celebrated by the new breed of urban realist painters. Arts and letters were a veritable kaleidoscope of bright new ideas and sentiments from the poets of the Chicago Renaissance, the irreverent cartoonists of *The Masses,* and avant-garde artists saluting the iconoclasm of the Cubists. Against the prevailing chaos of "drift," Lippmann urged what a growing chorus of contemporaries demanded, a commanding strategy of "mastery."

No longer could Yankee Protestant elites be complacent about their place atop the social hierarchy. The unwanted children of nineteenth-century American society were in revolt against the parent, and their revolt called into question the existing relation between state and society. From 1912 through 1916 the key battles were fought out around the trust, industrial democracy, and social justice, all of which were forced upon an otherwise unwilling national leadership by popular movements originating in the working and middle classes. . . .

Alan Dawley, *Struggles for Justice: Social Responsibility and the Liberal State* (Cambridge, Mass.: Harvard University Press, 1991), 141–150, 171–172. Copyright © 1991 by the President and Fellows of Harvard College.

The trust question dominated Wilson's first two years as President. The rise of the giant corporation threw a huge monkey wrench into the inherited governing system. Corporations as big as United States Steel did not play by the same competitive rules as small proprietary firms. They did not link up with family ownership and inheritance in the same way as individual entrepreneurs. They did not hire or supervise their thousands of employees in the same way as the on-site boss in his own shop. Yet they continued to be governed by the same legal rules that applied to the competitive marketplace. This underlying contradiction between the actual relations of production and the ideological-legal form of property came to the surface in political battles around the trust in which nearly every economic group had a stake. Wall Street wanted a private central bank; shippers wanted lower freight rates; farmers wanted cheaper credit; small manufacturers wanted competitive advantages; technocrats wanted efficiency; and workers wanted greater leverage. Out of this tangle of competing interests, a daunting possibility arose: what would happen if all those who had been gored by the plutocratic ox made common cause? The pursuit of social justice had already brought workers and middle-class elements together; could the same groups draw upon the legacy of the Knights of Labor and the Populists to forge a new antimonopoly alliance against the trusts?

The term *trust* was a holdover from nineteenth-century populism, and it came freighted with faintly evil connotations. It was easier to define the enemy in rhetoric than in fact. Contemporaries applied the term to everything from monopolies such as the American Telephone and Telegraph Corporation to oligopolies such as the handful of giant meatpackers and, for that matter, to just about any other big business. Though imprecise, it reflected the need for some generic term to cover the emergence of large-scale enterprise whose characteristic industrial structure was neither monopoly nor competition, but something in between named oligopoly. The rise of industrial goliaths such as U.S. Steel, Armour, and the American Tobacco Company was the result of convergence of changes at several levels, including the emergence of mass-production techniques and mass consumption, along with the legal prohibition on cartels embodied in the Sherman Act.

In terms of the mode of production, the key was vertical integration, that is, the linkage of mass production with mass distribution. Integration was both a matter of new technologies, such as the integrated steel mill, which turned iron ore into steel girders, and business reorganization, in which a single firm took control of purchasing, production, and marketing. Coordinating these complex operations called forth an elaborate internal managerial apparatus in each of the giant firms. Where once separate firms had bought and sold, now functional divisions, each under its own vice-president, coordinated purchasing, production, and marketing. In short, the corporation turned the competitive markets of the proprietary era into their opposite, managed markets.

Mass production and distribution would not have been possible without changes in social reproduction. To move beyond the pioneering stage of illustrious inventors such as Thomas Edison toward the systematic exploitation of scientific discoveries, it was necessary, particularly for new electrical and chemical industries, to have at their disposal an expanding corps of engineers and scientists coming from the Massachusetts Institute of Technology and other polytechnic training grounds. By the same token, to manage markets properly required a corps of college-educated planners whose decisions were recorded and communicated by legions of high-school-trained office clerks, the same feminized work force that also made mass distribution possible through their low-paid work as telephone operators and sales clerks. Mass education inculcated the skills and work habits that prepared the rising generation for the discipline and tedium of the office routine. Absent these changes in the reproduction of daily life, the evolution of twentieth-century society with the giant corporation at the hub simply could not have gone forward.

Presiding over these wide-ranging developments, investment bankers and big stockholders were converting proprietary ownership into corporate ownership. The advantages of limited liability quickly proved themselves in manufacturing, where 87 percent of wage earners toiled for a corporate employer by 1919. Although most of the several million employers in the United States were small, a large share of corporate property was being concentrated in a few hands. By 1914 a mere 2.2 percent of all establishments produced more than $1 million worth of goods, but these same firms employed 35 percent of all wage earners in manufacturing, and the proportion rose to more than half after the First World War. No nineteenth-century coal baron or railroad tycoon could match the $1 billion capitalization of U.S. Steel, and soon other manufacturing combines, investment banks, and insurance companies surpassed railroads as the largest concentrations of wealth. . . .

Such were the agglomerations of wealth that came under attack for being "trusts." Seen as standing conspiracies against the public interest, the trusts gained notoriety in the great merger wave of 1898–1904, when hundreds of horizontal competitors were consolidated into a relative handful of large corporations a few of which controlled over 70 percent of their markets (Du Pont, International Harvester) and others over 40 percent (U.S. Steel, American Smelting and Refining, National Biscuit). Maverick economist Thorstein Veblen contended that these mergers were a parasitic incubus on the underlying productive system, and in *Theory of Business Enterprise* (1904) he pressed the case for a conflict between the technical efficiency of the modern machine process and the "pecuniary motivation" of property owners. Damning the corporate investor with faint praise, he wrote, "the captain of industry works against, as well as for, a new and more efficient organization." In a more popular vein, Upton Sinclair indicted the Beef Trust for its careless disregard of public health and brutal exploitation of immigrant workers in *The Jungle* (1906). In defending supposedly "soulless corporations" against "demagogues" and socialists, John Moody ironically gave ammunition to the critics in *The Truth about the Trusts* (1904), which depicted a steep pyramid of wealth topped by two rival groups of finance capitalists around the Rockefeller and Morgan interests. The Wall Street Panic of 1907 only confirmed public anxiety about the machinations of high finance.

In this highly charged atmosphere, government efforts to resolve the contradiction between the corporation and the legal tradition of antimonopoly only succeeded in further politicizing the issue. President Roosevelt won a reputation as a "trustbuster" largely on the strength of a single successful prosecution under the Sherman Anti-Trust Act of the Northern Securities railroad empire. His successor, President Taft, initiated more prosecutions but left the deciding influence in the hands of the Supreme Court. For its part, the Court tried to take the trust issue out of politics in announcing the "rule of reason" doctrine in 1911, under which only "unreasonable" combinations in restraint of trade would run afoul of the law. Although the Court actually struck a blow against monopoly by breaking up Standard Oil and the American Tobacco Company, the result tended to promote not free competition but oligopoly. . . .

By the election of 1912, antitrust feeling was running high. Eugene Debs resolved to bring the system of property ownership into line with already socialized production through nationalization of big capital, while "Bull Moose" Progressives talked about thoroughgoing government regulation under their New Nationalism. Woodrow Wilson, for his part, solemnly announced with Delphic ambiguity, "I am for big business and I am against the trusts." To the consternation of conservatives, the atmosphere was reminiscent of the great battles of the Gilded Age over money inflation and the protective tariff. There was no guarantee that a Congress susceptible to democratic enthusiasms would not do something drastic such as taking public control of the banking system or putting teeth into the Sherman Act. The trust question, broadly defined, was the most pressing business faced by the incoming Wilson administration, and it was clear that a solution would require statecraft of the highest order.

There is enough conflicting evidence about the president to suggest that upon coming to office he simply did not know what he was doing, or at least he did not know exactly how to proceed. He fully accepted the rise of big business as "normal and inevitable" and in common with progressive opinion believed that some middle way in the law would have to be found between extreme individualism and public ownership. Yet he had also accepted Louis Brandeis' prescriptions for restoring competition and had campaigned as a Victorian liberal devoted to free trade and what he called "the men who are on the make rather than the men who are already made." Such rhetoric placated the Bryan wing of the Democratic party and other legatees of the nineteenth-century antimonopoly agitation, who were also gratified by Wilson's first major action as president in support of the Underwood Tariff, which reduced import duties from 40 percent to around 25 percent.

Having shown his gentlemanly independence from the bribery and intrigue of high-tariff lobbies, Wilson next tackled the thorny problem of currency and banking. The popular clamor for "people's money" had revived after lying dormant since Bryan's defeat in 1896. Agrarians of the Southwest and militant midwestern followers of Robert La Follette, plus the handful of surviving inflationists who had once wept with Bryan to see mankind crucified upon a "cross of gold" all demanded public currency and public control over private bankers. . . . The revival of the antimonopoly hatred for the "money power" received a big boost in 1912 from the Pujo Committee, named after a Louisiana congressman, whose investigations of the "money trust" were condensed by Louis Brandeis into a muckraking classic, *Other People's Money* (1914). These attacks indicted finance capitalists for a vast conspiracy of interlocking directorates and behind-the-scenes banker control of industry.

Money trust or not, Wall Streeters sought to insulate themselves against just this sort of "agrarianism," not to mention socialism. They came forward with the Aldrich Plan under what amounted to a revival of the old Bank of the United States, which they also hoped would prevent a recurrence of the Panic of 1907. That was too much centralized banking for Carter Glass, a Virginia senator who was thoroughly conservative on every point except his antipathy to New York banks. Although Glass was the principal author of the administration's bill, Brandeis contributed the key progressive innovations—government currency and a Federal Reserve Board to oversee private banks. In its final form, the bill contained only weak antimonopoly provisions, which enabled a large body of big bankers to support it in the expectation that real power would lie not in the Federal Reserve Board but in the officers of the member banks themselves.

What emerged as the Federal Reserve System in 1913 was an exquisite political compromise that satisfied advocates of both centralized and decentralized banking, as well as supporters of private and public control. It created a dozen federal reserve banks with New York as the first among equals; banks could issue Federal Reserve notes in small denominations backed by the U.S. Treasury; the system was overseen by a federal bank board appointed by the president but presumably drawn from the leading men of the banking community. It also created the statutory basis for U.S. branch banking overseas. In all it was a remarkable balancing act that expanded the federal government's regulatory role without resorting to statist control and built on decentralized, federal structures congenial to small property while recognizing the primacy of New York banks and their leadership in foreign investment. It edged away from the "drift" of laissez faire while lodging "mastery" not in a public bureaucracy but in a regulatory-corporate complex that left the main decisions in private hands. As a consequence, currency and banking disappeared as major issues until the Great Depression.

With respect to giant industrial combines, progressive statecraft followed the same lines of finely balanced compromise. The most drastic proposals came from latter-day populists, Bryan Democrats, and southwestern agrarians who wanted nothing less than destruction of oligopoly itself in the name of free enterprise. To that end they called for strict government regulation of the stock exchange, abolition of the "rule of reason," and outright prohibition on corporate interlocks of the sort uncovered by the Pujo investigation. By comparison, the socialist prescription for public ownership of concentrated capital, though a radical transformation in property relations, would have resulted in less disruption in the actual day-to-day processes of production and distribution. Keeping both of these drastic remedies at bay became the first aim of progressive policy. Taft's preferred method had been to refer the trust question to the courts, the branch of government most shielded from popular influence. In Roosevelt's case, the preference was for hands-on administrative regulation through a commission that would police the activities of big business, a position that accorded well with the tripartite, protocorporatist proposals of the National Civic Federation. Wilson, on the other hand, was more elusive. As a professor of government at Princeton, Wilson had accepted the big corporation as a legitimate fact of life, but as a presidential candidate he had talked like a latter-day Jeffersonian about a New Freedom in support of small property and against monopoly control.

In the event, progressive statecraft was based not on campaign rhetoric or presidential whim but on the balance of political forces. It was clear that the socialist proposal for government ownership fell beyond the pale of liberal ideology and that the agrarian proposal for dissolution of the trusts was also unacceptable. Both were ruled out when Wilson reassured businessmen at the start of the 1914 legislative session that "the antagonism between business and government is over." At the same time, the government could not simply continue drifting on a laissez-faire course, because doing so had only raised the popular temperature to a fever level. In the end, the administration and Congress charted a course between radical change and the status quo. They established the Federal Trade Commission (FTC), which was empowered to set rules for fair competition, issue cease-and-desist orders against infractions, and collect information on trade conditions.

This compromise was enough to placate both the New Nationalists, who welcomed clarification of the rules of oligopolistic competition, and New Freedomites, who hoped that small competitors would be protected against monopoly pricing. Even Taft conservatives were mollified by having FTC decisions made subject to judicial review in courts that were well beyond the reach of the people's elected tribunes. To guide judicial decisions, the Clayton Act defined "unfair" competition in terms of price discrimination, tying contracts, and some kinds of interlocking directorships and stockholding. When all was said and done, business leaders were in agreement with Wilson that antagonism between business and government was over. The U.S. Chamber of Commerce spoke for most in supporting the new arrangements for what it called industrial "self-regulation," a necessary euphemism cloaking the reality of expanded government regulation. A Missouri senator was closer to the mark in saying that the Clayton Act started out as "a raging lion with a mouth full of teeth. It has degenerated to a tabby cat with soft gums, a plaintive mew, and an anemic appearance."

Wage earners had an immense stake in the trust question. Their ability to organize for self-protection was deeply affected by the way property relations were being redefined to keep up with the rise of the corporation. President Cleveland's use of the Sherman Act against the American Railway Union in the 1894 railroad strike was the opening gun of the era of the injunction, which lasted until the Norris-Laguardia Act of 1932. Although courts had long since stopped holding unions and strikes to be illegal per se, the broader forms of worker solidarity ran afoul of antitrust law, including the industrywide strike (*In re Debs,* 1895), the consumer boycott in support of a strike (*Loewe v. Lawlor,* 1908), and publication of a list of "foul" employers (*Bucks Stove,* 1911). In fact, most of the early prosecutions of "illegal combinations in restraint of trade" went against unions, no matter how much the American Federation of Labor invoked the free speech protections of the Bill of Rights.

With the National Association of Manufacturers crowing over this string of courtroom victories, the AFL set out to break the potent alliance between business and the judiciary. AFL strategy was geared to the system of constitutional checks and balances and was aimed at electing "friends of labor" to Congress and the White House. Gompers supported Wilson in 1912 and used every ounce of his rather puny congressional muscle to win exemption for unions under the Clayton Act. For all his pains, the only outcomes were a pious reiteration of common legal doctrine that unions were not illegal and an eloquent but empty proclamation that "human labor is not a commodity." Grasping for any straw of legitimacy, Gompers nonetheless embraced the new law as "labor's Magna Carta." He lived to eat those words. In the ensuing fifteen years, the courts handed down more antiunion injunctions than in the twenty-four years before Clayton. Although open-shop industry enjoyed steady injunctive relief from trade unionism, it was not until the Great Depression that the balance was partially redressed and unions got some relief.

In purely political terms the progressive answer to the trust question was a masterful compromise. It gave just enough to Bryan Democrats and "friends of labor" for them to stand with conservative Democrats, Taft Republicans, and Bull Moosers behind the new regulations on banking and corporate practices. It harmonized the three branches of government insofar as Congress gave a statutory basis to the executive's Federal Trade Commission and Federal Reserve Board, while providing for judicial review of FTC decisions. It tended toward centralized control, but it left enough regional autonomy, for example, in the dozen Federal Reserve districts, for continuity with federalist tradition. It modified the liberal state in the direction of government regulation of the market, but instead of erecting a state bureaucracy, it lodged real power in a kind of parastate, that is, a nexus of private-public authority that combined corporate management with government regulation. As a result, it took the trust question out of politics in both senses. That is, it silenced much popular clamor, removing trust-busting as an issue in the next presidential election; and it referred future issues of corporate malfeasance to "nonpolitical" bodies of experts.

This harmonious political resolution of the trust question should not be mistaken for a resolution of social antagonism. Contrary to the aims of social-justice advocates at the grass roots, progressive statecraft at the national level favored capital against workers and large capital over small. The consequence of federal action at the height of progressive influence was to reshape property relations by helping to redefine the legal norms of ownership. The formal cartel arrangements among oligopolistic firms of the sort common in German industry—price fixing, exclusive contracts, direct government promotion—were put out of bounds, and true monopoly was discouraged. But the tight oligopoly of a handful of separate corporations was fully accepted, so long as they refrained from "unreasonable" collusion. The Supreme Court made it official in 1920 by upholding the legality of the United States Steel Corporation under the "rule of reason," leaving the steel industry in possession of a few firms that preferred stability to competition and were therefore willing to follow the lead of Judge Elbert Gary and his "Steel Trust." It was crystal clear that the new balance favored open-shop employers in their battle against the unions, a fact that would be resoundly confirmed in the defeat of the great 1919 steel strike. Thus the progressive corporate-regulatory complex altered the relation between state and society in ways that helped transform the corporate elite into the dominant class and legitimate their leadership in society at large. . . .

Wilsonian statecraft brought to a close the first chapter in the emergence of twentieth-century liberalism. The social movements of workers, women, and middle-class reformers had forced their issues into the public arena around calls for industrial democracy, feminism, and social reform, many of which were embodied in the spirited Progressive and Socialist party campaigns of 1912. But campaigning is not governing, and although American parties were responsible for putting people into elective office, they were not responsible for running the country, at least not in the same way as British, French, and, after 1918, German parliamentary parties. That cardinal difference gave President Wilson the flexibility he needed to include elements outside his own party in fashioning a program of reform. Elected as a Victorian liberal who advocated free trade and open competition, he adroitly stole regulatory and social justice planks from Roosevelt's Progressive party, thereby co-opting the social-justice wing of progressivism and, much more distantly, co-opting socialism. And if his program *contained* socialism and social reform in the inclusive sense, it also did so in the exclusive sense, making sure that there would be no significant experiments in state paternalism. Certainly, the southern wing of the Democratic party in conjunction with Republican business conservatives set severe restrictions on how far he could go toward aiding the poor.

Thus even at its highwater mark, progressive statecraft at the national level stopped far short of the kind of statist authority found in Germany. Instead of a German-style welfare state, President Wilson supported women's protective legislation on the state level and the federal child labor act, but scarcely anything more. Instead of full-scale federal mediation of industrial relations, he supported the exercise in public relations known as the Commission on Industrial Relations and the Adamson Act, but, again, little else. Instead of extensive state controls on central banking, Wilson set up the Federal Reserve System under private management with minimal federal oversight, and he appointed friends of business to the Federal Trade Commission. In short, instead of a statist bureaucracy, he constructed a corporate-regulatory complex within the liberal state that left society supreme over the state. As a consequence, the most powerful element in the market—that is, big business—remained supreme in society.

The corporate-regulatory complex pointed the way toward a new governing system in which corporate property and a new form of the nuclear family oriented toward consumption instead of production might be better secured than in the increasingly outmoded shell of laissez-faire liberalism. Certainly, the Federal Reserve helped legitimate Wall Street's finance capitalists at a time when their trusts had come under strong public censure. Likewise, protective legislation came to the support of the family ideal of husband-breadwinner/wife-homemaker, which legitimated women's subordination at a time when radical voices had been raised in favor of equality between the sexes. In addition, the new corporate order increased inequalities of wealth and income to the point that a higher share of income went to the top than ever before in American history; several combined studies show that inequality of income distribution peaked in 1916. In sum, the achievement of Wilson's progressive statecraft was to remake the liberal state so that liberalism could continue as the dominant tradition in altered form, and also as a tradition that upheld the dominance of rich, white men.

This does not mean that social antagonism was adjourned, or that the great questions of the day had been answered, or that there would never be another attempt to remake the liberal state. But it did mean that progressivism would never get another chance; for even as the Wilsonians were putting the finishing touches on their work, a new dynamic took command of events as more and more the United States was drawn into the vortex of the Great War in Europe.

Freedom and the Progressive State

ERIC FONER

Whether the aim was to regulate or destroy the power of the trusts, protect consumers, civilize the marketplace by eliminating cutthroat competition, or guarantee "industrial freedom" at the workplace, Progressives assumed that the modern era required a fundamental rethinking of the functions of government. The national

Eric Foner, *The Story of American Freedom* (New York: W. W. Norton, 1998), 152–161. Copyright © 1998 by Eric Foner. Used by permission of W. W. Norton & Company, Inc.

state, noted one Progressive commentator, was "a moral agent," which should set the rules under which society conducted its affairs.

Most of the era's reform legislation, including changes in voting requirements, regulation of corporations, and the overseeing of safety and health conditions in factories, was enacted at the municipal and state levels. But the most striking development of the early twentieth century was the rise of the nation-state, complete with administrative agencies, independent commissions, and laws establishing the parameters for labor relations, business behavior, and financial policy, and acting as a broker among the disputatious groups whose conflicts threatened to destroy social harmony. These were the years when the Federal Reserve Board, the Federal Trade Commission, and other agencies came into existence, and when the federal government, through measures like the Pure Food and Drug Act (1906), sought to set basic rules for market behavior and protect citizens from market abuses.

To most Progressives, the tradition of localism and states' rights seemed an excuse for parochialism, an impediment to a renewed sense of national purpose. Poverty, economic insecurity, and lack of industrial democracy were national problems that demanded national solutions. As for laissez-faire, this, observed the Progressive social scientist Horace Kallen, had become "anathema among lovers of liberty." Many Progressives believed that economic evolution, rather than the misconduct of capitalists, had produced the large corporation acting nationally and even internationally. The same kind of process, they concluded, had made the national state the natural unit of political action. Only energetic government could create the social conditions for freedom. The democratic state, wrote Herbert Croly, embodied an alterative to control of Americans' lives by narrow interests that manipulated politics or by the all-powerful corporations. To achieve the "Jeffersonian ends" of democratic self-determination and individual freedom, he insisted, it was now necessary to employ the "Hamiltonian means" of a government-directed economy.

Progressives could reject the traditional assumption that a powerful government posed a threat to freedom because their understanding of freedom was itself in flux. In a lecture in 1880 that would exert a powerful influence on Progressive social thought, the British philosopher T. H. Green had argued that freedom was a positive concept, a matter, ultimately, of "power." Green's call for a new definition of freedom was taken up throughout Progressive America. "Effective freedom," wrote John Dewey, who pondered the question from the 1890s until his death in 1952, was far different from the "highly formal and limited concept of liberty" as a preexisting possession of autonomous individuals that needed to be protected from outside restraint. It meant "effective power to do specific things," and as such was a function of "the *distribution* of powers that exists at a given time." Thus, freedom was "always a *social* question" and inevitably also a political issue. Freedom—and the individual endowments, powers, and desires it embodied—was constructed by and enjoyed through social institutions and democratic citizenship. "Freedom," wrote Dewey's brilliant young admirer Randolph Bourne, "means a democratic cooperation in determining the ideals and purposes and industrial and social institutions of a country."

What the nineteenth century had called autonomy appeared to Progressives like Dewey and Croly mere isolation; real freedom, they believed, involved the constant growth entailed by a lifetime of interaction with others. In seeing freedom as an ongoing process of self-realization, to be sure, they harked back to the Emersonian notion of personal fulfillment and even to Jefferson's natural right to "the pursuit of happiness." But to traditional notions of individualism and autonomy. Progressives wedded the idea that such freedom required the conscious creation of the social conditions for full human development. To Croly, this suggested that the state must become responsible for "a morally and socially desirable distribution of wealth." For Dewey, it meant equipping Americans with the intellectual resources required to understand the modern world, and empowering the state to combat economic deprivation and disempowerment. Progressivism, said the social scientist William F. Willoughby, "looks to state action as the . . . only practicable means now in sight, of giving to the individual, all individuals, not merely a small economically strong class, real freedom."

Yet while Progressive intellectuals developed a new conception of the national state, their "new democracy" (the title of Walter Weyl's influential book) had a highly ambiguous relationship to the inherited definition of political freedom as democratic participation in governance. Enhancing the power of the state made it all the more important to identify the boundaries of political participation. During the Progressive era, a host of changes were implemented in the electoral process and political arena, many seemingly contradictory in purpose. The electorate was simultaneously expanded and contracted, empowered and removed from direct influence on many functions of government. The era witnessed the massive disenfranchisement of blacks in the South (a process begun in Mississippi in 1890 and completed in Georgia in 1908), and a constitutional amendment enfranchising women—the largest expansion of democracy in U.S. history. It saw the adoption of measures like the initiative, referendum, and recall, designed to allow the electorate to propose and vote directly on legislation and remove officials from office, and the widespread replacement of elected mayors by appointed city managers. It saw literacy tests (increasingly common in the North as well as the South) expanded, and new residency and registration requirements implemented in the hope of limiting the franchise among the poor.

Taken as a whole, the electoral changes of the Progressive era represented a significant and ironic reversal of the nineteenth-century trend toward manhood suffrage and a rejection of the venerable idea that voting was an inalienable right of American citizenship. To most Progressives, the "fitness" of voters, not their absolute numbers, defined a functioning democracy. In the name of improving democracy, millions of men—mostly blacks, immigrants, and other workers— were eliminated from the voting rolls, even as millions of white women were added. The more egalitarian Progressives, like Dewey, believed that given the necessary opportunities and resources, all citizens were capable of mastering the spirit of disinterested inquiry and of applying themselves to finding pragmatic, "scientific" solutions to social problems. Thus, government could safely be removed from the control of trusts and machines and placed in the hands of "the people." Yet most Progressive thinkers were highly uncomfortable with the real world of politics, which seemed to revolve around the pursuit of narrow class, ethnic, and regional interests. Indeed, one reason for many Progressives' support for women's suffrage was the belief—encouraged by feminists—that as an independent, non-partisan force, women voters could help rescue politics from politicians and partisanship and reorient it toward the pursuit of the common good.

"He didn't believe in democracy; he believed simply in government." H. L. Mencken's quip about Theodore Roosevelt came uncomfortably close to the mark for many Progressive advocates of an empowered national state. The government could best exercise intelligent control over society through a "democracy" run by impartial experts and in many respects unaccountable to the citizenry. This technocratic impulse toward order, efficiency, and centralized management—all, ostensibly, in the service of social justice—was an important theme of Progressive reform. The title of Walter Lippmann's influential work of social commentary, *Drift and Mastery* (1914), posed the stark alternatives facing the nation. "Drift" meant continuing to operate according to the outmoded shibboleth of individual autonomy; "mastery," recognition that society could be remade by the application of rational inquiry to social problems and conflicts. "The scientific spirit," Lippmann wrote, was "the outlook of a free man." But, Lippmann feared, ordinary citizens, attached to antiquated ideas and parochial concerns, were ill-prepared to embrace it. . . . The new generation of corporate managers and educated professionals could be trusted to address creatively and efficiently America's deep social problems. For Lippmann, political freedom was less a matter of direct participation in governance than of proper policy outcomes.

But alongside this elitist administrative politics arose a more democratic Progressive vision of the activist state. As much as any other group, organized women reformers were its midwives. In the first two decades of the century, as women's suffrage for the first time became a mass movement, it moved beyond the elitism of the 1890s to engage a broad coalition, ranging from middle-class club women to unionists, socialists, and settlement house workers, and its rhetoric became more democratic and less nativist. Among the reasons for the movement's expanding base was that it became linked to the broad demand for state intervention on behalf of economic freedom. The immediate catalyst was a growing awareness of the plight of the immigrant poor among women involved in the settlement house movement, and the emergence of the condition of women and child laborers as a major focus of public concern.

Still barred from political participation in most states, women nonetheless were central to the era's political history. The effort of middle-class women to uplift the poor, through clubs, settlement houses, and other agencies, and of laboring women to uplift themselves, helped shift the center of gravity of political discourse toward activist government. Well-educated middle-class women not only found a calling in providing social services and education to poor families, but discovered the severe limitations of laissez-faire orthodoxy as an explanation for urban poverty and the failure of even well-organized social work to alleviate the problems of inadequate housing, income, and health. Out of the settlement houses came not only Jane Addams and Florence Kelley but also Julia Lathrop, the first woman to head a federal agency (the Children's Bureau, established in 1912 to investigate the conditions of mothers and children and advocate their interests), and Frances Perkins, secretary of labor during the 1930s. In turning for assistance to the state, Progressive women helped to launch a mass movement for governmental regulation of working conditions and direct state assistance to improve the living standards of the poor.

"We need the ballot," said labor leader Leonora O'Reilly, "to do justice to our work as home-keepers. Children need pure milk and good food, good schools and playgrounds, sanitary homes and safe streets." What historians have called "maternalist" reform—based on the assumption that the state had an obligation to encourage women's unique capacity for childbearing and childrearing—inspired many of the era's experiments in governmental policy. Ironically, those who sought to exalt women's role within the home helped to inspire the state-building process during the Progressive era.

By the time the United States entered World War I in 1917, Progressives had succeeded in bringing governmental power to bear in seeking to enhance the conditions of women's freedom, at work and at home. Laws providing for mothers' pensions (state aid to mothers of young children who lacked male support) spread rapidly after 1910. Although the pensions tended to be meager and local eligibility requirements opened the door to discrimination in application (white widows were always the primary beneficiaries, single mothers were widely discriminated against, and only 3 percent of the recipients nationally were black), the laws recognized the government's responsibility to enable women to devote themselves to their children and be economically independent at the same time. . . . Laws prohibiting child labor, a major issue at a time when an estimated 2 million children under the age of fifteen were gainfully employed, represented another "maternalist" reform (although these laws were often opposed by poor families for whom income earned by children was essential for family survival).

Other Progressive legislation recognized that large numbers of women did in fact work outside the home, but defined them as a dependent group (analogous to children) in need of state protection in ways male workers were not. In 1908, in the landmark case of *Muller* v. *Oregon,* the Supreme Court unanimously upheld the constitutionality of a maximum hours law for women. In his famous brief supporting the Oregon measure, Louis Brandeis invoked a battery of scientific and sociological studies to demonstrate that because they had less strength and endurance than men, long hours of labor were especially dangerous for women, while their unique ability to bear children gave the state a legitimate interest in their working conditions. Thus, three years after the notorious *Lochner* decision invalidating a state law limiting the working hours of bakers, the Court created the first large breach in liberty of contract orthodoxy. But the cost was high: at the very time that women in unprecedented numbers were entering the labor market and earning college degrees, Brandeis's brief and the Court's opinion solidified the idea that women workers were weak, dependent, and incapable of enjoying the same economic freedom as men. By 1914, twenty-seven states had enacted laws limiting the hours of labor of female workers.

While the maternalist agenda built gender inequality into the early foundations of the welfare state, the very use of government to regulate working conditions called into question basic assumptions concerning laissez-faire and the sanctity of the labor contract. . . . Although not all reformers were willing to take the step, it was easy to extend the idea of protecting women to demand that government better the living and working conditions of men by insuring them against the vagaries of unemployment, old age, ill health, and disability. Brandeis himself insisted that a broad definition of social welfare formed part of the "liberty" protected by the Fourteenth Amendment and that government should concern itself with the health, income, and future prospects of all its citizens. . . .

Brandeis . . . envisioned a different welfare state from that of the maternalist reformers, one rooted less in the social work tradition and visions of healthy mother-hood than in the idea of universal economic entitlements, including the right to a decent income and protection against unemployment and injury on the job. This vision, too, enjoyed considerable support in the Progressive era. By 1920, nearly all the states had enacted workmen's compensation laws, the entering wedge for broader programs of social insurance. But state minimum wage laws and most laws regulating working hours applied only to women. The provision of a basic liv-ing standard and a set of working conditions beneath which no individual should fall would await the coming of the New Deal.

All the cross-currents of Progressive-era thinking about what *McClure's Mag-azine* called "the problem of the relation of the State and the corporation" came together in the presidential campaign of 1912. A "year with supreme possibilities," as Eugene V. Debs put it, 1912 witnessed a four-way contest between Republican president William Howard Taft, former president Theodore Roosevelt, now run-ning as candidate of the Progressive Party, Democrat Woodrow Wilson, and Debs himself, representing a Socialist Party at the height of its influence. The campaign became an extended national debate on the relationship between political and eco-nomic freedom in the age of the large corporation. At one end of the political spec-trum stood the president, a bona fide Progressive, although in 1912 he stressed that economic individualism could remain the foundation of the social order so long as government and private entrepreneurs cooperated in addressing social ills. At the other end was Debs, the only candidate to demand a complete change in the eco-nomic structure to propel the nation "from wage slavery to free cooperation, from capitalist oligarchy to industrial democracy." Relatively few Americans adhered to the party's goal of abolishing the "capitalistic system" altogether, but its immediate demands—including public ownership of the railroads and banking system, gov-ernment aid to the unemployed, legislation establishing shorter hours and a min-imum wage, and a graduated income tax—summarized the most forward-looking Progressive thought.

But it was the battle between Wilson and Roosevelt over the meaning of free-dom and the role of the state in securing it that galvanized public attention in 1912. The two differed on many issues, notably the dangers of governmental power and the inevitability of economic concentration, but both believed increased state ac-tion was necessary to preserve individual freedom. Though representing a party thoroughly steeped in states' rights and laissez-faire ideology, Wilson was deeply imbued with Progressive ideas. "Of course, we want liberty," he had declared in 1911, "but what is liberty?" "Old words . . . consecrated throughout many genera-tions," he insisted, needed to be "translated into experience," and as governor of New Jersey, he had presided over the implementation of workmen's compensation and state regulation of utilities and railroads. Nonetheless, Wilson's 1912 "pro-gram of liberty," or the "New Freedom," as he came to call it, was heavily indebted to traditional Democratic ideology. Government, he insisted, was the antagonist of freedom: "the history of liberty is a history of the limitation of governmental power, not the increase of it. "Yet freedom, Wilson maintained, meant more than in Jefferson's time, and government had a responsibility to promote it: "freedom today is something more than being let alone. The program of a government of freedom must in these days be positive, not negative merely." Strongly influenced by Brandeis, with whom he consulted frequently during the campaign, Wilson insisted that freedom was "an economic idea" as well as a political one, and that the way to reinvigorate democracy was to restore market competition by freeing government from subservience to big business. Freedom could only thrive in a decentralized economy that bred independent citizens and restored self-government to local communities—goals the federal government could pursue by strengthening antitrust laws, protecting the right of workers to unionize, and actively encouraging small entrepreneurs.

In retrospect, it seems clear that Wilson had little understanding of the myriad sources of corporate hegemony in a modern economy. But his warning that consolidated economic power might join with concentrated political power to the detriment of ordinary citizens was remarkably prescient, especially given the confidence of so many Progressives that the state could be counted upon to act as a disinterested arbiter of the nation's social and economic purposes. To Roosevelt's supporters, however, Wilson seemed a relic of a bygone era, whose program served the needs of small businessmen but ignored the interests of professionals, consumers, and labor. The New Freedom, wrote Lippmann, meant "freedom for the little profiteer, but no freedom for the nation from the narrowness, the . . . limited vision of small competitors." Wilson and Brandeis spoke of the "curse of bigness"; what the nation actually needed, Lippmann countered, was frank acceptance of the inevitability and benefits of bigness, coupled with the active intervention of government to counteract its abuses while guiding society toward common goals. Lippmann was articulating the core of the New Nationalism, Theodore Roosevelt's alternative vision of 1912. Wilson's statement that limits on governmental power formed the essence of freedom, Roosevelt pointedly remarked, "has not one particle of foundation in the facts of the present day." It was a recipe for "the enslavement of the people by the great corporations who can only be held in check by the extension of governmental power"; only the "regulatory, the controlling, and directing power of the government" could represent "the liberty of the oppressed."

Where Wilson opposed extensive social welfare programs for making citizens dependents of the state, the Progressive Party platform offered a myriad of proposals to promote social justice. Inspired by a group of settlement house feminists, labor reformers, and Progressive social scientists, the platform laid out a blueprint for a modern, democratic welfare state, complete with women's suffrage, federal supervision of corporate enterprise, national labor and health legislation for women and children, an eight-hour day and a "living wage" for all workers, the right of workers to form unions, and a national system of social insurance covering unemployment, medical care, and old age. Roosevelt called it the "most important document" since the end of the Civil War, and the platform brought together many of the streams of thought and political experience that flowed into Progressivism. Roosevelt, of course, lost the election (although once in office, Wilson often seemed to act as a New Nationalist). But his campaign helped give freedom a modern social and economic content and established an agenda that would continue to define political liberalism for much of the rest of the century.

Indeed, by 1916, writers like Herbert Croly were consciously attempting to redefine the venerable term "liberalism," previously shorthand for limited government and laissez-faire economics, to describe belief in an activist, socially conscious state. This would become the word's meaning for most of the twentieth century. Modern liberalism, however, has other features conspicuously absent from the Progressive agenda: an overriding preoccupation with civil liberties, including the right to personal privacy and the free expression of ideas, and a pluralist concern for the rights of racial and ethnic minorities. With its impulse toward social cohesiveness and homogeneity, and its exaltation of the national state as the embodiment of democracy, mainstream Progressivism was not attuned to these understandings of freedom. Their origins lay elsewhere—among the radicals and cultural bohemians of Progressive America.

 # F U R T H E R   R E A D I N G

Eileen Boris, *Home to Work: Motherhood and the Politics of Industrial Homework in the United States* (1994)

John Milton Cooper, Jr., *The Warrior and the Priest: Woodrow Wilson and Theodore Roosevelt* (1983)

Morton Keller, *Regulating a New Economy: Public Policy and Economic Change in America, 1900–1933* (1990)

Arthur S. Link, *Woodrow Wilson and the Progressive Era* (1963)

Richard L. McCormick, *From Realignment to Reform: Political Change in New York State, 1893–1910* (1981)

———, *Progressivism* (1983)

Edmund Morris, *The Rise of Theodore Roosevelt* (1979)

Bruno Ramirez, *When Workers Fight: The Politics of Industrial Relations in the Progressive Era, 1898–1916* (1978)

John F. Reynolds, *Testing Democracy: Electoral Behavior and Progressive Reform in New Jersey, 1880–1920* (1988)

Bradley R. Rice, *Progressive Cities: The Commission Government Movement in America, 1901–1920* (1977)

Martin J. Schiesl, *The Politics of Efficiency* (1977)

Stephen Skowronek, *Building a New American State* (1982)

David P. Thelen, *Robert La Follette and the Insurgent Spirit* (1976)

Melvin I. Urofsky, *Louis Brandeis and the Progressive Tradition* (1981)

James Weinstein, *The Cooperate Ideal in the Liberal State, 1900–1918* (1968)

Nature Without Nurture:

Progressives Confront

Environmental Destruction

Environmentalism emerged as an important progressive cause, affecting attitudes and public policies toward the cities as well as the countryside. Its emergence indirectly resulted from a general retreat from explanations of social behavior (especially poverty and social "breakdown") in terms of individual character and moral purity toward more collective, behaviorist terms of reference. If "outside" influences significantly conditioned human actions, as social scientists universally proclaimed, then the "control" of those influences became paramount. In the cities, this basic behaviorist argument could be used to promote parks and playgrounds as well as sanitation campaigns.

Better known is the rise of the modern conservationist movement, closely associated with President Theodore Roosevelt and his chief of the U.S. Forest Service, Gifford Pinchot. In this form, "conservationism" is distinguished from "preservationism": the former sought the application of science and engineering to the responsible development of natural resources; the latter, attracting Sierra Club founder John Muir, emphasized the aesthetic and spiritual virtues of the unspoiled wilderness. In 1913, the two positions collided in the fight over the Hetch Hetchy Dam, a project that would alleviate a water shortage in San Francisco—at the cost of a section of Yosemite National Park.

 D O C U M E N T S

The following selections highlight the basic conflict confronting Progressive-Era Americans between development and preservation and explore the emerging logic of the newfound conservationist ethos. Document 1, President Theodore Roosevelt's pathbreaking address to the Congress in 1907, cogently elaborates the argument for the federal government's conservation of natural resources. Roosevelt makes a case both for preservation and long-term *use* of resources. The polarities of the contemporary political debate over conservation are also on display in Document 2 in which a California lumber executive cites the need for treating trees like any other renewable resource, while preservationist Enos Mills, a disciple of John Muir, offers a poignant tribute (Document 3) to an ancient pine tree felled by developers. Document 4 further documents such differences, as claimed in congressional testimony concerning the Hetch Hetchy Dam, a project that stirred up a classical confrontation between utilitarian conservationists on the one and wilderness preservationists on the other. The controversy pitted former Chief Forester Gifford Pinchot, together with former San Francisco mayor James D. Phelan, against the Society for the Protection of National Parks, represented by Boston lawyer Edmund A. Whitman and poet Robert Underwood Johnson. In Document 5, reformer Jane Addams suggests the urban side of the new environmentalist consciousness—an angle that also indicated an enhanced role for women in public affairs.

1. President Theodore Roosevelt's Conservation Message, 1907

To the Senate and House of Representatives:

. . . The conservation of our natural resources and their proper use constitute the fundamental problem which underlies almost every other problem of our national life. . . . As a nation we not only enjoy a wonderful measure of present prosperity but if this prosperity is used aright it is an earnest of future success such as no other nation will have. The reward of foresight for this nation is great and easily foretold. But there must be the look ahead, there must be a realization of the fact that to waste, to destroy, our natural resources, to skin and exhaust the land instead of using it so as to increase its usefulness, will result in undermining in the days of our children the very prosperity which we ought by right to hand down to them amplified and developed. For the last few years, through several agencies, the government has been endeavoring to get our people to look ahead and to substitute a planned and orderly development of our resources in place of a haphazard striving for immediate profit. Our great river systems should be developed as national water highways, the Mississippi, with its tributaries, standing first in importance, and the Columbia second, although there are many others of importance on the Pacific, the Atlantic, and the Gulf slopes. The National Government should undertake this work, and I hope a beginning will be made in the present Congress; and the greatest of all our rivers, the Mississippi, should receive special attention. From the Great Lakes to the mouth of the Mississippi there should be a deep waterway, with deep waterways leading from it to the East and the West. Such a waterway would practically mean the extension of our coastline into the very heart of our country. It would be of incalculable benefit to our people. If begun at once it can be carried through in time appreciably to relieve the congestion of our great freight-carrying lines of railroads. The work should be systematically and continuously carried forward in accordance with some well-conceived plan. The main streams should be improved to

Congressional Record, 60th Cong. 1st sess., 74–76.

the highest point of efficiency before the improvement of the branches is attempted; and the work should be kept free from every taint of recklessness or jobbery. The inland waterways which lie just back of the whole Eastern and Southern coasts should likewise be developed. Moreover, the development of our waterways involves many other important water problems, all of which should be considered as part of the same general scheme. The government dams should be used to produce hundreds of thousands of horse-power as an incident to improving navigation; for the annual value of the unused water-power of the United States perhaps exceeds the annual value of the products of all our mines. As an incident to creating the deep waterways down the Mississippi, the government should build along its whole lower length levees which, taken together with the control of the headwaters, will at once and forever put a complete stop to all threat of floods in the immensely fertile delta region. The territory lying adjacent to the Mississippi along its lower course will thereby become one of the most prosperous and populous, as it already is one of the most fertile, farming regions in all the world. I have appointed an inland waterways commission to study and outline a comprehensive scheme of development along all the lines indicated. Later I shall lay its report before the Congress.

Irrigation should be far more extensively developed than at present, not only in the States of the great plains and the Rocky Mountains, but in many others, as, for instance, in large portions of the South Atlantic and Gulf States, where it should go hand in hand with the reclamation of swampland. The Federal Government should seriously devote itself to this task, realizing that utilization of waterways and water-power, forestry, irrigation, and the reclamation of lands threatened with overflow, are all interdependent parts of the same problem. The work of the Reclamation Service in developing the larger opportunities of the Western half of our country for irrigation is more important than almost any other movement. The constant purpose of the government in connection with the Reclamation Service has been to use the water resources of the public lands for the ultimate greatest good of the greatest number; in other words, to put upon the land permanent homemakers, to use and develop it for themselves and for their children and children's children. . . .

Some such legislation as that proposed is essential in order to preserve the great stretches of public grazing-land which are unfit for cultivation under present methods and are valuable only for the forage which they supply. These stretches amount in all to some 30,000,000 acres, and are open to the free grazing of cattle, sheep, horses, and goats, without restriction. Such a system, or lack of system, means that the range is not so much used as wasted by abuse. As the West settles, the range becomes more and more overgrazed. Much of it cannot be used to advantage unless it is fenced, for fencing is the only way by which to keep in check the owners of nomad flocks which roam hither and thither, utterly destroying the pastures and leaving a waste behind so that their presence is incompatible with the presence of home-makers. The existing fences are all illegal. . . . All these fences, those that are hurtful and those that are beneficial, are alike illegal and must come down. But it is an outrage that the law should necessitate such action on the part of the Administration. The unlawful fencing of public lands for private grazing must be stopped, but the necessity which occasioned it must be provided for. The Federal Government should have control of the range, whether by permit or lease, as local necessities may determine. Such control could secure the great benefit of legitimate fencing, while at the same time securing and promoting the settlement of the country. . . . The government should part with its title only to the actual home-maker, not to the profit-maker who does not care to make a home. Our prime object is to secure the rights and guard the interests of the small ranchman, the man who ploughs and pitches hay for himself. It is this small ranchman, this actual settler and home-maker, who in the long run is most hurt by permitting thefts of the public land in whatever form.

Optimism is a good characteristic, but if carried to an excess it becomes fool-ishness. We are prone to speak of the resources of this country as inexhaustible; this is not so. The mineral wealth of the country, the coal, iron, oil, gas, and the like, does not reproduce itself, and therefore is certain to be exhausted ultimately; and wastefulness in dealing with it today means that our descendants will feel the exhaustion a generation or two before they otherwise would. But there are certain other forms of waste which could be entirely stopped—the waste of soil by washing, for instance, which is among the most dangerous of all wastes now in progress in the United States, is easily preventable, so that this present enormous loss of fertility is entirely unnecessary. The preservation or replacement of the forests is one of the most important means of preventing this loss. . . . We should acquire in the Appalachian and White Mountain regions all the forest-lands that it is possible to acquire for the use of the nation. These lands, because they form a national asset, are as emphatically national as the rivers which they feed, and which flow through so many States before they reach the ocean.

2. A Lumberer's Perspective on the California Redwoods, 1884

Twenty-five or thirty years ago—long before the era of Continental Railways—our Eastern and trans-Atlantic cousins read in letters from our people of California, of its wonderful scenery, climate and productions, with incredulity; they believing, perhaps, that the then wanderers from the old homes and hearthstones to the jump-ing off place on the American continent had produced a sort of epidemic in the way of boasting of the new Eldorado. . . .

Of all that has been told or written by travellers and correspondents concern-ing California scenery, its huge growth of beets, melons, squash, pears, and fruits of all descriptions, the least attention has been called to our grand forests of Red-wood. This, however, is not much a matter of surprise, as the facilities for a careful inspection of this favorite building material are quite or nearly as primitive as during the early settlement of the State. Especially is this the case in the northern section of the State, where the redwood belt has greater width, and from climatic causes has developed a heavier growth of timber. Not only are the trees in this northern section larger in circumference, but they attain a much greater height, and withal

C. G. Noyes, *Redwood and Lumbering in California Forests* (San Francisco: Edgar Cherry & Co., 1884), 3–4, 14–18, 34–35, 75. As edited in Carolyn Merchant, ed., *Major Problems in American Environmental History: Documents and Essays* (Lexington, Mass.: D. C. Heath, 1993), 387–398. Reprinted by permission of Houghton Mifflin Company.

give a product to the millmen that is far superior in quality to that obtained in the southern extremity of the redwood belt. . . .

The California Redwood Company (the largest in this line on the coast) has already taken the initiative step looking to a supply of clear seasoned lumber for the Eastern market. At Tormey Station just below Port Costa, and convenient for shipping both by rail and sea to all parts of the world, they have built wharves and opened a yard covering some twenty acres, where their lumber can be seasoned properly before being offered to the markets abroad. . . . Once let builders at the East be thoroughly convinced, as we are, that redwood is superior for interior finish, and our local market will seldom become glutted with an over-product.

Many will argue—and justly, too—that it would be better for the country that a demand which causes such a draft upon its lumber resources should, by some manner of means, be restricted, and that if high rates of freight will prevent the rapid denudation of our forest, they had better be maintained by the railroad corporations. Others can argue, however, that owners of timber lands can assist in reproduction by a slight effort in the way of timber culture, and thereby extend the supply to an indefinite period. . . . We have often thought that should the Government offer as great inducements in the reproduction of redwoods as it is doing to encourage timber culture in parts where it is unnatural for forests to thrive, that the redwoods would never become exterminated, as has so frequently been predicted. One must confess, however, that the matter of cultivating this tree with a view to growing timber like anything of its present size, would require a people possessing a higher regard for generations a hundred or more years hence than the mind of an average American can comprehend.

The Government map . . . shows that the really valuable portion of the belt (from Russian River to the northern limit) covers about two hundred and seventy miles from north to south. . . . The Government estimate (board measure) of timber standing in this belt in the census year 1880 was 25,825,000,000 feet. This was made up from estimates furnished by a few lumbermen, whose opportunities for making a fair estimate cannot be questioned. But it is also true that many others, including millmen and lumbermen, estimate from 50 to 100 per cent higher; and taking the estimated area of the belt from Russian River to the Oregon line with the estimate of timber standing, we shall find even their figures largely increased. The 275 miles covered by this portion of the belt multiplied by the least estimated width (15 miles) gives 4125 miles. A square mile contains 640 acres, and the average yield per acre (according to government estimate) is 50,000 feet, which would give 32,000,000 feet to the square mile. This would give us a total for the 4125 square miles 132,000,000,000 feet of standing timber. . . .

Economy in the manufacture of redwood lumber is a matter in which the pioneer millmen of the Pacific Coast have taken but little interest until within the past three or four years. This could hardly be expected to have been otherwise, for the reason that the supply seemed to them unlimited and inexhaustible. The interest manifested by foreign investors and eastern capitalists in the timber reserves of America, however, has of late checked the inclination to waste which our old lumbermen inconsiderately indulged in for years. This check upon waste is commendable, more especially in the redwoods, because of its adaptability for building purposes, where white pine and the softer woods of the eastern forests are considered indispensable.

And that the redwood is largely to fill the demand which has caused the almost entire destruction of the pineries of Maine, Michigan, Wisconsin, and Canada, there is not the least doubt among observant lumbermen of the eastern States. As corroboration of this statement, we may here refer to the large number of agents sent into the counties of Humboldt and Mendocino during the past two years by eastern capitalists, as well as from England and Scotland, to purchase tracts of redwood timber ranging from three thousand to ten thousand acres. . . .

Almost the first thought passing in one's mind, as he enters a virgin forest of redwoods, is one of pity that such a wonderful creation of nature should be subject to the greed of man for gold. The same feelings of awe pervade one's being upon his first introduction to this apparently exhaustless army of giants, that impress the beholder of Niagara, Yosemite, and the near relatives of the redwoods—the Big Trees of Calaveras and Merced. . . .

When transportation facilities are complete, either by rail or by water, . . . as they certainly will be within a few years, it needs no prophet to predict that the California Redwood will, in the near future, have no rival in the lumber marts of the world.

Within a generation to come the question will be asked: "How long will the Redwoods last? A few years at most. But in that brief time men will build their castles and their thrones of power upon the mighty race of giants, with the one regret that there are no more to conquer."

3. Enos Mills Mourns the Death of a One-Thousand-Year-Old Pine, 1914

I

The peculiar charm and fascination that trees exert over many people I had always felt from childhood, but it was that great nature-lover, John Muir, who first showed me how and where to learn their language. Few trees, however, ever held for me such an attraction as did a gigantic and venerable yellow pine which I discovered one autumn day several years ago while exploring the southern Rockies. It grew within sight of the Cliff-Dwellers' Mesa Verde [Colorado], which stands at the corner of four States, and as I came upon it one evening just as the sun was setting over that mysterious tableland, its character and heroic proportions made an impression upon me that I shall never forget, and which familiar acquaintance only served to deepen while it yet lived and before the axeman came. Many a time I returned to build my camp-fire by it and have a day or a night in its solitary and noble company. I learned afterwards that it had been given the name "Old Pine," and it certainly had an impressiveness quite compatible with the age and dignity which go with a thousand years of life.

When, one day, the sawmill-man at Mancos wrote, "Come, we are about to log your old pine," I started at once, regretting that a thing which seemed to me so human, as well as so noble, must be killed.

Enos Mills, *The Story of a One-Thousand Year Pine* (New York: Houghton Mifflin, 1914), selections.

I went with the axemen who were to cut the old pine down. . . . Never have I seen so much individuality, so much character, in a tree. Although lightning had given him a bald crown, he was still a healthy giant, and was waving evergreen banners more than one hundred and fifteen feet above the earth. His massive trunk, eight feet in diameter at the level of my breast, was covered with a thick, rough, golden-brown bark which was broken into irregular plates. Several of his arms were bent and broken. Altogether, he presented a timeworn but heroic appearance. . . .

Trees, like people, struggle for existence, and an aged tree, like an aged person, has not only a striking appearance, but an interesting biography. I have read the auto-biographies of many century-old trees, and have found their life-stories strange and impressive. The yearly growth, or annual ring of wood with which trees envelop themselves, is embossed with so many of their experiences that this annual ring of growth literally forms an autobiographic diary of the tree's life.

I wanted to read Old Pine's autobiography. A veteran pine that had stood on the southern Rockies and struggled and triumphed through the changing seasons of hundreds of years must contain a rare life-story. . . . Many a wondrous secret he had locked within his tree soul. Yet, although he had not recorded what he had *seen,* I knew that he had kept a fairly accurate diary of his own personal experience. This I knew the saw would reveal, and this I had determined to see. . . .

II

Two loggers swung their axes: at the first blow a Frémont squirrel came out of a hole at the base of a dead limb near the top of the tree and made an aggressive claim of ownership, setting up a vociferous protest against the cutting. . . . From time to time he came out on the top of the limb nearest to us, and, with a wry face, fierce whiskers, and violent gestures, directed a torrent of abuse at the axemen who were delivering death-blows to Old Pine.

The old pine's enormous weight caused him to fall heavily, and he came to earth with tremendous force and struck on an elbow of one of his stocky arms. The force of the fall not only broke the trunk in two, but badly shattered it. The damage to the log was so general that the sawmill-man said it would not pay to saw it into lumber and that it could rot on the spot. . . . Receiving permission to do as I pleased with his remains, I at once began to cut and split both the trunk and the limbs, and to transcribe their strange records. Day after day I worked. I dug up the roots and thoroughly dissected them, and with the aid of a magnifier I studied the trunk the roots, and the limbs.

I carefully examined the base of his stump, and in it I found ten hundred and forty-seven rings of growth! He had lived through a thousand and forty-seven memorable years. As he was cut down in 1903, his birth probably occurred in 856.

In looking over the rings of growth, I found that few of them were much thicker than the others; and these thick rings, or coats of wood, tell of favorable seasons. There were also a few extremely thin rings of growth. In places two and even three of these were together. These were the results of unfavorable seasons,— of drought or cold. . . . The somewhat kinked condition of several of the rings of growth, beginning with the twentieth, shows that at the age of twenty he sustained an injury which resulted in a severe curvature of the spine, and that for some years he was somewhat stooped. I was unable to make out from his diary whether this injury was the result of a tree or some object falling upon him and pinning him down, or whether his back had been overweighted and bent by wet, clinging snow. . . . However, after a few years he straightened up with youthful vitality and seemed to outgrow and forget the experience

A century of tranquil life followed, and during these years the rapid growth tells of good seasons as well as good soil. This rapid growth also shows that there could not have been any crowding neighbors to share the sun and the soil. The tree had grown evenly in all quarters, and the pith of the tree was in the center. . . .

When the old pine was just completing his one hundred and thirty-fifth ring of growth, he met with an accident which I can account for only by assuming that a large tree that grew several yards away blew over, and in falling, stabbed him in the side with two dead limbs. His bark was broken and torn, but this healed in due time. . . .

A year or two later some ants and borers began excavating their deadly winding ways in the old pine. They probably started to work in one of the places injured by the falling tree. . . . Both the borers and the ants succeeded in establishing colonies that threatened injury and possible death.

Fortunately relief came. One day the chief surgeon of all the Southwestern pineries came along. This surgeon was the Texas woodpecker. . . . After a brief examination, holding his ear to the bark for a moment to get the location of the tree's deadly foe beneath, he was ready to act. He made two successful operations. . . . The wounds finally healed, and only the splitting of the affected parts revealed these records, all filled with pitch and preserved for nearly nine hundred years.

Following this, an even tenor marked his life for nearly three centuries. This quiet existence came to an end in the summer of 1301, when a stroke of lightning tore a limb out of his round top and badly shattered a shoulder. He had barely recovered from this injury when a violent wind tore off several of his arms. During the summer of 1348 he lost two of his largest arms. These were sound, and more than a foot in diameter at the point of breakage. . . .

It is doubtful if there is any portion of the earth upon which there are so many deadly struggles as upon the earth around the trunk of a tree. Upon this small arena there are battles fierce and wild; here nature is "red in tooth and claw." . . . Around the tree are daily almost merciless fights for existence. These death-struggles occur not only in the daytime, but in the night. Mice, rats, and rabbits destroy millions of young trees. . . . The owl, the faithful night-watchman of trees, often swoops down at night, and as a result some little tree is splashed with the blood of the very animal that came to feed upon it.

The lower section of Old Pine's trunk contained records which I found interesting. One of these in particular aroused my imagination. I was sawing off a section of this lower portion when the saw, with a *buzz-z-z-z,* suddenly jumped. The object struck was harder than the saw. I wondered what it could be, and, cutting the wood carefully away, laid bare a flint arrowhead. . . . The outer ring which these arrowheads had pierced was the six hundred and thirtieth, so that the year of this occurrence was 1486.

Had an Indian bent his bow and shot at a bear that had stood at bay backed up against this tree? Or was there around this tree a battle among Indian tribes? Is it possible that at this place some Cliff-Dweller scouts encountered their advancing foe from the north and opened hostilities? It may be that around Old Pine was fought the battle that is said to have decided the fate of that mysterious race, the Cliff-Dwellers. . . .

III

After I had finished my work of splitting, studying, and deciphering the fragments of the old pine, I went to the sawmill and arranged for the men to come over that evening after I had departed, and burn every piece and vestige of the venerable old tree. I told them I should be gone by dark on a trip to the summit of Mesa Verde, where I was to visit a gnarled old cedar. Then I went back and piled into a pyramid every fragment of root and trunk and broken branch. Seating myself upon this pyramid, I spent some time that afternoon gazing through the autumn sun-glow at the hazy Mesa Verde, while my mind rebuilt and shifted the scenes of the long, long drama in which Old Pine had played his part and of which he had given us but a few fragmentary records. I lingered there dreaming until twilight. I thought of the cycles during which he had stood patient in his appointed place, and my imagination busied itself with the countless experiences that had been recorded, and the scenes and pageants he had witnessed but of which he had made no record. . . . More than a thousand times he had beheld the earth burst into bloom amid happy songs of mating birds; hundreds of times in summer he had worn countless crystal rain-jewels in the sunlight of the breaking storm, while the brilliant rainbow came and vanished on the near-by mountain-side. Ten thousand times he had stood silent in the lonely light of the white and mystic moon.

Twilight was fading into darkness when I arose and started on my night journey for the summit of Mesa Verde. When I arrived at the top of the Mesa, I looked back and saw a pyramid of golden flame standing out in the darkness.

4. The Pros and Cons of the Great Hetch Hetchy Dam Debate, 1913

Mr. Pinchot. . . . We come now face to face with the perfectly clean question of what is the best use to which this water that flows out of the Sierras can be put. As we all know, there is no use of water that is higher than the domestic use. Then, if there is, as the engineers tell us, no other source of supply that is anything like so reasonably available as this one; if this is the best, and within reasonable limits of cost, the only means of supplying San Francisco with water, we come straight to the question of whether the advantage of leaving this valley in a state of nature is greater than the advantage of using it for the benefit of the city of San Francisco.

Now, the fundamental principle of the whole conservation policy is that of use, to take every part of the land and its resources and put it to that use in which it will best serve the most people, and I think there can be no question at all but that in this case we have an instance in which all weighty considerations demand the passage

U.S. House Committee on the Public Lands, *Hetch Hetchy Dam Site,* 63rd Cong., 1st sess., June 25–28, July 7, 1913, 25–26, 28–29, 165–166, 213–214, 235–238. This document can also be found in Roderick Nash, ed., *The Call of the Wild* (New York: G. Braziller, 1970), 86–96.

of the bill. There are, of course, a very large number of incidental changes that will arise after the passage of the bill. The construction of roads, trails, and telephone systems which will follow the passage of this bill will be a very important help in the park and forest reserves. The national forest telephone system and the roads and trails to which this bill will lead will form an important additional help in fighting fire in the forest reserves. As has already been set forth by the two Secretaries, the presence of these additional means of communication will mean that the national forest and the national park will be visited by very large numbers of people who cannot visit them now. I think that the men who assert that it is better to leave a piece of natural scenery in its natural condition have rather the better of the argument, and I believe if we had nothing else to consider than the delight of the few men and women who would yearly go into the Hetch Hetchy Valley, then it should be left in its natural condition. But the considerations on the other side of the question to my mind are simply overwhelming, and so much so that I have never been able to see that there was any reasonable argument against the use of this water supply by the city of San Francisco. . . .

Mr. Raker [U.S. Congressman from California]. Taking the scenic beauty of the park as it now stands, and the fact that the valley is sometimes swamped along in June and July, is it not a fact that if a beautiful dam is put there, as is contemplated, and as the picture is given by the engineers, with the roads contemplated around the reservoir and with other trails, it will be more beautiful than it is now, and give more opportunity for the use of the park?

Mr. Pinchot. Whether it will be more beautiful, I doubt, but the use of the park will be enormously increased. I think there is no doubt about that.

Mr. Raker. In other words, to put it a different way, there will be more beauty accessible than there is now?

Mr. Pinchot. Much more beauty will be accessible than now.

Mr. Raker. And by putting in roads and trails the Government, as well as the citizens of the Government, will get more pleasure out of it than at the present time?

Mr. Pinchot. You might say from the standpoint of enjoyment of beauty and the greatest good to the greatest number, they will be conserved by the passage of this bill, and there will be a great deal more use of the beauty of the park than there is now.

Mr. Raker. Have you seen Mr. John Muir's criticism of the bill? You know him?

Mr. Pinchot. Yes sir; I know him very well. He is an old and very good friend of mine. I have never been able to agree with him in his attitude toward the Sierras for the reason that my point of view has never appealed to him at all. When I became Forester and denied the right to exclude sheep and cows from the Sierras, Mr. Muir thought I had made a great mistake, because I allowed the use by an acquired right of a large number of people to interfere with what would have been the utmost beauty of the forest. In this case I think he has unduly given away to beauty as against use. . . .

Mr. Phelan [former mayor of San Francisco] . . . I will only emphasize the fact that the needs of San Francisco are pressing and urgent. San Francisco is expanding with tremendous rapidity due to the development of the interior of California and to the prospect of the early opening of the canal and the building of the exposition, and already, not withstanding the threat of a water famine, the outlying district, which never before was developed, is being cut up into suburban tracts.

A large number of our population has been lost to Oakland, Alameda, and Berkeley, by reason of the fact that we have never had adequate facilities either of transportation or of water supply to meet what would otherwise be a demand for residences on the peninsula. There are disadvantages in crossing the bay. So San Francisco, the chief Federal city on the Pacific coast, asks the Federal Government for assistance in this matter of grant and not by money. It has obligated itself to pay $70,000,000 for a water supply. We have endeavored to satisfy the needs of the irrigationists in good faith, as well as the local water monopoly, and we come this year to Washington, I think, with the good will of those heretofore opposed, possibly with the exception of the gentlemen who are devoted to the preservation of the beauties of nature.

As Californians, we rather resent gentlemen from different parts of the country outside of California telling us that we are invading the beautiful natural resources of the State or in any way marring or detracting from them. We have a greater pride than they in the beauties of California, in the valleys, in the big trees, in the rivers, and in the high mountains. We have the highest mountain in the United States in California, Mount Whitney, 15,000 feet above the sea, as we have the lowest land, in Death Valley, 300 feet below the sea. We have the highest tree known in the world, and the oldest tree. Its history goes back 2,000 years, I believe, judged by the internal evidences; as we have the youngest in the world, Luther Burbank's plumcot.

All of this is of tremendous pride, and even for a water supply we would not injure the great resources which have made our State the playground of the world. By constructing a dam at this very narrow gorge in the Hetch Hetchy Valley, about 700 feet across, we create, not a reservoir, but a lake, because Mr. Freeman, who has studied the situation in Manchester or Birmingham, where there is a similar case, has shown that by planting trees or vines over the dam, the idea of a dam, the appearance of a dam, is entirely lost; so, coming upon it will look like an emerald gem in the mountains; and one of the few things in which California is deficient, especially in the Sierras, is lakes, and in this way we will contribute, in large measure, to the scenic grandeur and beauty of California. I suppose nature lovers, suspecting a dam there not made by the Creator, will think it of no value, in their estimation, but I submit, man can imitate the Creator—a worthy exemplar. . . .

Mr. Graham [U.S. Congressman from Illinois]. In that they are mistaken by a dam site?

Mr. Phelan. They are mistaken by a dam site, and after it is constructed, as somebody said, not wishing to be outdone in profanity, "It will be the damdest finest sight you ever saw."

I remember the story of John Hay's Little Breeches, which describes the old fellow, who, believing in nothing that was religious or good, and having been told, after his child recovered, that he had wandered away in the woods and must have been restored by the angels, said:

> To restore the life of a little child and to bring him back to his own,
> Is a darn sight better business than loafing 'round the throne.

To provide for the little children, men, and women of the 800,000 population who swarm the shores of San Francisco Bay is a matter of much greater importance than encouraging the few who, in solitary loneliness, will sit on the peak of the Sierras loafing around the throne of the God of nature and singing His praise. A benign father loves his children above all things. There is no comparison between the highest use of the water—the domestic supply—and the mere scenic value of the mountains. When you decide that affirmatively, as you must, and then, on top of that, that we are not detracting from the scenic value of the mountains, but enhancing it, I think there is nothing left to be said. That is all. . . .

Mr. Whitman [U.S. Congressman from Washington]. You are asked to consider this park as it is at present, with almost nobody using it. Very little attention has been given to what may happen to this park by the year 2000. On the other hand, the city desires to focus your attention to the year 2000 for its water supply. They are getting along and can get along perfectly comfortably for a good many years for their local supply, but it is the year 2000 they want you to look to. If you look to the year 2000 in one way, I pray you to look to it in the other. What will that park be and what will the use of it be to the American public, winter and summer, in the year 2000?

Now, I have said nothing about nature. I have tried to put this thing on a practical ground, which will appeal to the American citizen, and I do not want to add anything as to nature. But I have a letter here addressed to the chairman of this committee from Robert Underwood Johnson, who was, with Mr. John Muir, the original cause of the establishment of this park, and he has put this matter so admirably in his letter that, as a few concluding words, I should like to read it. There is not very much of it. He says:

New York, June 25, 1913

Hon. Scott Ferris, M. C.,
Chairman House Committee on the Public Lands,
Washington, D.C.

What is at stake is not merely the destruction of a single valley, one of the most wonderful works of the Creator, but the fundamental principle of conservation. Let it be established that these great parks and forests are to be held at the whim or advantage of local interests and sooner or later they must all be given up. One has only to look about to see the rampant materialism of the day. It can only be overcome by a constant regard for ideas and for the good of the whole country now and hereafter. The very sneers with which this type of argument is received are a proof of the need of altruism and imagination in dealing with the subject. The time has not yet come to substitute for our national motto those baleful words, "let us eat, drink, and be merry, for to-morrow we die."

The opponents of the Hetch Hetchy scheme maintain that their position is not inimical to the true interests of San Francisco. They say if there were no other source of good and abundant water for the city they would willingly sacrifice the valley to the lives and the health of its citizens. The records of the hearing before the Senate Committee on Public Lands two or three years ago show that two official representatives of the city (one, ex-Mayor Phelan) confessed that the city could get water anywhere along the Sierra if she would pay for it. This is the crux of the whole matter. The assault upon the integrity of the park has this purpose—to get something for nothing. Mr. Freeman, the engineer employed by the city, has also stated that it is physically possible to get water anywhere along the Sierra. The elaborate published examination of the Hetch Hetchy resources bears the proportion, let us say, of 30 or 50 to 1 to all the information concerning other sources. It has not been demonstrated that Hetch Hetchy is the only available source, but only that it might be the cheapest. On this point we hold that while we are willing to die for the lives or the health of the citizens of San Francisco, we are not willing to die for their pockets.

We believe, moreover, that a larger measure of attention should be given to the question of filtration. I have already called your attention to the system in operation at Toledo, under which typhoid fever has almost disappeared, and to the abandonment by the city of London of its project of a supply from the Welsh Mountains in favor of the same system of filtration. I earnestly suggest that the advantages of this method be made the subject of an official examination during the present summer by United States Government experts, for if such a system be feasible, it would be folly to destroy the valley and dismember the park to have it discovered later that they must, after all, be abandoned for a method both better and cheaper.

The opponents of the bill invite your careful attention to the fact that whereas at first the scheme was put forward as one appealing to humane instincts—to provide a great city with potable water—it is now clearly seen to be aiming at quite another purpose— the production of power for use and for sale. This is commercialism pure and simple, and the far-reaching results of this disposition of the national parks when the destruction of their supreme features is involved, is something appalling to contemplate.

I have not yet spoken of the great recreative, curative, and hygienic uses of the park. It contains three considerable camping spots—the Yosemite Valley, now greatly crowded every summer; the Tuolumne Meadows, and the Hetch Hetchy. The second is much more difficult of access than the third, and both would be withdrawn from public use by the operation of the proposed bill, for it would be idle to take the valley for a reservoir without giving to the city full control of the watershed, since a single case of typhoid infection would endanger the health of the city. The population of the San Joaquin Valley, in the hot and dusty summer, increasingly frequent the park as campers. These would be deprived of the use of these wonderful scenes. As for the general public of travelers, that take so much money to California in quest of beauty—for it, there would be only a phantom valley, sunken, like the fabled city of Brittany, while the 20 miles of the most wonderful rapids in the world, the cascades of the Tuolumne, would be virtually eclipsed. I am aware that in certain quarters one who contends for the practical value of natural beauty is considered a "crank," and yet the love of beauty is the most dominant trait in mankind. The moment anyone of intelligence gets enough to satisfy the primal needs of the physical man, he begins to plan for something beautiful— house, grounds, or a view of nature. Could this be capitalized in dollars, could some alchemy reveal its value, we should not hear materialists deriding lovers of nature, with any effect upon legislators. Without this touch of idealism, this sense of beauty, life would only be a race for the trough.

I have only time for one other point. In 1890 when I appealed to Senator George Hearst to support the bill creating the Yosemite National Park, a project which, as is well known, was first proposed by me to Mr. Muir in 1889, and was jointly urged by us upon Congress, that practical Senator assented with alacrity, and in effect said: "The chief use of that region is for water for irrigation purposes and for its scenery. It has been prospected over many times and there are no precious metals worth speaking of. The forests are more valuable to hold water for irrigation than as timber. Indeed I should favor reserving the whole of the Sierra down to Mount Whitney." I reported this last remark to Gen. Noble, President Harrison's Secretary of the Interior, and toward the close of the administration the whole of that region was reserved. I believe California would not consent to give up the great reservations. Moreover, I believe that the people of the State are opposed to the destruction of the Hetch Hetchy, and that this can be demonstrated if the bill can be delayed until the December session.

I have the honor to remain, respectfully yours,

Robert Underwood Johnson

5. Jane Addams Offers an Example of Municipal Housekeeping in Chicago, 1910

One of the striking features of our neighborhood twenty years ago, and one to which we never became reconciled, was the presence of huge wooden garbage boxes fastened to the street pavement in which the undisturbed refuse accumulated day by day. The system of garbage collecting was inadequate throughout the city but it became the greatest menace in a ward such as ours, where the normal amount of waste was much increased by the decayed fruit and vegetables discarded by the Italian and Greek fruit peddlers, and by the residuum left over from piles of filthy rags which were fished out of the city dumps and brought to the homes of the rag pickers for further sorting and washing.

The children of our neighborhood twenty years ago played their games in and around these huge garbage boxes. They were the first objects that the toddling child learned to climb; their bulk afforded a barricade and their contents provided missiles in all the battles of the older boys; and finally they became the seats upon which absorbed lovers held enchanted converse. We are obliged to remember that all children eat everything which they find and that odors have a curious and intimate power of entwining themselves into our tenderest memories, before even the residents of Hull-House can understand their own early enthusiasm for the removal of these boxes and the establishment of a better system of refuse collection.

It is easy for even the most conscientious citizen of Chicago to forget the foul smells of the stockyards and the garbage dumps, when he is living so far from them that he is only occasionally made conscious of their existence but the residents of a Settlement are perforce constantly surrounded by them. During our first three years on Halsted Street, we had established a small incinerator at Hull-House and we had many times reported the untoward conditions of the ward to the city hall. We had also arranged many talks for the immigrants, pointing out that although a woman may sweep her own doorway in her native village and allow the refuse to innocently decay in the open air and sunshine, in a crowded city quarter, if the garbage is not properly collected and destroyed, a tenement-house mother may see her children sicken and die, and that the immigrants must therefore, not only keep their own houses clean, but must also help the authorities to keep the city clean.

Possibly our efforts slightly modified the worst conditions but they still remained intolerable, and the fourth summer the situation became for me absolutely desperate when I realized in a moment of panic that my delicate little nephew for whom I was guardian, could not be with me at Hull-House at all unless the sickening odors were reduced. I may well be ashamed that other delicate children who were torn from their families, not into boarding school but into eternity, had not long before driven me to effective action. Under the direction of the first man who came as a resident to Hull-House we began a systematic investigation of the city

Jane Addams, *Twenty Years at Hull-House* (New York: Macmillan, 1930 [1910]), 281–287, 293–294. As edited in Carolyn Merchant, ed., *Major Problems in American Environmental History: Documents and Essays* (Lexington, Mass.: D. C. Heath, 1993), 418–420. Reprinted by permission of Houghton Mifflin Company.

system of garbage collection, both as to its efficiency in other wards and its possible connection with the death rate in the various wards of the city.

The Hull-House Woman's Club had been organized the year before by the resident kindergartner who had first inaugurated a mothers' meeting. The members came together, however, in quite a new way that summer when we discussed with them the high death rate so persistent in our ward. After several club meetings devoted to the subject, despite the fact that the death rate rose highest in the congested foreign colonies and not in the streets in which most of the Irish American club women lived, twelve of their number undertook in connection with the residents, to carefully investigate the condition of the alleys. During August and September the substantiated reports of violations of the law sent in from Hull-House to the health department were one thousand and thirty-seven. For the club woman who had finished a long day's work of washing or ironing followed by the cooking of a hot supper, it would have been much easier to sit on her doorstep during a summer evening than to go up and down ill-kept alleys and get into trouble with her neighbors over the condition of their garbage boxes. It required both civic enterprise and moral conviction to be willing to do this three evenings a week during the hottest and most uncomfortable months of the year. Nevertheless, a certain number of women persisted. . . .

With the two or three residents who nobly stood by, we set up six of those doleful incinerators which are supposed to burn garbage with the fuel collected in the alley itself. The one factory in town which could utilize old tin cans was a window weight factory, and we deluged that with ten times as many tin cans as it could use—much less would pay for. We made desperate attempts to have the dead animals removed by the contractor who was paid most liberally by the city for that purpose but who, we slowly discovered, always made the police ambulances do the work, delivering the carcasses upon freight cars for shipment to a soap factory in Indiana where they were sold for a good price although the contractor himself was the largest stockholder in the concern. Perhaps our greatest achievement was the discovery of a pavement eighteen inches under the surface in a narrow street. . . . This pavement became the *casus belli* between myself and the street commissioner when I insisted that its restoration belonged to him, after I had removed the first eight inches of garbage. The matter was finally settled by the mayor himself, who permitted me to drive him to the entrance of the street in what the children called my "garbage phaëton" and who took my side of the controversy.

. . . Perhaps no casual visitor could be expected to see that these matters of detail seemed unimportant to a city in the first flush of youth, impatient of correction and convinced that all would be well with its future. The most obvious faults were those connected with the congested housing of the immigrant population, nine tenths of them from the country, who carried on all sorts of traditional activities in the crowded tenements. That a group of Greeks should be permitted to slaughter sheep in a basement, that Italian women should be allowed to sort over rags collected from the city dumps, not only within the city limits but in a court swarming with little children, that immigrant bakers should continue unmolested to bake bread for their neighbors in unspeakably filthy spaces under the pavement, appeared incredible to visitors accustomed to careful city regulations.

🌉 *E S S A Y S*

The following essays reflect this chapter's dual focus on natural and urban environmentalism. Historian William J. Cronon of the University of Wisconsin at Madison
neatly dissects the destructive effects of the urban marketplace on once-flourishing
Midwestern forests. In the second selection, historian Roderick Nash of the University
of California at Santa Barbara considers the motives of the main actors in the Hetch
Hetchy controversy and assesses the impact of their battle on federal conservation
policy. In the final essay (which neatly extends the Maury Klein–Harvey A. Kantor
argument of Chapter 5), Martin V. Melosi, a historian at the University of Houston,
describes the belated public alarm and the first steps taken to ameliorate the environmental crisis caused by urban technology.

Economic Gain and Environmental Loss: Lumber

WILLIAM J. CRONON

Beneath the geography of capital, underpinning it and sustaining it even as the two
transformed each other, there was still the geography of first nature. To explain
why Chicago lost its wholesale lumber trade, one must ultimately turn to that older
geography. Behind the retailers' resentment of the Chicago drummers, behind the
millowners' efforts to escape the influence of the cargo market, behind the competition of other regions and the coming of yellow pine, behind even the proliferation
of the railroads, there remained the forest itself. Without it, none of the others
would have mattered. Chicago lost its lumber trade because the forest was finally
exhausted by the effort to bring it to market.

Even as late as the early 1870s, few had believed this possible. "*Will* our pine
timber soon be exhausted?" asked a journalist in a popular Chicago magazine in
1870. "We say no. None of our generation will see our pine forests decimated."
Efforts by early conservationists to suggest that the forests of Michigan, Wisconsin,
and Minnesota were finite and should be used more carefully were greeted with
scorn by the lumber press. A case in point was the reaction to James S. Little, a
wealthy Canadian lumberman unusually concerned about preserving forest resources, who wrote a long article in 1876 on the timber supply of the United States
and Canada. In it, he suggested that Great Lakes loggers were "not only burning
the candle at both ends . . . but cutting it in two, and setting the match to the four
ends to enable them to double the process of exhaustion." In the face of Little's estimates, the editors of the *Northwestern Lumberman* simply argued that his statistics
were inadequate and his economic assumptions naive. They showed no real concern
about whether he might be right in the long run about the potential destruction of
the forest. They were equally hostile to the special report on the nation's forests
published in the 1880 census, and devoted many columns to refuting its pessimistic
estimates of the remaining timber supply.

During the 1880s, however, as Chicago lumbermen reeled from one bad piece
of news after another, there were more signs that the white pines might in fact be

giving out. For instance, sawlog prices, along with the prices of forested real estate, were steadily rising. Michigan sawlogs in 1879 were selling for $14 per thousand feet, when just four years earlier even fully milled coarse lumber had not cost as much. Just as worrisome was the general decline in the quality of trees that loggers were cutting. In 1870, the typical sawlog reaching a Michigan mill town measured sixteen to eighteen inches in diameter, and no one considered a tree worth cutting if it was not at least a foot wide. Ten years later, the minimum size had fallen to six to eight inches, so the average log contained far less lumber than before. The costs of logging rose accordingly. By 1883, loggers in the Muskegon district were cutting trees higher into the branches than they ever had before; they cut almost the entire tree into logs. To make matters worse, trees still worth cutting were located farther and farther from the lumber streams. In 1879, for instance, the *Lumberman* reported, "There is not to-day a navigable creek in the state of Michigan or Wisconsin and we may, with little risk, add Minnesota, upon whose banks, to the head waters, the better grade of timber is still standing within a distance of two to three miles."

Many of the technological and economic changes sweeping the western lumber trade were responses to these fundamental shifts in the nature of the forest. With suitable trees no longer in easy reach of the watercourses, logging railroads became an ever more necessary, if expensive, investment. The rising sale of hardwood lumber from Michigan and elsewhere occurred partly because railroads could now carry such wood, but also because there was so little white pine lumber left to compete with it. The rapid disappearance of uncut pine land led lumbermen to realize they were running out of timber, and many of them therefore began looking to the uncut forests of the South and the Pacific Northwest. Frederick Weyerhaeuser's decision to move his chief field of activity to Idaho and Washington was only the most celebrated of these movements, for the rise of the southern yellow pine industry also followed the search of Great Lakes capital for new timber investments.

The ability of yellow pine to compete at all in the heart of white pine country was among the most telling signs that the best of the white pine was already gone. When Chicago wholesalers started having trouble obtaining the higher grades of white pine, it was not just because manufacturers were holding back those grades to sell directly from the mill but also because higher grades no longer existed. In 1890, sawmill operators in the Mississippi Valley met to suggest that regional grading scales be shifted downward so that lower-quality wood could be graded higher than before. In the very act of trying to obscure the truth, they acknowledged that their forests were disappearing. By the 1880s, that realization was dawning on even the most skeptical. As early as 1881, the *Northwestern Lumberman* was admitting that "the old prophets must be accredited with a remarkably correct appreciation of the timber supply." By 1887, its editors had joined the prophets of doom to declare that "the end of the, at one time supposed inexhaustible, supply of white and norway pine timber is altogether too near."

Lumber production in the Great Lakes peaked in the early 1890s, and began to decline precipitously thereafter. The Michigan white pines gave out first, followed by those in Wisconsin and finally by those in Minnesota. As the loggers finished their work in the forests they had consumed, they left behind a literal wasteland. Great piles of slash—small timber, branches, and other debris that had little economic value—remained on the ground where they fell, sometimes in piles ten to fifteen feet high. They accumulated over a vast area, turned brown in the summer heat, and waited for the dry season, when a spark might set them alight.

Fires had long been common in the Great Lakes forests. Indeed, fires were an important reason why the white pine was so abundant in the region, for the tree was adapted to reproduce most effectively in newly burned-over lands. The most extensive stands of white pines were often on the sites of old forest fires. But the fires that followed in the wake of the loggers were not like earlier ones. As the loggers cleared the forest, farmers—believing the old theory that the plow followed the ax—moved onto the newly cleared land to plant their crops. To remove the loggers' debris and to ready their fields for plowing they typically followed the pioneer practice of setting fire to the ground in the fall. In so doing, aided by an occasional spark from the logging railroads, they ignited the immense tracts of clear-cut land to produce some of the worst forest fires in American history. The 1871 fire at Peshtigo, Wisconsin, killed perhaps fifteen hundred people, far more than died in Chicago during the fire that burned down the city at almost the same time. Comparable holocausts occurred in Michigan in 1881, at Hinckley, Minnesota, in 1894, and—the last of the great slash fires—at Cloquet, Minnesota, in 1918.

But human deaths and the destruction of would-be farming communities were not the only consequences of the great fires. They killed much of the remaining white pine forest as well. The tree's ability to flourish in the wake of natural fires depended on the seeds its cones released after undergoing the intense heat of burning. After a fire, tall parent trees ordinarily released their seeds to the newly cleared, now sunny ground beneath them, where young trees thrived and achieved maximum growth. In logged areas, few parent trees remained to reseed after a burn. As a result, other species, especially the deciduous aspens and birches with their ability to reproduce from stumps and suckers, began to invade the pine's old territory. They were aided in this at the end of the nineteenth century when people accidentally introduced to North America a European plant disease, the white pine blister rust. Fatal to a majority of white pines in moist areas like the north woods, the rust had reached the Great Lakes forest by the second decade of the twentieth century, and it diminished still further the chances that the white pine forest would ever fully reproduce itself. Aspen and birch, in alternation with balsam fir, appear to have permanently replaced the pines in areas where the forest has been left to its own devices. In many places, however, people in the twentieth century have systematically replanted pines and other desirable tree species, so stands of pines do still exist in many areas of the north woods.

The dream that the "Cutover" district would become a fertile agricultural landscape proved within two or three decades to be an illusion. Clear-cutting and the fires that followed it reduced what little natural fertility the soil already had, and contributed to problems of erosion and flooding. More important, the poorly drained, heavily glaciated soils typical of the northern forests were inherently inhospitable to agriculture, as was the climate. Farmers who tried to earn a livelihood amid the stumps of the old pines quickly discovered that doing so was very hard indeed. Potatoes might survive in the poor soil, but few other crops did well there. Already by the late 1890s, a government report could foresee "no prospect that our denuded lands will be put to agricultural uses." Old pinelands, whether abandoned by lumbermen or farmers or both, became an increasing burden on county and state tax rolls as their owners went into arrears and let the government claim the lands. The problem of what to do with the resulting depopulated landscape continued to haunt Great Lakes states well into the twentieth century. As time went on, the north woods found new economic possibilities in the rise of the paper industry, which made good use of fast-growing species like birch and aspen; and the regrowing forests also became prime recreational country for Chicagoans and other inhabitants of the Great Lakes region. All of that lay in the future. In 1900, the Cutover was just that: cut over, and abandoned.

The newly treeless countrysides of northern Michigan and Wisconsin were far from the minds of most Chicagoans by the 1890s. Even though the city's wholesalers were abandoning their old western haunts to new competitors, they never lost their home market. Ever since the Civil War, people in Chicago itself had consumed a gradually rising share of the lumber that entered its yards. This home consumption eventually became the mainstay of the lumber trade, with regional wholesalers shifting toward a local retail business. No one feared that Chicago itself would run out of wood, for the city was now attracting lumber from across the entire nation. The demise of the white pine forest thus posed no permanent problem for the Chicago lumber trade.

The internal growth of the city had replaced the settlement of the prairies as the driving force behind lumber sales. Some even saw in the wholesalers' adversity the signs of future opportunity: by losing the trade of western farmers, hadn't the lumbermen acquired the much more profitable trade of the new metropolis? "The time is rapidly approaching," wrote the *Northwestern Lumberman* in 1889, "when the city demand will be much more important than that in the rural districts." Cities, and especially Chicago, had become the centers for great concentrations of wealth, and the wealthy were likely to spend huge sums on mansions and other expensive structures for which white pine was hardly needed. How fortunate, then, that just as the northern forests were disappearing, "hardwoods have come in and pine has been in a great measure ruled out"—a wood unworthy of the new urban elite. Demand for cheaper lumber would continue to come from people building the growing numbers of working-class houses in the city, as well as the prosperous farmers living in the immediate vicinity of Chicago, so lumber dealers could look forward to ongoing business from those markets as well.

And what of the ravaged pinelands to the north? What was their relationship to this new vision of urban harmony and grandeur? Presumably those Chicagoans who thought about it, like most other Americans, saw the vanished forests as a worthy sacrifice to the cause of civilization. The fate of those forests had been prophesied as early as 1868, when a visitor to upper Michigan could declare in a remarkable passage, "The waste of timber is inevitable." He went on.

> The pioneer is insensible to arguments touching the future supply; to him the forest is only fit to be exterminated, as it hinders his plough and obstructs his sunlight. When Northern Michigan becomes, like Southern Illinois, a great rolling prairie of grass and grain, whose horizon is unbroken as the horizon of the ocean, the want of foresight that permitted the destruction of these magnificent forests will be bitterly lamented. But the lament will come from the next generation: the people of this will only boast the swift change of the wood and the wilderness to the fertile field, and exult in the lines of towns and cities which spring up along its watercourses and overlook its lakes.

What made this vision so remarkable was its partial truth. The deaths of the forest trees had indeed built farms on great rolling prairies, and towns and cities had indeed sprung up as a result of the white pines' sacrifice—but not on the forest soil itself. The wealth that the northern pines had stored as natural capital had been successfully transformed into a more human form of wealth, but the vast bulk of it had been moved to another soil, another landscape, another ecosystem. The forest had been consumed in pursuit of a vision that would triumph in the grasslands and, even more, in the city of Chicago—but not in the Cutover. The old blackened stumps would continue to serve as reminders, like the gray stones in an abandoned churchyard, that the city and its hinterland had originally been the products of a kind of theft that few now wished to remember. A sizable share of the new city's wealth was the wealth of nature stolen, consumed, and converted to human ends. The task of forgetting that fact was easier the farther one traveled from the north country, and easiest of all when one stood in the shadows of the tall stone buildings of Chicago's Loop.

A few remembered nonetheless. Toward the end of his life, Isaac Stephenson, one of the most successful of the Marinette-Menominee lumbermen, would write in his autobiography,

> The habitual weakness of the American people is to assume that they have made themselves great, whereas their greatness has been in large measure thrust upon them by a bountiful providence which has given them forests, mines, fertile soil, and a variety of climate to enable them to sustain themselves in plenty. . . .

From the wealth of nature, Americans had wrung a human plenty, and from that plenty they had built the city of Chicago. Chicago's relationship to the white pines had been exceedingly intricate, emerging from ecological and economic forces that for a brief time had come together into a single market, a single geography. The tensions in that market and that geography finally destroyed the distant ecosystem which had helped create them—but by then it no longer mattered. Perhaps the greatest irony was that by surviving the forests that had nurtured its growth, Chicago could all too easily come to seem a wholly human creation.

The Hetch Hetchy Controversy

RODERICK NASH

> As to my attitude regarding the proposed use of Hetch Hetchy by the city of San Francisco . . . I am fully persuaded that . . . the injury . . . by substituting a lake for the present swampy floor of the valley . . . is altogether unimportant compared with the benefits to be derived from its use as a reservoir.
>
> Gifford Pinchot, 1913

> These temple destroyers, devotees of ravaging commercialism, seem to have a perfect contempt for Nature, and instead of lifting their eyes to the God of the Mountains, lift them to the Almighty Dollar.
>
> John Muir, 1912

Situated on a dry, sandy peninsula, the city of San Francisco faced a chronic fresh-water shortage. In the Sierra, about one hundred and fifty miles distant, the erosive action of glaciers and the Tuolumne River scooped the spectacular, high-walled Hetch Hetchy Valley. As early as 1882, city engineers pointed out the possibility of damming its narrow, lower end to make a reservoir. They also recognized the opportunity of using the fall of the impounded water for the generation of hydro-electric power. In 1890, however, the act creating Yosemite National Park designated Hetch Hetchy and its environs a wilderness preserve. Undaunted, San Francisco's mayor James D. Phelan applied for the valley as a reservoir site shortly after the turn of the century. Secretary of the Interior Ethan A. Hitchcock's refusal to violate the sanctity of a national park was only a temporary setback, because on April 18, 1906, an earthquake and fire devastated San Francisco and added urgency and pub-lic sympathy to the search for an adequate water supply. The city immediately reapplied for Hetch Hetchy, and on May 11, 1908, Secretary James R. Garfield ap-proved the new application. "Domestic use," he wrote, "is the highest use to which water and available storage basins . . . can be put."

John Muir, Robert Underwood Johnson, and those whom they had won to the cause of wilderness preservation disagreed. Secretary Garfield's approval stimu-lated them to launch a national protest campaign. Given the flourishing cult of wilderness on the one hand and the strength of traditional assumptions about the desirability of putting undeveloped natural resources to use on the other, the battle over Hetch Hetchy was bound to be bitter. Before Congress and President Woodrow Wilson made a final decision in 1913, the valley became a *cause célèbre.* The principle of preserving wilderness was put to the test. For the first time in the American experience the competing claims of wilderness and civilization to a spe-cific area received a thorough hearing before a national audience.

When the preservationists first learned of San Francisco's plans for Hetch Hetchy, Theodore Roosevelt occupied the White House, and the choice of reservoir or wilderness placed him in an awkward position. There were few Americans so committed to a belief in the value of wild country. Yet Roosevelt appreciated the importance of water, lumber, and similar commodities to national welfare and as President felt responsible for providing them. The result of this ambivalence was inconsistency in Roosevelt's early policy statement. In 1901 he declared in his first annual message that "the fundamental idea of forestry is the perpetuation of forests by use. Forest protection is not an end in itself; it is a means to increase and sustain the resources of our country and the industries which depend on them." But later in the message, he revealed his hope that some of the forest reserves could be made "preserves for the wild forest creatures." . . .

In this seesaw manner Roosevelt hoped to hold the two wings of the conserva-tion movement together on a united front. The task was formidable: Muir already had found his position incompatible with Gifford Pinchot's. But after 1905 Pinchot was Chief Forester and the principal spokesman of the utilitarian conception of conservation. Moreover, he enjoyed a close friendship with Roosevelt. According to Johnson, the President went so far as to declare that " 'in all forestry matters I have put my conscience in the keeping of Gifford Pinchot.' " And Pinchot favored converting Hetch Hetchy into a reservoir. Yet Roosevelt had camped in Yosemite with Muir and appreciated the growing political strength of the preservationist position. Early in September 1907, he received a letter from Muir that brought the issue to a head. Reminding the President of their 1903 trip into the Sierra wilderness, Muir expressed his desire that the region "be saved from all sorts of commercialism and marks of man's works." While acknowledging the need for an adequate municipal water supply, he maintained that it could be secured outside "our wild mountain parks." Concluding the letter, Muir expressed his belief that over ninety per cent of the American people would oppose San Francisco's plans if they were apprised of their consequences.

Roosevelt's initial reaction, made even before Muir's communication, was to seek advice from engineers about alternative reservoir sites. The report, however, was that Hetch Hetchy offered the only practical solution to San Francisco's problem. Reluctantly Roosevelt made up his mind. While assuring Muir that he would do everything possible to protect the national parks, the President reminded him that if these reservations "interfere with the permanent material development of the State instead of helping . . . the result will be bad." Roosevelt ended with an expression of doubt that the great majority would take the side of wilderness in a showdown with the material needs of an expanding civilization. . . . Still Roosevelt was not comfortable in his decision against wilderness, and confessed to Johnson that Hetch Hetchy was "one of those cases where I was extremely doubtful."

In spite of his doubts Roosevelt had made a choice, and in the spring of 1908 the Garfield permit opened the way for the development of the valley. Muir was discouraged but not defeated. He believed it still was possible to arouse a national protest and demonstrate to federal authorities that Roosevelt was mistaken in his judgment about the lack of public sentiment for keeping Hetch Hetchy wild. But Muir fully realized that "public opinion is not yet awakened." The first task of the preservationists was to capitalize on the wilderness cult and replace ignorance with anger. Telling arguments against the reservoir were needed. As the basis for their protest, the friends of wilderness turned to the old Romantic case against "Mammon." They made Hetch Hetchy into a symbol of ethical and aesthetic qualities, while disparaging San Francisco's proposal as tragically typical of American indifference toward them. This line of defense took advantage of national sensitivity to charges of being a culture devoted entirely to the frantic pursuit of the main chance. It criticized the commercialism and sordidness of American civilization, while defending wilderness.

John Muir opened the argument for the Valley on aesthetic grounds with an article in [the radical magazine] *Outlook*. After describing its beauties, he declared that its maintenance as a wilderness was essential, "for everybody needs beauty as well as bread, places to play in and pray in where Nature may heal and cheer and give strength to body and soul alike." . . .

[The] president of the American Civic Association, J. Horace McFarland, . . . believed the aesthetic should have a place in the conservation movement, and in 1909 expressed his displeasure at its concentration on utilitarian aims. In the same year he told Pinchot that "the conservation movement is now weak, because it has failed to join hands with the preservation of scenery." For McFarland, Hetch Hetchy was a test case, and he spoke and wrote widely in its defense. If even national parks were to be given over to utilitarian purposes, there was no guarantee that ultimately all the beauty of unspoiled nature would be destroyed. Speaking before the Secretary of the Interior on the Hetch Hetchy question, McFarland contended that such undeveloped places would become increasingly valuable for recreation as more and more Americans lived in cities. Yet when the preservation of wilderness conflicted with "material interests," those financially affected cried: "'that is sentimentalism; that is aestheticism; that is pleasure-loving; that is unnecessary; that is not practical.'" Usually such resistance carried the day and wildness was sacrificed. McFarland objected because "It is not sentimentalism, Mr. Secretary; it is living." . . .

Lyman Abbott, the editor of *Outlook,* also felt it was a mistake "to turn every tree and waterfall into dollars and cents." His magazine found most of its readers among a class of people concerned over what they thought was the eclipse of morality, refinement, and idealism by urbanization, industrialization, and an emphasis on business values. The defense of wilderness attracted them because it permitted making a positive case—they could be for something (wilderness) rather than merely against amorphous forces. Protecting the wild from an exploitative civilization, in short, represented the broader struggle to maintain intangibles against the pressure of utilitarian demands. . . .

Another tactic of the preservationists emphasized the spiritual significance of wild places and the tendency of money-minded America to ignore religion. Hetch Hetchy became a sanctuary or temple in the eyes of the defenders. John Muir, for one, believed so strongly in the divinity of wild nature that he was convinced he was doing the Lord's battle in resisting the reservoir. The preservationists' innumerable puns about "damning" Hetch Hetchy were only partly in jest. John Muir and his colleagues believed they were preaching "The Tuolumne gospel." San Francisco became "the Prince of the powers of Darkness" and "Satan and Co." Muir wrote: "we may lose this particular fight but truth and right must prevail at last. Anyhow we must be true to ourselves and the Lord." . . .

Using these arguments, and the especially effective one (unrelated to wilderness) that the valley as part of Yosemite National Park was a "public playground" which should not be turned over to any special interest, the preservationists were able to arouse considerable opposition to San Francisco's plans. Members of the Sierra and Appalachian Mountain Clubs took the lead in preparing pamphlet literature for mass distribution. *Let All the People Speak and Prevent the Destruction of the Yosemite Park* of 1909, for example, contained a history of the issue, reprints of articles and statements opposing the dam, a discussion of alternative sources of water, and photographs of the valley. Preservationists also obtained the sympathies of numerous newspaper and magazine editors in all parts of the nation. Even Theodore Roosevelt retreated from his earlier endorsement of the reservoir and declared in his eighth annual message of December 8, 1908, that Yellowstone and Yosemite "should be kept as a great national playground. In both, all wild things should be protected and the scenery kept wholly unmarred."

Evidence of the effectiveness of the protest appeared in the action of the House after its 1909 hearings. Although the Committee on the Public Lands had approved the grant in a close vote, a strong minority report dissented on the grounds that such action would deny the public's right to the valley for recreational purposes. Testifying to the amount of popular opposition, the report observed that "there has been an exceedingly widespread, earnest, and vigorous protest voiced by scientists, naturalists, mountain climbers, travelers, and others in person, by letters, and telegrams, and in newspaper and magazine articles." In the face of this expression of public opinion, the House pigeonholed and killed San Francisco's application in the Sixtieth Congress.

San Francisco was bewildered and incensed at the public unwillingness that it should have Hetch Hetchy as a reservoir. Was not supplying water to a large city a worthy cause, one that certainly took priority over preserving wilderness? The *San Francisco Chronicle* referred to the preservationists as "hoggish and mushy esthetes," while the city's engineer, Marsden Manson, wrote in 1910 that the opposition was largely composed of "short-haired women and long-haired men." San Francisco argued that the beauties of wilderness were admirable, but in this case human health, comfort, and even human life were the alternatives. Phrased in these terms, even some of the members of the Appalachian Mountain Club and the Sierra Club felt compelled to place the needs of civilization ahead of protecting wild country. In the Sierra Club, Warren Olney, one of the founders, led a faction which supported the city. In 1910 the Club held a referendum in which preservation won 589 to 161, but in order to prosecute the defense of Hetch Hetchy, the preservationists were obliged to act in a separate organization: the California Branch of the Society for the Preservation of National Parks. The wilderness enthusiasts in the Appalachian group formed an Eastern Branch of the Society.

At every opportunity the proponents of the dam expressed their belief that a lake in Hetch Hetchy would not spoil its beauty but, rather, enhance it. A prominent engineer reported on the City's behalf that roads and walks could be built which would open the region for public recreation in the manner of European mountain-lake resorts. Since the preservationists frequently based their opposition on the need to maintain a "scenic wonder" or "beauty spot," and on the desirability of maintaining a public playground, the claims of San Francisco were difficult to dismiss. If, instead, more attention had been paid specifically to the wilderness qualities of Hetch Hetchy—which *any* man-made construction would have eliminated—San Francisco's point about the scenic attraction of an artificial lake could have been more easily answered. As it was, this tactical error cost the preservationists considerable support.

The Hetch Hetchy controversy entered its climactic stage on March 4, 1913, when the Woodrow Wilson administration took office. San Francisco's hopes soared, because the new Secretary of the Interior, Franklin K. Lane, was a native, a former attorney for the city, and a proponent of the reservoir. But Lane upheld the policy of previous Secretaries that in cases involving national parks Congress must make the final decision. On behalf of San Francisco, Representative John E. Raker immediately introduced a bill to the Sixty-third Congress approving the grant. The preservationists prepared to send protest literature to 1418 newspapers and to make known their views before Congress. Robert Underwood Johnson distributed an *Open Letter to the American People* in which he declared Hetch Hetchy to be "a veritable temple of the living God" and warned that "again the money changers are in the temple." The stage was set for a showdown.

On June 25 the House Committee on the Public Lands opened hearings on the Hetch Hetchy issue, with Gifford Pinchot as the star witness. Pinchot simplified the question into "whether the advantage of leaving this valley in a state of nature is greater than . . . using it for the benefit of the city of San Francisco." He admitted that the idea of preserving wilderness appealed to him "if nothing else were at stake," but in this case the need of the city seemed "overwhelming." . . . Former San Francisco mayor James D. Phelan told the Committee that the criteria for a decision should be the needs of the "little children, men and women . . . who swarm the shore of San Francisco Bay" rather than the few who liked "solitary loneliness" and "the mere scenic value of the mountains."

Since the House hearings were called on short notice, Edmund D. Whitman of the Appalachian Mountain Club was the only preservationist to testify. He attempted to show that the reservoir would substantially reduce the value of Yosemite National Park as a public recreation ground and beauty spot. But Whitman did not bring out the fact that wilderness was at stake in Hetch Hetchy. As a result Phelan's rejoinder that San Francisco would cover the dam with moss, vines, and trees and would build picnic spots and trails around the reservoir seemed to answer his objections. . . .

On the basis of the June hearings, the Committee submitted a report unanimously endorsing the reservoir plans. When the bill reached the floor of the House on August 29, 1913, strong support immediately developed for its passage. Applying the time-honored utilitarian yardstick to the problem, Representative Raker of California asserted that the "old barren rocks" of the valley have a "cash value" of less than $300,000 whereas a reservoir would be worth millions. But most proponents of the dam were not so positive. They prefaced their support of the dam with a declaration of their love of wilderness and reluctance to have it destroyed. Finly H. Gray of Indiana, for example, explained: "Mr. Chairman, much as I admire the beauties of nature and deplore the desecration of God's Creation, yet when these two considerations come in conflict the conservation of nature should yield to the conservation of human welfare, health, and life."

The choice Representative Gray made between wilderness and the needs of civilization was especially difficult for William Kent, a Representative from California. Independently wealthy, he had chosen a career as a reformer in politics, first in Chicago and after 1906 in Marin County, north of San Francisco, where he had lived as a boy. Kent's devotion to wild country had the same characteristics as Theodore Roosevelt's. "My life," he declared in an autobiographical fragment, "has been largely spent outdoors . . . I have ridden the prairies, the mountains and the desert." A skilled hunter who deprecated the softness of his contemporaries, Kent called for a revitalization of the savage virtues. Understandably, he believed in the wisdom of preserving wilderness, and in 1903 bought several hundred acres of virgin redwood forest on the shoulder of Marin County's Mt. Tamalpais. In December 1907 Kent informed the Secretary of the Interior of his desire to give this land to the federal government as a national monument under the provisions of the Antiquities Act. His purpose was to keep in a primitive condition "the most attractive bit of wilderness I have ever seen." Kent requested the area be named in honor of John Muir, and on January 9, 1908, President Roosevelt issued a proclamation designating the Muir Woods National Monument.

In view of this record, preservationists believed they had found a champion in William Kent. The Sierra Club made him an honorary member while letters poured in from all parts of the country applauding him for upholding aesthetic and spiritual values in a materialistic age. . . . Protecting the redwoods, Muir thought, was "a much needed lesson to saint and sinner alike, and a credit and encouragement to God." It astonished Muir that "so fine divine a thing should have come out of money-mad Chicago." . . .

A few weeks after arriving in Washington in 1911 to begin his first term as a California Congressman, William Kent received a letter from his friend John Muir about Hetch Hetchy. Assuming that Kent, the donor of Muir Woods, would champion the cause of wilderness preservation, Muir simply encouraged him to follow the Hetch Hetchy issue and "do lots of good work." But for Kent the matter was not so simple. While he realized that Hetch Hetchy was valuable as wilderness and part of a national park, he also knew that the powerful Pacific Gas and Electric Company wanted the valley as a step toward consolidating its control over California hydro-electric resources. Municipal control of Hetch Hetchy's water by San Francisco would block this plan, be a significant victory for the ideal of public ownership, and, beyond that, assert the democratic principle. Moreover, Kent had decided with his political friend Gifford Pinchot that "real conservation meant proper use and not locking up of natural resources." The sacrifice of Hetch Hetchy's wilderness qualities, Kent concluded, was regrettable but in this case necessary for a greater good. Answering Muir indirectly in a letter to Robert Underwood Johnson, Kent stated his conviction that conservation could best be served by granting the valley to San Francisco.

In 1913, as a key member of the House Committee on the Public Lands, William Kent was in a position to exert considerable influence. He began by helping draft a bill permitting San Francisco to build its reservoir; then opened his home to the city's supporters as a campaign headquarters. The fact that Kent was widely known as the donor of Muir Woods lent extra weight to his opinions. Certainly *he* would not dismiss the claims of wilderness preservation lightly. Kent exploited this advantage fully. When the Hetch Hetchy bill came to the floor of the House, he stated simply: "I can lay claim to being a nature lover myself. I think that is a matter of record." . . .

It remained for Kent, as an acknowledged admirer of Muir, to provide public explanation for their divergence over Hetch Hetchy. He did so in the summer of 1913 in a series of letters to his Congressional colleagues. To Representative Sydney Anderson of Minnesota he wrote: "I hope you will not take my friend, Muir, seriously, for he is a man entirely without social sense. With him, it is me and God and the rock where God put it, and that is the end of the story. I know him well and as far as this proposition is concerned, he is mistaken." Similarly, Kent wired Pinchot that the Hetch Hetchy protest was the work of private waterpower interests using "misinformed nature lovers" as their spokesmen. In October Kent told a meeting in California that because Muir had spent so much time in the wilderness he had not acquired the social instincts of the average man.

It was not the case that Kent changed his mind about the value of wilderness between 1908 and 1913. In fact, at the very time he was advocating development of Hetch Hetchy, he asked Gifford Pinchot for a statement in support of a state park on Mt. Tamalpais. . . . Kent's problem was that the necessity of deciding about Hetch Hetchy left no room for an expression of his ambivalence. The valley could not be a wilderness and a publicly owned reservoir simultaneously. And, ultimately,

Kent and Muir gave wilderness preservation a different priority at the price of their earlier friendship.

As the consideration of the Hetch Hetchy question in the House continued into September, 1913, the sentiments of William Kent and other supporters of San Francisco encountered stiffer opposition. Halvor Steenerson of Minnesota declared it was nonsense to claim that an artificial lake would add to the beauty of the valley. "You may as well improve upon the lily of the field by handpainting it," he pointed out, and added that all the city offered was a power plant making a "devilish hissing noise" and a "dirty muddy pond." Concluding his remarks, Steenerson spoke in the agrarian tradition, deploring the tendency of Americans to live in cities, and in the Romantic manner, hoping that some day a poet would use the "pristine glory" of Hetch Hetchy "to produce something more valuable than money." . . .

On September 3 the House passed the Hetch Hetchy bill 183 to 43, with 203 Representatives not voting. No Congressman from a Western state voted against it. Most of its support came from Southern and Middle Western Democrats. In fact, the bill was rumored to be an administration measure, connected, in some minds, with the votes California had given to Wilson in the recent election. . . .

Between the time of the House passage and early December when the Senate began its debate, the destruction of the wilderness qualities of Hetch Hetchy Valley became a major national issue. Hundreds of newspapers throughout the country, including such opinion leaders as the New York *Times,* published editorials on the question, most of which took the side of preservation. Leading magazines, such as *Outlook, Nation, Independent,* and *Collier's,* carried articles protesting the reservoir. A mass meeting on behalf of the valley took place at the Museum of Natural History in New York City. Mail poured into the offices of key Senators: Reed Smoot of Utah estimated late in November that he had received five thousand letters in opposition to the bill, and other Senators were likewise besieged. The protests came from women's groups, outing and sportsmen's clubs, scientific societies, and the faculties of colleges and universities as well as from individuals. The American wilderness had never been so popular before.

The arguments the preservationists used against the dam followed the lines laid down in the earlier stages of the controversy. The issue was represented to be between the intangible values of wilderness and the insensitivity of utilitarianism. . . . Frederick Law Olmsted, Jr., who had succeeded to his father's place as a leader in the field of landscape architecture, also published a defense of the valley. After distinguishing between the "beauty-value" and the "use-value" of nature, he observed that the previous century "has shown . . . an enormous increase in the appreciation of and resort to the wilder and less man-handled scenery as a means of recreation from the intensifying strain of civilization." As a consequence, Olmsted contended wildernesses like Hetch Hetchy had great importance to modern society. . . .

The wilderness advocates looked forward hopefully to the Senate debate and vote. They had succeeded in demonstrating that a large number of Americans resented the proposed alteration of Yosemite National Park. In mid-November 1913, Muir cheered the hard-working Johnson: "we're bound to win, enemy badly frightened, Up and smite em!" But when the Senate began its consideration of the bill on December 1, it was apparent that San Francisco's representatives, who had not campaigned nationally but rather lobbied quietly in Washington, had done effective work. As was the case with many Representatives, most Senators first made clear that they too appreciated the values of unspoiled nature but went on to support the dam. "I appreciate the importance of preserving beautiful natural features of a landscape as much as anybody else," Frank B. Brandegee of Connecticut declared. Yet ultimately civilization won out because the "mere preservation of a beautiful, romantic, and picturesque spot   for esthetic purposes" could not conceivably take precedence over "the urgent needs of great masses of human beings for the necessities of life." . . ,

A decision had been made to vote on December 6, and when the Senators entered their chamber that morning they found copies of a "Special Washington Edition" of the San Francisco *Examiner* on their desks. Skillful drawings showed how the valley might appear as a man-made lake with scenic drives for automobiles and boating facilities for happy family groups. The *Examiner* also published experts' testimony justifying the grant in a variety of ways. In comparison, the preservationists' campaign literature was considerably less impressive.

At three minutes before midnight on December 6, the Senate voted. Forty-three favored the grant, twenty-five opposed it, and twenty-nine did not vote or were absent. Eighteen votes from Southern Democrats were the decisive factor, and suggested, as in the case of the House, that the Wilson administration was behind San Francisco. Only nine of the "yeas" came from Republicans.

A Presidential veto was the last hope of the preservationists. After the Senate passage, Wilson received numerous letters calling upon him to defend Yosemite National Park. Robert Underwood Johnson wrote, characteristically, that "God invented courage for just such emergencies. The moral effect of a veto would be immense." He even called in person on the President, but when he left the office, William Kent was waiting to enter! On December 19, 1913, Wilson approved the Hetch Hetchy grant. In signing he declared that "the bill was opposed by so many public-spirited men . . . that I have naturally sought to scrutinize it very closely. I take the liberty of thinking that their fears and objections were not well founded."

The preservationists had lost the fight for the valley, but they had gained much ground in the larger war for the existence of wilderness. A deeply disappointed John Muir took some consolation from the fact that "the conscience of the whole country has been aroused from sleep." Scattered sentiment for wilderness preservation had, in truth, become a national movement in the course of the Hetch Hetchy controversy. Moreover, the defenders of wilderness discovered their political muscles and how to flex them by arousing an expression of public opinion, and in Hetch Hetchy they had a symbol which, like the *Maine,* would not easily be forgotten. In fact, immediately after the Hetch Hetchy defeat the fortunes of wilderness preservation took an abrupt turn for the better. Early in 1915 Stephen T. Mather, a highly successful businessman and wilderness enthusiast, became director of the national parks. Along with Horace M. Albright, Robert Sterling Yard, J. Horace McFarland, and the Sierra Club, Mather generated a campaign on the park's behalf that resulted in the enactment in 1916 of the National Park Service Act. The publicity that accompanied its passage did much to increase the national interest in preserving wilderness that the Hetch Hetchy fight had aroused.

Near the close of the Senate debate on Hetch Hetchy, James A. Reed of Missouri arose to confess his incredulity at the entire controversy. How could it be, he wondered, that over the future of a piece of wilderness "the Senate goes into profound debate, the country is thrown in a condition of hysteria." Observing, accurately, that the intensity of resistance to the dam increased with the distance from Yosemite, he remarked that "when we get as far east as New England the opposition has become a frenzy." . . .

Indeed the most significant thing about the controversy over the valley was that it occurred at all. One hundred or even fifty years earlier a similar proposal to dam a wilderness river would not have occasioned the slightest ripple of public protest. Traditional American assumptions about the use of undeveloped country did not include reserving it in national parks for its recreational, aesthetic and inspirational values. The emphasis was all the other way—on civilizing it in the name of progress and prosperity. Older generations conceived of the thrust of civilization into the wilderness as the beneficent working out of divine intentions, but in the twentieth century a handful of preservationists generated widespread resistance against this very process. What had formerly been the subject of national celebration was made to appear a national tragedy.

Responding to the Urban Environmental Crisis

MARTIN V. MELOSI

By the late nineteenth century, the saturation of cities and suburbs with air, water, refuse, and noise pollution finally produced an environmental consciousness among the complacent citizenry. Until this time, almost everyone had ignored questions of environmental quality. . . . However, it soon became evident that industrial expansion, which made urban centers advantageous places to work, also made them unbearable places to live. Predictably, frustration over the quality of life in the cities was greatest for those who did not have the means of separating their working environment from their residential environment. However, even those who fled the inner city for the suburbs could not be assured of escaping pollution. . . . Early protests against pollution, therefore, tended to be responses to the obvious irritations, such as bad-tasting water, eye-smarting smoke, stench-ridden garbage, or noisy machinery. The concept of pollution as "nuisance" dominated these early complaints. Indeed, "nuisance" was a popular contemporary term, which urbanites applied indiscriminately to any more serious environmental problems. Contemporary observers often referred to all manner of ills in this way: "the noise nuisance," "hooting nuisance," "the garbage nuisance," "the smoke nuisance." As the noted sanitarian, John S. Billings, stated,

> The great majority of the dwellers in our cities have not, heretofore, taken any active personal interest in the sanitary condition of their respective towns. They may grumble occasionally when some nuisance is forced on their notice, but, as a rule, they look on the city as a sort of hotel, with the details of the management of which they have no desire to become acquainted.

Their ignorance, as well as their acceptance of unrestrained industrial growth as a positive good, produced the urbanites' initial mild response to pollution. Few city dwellers possessed a broad ecological perspective about pollution problems because such an outlook did not exist at the time, even within the scientific community. . . . Not until the twentieth century did the scientific community begin to acquire sophisticated notions about the relationship between pollutants and health problems. . . . Social scientists had yet to analyze the complex interrelationships between urban/industrial growth and environmental degradation. No wonder most Americans were unprepared to confront urban pollution—no one had a total grasp of the problem.

By the turn of the century, however, sporadic protests against the irritations of a dirty city led to individual and group efforts to deal with smoke, sewage, garbage, and noise. Demands for cleansing the environment grew out of citizens' complaints for the most part, but reformers occasionally pursued substantive changes in nuisance laws, industrial operations, municipal services, and even public behavior and conduct. Sometimes reform came from within municipal health and public works departments. Environmental reform never took the shape of a permanent or comprehensive movement during the period. Instead, it was an outgrowth of protests against specific problems, usually on the local level, but occasionally state-, region-, or nationwide. . . .

By the 1890s, . . . reformers were beginning to see pollution not simply as an irritant but as an unwanted by-product of industrialization. However, pollution was linked with wastefulness and inefficiency in such a way as to avoid the conclusion that industrial activity was intrinsically responsible for despoiling the environment. Smoke abatement advocates, for example, often charged that air pollution not only produced a health hazard but graphically demonstrated the squandering of natural resources. One observer, extolling the virtues of technical improvements made to a furnace of the Power Building in Cincinnati, stated: "The large Power Building at Eighth and Sycamore for the past year has been a standing monument of what a good appliance and careful firing will do. The stack has been and is absolutely smokeless, and the saving in coal bills has been over twenty-five percent." Anti-noise advocates also drew ammunition from the link between pollution and inefficiency. They often argued that excessive noise in factories worked against high productivity by employees. As Raymond Smilor suggests, "Noise was a liability in business; it cost money. Although it failed to appear on the balance sheet, noise showed in the profit-and-loss statement as an unrealized economy. . . .

. . . To many reformers, the curtailing of pollution was one measure of civilization. The "White City" of the 1893 Chicago World's Fair and "Hygeia," the mythical Victorian city of health, were standards toward which to strive. After all, the city was supposed to put in order what was chaotic in nature. Citizens who littered the streets or defiled their physical surroundings were classified with cavemen or even animals. The interest in the City Aesthetic, best expressed in the City Beautiful movement of the 1890s, was a very subjective indictment of pollution. Many people continued to equate pollutants, such as factory smoke, with material progress. But advocacy of the aesthetic elevated concern about the environment from the purely utilitarian realm.

What gave environmental reform a broader appeal and national attention was its almost inevitable association with progressivism in the 1890s and beyond. Since progressive reform was rooted in the industrial city, environmental protesters had little trouble associating themselves with the larger movement. Despite the diversity of the Progressives, they shared several common beliefs and values that environmental reformers could readily accept. Progressives were trying to bring order out of the chaos caused by the transition of the United States from a rural/agrarian to an urban/industrial society. They had faith in the inherent good of humankind and believed progress was possible by eliminating evils produced by the physical and social environment. They placed great confidence in the ability to measure problems scientifically and to resolve them through the efforts of an expert elite. Of course, the Progressives' limitations were as unbounded as their optimism. . . . Their faith in simplistic solutions to complex problems was naive at best, and, although they decried poverty, injustice, and corruption, they were paternalistic and even hostile to those who fell outside their societal norms.

Yet the conviction of Progressives that the environment in which humans lived could be improved and their adherence to scientific solutions gave substantial support to the protest against urban degradation. Several leading Progressives, especially those with strong interests in urban affairs, were important advocates of environmental reform. Among these were Theodore Roosevelt; Albert Shaw, editor of *Review of Reviews;* Hazen Pingree, mayor of Detroit and governor of Michigan; "Golden Rule" Jones, mayor of Toledo; and Tom Johnson, mayor of Cleveland. Likewise, environmental reformers often became strong adherents to various progressive reforms. The link to progressivism is clear in the following statement by municipal engineer William Mayo Venable:

> . . . The same spirit that leads men to realize the corruption of politics and business, and to attempt to remedy those conditions by adopting new methods of administration and new laws, also leads to a realization of the primitiveness of the methods of waste disposal still employed by many communities, and to a consequent desire for improvement.

By the early twentieth century, environmental protest had undergone some important changes. . . . Major cities began to grapple with the problems of sewage and garbage collection and disposal. Civic and professional organizations, including smoke and noise abatement committees, were putting pressure on city government for change. And the association of environmental reform with progressivism had brought some national attention to several urban problems. Yet environmental reform had serious limitations during this period. . . . The most severe restriction was the lack of what might be called "environmental perspective." Pollution problems were most often approached as isolated cases. The smoke problem was considered independent of the noise problem and the noise problem independent of the sewage problem. Rarely did environmental protest groups confront pollution comprehensively, as part of an overall urban crisis. In fact, other than civic reform groups, which developed interests in many phases of urban life, there were no organizations that were broadly concerned with environmental quality. Urban reformers had yet to consider pollution in terms of its root causes—the processes of urbanization and industrialization; instead, they concentrated on the results and consequences of pollution. As commendable as their efforts were, the reformers, as the well-worn cliché states, "could not see the forest for the trees." . . .

Rallying to combat the most flagrant pollution problems, protesters and reformers rarely found it easy to agree on solutions. As stated above, environmental
reformers shared many of the characteristics of the middle-class reformers of the
period. Various factors, especially occupation, influenced the environmental goals
of the reformers and often limited collective action. Sanitarians and public health
officials, who played a central role in many reform efforts, tended to give priority
to high standards of health as a goal of pollution control. . . . Civic reform groups,
especially those dominated by women, represented the nonspecialist's interest in
the health question; they generally accepted the efficacy of a technical solution to
pollution and placed substantial emphasis upon aesthetic benefits of improving the
urban environment. . . . Similarly, the occupational interests of other groups dictated their behavior. For instance, political leaders had to consider environmental
issues that would appease their constituencies, and businessmen sought to protect
their special interests. Efforts at compromise were always difficult. Overlapping
interests made clear environmental goals almost impossible to achieve.

Of all those involved with environmental problems, *city planners* seemed the
most likely group to combine the myriad interests of reformers and devise a plan of
action. But even this group contributed little to a comprehensive solution to environmental problems between 1870 and 1920. . . . Planners, of course, were deeply
involved in housing reform, land-use controls, and social manipulation in the form
of zoning regulations, but not as chief architects of a comprehensive anti-pollution
plan. After 1920, the profession was gradually transforming the planners' role from
that of reformer to that of technician. As Roy Lubove argues:

> Increasingly . . . the professional planner evolved into a technician who minimized nor-
> mative goals—structural or institutional innovation—and became the prophet of the
> "City Scientific" or "City Efficient." Technical matters relating to zoning, law, finance,
> capital expenditure, and transportation became his province. He did not seek funda-
> mental changes in urban form and structure, but projected existing demographic and
> institutional trends into the future as a basis for planning.

. . . Reform was worthless without implementation, and implementation was
difficult at a time when the line between individual and municipal responsibility
was still unclear. Few government officials could make a distinction between environmental degradation as a citywide problem requiring community action and as a
problem of personal discomfort requiring private action. Between 1870 and 1920,
many cities were just attempting to establish home rule in basic areas of governance.
In the 1850s, rural-dominated state legislatures began to exercise extensive control
over the major cities in their states, especially by creating independent departments
and boards as a means of decentralizing authority. The industrial cities were not very
successful in restoring home rule and often were vulnerable to control by political
machines that simply overlooked the directives of the legislatures. Machine—or
boss—rule was based upon personal loyalties. Bosses actually sustained themselves
through the disorder of the industrial cities and used political power as a marketable
commodity, with patronage going to the highest bidder. In this kind of system, large-
scale environmental reform, based on notions of community responsibility, was
virtually impossible. Even with the establishment of so-called reform governments,
a solution to environmental problems was no easy task. Commission and city manager systems of government, for instance, which were intended to allow efficient

execution of municipal responsibilities, often swapped the working-class constituency of the boss for a middle- or upper-class constituency. . . . The special interests that influenced most municipal governments of the period played a large part in determining municipal priorities and could work against communitywide solutions. . . .

. . . Most cities responded fairly rapidly and effectively in those areas where solutions had to be found in order to avoid rampant health hazards. This was especially true with respect to the search for pure water supplies and improved sewerage systems. However, water pollution per se was not eliminated; industrial wastes and raw household sewage continued to pour into waterways without proper treatment or filtration Numerous cities adopted new methods of collection and disposal of refuse, but these methods did nothing to reduce ever-growing quantities of solid waste and often created alternate forms of pollution, such as smoke from incineration of rubbish. . . . The successes of environmental reform efforts, therefore, were often ephemeral or incomplete. A comprehensive solution to environmental blight in the cities was still a dream. Yet it would be unfair to overlook the major accomplishment of environmental protests of the era—a heightened environmental awareness or consciousness that made urbanites take notice of many of the threats posed by this first environmental crisis in the cities.

 F U R T H E R   R E A D I N G

Kendall E. Bailes, ed., *Environmental History* (1985)
Robert F. Berkhofer, Jr., *The White Man's Indian* (1978)
Michael P. Cohen, *The Pathless Way: John Muir and the American Wilderness* (1984)
William Cronon, *Nature's Metropolis: Chicago and the Great West* (1991)
Harry Sinclair Drago, *The Great Range Wars* (1985)
Samuel P. Hays, *Conservation and the Gospel of Efficiency* (1975)
Suellen Hoy, *Pollution and Reform in American Cities, 1870–1930* (1980)
Melvin Kalfus, *Frederick Law Olmsted* (1990)
Martin V. Melosi, ed., *Pollution and Reform in American Cities, 1870–1930* (1980)
Carolyn Merchant, "Women of the Progressive Conservation Movement," *Environmental Review* (1984)
Roderick Nash, *The American Environment* (1973)
———, *The Call of the Wild* (1970)
———, *Wilderness and the American Mind* (1973)
David Schuyler, *The New Urban Landscape* (1986)

America and the

Great War

The First World War captured in sharp relief both the material benefits and the social cost of America's Great Leap Forward since 1880. When the United States finally entered the war in 1917, the unsurpassed productive capacity and technical efficiency of the world's largest democracy was vividly on display; so too was the lagging, but rapidly improving administrative capacity of its government. By the time the war ended, on November 11, 1918, some 2 million American soldiers were in France. Although they had provided a key resource in dislodging exhausted German troops from their entrenched positions, the Americans had been spared the horrors of sustained trench warfare that had lain waste to both the Allied and German armies. American casualties during the eighteen months of wartime action—48,000 battle-related deaths and another 27,000 deaths from other causes, including the influenza epidemic of 1918–1919—were minimal compared to the 8 million soldiers lost by the Allies and Central Powers. Perhaps, then, it is not surprising that many members of the American Expeditionary Force (AEF) described their experience in France in the romantic terms of medieval chivalry. Wartime service, to be sure, was a more complicated experience for the quarter-million African Americans who volunteered or were drafted in World War I. Assigned largely to menial positions (and denied entry into the Marines altogether) and implored by enemy propaganda to cross over to the German lines, black soldiers nevertheless not only fought and served with distinction but also enjoyed a warm and relatively egalitarian reception from their French hosts—an experience they would not forget when they returned home.

Victorious on the battlefront, the Americans faced a bigger challenge in managing the wartime mobilization and its aftermath on the political front. The peculiarity of the United States' political culture—mixing devout moralism with narrow self-interest, social pluralism with coercive conformity—left multiple casualties, ranging from violently persecuted wartime dissenters to a weakened American president, unable either to tame the postwar appetites of vengeful Allies abroad or to secure congressional support for what was supposed to be the crowning achievement of a "war for democracy," the League of Nations.

DOCUMENTS

The main arguments that brought the United States into the war and the key domestic issues triggered by a wartime mobilization are treated in the following selections. In Documents 1 and 2, respectively, President Woodrow Wilson reluctantly declares war against Germany, and Senator Robert M. La Follette of Wisconsin unhesitatingly dissents. In Document 3, George Creel, head of the Committee on Public Information, recalls the government's unprecedented effort to rally pro-war opinion. Those groups like the radical Industrial Workers of the World, or "Wobblies," who resisted such mobilization efforts, faced a variety of both legal and extralegal punishments, including vigilante "justice," as indicated in Document 4. Formal suspension of wartime civil liberties arrived with the Espionage Act of 1918 (Document 5). Document 6 sheds light on another source of domestic tension, the treatment of African American soldiers in segregated U.S. Army units. While a divisional commander at an army base in Kansas tries to hush discussion of the race question, German propaganda attempts to take full advantage of the racial divide amongst American troops. Finally, Document 7 presents President Wilson's Fourteen Points for world peace, the program that would become the controversial basis for a postwar world order.

1. President Woodrow Wilson's War Message, 1917

When I addressed the Congress on the twenty-sixth of February last I thought that it would suffice to assert our neutral rights with arms, our right to use the seas against unlawful interference, our right to keep our people safe against unlawful violence. But armed neutrality, it now appears, is impracticable. Because submarines are in effect outlaws when used as the German submarines have been used against merchant shipping, it is impossible to defend ships against their attacks as the law of nations has assumed that merchantmen would defend themselves against privateers or cruisers, visible craft giving chase upon the open sea. It is common prudence in such circumstances, grim necessity indeed, to endeavor to destroy them before they have shown their own intention. They must be dealt with upon sight, if dealt with at all. The German Government denies the right of neutrals to use arms at all within the areas of the sea which it has proscribed, even in the defense of rights which no modern publicist has ever before questioned their right to defend. The intimation is conveyed that the armed guards which we have placed on our merchant ships will be treated as beyond the pale of law and subject to be dealt with as pirates would be. Armed neutrality is ineffectual enough at best; in such circumstances and in the face of such pretensions it is worse than ineffectual; it is likely only to produce what it was meant to prevent; it is practically certain to draw us into the war without either the rights or the effectiveness of belligerents. There is one choice we cannot make, we are incapable of making; we will not choose the path of submission and suffer the most sacred rights of our nation and our people to be ignored or violated. The wrongs against which we now array ourselves are no common wrongs; they cut to the very roots of human life.

Congressional Record, 65th Cong., 1st sess.,102–104.

With a profound sense of the solemn and even tragical character of the step I am taking and of the grave responsibilities which it involves, but in unhesitating obedience to what I deem my constitutional duty, I advise that the Congress declare the recent course of the Imperial German Government to be in fact nothing less than war against the Government and people of the United States; that it formally accept the status of belligerent which has thus been thrust upon it; and that it take immediate steps not only to put the country in a more thorough state of defense, but also to exert all its power and employ all its resources to bring the Government of the German Empire to terms and end the war. . . .

While we do these things, these deeply momentous things, let us be very clear, and make very clear to all the world, what our motives and our objects are. My own thought has not been driven from its habitual and normal course by the unhappy events of the last two months, and I do not believe that the thought of the nation has been altered or clouded by them. I have exactly the same things in mind now that I had in mind when I addressed the Senate on the twenty-second of January last; the same that I had in mind when I addressed the Congress on the third of February and on the twenty-sixth of February. Our object now, as then, is to vindicate the principles of peace and justice in the life of the world as against selfish and auto-cratic power, and to set up among the really free and self-governed peoples of the world such a concert of purpose and of action as will henceforth ensure the obser-vance of those principles. Neutrality is no longer feasible or desirable where the peace of the world is involved and the freedom of its peoples, and the menace to that peace and freedom lies in the existence of autocratic governments, backed by organized force which is controlled wholly by their will, not by the will of their people. We have seen the last of neutrality in such circumstances. We are at the be-ginning of an age in which it will be insisted that the same standards of conduct and of responsibility for wrong done shall be observed among nations and their governments that are observed among the individual citizens of civilized States.

We have no quarrel with the German people. We have no feeling towards them but one of sympathy and friendship. It was not upon their impulse that their gov-ernment acted in entering this war. It was not with their previous knowledge or approval. It was a war determined upon as wars used to be determined upon in the old, unhappy days when peoples were nowhere consulted by their rulers and wars were provoked and waged in the interest of dynasties or of little groups of ambi-tious men who were accustomed to use their fellow-men as pawns and tools. . . .

We are accepting this challenge of hostile purpose because we know that in such a government, following such methods, we can never have a friend; and that in the presence of its organized power, always lying in wait to accomplish we know not what purpose, there can be no assured security for the democratic governments of the world. We are now about to accept the gauge of battle with this natural foe to liberty and shall, if necessary, spend the whole force of the nation to check and nul-lify its pretensions and its power. We are glad, now that we see the facts with no veil of false pretense about them, to fight thus for the ultimate peace of the world and for the liberation of its peoples, the German peoples included; for the rights of nations, great and small, and the privilege of men everywhere to choose their way of life and of obedience. The world must be made safe for democracy. Its peace must be planted upon the tested foundations of political liberty. We have no selfish ends to serve. We desire no conquest, no dominion. We seek no indemnities for ourselves, no material compensation for the sacrifices we shall freely make. We are but one of the champions of the rights of mankind. We shall be satisfied when those rights have been made as secure as the faith and the freedom of nations can make them. . . .

It is a distressing and oppressive duty, Gentlemen of the Congress, which I have performed in thus addressing you. There are, it may be, many months of fiery trial and sacrifice ahead of us. It is a fearful thing to lead this great peaceful people into war, into the most terrible and disastrous of all wars, civilization itself seeming to be in the balance. But the right is more precious than peace, and we shall fight for the things which we have always carried nearest our hearts—for democracy, for the right of those who submit to authority to have a voice in their own governments, for the rights and liberties of small nations, for a universal dominion of right by such a concert of free peoples as shall bring peace and safety to all nations and make the world itself at last free. To such a task we can dedicate our lives and our fortunes, everything that we are and everything that we have, with the pride of those who know that the day has come when America is privileged to spend her blood and her might for the principles that gave her birth and happiness and the peace which she has treasured. God helping her, she can do no other.

2. Senator Robert M. La Follette's Antiwar Dissent, 1917

The poor, sir, who are the ones called upon to rot in the trenches, have no organized power, have no press to voice their will upon this question of peace or war; but, oh, Mr. President, at some time they will be heard. I hope and I believe they will be heard in an orderly and a peaceful way. I think they may be heard from before long. I think, sir, if we take this step, when the people to-day who are staggering under the burden of supporting families at the present prices of the necessaries of the life find those prices multiplied, when they are raised a hundred percent, or 200 percent, as they will be quickly, aye, sir, when beyond that those who pay taxes come to have their taxes doubled and again doubled to pay the interest on the nontaxable bonds held by Morgan and his combinations, which have been issued to meet this war, there will come an awakening; they will have their day and they will be heard. It will be as certain and as inevitable as the return of the tides, and as resistless, too. . . .

Just a word of comment more upon one of the points in the President's address. He says that this is a war "for the things which we have always carried nearest to our hearts—for democracy, for the right of those who submit to authority to have a voice in their own government." In many places throughout the address is this exalted sentiment given expression.

It is a sentiment peculiarly calculated to appeal to American hearts and, when accompanied by acts consistent with it, is certain to receive our support; but in this same connection, and strangely enough, the President says that we have become convinced that the German Government as it now exists—"Prussian autocracy" he calls it—can never again maintain friendly relations with us. His expression is that

Congressional Record, LV (April 4, 1917), Part 1, 226, 228. As edited in Thomas G. Paterson, *Major Problems in American Foreign Policy: Documents and Essays* (Lexington, Mass.: D.C. Heath, 1989), 55–56.

"Prussian autocracy was not and could never be our friend," and repeatedly through-out the address the suggestion is made that if the German people would overturn their Government it would probably be the way to peace. So true is this that the dis-patches from London all hailed the message of the President as sounding the death knell of Germany's Government.

But the President proposes alliance with Great Britain, which, however liberty-loving its people, is a hereditary monarchy, with a hereditary ruler, with a heredi-tary House of Lords, with a hereditary landed system, with a limited and restricted suffrage for one class and a multiplied suffrage power for another, and with grind-ing industrial conditions for all the wageworkers. The President has not suggested that we make our support of Great Britain conditional to her granting home rule to Ireland, or Egypt, or India. We rejoice in the establishment of a democracy in Russia, but it will hardly be contended that if Russia was still an autocratic Government, we would not be asked to enter this alliance with her just the same. Italy and the lesser powers of Europe, Japan in the Orient; in fact all of the countries with whom we are to enter into alliance, except France and newly revolutionized Russia, are still of the old order—and it will be generally conceded that no one of them has done as much for its people in the solution of municipal problems and in securing social and industrial reforms as Germany.

Is it not a remarkable democracy which leagues itself with allies already far overmatching in strength the German nation and holds out to such beleaguered nation the hope of peace only at the price of giving up their Government? I am not talking now of the merits or demerits of any government, but I am speaking of a profession of democracy that is linked in action with the most brutal and domineer-ing use of autocratic power. Are the people of this country being so well repre-sented in this war movement that we need to go abroad to give other people control of their governments? Will the President and the supporters of this war bill submit it to a vote of the people before the declaration of war goes into effect? Until we are willing to do that, it ill becomes us to offer as an excuse for our entry into the war the unsupported claim that this war was forced upon the German people by their Government "without their previous knowledge or approval."

Who has registered the knowledge or approval of the American people of the course this Congress is called upon in declaring war upon Germany? Submit the question to the people, you who support it. You who support it dare not do it, for you know that by a vote of more than ten to one the American people as a body would register their declaration against it.

In the sense that this war is being forced upon our people without their knowing why and without their approval, and that wars are usually forced upon all peoples in the same way, there is some truth in the statement; but I venture to say that the response which the German people have made to the demands of this war shows that it has a degree of popular support which the war upon which we are en-tering has not and never will have among our people. The espionage bills, the con-scription bills, and other forcible military measures which we understand are being ground out of the war machine in this country is the complete proof that those responsible for this war fear that it has no popular support and that armies sufficient to satisfy the demand of the entente allies can not be recruited by volun-tary enlistments.

3. George Creel Looks Back on the Selling of the War, 1920

Back of the firing-line, back of armies and navies, back of the great supply-depots, another struggle waged with the same intensity and with almost equal significance attaching to its victories and defeats. It was the fight for the *minds* of men, for the "conquest of their convictions," and the battle-line ran through every home in every country. . . .

We strove for the maintenance of our own morale and the Allied morale by every process of stimulation; every possible expedient was employed to break through the barrage of lies that kept the people of the Central Powers in darkness and delusion; we sought the friendship and support of the neutral nations by continuous presentation of facts. We did not call it propaganda, for that word, in German hands, had come to be associated with deceit and corruption. Our effort was educational and informative throughout, for we had such confidence in our case as to feel that no other argument was needed than the simple, straightforward presentation of facts.

There was no part of the great war machinery that we did not touch, no medium of appeal that we did not employ. The printed word, the spoken word, the motion picture, the telegraph, the cable, the wireless, the poster, the sign-board— all these were used in our campaign to make our own people and all other peoples understand the causes that compelled America to take arms. All that was fine and ardent in the civilian population came at our call until more than one hundred and fifty thousand men and women were devoting highly specialized abilities to the work of the Committee, as faithful and devoted in their service as though they wore the khaki.

While America's summons was answered without question by the citizenship as a whole, it is to be remembered that during the three and a half years of our neutrality the land had been torn by a thousand divisive prejudices, stunned by the voices of anger and confusion, and muddled by the pull and haul of opposed interests. These were conditions that could not be permitted to endure. What we had to have was no mere surface unity, but a passionate belief in the justice of America's cause that should weld the people of the United States into one white-hot mass instinct with fraternity, devotion, courage, and deathless determination. The *war-will,* the will-to-win, of a democracy depends upon the degree to which each one of all the people of that democracy can concentrate and consecrate body and soul and spirit in the supreme effort of service and sacrifice. What had to be driven home was that all business was the nation's business, and every task a common task for a single purpose. . . .

. . . A speaking division toured great groups like the Blue Devils, Pershing's Veterans, and the Belgians, arranged mass-meetings in the communities, conducted forty-five war conferences from coast to coast, coordinated the entire speaking

George Creel, *How We Advertised America* (New York: Harper and Brothers, 1920), 3–8.

activities of the nation, and assured consideration to the crossroads hamlet as well as to the city.

The Four Minute Men, an organization that will live in history by reason of its originality and effectiveness, commanded the volunteer services of 75,000 speakers, operating in 5,200 communities, and making a total of 755,190 speeches, every one having the carry of shrapnel.

With the aid of a volunteer staff of several hundred translators, the Committee kept in direct touch with the foreign-language press, supplying selected articles designed to combat ignorance and disaffection. It organized and directed twenty-three societies and leagues designed to appeal to certain classes and particular foreign-language groups, each body carrying a specific message of unity and enthusiasm to its section of America's adopted peoples.

It planned war exhibits for the state fairs of the United States, also a great series of interallied war expositions that brought home to our millions the exact nature of the struggle that was being waged in France. In Chicago alone two million people attended in two weeks, and in nineteen cities the receipts aggregated $1,432,261.36.

The Committee mobilized the advertising forces of the country—press, periodical, car, and outdoor—for the patriotic campaign that gave millions of dollars' worth of free space to the national service.

It assembled the artists of America on a volunteer basis for the production of posters, window-cards, and similar material of pictorial publicity for the use of various government departments and patriotic societies. A total of 1,438 drawings was used.

It issued an official daily newspaper, serving every department of government, with a circulation of one hundred thousand copies a day. For official use only, its value was such that private citizens ignored the supposedly prohibitive subscription price, subscribing to the amount of $77,622.58.

It organized a bureau of information for all persons who sought direction in volunteer war-work, in acquiring knowledge of any administrative activities, or in approaching business dealings with the government. In the ten months of its existence it gave answers to eighty-six thousand requests for specific information.

It gathered together the leading novelists, essayists, and publicists of the land, and these men and women, without payment, worked faithfully in the production of brilliant, comprehensive articles that went to the press as syndicate features.

One division paid particular attention to the rural press and the plate-matter service. Others looked after the specialized needs of the labor press, the religious press, and the periodical press. The Division of Women's War Work prepared and issued the information of peculiar interest to the women of the United States, also aiding in the task of organizing and directing.

Through the medium of the motion picture, America's war progress, as well as the meanings and purposes of democracy, were carried to every community in the United States and to every corner of the world. "Pershing's Crusaders," "America's Answer," and "Under Four Flags" were types of feature films by which we drove home America's resources and determinations, while other pictures, showing our social and industrial life, made our free institutions vivid to foreign peoples.

4. Wobbly Testifies to Vigilante Attack, 1917

"On the night of November 5, 1917, while sitting in the hall at No. 6 W. Brady Street, Tulsa, Okla. (the room leased and occupied by the Industrial Workers of the World, and used as a union meeting room), at about 8:45 P.M., five men entered the hall, to whom I at first paid no attention, as I was busy putting a monthly stamp in a member's union card book. After I had finished with the member, I walked back to where these five men had congregated at the baggage-room at the back of the hall, and spoke to them, asking if there was anything I could do for them.

"One who appeared to be the leader, answered 'No, we're just looking the place over.' Two of them went into the baggage-room flashing an electric flashlight around the room. The other three walked toward the front end of the hall. I stayed at the baggage-room door, and one of the men came out and followed the other three up to the front end of the hall. The one who stayed in the baggage-room asked me if I was 'afraid he would steal something.' I told him we were paying rent for the hall, and I did not think anyone had a right to search this place without a warrant. He replied that he did not give a damn if we were paying rent for four places, they would search them whenever they felt like it. Presently he came out and walked toward the front end of the hall and I followed a few steps behind him.

"In the meantime the other men, who proved to be officers, appeared to be asking some of our members questions. Shortly after, the patrol-wagon came and all the members in the hall—10 men—were ordered into the wagon. I turned out the light in the back end of the hall, closed the desk, put the key in the door and told the 'officer' to turn out the one light. We stepped out, and I locked the door, and at the request of the 'leader of the officers,' handed him the keys. He told me to get in the wagon, I being the 11th man taken from the hall, and we were taken to the police station. . . .

After some argument by both sides the cases were continued until the next night, November 8th, and the case against Gunnard Johnson, one of our men, was called. After four and a half hours' session the case was again adjourned until November 9th at 5 P.M., when we agreed to let the decision in Johnson's case stand for all of us. . . .

"Johnson said he had come into town Saturday, November 3d, to get his money from the Sinclair Oil & Gas Co. and could not get it until Monday, the 5th, and was shipping out Tuesday, the 6th, and that he had $7.08 when arrested. He was reprimanded by the judge for not having a Liberty Bond, and as near as anyone could judge from the closing remarks of Judge Evans, he was found guilty and fined $100 for not having a Liberty Bond.

"Our lawyer made a motion to appeal the case and the bonds were then fixed at $200 each. I was immediately arrested, *as were also five spectators in the open court-room,* for being I. W. W.'s. One arrested was not a member of ours, but a property-owner and citizen. I was searched and $30.87 taken from me, as also was the receipt for the $100 bond, and we then were all placed back in the cells.

"In about forty minutes, as near as we could judge about 11 P.M., the turnkey came and called 'Get ready to go out you I. W. W. men.' We dressed as rapidly as possible, were taken out of the cells, and the officer gave us back our possessions,

From the sworn testimony of the secretary of the Industrial Workers of the World local, Tulsa, Oklahoma, November 1917, from the *Liberator,* April 1918.

Ingersoll watches, pocketknives and money, with the exception of $3 in silver of mine which they kept, giving me back $27.87. I handed the receipt for the $100 bond I had put up to the desk sergeant and he told me he did not know anything about it, and handed the receipt back to me, which I put in my trousers' pocket with the 87 cents. Twenty-seven dollars in bills was in my coat pocket. We were immediately ordered into automobiles waiting in the alley. Then we proceeded one block north to 1st Street, west one-half block to Boulder Street, north across the Frisco tracks and stopped.

"Then the masked mob came up and ordered everybody to throw up their hands. Just here I wish to state I never thought any man could reach so high as those policemen did. We were then bound, some with hands in front, some with hands behind, and others bound with arms hanging down their sides, the rope being wrapped around the body. Then the police were ordered to 'beat it,' which they did, running, and we started for the place of execution.

"When we arrived there, a company of gowned and masked gunmen were there to meet us standing at 'present arms.' We were ordered out of the autos, told to get in line in front of these gunmen and another bunch of men with automatics and pistols, lined up between us. Our hands were still held up, and those who were bound, in front. Then a masked man walked down the line and slashed the ropes that bound us, and we were ordered to strip to the waist, which we did, threw our clothes in front of us, in individual piles—coats, vests, hats, shirts and undershirts. The boys not having had time to distribute their possessions that were given back to them at the police stations, everything was in the coats, everything we owned in the world.

"Then the whipping began, a double piece of new rope, $\frac{5}{8}$ or $\frac{3}{4}$ hemp, being used. A man, 'the chief' of detectives, stopped the whipping of each man when he thought the victim had had enough. After each one was whipped another man applied the tar with a large brush, from the head to the seat. Then a brute smeared feathers over and rubbed them in.

"After they had satisfied themselves that our bodies were well abused, our clothing was thrown into a pile, gasoline poured on it and a match applied. By the light of our earthly possessions, we were ordered to leave Tulsa, and leave running and never come back. The night was dark, the road very rough, and as I was one of the last two that was whipped, tarred and feathered, and in the rear when ordered to run, I decided to be shot rather than stumble over the rough road. After going forty or fifty feet I stopped and went into the weeds. I told the man with me to get in the weeds also, as the shots were coming very close over us and ordered him to lie down flat. We expected to be killed, but after 150 or 200 shots were fired they got in their autos.

"After the last one had left, we went through a barbed-wire fence, across a field, called to the boys, collected them, counted up, and had all the 16 safe, though sore and nasty with tar. After wandering around the hills for some time—ages it seemed to me—we struck the railroad track. One man, Jack Sneed, remembered then that he knew a farmer in that vicinity, and he and J. F. Ryan volunteered to find the house. I built a fire to keep us from freezing.

"We stood around the fire expecting to be shot, as we did not know but what some tool of the commercial club had followed us. After a long time Sneed returned and called to us, and we went with him to a cabin and found an I. W. W. friend in the shack and 5 gallons of coal oil or kerosene, with which we cleaned the filthy stuff off of each other, and our troubles were over, as friends sent clothing and money to us that day, it being about 3 or 3:30 A.M. when we reached the cabin.

"The men abused, whipped and tarred were Tom McCaffery, John Myers, John Boyle, Charles Walsh, W. H. Walton, L. R. Mitchell, Jos. French, J. R. Hill, Gunnard Johnson, Robt. McDonald, John Fitzsimmons, Jos. Fischer, Gordon Dimikson, J. F. Ryan, E. M. Boyd, Jack Sneed (not an I. W. W.).

"This is a copy of my sworn statement and every word is truth."

"It was very evident that the police force knew what was going to happen when they took us from jail, as there were extra gowns and masks provided *which were put on by the Chief of Police and one detective named Dlaine, and the number of blows we received were regulated by the Chief of Police himself, who was easily recognizable by six of us at least.*"

5. The U.S. Government Punishes War Protestors: The Espionage Act, 1918

Be it enacted by the Senate and House of Representatives of the United States of America in Congress assembled, That section three of title one of the Act entitled, "An Act to punish acts of interference with the foreign relations, the neutrality, and the foreign commerce of the United States, to punish espionage, and better to enforce the criminal laws of the United States, and for other purposes," approved June fifteenth, nineteen hundred and seventeen, be, and the same is hereby, amended so as to read as follows:

"SEC. 3. Whoever, when the United States is at war, shall willfully make or convey false reports or false statements, with intent to interfere with the operation or success of the military or naval forces of the United States, or to promote the success of its enemies, or shall willfully make or convey false reports or false statements, or say or do anything except by way of bona fide and not disloyal advice to an investor or investors, with intent to obstruct the sale by the United States of bonds or other securities of the United States or the making of loans by or to the United States, and whoever, when the United States is at war, shall willfully cause or attempt to cause, or incite or attempt to incite, insubordination, disloyalty, mutiny, or refusal of duty, in the military or naval forces of the United States, or shall willfully obstruct or attempt to obstruct the recruiting or enlistment service of the United States, and whoever, when the United States is at war, shall willfully utter, print, write, or publish any disloyal, profane, scurrilous, or abusive language about the form of government of the United States, or the Constitution of the United States, or the military or naval forces of the United States, or the flag of the United States, or the uniform of the Army or Navy of the United States, or any language intended to bring the form of government of the United States, or the Constitution of the United States, or the military or naval forces of the United States, or the flag of the United States, or the uniform of the Army or Navy of the United States into contempt, scorn, contumely, or disrepute, or

U.S. Statutes at Large, Vol. XL, p. 553ff.

shall willfully utter, print, write, or publish any language intended to incite, provoke, or encourage resistance to the United States, or to promote the cause of its enemies, or shall willfully display the flag of any foreign enemy, or shall willfully by utterance, writing, printing, publication, or language spoken, urge, incite, or advocate any curtailment of production in this country of any thing or things, product or products, necessary or essential to the prosecution of the war in which the United States may be engaged, with intent by such curtailment to cripple or hinder the United States in the prosecution of the war, and whoever shall willfully advocate, teach, defend or suggest the doing of any of the acts or things in this section enumerated, and whoever shall by word or act support or favor the cause of any country with which the United States is at war or by word or act oppose the cause of the United States therein, shall be punished by a fine of not more than $10,000 or imprisonment for not more than twenty years, or both. . . .

Title XII of the said Act of June fifteenth, nineteen hundred and seventeen, be, and the same is hereby, amended by adding thereto the following section:

"SEC. 4. When the United States is at war, the Postmaster General may, upon evidence satisfactory to him that any person or concern is using the mails in violation of any of the provisions of this Act, instruct the postmaster at any post office at which mail is received addressed to such person or concern to return to the postmaster at the office at which they were originally mailed all letters or other matter so addressed, with the words 'Mail to this address undeliverable under Espionage Act' plainly written or stamped upon the outside thereof, and all such letters or other matter so returned to such postmasters shall be by them returned to the senders thereof under such regulations as the Postmaster General may prescribe."

Approved, May 16, 1918.

6. Two Treatments of the Color Question During Wartime, 1918

A U.S. Divisional Commander in Kansas Counsels Against Race Discussions

HEADQUARTERS 92ND DIVISION,
CAMP FUNSTON, KAN.
MARCH 28, 1918.

Bulletin No. 35.

1. It should be well known to all colored officers and men that no useful purpose is served by such acts as will cause the "Color Question" to be raised. It is not a question of legal rights, but a question of policy, and any policy that tends to bring about a conflict of races, with its resulting animosities, is prejudicial to the military interests of the 92nd Division, and therefore prejudicial to an important interest of the colored race.

Addie W. Hunton, *Two Colored Women with the American Expeditionary Forces* (New York: Brooklyn Eagle Press, 1920), 46–47, 55–56, 53–54.

2. To avoid conflicts the Division Commander has repeatedly urged that all colored members of his command, and especially the officers and non-commissioned officers should refrain from going where their presence will be resented. In spite of this injunction, one of the sergeants of the Medical Department has recently precipitated the precise trouble that should be avoided, and then called on the Division Commander to take sides in a row that should never have occurred, and would not have occurred had the sergeant placed the general good above his personal pleasure and convenience. This sergeant entered a theatre, as he undoubtedly had a legal right to do, and precipitated trouble by making it possible to allege race discrimination in the seat he was given. He is entirely within his legal rights in the matter, and the theatre manager is legally wrong. Nevertheless the sergeant is guilty of the greater wrong in *doing* anything, no matter how legally correct, that will provoke race animosity.

3. The Division Commander repeats that the success of the Division with all that that success implies, is dependent upon the good will of the public. That public is nine-tenths white. White men made the Division, and can break it just as easily as it becomes a trouble maker.

4. All concerned are again enjoined to place the general interest of the Division above personal pride and gratification. Avoid every situation that can give rise to racial ill-will. Attend quietly and faithfully to your duties, and don't go where your presence is not desired.

5. This will be read to all organizations of the 92nd Division.

By Command of Major General Ballou.

ALLEN J. GREER,

Lieutenant Colonel General Staff,
Chief of Staff.

German Propaganda Circular Targets the African American Soldier

TO THE COLORED SOLDIERS OF THE UNITED STATES ARMY

"Hello, boys, what are you doing over here? Fighting the Germans? Why? Have they ever done you any harm? Of course some white folks and the lying English-American papers told you that the Germans ought to be wiped out for the sake of humanity and Democracy. What is Democracy? Personal freedom; all citizens enjoying the same rights socially and before the law. Do you enjoy the same rights as the white people do in America, the land of freedom and Democracy, or are you not rather treated over there as second class citizens?

Can you get into a restaurant where white people dine? Can you get a seat in a theatre where white people sit? Can you get a seat or a berth in a railroad car, or can you even ride in the South in the same street car with the white people?

And how about the law? Is lynching and the most horrible crimes connected therewith, a lawful proceeding in a Democratic country? Now all this is entirely different in Germany, where they do like colored people; where they treat them as gentlemen and as white men, and quite a number of colored people have fine positions in business in Berlin and other German cities. Why, then, fight the Germans only for the benefit of the Wall Street robbers, and to protect the millions that they have loaned to the English, French, and Italians?

7. Wilson's Fourteen Points for World Peace, 1918

Gentlemen of the Congress:

. . . It will be our wish and purpose that the processes of peace, when they are begun, shall be absolutely open and that they shall involve and permit henceforth no secret understandings of any kind. The day of conquest and aggrandizement is gone by; so is also the day of secret covenants entered into in the interest of particular governments and likely at some unlooked-for moment to upset the peace of the world. It is this happy fact, now clear to the view of every public man whose thoughts do not still linger in an age that is dead and gone, which makes it possible for every nation whose purposes are consistent with justice and the peace of the world to avow now or at any other time the objects it has in view.

We entered this war because violations of right had occurred which touched us to the quick and made the life of our own people impossible unless they were corrected and the world secured once for all against their recurrence. What we demand in this war, therefore, is nothing peculiar to ourselves. It is that the world be made fit and safe to live in; and particularly that it be made safe for every peace-loving nation which, like our own, wishes to live its own life, determine its own institutions, be assured of justice and fair dealing by the other peoples of the world as against force and selfish aggression. All the peoples of the world are in effect partners in this interest, and for our own part we see very clearly that unless justice be done to others it will not be done to us. The program of the world's peace, therefore, is our program; and that program, the only possible program, as we see it, is this:

I. Open covenants of peace, openly arrived at, after which there shall be no private international understandings of any kind but diplomacy shall proceed always frankly and in the public view.

II. Absolute freedom of navigation upon the seas, outside territorial waters, alike in peace and in war, except as the seas may be closed in whole or in part by international action for the enforcement of international covenants.

III. The removal, so far as possible, of all economic barriers and the establishment of an equality of trade conditions among all the nations consenting to the peace and associating themselves for its maintenance.

IV. Adequate guarantees given and taken that national armaments will be reduced to the lowest point consistent with domestic safety.

V. A free, open-minded, and absolutely impartial adjustment of all colonial claims, based upon a strict observance of the principle that in determining all such questions of sovereignty the interests of the populations concerned must have equal weight with the equitable claims of the government whose title is to be determined.

VI. The evacuation of all Russian territory and such a settlement of all questions affecting Russia as will secure the best and freest cooperation of the other nations of the world in obtaining for her an unhampered and unembarrassed opportunity for the independent determination of her own political development and national policy and assure her of a sincere welcome into the society of free nations under institutions of her own choosing; and, more than a welcome, assistance also of every kind that she

Supplement to the Messages and Papers of the Presidents Covering the Second Administration of Woodrow Wilson, 8421 ff. This document can also be found in Henry Steele Commager, *Documents of American History* (New York: Meredith Publishing Co., 1963), 137–139.

may need and may herself desire. The treatment accorded Russia by her sister nations in the months to come will be the acid test of their good will, of their comprehension of her needs as distinguished from their own interests, and of their intelligent and unselfish sympathy.

VII. Belgium, the whole world will agree, must be evacuated and restored, without any attempt to limit the sovereignty which she enjoys in common with all other free nations. No other single act will serve as this will serve to restore confidence among the nations in the laws which they have themselves set and determined for the government of their relations with one another. Without this healing act the whole structure and validity of international law is forever impaired.

VIII. All French territory should be freed and the invaded portions restored, and the wrong done to France by Prussia in 1871 in the matter of Alsace-Lorraine, which has unsettled the peace of the world for nearly fifty years, should be righted, in order that peace may once more be made secure in the interest of all.

IX. A readjustment of the frontiers of Italy should be effected along clearly recognizable lines of nationality.

X. The peoples of Austria-Hungary, whose place among the nations we wish to see safe-guarded and assured, should be accorded the freest opportunity of autonomous development.

XI. Rumania. Serbia, and Montenegro should be evacuated; occupied territories restored; Serbia accorded free and secure access to the sea; and the relations of the several Balkan states to one another determined by friendly counsel along historically established lines of allegiance and nationality; and international guarantees of the political and economic independence and territorial integrity of the several Balkan states should be entered into.

XII. The Turkish portions of the present Ottoman Empire should be assured a secure sovereignty, but the other nationalities which are now under Turkish rule should be assured an undoubted security of life and an absolutely unmolested opportunity of autonomous development, and the Dardanelles should be permanently opened as a free passage to the ships and commerce of all nations under international guarantees.

XIII. An independent Polish state should be erected which should include the territories inhabited by indisputably Polish populations, which should be assured a free and secure access to the sea, and whose political and economic independence and territorial integrity should be guaranteed by international covenant.

XIV. A general association of nations must be formed under specific covenants for the purpose of affording mutual guarantees of political independence and territorial integrity to great and small states alike.

In regard to these essential rectifications of wrong and assertions of right we feel ourselves to be intimate partners of all the governments and peoples associated together against the Imperialists. We cannot be separated in interest or divided in purpose. We stand together until the end.

For such arrangements and covenants we are willing to fight and to continue to fight until they are achieved; but only because we wish the right to prevail and desire a just and stable peace such as can be secured only by removing the chief provocations to war, which this program does not remove. We have no jealousy of German greatness, and there is nothing in this program that impairs it. We grudge her no achievement or distinction of learning or of pacific enterprise such as have made her record very bright and very enviable. We do not wish to injure her or to block in any way her legitimate influence or power. We do not wish to fight her either with arms or with hostile arrangements of trade if she is willing to associate herself with us and the other peace-loving nations of the world in covenants of justice and law and fair dealing. We wish her only to accept a place of equality among the peoples of the world,—the new world in which we now live,—instead of a place of mastery.

Neither do we presume to suggest to her any alteration or modification of her institutions. But it is necessary, we must frankly say, and necessary as a preliminary to any intelligent dealings with her on our part, that we should know whom her spokesmen speak for when they speak to us, whether for the Reichstag majority or for the military party and the men whose creed is imperial domination.

We have spoken now, surely, in terms too concrete to admit of any further doubt or question. An evident principle runs through the whole program I have outlined. It is the principle of justice to all peoples and nationalities, and their right to live on equal terms of liberty and safety with one another, whether they be strong or weak. Unless this principle be made its foundation no part of the structure of international justice can stand. The people of the United States could act upon no other principle; and to the vindication of this principle they are ready to devote their lives, their honor, and everything that they possess. The moral climax of this the culminating and final war for human liberty has come, and they are ready to put their own strength, their own highest purpose, their own integrity and devotion to the test.

 *E S S A Y S*

The three essays continue this chapter's focus on the precarious balance between American ideals and actions, both at home and abroad. In the first, historian Barry D. Karl of the University of Chicago suggests that wartime management provided a superficially successful but ultimately failed experiment in governmental centralism. In the second essay, Stanford University Professor David M. Kennedy analyzes the American soldier's peculiarly romantic view of the Great War. In the final selection, historian Arthur S. Link of Princeton University argues that President Wilson's moral diplomacy was more realistic and effective than posterity has acknowledged.

Managing War

BARRY D. KARL

The outbreak of war in Europe in August 1914 was not looked on by most Americans as an event that urgently affected the interests of the United States. Businessmen involved in international trade of course wondered what the consequences of so widespread a conflict might be, and when they saw foreign trade come to a virtual halt in the first few months of the war, they became intensely concerned. The general public

Barry D. Karl, *The Uneasy States from 1915 to 1945* (Chicago: University of Chicago Press, 1983), 34–49. Copyright © 1983, reprinted by permission of the University of Chicago Press.

followed the war in the newspapers, but it was probably more troubled by disturbances immediately to our southwest, where Mexican revolutions seemed threatening. Few serious observers would have predicted that in less than two and a half years
American soldiers, drafted by an aroused and angry citizenry, would be crossing the
Atlantic to fight on European soil. The transformation of popular attitudes in so brief
a period of time was as remarkable as the experience of the war itself. American interest in international affairs entered a new phase as public opinion shifted from its
familiar focus on protection of "our" hemisphere to salvation of the world. . . .

On 7 May 1915 a German submarine sank the British ship *Lusitania.* Among
the 1,198 passengers and crew who died were 128 Americans. The fact that the
vessel was British and hence, by German definition, an "enemy" did not mollify
American feelings, which ran high. It was, moreover, a passenger vessel, not a
purely merchant ship, a fact that occasioned much argument, not only in the United
States but within the German General Staff, where it was clear that the novelty of
the submarine as a weapon had reduced many of the formal definitions to rubble.
The ship had been sunk without warning, despite the fact that it was unarmed. No
effort had been made to find out what, in fact, it might have been carrying.

For Americans the event could be distinguished even from the sinking of vessels
known to be carrying goods and supplies. The *Lusitania,* whatever its cargo, was
loaded with passengers; and the freedom of Americans to travel the seas, even on
the ships of nations at war, became the issue that galvanized popular response and
began the crucial shift in the official position, which was no longer to be based on
the freedom of neutral states to engage in trade in wartime but on the freedom of
American citizens to travel as they chose. . . .

The debate that raged from May 1915 to the American declaration of war on 6
April 1917 reveals the gradual escalation of emotions on all sides. Great Britain
was growing increasingly dependent on American supplies. Germany could not continue to allow its enemies to be supported by a supposed neutral. German strategy,
dependent as it was on speed and surprise, could not be maintained indefinitely.
The stalemated war in the trenches of Europe had developed into a ghastly inferno,
where soldiers crawled in mud and darkness, lit only by the rocket flares, to achieve
little but mutual destruction. The German decision to engage in unrestricted submarine warfare was based on an acceptance of the fact that the United States would
probably intervene; but the Germans also calculated that internal divisions in the
United States and the disorganized state of American industry, already revealed by
Wilson's efforts at "preparedness," would render America's entry irrelevant. The
benefits of halting Atlantic shipping, they reasoned, would outweigh any direct
American involvement.

The Germans should have been right. The fact that they were not—and the reasons why they were not—reveals important aspects both of America's experience
in the war and of the ways that experience affected postwar American thought. The
sinking of the *Lusitania* had shown the inherent weaknesses of "neutrality," but
Wilson's attempts to persuade Americans to prepare themselves by adopting even a
limited form of military conscription, like his attempts to get American industry to
organize itself voluntarily for war production, had demonstrated the profound limits
of presidential power over the nation's industrial system. What is more, it revealed
that there was no national system capable of centralized management.

Readers of American newspapers and journals of various political persuasions and ethnic identifications would also have noted deep divisions in public opinion. It was, initially at least, not easy to hate the Germans. After all, they were Anglo-Saxons, like the English. Their contributions to American intellectual development were clear, not only to Americans of German origin but to the generation of American scientists and social scientists who had gone to Germany to work for higher degrees. Moreover, the American Irish sympathized with the Irish revolutionaries, who were seeking to win independence from Great Britain; they were contributing money as well as young fighters to what had become a bloody battle for the kind of freedom Americans of older English stock felt they had won from the mother country. Their concern for British interests on the continent of Europe were obviously very limited. . . . All in all, observers of the American scene from abroad would have had difficulty in detecting a national consensus on the war.

The American war machine gradually took shape, but it did so like a lumbering leviathan, willing to respond to the demands the new age was making upon it but slow and clumsy in its efforts to do so. The assumption that so vast a national program could be built on a voluntary basis, that Americans, from the top industrial managers down to the lowliest factory laborers, would organize themselves to serve the national war purpose, required the creation of a national will far more purposeful and far more self-sacrificing than Americans had ever before been asked to sustain. The insistence, too, that a significant portion of the cost of the war should be borne by public subscription through the sale of bonds also required a national consciousness different from that demanded by any previous crisis. The belief that all such things could be done with the minimum of legal coercion rested on a willingness to use the maximum of rhetorical persuasion and popular pressure to bring them about. Yet, long before the American decision to intervene, the tone had been irrevocably set. The war that no one could justify in 1914 had become a national crusade for aims no one could define in 1917; but everyone knew they were right. . . . The Great War had been transformed. A puzzle in international power relationships had become a new democratic revolution; for the world, as Wilson put it, was going to be made "safe for democracy."

The American declaration of war against Germany on 7 April 1917 could be viewed as the culmination of one process of development and its transformation into something else. . . . By asserting its rights not only to protect its own interests but to change the basic international structures that had presumably placed those interests under threat in the first place, the United States was seeking a new role for itself in international affairs, a role much closer to that of the sympathetic revolutionary state it had so often tried to be in nineteenth-century international politics. Whether Wilson and the military-industrial state he assembled reflected a national consensus was, as we have seen, highly questionable, but it was absolutely necessary that such a state be created, consensus or not. In fact, it became necessary that the consensus itself be created. Wilson's speeches were all calculated to produce a fervent national agreement, to call upon all Americans to help him fight not only the war but internal opposition to it. The Allied victory was produced by the power of an American industrial system created specifically for that purpose and placed under the command of a national administration with powers the United States had never before granted to its federal government. While the process of getting the system

In place was slow and awkward, at the peak of its power, from December 1917 to November 1918, it exercised extraordinary control over American industrial life.

Wilson's decision to staff the war administration with volunteers recruited from the nation's industries was crucial not only to the way the war effort was ultimately organized but to the American approach to the war itself. Selecting leaders from the nation's railroad industry and its clothing and manufacturing concerns, as well as key figures in banking and finance, meant that Wilson would have an experienced cadre of industrial managers to work with. Given the fact that there was no alternative group in the federal government itself, the decision was less a matter of choice than a quickness to take advantage of the options open to him. These leaders in turn brought a younger group of executives with them. The top echelon consisted of men who, wealthy in their own right, could work for the government for "a dollar a year," the phrase used to characterize their patriotism.

Equally important, the private managerial system was inspired by a nationalism just as intense in its control of the life of the nation as the patriotism that justified wartime service. The need to "win the war" produced a sense of urgency that veiled a fear, not simply that the war might be lost or that the consequences of losing it would be dire, but that the cause of failure would be the internal divisions that the years from 1914 to 1917 had revealed so clearly. The war abroad had to be won; but that victory seemed to many to depend on winning the other war—the war at home.

On 14 April 1917, a week after his address requesting a declaration of war, President Wilson issued an executive order creating the Committee on Public Information. Headed by a newspaperman and magazine writer, George Creel, the committee was intended to organize the distribution of information required to keep the public properly informed on the course of the war. . . . The committee . . . became a propaganda agency; . . . it assumed responsibility not only for informing public opinion but for controlling it. Members of the new advertising industry joined with journalists and academicians to promote the war effort. The public schools were provided with pamphlets to distribute to schoolchildren, explaining America's role in the war and the need for loyalty to the American cause. Local committees tapped citizen volunteers to speak on behalf of the war effort to schoolchildren, clubs, and other organized citizen groups and in movie theaters between the end of the film and the beginning of the vaudeville acts. Such "four-minute men," as they were called (partly because they promised to speak for only four minutes and partly to recall the volunteer fighters of Revolutionary days), exhorted audiences to all forms of engagement in the war, from military service to volunteer activity. . . .

The promotion of Americanism and a spirit of wartime loyalty inevitably focused on the dissenters, the un-American and the disloyal, who opposed the war for whatever reason. . . . Freedom of the seas, rights of neutrals, competition of national empires for world markets—all of the issues that had been central to the debates of the previous three years—were pushed aside in the turmoil of the war effort, replaced now by a rage against Germans and things German. The German language was removed from school curricula, German operas and symphonies were cut from repertoires, German street names were changed, often being replaced with some form of the term "Liberty," and "von" vanished from family names, where it had once signified some proudly remembered identification with nobility. The

British royal family of Saxe-Coburg-Gothas became Windsors, the Battenbergs became Mountbattens, and Americans with German names followed suit.

The actual organization of the war effort itself brought many of the progressives' arguments to the fore. . . . The possibility that the war would become dependent on the American public for funding was not seriously considered in advance. The income tax was still a novelty, and the initial rates were still set by the compromises made by the progressives. Thus it did not weigh heavily on the wealthy, and it bypassed all Americans with incomes of less than $4,000—the vast majority. By 1916, increases in military expenditures had begun to produce a national deficit, but Congress was unwilling to increase taxes.

The War Revenue Act of 4 October 1917 was in some respects a progressive triumph. It authorized a graduated income tax beginning at 4 percent on personal incomes of more than $1,000, raised the corporation tax, and placed an excess-profits tax on corporate and personal income. Excise taxes on alcohol and tobacco were increased, and new excise taxes were levied on luxuries, amusements, and transportation. This triumph was short-lived, but the progressive principle was nonetheless established: almost three-quarters of the cost of the war was to be borne by corporations and those with large incomes, not by the consumption taxes conservatives had tried to promote. The costs skyrocketed far beyond what was envisaged at the beginning. Ultimately, a third of the money came from war-bond subscriptions; the rest was charged to future generations of Americans. War-financing was a mixed experience, and few on either the progressive or the conservative side of the debate were satisfied. The issue was destined to return in the aftermath of the war as critics reexamined the experience and tried to assess its meaning.

The effective management of the war was again a subject of dispute. It was clear by the winter of 1917 that volunteerism was not working. The collapse of the nation's railroad system was the most threatening sign. It was also the oldest and most familiar example of American industrial inefficiency. . . . Reluctant pioneers, [the railroads] had been forced to face the development of a national labor force, the pressures of regional customer demand, the puzzles of technological innovation in materials and equipment, and above all, the impact of federal regulation well ahead of their companions in the American technological revolution. They had also served as the most logical target of those who called for government ownership of public utilities. Even William Jennings Bryan had returned from Europe convinced that public ownership of the railroads was a national need, and, by the eve of the war, that conviction was shared by a sizable segment of informed public opinion.

By 1917, the American railroads had experienced almost thirty years of federal regulation, but this had been administered, by and large, with their advice and consent. As critics had been pointing out for more than two decades, railroad ownership had become centralized to a degree that had disturbed trust-busters without eliciting clear judicial decisions on what the government's response ought to be. The American railroad system was not a "system" in any serious sense. The lack of standardization in such obvious mechanisms as the couplings that attached one car to another made it impossible to ship a loaded car across the country without several reloadings into cars of different lines. Shippers complained about rates, while local railyards maintained platoons of workers whose job it was to reload cars. . . . The United States had a national railroad system in one sense only: the rail lines spanned the nation.

The war effort compelled the adoption of a national system. Shipments of troops and materials had to be organized for one basic purpose: support of the war effort. The demands of war exposed the inner workings of the rail system as they had never been seen before, and the strain on the system was already very great when the weather—December 1917 was an unusually snowy month—produced the straw that broke the old camel's back. The federal government took over the running of the railroads the day after Christmas. Secretary of the Treasury William Gibbs McAdoo became director-general of the Railroad Administration, which controlled almost 400,000 miles of track operated by 3,000 companies. The progressives cheered. Innovative managers moved in. They introduced technical improvements, modernized the system, rationalized rates, and raised wages, not only to keep the system going but to keep it going well. But again the progressives, who had seen all this as a needed revolution, turned out to be wrong; for the government did not choose to go on managing the reformed system after the war. The Transportation Act of 1920, against president Wilson's advice, returned the system to its private owners, much improved, more efficient, and more profitable. The war, and the public, had bailed out the railroads. They had also created the necessary transportation system for making the war effort work, and that, when all was said and done, was all they had intended to do.

The War Industries Board, established in July 1917, is another example of a centralized administrative control replacing a failed volunteer effort. In March 1918, President Wilson authorized a sweeping reorganization that placed financier Bernard M. Baruch in charge of the group that controlled war industry, set priorities, and fixed prices. Congress had already authorized strict presidential control over food production and fuel, and it moved now to take over patents and other property of enemy aliens and to control all trade with enemy nations. The creation of a War Finance Corporation to lend money to financial institutions, who would in turn lend money to industries engaged in war work, was another dramatic step in the process of government intervention, while the National War Labor Board and the War Labor Policies Board were presidential efforts to resolve labor disputes in war industries.

Progressives pressed all of the industrial boards and committees to follow progressive principles and to use their power to institute the reforms that progressives had long been advocating. Economists on the War Industries Board had their first opportunity to acquire systematic information on the economics of national industrial production and to push for standardized reporting. The Labor Board, under the joint chairmanship of Frank P. Walsh and former president William Howard Taft, committed itself to the ideal of a living wage, carrying a significant step further the argument against the treatment of labor as a commodity in the production system whose compensation was determined only by the law of supply and demand. . . . Presidential threats to use war power to take over industries whose management refused to negotiate with labor were effective in forcing bargaining and in gaining support from the leaders of the labor movement. Yet, as the experience in the twenties was to demonstrate, the balance between wartime fervor and commitment to progressive ideals was considerably more uneven than even the most knowledgeable of the progressives were inclined to believe in the heat of what some preferred to see as a wartime revolution. At the same time, the experience was there. It was intense, and it was available for later use in the New Deal decades. Even so, it was the sense of emergency, one could argue, that could be appealed to, not any commitment to reform. . . .

All in all, the war was a disruptive experience that swept across the American landscape like a firestorm feeding on every source of energy it touched. Prohibition had been an issue for more generations than anyone could remember. Wartime morality, plus the belief that most American manufacturers of alcohol were German, gave the Eighteenth Amendment movement the edge it needed. The intensity of the need to create and sustain a national sentiment in favor of the war was based on a fear that failure to do so would make victory impossible; but it led to repressive legislation that severely limited any criticism of the war or of the nation's conduct of it. The Espionage Act of June 1917 was intended to control treasonable or disloyal activities, and the coupling of treason and loyalty is the key to the difficulties that were encountered in interpreting and administering the law. Treason could be defined by forms of behavior determinable by law as treasonous. The same standard could not be applied to loyalty, a concept that depended on beliefs and on statements in speech or writing. The act empowered the postmaster general to exclude from the mails anything he deemed treasonable or seditious. Its constitutionality was upheld by the Supreme Court, even though Oliver Wendell Holmes's ringing dissent became the standard, ultimately, by which the Court would defend free speech. Before the war was over, the act was amended to make it even more severe, particularly in its penalties against socialists and pacifists.

Faced with congressional pressures to create a national war cabinet to build a more effective war machine, Wilson himself wrote the legislation that became the Overman Act of 1918, which granted the president greater administrative authority than any previous president had ever had. Passed in May 1918, the Overman Act gave Wilson enormous powers of reorganization and concentration of government where war activities were concerned. The American war machine had reached its peak. It could now win the war, but it would do so at a price that many were beginning to consider much more costly than anyone had anticipated. Americans had nationalized themselves to face threats that had gradually become more internal than external, although it grew increasingly difficult to see the distinction. . . . The enemy at home became the most visible enemy to attack.

The transformation of Wilson's attitude toward the war from "peace without victory" to "the war to end war" and then to a "war to make the world safe for democracy" was a transformation from the instrumental realism of much of the nineteenth century to a dramatic idealism that became much more of a religious crusade. Nor was this simply an American aberration, traceable to a unique American idealism or to Wilson's personal naïveté. Russia's withdrawal from the war, following the November 1917 revolution, led to the enunciation of similar criticisms of the aims of the war. Couched in Marxist terms, they held little appeal for Americans, even though they spoke to some of the same issues of international politics and to the ultimate uselessness of war as a policy instrument. Instead of arousing American sympathies, the Bolshevik position exacerbated American fears; for Russia's withdrawal liberated German troops for service on the Western front and underscored the growing fear that the antiwar movement, led by socialist and pacifist groups in other countries, would lead other allies to withdraw. . . . In the United States the hostility to socialism and to immigrant groups who were identified, rightly or wrongly, with leftist ideological positions came to be tied directly to the commitment to winning the war. It appeared to be a simple step in logic to argue that socialism and communism alike were pro-German.

The entry of the United States determined the outcome of the war; but the United States did not win the war. The victory went to the Allies, who dictated the terms of the peace. Germany had agreed to an armistice on the understanding that the United States would dictate the terms of the peace and that Wilson's Fourteen Points would serve as the basis of the terms. But Wilson joined the Versailles Conference as only one of the four heads of state who drafted the terms, and his influence was limited, especially given his inexperience and given the fact that the election in November 1918 had turned control of Congress over to the Republicans. Those who considered the election results a repudiation of Wilson seemed to forget that none of Wilson's political victories had been clear-cut. The Democrats had not been a majority party in 1912 and they were not one in 1918. The factors that had given them their slender margins had quite possibly been balanced by the experience of the war. The return to normal politics was on the way, and normal politics meant Republican majorities at the polls.

For so brief an experience, even if one dates it from 1914 rather than 1917, the American involvement in World War I was as intense and as significant as any since the Civil War. The regular army in 1917 consisted of about two hundred thousand men. By 1919 that number had reached more than four million, over two million of whom had gone to France. . . .

That Americans were fighting on the battlefields of Europe was something new and shocking, both for those who went and for those who joined the labor force to serve the nation's industrial needs. American industry responded, too, to its first major taste of government intervention; but even that was an experience of gradual escalation of control. One could remember the voluntary beginnings or the coercive last months and be remembering something quite different. The new industrial efficiency, developed along lines recommended by Frederick Winslow Taylor, gave some an opportunity to see what might come of scientific management; but the tests were too sporadic and too incomplete for anyone to draw clear conclusions.

The introduction of psychological testing brought professionals from a new academic field into consulting positions where industrial managers could see the possible effects of their methods. An experimental field hospital funded by the Rockefeller Foundation advanced medical knowledge of burn and wound treatment. . . . Yet, in virtually every field, the lesson was always the same. From the economists who worked for the War Industries Board to the historians and political scientists who advised the president at Versailles, the issue boiled down to one basic problem: American specialization in such fields was essentially in its infancy. American energy was great. The creation of the industrial machine that won the war had supplied an undeniable demonstration of that energy. But efficient management of the machine had depended entirely on the emergency of the war, on the fear of losing it, and on the support of a popular fervor the government worked desperately to sustain. The speed with which Congress dismantled the machine at the war's end, to the point of leaving Washington office workers to find money for their passage home when federal funds were abruptly cut off, suggests that national management was basically viewed as something temporary, even dangerous.

Yet progressives had argued, long before the war emergency gave them what they took to be their opportunity, that American society was seriously threatened by its inability to organize its resources and rationalize its industrial system. From the conservationists to the scientific industrial managers, the depth of concern was profound. The war had revealed the precarious condition of the American industrial system. Concerned Americans who lamented the closing of the frontier, the disorganization of the industrial labor force, the weaknesses of the transportation system, the pointless duplications and inefficiencies in agricultural and industrial production methods, the pockets of illiteracy and substandard health among the young, and the lack of technical information on national finance and industry found that they had indeed been correct in their assessment of conditions. They looked to the war to make their point for them, to prove to public opinion and even the most backward congressmen that their prescriptions would have to be followed. Nothing could have been further off the mark. All down the line, from their conviction that the new wave of American internationalism could not now be turned back to their belief that the war had put industrial management on a new course, with government firmly in command, the progressives simply turned out to be wrong.

The war had become a reform movement of its own, sweeping up all of the reform interests in one way or another but turning them to the one central purpose, winning the war. Still, what really destroyed the reform movement was not just the excesses generated by that purpose by the exhaustion produced by the war effort itself. Trench warfare had been a nightmare. As if to be certain that civilian populations would share the nightmare, an influenza pandemic, which originated on the Western front, spread to the United States with extraordinarily devastating effect in the winter of 1918–19. The high mortality rate from the disease accounted for more than half of the 112,432 American war fatalities and for thousands more at home.

The failure to consolidate, let alone to extend, wartime gains was nowhere more apparent than in the American labor movement. Spurred by an immediate postwar inflation, which by 1919 had driven the cost of living 77 percent above its prewar level, labor unions began to organize strikes. The most dramatic were the strike in the steel industry, where workers had for years suffered conditions among the worst in American industry, and the strike of the Boston police. Public reaction to both was colored by the antiradical hysteria of the period. Violence in the steel strike and the threat of violence in the police strike touched old nerves in the American public's general suspicion of unionization and its association with radical ideas. Yet these two were among 2,665 strikes involving more than four million workers, while the cost of living rose to 105 percent above prewar levels by 1920. Faced with the opposition first of state officials and ultimately of the United States attorney general, labor backed down. That it was forced to do so during the immediate period of postwar prosperity suggests something markedly antilabor in the public response. The Boston police strike became the symbol. Public protectors had no right to strike; they must have been led to do so by insidious forces. . . .

Former wartime managers, when writing of their part in the war effort, continued to extol the voluntarism with which Americans had joined together to forget their differences and win the war; but even many of those who praised that victory still insisted that the national industrial system should not be required to undertake such a burden again. Businessmen and labor leaders had not found government intervention in their interest, and neither side thought that the government had been even-handed. . . . The progressives' use of the war as an occasion for achieving the reforms they had failed to achieve in peacetime was more than a failure; for by linking the war with a fearful centralization, they proved the point about reformers that their critics had so often made: they were seen as oppressive zealots seeking to impress a national unity on an inherently free people. In the years to come, Prohibition would be taken as another proof of this point. And when the crisis of the thirties began, the reluctance to go back to wartime measures of national control was based in part on recollection of what had happened before. The fear that leaders used emergencies to justify the imposition of state controls was part of a historical experience with war that had nothing to do with voluntarism. Like children whistling past a cemetery, postwar memoirists praised voluntarism, but there was always a gnawing fear that it had not really worked. The truth of the matter was that it hadn't.

Over There: Interpreting Wartime Experiences Abroad

DAVID M. KENNEDY

Two million men served in the AEF [American Expeditionary Force]. The experience struck nearly all of them as an extraordinary moment in their lives—while they passed through it, and when they later remembered it. That they considered it an extraordinary interlude at the time is evidenced by the diaries and journals and strikingly "literary" letters so many of them wrote during their period of service. Americans in 1917, especially those of the age and class who qualified for the AEF, were not the diary-keeping people they had once been. Yet thousands of men who had never before recorded in writing their daily doings, and never would again, faithfully kept journals while they were in the Army. Most of these records began with induction and ended with discharge, neatly delineating the time spent in uniform as a peculiar interval, a moment stolen from ordinary life and forever after sealed off in the memory as a bundle of images that sharply contrasted with "normal" experience. The reactions to France and to war were, of course, as varied as the men who recorded them. But even a modest sampling of the personal documents left behind—a few of them published, many deposited in libraries, more still passed down reverently as family heirlooms to later generations—reveals common responses to the shared enterprise, and common conventions of perception and language to which these men resorted in the effort to comprehend their experience and relate it to others.

They were, first of all, as much tourists as soldiers. Later reflections governed by the masculine need to emphasize prowess at martial exploits, would tend to blot that fact from the record. But the average doughboy spent more peacetime than wartime in France. And, though as many as 1.3 million Americans came under enemy fire, few saw sustained or repeated battle. Virtually none was subjected to the horror and tedium of trench warfare for years on end, the typical lot of the European soldier. The Americans fought no major defensive battles. Their two chief engagements were relatively brief, mobile attacks in the closing weeks of the conflict.

Hence, to a remarkable extent—remarkable at least when compared with the war writings of European combatants—the doughboys' accounts deal with topics other than war. It was AEF policy to rotate leave zones "in order to give all an equal chance to see as much of France as possible." Most coveted of all were the pink tickets that permitted a trip to Paris. *Stars and Stripes* felt obliged to caution arriving troops against the "oo-la-la" idea of France as a great tourist playground. Too many men, said the journal, came over "expecting to find a sort of international Coney Island, a universal pleasure resort." "We have been all over France and seen and learn [*sic*] a lot," said one awestruck New Yorker. After the Armistice, the Army organized sporting events and provided educational opportunities for the idle troops. It also endlessly compelled them to solve "problems"—sham attacks against an imaginary enemy. Many men fought more of these mock battles than real ones. One long-suffering soldier reported in April 1919 that "every hill in this vicinity has been captured or lost at least ten times." But the same enlisted man spoke the sentiments of many when, describing his post-Armistice leave to Nice and Monte Carlo, he called it "the most important event in my life over here (from a social standpoint)."

Like previous generations of their traveling countrymen, the doughboys were impressed with the *age* of the Old World. "Its old cathedrals, chateaux and ancient towns have been quite wonderful to my eyes so accustomed to the look of the New World," said one. In countless diaries and letters the soldiers dwelt on the quaint antiquity of this town, or that church or chateau, their imaginations especially fired by the evocation of names from the history books. "The church here," wrote another doughboy, "is very, very old, probably built sometime in the 12th or 13th century. Saint Louis the Crusader, King of France, attended service there on three occasions and Jeanne d'Arc was there several times." "The architecture for the most part seems to represent a period several hundred years past," wrote another. "We are living, for the present, in barracks built about the time of Louis XIV, though no one here knows anything about them prior to Napoleon."

The France they described was rich with history, an old country inhabited by old people. No observation of French life was more common than remarking the elderly women in black who seemed to be the only residents of the ruined towns behind the front. A tired people in a blighted land, the French pursued antiquated ways. "My but the people are old fashioned," observed one enlisted man. "They still harvest with cradles and sickles. Once in a while you see a binder or mower. I've never saw [*sic*] a real wagon, they use carts." All signs, in short, confirmed the American myth of the Old World as an exhausted place, peopled by effete and even effeminate races. All this, of course, served as a useful foil for the image of American energy and "pep." "What an impression our boys are making on the French," enthused Raymond Fosdick, head of the Commission on Training Camp Activities. "They are the greatest lot of sheer boys you ever saw. . . . The French, who love to sit and meditate, are constantly gasping at the exuberance and tirelessness of our fellows." "Never was there such a spectacle in all history," exclaimed a *New York Times* correspondent, "as that of the fresh millions of free Americans flocking to the rescue of beleaguered and exhausted Europe."

But if Europe was exhausted, it was still splendid to behold. Numerous accounts expressed rapt wonder at the sheer physical beauty of France. "Picturesque" was perhaps the most commonly used word in these descriptions. One is struck too by the frequency of panoramic portraits of nature, of efforts to translate a long sweep of the eye into a string of words. If sunrise and sunset were the characteristic themes in the writings of trench-bound British troops in Flanders, as Paul Fussell has observed in his study *The Great War and Modern Memory*, it was the panoramic landscape that most attracted the eye of Americans.

There were good reasons for these divergent motifs. In the flatness of Flanders, sunup and sundown provided the only natural relief from the monotonous landscape. And twice-a-day British stand-to's on the trench firing step, year after year, in season and out, were timed to take advantage of the long silhouetting light when the sun was low on the horizon. But the American troops, by contrast, were doubly "summer soldiers." They were not only civilians temporarily in uniform, but the bulk of them came to France in the late spring and summer months of 1918. Behind the front, at least, the forests were indeed verdant, the fields aripple with grain, the roadsides in bloom. "The country is green and covered with flowers. It is a continuous garden," said a soldier who arrived in April 1918. Moreover, again unlike the British, the American troops were on the move, all the way across France from ports on the Bay of Biscay to their training areas in the north and east. They traversed the rolling country of north-central France, and when they at last saw their assigned portion of the front, it ran along the undulating hills from Verdun to the Vosges. From the prominence of Montfaucon, for example, one could easily see in clear weather virtually the entire American battle line on the Romagne heights, stretching several miles from east to west. Even the seasons and the terrain conspired to sustain an image of France as a kind of grand open-air arena suited to staging battles of operatic movement and theatrical visibility.

Common to many Americans' perceptions of France was a sense of ceremony, which often had religious overtones. *Stars and Stripes* declared that France was "holy ground," and that more than once in history the French "at Chalons, at Tours, at the Marne—'saved the soul of the world.' To many of the doughboys, the great war in which they were now engaged amounted to a ritual reenactment of those historic dramas. To the largely Protestant Americans, the exotic rites of French Catholicism fittingly exemplified the ceremonial attitude they deemed appropriate to the occasion. Alan Seeger had noted that "the Catholic religion with its idealization of the spirit of sacrifice makes an almost universal appeal in these times," and many members of the AEF agreed with him. The "Marseillaise," too, had the power to "set you quivering." When French religion and patriotic music were combined, the effect was deeply moving. One American soldier attended high mass on Bastille Day, 1918, and a band at the flag-draped church played the "Marseillaise": "Rene, talk about throwing up your hat and shouting 'To Hell with the Kaiser.' The scene and music impressed me so much that I could hardly get my breath. I cannot describe how grand the whole thing was."

Time and again in the personal narratives of these touring provincials one suddenly hears a different voice. The rough and often wise-cracking American idiom abruptly gives way to a grandiloquent tone that speaks, for example, of the "red-tiled roofs resplendent in the sunlight, resembling huge cameos set conspicuously on the vine covered slopes." This strange diction was the language of the tourist brochures, or of the ubiquitous YMCA guides who shepherded the gawking troops about the various sights. It was not a natural voice. Those wondrous foreign scenes often exceeded the native American capacity for authentic speech, and the confrontation with the unfamiliar was thus almost automatically rendered in clichés and highly stylized prose. To a significant degree, the same was true of descriptions of the war itself.

Reverence toward France and the "cause" was not carried over to the Army. Fellowship of arms gave certain consolation, but the physical conditions of life and the restrictions of the military regime were constant causes of complaint. Most pestiferous were the lice—"cooties"—that occasioned frequent trips to the delousing stations, and almost daily "shirt readings," or close inspections of clothing for nits. Equally wearing on men's bodies and spirits was army food—or lack of it. In vivid contrast with the wooden descriptions of tourist sights are the lively and lavish descriptions of those rare meals eaten somewhere—anywhere—other than the military mess. The careful recording of menus, indeed, took up a great deal of space in many soldiers' diaries and letters. Men frequently noted losses of more than ten percent of their body weight in the weeks after arrival in France. These accounts confirmed Field Marshal Haig's observation that the Americans "hardly knew how to feed their troops." They also suggest that undernourishment may have dulled the fighting effectiveness of the AEF.

But the worst feature of military life was the discipline. Military hierarchy and subordination chafed against ingrained American values of equality and individualism. Anti-German propaganda harped on the supposedly slavish subservience of the "Hun" in order to enhance an image of the German soldier as an eminently bayonetable alien. The American resentment of martial authority could be found in all ranks, and sometimes manifested itself in striking ways. Even a pillar of traditional authority such as once and future Secretary of War Henry L. Stimson complained to his diary, while a staff officer in France, that "I am getting a little tired of kow-towing to regulars just because they are regulars." On the returning troop carriers in 1919, the doughboys enacted a ritual "funeral of Sam Browne." To the throaty cheers of the enlisted men, the officers solemnly marched to the ship's rail and threw their leather girth-and-shoulder "Sam Browne" belts, hated symbols of military caste, into the sea. Even the hierarchy of different services prompted resentment, as infantry officers often took potshots at airborne American pilots, the elite and haughty "Knights of the Air." "It is just a gesture of irritation at the air service," opined the commander of an observation balloon squadron, "something like boys throwing a rock at a limousine which is dashing by when they are having to work."

Long idle behind the lines, and then only briefly exposed to battle, the great mass of the American soldiers in France were spectators in the theater of war. They had come to see the "Big Show," and were not disappointed. Nothing in that show was more exciting than the aerial battles. Men approaching the front strained their eyes and ears for signs of aircraft, more out of curiosity than fear. Always they referred to aerial "duels," or "wonderful air battles," or "thrilling air fights." One balloonist described seeing "Richthofen's *circus*." The famed "Red Baron's" formation approached, "some of the planes with red bodies, and they fly along with some planes climbing and some dropping and give the effect of being on the rim of a giant wheel which is rolling thru the sky."

Artillery fire, too, provided visual spectacle on a colossal scale. In the rear training area, reported one young officer, "the most fun is going out to the artillery range." There, secure in a bomb-proof observation shelter near the target, "you can see the shot appear as a little black speck and follow it down to the earth when it bursts." In the battle area, the long-range guns were usually registered on specific targets, and their effects could be safely observed from beyond the target perimeter. Seen from this distance, the discharge noise partly dissipated, the artillery blasts blended into the natural beauty of the landscape itself: "Later another boy and I from section C walked out to the tip of the strip of woods, where we could see the French guns firing and watch the German replies. The shrapnel was exploding harmlessly over a meadow perhaps 500 yards away from us. In the air you would see a sudden noiseless puff of brown smoke which hung very close together for some time after the explosion, then quite a perceptible time later would come the whistle and then the report. It was all very unreal and spectacular."

But the big guns also brought death. Worse, they brought it without warning, from an unseen distance. In descriptions of shelling, one occasionally finds the faintly dawning realization that modern military combat was something quite different from what the eager troops had been led to expect. And its worst feature was its impersonality. Many men wrote of their sense of outraged helplessness while being shelled. Indeed, "shell shock" may have had as much to do with this feeling of impotence as it did with the physical effects of concussion. Even the irrepressible Alan Seeger found bombardment "distressing," because he was "being harried like this by an invisible enemy and standing up against all the dangers of battle without any of its exhilaration or enthusiasm." William Langer wrote that shellfire "has always seemed a bit unfair to me. Somehow it makes one feel so helpless, there is no chance of reprisal for the individual man. The advantage is all with the shell, and you have no comeback." Enduring shellfire often prompted fantasies of bloody personal reprisal. As one draftee wrote: "we cannot fight artillery. Jerry is a rotten sport. . . . Poor Frank Carr, he was hit with a shell and broken all up. I'll remember that and when it comes my time to run a bayonet into one of the skunks I'll look to heaven and cry out to Frank to watch me do the job up."

But negative notes in the contemporary reactions to the war were relatively rare. What most strikes the reader of these personal war records is their unflaggingly positive, even enthusiastic, tone. Seeger's sanguine reflection that war was affording him "the supreme experience" was reiterated countless times by those who followed him to France. Raymond Fosdick, arriving overseas during the German offensive in the spring of 1918, wrote that he was "having an experience . . . which dwarfs anything I have ever lived through or seen before. . . . I am just back from a four days' trip at the Front. . . . Needless to say I had a wonderful time—a most exhilarating time—at moments, a most exciting time." One volunteer wrote from France in mid-1917 that "I never enjoyed life as much as I have since I have been over here and if one must be killed to enjoy life—Well. It has already been a wonderful thing for me." After the Armistice the same man could only reflect "what a glorious adventure it has all been to me."

These expressions of exhilaration, wonder, and glory are notable not only for what they say but also for the way in which they say it. The sights of France elicited mostly tourist-brochure boilerplate from the doughboy writers. Similarly, the war itself seemed to overwhelm the power of the imagination to grasp directly, and of language to describe authentically. It is not especially surprising to find *Stars and Stripes* assuring a soldier-reader that he was the "spiritual successor" to "the Knights of King Arthur's Round Table." But it is to be remarked when countless common soldiers wrote privately of themselves in the same vein. American war narratives, with unembarrassed boldness, speak frequently of "feats of valor," of "the cause" and the "crusade." The memoirs and missives penned in France are shot through with images of knight-errantry and of grails thrillingly pursued. A truck driver in the aviation section of the AEF exclaimed that "war's great caldron of heroism, praise, glory poetry, music, brains, energy, flashes and grows, rustles and roars, fills the heavens with its mighty being. . . . Oh! War as nothing else brings you back to the adventurous times of old." One of Lillian Wald's "boys" from the Henry Street Settlement proudly announced his enlistment in the "battle to throw down the shackles of Honensollern [*sic*] and Junkerism."

. . . Faced with the unfamiliar reality of modern war, many young American soldiers tried to comprehend it in the comfortably familiar verbal formulae of their childhood storybooks. In the homeliest lines scribbled by the humblest privates, the war was frequently couched in language that appears to have been lifted verbatim from the pages of G. A. Henty or, more often, those of Sir Walter Scott. That language echoed, however pathetically, the epic posturings of George Creel and the elaborately formal phrasing of Woodrow Wilson. Those accents may ring strangely in the modern ear, but they flowed easily from the tongues and pens of the doughboys in 1918. The ubiquity of that idiom, from the White House to the trenches, suggested a widely made equation between the official and the personal definitions of the war's significance. If the war was to redeem Europe from barbarism, it would equally redeem individual soldiers from boredom; if the fighting in France was the "Great Adventure," the doughboys were the great adventurers; if Creel and Wilson could speak of the "Crusade," then it followed that American troops were crusaders. Not only did many doughboys accept without reflection the official definition of the war's meaning, but, perhaps more important, they translated that meaning into their understanding of their personal experiences, and described those experiences in language transported directly from the pious and inflated pronouncements of the spokesmen for traditional culture. That language pervaded all the vast "literature" produced during the war by members of the AEF.

British troops, eager and exuberant in 1914 and 1915, had at first written of the war in much the same archaic idiom. But they were soon made to see the skull of death beneath the smiling skin of life. As Paul Fussell writes, that "innocent army fully attained the knowledge of good and evil at the Somme on July 1, 1916." There, the Germans inflicted nearly 60,000 casualties on the first day of the British attacks; succeeding weeks of the abortive campaign would see casualty lists climb to ten times that number on each side. Haig thereafter settled his armies into the appallingly costly warfare of attrition that the French and Germans had already made infamous at Verdun, and "the possibility that the war might be endless began to tease the mind near the end of 1916."

One of the casualties of that warfare was a manner of speech, language itself, the very medium of thought and expression used to comprehend war. The formal phraseology with which the earlier English writers had described battle began to give way. In its place came new images, new diction—indeed, suggests Fussell, a wholly new phase of the literary cycle, in which irony displaced mimesis as the dominant form of understanding. . . .

Fussell additionally observes that British war writing was couched in the conventions of proscenium theater, conventions appropriate "for a war settled for years into fixed positions." All three of the great English war memoirists—Robert Graves, Edmund Blunden, and Siegfried Sassoon—confessed "to entertaining the idea or the image of the war's literally lasting forever."

Those developments on British battlefields and in British literature had no American analogues. . . . Almost never in the contemporary American accounts do the themes of wonder and romance give way to those of weariness and resignation, as they do in the British. The narrative devices most characteristic of American war novels were adopted not from proscenium theater but from cinematic film—a source more appropriate to the American experience of movement and rapt incredibility. And while the American narratives may occasionally reflect on the immenseness and incomprehensibility of the war's evil, they much more often crackle with positive excitement—what the authors themselves would be likely to call "zest" or "peptomism." "Our boys went [to] the battle field last night singing," recorded a Regular Army veteran; "you can't beat them they are surely [a] game and happy bunch."

No doubt the objective circumstances of the AEF's relation to the war helped to sustain this cheerful attitude: the season and the terrain, the lateness and brevity of American belligerency, the relatively open warfare that characterized action all along the front in the final weeks when the American army at last saw combat. But one should note, too, the precise character of American good cheer, the imaginative constructs in which it found expression. English war writing showed the heavy impress of the long and rich tradition of English literature. *The Oxford Book of English Verse* traveled in many a Tommy's rucksack to the trenches, and provided a fund of literary models and allusions in which the scene at the front could be mentally encompassed. By contrast, says Paul Fussell, "American writing about the war tends to be spare and one-dimensional," devoid of allusion, without the shaping mold of tradition to give it proper form. Of Seeger's most famous poem, "I Have a Rendezvous with Death," Fussell notes that it "operates without allusion, without the social instinct to invite a number of canonical poems into its vicinity for comparison or ironic contrast."

This is a telling observation, but it can be carried too far. The canon of English literature, after all, had not been embargoed in the British Isles. It had been exported in bulk to the United States, and consumed avidly by generations of readers. . . . Thus, in one sense American war writing was different from British only in that its life cycle was truncated. It sprang from the same sources but never, or only later, completed the cyclical devolution from mimesis to irony that British writing accomplished. In another sense, the contemporary American war literature was more attenuated than the British: it drew on a narrower range of allusions, traced its literary lineage to fewer forebears. Why this should have been so is a question whose pursuit would carry well beyond the boundaries of the present subject. But suffice it to say that Fussell notwithstanding, the contemporary American imaginative response to the war unmistakably took its inspiration from a branch of English literature: the medieval romantic tale. To be sure, the immediate source of this inspiration was most often the nineteenth-century author Sir Walter Scott, a "popular" writer perhaps not of "canonical" stature. But at the level of popular culture, the mind-set of the great mass of doughboys, Scott's influence was prodigious—and lasting.

Raymond Fosdick showed Scott's tutelage, for example, when he wrote: "I saw one of our divisions going into action the other afternoon. . . . The men had decorated their helmets with red poppies from the fields and they swept by like plumed knights, cheering and singing. I could have wept not to be going with them." Heywood Hale Broun, a correspondent for the New York *Tribune,* was still more explicit: "Verdun and Joffre, and 'they shall not pass,' and Napoleon's tomb, and war bread, and all the men with medals and everything. Great stuff! There'll never be anything like it in the world again. I tell you it's better than 'Ivanhoe.' Everything's happening and I'm in it."

Graphic attempts to invest the war with meaning drew from a similar stock of imagery. Cartoons and posters depicted the spike-helmeted Germans as human gargoyles. Against them stood the lantern-jawed doughboys, fighting for the honor of a fair lady—Dame Victory and Dame Liberty were favorites of *Stars and Stripes,* which also counseled its readers "to hold all women as sacred." . . .

By war's end, in November 1918, little had happened to dislodge the American imagination from that exotic territory. The Armistice had come so swiftly after Pershing's army at last took the field that many troops in fact registered a desire to continue to dwell in that fantastic landscape. "I have a rather peculiar feeling," wrote one doughboy the day after the Armistice. "Heaven knows I am enormously thankful the war is over, but nevertheless I feel as tho [*sic*] my occupation was entirely gone, and the idea of turning back to civilian life seems like an awful jump. I really have got accustomed to fighting, life in the open, running a balloon company with a lot of men, trucks, etc., and it is going to leave a rather gone feeling for a while." A year later, a marine wrote: "I know how we all cried to get back to the States. . . . But now that we are here, I must admit for myself at least that I am lost and somehow strangely lonesome. These our own United States are truly artificial and bare. There is no romance or color here, nothing to suffer for and laugh at."

For men like these, the war had provided a welcome relief from ordinary life. It had in large measure lived up to the romantic expectations encouraged by spokesmen for traditional culture like Holmes and Roosevelt. Like the legendary American West, wartime France was a place where men lived in the open, on the move, in the intensely male comradery of adventure and misery and threatening violence. Like the frontier West, "over there" was a distant land, where men could give vent to dangerous impulses that must be suppressed in civil society. For women, by contrast, wartime heroism consisted in preserving their civilian demeanor. Thus did Raymond Fosdick praise the YMCA girls and the "Salvation Army lassies" for being "just as cool and calm as if they were pouring tea at home." This constancy, frequently attributed to women at the front, bespoke an ideal vision of the true feminine character. But for many men, the true male character, including the fancied immemorial imperatives to hunt and to kill, could only be released in war. The mystery and allure of the battleground derived largely from the fact that it was *not* home. France figured as a kind of equivalent to Huck Finn's "Territory," a place to light out to in flight from the artificial constraints of civilized life.

Wilson and the War for Democracy

ARTHUR S. LINK

There was much truth in a British contemporary's quip that Wilson was talking more like a mediator than a belligerent. He certainly hoped all through 1917 that the moderate forces in the Reichstag (the German parliament) and the civilian leaders in the Imperial government would take control from the High Command and appeal for a peace conference. Wilson correctly regarded the Kaiser as a figure-head of the military. Had such a turnover of power occurred in Berlin, then Wilson almost certainly would have responded eagerly, even if Allied refusal to cooperate had resulted in a separate peace between the United States and Germany.

Wilson had no fears of any such rupture with the Allies. He had great faith in his own ability to marshal world opinion behind a generous settlement. As he warned in his address of December 4, 1917:

> Statesmen must by this time have learned that the opinion of the world is everywhere wide awake and fully comprehends the issues involved. No representative of any self-governed nation will dare disregard it by attempting any . . . covenants of selfishness and compromise. . . . The congress that concludes this war will feel the full strength of the tide that runs now in the hearts of consciences of free men everywhere.

There was, besides, the reassuring fact that the Allies were absolutely dependent economically and were growing militarily dependent upon the United States. Indeed, no one could foresee victory on the western front without a large American army to break the stalemate in the trenches. This meant, as Wilson wrote to Colonel House in July 1917, "When the war is over we can force them to our way of thinking, because by that time they [the Allies] will, among other things, be financially in our hands."

Growing confidence in his own power and leadership, evidence of war weariness everywhere in Europe (mutinies broke out in sixteen corps of the French army in the spring of 1917), and signs of revolt in the Reichstag against the High Command (the Reichstag adopted a no-annexation, no-indemnities resolution on July 19, 1917) all stimulated in Wilson the desire to strike for peace in some dramatic way. . . .

The opportunity, indeed the necessity, for a peace move came almost as soon as House arrived in London. The Bolsheviks seized control of the Russian government on November 7 and appealed to the Allies to begin negotiations at once looking toward a peace based upon the principles of no annexations and no indemnities. In Paris, House pleaded with the British and French leaders to approve a preliminary

Arthur S. Link, *Woodrow Wilson: Revolution, War and Peace* (Arlington Heights, Ill.: Harlan Davidson, 1979), 72–92, 97–103. Reprinted by permission of Harlan Davidson, Inc.

reply in the form of a simple announcement of liberal war aims. That, House urged, might at least persuade the Bolshevik authorities to try to maintain the Russian war effort. . . . The British and French were adamant. They would not even approve an innocuous declaration of war aims. . . .

Events of the next two weeks convinced Wilson that he himself would have to make an authoritative statement. The Bolsheviks signed a separate armistice with the Central Powers on December 15 and appealed for the assembling of a *general* peace conference at once. The new Russian leaders also published the secret treaties between the czarist government and the Allies negotiated since the beginning of the war; they pointed to the refusal of the Entente powers to join a peace conference as proof of their perfidious ambitions. Czernin, the Austrian Foreign Minister, speaking on Christmas Day, echoed the Bolshevik appeal and declared that the Central Powers desired no forcible annexations, would deprive no country of its independence, and wanted minorities to enjoy the right of self-determination. Liberals, idealists, labor leaders, and Socialists in the United States and Great Britain were excited. They denounced Allied intransigence, declared that the time for peace had come, and demanded that a frank reply be sent to the Russian and Austrian overtures.

It was in these circumstances that Wilson set to work with Colonel House on January 4, 1918, on what was to become the Fourteen Points Address. . . . He hammered out on his own typewriter a statement intended to appeal to German and Austrian moderates, to reply to the Bolsheviks, and, above all, to make clear to all the world the aspirations and ideals for which the American people were fighting.

The address was completed on January 7, and Wilson read it to a joint session of Congress on the following day. . . . It was evident, Wilson said, that the German military masters were bent upon the conquest and subjugation of the helpless Russian people. Therefore, the time had come for the peace-loving nations to avow their ideals and objectives, and these he summarized in fourteen points.

On the one hand there were the general points promising open diplomacy; . . . limitation of armaments to the lowest level consistent with domestic safety; the removal, insofar as possible, of barriers to international trade; an absolutely impartial and open-minded settlement of colonial claims; . . . and the establishment of a league of nations to protect great and small states alike.

On the other hand there were the points relating to specific issues. Two of these—the evacuation and restoration of Belgium and the evacuation of Russia and the self-determination of the Russian people—were, like the general points, indispensable to a peace settlement. The remaining six points were not quite as important, for in defining them Wilson said that they "should" rather than "must" be achieved. They were, presumably, negotiable. They were the return of Alsace-Lorraine to France. Wilson had great difficulty in framing this point—the chief French war objective—and in deciding whether to include it. House wanted him to leave it out altogether! The other five were autonomy for the subject peoples of the Austro-Hungarian Empire; a readjustment of Italy's boundary along clearly recognizable lines of nationality; the evacuation of the Balkans and free development for the states of that region; security for the Turkish portions of the Ottoman Empire, but autonomy for the subject peoples of that empire and internationalization of the Dardanellles; and the creation of an independent Polish state with access to the sea and international guarantees of its independence.

There was an implied fifteenth point, one as important as any of the fourteen—
that the United States had no jealousy of Germany's greatness and no desire to do
her any injury. . . .

. . . The United States would be willing to go at once to the peace table if the
Germans would accept the fourteen points as the basis for a settlement. It was not
even necessary, Wilson said, for the Germans to alter their political institutions.
But it was necessary for the United States to know who spoke for Germany—the
majority of the Reichstag, or the military party whose creed was domination. The
moral climax of the war had now come, and the American people were ready for
the test. Germany, Wilson was saying, could obtain a generous settlement if she
wanted one. . . .

. . . The Fourteen Points Address . . . immediately became the moral standard to
which liberals, labor leaders, and Socialists in the United States and Europe rallied.
British Labourites hailed Wilson as their own spokesman. The entire French Left, as
one authority has written, were "galvanized into the President's most ardent supporter in the Entente." Even V. I. Lenin, head of the Bolshevik government, warmly
responded that the address was "a potential agency promoting peace"; the address
was printed in *Izvestiya,* the official Bolshevik daily, and distributed widely throughout Russia.

For a time it seemed that Wilson had begun transatlantic conversations that
might lead to an armistice and peace negotiations. Czernin responded in an address
. . . on January 24 . . . That the Austro-Hungarian government agreed for the most
part with Wilson, and that the fourteen points provided an acceptable basis for peace
negotiations. The new German Chancellor, Count Georg F. von Hertling, . . . said
[that Germany], could certainly agree with many of the President's general points,
but it would brook no interference in its negotiations with Russia. Hertling was
evasive about Belgium, and said that Germany would never return Alsace-Lorraine
to France. . . .

The brief transatlantic dialogue came to an abrupt end on March 3, 1918,
when the Germans imposed a Carthaginian peace upon the Russians at Brest-
Litovsk. Wilson expressed his disillusionment and despair in a speech at Baltimore
on April 6. He had tried, he said, to judge Germany's purposes without hatred or
vindictiveness. . . . The Treaty of Brest-Litovsk had revealed that Germany's real
masters sought the domination of Europe. . . . He cried out that there was only one
response that the American people could give: "Force, Force to the utmost, Force
without stint or limit, the righteous and triumphant Force which shall make Right
the law of the world, and cast every selfish dominion down in the dust."

The poignancy of Wilson's consternation at the Treaty of Brest-Litovsk becomes clearer when one recalls what that treaty portended. It meant that peace
could be won only by smashing the power of the German military machine. This, in
turn, meant a settlement, not negotiated among equals, but imposed by the victors—
in short a situation of grave difficulty for the man who knew that it would be as
necessary to restrain the ambitions of his associates as to defeat those of his enemies.
But peace without victory was no longer possible after March 1918. With Russia
prostrate, the German High Command decided to go for all-out victory on the
western front. It transferred some forty divisions from the eastern front and launched
a gigantic offensive to knock France out of the war before the trickle of American
reinforcements could become a mighty stream. . . .

The French defenses held before Paris in mid-July. Soon afterward, with the help of an ever growing American Expeditionary Force, the supreme Allied commander, Marshal Ferdinand Foch, began a counteroffensive. By October 1, the combined Allied and American armies had broken the Hindenburg Line and were nearing the Belgian and German frontiers. Panic-stricken, General Erich von Ludendorff then demanded that the Imperial government obtain an immediate armistice. . . .

The German government responded by appealing to Wilson, *not* to the Allied governments, for an armistice on the basis of the Fourteen Points and Wilson's subsequent war addresses. Wilson was not taken in by the German leaders. He deftly maneuvered them into acknowledgement of defeat and agreement to accept an armistice that would render them powerless to resume *offensive* operations. However, he wanted to maintain enough German power to serve as a counterbalance to Allied might. "It is certain," he advised Colonel House on October 28, "that too much success or security on the part of the Allies will make a genuine peace settlement exceedingly difficult, if not impossible." . . .

Wilson's decision to go forward with armistice negotiations carried heavy risks at home and abroad. In the United States, Theodore Roosevelt led the chorus demanding a drive to Berlin and a dictated peace. Abroad, the Allies were naturally reluctant to promise Germany to make peace upon a basis of the fourteen points and Wilson's later pronouncements, when total victory was so near.

Determined to end the bloodshed, Wilson sent Colonel House to Paris in mid-October to force a final showdown before the collapse of German resistance had emboldened the Allied leaders into taking peace negotiations into their own hands. From October 29 through November 4, House confronted the Allied prime ministers in a series of stormy meetings. When they threatened to repudiate the fourteen points, House countered with the warning that Wilson was prepared to make a separate peace. The result was an agreement to promise Germany terms as stipulated in the Fourteen Points Address. . . .

House, in a telegram to Wilson on November 5, boasted of his "great diplomatic victory," and so it was in a sense. However, Foch, aided by General John J. Pershing, . . . imposed such military and naval terms, most importantly, French occupation of the Rhineland and the internment of the German navy, as to put Germany completely at the mercy of the British and French. Thus the armistice signed on November 11 was a shadow victory for House and a substantive victory for the Allies, particularly France. Although Wilson had questioned the necessity of occupying Alsace-Lorraine and opposed the occupation of the Rhineland, now he had no alternative but to accept the package that was known as the Pre-Armistice Agreement.

The opportunity for which Wilson had waited since 1914 was now almost at hand. . . . He had decided to go to Paris as the head of the American delegation. . . . No leader in history ever embarked upon a fateful undertaking with higher hopes or nobler ambitions. However, his bargaining position had been additionally weakened by the time he sailed for France on December 4, 1918. On October 25, he had made a frankly partisan appeal for the election of a Democratic Congress and had said that a Republican victory "would . . . certainly be interpreted on the other side of the water as a repudiation of my leadership." Republicans had won both houses of Congress, and their leaders were now saying that Wilson did not represent the American people on his fateful mission to France. Second, all of western Europe was in a state of nearly psychotic shock after more than four years of bloodletting. Passions of hatred and revenge were surging through the British, French, and Italian peoples and inevitably infected their spokesmen. These primeval forces, beyond Wilson's control, boded ill for one who wanted only to do what was right and just. Among other things, his suggestion that Germany be represented at the peace conference was rejected peremptorily.

The first stage of the Paris Peace Conference began when it opened on January 18, 1919, and ended when Wilson left for a visit to the United States on February 14. . . . The second stage lasted from Wilson's departure to his return to Paris on March 14. . . . The third stage lasted from March 24 until about May 7, when agreement on a treaty with Germany was reached. During this period, Wilson had his hardest struggles and made his most important compromises. The final stage lasted from May 7, when the Treaty was presented to the German delegation, to June 28, when it was signed in the Hall of Mirrors at Versailles. . . .

The overshadowing issue of the Paris Peace Conference was security for France against future German aggression. Wilson offered security in a Reich that was reformed because now democratic, and in the League of Nations that would provide machinery to prevent future German aggression. Such assurances were not enough for the French. Their territory had been invaded twice by Germany in less than half a century; France was still, in 1919, inferior in manpower, resources, and industry to Germany. The French were determined to destroy the German colossus once and for all and to guarantee their safety in the future. Thus Clemenceau followed plans devised by Marshal Foch and approved even before the United States had entered the war. These included, in addition to the recovery of Alsace-Lorraine, tearing the west bank of the Rhine from Germany and the establishment of one or more autonomous Rhenish republics under French control.

Wilson opposed this plan with grim determination. He argued that the dismemberment of Germany in the West would outrageously violate the Pre-Armistice Agreement and create a wound that would fester until it produced another war. The tension reached its climax during late March and early April. Clemenceau accused Wilson of being pro-German; Wilson ordered his ship to raise steam and be prepared to take him back to the United States.

Compromise was the only alternative to the disruption of the conference. In the showdown, it was Clemenceau who made the vital concession—by yielding his demand for the creation of the Rhenish republics and permanent French occupation of the Rhineland. In return, Wilson and David Lloyd George, the British Prime Minister (who gave Wilson indispensable support at this juncture), agreed to permit a fifteen-year occupation of the Rhineland and signed with Clemenceau treaties promising that, for a limited period, the United States and Great Britain would come to France's aid if she was attacked by Germany. . . .

The issue of reparations and indemnities provoked the most protracted debates at the conference and the greatest bitterness in Germany afterward. In cynical disregard of the Pre-Armistice Agreement, which strongly implied that Germany should be liable only for civilian damages, Clemenceau and Lloyd George, under heavy pressure from their own peoples, demanded that Germany be made to shoulder the entire costs of the war to the Allied peoples as well as its partial costs to their governments. Wilson made his most important concessions at Paris on this issue.

First, he agreed that Germany should be forced to bear the costs of disability pensions to Allied veterans and their families, on the ground that these were really civilian damages. Second, he agreed that the French should have the right to occupy the Rhineland if the Germans failed to meet their reparations obligations. The French demanded ownership of the Saar Valley in compensation for the wanton destruction wrought in France by the retreating German armies. Wilson fought this demand bitterly and successfully on the ground that the Saar was German territory. However, he did agree to French ownership of the Saar coal mines and French administration of the territory for fifteen years under the supervision of the League of Nations. . . . In addition, Wilson consented to the immediate seizure of some $5 billion worth of German property. Finally, Wilson agreed to the inclusion of the much-controverted Article 231 in the treaty, by which Germany and her allies acknowledged legal responsibility for all losses incurred during the war by the Allied peoples and governments. . . .

Perhaps Wilson made this, his most important concession at the conference, in the conviction that it would not matter much in the long run. He knew that the Allies would never be able to collect the astronomical sums that they expected. He knew that the Allies could not collect huge sums without bankrupting the German economy, the well being of which was absolutely essential to the prosperity of western Europe. He also knew that passions would eventually cool. And he must have thought that the Reparations Commission, under American leadership, would gradually handle the reparations problem in a sensible and realistic way. This, in fact, is what did occur in the 1920s with the establishment of the Dawes and Young commissions of 1923–1924 and 1929. Finally, in 1932, the European powers meeting in Lausanne, Switzerland, ended the problem altogether. They reduced Germany's obligations to some $700 million and tacitly acknowledged that this sum would never have to be paid. . . .

[A] large problem was disarmament, the key, Wilson believed, to peace and security in the future. Wilson proposed that the victors accept virtually the same limitations on ground forces that they were imposing upon the Germans and agree in the peace treaty itself to abolish conscription, prohibit private manufacture of the implements of war, and maintain armies sufficient only to preserve domestic order and fulfill international obligations. He encountered insuperable opposition from the French and won only a vague promise to undertake general disarmament in the future. He did not propose to restrict navies because, for one reason, he was forced to use the threat of American naval expansion as a bargaining tool to win British support for the League of Nations. He was also deeply suspicious of Japanese imperialism and did not want to weaken the chief potential deterrent to Japanese ambitions.

The issue that took precedence over all the others in Wilson's plans and purposes—the question of the League of Nations—is mentioned last because it was so pervasively involved in all the discussions at Paris. There were two divergent concepts of what the League should be and do, and they cast a revealing light upon the motives and objectives of the opposing forces at Paris. One was the French concept of a league of victors, which would be used to guarantee French military domination of the Continent. The French plan was embodied in a draft presented at the first meeting of the League of Nations Commission on February 3, 1919. It envisaged the creation of an international army and a general staff with startling supranational powers, not unlike those later given to NATO. The other was Wilson's concept of a league of *all* nations, the vanquished as well as the victors—a universal alliance for the purpose of creating a concert of power, not really a supranational agency, but one depending upon the leadership of the great powers, the cooperation of sovereign states, and the organized opinion of mankind for its effectiveness.

As chairman and with strong British support, Wilson controlled the meetings of the commission that drafted the Covenant, or constitution, of the League. The crucial conflicts came when the French, Italians, Japanese, and even the British at times, ruthlessly threatened to refuse to support Wilson's league in order to exact concessions on other issues. Time and again Wilson did retreat, but by thus yielding he won the larger goal a League of Nations constructed almost exactly as he wanted it.

The Covenant of the League was firmly embedded in all the treaties signed at Paris; it bound its signatory members in an alliance of nonaggression and friendship; and it created the machinery for international cooperation in many fields and for the prevention of war. . . .

The structure erected was the League itself: an international parliament with an Assembly, in which all members were represented, and an executive Council, in which the great powers shared a larger responsibility with a minority of smaller states. In addition, there was a separate and independent judicial branch—a Permanent Court of International Justice, and an administrative arm—a Secretariat and various commissions charged with the responsibility to execute the peace treaties and to promote international cooperation in economic and social fields. It was, Wilson said when he first presented the Covenant to a full session of the conference, "a living thing . . . a definite guarantee of peace . . . against the things which have just come near bringing the whole structure of civilization into ruin."

Did Wilson fail at Paris? This is a question that has been asked and answered a thousand times by statesmen and scholars since the Versailles Treaty was signed in 1919. It will be asked so long as men remember Woodrow Wilson and the world's first major effort to prevent future aggressions and wars. The answer that one gives depends, not only upon the circumstances and mood prevailing at the time it is given, but also upon the view that one takes of history and of the potentialities and limitations of human endeavor. That is to say, it makes a great deal of difference whether one judges Wilson's work by absolute so-called moral standards, or whether one views what he did while remembering the obstacles that he faced, the pressures under which he labored, what was possible and what impossible to achieve at the time, and what would have happened had he not been present at the conference.

The Versailles Treaty, measured by the standards that Wilson had enunciated from 1916 to 1919, obviously failed to fulfill entirely the liberal peace program. It was not, as Wilson had demanded in his "Peace without Victory" speech and implicitly promised in the Fourteen Points Address, a peace among equals. It was, rather, as the Germans contended then and later, a *diktat* imposed by victors upon a beaten foe. It shouldered Germany with a reparations liability that was both economically difficult for Germany to satisfy and potentially a source of future international conflict. It satisfied the victors' demands for a division of the enemy's colonies and territories. In several important instances, it violated the principle of self-determination. Finally, it was filled with pinpricks, like Article 231 and the provision for the trial of the former German Emperor, that served no purpose except to humiliate the German people. It does not, therefore, require much argument to prove that Wilson failed to win the settlement that he had demanded and that the Allies had promised in the Pre-Armistice Agreement.

To condemn Wilson because he failed in part is, however, to miss the entire moral of our story. That moral is a simple one: The Paris peace settlement reveals more clearly than any other episode of the twentieth century both the tension between the ideal and the real in history, and the truth of the proposition that failure inheres in all human striving. It does not make much sense merely to list Wilson's failures. We can see their meaning only when we understand *why* he failed to the extent that he did.

Wilson did not succeed wholly at Paris because he did not fight with all his mind and strength for the liberal peace program. Never before had he fought more tenaciously or pleaded more eloquently. Nor did he fail because he was incompetent, uninformed, and "bamboozled" by men of superior wit and learning, as John Maynard Keynes, in *The Economic Consequences of the Peace,* and Harold Nicolson, in *Peacemaking 1919* (1933), have portrayed him in their unkind caricatures. Indeed, the records of the deliberations at Paris demonstrate conclusively that Wilson was the best-informed and on the whole the wisest man among the statesmen assembled there.

Wilson failed as he did because his handicaps and the obstacles he fought against made failure inevitable. First and foremost, he had lost most of his strategic advantages by the time the peace conference opened. German military power, upon which he had relied as a balance against Allied ambitions, was not totally gone. Wilson had no lever to use against Britain and France, for they were no longer dependent upon American men and resources for survival. His only recourse— withdrawal from the conference—would have resulted in a Carthaginian peace imposed by the French, as the British alone could have prevented the French from carrying out their plans to destroy Germany. In these circumstances, compromise was not merely desirable; it was a compelling necessity to avert, from Wilson's point of view, a far worse alternative.

To compound Wilson's difficulties, his claim to the right to speak in the name of the American people, already seriously weakened by the election of a Republican Congress in November 1918, was denied during the peace conference itself by Republican leaders like Senator Henry Cabot Lodge. In addition, Colonel House, upon whom Wilson had relied as his strong right arm, had failed to support liberal peace ideals during that period of the conference when he was still the President's spokesman. Not only did House become a captive of Clemenceau, he was so eager for harmony that he seriously undercut and compromised Wilson on several crucial occasions.

The character of Wilson's antagonists at Paris also posed a formidable obstacle. Clemenceau, Lloyd George, Orlando, Baron Sonnino, and the Japanese delegates were all tough and resourceful negotiators, masters of the game of diplomacy, quick to seize every advantage that the less experienced American offered.

To overcome such opposition, Wilson had at his command the threat of withdrawal, the promise of American support for the right kind of settlement and of leadership in the League of Nations, and the fact that he did speak for liberal groups, not only in his own country, but throughout the world as well. These were sources of considerable strength, to be sure, but they were not enough to enable Wilson to *impose his own settlement. . . .*

In spite of it all, Wilson won a settlement that honored more of the fourteen points than it violated and which to a large degree vindicated his liberal ideals. Belgium was restored, Alsace-Lorraine was returned to France, and an independent Poland with access to the sea was created. The claims of the Central European and Balkan peoples to self-determination were satisfied. German military power was destroyed, at least for a time. Most important, the Paris settlement provided machinery for its own revision through the League of Nations and the hope that the passing of time and American leadership in the League would help to heal the world's wounds and build a future free from fear.

As it turned out, many of Wilson's expectations were fulfilled even though the American people refused to play the part assigned to them. As intimated earlier, the reparations problem was finally solved in the 1920s and early 1930s in a way not dissimilar from the method that Wilson had proposed. Germany was admitted to the League in 1926, and that organization then ceased to be a mere league of victors. Substantial naval disarmament and limitation were accomplished in 1921 and 1930. Even the great and hitherto elusive goal of land disarmament and the recognition of Germany's right to military equality were seriously sought by international action in the early 1930s. In brief, the Paris settlement, in spite of its imperfections, did create a new international order that functioned reasonably well, relatively speaking.

It is time to stop perpetuating the myth that the Paris settlement made inevitable the rise to power of Mussolini, the Japanese militarists, and Hitler, and hence the Second World War. That war was primarily the result of the Great Depression, which wrought great havoc particularly in Japan and Central Europe and devastated the international economy. In turn, the depression caused all nations to follow selfish policies and eschew international cooperation. The Second World War was also caused by the failure of the United States and Great Britain, in the midst of the depression, to stop Japanese aggression in Manchuria in 1931, and by the loss of British and French nerve in dealing with Hitler from 1935 to 1938. It was, additionally, caused by British fear of the Soviet Union and the delusion that Hitler might be used as a counterweight to the Soviets. . . .

The Paris settlement . . . was not inevitably a "lost peace." On the contrary, it established the foundation of what could have been a viable and secure world order, if only the victors had maintained the will to build upon it.

FURTHER READING

Michael C. Adams, *The Great Adventure: Male Desire and the Coming of World War I* (1990)

John Whiteclay Chambers II, *To Raise an Army: The Draft Comes to Modern America* (1987)

Melvyn Dubofsky, *We Shall Be All: A History of the Industrial Workers of the World* (1969)

Robert H. Ferrell, *Woodrow Wilson and World War I* (1985)

Paul Fussell, *The Great War and Modern Memory* (1975)

Lloyd C. Gardner, *Safe for Democracy: The Anglo-American Response to Revolution, 1913–1923* (1984)

Maurine W. Greenwald, *Women, War and Work* (1980)

Ellis W. Hawley, *The Great War and the Search for a Modern Order* (1979)

Arthur S. Link, *Wilson the Diplomat* (1965)

Paul L. Murphy, *World War I and the Origin of Civil Liberties in the United States* (1979)

Richard Polenberg, *Fighting Faiths: The Abrams Case, the Supreme Court, and Free Speech* (1987)

William Preston, Jr., *Aliens and Dissenters: Federal Suppression of Radicals, 1903–1933* (1966)

Dorothy and Carl J. Schneider, *Into the Breach: American Women Overseas in World War I* (1991)

Joe William Trotter, ed., *The Great Migration in Historical Perspective* (1991)

Arthur Walworth, *Wilson and His Peacemakers: American Diplomacy at the Paris Peace Conference, 1919* (1986)

J. M. Winter, *The Experience of World War I* (1989)